Welcome to

McGraw-Hill Education
GMAT

*C*ongratulations! You've chosen the GMAT guide from America's leading educational publisher. You probably know us from many of the textbooks you used in school or in college. Now we're ready to help you take the next step—and get into the business school of your choice.

This book gives you everything you need to succeed on the test. You'll get in-depth instruction and review of every topic tested, tips and strategies for every question type, and plenty of practice exams to boost your test-taking confidence. To get started, read on to learn:

▶ How to Use This Book: Step-by-step instructions to help you get the most out of your test-prep program.

▶ Your GMAT Action Plan: Learn how to make the best use of your preparation time.

▶ Getting the Most from the Interactive Practice Tests: Download the Premium Practice Test App to your tablet or smartphone or visit the companion website for extensive test-taking practice.

▶ Information for International Test Takers: Find out everything you need to know if you live outside the United States and want to attend a U.S. business school.

ABOUT McGRAW-HILL EDUCATION

This book has been created by McGraw-Hill Education. McGraw-Hill Education is a leading global provider of instructional, assessment, and reference materials in both print and digital form. McGraw-Hill Education has offices in 33 countries and publishes in more than 65 languages. With a broad range of products and services—from traditional textbooks to the latest in online and multimedia learning—we engage, stimulate, and empower students and professionals of all ages, helping them meet the increasing challenges of the 21st century knowledge economy.

Learn more. McGraw Hill Education **Do more.**

How to Use This Book

Follow the steps below to work your way through this book, or develop your own personalized action plan (see the next page).

1 **Learn about the GMAT Test Format**

Don't skip the first two chapters. In them you'll meet the GMAT and learn about the structures of the test, including the different test sections, the number of questions in each section, and the section time limits. You'll also find valuable test-taking strategies and important information about how the test is scored.

2 **Take the Diagnostic Test**

Use the diagnostic test in Chapter 3 to determine your strengths and weaknesses. Doing so will help guide your study schedule.

3 **Get Ready for the Analytical Writing Assessment**

Chapter 4 contains information on how the Analytical Writing Assessment is scored as well as strategies and tips to help you maximize your score. You'll also find sample high-scoring responses to study.

4 **Learn All About Integrated Reasoning**

Chapter 5 covers the GMAT's unique Integrated Reasoning section. You'll see examples of these distinctive question types, which require you to reach conclusions from data presented in varied formats. You'll also get the opportunity to sharpen your reasoning skills with practice problems.

5 **Prepare for the Quantitative Section**

Chapters 6 and 7 introduce the types of questions—problem solving and data sufficiency—that you'll encounter in the Quantitative section of the test. In Chapters 8–11, you'll be able to brush up on the math skills required for the GMAT, including basic math, algebra, geometry, and working with word problems. In each chapter, there are plenty of GMAT practice questions to check your progress.

6 **Prepare for the Verbal Section**

Chapter 12 focuses on the Reading Comprehension portion of the test; use it to familiarize yourself with the format and question types you'll encounter in this section of the test. Chapter 13 provides the practice you'll need to do well on the critical reasoning questions of the GMAT. Chapter 14 contains a basic review of grammar and practice with sentence correction questions.

7 **Take the Practice Tests**

Get ready for the actual exam by taking the GMAT practice tests, both the ones in the book and the ones on the app or online. (See Getting the Most from the Interactive Practice Tests, page 8A.) Try to simulate actual testing conditions. You'll gain experience with the test format, and you'll learn to pace yourself so that you can earn your highest possible score.

Your GMAT Action Plan

To make the best use of your GMAT preparation time, you'll need a personalized action plan that's based on your needs and the time you have available. This book has been designed for flexibility; you can work through it from cover to cover, or you can move around from one chapter to another in the order you want based on your own priorities and needs. However, before you jump in, maximize the effectiveness of your preparation time by spending a few minutes to develop a realistic plan of action that focuses on the areas where you are weakest, takes into account the time you have, and provides the discipline you need to pace yourself and achieve your goals.

Components of a Good Preparation Strategy

Make sure your action plan includes all the areas you need to cover. There are three broad areas you need to consider in any well-rounded action plan to master the GMAT.

1. Knowledge and Skills

You'll need a combination of knowledge and skills to determine the correct answers to GMAT questions. Chapters 4–14 give specific guidance on knowledge and skill areas required. Here is a broad summary:

▶ Math skills: Basic mathematics, algebra, geometry, probability, etc. The GMAT covers everything from fractions to permutations and combinations.

▶ Reading skills: Reading quickly, understanding what you read, scanning a passage for specific information, etc. You'll need to be able to quickly read various types of passages with a good comprehension of what you have read.

▶ Analytical skills: Identifying issues, understanding how evidence is used to support or weaken an argument, recognizing inferences, finding inconsistencies, etc. The Analytical Writing Assessment and the Critical Reasoning and Integrated Reasoning sections of the test require sound analytical skills.

▶ Grammar skills: Word usage, sentence construction, punctuation, grammar, etc. There are more sentence correction questions in the GMAT Verbal section than any other kind of question.

▶ Writing skills: Paragraph construction, clarity, organization, transition, etc. The first half hour of the test requires a written essay, so you'll need good writing skills to do well.

2. Pacing and Endurance

The GMAT is both a sprint and a marathon. You have less than two minutes, on average, for each Verbal question and about two minutes for each Quantitative or Integrated Reasoning question, so it is essential to develop the ability to work through these questions quickly and efficiently. Speed is not enough; at nearly four hours in length, the GMAT requires that you have extraordinary mental stamina so that you can stay focused throughout the test. The best way to prepare yourself is to take practice tests observing strict time limits.

3. Test-Taking Strategies

To maximize your performance on the GMAT, you need to have a good understanding of the test, including all the question types you'll encounter. In Chapters 4–14 there are tips and strategies for approaching each of the different question types. Before you take the test, be sure you know the instructions for each part of the test and have no confusion about the tasks you'll be asked to perform. Knowing the instructions will save valuable time during the test.

You'll also need a good guessing strategy. You must answer each question you're given in order to move on to the next question, which means that you and all other test takers will have to guess at some point in the GMAT. What differentiates great test takers from merely good ones is the ability to guess in such a way as to maximize the chances for a correct answer. If you don't know the correct answer, try to eliminate incorrect answers. You can increase your odds of guessing correctly from the 20 percent of a completely random guess to 25, 33, or even 50 percent, depending on how many answer choices you're able to eliminate.

Creating Your Personalized Action Plan

Every GMAT prep plan should devote some time to knowledge and skills, pacing and endurance, and test-taking strategies. But every action plan will be different since it depends on the needs of each individual test taker. Spend a few minutes to devise your plan of attack.

Step 1: Identifying Your Needs

You probably already have a pretty good idea what areas you feel are your weakest ones from previous standardized tests you've taken. But the GMAT is unique and has some question types you may never have encountered before. So it's a very good idea to take the book's diagnostic test, find out exactly what the GMAT entails, and see on which areas of the test you'll need to focus your preparation.

Step 2: Managing Your Time

How many weeks do you have before the test? Whether you have months or only a couple of weeks, you can develop an action plan to improve your score. If you have only a few weeks, try to work some serious prep time into your schedule. But whether you have months or only weeks, it's a good idea to plot out specific time periods each week and reserve them for GMAT prep.

Step 3: Maximizing Effectiveness

Where and when do you study best? Assess when and where you can study most effectively. You know what will work best for you. If you like flash cards, make some. If you work best alone in the library, go there. Whatever you do, make a concrete plan and assess your progress frequently.

Resources for Your Action Plan

This book has the content review, practice questions, practice tests, and strategies you'll need for your personalized action plan. However, in addition to using this book, be sure to take advantage of the free materials available at www.mba.com, the official website of the organization (GMAC) that creates and administers the GMAT. While preparation tools available on this site are limited, be sure to use the two practice tests provided. These use the actual test delivery software and real, previously used GMAT questions. In addition, you'll get accurate GMAT scores for these practice tests so you can see exactly how well you are doing. However, no explanations are provided, so you'll have to figure out on your own why you missed the questions you did.

Sample Action Plans

The one thing that limits you is time. Your GMAT preparation strategy will depend on how much time you have to prepare. The more time and energy you devote to preparation, the better your odds are of achieving your goals. The following pages show two sample action plans—one if you have two months to prepare and one if you have only two weeks.

Sample Action Plan 1—If You Have Two Months to Prepare

Two months is an adequate time for most people to prepare for the GMAT, but the time you'll need depends on how busy you are with work or personal commitments and on how much of an effort you'll need to reach your target score.

Two months until test day

▶ Take the diagnostic test in this book. Evaluate how you did on the different content areas and the different types of questions. Since you have two months to prepare, you can probably focus on each area of the test in depth, but you should start with your weaknesses. Reading Comprehension in particular tends to require longer-term work, so if this is an area you have identified as a weakness, it may be a good idea to start working on the Reading Comprehension chapter (Chapter 12). If there is any math content that consistently gives you trouble—geometry, perhaps, or quadratic equations—start brushing up on it as well. Similarly, certain question types may be problematic; Data Sufficiency and Integrated Reasoning questions are unfamiliar to most test takers before taking the GMAT, so they may be a weakness. Identify three key areas to work on first.

▶ Schedule time over the following month to work on the chapters in this book that correspond to those three key areas. Be sure you read and review each whole chapter, in addition to working the drills at the end of the chapter. For best retention, read the chapter and work half of the practice problems in one study session, then review the chapter and work the remainder of the practice problems in the next study session.

▶ Set aside time to take another of the practice tests sometime during this first month. Take the entire test in one sitting, if possible. Review the explanations not only for the questions you missed, but also for the questions you got right but found difficult.

One month until test day

▶ Take another GMAT practice test to check your progress. Chances are you've improved in your weaker areas, but there are still areas in which you need to do more work.

▶ Schedule time in the next three weeks to complete the chapters you have not worked on and take two more practice tests. For chapters that cover material with which you are already proficient, start with the practice questions at the end of the chapter. Do half of them and check your accuracy. If you've made any mistakes, review the explanations and use the chapter to brush up on your skills. Then complete the rest of the end-of-chapter questions.

Two weeks until test day

▶ Take another GMAT practice test and check your progress. If needed, re-evaluate your study schedule for this week to accommodate any additional areas you need to review or practice.

One week until test day

▶ Take at least one more GMAT practice test to check your progress and practice your pacing; taking additional practice tests is optional, depending on how confident you feel.

▶ Keep your mind focused and ready by doing some review work each day, but don't cram. Above all else, don't get stressed out. Visualize yourself succeeding and try to relax.

▶ Make sure you're not in for any surprises on test day. For example, it's a good idea to actually go to the test center location so you know exactly how to get there.

Sample Action Plan 2—If You Have Only Two Weeks to Prepare

Successfully preparing for the GMAT in just a couple of weeks is an ambitious—and often stressful—project, but it has been done. You'll have to prioritize; focus on your weaknesses and take at least two or three practice tests. The more time and energy you can carve out for preparation for the GMAT, the better.

Two weeks until test day

▶ Take the diagnostic test in this book. Examine your performance and really home in on your weaknesses. You probably are not going to have time to study every chapter in this book in depth; you'll make the best use of your time by focusing on shoring up your weak areas. Decide what areas you need to focus on and prioritize.

▶ Schedule time over the next week to go through the chapters of this book that deal with the weak areas you have identified based on your performance on the diagnostic test. Work through no more than one chapter in a sitting. For best retention, read the chapter and work half of the practice problems in one study session, then review the chapter and work the remainder of the practice problems in a later study session.

One week until test day

▶ Take a GMAT practice test to check your progress.

▶ Schedule time over the several days to address the remaining chapters that you have not yet covered. Try a few questions from the practice problems at the end of each chapter and review what you need from the chapter to clear up any questions you might have.

▶ Above all else, don't get stressed out. Visualize yourself succeeding and try to relax.

▶ Make sure you're not in for any surprises on test day. For example, it's a good idea to actually go to the test center location so you know exactly how to get there, how long it might take, and where you will park (if you are driving).

Three days until test day

▶ Take one more practice test to build your confidence level and practice pacing.

The Day Before the Test (for both sample plans)

No matter what preparation schedule you've chosen, your plan for the day before the test should be the same.

- Try to schedule some relaxing activity so that you keep the stress level low. A brisk walk or other physical activity is great for relieving stress. The goal is to get a good night's sleep. Visualize yourself succeeding on the test and try to avoid getting stressed out.

- Don't cram and don't stay up late. Eat healthy foods and don't do anything to dehydrate yourself. Obviously, drinking a lot of alcohol is not advisable even if it might help reduce stress.

Test Day Strategy

Ready or not, the day for your face-to-face encounter with the GMAT will arrive. Your test-day strategy should include the following:

- Stick to whatever routine will make you most comfortable before you walk into the test center. For example, if you have coffee every morning, have it on the morning before you take the test.

- It is a good idea to eat a healthy breakfast, but don't eat too much, especially if you don't usually eat a substantial breakfast. You don't want to get hungry, but you don't want to feel sluggish either. Bring snacks that you can eat during your two optional timed breaks.

- Keep track of your pace during the test. Pace yourself and do not spend too much time on any particular question. If you don't know an answer, try to quickly eliminate answer choices, make a selection, and move on. Remember that about 20 percent of the questions you see will not affect your score at all; they are used as experimental questions to help in developing new tests. So don't waste time on a question; it may not even count.

- As far as whether you should guess on the GMAT goes—given that it's computer-adaptive—the best favor you can do for yourself is to focus on finishing each section on your practice tests in the given time limits so you can do the same on test day.

- Read each question carefully and completely. This will help you avoid silly mistakes on questions that you should get right.

Getting the Most from the Interactive Practice Tests

McGraw-Hill Education: GMAT gives you a number of options to practice for the exam. You can practice using this book, your tablet or smartphone, or your laptop or home computer. Whether you use a PC or a Mac or a tablet or smartphone with the Apple, Android, or Windows platform, you'll be able to practice on the device of your choosing.

In addition to the diagnostic test and two practice tests in this book, **six more practice tests** are available as part of the **Premium Practice Test App** and on the companion website, **MHE Practice Plus**.

Features of the Interactive Practice Tests

The interactive practice tests found on the mobile app and the companion website offer a number of features that will help you meet your study goals:

- The app and website include six additional practice tests that will enhance your preparation for the exam.

- You can choose whether to take a test section timed or open-ended, depending on your practice goals.

- When you finish a section of a test, you will immediately receive a score that shows the percentage of correct answers.

- Your scores will be saved so you can refer back to them and follow your progress.

- Review mode allows you to see your answer and the correct answer together. (We hope they're the same!) Here you'll find a concise and clear explanation for the answer. Moreover, you'll still be able to see the original question for reference.

- If you exit a test section before finishing it, you can simply return to where you left off at a later time.

Accessing the Premium Practice Test App

If you take the six practice tests on your tablet or smartphone, you will find the Premium Practice Test App to be the ideal companion to your study plans. Depending on the device you have, go to one of the following:

Apple → iTunes
Android → Google Play
Windows → Apps for Windows

Once you are at the appropriate app store, search "McGraw-Hill Education GMAT Premium Practice Test App" and download.

Accessing the Practice Tests Online

Visit http://www.mhpracticeplus.com/gmat.php to access the online version of the practice tests. Click on "Begin Practice Tests" and you will have access to the six practice tests to use on your laptop or home computer.

GMAT Information
for International Test Takers

More and more people taking the GMAT do not live in the United States. The largest numbers of non-U.S. citizens taking the GMAT come from India, China, Korea, Canada, and Taiwan.

Registering for the Test

Everyone—whether taking the test in the United States or some other country—has to register for the test in advance. The test is administered by the Graduate Management Admissions Council (GMAC), and information about the test and registration procedures is available at its site, www.mba.com.

Finding a Testing Center

With permanent testing centers in 98 countries, most applicants should not have trouble finding a place to take the test. If there are no centers near your home, you will need to travel to one. When you register for the GMAT, you will need to schedule a test appointment at a specific testing center. Go to www.mba.com for a complete listing of testing centers worldwide. The testing fee is the same at all test centers worldwide.

How to Register

When registering, you will enter your birth date in the order in which it tends to be written in the U.S.: month/day/year. You may register online, by telephone, by fax, or by mail. You will need to pay the testing fee by credit or debit card if registering online, by fax, or by phone. If you want to pay by check or money order, you must register by mail. To register online, you must sign up as a registered user at www.mba.com. If you wish to register by telephone, you may do so by calling the number provided below for your region. To register by fax, download the appropriate form from www.mba.com and fax it to the number for your region listed below.

The Americas

E-mail: GMATCandidateServicesAmericas@pearson.com
Telephone (toll-free within the U.S. and Canada): +1 (800) 717-GMAT (4628), 7 a.m. to 7 p.m. Central Time
Telephone: +1 (952) 681-3680, 7:00 a.m. to 7:00 p.m. Central Time
Fax: +1 (952) 681-3681

Asia and Pacific Region

Email: GMATCandidateServicesAPAC@pearson.com
Telephone: +852-3077-4926, 9 a.m. to 6 p.m. Australian Eastern Standard Time
In India: +91 120-439-7830, 9 a.m. to 6 p.m. Indian Standard Time
Fax: +91-120-4001660

China

Email: gmatservice@neea.edu.cn
Telephone: +86-10-82345675, Monday–Friday, 8:30 a.m. to 5 p.m. China Standard Time
Fax: +86-10-61957800

Email: GMATCandidateServicesEMEA@pearson.com
Telephone: +44 (0) 161 855 7219, 9 a.m. to 5 p.m. Greenwich Mean Time
Fax: +44 (0) 161 855 7301

It is important to register well in advance—especially good advice if you plan to take the test outside the United States. In some countries the number of people wishing to take the test may sometimes exceed test-center capabilities, resulting in a wait of three to five weeks. Also, keep in mind that you will want to start taking the GMAT early enough so that you have the option of retaking the test before submitting your applications. In nearly all cases, business schools will use only your best score. Thus many people—especially international students—take the test more than once.

Taking the Test

Testing centers around the world are similar and implement the same testing procedures. Everyone takes the test on a computer—gone are the days of the paper GMAT—but the computer skills required of test takers are minimal. You need to be able to use a mouse and word processor, enter responses, move to the next question, and access help. Keep in mind, however, that using the help function could steal valuable time from you during the test.

> The test is given on a standard English-language (QWERTY) computer keyboard; if you aren't used to this keyboard, make sure you practice on one before you arrive on test day. (This keyboard is also used for the TOEFL and PTE discussed below.)

Identification Requirements

On test day, you will be required to present proper identification in order to take your test. Your government-issued ID must have the following:

- Valid date (unexpired), legibility, and your name shown in the Roman alphabet exactly as you provided when you made your test appointment, including the order and placement of the names
- Your date of birth (must match the date provided when you registered for your test appointment)
- A recent, recognizable photograph
- Your signature

In most cases, the following are the only forms of identification that will be accepted at the test center.

- Passport (or green card if you are a permanent U.S. resident taking the test in the United States)
- Government-issued driver's license
- Government-issued national/state/province identity card
- Military ID card

Before you go to the test center, check online at www.mba.com to verify the latest requirements for identification. Note that if you are taking the GMAT in Bangladesh, China (including Hong Kong), India, Japan, Pakistan, Singapore, or South Korea, you must present your passport as identification.

Test Preparation for International Test Takers

GMAC makes sure that the GMAT is not biased against international test takers. The test makers pre-test all questions by including them in "experimental" test sections given to both U.S. and international test takers. If statistics prove that any of the new questions put international test takers at a disadvantage, those items never appear on the test. Still, international test takers face certain challenges.

Improving Your English

The most obvious difficulty for non-native English–speaking test takers is the language barrier. The entire test, including instructions and questions, is in English. Much of the test is focused on verbal skills, and part is a writing test, which requires not only an understanding of the language but a command of it. Your writing, reading comprehension, and grammar skills are directly tested on the GMAT.

Most experts advise non-native English speakers to read as much in English as they can in the months leading up to the test. Financial and business articles are particularly useful to get used to the business terms that might be on the exam.

Other activities that might help you are creating and using flash cards with difficult English words on them and practicing your English by communicating with others who speak the language. To improve your understanding of spoken English, you can watch American TV shows (often now available online). Keep a journal and express your thoughts about what you've read and seen in writing. Your goal should be to practice presenting evidence in a cohesive and interesting way to support your arguments in the writing section of the exam. When you read items from American publications, pay particular attention to how the writers gather evidence and present it because there are often subtle cultural differences at play. Remember that the quantitative part of the GMAT is also in English, so it's a good idea to review math formulas and glossaries in English.

Becoming Familiar with Standardized Tests

Getting acquainted with standardized tests is another must-do for international test takers. This type of exam is a part of the average American's educational experience but is not necessarily a cultural norm in other parts of the world. Some people outside the United States may be unfamiliar with multiple-choice questions. These are questions in which you must select the correct answer from several given choices. There are strategies for choosing the best one when you're not sure. For example, you can eliminate answers that you know are incorrect and then choose among the remaining choices. This is called "taking an educated guess," and it can improve your chances of picking the correct answer.

Timing is a very important part of standardized tests. Keeping calm is the first step to overcoming the pressure. Taking practice tests is key to learning how to pace yourself to maximize your performance in a limited time period. Taking practice tests will also help you become familiar with the test format. Understanding the instructions for each part of the test in advance can save you time during the exam because you won't have to spend time on the instructions in addition to the other reading you have to do.

Another Hurdle: Testing Your English Language Skills

If you received your undergraduate degree from an institution in a country whose official language is not English, the MBA program to which you are applying will likely require you to submit proof of your English proficiency along with your GMAT scores. Most institutions accept scores on either the TOEFL (Test of English as a Foreign Language) or the IELTS (International English Language Testing System); many now also accept scores on the newer PTE (Pearson Test of English). Check with the programs to which you are applying for information about their test requirements. There is no specific passing score on these tests; graduate institutions set their own requirements.

▶ TOEFL: The TOEFL iBT is an Internet-based test administered on 30 to 40 dates a year at more than 4,500 sites around the world. A paper-based version (TOEFL PBT) is still used but only in a few locations where Internet access is not reliable. For more information including the format of the test, scoring, and registration, visit www.ets.org/toefl. The TOEFL iBT captures the test taker's speech and uses this to measure English-speaking ability in a standardized manner. Multiple-choice questions are used to measure reading and listening abilities. Two essay questions are used to measure writing abilities.

▶ IELTS: The IELTS is a paper-based test created at Cambridge University in the UK. It consists of four modules—Listening, Reading, Writing, and Speaking. Question types include multiple choice, sentence completion, short answer, classification, matching, labeling, and diagram/chart interpretation. The Speaking test is a face-to-face interview with a certified examiner. IELTS has two versions: Academic and General Training. The Academic test is for those who want to study at a tertiary level in an English-speaking country. The General Training test is for those who want to do work experience or training programs, enroll in secondary school, or migrate to an English-speaking country. For more information, visit www.ielts.org.

▶ PTE: The PTE was developed by Pearson, an international educational testing and publishing company. Like the TOEFL iBT, it is administered at testing centers on a computer (there is no paper version). Visit www.pearsonpte.com for more information about the PTE and updated lists of the schools that accept it and the locations where it is given. Like the TOEFL, the PTE uses multiple-choice questions plus essay questions to measure reading, listening, and writing skills. A 30-second audio clip of the test taker's speech is sent to schools along with the test scores.

Preparing for English Language Tests

There are many products available to help you prepare for the TOEFL; the most reliable is ETS's own book, *The Official Guide to the TOEFL® Test* (published by McGraw-Hill Education), which includes a CD-ROM and sample tests. The TOEFL, IELTS, and PTE websites offer free test samples and, for a fee, additional practice materials.

The best preparation for English proficiency exams is simply to improve your abilities to communicate in English. (See "Improving Your English" above. Since the TOEFL, IELTS, and PTE are standardized tests characterized by time limits and multiple-choice questions, see also "Becoming Familiar with Standardized Tests" above.) If you need to take dramatic steps to get your English up to the level you need to attend an American university, a number of companies offer English-immersion courses, including courses in the United States and other English-speaking countries.

Admission to U.S. Business Schools

People who live outside the United States but are considering American business schools often have lots of questions about the application process. The following box shows some issues that come up frequently.

Business School Admissions: Fact or Fiction?

Certain parts of the application are weighted more than others by the business school's admissions committee.

FICTION. The overwhelming majority of admissions directors will tell you that they—and their colleagues—read each application cover to cover. Every section is important. They want to get a sense of who the applicant is and what he or she "brings to the table." Your GMAT score and GPA from undergraduate studies will tell them if you can handle the academic rigor of the institution. The TOEFL score will prove your English-language proficiency if you do not speak English as your native language. Recommendations will provide evidence from an objective third party who knows you and your work well. Your work experience will shed light on what you've been doing with your time since earning an undergraduate degree, or its equivalent. For insight into who you are as a person and the qualities you will bring to campus, your essays will be used.

Your application must show that you write well in English. There is no room for errors; spelling and grammar must be impeccable. Also, be sure you understand the questions being asked and that you are answering them directly. You do not have to be fancy or use flowery language. Keep your essays straightforward and to the point. Use simple language and lots of examples that support your thesis. Be honest and genuine. Having someone read your essay and offer his or her opinion is advisable. But do not have someone write the essay for you—and never plagiarize. If you have a question about something, pick up the phone or send an email to the admissions office; most offices are happy to take queries from potential students.

American business schools only accept a certain number of applicants from each region. Therefore, if many people from my country or region apply to a particular business school, I have less of a chance of getting accepted.

FACT and FICTION. While admissions committees deny having any sort of quota system, they admit that they seek diversity when trying to put together the next class for their business school. But they see diversity as more than just being about ethnic, cultural, and racial groups. The schools are also looking for people in different industries and functions with different aspirations for the future. To keep a competitive edge, you should focus in your application on what's unique about you so that you aren't seen as just another person out of the same mold.

You must write what you think the admissions committee wants to see in the application essays.

FICTION. Many international applicants mistakenly think that there is some sort of template or formula to writing an effective essay. While it is true that you must write in a straightforward, well-organized manner, you will most likely fail if you try to write what you think the admissions committee members want to see. If you pick up a book of essays from applications that had been accepted and try to mimic what someone else wrote, you risk having your application rejected. All school representatives really want to see is someone who has a passion for their program and has a plan for his or her life and career. They want to know why you have chosen to apply to their school and how their school will help you accomplish your future goals. The more specific you can get about what you'd like to do, when, how, and what role the school will play in this plan, the happier they will be. Of course, they want to see your unique perspective on the subject. Tell your story in an interesting way because they have to read hundreds—sometimes thousands—of these essays, and you want to keep them captivated. Authenticity combined with a dash of creativity will win every time.

The Business School Interview

Most American business schools require applicants to interview with someone from the school, usually a graduate or an administrator trained to conduct applicant interviews. Sometimes an interview may be optional. Every school is different, so you should look into this when you're filling out your application, to know what to expect.

You already know how important it is for non-native English speakers to gain fluency before applying to business school in the United States. Knowing the rules of a language or even having a good vocabulary is not enough. You also need to be able to carry on a conversation with native English speakers. This is particularly important when you are interviewing with business schools. Many of the interviews are behavioral, which means the school will be asking you questions about yourself, your experiences, and how you have handled particular situations. There are usually no trick questions. The interviewers simply want to know a little more about you and get a sense of the type of personality you will be bringing to campus.

Preparing for the Interview

To prepare for the interview, you should practice answering questions in English, preferably with an English-speaking person. You should probably think about specific examples of your leadership, management skills, and values. Seriously consider what drew you to this particular school, what its culture is like, why you would fit in there, and how the school can help you achieve your career goals. Also, come up with intelligent questions to ask about the school. Seize the opportunity. Refrain from asking questions whose answers will appear on the school's website, such as how many credits do I need to graduate, or what are the core requirements? Instead, ask about the workload you should expect or the events the school offers to unify the community.

Face-to-Face Versus Telephone Interviews

Schools tend to prefer face-to-face interviews, but those are not always possible for international applicants. Sometimes, applicants from abroad have to participate in the interview via telephone. If, however, you are planning a campus visit anyway, then you can try to schedule a face-to-face interview. For an in-person meeting, you should plan to dress in business attire. Keep it simple and conservative.

One Last Hurdle: The Student Visa

Nonresidents of the United States will need to obtain a visa to live in the United States. In the years following the September 11 terrorist attacks, there have been lots of rumors about who gets visas and who does not. The biggest change has been that every student must be officially cleared by the government before receiving a visa. This does not change the process for you, but you will need to give yourself plenty of time. Once you have been accepted to business school and have chosen an institution to attend, the process of obtaining a student visa must begin. At the very least, you should get started three months before you need the visa. Besides needing time to complete the requisite forms, you will also need to schedule an appointment for the required embassy consular interview, and waiting times for this vary and can be lengthy.

Visa Requirements

During the student visa process, you are expected to prove that you have adequate financing to study in the United States, ties to your home country, and a likelihood that you will return home after finishing your studies. In addition, you will have to participate in an ink-free, digital fingerprint scan and provide a passport valid for travel to the United States and with a validity date at least six months beyond your intended period of stay. The school will provide you with an I-20 form to complete. Your school will use this to register you with the Student and Exchange Visitor Information System (SEVIS), an Internet-based system that maintains accurate and current information on nonimmigrant students and exchange visitors and their families. You'll also need to submit a completed and signed nonimmigrant visa application with Form DS-160 and photo that meets the requirements outlined on the website. You'll find information on all this and more at the U.S. Department of State website:

http://travel.state.gov/content/visas/english/study-exchange.html

Transcripts, diplomas from previous institutions, scores from standardized tests such as the GMAT and TOEFL, and proof you can afford the school (such as income tax records, original bank books and statements) are things you should have on hand. If you have dependents, you will also need documents that prove your relationship to your spouse and children (think marriage license and birth certificates).

Obtaining the U.S. Visa

Dealing with a bureaucracy can get frustrating. It is important to stay calm and do your best to follow the instructions. Remember to call on your business school if you need help. Although meeting deadlines, starting early, and turning in all the paperwork does not guarantee that you will receive a visa, it does increase your chances of having an easier time. Anything you can do to streamline the application and entrance process into business school will serve you well as you move your life from one country to another.

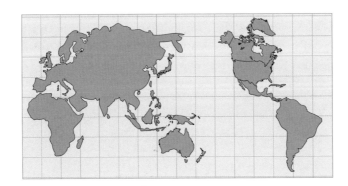

McGraw-Hill Education
GMAT*
2018

McGraw-Hill Education

GMAT*

2018

Sandra Luna McCune

Shannon Reed

New York Chicago San Francisco Athens London Madrid
Mexico City Milan New Delhi Singapore Sydney Toronto

1 2 3 4 5 6 7 8 9 0   LHS   21 20 19 18 17 (book for cross-platform prep course)
1 2 3 4 5 6 7 8 9 0   LHS   21 20 19 18 17 (book alone)

ISBN   978-1-260-01168-5   (cross-platform prep course)
MHID   1-260-01168-2

e-ISBN   978-1-260-01169-2   (e-book cross-platform prep course)
e-MHID   1-260-01169-0

ISBN   978-1-260-01166-1   (book alone)
MHID   1-260-01166-6

e-ISBN   978-1-260-01167-8   (e-book alone)
e-MHID   1-260-01167-4

GMAT is a registered trademark of Graduate Management Admission Council, which was not involved in the production of, and does not endorse, this product.

McGraw-Hill Education books are available at special quantity discounts to use as premiums and sales promotions or for use in corporate training programs. To contact a representative, please visit the Contact Us pages at www.mhprofessional.com.

Contents

PART 6   GMAT Math Review

PART 7   The GMAT Verbal Section

PART 8   GMAT Practice Tests

McGraw-Hill Education

GMAT*

2018

PART 1

Getting Started

CHAPTER 1

Introducing the GMAT

The Graduate Management Admission Council (GMAC) owns the GMAT. GMAC develops and delivers the exam in coordination with two service providers: Pearson VUE and ACT. ACT designs and develops the exam, which is delivered at Pearson VUE authorized test centers.

Structure and Format of the GMAT

The GMAT is a computer-based, three-and-a-half-hour writing and selected-response exam. For the writing section, you type a written response onto the computer screen using a word processing program. For the selected-response questions, you click an on-screen button or select from a drop-down menu to indicate your answer choices. Most of the selected-response questions are traditional multiple-choice questions with five response options.

The GMAT is divided into four sections: Analytical Writing Assessment (AWA), Integrated Reasoning (IR), Quantitative, and Verbal. The order, number of questions and types, and lengths of the sections are shown in the following table.

GMAT SECTION	NUMBER OF QUESTIONS	QUESTION TYPE	ALLOTTED TIME
AWA	1	Written response	30 minutes
IR	12	Various selected-response	30 minutes
Quantitative	37	Traditional multiple-choice	75 minutes
Verbal	41	Traditional multiple-choice	75 minutes

Total Allotted Testing Time $3\frac{1}{2}$ hours

In the **AWA section** you will have 30 minutes to write a written analysis of a presented argument. You will type your response on the computer screen using a basic word processing program.

The **Integrated Reasoning section** of the GMAT is designed to be presented electronically. This section will include 12 questions to be completed in 30 minutes. You may need to sort data in spreadsheets or make calculations with the help of an on-screen calculator.

The questions ask you to assess the truth of statements based on given information, decide whether certain conclusions reasonably can be drawn, complete statements correctly, and determine values of two variables. The questions are presented in clusters, with each cluster preceded by data, graphs, or other information on which the questions are based. The questions will have one of four formats: table analysis, graphics interpretation, multi-source reasoning, and two-part analysis. Table analysis questions present data in a spreadsheet-like format. You will be able to sort the data by clicking on the column headings. The questions ask you to choose yes or no, true or false, or consistent or inconsistent to statements based on the information in the table. Graphics interpretation questions present information in a graph or other visual representation. The questions ask you to choose from drop-down menus the correct word or phrase to make a given statement true. Multi-source reasoning questions present several sources of information, such as memos, e-mails, newspaper articles, or graphical material. Your task is to decide if the information supports the conclusions in the statements that follow. Two-part analysis questions describe a situation in which two related values are unknown, and you must indicate the value of each.

The multiple-choice Quantitative and Verbal sections are designed as computer-adaptive tests. You are presented with only one question at a time. Once you answer a question and move on, you can't go back to it. The computer gives you harder or easier questions depending on whether your previous responses were right or wrong.

The **Quantitative section** of the GMAT consists of 37 questions with a 75-minute time limit. Note: You will not be allowed to use a calculator for this section. The questions test your knowledge of and skills in arithmetic, basic probability and statistics, elementary algebra, and basic geometry. Two question types are presented in the Quantitative section: problem solving and data sufficiency. Problem-solving questions are multiple-choice questions with five answer choice options. You must select the one best answer choice. Data sufficiency are also multiple-choice questions with five answer choice options. However, as you will learn in Chapter 7, the five answer choice options are always the same from question to question. These questions are unique to the GMAT. You are presented with a question followed by two statements containing additional information. Your task is to determine whether the data given are sufficient to answer the question posed.

The **Verbal section** of the GMAT consists of 41 multiple-choice questions with a 75-minute time limit. The questions test your proficiency in reading and comprehending text-based materials, evaluating the strengths and weaknesses of arguments, and applying your knowledge of standard written English to correct errors in written material. Three question types are presented in the Verbal section: reading comprehension, sentence correction, and critical reasoning. All questions have five answer choice options from which you must select the one best answer choice.

How to Register

To register for the GMAT, either go online at www.mba.com or call GMAT Customer Service in your region. (More detailed information on registration for international students is available in the front "insert" to this book.) The current registration fee is US $250. Call several weeks ahead of time in order to get the date and time of day you want. You can choose either a morning or an afternoon slot, so pick the time of day when you think you will perform at your best. You can reschedule or cancel your exam online or by phone except that *changes cannot be made within 24 hours of your appointment.* Cancellation refunds and/or rescheduling fees will apply. For additional information about registering for the exam, test fees, and policies and procedures, download the *GMAT Handbook* at http://www.mba.com/us/the-gmat-exam/prepare-for-the-gmat-exam/test-prep-materials/gmat-handbook.aspx.

When to Take the GMAT

If you want to pursue a graduate degree in business, you should apply early to the school of your choice. Make sure to schedule your GMAT so that you will have your score report in time to meet application deadlines. To be practical, you should factor in enough time to retake the exam if you are not satisfied with your score.

Taking the GMAT More Than Once

Business schools expect that you might take the GMAT more than once. You should try to achieve a score in the upper 600s or better. For consideration in the top business schools a score of 700 or better should be your goal. Schools accept only your highest reported score. So, it is doubtful that taking the test more than once will hurt your chances of admission.

Scoring of the GMAT

When you complete your exam, you will be shown your unofficial GMAT Integrated Reasoning, Quantitative, Verbal, and Total scores. (Your score on the Analytical Writing Assessment requires a human grader, so it will arrive in the mail a few weeks after you take the GMAT.) You will have two minutes to decide whether to cancel or accept your scores. After two minutes, your scores will be canceled automatically. If your scores are canceled, you will not be able to view them again. If you accept your scores, you will pick up a printed copy of your unofficial score report from the test administrator before you leave the testing center. The following table shows the scoring range and scoring guidelines for the exam sections.

GMAT SECTION	SCORE RANGE	SCORING GUIDELINES
AWA	0.0 to 6.0	Each response is scored at least twice. The section score is the average, reported in increments of 0.5.
IR	1 to 8	The score is based on the number of questions answered correctly. Candidates receive credit for questions with multiple parts *only* if all parts of the question are answered correctly.
Quantitative	0 to 60	The score is based on the number of questions answered, the number of correct answers, and the difficulty level of the questions answered. Scores are reported in increments of 1.
Verbal	0 to 60	The score is based on the number of questions answered, the number of correct answers, and the difficulty level of the questions answered. Scores are reported in increments of 1.
Total	200 to 800	The score is a scale score based on the raw scores from the Quantitative and Verbal sections, reported in increments of 10.

How Business Schools Use Your GMAT Score

More than 5,000 programs around the world use the GMAT exam to help in making admission decisions about students. Of course, your GMAT score is one of many factors such as GPA, professional experience, letters of recommendation, and activities and awards that are considered. Nevertheless, your GMAT scores give recruiters and admissions officers information they use to judge whether you can be successful in their graduate programs. After all, you are competing with other candidates for a spot in the business school of your choice. You will be compared to each of them, so you want to achieve a strong score that will give you a competitive edge over other candidates. This book is designed to help you do just that.

GMAT CAT: Questions and Answers

Which Sections on the GMAT Use Computer Adaptive Testing (CAT)?

Only the Quantitative and Verbal sections use CAT. The Analytical Writing section requires you to write a critique of an argument. The Integrated Reasoning section presents a fixed set of items for all test takers.

Are All GMAT CAT Questions the Same from Test Taker to Test Taker?

No. GMAT CAT questions are uniquely selected for each test taker. CAT is a computer-based assessment method that uses an algorithm to target test-question difficulty to a test taker's estimated ability. Accordingly, it is highly improbable that another test taker will see exactly the same combination of CAT questions that you do.

How Does CAT Work?

When you begin a given section, the computer starts with a mid-range ability estimate and presents you with a question of medium difficulty. The way you answer question 1 determines the difficulty level of question 2. If you answer question 1 correctly, question 2 is more difficult. If you answer incorrectly, question 2 is easier. This process is repeated as you proceed through the test. You are presented with only one question at a time. You cannot skip a question. Before you can go to the next question, you must select your answer and confirm it. Once you confirm your answer to a question, you must move on. *You are not allowed to revisit questions and change answers.*

How Is My Final Ability Estimate Determined?

The questions for your test are selected from a large question bank. After each question, a new *interim* ability estimate for you is calculated. The next question is selected based on this updated ability estimate and on constraints imposed on the test (such as content coverage). As you continue to answer questions, the difficulty level of subsequent questions oscillates, depending on whether you answer correctly (in which case the difficulty level goes up) or incorrectly (in which case the difficulty level goes down). Your estimated ability will also fluctuate up and down. Eventually, the computer settles on an estimated ability for you that takes into account all the questions you have answered. Thereafter, the computer presents questions closely matched to that new (less erratic) estimate. This process continues until a fixed number of questions have been presented or when time expires. At this point your final ability estimate is calculated and used to determine your score.

How Can I Maximize My GMAT CAT Score?

The computer determines your score using a procedure that takes into account the following information:

- *Number of questions you answer correctly*

  Every question counts. Come to the test prepared to do your best. Don't expect to do well by random guessing. Know the content and be familiar with the question types. Practice, practice, practice!

- *Difficulty level of the questions you answer*

  As you answer questions correctly, you are presented with questions of increasing difficulty. The more of these difficult questions you answer, the higher your final score. In addition, you are awarded more points for responding correctly to a difficult question than for answering an easier question correctly.

- *Number of questions you answer*

  You incur a severe scoring penalty for leaving questions unanswered at the end of a section. Leaving five questions blank can drop you as many as 15 percentile points. Manage your time wisely, so that you do not run out of time at the end.

What Else Should I Know About CAT?

Here is some additional advice.

- *Don't waste mental energy trying to identify questions as easy or difficult.*

  There's no way for you to know for sure the difficulty level of a particular question. A question can be easy for you yet be one that is designated as difficult in the test bank, and vice versa.

- *Avoid spending too much time on any one question.*

  If a question is taking up too much time, eliminate answer choices that you know are wrong, and then make your best guess from among the remaining choices. By guessing and moving on, you give yourself time to answer upcoming questions that you might get right.

- *Don't be upset about guessing.*

  Expect to have to guess on some questions. Just about everyone who takes the GMAT has to guess. Just make sure you guess cleverly by using elimination strategies.

- *Don't think you can outsmart the test.*

  You may have heard or read that devoting more time to the first 5 to 10 questions will up your score. Although the computer does use the first few questions as a basis for its initial estimate of your ability, as you are presented with additional questions, your ability estimate is continually updated. Your score is based on what your ability estimate is at the end of the section. It is certainly okay to give an adequate amount of time and attention to those first questions, the same as you should to every question. *The most effective strategy for a successful outcome on the GMAT is to answer <u>every</u> question you see to the best of your ability!*

CHAPTER 2

GMAT Test-Taking Strategies

Now that you have a clear understanding of what the GMAT is and why business schools want you to take it, it's time to think about preparing for the test itself. Of course, this book will guide you through getting ready for every section of the test, but in this chapter, we'll cover general test-taking tips, as well as how to pace yourself once the big day has arrived. Finally, we'll review what to do the day of the test.

General Strategies

Approaches for specific question types form the bulk of the rest of the book. It's important to understand each section of the test so you'll be able to quickly get to the business of answering questions on the real test without reading the instructions for the first time. Practicing with the problem-solving drills we've provided, as well as taking the practice tests, will also help. Here, let's look at general test-taking suggestions that should prove helpful to you.

Make Good Use of Your Time

The GMAT is a marathon; the test takes nearly four hours to complete. But it's also a sprint; on average, you have less than two minutes for each Verbal question, and about two minutes for each Quantitative or Integrated Reasoning question. Time is of the essence. Once you begin the test, a clock appears on your computer screen. It will count down the amount of time you have left. While you can hide the clock if it's too stressful or distracting, it's worth checking it every now and again to make sure you're not lingering over a problem too long.

The clock that's programmed to appear on your computer screen will reappear when there are five minutes left in the section. If you think worrying about it popping up will distract you, practice with an on-screen clock at home. You can either have the clock on screen at all times, or set it on a timer so it appears at five minutes until the end.

Make Your Best Guess and Move On

You don't want to guess blindly throughout the test. Your score will be affected if you do. But because of the way the test is set up, your score will suffer much more if you do not complete the exam. So try to eliminate the answers that are clearly wrong, make your best guess, and keep moving! If you have guessed incorrectly, the software is likely to offer you an easier question next—and that's not the worst thing in the world.

Read All the Directions

Yes, you'll have read similar instructions in this practice book. Still, you should skim the instructions for each section before you begin, and click on the "Help" button during the test if you want to review them again. There's no benefit to blindly answering questions without really being sure of what you're being asked to do!

Read All Questions Carefully

Don't skim the questions themselves, as tempting as it may be. The test makers love to trip you up with trickily worded questions. As stressful as it is to be so rushed for time, slow down and read the questions—and their possible answers—very carefully.

Just as you read the questions carefully, you should read all of the possible answers carefully. Mixing up 100 and 1000 could sink the answer for you. So could reading *egregious* for *erudite*. Make sure you're reading what's on the page, not just what your brain has already decided is the correct answer!

Don't Confirm Your Answer Until You're Sure

Many sections of the test will ask you to "confirm" your answer before you move on to the next response. Keep in mind that once you click "confirm," you can't go back to the question and reconsider it. Similarly, the test may present several questions to you on one page. While you can move around within that page to answer the questions as you choose, once you move on to the next screen, you can't go back. So be sure!

Outline Your Essay First

We'll cover the Analytical Writing Assignment in great depth in Part 3, but it's worth remembering now: always outline your essay before you begin writing. Take the time to read and understand the question's premise, jot down a few notes about the response you want to make, and organize your ideas. It will make a huge difference in your final score by helping you to write a clear, organized essay.

Timing and Pacing

The GMAT consists of four sections, each of which is separately timed. The Analytical Writing Assessment—more commonly known as the essay or the AWA—comes first. You'll get only one question for this section, and 30 minutes to answer it. That's enough time, if you work with focus, to read the question carefully, outline a response, and type the essay into the computer.

The AWA is followed by a 30-minute Integrated Reasoning section, including 12 questions in four different formats. This section is followed by an optional timed break. Our advice is to take that break, even if you don't feel like you need it. You'll be only an hour or so in at this point, with over half of the test still to come. Pace yourself.

The break is followed by the Quantitative section, which asks 37 questions in 75 minutes. There's a chance for another quick break after it. If you know it will serve you well to take your eyes off the keyboard, stretch, and use the facilities, do so. Whatever you do, don't start rushing—that's the way mistakes happen.

We can't tell you what to do, but taking the breaks offered to you makes good sense. If you skip them, you're done about 15 minutes sooner, which isn't much of a time saver. But if you take them, you'll probably feel better. After all, you'll take care of your bodily needs and clear your head before digging in again.

The test ends with a 41-question Verbal section, again lasting 75 minutes. And then, after a little housekeeping, you're free!

Move through the test with focus, but don't try to race the clock. Yes, you do want to finish before the section's time is up, because not finishing a section will adversely affect your score. But there's no point in racing through questions to find that you have five minutes left in a section. You won't be able to go back to prior questions except the last one, if you haven't submitted it. You could've used that time on the questions!

While an almost four-hour test does sound incredibly intimidating—and isn't any fun while you're there—it's helpful to keep in mind that this is a one-shot (okay, possibly two-shot) opportunity. Let's be honest: you don't want to come back to take this test over and over. You want to do well the first time. Take your time and pace yourself so that your first GMAT is also your best GMAT.

The Day of the Test

- Don't stay up late the night before cramming or blowing off steam. Eat healthy foods for the entire day before the test, and stay away from caffeine and alcohol, which could impair your sleep. You don't want to be dehydrated, either, so make sure you drink plenty of water.
- Don't change your routine the day of the test. If you always have a bowl of cereal for breakfast, have a bowl of cereal. There's no point in stressing yourself out more by preparing a fruit smoothie for the first time, just because you think it'll help your cognitive ability.
- Understand what time you need to be at the testing center. This may be considerably earlier than the time your test is scheduled to begin.
- Know how to get to the testing facility, and leave in plenty of time to get there. If you're driving, make sure you know where to park. If you're taking public transportation, check schedules for arrival times and delays. If a friend or family member is driving

you, send him or her a text in the morning to make sure the person is up and ready to get you. Many testing centers will not allow you to reschedule without an additional fee, so you need to be there on time.

- Pack a snack that you can eat during your breaks. You get about eight minutes, and that's enough time for a granola bar or apple.

- Wear comfortable clothes. This isn't a fashion show, so wear whatever will be least distracting to you. Watch out for belts that cut into your waist. You may want to bring a light sweater or non-outerwear jacket if the testing center has the possibility of being too air-conditioned. If you're taking the test in the winter, you may want to dress in layers just in case it's overheated or not heated enough.

- Try to remember that the people who run the testing center must deal with dozens of very nervous people every day. They may not respond as quickly as you would like. But don't get frazzled. Everything will work out, and a smile and a kind word always go a long way.

- Don't make plans for immediately after the test. You don't want to feel like you have to rush to meet up with a friend if the testing center can't start your test immediately for some reason.

- While you can't take anything into the testing area with you, you may want to stash some aspirin or other pain reliever in your bag for after you finish—it's not uncommon to have a headache at the end!

PART 2

Diagnostic Test

CHAPTER 3
Take a Diagnostic Test

Take a Diagnostic Test

How to Use the Diagnostic Test

This chapter presents a sample GMAT diagnostic test. The test is the same length as the GMAT. Its questions have been designed to match real GMAT questions as closely as possible in terms of format and degree of difficulty. You should use this test as a launch point to determine your strengths and weaknesses, and to identify how far your current score is from your score goal.

1. **Take the diagnostic test under test-like conditions.** Find a quiet place where you will not be disturbed. Take the test as if it were the actual GMAT. Work through the test from beginning to end in one sitting. Mark your answers directly on the test pages. Observe the time limit given at the start of each section. If you have not finished a section when time runs out, mark the last question you answered and note how much longer it takes you to complete the section. This will tell you if you need to speed up your pace, and if so, by how much.

2. **Answer every question.** On the real GMAT, there is no added penalty for wrong answers, so it makes sense to answer every question, even if you have to guess. If you don't know an answer, see if you can eliminate one or more of the answer choices. The more choices you can eliminate, the better your chance of guessing correctly.

3. **Check your answers**. Go to the Answers and Explanations section at the end of the test. Pay particular attention to the explanations for questions you missed.

4. **Fill out the evaluation charts.** These charts are located after the Answers and Explanations section. Mark the numbers of the questions you missed, and the charts will show you which sections of this book you need to spend the most study time on.

DIAGNOSTIC TEST

Analytical Writing Assessment

Analysis of an Argument

Time—30 minutes

Directions: In this section, you will be asked to write a critique of the argument presented below. You may, for example, consider what questionable assumptions underlie the thinking, what alternative explanations or counterexamples might weaken the conclusion, or what sort of evidence could help strengthen or refute the argument.

Read the argument and the instructions that follow it, and then make any notes that will help you plan your response. Write your response on a separate sheet of paper. If possible, type your essay on a computer or laptop. Observe the 30-minute time limit.

The following letter was printed in a medical journal:

Many nonprescription drugs can cause serious side effects, particularly when taken in conjunction with other drugs or in large quantities. If these potentially harmful nonprescription drugs were sold only by prescription, then a doctor or pharmacist would be able to explain the possible side effects of the drug and would also be able to monitor the quantity of the drug purchased, thereby decreasing the chance that a person would take too much of the drug. Therefore, any drug with potentially serious side effects should be sold only by prescription.

Discuss how well-reasoned you find this argument. In your discussion, be sure to analyze the line of reasoning and the use of evidence in the argument. For example, you may need to consider what questionable assumptions underlie the thinking and what alternative examples or counterexamples might weaken the conclusion. You can also discuss what sort of evidence would strengthen or refute the argument, what changes in the argument would make it more logically sound, and what, if anything, would help you better evaluate its conclusion.

Integrated Reasoning

Time—30 minutes

Select the best answer or answers for the questions below. You may use a calculator for this section of the test only.

> On the actual test, you will be provided with an online calculator. You will NOT be permitted to bring your own calculator to the test.

1. Practice Tech currently offers 2,000 courses per year, and Jameson Vocational currently offers 3,200 courses per year. The number of courses offered by each school increases each year at a constant rate. If each of these schools continues to offer an increased number of courses annually at its constant rate, in three years both schools will offer the same number of courses for the first time. Each year after three years, Practice Tech will offer more courses per year than Jameson Vocational. In the table below, identify the rates of increase, in annual courses offered, for each school that together meet the course offering forecasts described above. Select only one option in each column.

PRACTICE TECH	JAMESON VOCATIONAL	RATE OF INCREASE (COURSES PER YEAR)
○	○	250
○	◉	400
○	○	540
○	○	600
○	○	760
◉	○	800

2. The following graph is a scatter plot with 64 points, each representing the average number of publication subscriptions per month received over the previous five years by 64 households in a focus group and the corresponding annual income for each household. The annual income, measured in thousands of dollars, was reported for the tax year immediately before the focus group was held. The solid line is the regression line. Select the best answer to fill in the blank for each of the following statements, based on the data shown in the graph.

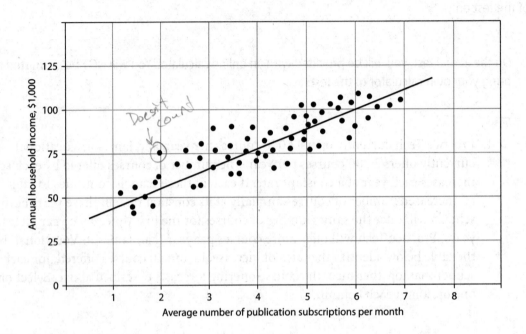

The number of households that average less than three subscriptions per month and have incomes greater than $75,000 is _____ .

correct Answer

(A) 2

(B) 3

(C) 4

It can be inferred from the scatter plot that the correlation between the average number of subscriptions and annual income is _____ .

(A) negative

(B) zero

(C) positive

3. The table gives information on the total inventory in 2016 and the total items sold by a national doll importer over a five-year period, from 2012 through 2016. The 20 dolls were included in the table because they fall among the top 25 items imported for sale by the company in terms of both total inventory and total items sold. In addition to listing the total inventory and the total number sold for each doll type, the table also gives the percent of increase or decrease over the 2015 inventory, the 2007–2011 sales numbers, and the rank of each doll type for total inventory and total items sold.

> On the actual exam, you will be able to sort the table by any of its columns. (Columns can be sorted in ascending order only.) The following table is shown sorted in different ways to mirror the test.

Sorted by Material (Column 2)

DOLL			INVENTORY			NUMBER SOLD		
NAME	MATERIAL	OUTFIT	NUMBER	% CHANGE	RANK	NUMBER	% CHANGE	RANK
Sue Good	Cloth	Nightgown	198,621	3.7	11	1,295,682	3.9	4
Oliver Oh	Cloth	Overalls	254,030	−3.0	3	1,142,367	0.1	10
Raggedy Jane	Cloth	Dress	169,545	3.2	16	1,121,738	1.2	12
Mighty Pete	Cloth	Overalls	238,772	−2.9	5	1,001,490	7.0	22
Henry Bee	Hard plastic	Overalls	190,453	1.8	12	1,290,757	8.6	5
Suzie Belle	Hard plastic	Dress	253,908	1.2	4	1,239,008	−0.7	7
Justin	Hard plastic	Uniform	173,009	2.5	14	1,156,374	−1.3	9
Rogelio Rojas	Hard plastic	Overalls	161,294	−0.9	17	1,109,334	4.2	13
Mr. Fixit	Hard plastic	Overalls	203,776	−4.0	9	1,100,768	0.2	15
Jennifer	Hard plastic	Uniform	145,321	0.3	22	1,001,893	0.4	21
Mallory	Paper	Dress	190,009	−0.5	13	1,272,314	−5.8	6
Handy Man	Paper	Overalls	146,812	0.2	19	1,008,452	−4.0	16
Clara Bow	Porcelain	Dress	216,592	9.0	7	1,332,105	0.6	2
Mama Jean	Porcelain	Dress	158,339	4.3	18	1,102,938	−4.8	14
Molly McGee	Resin	Overalls	235,114	−2.5	6	1,429,764	−5.2	1
Chef Pierre	Resin	Uniform	143,729	−2.7	20	1,006,845	−4.8	17
Madison	Resin	Dress	132,867	0.6	21	1,002,377	2.2	20
Joanie	Soft plastic	Dress	208,322	−3.6	8	1,300,982	3.4	3
Pretty Baby	Soft plastic	Nightgown	276,558	5.3	2	1,132,008	0.4	11
Miss Cindie	Soft plastic	Nightgown	287,905	2.1	1	1,002,389	−2.0	18

GO ON TO NEXT PAGE ➤

Sorted by Outfit (Column 3)

	DOLL		INVENTORY			NUMBER SOLD		
NAME	MATERIAL	OUTFIT	NUMBER	% CHANGE	RANK	NUMBER	% CHANGE	RANK
Clara Bow	Porcelain	Dress	216,592	9.0	7	1,332,105	0.6	2
Joanie	Soft plastic	Dress	208,322	−3.6	8	1,300,982	3.4	3
Mallory	Paper	Dress	190,009	−0.5	13	1,272,314	−5.8	6
Suzie Belle	Hard plastic	Dress	253,908	1.2	4	1,239,008	−0.7	7
Raggedy Jane	Cloth	Dress	169,545	3.2	16	1,121,738	1.2	12
Mama Jean	Porcelain	Dress	158,339	4.3	18	1,102,938	−4.8	14
Madison	Resin	Dress	132,867	0.6	21	1,002,377	2.2	20
Sue Good	Cloth	Nightgown	198,621	3.7	11	1,295,682	3.9	4
Pretty Baby	Soft plastic	Nightgown	276,558	5.3	2	1,132,008	0.4	11
Miss Cindie	Soft plastic	Nightgown	287,905	2.1	1	1,002,389	−2.0	18
Molly McGee	Resin	Overalls	235,114	−2.5	6	1,429,764	−5.2	1
Henry Bee	Hard plastic	Overalls	190,453	1.8	12	1,290,757	8.6	5
Oliver Oh	Cloth	Overalls	254,030	−3.0	3	1,142,367	0.1	10
Rogelio Rojas	Hard plastic	Overalls	161,294	−0.9	17	1,109,334	4.2	13
Mr. Fixit	Hard plastic	Overalls	203,776	−4.0	9	1,100,768	0.2	15
Handy Man	Paper	Overalls	146,812	0.2	19	1,008,452	−4.0	16
Mighty Pete	Cloth	Overalls	238,772	−2.9	5	1,001,490	7.0	22
Justin	Hard plastic	Uniform	173,009	2.5	14	1,156,374	−1.3	9
Chef Pierre	Resin	Uniform	143,729	−2.7	20	1,006,845	−4.8	17
Jennifer	Hard plastic	Uniform	145,321	0.3	22	1,001,893	0.4	21

Sorted by Rank in Inventory (Column 6)

	DOLL		INVENTORY			NUMBER SOLD		
NAME	MATERIAL	OUTFIT	NUMBER	% CHANGE	RANK	NUMBER	% CHANGE	RANK
Miss Cindie	Soft plastic	Nightgown	287,905	2.1	1	1,002,389	−2.0	18
Pretty Baby	Soft plastic	Nightgown	276,558	5.3	2	1,132,008	0.4	11
Oliver Oh	Cloth	Overalls	254,030	−3.0	3	1,142,367	0.1	10
Suzie Belle	Hard plastic	Dress	253,908	1.2	4	1,239,008	−0.7	7
Mighty Pete	Cloth	Overalls	238,772	−2.9	5	1,001,490	7.0	22
Molly McGee	Resin	Overalls	235,114	−2.5	6	1,429,764	−5.2	1
Clara Bow	Porcelain	Dress	216,592	9.0	7	1,332,105	0.6	2
Joanie	Soft plastic	Dress	208,322	−3.6	8	1,300,982	3.4	3
Mr. Fixit	Hard plastic	Overalls	203,776	−4.0	9	1,100,768	0.2	15
Sue Good	Cloth	Nightgown	198,621	3.7	11	1,295,682	3.9	4

(continued)

Sorted by Rank in Inventory (Column 6) (*continued*)

| DOLL | | | INVENTORY | | | NUMBER SOLD | | |
NAME	MATERIAL	OUTFIT	NUMBER	% CHANGE	RANK	NUMBER	% CHANGE	RANK
Henry Bee	Hard plastic	Overalls	190,453	1.8	12	1,290,757	8.6	5
Mallory	Paper	Dress	190,009	−0.5	13	1,272,314	−5.8	6
Justin	Hard plastic	Uniform	173,009	2.5	14	1,156,374	−1.3	9
Raggedy Jane	Cloth	Dress	169,545	3.2	16	1,121,738	1.2	12
Rogelio Rojas	Hard plastic	Overalls	161,294	−0.9	17	1,109,334	4.2	13
Mama Jean	Porcelain	Dress	158,339	4.3	18	1,102,938	−4.8	14
Handy Man	Paper	Overalls	146,812	0.2	19	1,008,452	−4.0	16
Chef Pierre	Resin	Uniform	143,729	−2.7	20	1,006,845	−4.8	17
Madison	Resin	Dress	132,867	0.6	21	1,002,377	2.2	20
Jennifer	Hard plastic	Uniform	145,321	0.3	22	1,001,893	0.4	21

Sorted by Rank in Number Sold (Column 9)

| DOLL | | | INVENTORY | | | NUMBER SOLD | | |
NAME	MATERIAL	OUTFIT	NUMBER	% CHANGE	RANK	NUMBER	% CHANGE	RANK
Molly McGee	Resin	Overalls	235,114	−2.5	6	1,429,764	−5.2	1
Clara Bow	Porcelain	Dress	216,592	9.0	7	1,332,105	0.6	2
Joanie	Soft plastic	Dress	208,322	−3.6	8	1,300,982	3.4	3
Sue Good	Cloth	Nightgown	198,621	3.7	11	1,295,682	3.9	4
Henry Bee	Hard plastic	Overalls	190,453	1.8	12	1,290,757	8.6	5
Mallory	Paper	Dress	190,009	−0.5	13	1,272,314	−5.8	6
Suzie Belle	Hard plastic	Dress	253,908	1.2	4	1,239,008	−0.7	7
Justin	Hard plastic	Uniform	173,009	2.5	14	1,156,374	−1.3	9
Oliver Oh	Cloth	Overalls	254,030	−3.0	3	1,142,367	0.1	10
Pretty Baby	Soft plastic	Nightgown	276,558	5.3	2	1,132,008	0.4	11
Raggedy Jane	Cloth	Dress	169,545	3.2	16	1,121,738	1.2	12
Rogelio Rojas	Hard plastic	Overalls	161,294	−0.9	17	1,109,334	4.2	13
Mama Jean	Porcelain	Dress	158,339	4.3	18	1,102,938	−4.8	14
Mr. Fixit	Hard plastic	Overalls	203,776	−4.0	9	1,100,768	0.2	15
Handy Man	Paper	Overalls	146,812	0.2	19	1,008,452	−4.0	16
Chef Pierre	Resin	Uniform	143,729	−2.7	20	1,006,845	−4.8	17
Miss Cindie	Soft plastic	Nightgown	287,905	2.1	1	1,002,389	−2.0	18
Madison	Resin	Dress	132,867	0.6	21	1,002,377	2.2	20
Jennifer	Hard plastic	Uniform	145,321	0.3	22	1,001,893	0.4	21
Mighty Pete	Cloth	Overalls	238,772	−2.9	5	1,001,490	7.0	22

GO ON TO NEXT PAGE ➤

Review each of the statements below. Based on the information provided in the table, indicate whether the statement is true or false.

True	False	
○	◉	More than half of the hard plastic dolls experienced a decrease in total items sold.
○	◉	The lowest-selling doll in a nightgown sold more than the highest-selling doll in a uniform.
◉	○	Overall, fewer than 3,500,000 of the resin dolls listed above were sold.
○	◉	More than 1,000,000 of the Madison dolls were sold in 2007–2011.

Read the sources below answering the question that follows.

Source #1: Appraisal Letter

Dear Mr. and Mrs. Brown:

We again want to thank you for choosing to work with the experts at Coin and Gem to settle your mother's estate. After careful review of the coin collection in question, we found a total of 187 coins. Each coin has been appraised, packaged, and marked according to its grade.

Each coin was ranked on a scale of 1 to 70 according to the Sheldon Scale of coin grading. We estimate the total value of the collection to be about $27,000. Most of the value resides in a few very rare U.S. coins, which are in mint condition.

We would be happy to further assist you in deciding how to handle this aspect of your mother's estate. Please contact us with any questions or concerns you may have.

Attached is a detailed appraisal that inventories each coin, its condition, and its value.

Sincerely yours,
Charles Barker, Owner and Appraisal Expert
Coin and Gem

Source #2: Inventory Appraisal: Very Fine and Mint Pieces

COIN	CONDITION	VALUE
Draped Bust Half Cent—1803	Extremely Fine	$639
Liberty Capped Half Cent—1794	Extremely Fine	$4,425
Buffalo Nickel—1913 STYPE2	Mint	$512
1863–1865 Three-Cent Pieces (4)	Extremely Fine	$351 each
Mercury Dime—1921 D	Mint	$887
Mercury Dime—1926 S (2)	Extremely Fine	$151 each
Bust Quarter—1807	Mint	$7,665
Seated Liberty Half Dollar—1848 O	Mint	$1,294
Franklin Half Dollar—1897 S	Extremely Fine	$869
Indian Head Penny—1872	Mint	$800

Source #3: Letter of Recommendation

Dear Mr. and Mrs. Brown:

We highly recommend that the Extremely Fine and Mint pieces valued more than $350.00 each be sold at auction, with a reserve price that falls only slightly below their appraised value. Collectors will pay dearly for rare pieces in mint condition, especially if they will complete a collection.

The remaining pieces of high value, 80 coins valued at $100.00 to $300.00 each, should be handled by a broker and sold individually. We would be more than willing to handle the sale of these pieces, at a commission of 2.7%.

Finally, I recommend that the coins you have many of—like the wheat penny, which have a relatively low sale value—be sold off in lots. You will receive more for these coins from a prospector who wants to look through the lot for a specific coin of value than you would by selling them individually.

Let us know of any way we can assist you in this matter.

Sincerely,
Charles Barker, Owner and Appraisal Expert
Coin and Gem

GO ON TO NEXT PAGE ➤

4. Consider each of the following statements. Does the information in the three sources support the inference as stated?

Yes	No	
○	●	The appraiser does not believe that the Browns will obtain full value for their coin collection if the pieces are sold.
○	●	If the Browns follow the appraiser's recommendations, they will most likely sell all of their Extremely Fine coins at auction.
●	○	More than half of the coins in the Browns' collection are valued at less than $100 each.

5. At Acme University, there are 65 students who are taking finance and 55 students who are taking economics.

   In the table that follows, select two numbers among the numbers listed that are consistent with the information given. In the first column, select the largest number of students at Acme University who are taking either finance or economics, and in the second column, select the largest number of students at Acme University who are taking both finance and economics. Select only one option in each column.

TAKING EITHER FINANCE OR ECONOMICS	TAKING BOTH FINANCE AND ECONOMICS	NUMBER OF STUDENTS
○	○	23
○	●	30
○	○	70
○	○	85
●	○	110
○	○	125

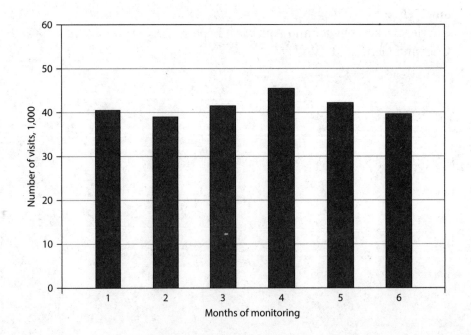

6. The graph above is a bar graph with six bars, each representing the number of website visits received by an Internet company monitoring its advertising efficacy. The website received visits anywhere from one to six months after the ad campaign was initiated. The ads were grouped by advertising channel, and the number of site visits was recorded each month over a six-month period. Select the best answer to fill in the blanks for each of the statements below, based on the data shown in the graph.

The percent change between the number of visits after one month and the number of visits after six months is closest to _____.

(A) 0
(B) 50
(C) 100

The number of visits after four months is closest to _____% of the number of visits after one month.

(A) 40
(B) 45
(C) 90
(D) 105
(E) 110

This table displays data on a Los Angeles department store in 2017.

> On the actual exam, you will be able to sort the table by any of its columns. (Columns can be sorted in ascending order only.) The table is shown sorted in different ways to mirror the test.

Sorted by Item (Column 1)

ITEM	IN-STORE SALES, STATE SHARE (%)	IN-STORE SALES, STATE RANK	ONLINE SALES, STATE SHARE (%)	ONLINE SALES, STATE RANK
Accessories	17	3	24	2
Children's apparel	22	2	37	1
Cosmetics	14	4	33	1
Housewares	6	4	5	3
Jewelry	40	1	10	1
Luggage	3	5	16	4
Men's apparel	27	2	37	2
Shoes	52	1	73	1
Women's apparel	46	1	80	1

Sorted by In-Store Sales, State Share (Column 2)

ITEM	IN-STORE SALES, STATE SHARE (%)	IN-STORE SALES, STATE RANK	ONLINE SALES, STATE SHARE (%)	ONLINE SALES, STATE RANK
Luggage	3	5	16	4
Housewares	6	4	5	3
Cosmetics	14	4	33	1
Accessories	17	3	24	2
Children's apparel	22	2	37	1
Men's apparel	27	2	37	2
Jewelry	40	1	10	1
Women's apparel	46	1	80	1
Shoes	52	1	73	1

Sorted by Online Sales, State Share (Column 4)

ITEM	IN-STORE SALES, STATE SHARE (%)	IN-STORE SALES, STATE RANK	ONLINE SALES, STATE SHARE (%)	ONLINE SALES, STATE RANK
Housewares	6	4	5	3
Jewelry	40	1	10	1
Luggage	3	5	16	4
Accessories	17	3	24	2
Cosmetics	14	4	33	1
Children's apparel	22	2	37	1
Men's apparel	27	2	37	2
Shoes	52	1	73	1
Women's apparel	46	1	80	1

7. For each of the following statements, select *Yes* if the statement can be shown to be true based on information in the table. Otherwise, select *No*.

Yes	No	
●	○	This store ranks first in the state in both online and in-store sales in three departments.
○	●	This store has more than half of the in-store sales in the state in women's and men's apparel combined.
○	●	This store made more online sales than in-store sales in the cosmetics department.

The sources that follow accompany questions 8, 9, and 10.

Source #1: Excerpt from a news report in a popular major newspaper

In 2015, the Chinese government proclaimed the end of its one-child policy for families. Now restricted couples are allowed to have two children for the first time since the policy was first announced in 1979. A leading criticism of the policy is that it contributed to discrimination against females. Because families want a male heir, from the 1980s to 2015, the sex-ratio at birth gradually changed from 108:100 to 116:100 in favor of male births. This latter ratio means that in 2015 for every 116 boys only 100 girls were born in China.

Source #2: Interview with demographic expert

China's one-child policy, first put into effect in the 1980s, was designed to slow the rapid growth of the Chinese people, as that growth was causing severe overcrowding. Leaders believed the policy would protect the country's resources and improve productivity. Unfortunately, they did not foresee that the long-held preference for male heirs would lead to a substantial gender imbalance.

Since the introduction of the policy, the fertility rate among Chinese women dropped from approximately 2.8 births per woman to about 1.4 in 2015. It is estimated that even though the country reduced births by roughly 40 percent in 2015, there were still many more children born each week than people dying, creating a steady increase in population in spite of the law.

Source #3: Commentary on a social side effect of China's one-child policy

China's one-child policy, which was in effect for over three decades, produced noticeable side effects. One hapless side effect is male-biased sex ratios. Unfortunately, Chinese authorities did not foresee that the long-held preference for male heirs among Chinese people would lead to a substantial gender imbalance. This gender imbalance means millions of Chinese men will never find a mate.

Furthermore, the imbalance causes men who know they are unlikely to form strong family ties to become vagrants. The nation has experienced an increased crime rate that is frequently linked to a large transient population of about 80 million unmarried, low-status, adult males. Not uncommonly, these individuals are willing to resort to crime to improve their situations, given they have no family ties and perceive that they have nothing to lose.

GO ON TO NEXT PAGE ➤

8. Consider each of the items listed below. Select *Yes* if the item can be determined based on the information given in the three sources. Otherwise, select *No*.

Yes	No	
○	◉	The number of women vagrants in the Chinese population
◉	○	As of 2015, the approximate percent decrease in the fertility rate of Chinese women since the introduction of the one-child policy
○	◉	The number of female children expected to be born in China in 2020

9. Consider each of the items listed below. Select *Yes* if the item can be determined based on the information given in the three sources. Otherwise, select *No*.

Yes	No	
◉	○	The ratio of male births to female births in 2015
○	◉	The number of permanent bachelors expected to be living in China in 2030
○	◉	The economic influences that predispose a woman to give birth to a female child

10. Suppose that in China over the next 10 years, for every 100 female children born the number of male births decreases to 110. If all of the information in the three sources is accurate, the percent change since 2015 in the number of male births for every 100 female births would be closest to which of the following?

- ◉ 5 %
- ○ 6 %
- ○ 7 %
- ○ 8 %
- ○ 9 %

11. In-Style Interiors is considering buying two new paint bases that have become extremely popular as interior décor paints, because they lend themselves well to texturing. Quality Touch costs $13 a gallon, and it requires two coats. Something Irresistible costs $31 per gallon and is guaranteed to create a one-coat cover.

    In the table below, identify the cost (to the nearest rounded dollar) of using each paint type to cover a wall measuring 24 feet × 18 feet. Each gallon will complete a single coat of 350 square feet, and paint can be purchased in full gallons only. Select only one option in each column.

QUALITY TOUCH	SOMETHING IRRESISTIBLE	PAINT COST
○	○	$13.00
○	○	$31.00
◉	○	$39.00
○	○	$52.00
○	◉	$62.00
○	○	$93.00

The table that follows accompanies question 12.

> On the actual exam, you will be able to sort the table by any of its columns. (Columns can be sorted in ascending order only.) The table is shown sorted in different ways to mirror the test.

Percentage of Art Exhibits Displaying Selected Media, Single Year

Sorted by City (Column 1)

CITY	PAINTING	SCULPTURE	MIXED MEDIA	PHOTOGRAPHY
Boston	81	58	46	14
Chicago	55	34	68	76
Dallas	20	9	24	13
Los Angeles	42	28	46	14
New York	73	89	78	92
San Francisco	64	10	25	33
Washington, D.C.	55	87	36	75

Sorted by Percentage of Exhibits with Paintings (Column 2)

CITY	PAINTING	SCULPTURE	MIXED MEDIA	PHOTOGRAPHY
Dallas	20	9	24	13
Los Angeles	42	28	46	14
Chicago	55	34	68	76
Washington, D.C.	55	87	36	75
San Francisco	64	10	25	33
New York	73	89	78	92
Boston	81	58	46	14

Sorted by Percentage of Exhibits with Sculptures (Column 3)

CITY	PAINTING	SCULPTURE	MIXED MEDIA	PHOTOGRAPHY
Dallas	20	9	24	13
San Francisco	64	10	25	33
Los Angeles	42	28	46	14
Chicago	55	34	68	76
Boston	81	58	46	14
Washington, D.C.	55	87	36	75
New York	73	89	78	92

Sorted by Percentage of Exhibits with Mixed Media Works (Column 4)

CITY	PAINTING	SCULPTURE	MIXED MEDIA	PHOTOGRAPHY
Dallas	20	9	24	13
San Francisco	64	10	25	33
Washington, D.C.	55	87	36	75
Los Angeles	42	28	46	14
Boston	81	58	46	14
Chicago	55	34	68	76
New York	73	89	78	92

Sorted by Percentage of Exhibits with Photography (Column 5)

CITY	PAINTING	SCULPTURE	MIXED MEDIA	PHOTOGRAPHY
Dallas	20	9	24	13
Los Angeles	42	28	46	14
Boston	81	58	46	14
San Francisco	64	10	25	33
Washington, D.C.	55	87	36	75
Chicago	55	34	68	76
New York	73	89	78	92

12. For each of the following statements, select *Would help explain* if it would, if true, help explain some of the information in the table. Otherwise select *Would not help explain*.

Would help explain	Would not help explain	
●	○	In Dallas, textiles and fiber arts are the most popular medium.
●	○	New York critics prefer art shows with a great deal of variety.
○	●	Photographers don't consider Boston an interesting city to photograph.

—— STOP. ——

Quantitative

Time—75 minutes

Solve the problem and indicate the best of the answer choices given.

NUMBERS: **All numbers used are real numbers.**

FIGURES: A figure accompanying a problem-solving question is intended to provide information useful in solving the problem. Figures are drawn as accurately as possible EXCEPT when it is stated in a specific problem that its figure is not drawn to scale. Straight lines may sometimes appear jagged. All figures lie in a plane unless otherwise indicated.

1. Greg sells gaskets. On three sales, Greg has received commissions of $385, $70, and $190, and he has one additional sale pending. If Greg is to receive an average (arithmetic mean) commission of exactly $220 on the four sales, then the fourth commission must be:

    (A) $135
    (B) $155
    (C) $220
    (D) $235
    (E) $645

2. In an effort to plan out expenses, the Roberts family is representing its annual budget as a circle graph. Each sector of the graph is proportional to the amount of the budget it represents. If "clothes and shoes" takes up 54° of the graph, how much of the Roberts' $20,000 annual budget is dedicated to clothes and shoes?

    (A) $1,500
    (B) $3,000
    (C) $4,500
    (D) $5,000
    (E) $5,400

3. What is the value of $3x^2 - 1.8x + 0.3$ for $x = 0.6$?

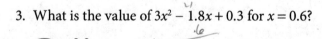

    (A) −0.3
    (B) 0
    (C) 0.3
    (D) 1.08
    (E) 2.46

4. Over a three-week period, the price of an ounce of gold increased by 25% in the first week, decreased by 20% in the following week, and increased by 5% in the third week. If the price of gold was G dollars per ounce at the beginning of the three weeks, what was the price, in terms of G, at the end of the three weeks?

(A) $0.95G$
(B) G
(C) $1.05G$
(D) $1.1G$
(E) $1.15G$

5. If a cube has a total surface area of 96, what is its volume?

(A) 16
(B) 36
(C) 64
(D) 81
(E) 96

6. The table below shows the enrollment in various classes at a certain college.

CLASS	NUMBER OF STUDENTS
Biology	50
Physics	35
Calculus	40

Although no student is enrolled in all three classes, 15 are enrolled in both Biology and Physics, 10 are enrolled in both Biology and Calculus, and 12 are enrolled in both Physics and Calculus. How many different students are in the three classes?

(A) 51
(B) 88
(C) 90
(D) 125
(E) 162

7. In a nationwide poll, P people were asked 2 questions. If $\frac{2}{5}$ answered "yes" to question 1, and of those $\frac{1}{3}$ also answered "yes" to question 2, which of the following represents the number of people polled who did not answer "yes" to both questions?

(A) $\frac{2}{15}P$
(B) $\frac{3}{5}P$
(C) $\frac{3}{4}P$
(D) $\frac{5}{6}P$
(E) $\frac{13}{15}P$

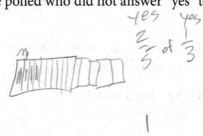

The following <u>data sufficiency</u> problems consist of a question and two statements, labeled (1) and (2), in which certain data are given. You have to decide whether the data given in the statements are sufficient for answering the question. Using the data given in the statements plus your knowledge of mathematics and everyday facts (such as the number of days in July or the meaning of *counterclockwise*), you must indicate whether

- Ⓐ Statement (1) ALONE is sufficient, but statement (2) alone is not sufficient.
- Ⓑ Statement (2) ALONE is sufficient, but statement (1) alone is not sufficient.
- Ⓒ BOTH statements TOGETHER are sufficient, but NEITHER statement ALONE is sufficient.
- Ⓓ EACH statement ALONE is sufficient.
- Ⓔ Statements (1) and (2) TOGETHER are NOT sufficient.

NUMBERS: All numbers used are real numbers.

FIGURES: A figure accompanying a data sufficiency problem will conform to the information given in the question, but will not necessarily conform to the additional information given in statements (1) and (2). Lines shown as straight can be assumed to be straight, and lines that appear jagged can also be assumed to be straight. You may assume that the position of points, angles, regions, etc., exist in the order shown and that angle measures are greater than zero. All figures lie in a plane unless otherwise indicated.

NOTE: In data sufficiency problems that ask for the value of a quantity, the data given in the statements are sufficient only when it is possible to determine exactly one numerical value for the quantity.

8. A certain salad dressing made only of oil and vinegar is premixed and sold in the grocery store. What is the ratio of oil to vinegar in the mix?

   (1) An 18.6-ounce bottle of the salad dressing contains 12.4 ounces of vinegar.
   (2) In a 32-ounce bottle of the salad dressing, there is half as much oil as there is vinegar.

9. At a certain pancake festival with 600 attendees in which every attendee ate at least one pancake, how many people had only one pancake?

   (1) At the festival there were 1,200 pancakes served, and no person had more than three pancakes.
   (2) Seventy-two percent of the attendees at the festival had two or more pancakes.

10. A rectangle is equal in area to that of a square with sides of length 12. Is the diagonal of the rectangle greater in length than 20?

   (1) The rectangle has a length of 16.
   (2) The rectangle has a width of 9.

11. A type of candy comes in two flavors, sweet and sour, and in two colors, yellow and green. The color and flavor of the individual pieces of candy are not related. If in a certain box of this candy $\frac{1}{4}$ of the yellow pieces and $\frac{5}{7}$ of the green pieces are sour, what is the ratio of the number of yellow pieces to the number of green pieces in the box?

   (1) In the box, the number of sweet yellow pieces is equal to the number of sour green pieces.
   (2) In the box, the number of green pieces is two less than the number of yellow pieces.

12. In isosceles triangle *ABC*, what is the value of ∠*C* ?

   (1) The measure of ∠*B* is 42°.
   (2) The measure of ∠*A* is 96°.

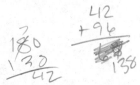

Solve the problem and indicate the best of the answer choices given.

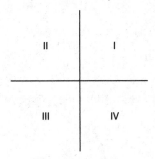

13. In the rectangular quadrant system shown above, which quadrant, if any, contains no point (*x*, *y*) that satisfies the equation $3x + 5y = -2$?

   Ⓐ none
   Ⓑ I
   Ⓒ II
   Ⓓ III
   Ⓔ IV

14. If a copier makes 3 copies every 4 seconds, then continues at this rate, how many minutes will it take to make 9,000 copies?

   Ⓐ 60
   Ⓑ 100
   Ⓒ 120
   Ⓓ 200
   Ⓔ 3,000

15. To be considered grade AA, an egg must weigh between 75 and 90 grams, including the shell. Shells of grade AA eggs weigh between 3 and 5 grams. What is the smallest possible mass, in grams, of a 12-egg omelet, assuming that only grade AA eggs are used, the shells are all discarded, and no mass is lost in the cooking process?

    (A) 800
    (B) 840
    (C) 864
    (D) 900
    (E) 1,080

16. $\dfrac{(0.2)^8}{(0.2)^5} =$

    (A) 0.0008
    (B) 0.001
    (C) 0.008
    (D) 0.04
    (E) 0.08

17. What is the ratio of $\left(\dfrac{1}{3}\right)^2$ to $\left(\dfrac{1}{3}\right)^4$?

    (A) 9:1
    (B) 3:1
    (C) 1:3
    (D) 1:9
    (E) 1:27

18. A group of 7 fishermen chartered a boat for a day to fish for flounder. The boat costs x dollars per day to rent. If the group can find 3 more fishermen on the docks who are willing to come aboard and share the rental costs, how much less will the rental cost be per person in terms of x?

    (A) $x/70$
    (B) $x/35$
    (C) $3x/70$
    (D) $3x/10$
    (E) $3x/7$

19. The size of a flat-screen television is given as the length of the screen's diagonal. How many square inches greater is the screen of a square 34-inch flat-screen television than a square 27-inch flat-screen television?

    (A) 106.75
    (B) 213.5
    (C) 427
    (D) 729
    (E) 1,156

The following <u>data sufficiency</u> problems consist of a question and two statements, labeled (1) and (2), in which certain data are given. You have to decide whether the data given in the statements are sufficient for answering the question. Using the data given in the statements plus your knowledge of mathematics and everyday facts (such as the number of days in July or the meaning of *counterclockwise*), you must indicate whether

(A) Statement (1) ALONE is sufficient, but statement (2) alone is not sufficient.

(B) Statement (2) ALONE is sufficient, but statement (1) alone is not sufficient.

(C) BOTH statements TOGETHER are sufficient, but NEITHER statement ALONE is sufficient.

(D) EACH statement ALONE is sufficient.

(E) Statements (1) and (2) TOGETHER are NOT sufficient.

20. What is the value of n?

    (1) $n^4 = 256$
    (2) $n^3 > n^2$

21. An employee at a company was given the task of making a large number of copies. He spent the first 45 minutes making copies at a constant rate on copier A, but copier A broke down before the task was completed. He then spent the next 30 minutes finishing the task on copier B, which also produced copies at a constant rate. How many total minutes would the task have taken had copier A not broken down?

    (1) Copier A produced twice as many copies in its first 5 minutes of operation as copier B produced in its first 15 minutes.
    (2) Copier B produces 10 copies per minute.

22. If $ab \neq 0$, is c an integer?

    (1) $c = 5a - 2b$
    (2) $a = 2b$

23. $x = 0.57y9$. If y denotes the thousandth digit in the decimal representation of x above, what digit is y?

    (1) If x were rounded to the nearest tenth, the result would be 0.6.
    (2) If x were rounded to the nearest hundredth, the result would be 0.58.

24. Is integer $y > 0$?

    (1) $-(2 + y) > 0$
    (2) $(2 + y)^2 > 0$

Solve the problem and indicate the best of the answer choices given.

25. If 4 and 11 are the lengths of two sides of a triangular region, which of the following can be the length of the third side?

 I. 5
 II. 13
 III. 15

    Ⓐ I only
    Ⓑ II only
    Ⓒ I and II only
    Ⓓ II and III only
    Ⓔ I, II, and III

26. A certain truck uses 18 gallons of diesel fuel in traveling 270 miles. In order for the truck to travel the same distance using 10 gallons of diesel fuel, by how many miles per gallon must the truck's fuel mileage be increased?

    Ⓐ 8
    Ⓑ 9
    Ⓒ 12
    Ⓓ 15
    Ⓔ 27

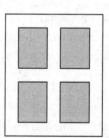

27. The figure above represents a window, with the shaded regions representing openings for glass and the pale regions representing the wood panels between and around the glass. If the window is 4.5 feet high by 2.5 feet wide, and if each of the wooden panels is exactly 4 inches in width what is the total surface area, in square inches, of glass in the window? (1 foot = 12 inches; figure not drawn to scale)

    Ⓐ 189
    Ⓑ 378
    Ⓒ 448
    Ⓓ 756
    Ⓔ 1,620

28. If $3(x^2 + x) - 7 = x^2 + 2(4 + x^2)$, then $x =$

    (A) 5
    (B) 6
    (C) 9
    (D) 15
    (E) 25

29. Suzie's Discount Footwear sells all pairs of shoes for one price and all pairs of boots for another price. On Monday the store sold 22 pairs of shoes and 16 pairs of boots for $650. On Tuesday the store sold 8 pairs of shoes and 32 pairs of boots for $760. How much more do pairs of boots cost than pairs of shoes at Suzie's Discount Footwear?

    (A) $2.50
    (B) $5.00
    (C) $5.50
    (D) $7.50
    (E) $15.00

30. For any 3 given numbers, which of the following is always equivalent to adding the 3 numbers together and then dividing the sum by 3?

    I. Ordering the 3 numbers numerically, from highest to lowest, and then selecting the middle number.
    II. Dividing each of the numbers by 3 and then adding the results together.
    III. Multiplying each number by 6, adding the resulting products together, and then dividing the sum by 9.

    (A) I only
    (B) II only
    (C) I and II only
    (D) II and III only
    (E) None of the above

31. A hat company ships its hats, individually wrapped, in 8-inch by 10-inch by 12-inch boxes. Each hat is valued at $7.50. If the company's latest order required a truck with at least 288,000 cubic inches of storage space in which to ship the hats in their boxes, what was the minimum value of the order?

    (A) $960
    (B) $1,350
    (C) $1,725
    (D) $2,050
    (E) $2,250

32. Chauncy, an English bulldog, received 1,618 votes in the Mr. Bulldog USA competition, giving him approximately 20 percent of the vote. Approximately what percent of the remaining votes would he have needed to receive in order to win 30 percent of the total votes?

    (A) 10%
    (B) 12.5%
    (C) 15%
    (D) 17.5%
    (E) 20%

The following <u>data sufficiency</u> problems consist of a question and two statements, labeled (1) and (2), in which certain data are given. You have to decide whether the data given in the statements are sufficient for answering the question. Using the data given in the statements plus your knowledge of mathematics and everyday facts (such as the number of days in July or the meaning of *counterclockwise*), you must indicate whether

    (A) Statement (1) ALONE is sufficient, but statement (2) alone is not sufficient.
    (B) Statement (2) ALONE is sufficient, but statement (1) alone is not sufficient.
    (C) BOTH statements TOGETHER are sufficient, but NEITHER statement ALONE is sufficient.
    (D) EACH statement ALONE is sufficient.
    (E) Statements (1) and (2) TOGETHER are NOT sufficient.

33. If 8 skiers raced down a course multiple times in one day, and each skier used a different pair of skis on each run, what is the total number of different pairs of skis used by the 8 skiers during the day?

    (1) No skier shared any skis with any other skier.
    (2) Each skier made exactly 12 runs during the day.

34. The symbol $\otimes$ represents one of the following standard arithmetic operations: addition, subtraction, multiplication, or division. What is the value of $7 \otimes 4$?

    (1) $4 \otimes 7 < 1$
    (2) $4 \otimes 3 > 1$

35. Salespeople at a certain car dealership are paid a $250 commission on every car they sell up to their monthly quota, and $500 for every car they sell over the quota. What is the monthly sales quota at this dealership?

    (1) One salesperson exceeded the quota by 8 cars and received a total monthly commission of $7,500.
    (2) One salesperson who achieved only half of the quota received a commission of $1,750.

36. If $a \neq -b$, is $\dfrac{a-b}{b+a} < 1$?

   (1) $b^2 > a^2$
   (2) $a - b > 1$

37. The hold of a fishing boat contains only cod, haddock, and halibut. If a fish is selected at random from the hold, what is the probability that it will be a halibut or a haddock?

   (1) There are twice as many halibut as cod in the hold, and twice as many haddock as halibut.
   (2) Cod account for 1/7 of the fish by number in the hold.

—————————————————————— **STOP.** ——————————————————————

41 QUESTIONS

Verbal

Time—75 minutes

For the following questions, select the best of the answer choices given.

1. Studies have shown that companies that present seminars on workplace safety to their employees actually have higher rates of workplace accidents than do companies which do not present such seminars to their employees. Despite this finding, it is still in the best interests of companies and their employees for companies to present these seminars.

   Which of the following, if true, provides the strongest support for the argument that the companies should continue to present these seminars?

   (A) Companies that present workplace safety seminars to their employees are likely to be in manufacturing industries or segments of the service sector that present more opportunities for workplace accidents than the average company.

   (B) A fast-food chain determined that the rate of workplace accidents remained the same at its franchises after all employees had viewed a 30-minute workplace safety video.

   (C) Workers are ultimately responsible for their own safety, and no amount of workplace education can alter their behavior.

   (D) A business research institute determined that workplace accidents reduce the productivity of manufacturing businesses by as much as 8 percent per year.

   (E) Many companies mistakenly believe that presenting workplace safety seminars to their employees relieves the company of legal liability in the event that employees are injured on the job.

2. For hundreds of years, pearl divers have gathered pearls directly from mollusks on the sea floor. This is an extremely risky profession, exposing the divers to risks of drowning, air embolism, and shark attacks. Still, as long as society demands authentic cultured pearls, these brave divers must continue to risk their lives.

   Which of the following statements, if true, most seriously weakens the conclusion above?

   (A) Shark attacks on pearl divers have decreased steadily over the last three decades because of declining shark populations.

   (B) Cultured pearls are generally considered more beautiful than those made by artificial means.

   (C) Robotic pearl harvesters can gather pearls faster and at less cost than human divers, although they may disturb aquatic communities.

   (D) Part of the value of cultured pearls derives from the exotic way in which they are obtained.

   (E) With the proper equipment and training, a diver employing scuba gear can harvest three times as many pearls per hour as can a free air diver.

3. An electronics company's two divisions showed consistent performance over the last two years. In each year, the audiovisual department accounted for roughly 30 percent of the company's sales and 70 percent of the company's profits over the period, while the home appliance division accounted for the balance.

   Which of the following statements regarding the last two years can be inferred from the statement above?

   (A) The audiovisual market is growing faster than is the home appliance division.
   (B) The home appliance division has realized lower profits per dollar of sales than has the audiovisual division.
   (C) Total dollar sales for each division has remained roughly constant for the last five years.
   (D) The company has devoted more money to research and development efforts in the audiovisual division than in the home appliance division.
   (E) To maximize profitability, the company should focus its resources on the home appliance division.

4. Gastric bypass surgery has been shown to be effective at helping extremely obese people lose weight. Some patients have lost as much as 300 pounds after undergoing the surgery, thereby substantially prolonging their lives. Despite the success of the treatment, most doctors have not embraced the surgery as a weight-loss option.

   Which of the following statements, if true, best accounts for the lukewarm reaction of the medical community to gastric bypass surgery?

   (A) Gastric bypass surgery carries a high risk of serious complications, including death.
   (B) Obesity is one of the leading contributors to heart disease and hypertension, two leading causes of death.
   (C) Obesity rates among the American population have been increasing consistently for the last three decades.
   (D) Many patients report that losing weight through diets is ineffective, since they usually gain the weight back within six months.
   (E) Most health insurance plans will cover the cost of gastric bypass surgery for morbidly obese patients at high risk of heart disease.

The questions in this group are based on the content of a passage. After reading the passage, choose the best answer to each question. Answer all questions following the passage on the basis of what is stated or implied in the passage.

While most people agree that the Golden Age of comic books began with the introduction of Superman in 1938 in *Action Comics #1*, there is less agreement about when exactly the Golden Age ended. There is a general consensus, however, about the factors that brought the Golden Age to a close: the rise of the horror comic book in the late 1940s, and the resulting backlash against comic books in the early 1950s.

Superhero comic books reached their peak of popularity in the early 1940s because of all the GIs in Europe and Japan who eagerly read about Superman, Batman, and The Spirit. When these soldiers came home, they still wanted to read comic books, but they sought out more adult content. William Gaines of EC Comics was happy to meet the market demand with such grim and gritty titles as *Weird Fantasy* and *The Crypt of Terror*. The creators of superhero comic books, not wanting to be left behind, responded by matching their protagonists against darker criminals in more violent encounters.

These darker comic books aroused the anger of child psychologist Fredric Wertham, who believed that comic books were leading the nation's youth into crime, violence, and drug abuse. Wertham's book, *The Seduction of the Innocent*, was a national best-seller that helped bring about congressional investigations into the corrupting influence of comic books. The Senate committee that reviewed Wertham's charges decided to create the Comics Code Authority, a regulatory body that prohibited comic books from mentioning sexuality, alcohol, drugs, criminal behavior, or any themes related to the horror genre.

These regulations had a numbing effect on the industry. EC Comics was nearly driven out of the comics business, and the other major players canceled many of their most prominent titles. The comics business did not recover until the Marvel revolution of the early 1960s ushered in the Silver Age.

5. This passage is primarily interested in which of the following?

    Ⓐ Investigating the factors that brought about the Marvel revolution and the Silver Age of comic books

    Ⓑ Reviewing the factors that brought about the end of the Golden Age of comic books

    Ⓒ Comparing and contrasting two eras in the history of comic books

    Ⓓ Condemning the horror comic book for its corrupting influence on the nation's youth

    Ⓔ Evaluating the historical legacy of William Gaines's EC Comics

6. According to the passage, which of the following was true of the creators of superhero comic books in the postwar years?

    Ⓐ They sought to head off the censorship of the Comics Code Authority by voluntarily prohibiting stories dealing with sexuality, drugs, or criminal behavior.

    Ⓑ They introduced characters such as Superman and The Spirit.

    Ⓒ They unintentionally laid the groundwork for the transition from the Golden Age of comic books to the Silver Age.

    Ⓓ They focused increasingly on flashy artwork and less on well-developed stories.

    Ⓔ They responded to the competitive pressure from horror comic books by increasing the amount of violence in their stories.

7. According to the passage, what can we infer to be the central message of Fredric Wertham's *The Seduction of the Innocent*?

   (A) Adults reading violent comic books were as likely to be corrupted by them as young people were.
   (B) The horror comic books of the late 1940s were inferior to the superhero comic books that gained popularity during World War II.
   (C) Comic books were leading the nation's youth into crime, violence, and drug abuse.
   (D) Creating a regulatory board to censor the comic book industry would drive the worst offenders out of the business.
   (E) Comic books would never be able to convey stories of any serious literary merit.

8. According to the final paragraph of the passage, what may we infer about the comic book companies of the Silver Age?

   (A) They were able to create popular comic books despite the regulations of the Comics Code Authority.
   (B) They achieved commercial success because of the popularity of characters such as Spider-Man, the Hulk, and the Fantastic Four.
   (C) They repeated the same mistakes as the comic book companies of the Golden Age.
   (D) They failed to succeed because of the numbing effect of the Comics Code Authority regulations.
   (E) Marvel Comics was the only major comic book company to survive from the Golden Age into the Silver Age.

9. In what light does the passage depict the efforts by Fredric Wertham to bring about regulation of the comic book industry?

   (A) As a fanatical crusade brought about by Wertham's inner demons
   (B) As a witch-hunt roughly analogous to the concurrent anti-Communist hearings by the House Committee on Un-American Activities
   (C) As a reasonable response to an industry that had gone too far
   (D) As an angry response to a trend in the subject matter of the comic book industry
   (E) As an inappropriate response to a phenomenon that was not actually hurting anyone

10. According to the passage, which of the following statements can be made about the content of *Weird Fantasy* and *The Crypt of Terror*?

    (A) Their adult-oriented content was not suitable for young readers.
    (B) Their grim and gritty content was a market response to the demands of soldiers home from World War II.
    (C) They frequently depicted violence and criminal behavior, but shied away from sexuality or drug abuse.
    (D) Their sales surpassed those of previous best-selling titles such as *Superman* or *Batman*.
    (E) The publication of *Weird Fantasy #1* coincided with the end of the Golden Age of comic books.

GO ON TO NEXT PAGE ➤

The following questions present a sentence, part of which or all of which is underlined. Beneath the sentence, you will find five ways of phrasing the underlined part. The first of these repeats the original; the other four are different. If you think the original is best, choose the first answer; otherwise choose one of the others.

These questions test correctness and effectiveness of expression. In choosing your answer, follow the requirements of standard written English; that is, pay attention to grammar, choice of words, and sentence construction. Choose the answer that produces the most effective sentence; this answer should be clear and exact, without awkwardness, ambiguity, redundancy, or grammatical error.

11. The way in which the mighty blue whale and the other baleen whales—the finback, gray, humpback, and right whales—<u>eats was discovered by</u> careful observation by biologists.

    Ⓐ eats was discovered by
    Ⓑ eat was discovered through
    Ⓒ eats were discovered by means of
    Ⓓ eat were discovered by
    Ⓔ eat was discovered resulting from

12. The eighteenth-century author Jonathan Swift once suggested in a satiric essay <u>Irish farmers could eat their children to address the twin problems of overpopulation and lack of food</u>.

    Ⓐ Irish farmers could eat their children to address the twin problems of overpopulation and lack of food
    Ⓑ that the twin problems of overpopulation and lacking food could be addressed by the eating of children by Irish farmers
    Ⓒ of the twin problems of Irish farmers, overpopulation and a lack of food, could be addressed by the eating of their children
    Ⓓ that Irish farmers could address the twin problems of overpopulation and lack of food by eating their children
    Ⓔ that Irish farmers, facing overpopulation and lacking food, could address the twin problems through eating their children

13. The stock market collapse of 1929 had far-reaching consequences for the national economy, causing a nationwide collapse in home values, putting millions out of work, <u>and by erasing</u> the investment savings of one-fifth of the population.

    Ⓐ and by erasing
    Ⓑ and erasing
    Ⓒ and having erased
    Ⓓ and erased
    Ⓔ by erasing

14. <u>No less remarkable than the invention of nuclear power</u> has been the way the technology has prompted governments to reevaluate the nature of international relations.

- (A) No less remarkable than the invention of nuclear power
- (B) What was as remarkable as the invention of nuclear power
- (C) Inventing nuclear power has been none the less remarkable than
- (D) The invention of nuclear power has been no less remarkable as
- (E) The thing that was as remarkable as inventing nuclear power

15. <u>Unlike the recognition of ethical lapses in others, many people are disinclined to perceive the same flaws in themselves.</u>

- (A) Unlike the recognition of ethical lapses in others, many people are disinclined to perceive the same flaws in themselves.
- (B) Unlike the perception of ethical flaws in themselves, many people are willing to recognize these same flaws in others.
- (C) Many people, willing to recognize ethical lapses in others, are disinclined to perceive the same flaws in themselves.
- (D) Many people are disinclined to perceive the same flaws in themselves, but are willing to perceive ethical lapses in others.
- (E) Although willing to recognize ethical lapses in others, many people in themselves are disinclined to perceive the same flaws.

For the following questions, select the best of the answer choices given.

16. The Elk City garbage dumps are so full that Elk City has been forced to pay a large sum to Caribou City to accept much of Elk City's garbage. The Elk City mayor has proposed paying for this garbage relocation by imposing a tax on manufacturing businesses in Elk City. MegaCorp, the largest manufacturing business in the area, protests that this tax is unfair because businesses should not have to pay for a garbage problem that has been created by homeowners.

Which of the following, if true, most weakens MegaCorp's argument?

- (A) MegaCorp already pays more than $10,000 per year in taxes and fees to Elk City.
- (B) MegaCorp employs more than 60 percent of the employed residents of Elk City.
- (C) A recycling program would address the garbage problem more effectively by reducing the overall quantity of waste.
- (D) MegaCorp's manufacturing processes produce more than 90 percent of the total waste that goes into Elk City's garbage dumps.
- (E) Caribou City is happy to receive the extra garbage because the fees it collects from Elk City have helped address a shortfall in education funding.

GO ON TO NEXT PAGE ➤

17. There are elected officials who say that the development of a space-based missile defense system will provide economic benefits only to military contractors. This claim is not true. A space-based missile defense system, even if it has no current applications for civilian businesses, will still benefit civilian businesses because those businesses will be able to find profitable uses for the government-developed technology in the future.

    Which of the following statements, if true, provides the most support for the argument that a space-based missile defense system could provide future economic benefits for civilian businesses?

    (A) Several new materials developed for the Apollo space program were later adapted to provide basic components of the modern computer and electronics industries.
    (B) The missile defense system in question will not require the development of any new technologies.
    (C) Space-based missile defense programs may be the only way to defend civilian populations against preemptive nuclear attacks.
    (D) Space-based missile defense programs, although more expensive than traditional land-based systems, are theoretically more effective than traditional land-based systems.
    (E) The scientists employed on the project could make extraordinary advances in the capabilities of intercontinental ballistic missiles used by the army.

18. The commissioner of a professional sports league dictated that teams could not put players on the field who had a greater than 20 percent chance of suffering a career-ending spinal injury during competition. The commissioner justified this decision as a way to protect players from injury while protecting the league from lawsuits.

    Which of the following, if true, would most undermine the effectiveness of the commissioner's new policy?

    (A) Spinal injuries can result in paralysis, loss of fine motor skills, and even death.
    (B) The previous year, more than seven players in the league suffered career-ending spinal injuries.
    (C) The players' union agrees that the risk of injury is an inevitable part of playing the game at a professional level.
    (D) There is no scientifically valid method for determining the likelihood of any player suffering a career-ending spinal injury at any given time.
    (E) Players barred from playing because of this new regulation will be entitled to compensation for lost wages at a level determined by the commissioner's office.

19. There are few things worse for a new parent than listening to a baby scream in hunger while a bottle of formula slowly warms up in a bowl of hot water. So why not just pop the bottle in the microwave and zap it in 20 seconds? Because microwaves heat fluids unevenly, and a hot pocket in the formula could seriously injure the baby.

Which of the following is presupposed in the argument against heating formula in the microwave?

(A) Babies generally refuse to eat formula that has been heated in a microwave.
(B) Microwave radiation might break down some of the proteins in formula that are vital to a baby's health.
(C) Different microwaves use different amounts of power, and consequently some models could heat a bottle to scalding temperature faster than others.
(D) Parents cannot be expected to consistently even out the temperature of a microwaved bottle by shaking it vigorously before giving it to the baby.
(E) Once formula has been heated, any leftover formula should be discarded, because otherwise the formula could spoil between feedings and make the baby sick.

20. Charlie's Chainsaw Company has reason to believe that one of its models of saw is defective. A recall of all of the saws would cost more than $5 million and would probably result in a loss in market share over the next quarter because of bad publicity. Still, a recall is the right economic decision.

Which of the following, if true, most supports the conclusion above?

(A) Defective chainsaws can seriously injure or even kill the people who use them.
(B) Charlie's chief rival has recalled two of its products within the past year.
(C) Product recalls often result in a perception by customers that a given product is permanently defective, even after the defect has been remedied.
(D) The stocks of publicly traded companies that announce product recalls often drop upon the announcement, but they generally return to the pre-announcement level within 12 months.
(E) Three years ago a rival company went out of business because of large punitive damages awarded to a plaintiff who had been injured by a defective chainsaw.

21. A dog enthusiast took home two puppies from the dog shelter. He fed one of the puppies super-premium canned dog food, while he fed the other a generic brand from the grocery store. The dog fed on the generic brand gained weight twice as fast as the dog fed the super-premium brand. Because of the difference in these results, the dog enthusiast concluded that the generic brand actually provided nutrition superior to that of the super-premium brand.

    Each of the following, if true, would weaken the evidence for the dog enthusiast's conclusion except for which of the following?

    (A) A dog will sometimes gain more weight when eating inferior-quality food because he must eat more of it to obtain the nutrients he needs.
    (B) The dogs were of mixed breeds and appeared to be descended from dogs of different sizes.
    (C) Both dogs ate all of the food given to them at each serving.
    (D) The dog enthusiast did not give the two dogs equal amounts of their respective foods.
    (E) The dog who received the super-premium dog food suffered from a digestive system disorder that hindered his growth.

The following questions present a sentence, part of which or all of which is underlined. Beneath the sentence, you will find five ways of phrasing the underlined part. The first of these repeats the original; the other four are different. If you think the original is best, choose the first answer; otherwise choose one of the others.

These questions test correctness and effectiveness of expression. In choosing your answer, follow the requirements of standard written English; that is, pay attention to grammar, choice of words, and sentence construction. Choose the answer that produces the most effective sentence; this answer should be clear and exact, without awkwardness, ambiguity, redundancy, or grammatical error.

22. A council of ecologists in Hawaii <u>have concluded that much of the currently uncontrolled invasive species on the island chain were arriving</u> in the holds of cargo ships.

    (A) have concluded that much of the currently uncontrolled invasive species on the island chain were arriving
    (B) has concluded that many of the currently uncontrolled invasive species on the island chain arrived
    (C) have concluded that many of the currently uncontrolled invasive species on the island chain have arrived
    (D) concluded that many of the currently uncontrolled invasive species on the island chain would arrive
    (E) has concluded that much of the currently uncontrolled invasive species on the island chain had arrived

23. Some people say that the answer to crime is to build more prisons, but more sensitive observers argue that instead we should address the sources of crime <u>through reduced poverty, a cut-off supply of illicit drugs, and by focusing on keeping kids in school</u>.

    (A) through reduced poverty, a cut-off supply of illicit drugs, and by focusing on keeping kids in school
    (B) by the reduction of poverty, cutting off the supply of illicit drugs, and to focus on keeping kids in school
    (C) by reducing poverty, cutting off the supply of illicit drugs, and focusing on keeping kids in school
    (D) by means of reducing poverty, cutting off the supply of illicit drugs, and through focusing on keeping kids in school
    (E) to reduce poverty, cut off the supply of illicit drugs, and to focus on keeping kids in school

24. <u>As automobiles replaced horses as the primary means of transportation, it was widely anticipated that</u> the time spent in transit by the average traveler would decrease.

    (A) As automobiles replaced horses as the primary means of transportation, it was widely anticipated that
    (B) Insofar as automobiles replaced horses as the primary means of transportation, it was anticipated widely
    (C) With horses being replaced by automobiles as the primary means of transportation, there was wide anticipation that
    (D) As the primary means of transportation replaced horses with automobiles, many anticipated that
    (E) Automobiles replacing horses as the primary means of transportation produced anticipation widely that

25. Intrigued by the new rules that favored quickness over strength, <u>the decision of the coach was to give more playing time to the team's smaller athletes</u>.

    (A) the decision of the coach was to give more playing time to the team's smaller athletes
    (B) the coach decided to give the team's smaller athletes more playing time
    (C) it was decided by the coach to give the team's smaller athletes more playing time
    (D) the team's smaller athletes were given more playing time by the coach
    (E) more playing time was given to the team's smaller athletes by the coach

26. At ground level, nitrous oxides are bad enough, <u>but when up high, atmospherically they</u> bond with free ions to create dangerous smog particles.

    (A) but when up high, atmospherically they
    (B) however, it is in the upper atmosphere in which it may
    (C) but in the upper atmosphere, they
    (D) however, but once in the upper atmosphere it is known to
    (E) as in the upper atmosphere they

GO ON TO NEXT PAGE ➤

For the following questions, select the best of the answer choices given.

27. Paleontologists hypothesize that modern birds evolved from the family of dinosaurs that included *Tyrannosaurus rex*. This hypothesis would be strongly supported if evidence that dinosaurs from this family had a body covering resembling feathers could be found, but so far no such evidence has been found.

    Which of the following, if true, would most help the paleontologists explain why no evidence of feathered dinosaurs has yet been found?

    (A) Fossilized dinosaurs have shown many birdlike characteristics, such as bone structure and winglike arms.
    (B) If birds are in fact the descendants of dinosaurs, then it can be argued that the dinosaurs never really died out.
    (C) Flying dinosaurs such as the *Pteranodon*, which is not thought to have been related to modern birds, do not appear to have had feathers.
    (D) Soft tissues such as skin and feathers do not fossilize like bones, and therefore are far less likely to have left permanent evidence in the fossil record.
    (E) The thousands of dinosaur fossils excavated by paleontologists represent only a tiny fraction of the billions of dinosaurs that once lived.

28. Esai and Linda are tired of the freezing cold days in Glenmont, so they are considering retiring to either Sunny Glen or Buena Vista. Esai points out that Sunny Glen has an average annual temperature 8 degrees Fahrenheit higher than that of Buena Vista. Linda insists, however, that Buena Vista would be the better choice.

    Which of the following, if true, best accounts for Linda's preference for Buena Vista?

    (A) Different people experience cold in different ways, so what seems cold to Linda may seem pleasantly cool to Esai.
    (B) Sunny Glen has a somewhat higher risk of hurricanes than does Glenmont.
    (C) Buena Vista has a range of cultural offerings, including an opera, a ballet, and three jazz clubs.
    (D) Living in a place that gets very hot, such as Sunny Glen, can have as many health risks as living in a place that gets very cold.
    (E) While Sunny Glen is warmer than Buena Vista in the summer, it also has more freezing cold days in the winter.

29. Although many people would not believe it, the mosquito is actually the most dangerous animal in Africa. While the bite of the black mamba is invariably lethal when untreated, this dreaded snake kills only a few dozen people per year. Hippopotami, with their immense strength and foul dispositions, kill hundreds of people per year in rivers and lakes, but the mosquito is still more dangerous. Mosquitoes bite hundreds of millions of people in Africa every year, and they infect over a million each year with malaria, a disease that is often fatal.

Which of the following questions would be most useful in evaluating the claim made above regarding the mosquito?

(A) Could a person survive an attack by a black mamba if that person received prompt medical attention?
(B) What criteria are used to determine which animal is the "most dangerous" animal?
(C) Could the incidence of mosquito bites be decreased through the judicious use of pesticides and insect repellent?
(D) Does malaria kill more people per year in Africa than tuberculosis?
(E) How does the percentage of people who survive hippopotamus attacks in Africa each year compare with the percentage of people who survive mosquito bites?

The questions in this group are based on the content of a passage. After reading the passage, choose the best answer to each question. Answer all questions following the passage on the basis of what is <u>stated</u> or <u>implied</u> in the passage.

Although hard statistics are difficult to come by, there is substantial anecdotal evidence that use of performance-enhancing drugs, or doping, is rampant in professional sports. Of perhaps greater significance to society are the estimated 1.5 million amateur athletes who use steroids, either to improve their appearance or to emulate the performance of their favorite professional athletes. This chemical epidemic is a pernicious threat to both the nation's health and our collective sense of "fair play."

Nonprescription anabolic steroids have been illegal in the United States since 1991, and most professional sports leagues have banned them since the 1980s. These bans are partly a matter of fairness—a talented athlete trained to the peak of her ability simply cannot compete with an equivalent athlete using steroids—but also based on issues of health. Anabolic androgenic steroids ("anabolic" means that they build tissues; "androgenic" means that they increase masculine traits) have been linked to liver damage, kidney tumors, high blood pressure, balding, and acne. They function by increasing the body's level of testosterone, the primary male sex hormone. In men, this dramatic increase in testosterone can lead to the shrinking of testicles, infertility, and the development of breasts; in women, it can lead to the growth of facial hair and permanent damage to the reproductive system. Steroids have also been linked to a range of psychological problems, including depression and psychotic rage.

The punishments for getting caught using steroids are severe, and the serious health consequences are well documented. Despite this, millions of professional and amateur athletes continue to use performance-enhancing drugs. Why is this?

One clear pattern is that many athletes will do whatever it takes to get an edge on the competition. Since the 1950s, Olympic athletes have played a cat-and-mouse game with Olympic Committee officials to get away with doping, because the drugs really do work. Athletes who dope are simply stronger and faster than their competitors who play fair. Professional athletes in football and baseball have found that steroids and human growth hormone can give them the edge to score that extra touchdown or home run, and in the modern sports market, those results can translate into millions of dollars in salary. For the millions of less talented athletes in gyms and playing fields across the country, drugs seem like the only way to approach the abilities of their heroes in professional sports.

The other clear pattern, unfortunately, is that it has been all too easy for abusers to get away with it. Steroid abuse is often regarded as a "victimless crime." One of the favored ways to trick the testers is to use "designer" steroids. There are thousands of permutations of testosterone, such as THG, that can be produced in a lab. Chemists have discovered that they can create new drugs that produce androgenic effects but do not set off the standard doping tests. Other methods have been to use the steroids but stop a few weeks before testing, to use other chemicals to mask the traces of steroids, or to switch in a "clean" sample of urine at the testing site. Other athletes use steroid precursors, such as androstenedione, that have androgenic effects similar to those of steroids but are not illegal because they are not technically steroids. The sad fact is that unless the government and professional sports organizations are willing to get tough on the steroid problem, the use of performance-enhancing drugs in sports is not going to end.

30. What appears to be the primary purpose of this passage?

   (A) To educate readers about the health threats involved in the use of performance-enhancing drugs
   (B) To analyze the ways in which professional athletes have eluded attempts to screen for performance-enhancing drugs
   (C) To discuss the reasons why performance-enhancing drugs are a dangerous and persistent problem for society
   (D) To complain about the inadequate efforts by government and professional sports organizations to eliminate the problem of performance-enhancing drugs
   (E) To argue that athletes, both professional and amateur, should not use performance-enhancing drugs on the grounds that they are both dangerous and unfair

31. According to the passage, all of the following are known potential consequences of steroid use except for which of the following?

   (A) Damage to reproductive organs
   (B) Decreased blood pressure
   (C) Increases in the user's strength and speed
   (D) Kidney tumors
   (E) Increased risk of depression

32. The author's attitude toward the problem of steroid abuse is best described as which of the following?

   (A) Cautious but optimistic
   (B) Judgmental but supportive
   (C) Ambivalent but resigned
   (D) Curious but subjective
   (E) Concerned but pessimistic

33. Which of the following can be inferred about a long-distance race in which both athletes who use performance-enhancing drugs and those who do not use these drugs compete?

   (A) The athletes using the drugs will be caught by the proper authorities and ejected from the race.
   (B) The athletes using the drugs will have a better chance of winning the race.
   (C) The athletes using the drugs will use steroid precursors that produce effects similar to those of androgenic drugs but are not technically steroids.
   (D) The athletes using the drugs are more likely to be professionals in their sport than the athletes who do not use such drugs.
   (E) The athletes using the drugs will be more likely to use any means possible to win the race, including intentional sabotage of the other racers' equipment.

34. The relationship of an athlete who does not use performance-enhancing drugs to an athlete who does use such drugs is most similar to which of the following?

   (A) The relationship of a farmer selling milk from cows that have been given bovine growth hormone, a legal drug that promotes greater than normal milk production, to a farmer selling milk from cows that have not been given bovine growth hormone
   (B) The relationship of a chess player to a competitor who uses psychological tricks in order to gain an advantage
   (C) The relationship of a boxer in the lightweight class to a boxer in the heavyweight class
   (D) The relationship of a person taking a standardized test according to the rules to a person taking the same test while using an illegal hidden calculator
   (E) The relationship of a person entering a pig in an agricultural contest to a person entering a guinea pig in the same contest

35. According to the passage, which of the following can be inferred about the "designer" steroid THG?

   (A) It can increase masculine traits in users without setting off standard doping tests.
   (B) It does not cause the health problems associated with traditional anabolic steroids.
   (C) Even if professional sports organizations could detect THG, they would take no action against those who use it.
   (D) It is a chemical permutation of progesterone, a hormone that has powerful effects on the human body.
   (E) Because it is a "designer" steroid, it is more expensive than generic steroids.

GO ON TO NEXT PAGE ➤

36. Which of the following best expresses the role of the third paragraph in the overall structure of the passage?

    (A) It redirects the theme of the passage from presenting a problem to explaining the reasons for the problem's severity.
    (B) It introduces a new concept that defines the rest of the passage.
    (C) It provides an answer to a question posed in the first two paragraphs.
    (D) It refutes the central hypothesis of the second paragraph and poses a question that is answered in the following paragraphs.
    (E) It narrows the focus of the passage from the general themes of the first two paragraphs to the more specific themes of the last two paragraphs.

The following questions present a sentence, part of which or all of which is underlined. Beneath the sentence you will find five ways of phrasing the underlined part. The first of these repeats the original; the other four are different. If you think the original is best, choose the first answer; otherwise choose one of the others.

These questions test correctness and effectiveness of expression. In choosing your answer, follow the requirements of standard written English; that is, pay attention to grammar, choice of words, and sentence construction. Choose the answer that produces the most effective sentence; this answer should be clear and exact, without awkwardness, ambiguity, redundancy, or grammatical error.

37. His opponent having sprained his wrist, Andrew could have won by exploiting this weakness, but he chose not to do it.

    (A) His opponent having sprained his wrist, Andrew could have won by exploiting this weakness, but he chose not to do it.
    (B) Andrew could have won by exploiting this weakness after his opponent sprained his wrist, but he chose not to do so.
    (C) Choosing not to do so, Andrew could have won after his opponent sprained his wrist by exploiting this weakness.
    (D) After his opponent sprained his wrist, Andrew could have won by exploiting this weakness, but he chose not to do so.
    (E) After his opponent sprained his wrist, Andrew could have, but chose not to do it, won by exploiting this weakness.

38. Since the average test score of students enrolled in charter schools were rising 7.5 percent in the spring, many educators concluded that the system was working.

    (A) Since the average test score of students enrolled in charter schools were rising 7.5 percent in the spring, many educators concluded
    (B) As the average test score of students enrolled in charter schools rose 7.5 percent in the spring, with many educators concluding
    (C) Because the average test score of students enrolled in charter schools rose 7.5 percent in the spring, many educators concluded
    (D) Because the average test score of students enrolled in charter schools were up 7.5 percent in the spring, many educators concluded
    (E) With average test scores rising by 7.5 percent among students enrolled in charter schools, and many educators concluded

39. The police chief argued that first-time offenders <u>who have no high school diploma but who have families with a record of crime</u> will probably break the law again.

    (A) who have no high school diploma but who have families with a record of crime
    (B) without a high school diploma and families having a criminal record
    (C) without a high school diploma whose families have a record of crime
    (D) whose families have criminal records and lacking high school diplomas
    (E) lacking high school diplomas and also having families having criminal records

40. Like the power-generating apparatus of a conventional car, <u>that of a hybrid car depends on</u> a combustible fuel to generate power.

    (A) that of a hybrid car depends on
    (B) hybrid cars depend on
    (C) hybrid cars' power-generating apparati are dependent on
    (D) that of a hybrid car's is dependent on
    (E) that of hybrid cars depend on

41. <u>Since red flags are likely to be raised at the IRS by the reporting of gambling income, business owners who declare their income as business revenue is less likely to receive an audit.</u>

    (A) Since red flags are likely to be raised at the IRS by the reporting of gambling income, business owners who declare their income as business revenue is less likely to receive an audit.
    (B) Because the reporting of gambling income is likely to raise red flags at the IRS, business owners can reduce their chances of receiving an audit by declaring that income as business revenue.
    (C) Business owners can reduce their chances of receiving an audit by declaring the income as business revenue, since the reporting of gambling income is likely to raise red flags at the IRS.
    (D) Their chances of receiving an audit are reduced by business owners who report that income as business revenue, because the reporting of gambling income is likely to raise red flags at the IRS.
    (E) The reporting of that income as business revenue can reduce the chances of business owners of receiving an audit, because of the red flags not having been raised at the IRS by the reporting of gambling income.

——————————— **STOP.** ———————————

Answer Key

See page 58 for answers to the Integrated Reasoning section.

1 QUANTITATIVE	1 VERBAL
1. D	1. A
2. B	2. C
3. C	3. B
4. C	4. A
5. C	5. B
6. B	6. E
7. E	7. C
8. D	8. A
9. B	9. D
10. D	10. B
11. A	11. B
12. B	12. D
13. B	13. B
14. D	14. A
15. B	15. C
16. C	16. D
17. A	17. A
18. C	18. D
19. B	19. D
20. C	20. E
21. A	21. C
22. E	22. B
23. E	23. C
24. A	24. A
25. B	25. B
26. C	26. C
27. D	27. D
28. A	28. E
29. B	29. B
30. B	30. C
31. E	31. B
32. B	32. E
33. C	33. B
34. C	34. D
35. D	35. A
36. A	36. A
37. D	37. D
	38. C
	39. C
	40. A
	41. B

Answers and Explanations

Analytical Writing Assessment
Model Response

This letter's author argues that any drug with potentially serious side effects should be sold only by prescription in order to decrease the chance of health risks due to overuse or adverse drug interactions with other medicines. While the author's concern for patient safety is well-placed, his argument is illogical and therefore reaches an incorrect conclusion. The actions proposed are only tangentially related to the desired outcome, making them an inefficient and likely an ineffective solution to the problem.

The author's argument relies heavily on the assumption that making potentially harmful drugs available exclusively by prescription will provide an opportunity to explain side effects and risks to patients. However, this argument also carries a number of unspoken assumptions, specifically that doctors and pharmacists will consistently take the time to explain side effects to their patients, and that patients will understand and appreciate the risks those side effects pose. Even if such perfect information transfer occurs, it still does not guarantee that patients will use the drugs correctly 100 percent of the time. Unless all of these steps occur flawlessly for perpetuity, some risk of serious side effects will persist. Thus information transfer cannot fully mitigate these health risks, making the shift to prescription-only distribution irrelevant.

Similarly, the author also claims that making these drugs available only by prescription will allow doctors to monitor the quantity purchased. Existing laws, prescription drug plans, and pharmaceutical practices already combine to monitor the rate at which many medications are purchased, but due to the availability of multiple doctors and pharmacy chains, the only complete picture of consumption patterns lies with the patient herself. As a result, it is practically impossible to effectively monitor the quantity and type of medication being purchased by a single patient. However, even if it were possible to monitor the combination and quantity of drugs being purchased by a patient, as the author proposes, it still would not solve the problem, because the author is falsely equating the quantity purchased with the quantity consumed. Patients will still be able to overdose on a drug, as they will have a full prescription's worth (generally 30 days) at their disposal.

Given the reasons above, the letter's arguments fall apart. In order to strengthen the argument, the author should have included statistics on the rate of serious side effects due to misuse for both prescription and nonprescription drugs in order to better demonstrate how successful this change might be. Additionally, in order to properly combat the risk of adverse drug side effects, the author should focus on finding ways to strengthen communication channels between doctors and patients, and increase patients' understanding of the importance of proper adherence.

Integrated Reasoning

1. The correct answer is **800** courses per year for Practice Tech and **400** courses per year for Jameson Vocational.

PRACTICE TECH	JAMESON VOCATIONAL	RATE OF INCREASE (COURSES PER YEAR)
○	○	250
○	●	400
○	○	540
○	○	600
○	○	760
●	○	800

If Practice Tech increases its course offerings by 800 courses per year, in three years it will offer 4,400 courses per year. If Jameson Vocational increases course offerings by 400 courses per year, in three years it will offer 4,400 courses per year as well. After the three-year mark, Practice Tech will offer more courses per year than Jameson Vocational.

2. The answer to the first blank is **A**. The number of households that have an average of less than three subscriptions per month and have incomes greater than $75,000 equals the number of points in the scatter plot to the left of 3 and above $75,000. There are two data points that are both to the left of 3 and above $75,000. Therefore, the correct answer is 2.

   The answer to the second blank is **C**. As income increases, the average number of subscriptions increases, so the correlation between the two is positive.

3. The correct answers are shown below.

True	False	
○	●	More than half of the hard plastic dolls experienced a decrease in total items sold.
○	●	The lowest-selling doll in a nightgown sold more than the highest-selling doll in a uniform.
●	○	Overall, fewer than 3,500,000 of the resin dolls listed above were sold.
○	●	More than 1,000,000 of the Madison dolls were sold in 2007–2011.

Of the six hard plastic dolls, only two (less than half) experienced a decrease in total items sold and the other four experienced an increase.

   All the dolls in nightgowns ranked higher in inventory than the dolls in uniforms, but they did not all rank higher in total items sold. The lowest-selling doll in a nightgown sold less than the highest-selling doll in a uniform.

   Three different resin dolls are listed in the table. Altogether, 3,438,986 of these three models were sold.

   About a million Madison dolls were sold in 2012–2016, and this was a 2.2% increase over the previous five years, so there were about 1,000,000/1.022, which is approximately 980,000, Madison dolls sold in the previous five years.

4. The correct answers are shown below.

Yes No

Yes	No	
○	●	The appraiser does not believe that the Browns will obtain full value for their coin collection if the pieces are sold.
○	●	If the Browns follow the appraiser's recommendations, they will most likely sell all of their Extremely Fine coins at auction.
●	○	More than half of the coins in the Browns' collection are valued at less than $100 each.

The first inference is not supported by the information in the three sources. The appraiser does not imply a belief that the Browns will not receive full value for their coins.

In Source #3, the appraiser recommends that pieces valued at more than $350 be sold at auction. Source #2 shows that some of the Browns' Extremely Fine coins are valued at $350 or less. These pieces would not be sold at auction.

Source #1 shows that the Browns' collection contains 187 coins. Source #2 lists 12 of these coins as valued at more than $350. Source #3 indicates that 80 coins have values from $100 to $300. That leaves 95 coins that are valued at less than $100. This is more than 50% of the collection.

5. The correct answers are **110** students taking either finance or economics, and **30** students taking both finance and economics.

TAKING EITHER FINANCE OR ECONOMICS	TAKING BOTH FINANCE AND ECONOMICS	NUMBER OF STUDENTS
○	○	23
○	●	30
○	○	70
○	○	85
●	○	110
○	○	125

There are 65 students taking finance and 55 students taking economics. Suppose no student is taking both courses, then the total number of students taking either finance or economics would be 65 + 55, or 120. The largest number listed in the table is 125, which is too large. The next largest number is 110. Of the numbers listed in the table, the largest number of students taking either finance or economics is 110.

If all of the students taking economics were also taking finance, there would be 55 students taking both courses. This is the largest number of students who could take both courses. However, the number 55 is not listed in the table, and 70 is too large. So of the numbers listed in the table, the largest number of Acme students who are taking both finance and economics is 30.

6. The answer to the first blank is **A**. The number of visits after six months is about the same as that after one month. Therefore, the percent change between the number of visits after one month and the number of visits after six months is closest to 0%.

The answer to the second blank is **E**. The number of visits after one month is about 40,000 and the number after four months is about 45,000, which is closest to 110 percent of 40,000.

7. The correct answers are as follows:

Yes   No

● ○   This store ranks first in the state in both online and in-store sales in three departments.

○ ●   This store has more than half of the in-store sales in the state in women's and men's apparel combined.

○ ●   This store made more online sales than in-store sales in the cosmetics department.

In jewelry, shoes, and women's apparel, the store ranks first in the state in both online and in-store sales.

The store has 27 percent of the sales in men's apparel and 46 percent of the sales in women's apparel, but without knowing the total sales figures for the state in both of those departments, you cannot determine exactly what percentage the store has of the total sales in both. However, since the store has less than half of the total sales in each, it definitely cannot have more than half of the total sales in both.

The store has a bigger share of the total sales in the state for online sales than for in-store sales, but without knowing the total number of both kinds of sales, you cannot determine whether the store actually made more sales online.

8. The correct answers are as follows:

Yes   No

○ ●   The number of women vagrants in the Chinese population

● ○   As of 2015, the approximate percent decrease in the fertility rate of Chinese women since the introduction of the one-child policy

○ ●   The number of female children expected to be born in China in 2020

Source #2 indicates that since the introduction of the one-child policy, the fertility rate among Chinese women dropped from approximately 2.8 births per woman to 1.4 births per woman. The percent decrease in the fertility rate can be determined based on this information. This is the only one of the three items that can be determined based on the sources provided.

9. The correct answers are shown below.

Yes   No

● ○   The ratio of male births to female births in 2015

○ ●   The number of permanent bachelors expected to be living in China in 2030

○ ●   The economic influences that predispose a woman to give birth to a female child

Source #1 provides the ratio of male to female births in 2015. This is the only one of the three items that can be determined based on the sources provided.

10. The correct answer is **5**.

The percent change is $[(116 - 110)/116] \times 100\% = [6/116] \times 100\%$, which is approximately 5 percent.

11. The correct answers are **$39.00** for Quality Touch and **$62.00** for Something Irresistible.

QUALITY TOUCH	SOMETHING IRRESISTIBLE	PAINT COST
○	○	$13.00
○	○	$31.00
●	○	$39.00
○	○	$52.00
○	●	$62.00
○	○	$93.00

The wall measures 24 feet × 18 feet, or 432 square feet. Quality Touch requires two coats, so paint will be needed for 432 × 2, or 864 square feet. Each gallon of paint provides one coat of 350 square feet, so three gallons of Quality Touch are required. At $13 per gallon, the total Quality Touch cost is $39.00.

Something Irresistible will cover the wall in one coat. One gallon covers 350 square feet, so two gallons are required. At $31.00 per gallon, the cost to use Something Irresistible is $62.00.

12. The correct answers are as follows:

Would help explain	Would not help explain	
●	○	In Dallas, textiles and fiber arts are the most popular medium.
●	○	New York critics prefer art shows with a great deal of variety.
○	●	Photographers don't consider Boston an interesting city to photograph.

The popularity of a medium not mentioned in the table would explain why the media that are mentioned in the table don't account for 100 percent of Dallas's art exhibits.

The high percentages of all four media in New York exhibits are only possible if many New York exhibits include more than one medium. Critics preferring more variety would help explain that tendency.

Artists often travel to create and show their art, so even if photographers did not take many pictures in Boston, that would not explain why they don't often bring their pictures to Boston to exhibit.

Quantitative

1. The correct answer is **D**. For the average of four commissions to be $220, the total must be $220 × 4 = $880. $880 minus the sum of the three listed commissions ($385 + $70 + $190 = $645) equals $235.

2. The correct answer is **B**. 54° is 15 percent of the 360° in a circle; 15 percent of $20,000 is $3,000.

3. The correct answer is **C**. The equation $3(0.6 \times 0.6) - 1.8(0.6) + 0.3 = 1.08 - 1.08 + 0.3 = 0.3$.

4. The correct answer is **C**. At the end of the first week, the price was $1.25 \times G = 1.25G$. At the end of the second week, it was $0.8 \times 1.25G = G$. At the end of the third week, the price was $1.05 \times G = 1.05G$.

5. The correct answer is **C**. A cube has six sides, so if the total surface area is 96, then the surface area of a square side is 96/6 = 16. The area of a square is the square of the length of its sides, so the length of a side is the square root of 16 = 4. The volume of a cube is the cube of the length of its sides, so $4 \times 4 \times 4 = 64$.

6. The correct answer is **B**. To find the total number of students, you must separate them into nonoverlapping groups so that no one is counted twice. The students taking only Biology are the 50 students minus the 15 also taking Physics and the 10 also taking Calculus, so there are 25 students taking just Biology. Using this same method, the number of students taking just Physics is 35 − 15 − 12 = 8, and the number taking just Calculus is 40 − 10 − 12 = 18. The total number, then, is 25 + 8 + 18 + 10 + 15 + 12 = 88.

7. The correct answer is **E**. The people who answered "yes" to both questions are 1/3 of $\frac{2}{5}P$, so $\frac{2}{15}P$. Therefore, the people who did not answer "yes" to both questions are
$$P - \frac{2}{15}P = \frac{13}{15}P.$$

8. The correct answer is **D**. (1) alone is sufficient, because if there are 12.4 ounces of vinegar, then there are 18.6 − 12.4 = 6.2 ounces of oil; 6.2/12.4 = 1:2. (2) alone is sufficient because it tells you directly that the ratio of oil to vinegar is 1:2.

9. The correct answer is **B**. (1) alone is not sufficient, because there could have been 300 people who had one pancake and 300 people who had three pancakes, or 600 people who had two pancakes. (2) alone is sufficient, because you can directly infer from the statement that 100 − 72 = 28 percent of attendees, or 168, had only one pancake.

10. The correct answer is **D**. Both (1) and (2) independently allow you to infer both the length and the width of the rectangle, because if the rectangle is equal in area to a square with sides of length 12, then its area = $12 \times 12 = 144$, and so the width is 144/16 = 9 and the length is 144/9 = 16. By the Pythagorean theorem, we can determine that the diagonal is equal to the square root of $9^2 + 16^2 = 337$. You do not have to determine the actual square root of 337 to determine that it is less than 20, because $20 \times 20 = 400$.

11. The correct answer is **A**. (1) alone is sufficient because it sets up a ratio between the colors and flavors; if $\frac{1}{4}$ of the yellow pieces are sour, then $\frac{3}{4}$ of the yellow pieces are sweet, and if $\frac{5}{7}$ of the green pieces are sour, then $\frac{2}{7}$ of the green pieces are sweet; if the number of sweet yellow pieces is equal to the number of sour green pieces, then $\frac{3}{4}$ of the number of yellow pieces is equal to $\frac{5}{7}$ of the number of green pieces; if y represents the number of yellows and g represents the number of greens, then the ratio can be represented as $3y/4 = 5g/7$, which can be restated as $21y = 20g$, or $y/g = 20/21$. Statement (2) alone is not sufficient, because it does not give sufficient information to determine the total number of either the greens or the yellows.

12. The correct answer is **B**. (1) alone is insufficient, because $\angle C$ could be the matching angle of the isosceles triangle with $\angle B$ at 42°, or it could match with $\angle A$ at 69°, or it could be the nonmatching angle at 96°. (2) alone is sufficient, because if $\angle A$ is 96°, then it cannot be one of the matching angles of the isosceles triangle, because two 96° angles cannot fit in a triangle, so $\angle C$ must be one of two 42° angles.

13. The correct answer is **B**. The equation describes a line that crosses the x axis at −2/3 and crosses the y axis at −2/5, so it never passes through quadrant I. You can plug in points from each axis to verify.

14. The correct answer is **D**. At three copies every four seconds, the copier will finish the batch in $(9{,}000/3) \times 4$ seconds, or 12,000 seconds. There are 60 seconds in a minute, so 12,000/60 = 200 minutes.

15. The correct answer is **B**. The smallest omelet will result from 75-gram eggs with shells of 5 grams each, resulting in 70 grams per egg added to the omelet. 70 grams/egg × 12 eggs = 840 grams.

16. The correct answer is **C**. $\dfrac{(0.2)^8}{(0.2)^5} = (0.2)^3 = 0.008$

17. The correct answer is **A**. $\left(\dfrac{1}{3}\right)^2$ equals $\dfrac{1}{9}$, while $\left(\dfrac{1}{3}\right)^4$ equals $\dfrac{1}{81}$.

    $\dfrac{1}{9}$ is nine times larger than $\dfrac{1}{81}$, so the ratio is 9:1.

18. The correct answer is **C**. The difference in cost is the difference between $x/7$ and $x/10$. $x/7 - x/10 = (10x - 7x)/70 = 3x/70$.

19. The correct answer is **B**. The question specifies that the televisions are square, so the diagonals are part of 45–45–90 triangles. This means that the side of such a television is the diagonal divided by $\sqrt{2}$. This would be an awkward number to deal with, but the question calls for areas, so you need to square the length of a side in order to get the area of the screen, thereby removing the square root. Set up the equation
$$\left(\frac{34}{\sqrt{2}}\right)^2 - \left(\frac{27}{\sqrt{2}}\right)^2 = \frac{1,156 - 729}{2} = \frac{427}{2} = 213.5$$

20. The correct answer is **C**. (1) alone is insufficient because n could equal either 4 or −4. (2) alone is insufficient, because although it tells us that $n > 1$, it does not give a value for n. If the statements are combined, $n = 4$ is the only solution to the stated criteria.

21. The correct answer is **A**. (1) alone is sufficient because it gives the relative rates of the two machines; if copier A can produce twice as many copies as copier B can produce in three times the time, then it could have finished the task in one-sixth the time it took copier B, or five minutes. (2) alone is insufficient because it does not allow you to determine the relative speeds of the two machines.

22. The correct answer is **E**. (1) alone is insufficient because it could give values for c that are both integers and nonintegers. (2) alone is insufficient because it says nothing about c. If the statements are combined, a and b could still take values that make c either an integer (e.g., 1, 2) or a noninteger (e.g., 1/3, 1/6).

23. The correct answer is **E**. (1) alone is insufficient because it gives us no new information about y. (2) alone is insufficient because it tells us only that $y \geq 5$, which is not sufficient to answer the question. Combining the statements yields no new information.

24. The correct answer is **A**. (1) alone is sufficient because this statement means that $y < -2$, which means that y is not greater than 0. (2) alone is insufficient, because the statement could work for values of y that are both greater and less than 0, such as 1 and −1.

25. The correct answer is **B**. A leg of a triangle cannot be greater than or equal to the sum of the other two legs. This principle eliminates both I (11 > 5 + 4) and III (4 + 11 = 15). Therefore, II is the only acceptable length.

26. The correct answer is **C**. If the truck travels 270 miles on 18 gallons, it is getting 270/18 = 15 miles per gallon. To travel 270 miles on 10 gallons, it would need to get 27 miles per gallon. 27 − 15 = 12.

27. The correct answer is **D**. For this problem, you could calculate the dimensions of each of the four pieces of glass, but it is probably simplest to calculate the area of glass as if the four pieces were just one rectangular area of glass. If the window is 4.5 feet high, then

it is $4.5 \times 12 = 54$ inches high. 54 inches minus the 3×4 inches for the wooden panels means that the glass in the window is $54 - 12 = 42$ inches high. The window is 2.5 feet wide = 30 inches; 30 inches minus 12 inches for the panels means that the glass is 18 inches wide. $42 \times 18 = 756$ square inches. Note that the figure is not drawn to the dimensions given in the question.

28. The correct answer is **A**. You can restate the equation as $3x^2 + 3x - 7 = 3x^2 + 8$, so $3x = 15$, and $x = 5$.

29. The correct answer is **B**. One approach to this question is to set up the two equations and then eliminate one variable to solve for the other. If s represents the price of shoes and b represents the price of boots, then $22s + 16b = 650$ and $8s + 32b = 760$. To eliminate b, multiply both sides of the first equation by 2 and then subtract the second equation from the modified first equation, and you get $44s - 8s + 32b - 32b = 1{,}300 - 760$; therefore, $36s = 540$, and shoes cost \$15. Plug this value into one of the equations and you get $b =$ \$20. $20 - \$15 = \$5$.

30. The correct answer is **B**. Choose any three numbers and test them on statements I, II, and III. You will quickly find that I and III are not always true. II is always true, because mathematically it and the process in the question are doing the same thing—summing the numbers and dividing by 3.

31. The correct answer is **E**. An $8 \times 10 \times 12$-inch box contains 960 cubic inches. 288,000 total cubic inches divided by 960 cubic inches per box equals 300 boxes. 300 boxes times \$7.50 per hat equals \$2,250.

32. The correct answer is **B**. If 1,618 was 20 percent of the vote, then there were approximately 8,090 votes ($1{,}618/0.2 = 8{,}090$). 30 percent of 8,090 would be 2,427. $2{,}427 - 1{,}618 = 809$ additional votes that Chauncy would have needed in order to reach 30 percent. $\dfrac{809}{8{,}090 - 1{,}618} = 0.125 = 12.5\%$

33. The correct answer is **C**. (1) alone is insufficient because it doesn't say how many times each skier raced the course. (2) alone is insufficient because it does not exclude the possibility of sharing; there could have been 12 pairs of skis shared among the eight skiers, or there could have been a total of $12 \times 8 = 96$ skis, or any number in between. If the statements are combined, we see that the number has to be $12 \times 8 = 96$ skis.

34. The correct answer is **C**. (1) alone is insufficient, because the statement could be true if the symbol represents either subtraction or division. (2) alone is insufficient, because the statement could be true if the symbol represents multiplication, division, or addition. If the statements are combined, the only common operation is division, so the answer is 7/4.

35. The correct answer is **D**. (1) alone is sufficient; we know the eight cars over the quota will receive a total of \$4,000 in extra commission ($8 \times \$500$), so divide the remaining money by \$250 per car to determine the quota—$3{,}500/\$250 = 14$ cars. (2) alone is sufficient; \$1,750 at \$250 per car means that he sold seven cars, and if seven is half of the quota, then the quota is 14.

36. The correct answer is **A**. (1) alone is sufficient; it states that the absolute value of b is greater than the absolute value of a, which means that $\dfrac{a - b}{b + a}$ is a negative number regardless of whether a and b are both positive, both negative, or a mix of positive and negative (plug in numbers to verify); since $\dfrac{a - b}{b + a}$ is a negative number, the answer to the question has to be "yes." (2) alone is insufficient, because if (a, b) equals $(4, 2)$, then

$\dfrac{a-b}{b+a}=\dfrac{1}{3}$ and the answer is "yes," but if (a, b) equals $(4, -3)$ then $\dfrac{a-b}{b+a}=7$, and the answer is "no."

37. The correct answer is **D**. (1) alone is sufficient because it means that if there is one cod, there are two halibut and four haddock, so halibut and haddock account for 6/7 of the fish in the hold, giving a probability of 6/7 of selecting one of these fish. (2) alone is sufficient, because the probability of selecting a cod is the complement of the probability of selecting one of the other two fish, or 6/7.

Verbal

1. The correct answer is **A**. To strengthen the argument, the answer must refute the apparent connection between workplace safety seminars and higher rates of accidents; answer A provides a plausible explanation for this phenomenon.

2. The correct answer is **C**. This answer provides an alternative means by which society can obtain cultured pearls without exposing divers to risk.

3. The correct answer is **B**. If the home appliance division accounted for 70 percent of sales but only 30 percent of profits, it is clearly generating less profit per dollar of sales than is the audiovisual division.

4. The correct answer is **A**. This answer provides a substantial reason—the operation's risk of serious complications and death—for doctors to refrain from recommending the gastric bypass surgery.

5. The correct answer is **B**. The introductory paragraph brings up the subject of the factors that brought the Golden Age to an end, and the next three paragraphs discuss these factors.

6. The correct answer is **E**. The passage states, "The creators of superhero comic books, not wanting to be left behind, responded by matching their protagonists against darker criminals in more violent encounters."

7. The correct answer is **C**. The sentence preceding the mention of Wertham's book states that he believed that comic books "were leading the nation's youth into crime, violence, and drug abuse."

8. The correct answer is **A**. The last paragraph states that the CCA regulations had a numbing effect on comic book publishers, but it concludes with the statement that the industry recovered in the Silver Age. Since the passage did not state that the CCA regulations were repealed, we can infer that the companies succeeded despite the regulations.

9. The correct answer is **D**. The passage describes the trend toward horror comics in neutral terms, and it states that horror comics "aroused the anger" of Wertham.

10. The correct answer is **B**. The second paragraph states: "When these soldiers came home, they still wanted to read comic books, but they sought out more adult content. William Gaines of EC Comics was happy to meet the market demand with such grim and gritty titles as *Weird Fantasy* and *The Crypt of Terror*."

11. The correct answer is **B**. The two subject-verb phrases in question here are "The way . . . was discovered" and "whales . . . eat"; only B and E present these verb forms properly. The construction "discovered resulting from" in E is awkward and unidiomatic; B is the best answer.

12. The correct answer is **D**. A and C fail to conform to the idiomatic construction "{subject} suggested that . . ."; B is awkward and is weakened by its use of the passive voice. In E, it is unclear that "twin problems" necessarily refers to overpopulation and lack of food. D is the clearest statement.

13. The correct answer is **B**. To maintain a parallel structure with "causing" and "putting," the verb in the final clause should be "erasing" without "by"; the presence of "by" in the phrase does not make sense with the rest of the sentence. B is the clearest and most idiomatic choice.

14. The correct answer is **A**. A is grammatically correct and idiomatic, and it is stylistically preferable to the other choices.

15. The correct answer is **C**. A and B incorrectly compare "people" with "recognition" and "perception," respectively. In D, it is unclear what "the same flaws" is referring to. The construction "many people in themselves" in E is unidiomatic. C is the best answer.

16. The correct answer is **D**. If MegaCorp produces the majority of the waste that goes into the overfull garbage dumps, the company cannot validly claim that the problem was "created by homeowners."

17. The correct answer is **A**. The example given demonstrates that a past technology developed by the government that did not have immediate civilian economic applications was later adapted to provide important economic benefits.

18. The correct answer is **D**. If there is no valid way to determine which players have a 20 percent chance of suffering such an injury, there will be no way to enforce the commissioner's new policy.

19. The correct answer is **D**. If parents could be expected to consistently even out the temperature of microwaved bottles, then the concern about hot pockets in the bottle would be unfounded.

20. The correct answer is **E**. Answer E suggests that the company has a justifiable concern that if the product is not recalled, the company could be involved in a damaging lawsuit that could even lead the company into bankruptcy; this concern provides a strong economic incentive to recall the chainsaws. Answer A could be correct if the passage referred to a "moral decision" or just "the right decision," but since the passage specifically refers to an "economic decision," answer E is the best choice.

21. The correct answer is **C**. All of the other answers provide alternative reasons that the dogs might show different growth rates, but C offers no explanation for the observed difference in growth.

22. The correct answer is **B**. The subject of the sentence is "council," so the plural verb "have concluded" in A and C is incorrect. The use of the conditional "would arrive" to describe species that are already "currently" on the island is illogical, so D is incorrect. E incorrectly uses "much" to describe the countable noun "species"; countable nouns require "many" instead of "much."

23. The correct answer is **C**. The best answer should present each of the three points in the same grammatical construction, if possible. C presents each point as a gerund modified by a single adverb, which is grammatically correct and stylistically superior to the other options.

24. The correct answer is **A**. The underlined passage is grammatically correct and stylistically superior to the other choices.

25. The correct answer is **B**. The introductory phrase "Intrigued by the new rules" makes sense only when it is applied to the coach, so B is the best answer.

26. The correct answer is **C**. The passage refers to "nitrous oxides" plural, so B and D are incorrect because they use the pronoun "it." Answer E does not make sense given the preceding clause, and A is awkwardly worded, so C is the best choice.

27. The correct answer is **D**. D provides an answer for the question of why, if feathered dinosaurs did exist, no evidence of their feathers has ever been found. Answer E also provides a partial answer—that the fossil record of dinosaurs is incomplete—but it is a weaker answer than D, because it does not directly address the question of feathers.

28. The correct answer is **E**. The passage specifically states that Esai and Linda are seeking to avoid freezing cold days, and answer E states that Buena Vista has fewer freezing cold days than Sunny Glen; this fact accounts for Linda's preference for Buena Vista, despite Sunny Glen's higher average temperature.

29. The correct answer is **B**. The claim about mosquitoes is that "the mosquito is actually the most dangerous animal in Africa." The argument then provides examples of other dangerous animals, but suggests that the mosquito is more dangerous because it attacks more people and infects a very large number of them with a potentially fatal disease. The answer to the question in choice B would allow us to determine whether the quantitative argument in the passage actually does make the mosquito the "most dangerous animal in Africa." If it was determined that the "most dangerous animal" was the one most likely to kill a person in a single encounter, then the black mamba or the hippopotamus might be considered more dangerous than the mosquito. Choice E could be a follow-up to the question in B, but on its own it is less useful than B for evaluating the claim in the passage.

30. The correct answer is **C**. The passage has two themes: presenting the dangers of performance-enhancing drugs, and then discussing the reasons why the problem is so hard to eliminate. The answer needs to address both of these themes. A and E address only the first of these themes, while B and D address only the second. C offers the most complete description of the passage's purpose.

31. The correct answer is **B**. The article specifically states in the second paragraph that steroids "have been linked to . . . high blood pressure." This is the opposite of what B suggests. There is support for all of the other answers in the passage.

32. The correct answer is **E**. The author is clearly concerned by the problem of steroid abuse; this attitude is seen in a statement such as: "This chemical epidemic is a pernicious threat to both the nation's health and our collective sense of 'fair play.'" The author's pessimism is seen in the final sentence: "The sad fact is that unless the government and professional sports organizations are willing to get tough on the steroid problem, the use of performance-enhancing drugs in sports is not going to end." A is incorrect because the author is not optimistic; B is incorrect because the author is not supportive; C is incorrect because the author is not ambivalent; and D does not capture the tone of the article.

33. The correct answer is **B**. The passage states: "the drugs really do work. Athletes who dope are simply stronger and faster than their competitors who play fair." There is no substantial evidence for any of the other answers.

34. The correct answer is **D**. D is the best answer because in both situations, the latter is using illegal means to gain an advantage over the former.

35. The correct answer is **A**. Referring to "designer" steroids, in the fifth paragraph the passage states: "Chemists have discovered that they can create new drugs that produce androgenic effects but do not set off the standard doping tests." In the second paragraph, the passage states: "'androgenic' means that they increase masculine traits." There is no substantial support in the passage for any of the other answers.

36. The correct answer is **A**. By posing the question "Why is this?" the third paragraph shifts the focus of the passage from a presentation of the problems caused by steroids to explanations of why large numbers of people use them despite the risks. Answer A captures this role best.

37. The correct answer is **D**. The problem with A is that it is unclear what the "it" at the end applies to: winning or exploiting the weakness. E has the same problem. The statements in B and C are presented in an illogical order, so it is more difficult to understand the meaning of the sentence. Of the choices, D is the clearest and conforms best to standards of written English.

38. The correct answer is **C**. "Score" is a single noun, so the statements "score . . . were rising" in A and "score . . . were up" in D suffer from noun-verb agreement errors. The constructions "as . . ., with" in B and "with . . ., and" in E do not convey the causal relationship between the first and second clauses of the sentence that the statements imply, so these choices are inferior to C, which is grammatically and stylistically acceptable.

39. The correct answer is **C**. C is the clearest and most concise choice. A is less concise, and it is unclear why "but" is used here; B implies that the offenders lack both diplomas and families; D implies that the families lack diplomas; and E is awkwardly worded.

40. The correct answer is **A**. A is grammatically and stylistically correct, and is superior to any of the alternatives.

41. The correct answer is **B**. A is incorrect because it makes an error of number—"business owners . . . is less likely." C, D, and E are all confusing because they do not specify what kind of income (gambling income) they are referring to until late in the sentence. B is grammatically correct and presents the information in the most logical order.

How to Use Your Diagnostic Test Scores

Once you have reviewed the answers and explanations to the GMAT diagnostic test and scored your performance, use that information to help you plan your GMAT study program.

Three charts follow for the Quantitative, Verbal, and Integrated Reasoning sections. For each question that you missed, find the item number in one of these three charts. Check the column on the left to see the test question type for that item. If you missed a particular question type more often, you need to focus on that type of question as you prepare for the GMAT. The chapters that provide explanations and practice questions for that question type are listed in the column on the right.

GMAT Diagnostic Test: Quantitative Section

QUESTION TYPE	QUESTION NUMBER	CHAPTERS TO REVIEW
Problem Solving	1, 2, 3, 4, 5, 6, 7, 13, 14, 15, 16, 17, 18, 19, 25, 26, 27, 28, 29, 30, 31, 32	6, 8, 9, 10, 11
Data Sufficiency	8, 9, 10, 11, 12, 20, 21, 22, 23, 24, 33, 34, 35, 36, 37	7, 8, 9, 10, 11

GMAT Diagnostic Test: Verbal Section

QUESTION TYPE	QUESTION NUMBER	CHAPTERS TO REVIEW
Analysis of an Argument	Opening Writing Assessment	4
Reading Comprehension	5, 6, 7, 8, 9, 10, 30, 31, 32, 33, 34, 35, 36	12
Critical Reasoning	1, 2, 3, 4, 16, 17, 18, 19, 20, 21, 27, 28, 29	13
Sentence Correction	11, 12, 13, 14, 15, 22, 23, 24, 25, 26, 37, 38, 39, 40, 41	14

GMAT Diagnostic Test: Integrated Reasoning Section

QUESTION TYPE	QUESTION NUMBER	CHAPTERS TO REVIEW
Table Analysis	3, 7, 12	5
Graphics Interpretation	2, 6	5
Multi-Source Reasoning	4, 8, 9, 10	5
Two-Part Analysis	1, 5, 11	5

PART 3

The GMAT Analytical Writing Section

CHAPTER 4

The Analytical Writing Assessment

Introduction

The Analytical Writing Assessment, which we'll call the AWA, is the very first section of the GMAT. This is good news! The AWA takes the most planning and sustained effort on the test, so it makes sense that it would come first. You'll have 30 minutes to complete this section. That 30 minutes includes the time to read the question, consider what argument the author is trying to make, and then write a persuasive essay that makes the author's argument clear before critiquing it. That last part is important: you are not writing your opinion on a topic. Instead, you're given someone else's argument, which you are going to explain in your essay. You'll test it for flaws and bias, and you will point out what the author has forgotten or ignored.

> The AWA is also called the Analysis of an Argument. That's a good reminder that your essay should consider the argument presented—you're *analyzing* someone else's argument, in other words, not concocting your own.

An erasable notepad and a marker are provided to use in outlining, and you'll type the entire essay into the simplified word processing program on the computer (so, no, you can't jazz it up with fancy fonts!). However, you will be able to cut, paste, undo, and redo. There will be icons on the screen that make these tasks clear.

You must keep reminding yourself of the following: The AWA is not about how creative a writer you are, nor about your ability to captivate your readers. After all, the GMAT is a test for those who want to enter business, and what matters most in that field is your ability to write clearly and precisely. The AWA isn't interested in your skill with metaphors or imagery. Instead, it asks you to take an argument and communicate it, as well as its strengths and weaknesses, effectively to your readers.

Okay, then. What kind of argument will you be analyzing? Well, you don't have to worry about being asked an extremely controversial question. It will be a topic of general interest, sometimes related to business, but not always. The question will not presuppose that you have some knowledge about business, though; in other words, it won't ask you for your opinion on an argument that's based on a particular stock sale from 2003.

How the AWA Is Used

The AWA is scored on a scale from 0 (the lowest) to 6 (the highest). If you arrange to have your GMAT scores sent to business schools, the schools will be able to see your AWA score along with a copy of your essay. Some people say that the AWA score isn't as important as the overall GMAT score, and that's certainly true at some schools. But others are genuinely interested in your ability to write well and will pay special attention to the AWA score. The bottom line is that you should do your best on this and every section of the test.

If the AWA worries you, remember that this is the kind of writing in which practice can make perfect. Try your hand at the sample essays presented here.

A good score on the AWA will help your application, but—be warned!—a poor score might raise some red flags for the admissions office. Admissions personnel may take the time to compare your application essays to your AWA essay, and if the former are much better than the latter, there might be concern that your essays were written by someone else. If all of your essays are equally subpar, your application could be in trouble.

How to Approach the AWA

The thought of writing an essay might freak you out, but please don't let your concerns keep you from preparing. No, you do not have enough time to become the next J. K. Rowling, but that's not what the raters are looking for anyway. The AWA asks for a very specific type of writing and grades it in an equally specific way. (More on that in a moment.) So long as your writing is clear and makes a sound critique of the argument you've been given, you'll do fine. In fact, flourishes won't help. Keep your writing simple, focused, and to the point. And watch your grammar!

First, read the entirety of the argument (the question, that is) you've been given. You might want to jot down your thoughts as you read it. Ask yourself questions as you read: What are the flaws of this argument? What does the argument assume without proof? What counterexamples might be raised against this argument? What else could be included in this argument to make it stronger?

You can expect the argument presented on your GMAT to be on a topic of general interest, often related to industry or entertainment. You will not be asked to write about anything that touches on particular political or religious views. If the topic you're assigned happens to dance close to your own political or religious views, do try your best not to bring them into what should be a fairly dry, impersonal essay.

Next try to come up with a thesis statement: a sentence that clearly states your critique of the argument you've been given. You don't have much time, so go with your gut. There's no need to find an obscure way to rebut some premise of the argument. Focus on the first thing that comes to mind: what do you want to say about this piece?

We've said it before, and we'll say it again: Outlining your essay before you begin writing is strongly recommended. Your first paragraph should introduce your critique, including your thesis statement. Get that down in your outline. Next, note what you'll put in your next paragraphs (no more than three, please, unless you type like the wind) that develop your critique. Use examples that illustrate your points. Figure out what you'll do to conclude your essay strongly, by restating your thesis and pointing out what should be done to make the argument stronger.

With your outline in hand, begin writing. Be concise and get to the point. You may not have time to proofread, so do your best to write clearly. Avoid tricky sentence structures and punctuation, such as dashes and semicolons, unless you're sure you can use them correctly.

Don't try to have it both ways by "agreeing and disagreeing" with the presented argument, even if that's how you really feel. Although you can make a gesture to a worthwhile opposing point that the argument makes or that could be made against it, you want to principally stick to one side of the argument.

If time permits, reread your essay. Don't cut large swaths of the essay unless you're sure you have time to retype or paste them before your half hour is up! Above all, make sure your essay reads well: full sentences, coherent logic, paragraphs, logical transitions, a clear introduction, and a conclusion.

It's almost impossible for test takers not to assume that a longer essay is a better essay. And sure, a two-paragraph essay will give readers pause. But don't keep writing just to fill up the screen. If you have only two strong supporting paragraphs, write those and move on to the conclusion.

How the AWA Is Scored

As mentioned, you'll receive a score between 0 and 6. This score comes from professional essay raters, some of whom are college and university faculty members and others graduate students. Not all will be in the field of management education. All of the raters are trained to be fair in evaluating your responses, although, of course, you should avoid anything that could cause offense. If you are a non-native writer of English, you should know that raters are particularly trained to be sensitive to your situation.

Your responses will be scored with these criteria in mind:

- The overall quality of your ideas
- Your ability to organize and express those ideas
- Your ability to logically support your ideas with relevant examples
- Your ability to write clearly and in grammatically correct form

An essay that receives a ranking of 6 is considered Outstanding: It's cogent, articulate, and full of relevant examples. It demonstrates a mastery of the elements of effective writing. On the other end of the scale, an essay that receives a 0 is off-topic, written in another language, merely copies the question given or is gibberish. The middle scores are Strong (5), Adequate (4), Limited (3), Seriously Flawed (2), and Fundamentally Deficient (1). You don't want to get lower than a 4.

All essays are read twice. Each rater is expected to spend no more than two minutes on each essay, and they'll read several hundred essays on exactly the same topic. If that sounds like they'll be skimming, yes, they will. They'll be looking for the logic of your summation and the flow of your essay—there's no time for flourishes, remember?

After the first read, your essay will be read again, this time by a rater with even less time. Oh, and also? That second rater is a computer. Yes, that's right. The ACT employs a specially designed computer program to scan your essay and give it a ranking based on predetermined criteria. If there's a discrepancy between the human rater and the computer, another human rater will read your essay to arbitrate.

All of this means that your writing is not going to get much time or attention. It's in your best interest to avoid being clever or creative. Write an essay that is organized and logical, and that employs good grammar. That's the kind of good writing an overtired human and an unhuman computer can appreciate. Let's take a look at those qualities.

Organization

A well-organized essay flows like water; the reader, running her tired eyes over your words, won't find any reason to stop reading. The thesis statement will be clear. The essay will be broken into paragraphs. The argument will be easy to follow. The conclusion will wrap everything up tidily. The good news is that composing a well-organized essay is a matter of logic and memorization.

Start by making sure you have a clear thesis statement. It should kick off, or at least be very close to, the opening of your essay. The easiest way to craft an organized essay is to draft a thesis statement that pushes against the argument you've been given. The rest of your paragraph should then list the reasons you'll use to prove your argument is superior to the one provided.

> Waiting until the end of your introductory paragraph to get to your thesis statement sounds like good writing—and it might be more enjoyable for the reader. But be sure you don't forget about the thesis statement before you rush on to the second paragraph. It should be crystal clear and easily spotted.

Write a paragraph for each supporting reason you have. If you start to run out of time, go ahead and cut back on your reasoning paragraphs, just don't forget to return to the opening paragraph and remove the cut reason there, as well. It's okay (although probably not going to get you a 6) to have only one supporting paragraph. More than three is asking a lot of your readers, although you certainly can write them if you have the wind in your sails (although maybe you should save that wind for the other 3½ hours of test ahead of you). Make sure that the supporting paragraphs, no matter how many, make well-argued points. Don't pad the essay to make it longer. Start your supporting paragraphs with whatever you feel is your strongest argument. That way, if you have to drop paragraphs toward the end, your strongest argument is in the paper.

You can also help the organization of your essay by giving the reader helpful transitions. These can both highlight arguments (such as "On the one hand …" or "Contrastingly …") and provide a structure ("First …" "Next …" "Last …"). These words denote an organized essay.

In your conclusion, restate that your argument is correct, and suggest what the author could have done to make his or her argument more persuasive. Make sure you write a conclusion. It's better to skip a supporting paragraph than the conclusion.

An essay written this way isn't going to set the world on fire, of course, but this structure is what the GMAT wants. It's what the computer (your second reader) is programmed to look for. Why disappoint them?

Please fight the temptation to make a unique argument, no matter how tempting. If you're fighting the urge to write a first-person narrative rebuff of the argument you've been given, just remind yourself that a computer—a computer!—will be reading this essay. Give it what it wants.

Logic

Logic is the heart of business. Decisions are supposed to be made for logical reasons. It makes sense that an essay on a test for entry into management would want you to employ logic. Thus, avoid making an overly personal and emotional appeal, even if you have an amazing personal anecdote that you think makes your whole case. It's okay to mention it, but don't leave it without surrounding airtight logic. Build your argument logically, one point building on the next. Nothing should make your reader stop to question what you're declaring.

To be logical doesn't mean that you can't be interesting. No matter what your thesis is, be sure you have an example or scenario that supports it. A little story can go a long way, even if you're using a hypothetical example. Do not make a point in support of your argument without providing reasoning around it. If you really can't think of anything to support your point, don't make it.

Good Grammar

The basics count, of course. You want to spell all words correctly, use the correct punctuation, and write sentences that match verbs and subjects. All the rules that you're going to review later in this book for the Sentence Correction questions will help.

But there's more: You want to write fluidly. This means that your sentences are not all in the same style or of the same length. Try to avoid using the same words over and over again (a particular glitch in business writing). Also, work to avoid putting words in the same order too often; too many subject-verb-object sentences in a row will read like an elementary school student's writing.

On the other hand, don't write to impress. Fancy words that you haven't used quite right; examples taken from Greek literature in which you've misremembered the moral; an anecdote about the time you scored the winning goal in your team's state championship (although you were in the band, never on the field)—those are all the type of thing that may make your essay seem like you're trying to show off or sell yourself instead of sticking to the task at hand. Not to mention, how embarrassing would it be if you're caught lying? Simple is best!

Try to avoid business clichés, such as "getting everyone on the same page" and "figuring out who's going to drive the bus." Sure, the readers might not care, but you don't want admissions counselors at your prospective school rolling their eyes at your writing.

Maximizing Your Score

Here are some tips we think will help you boost your essay score and also make it more appealing to the admissions office of the university of your choice.

Use Who You Are and What You Know

You have a unique voice and perspective—your own—and it's okay to make your essay stand out by making use of them. You might know a statistic that is relevant to the point at hand. If so, include it! Or you might be a whiz at connecting an argument to a historical event or a literary reference. If you can, make that connection! Or, best of all, you might happen to have specific personal experience that can be used to attack or bolster the argument being made. Definitely include that, if you can. Outside knowledge is a great way to make your essay pop out to the reader (the human one, anyway). Just be sure that it's relevant and correct, and not left on its own when it needs support.

Acknowledge the Argument of the Other Side

A good debater is rarely surprised by her opponent's arguments because she's taken the time to think through what he will say. She often even knows which counterarguments are the strongest or most convincing. You should do the same with your AWA. Consider what counterarguments can be made to what you're stating, reference them in your essay, and dismiss them as forcefully as you can. However, be careful that you don't come off as arguing both sides. Even if you truly think both sides of an argument have merit (which happens quite often), only forcefully argue the argument that you state in your thesis.

Don't Quit Early

Another gentle reminder: Write long *and* write well. No reader is going to award you a 6 simply because you've written about your cat for 1,000 words. But you shouldn't be done with your two-paragraph essay with 15 minutes of writing time to go. You should write as much as you can while keeping your argument clear and structured. Write the longest best essay you can!

Spelling

Does spelling matter? Well, yes and no. No, it's not factored into your scoring, and no, you're not expected to be perfect. That said, frequent errors or repetitive errors send subconscious signals to your human reader's brain: they say, "This person isn't detail-oriented and doesn't quite know what he's doing. Thus, he shouldn't get a 6." The computer reader is even trickier: if you misspell a word so that it can't understand your meaning, well, your essay's score is going to plummet. And there's no spellchecker on the GMAT word processing program to help you, sorry.

The bottom line is: If you know you have a tendency to make the same mistake frequently, now is the time to train yourself out of it. And if you possibly can, budget a minute at the end of the writing session to proofread.

Type Well

The GMAT obviously and clearly favors people who can type well and clearly. There's no way around it: slower typists are in trouble. Ideally, you'll practice typing your essays so that you'll get better, fast; there's really no point in practicing handwriting the AWA. If you're very concerned, at the very least you should practice your typing skills on a near-daily basis. Type e-mails, blog posts, letters, really, anything you can to improve. You'll need good typing skills in business school, anyway!

We can't help but emphasize that the practice tests and problem-solving drills included in this book will only be helpful to you if you take the time to make the conditions under which you're working similar to the test itself. If you give yourself an hour to handwrite the AWA, you're not much better prepared for when you take the test and must type the AWA in a half hour.

Understand the Schedule That Helps the Most

With all of the above in mind, here's what we suggest for the 30 minutes you have. By the way, keep the clock up on the screen for the essay; it really helps you know when you need to move on to the next step.

1. Read the argument you're given carefully (1 minute)
2. Choose your response and outline your essay (4–6 minutes)
3. Type your essay (22 minutes)
4. Proofread the essay for obvious typos (1 minute)

Notice that this asks you to spend about 7 minutes planning before you begin writing. This can seem like a long time, but planning is key! An outline helps you figure out what your main idea is, how you want to support it, and what reasons you're going to use to do so. If you just dive in and start writing, your argument is going to develop as you write, and you run a very strong risk of having to throw out your first paragraph by the time you've gotten through the second. Plus, remember that the essay is partially graded on how well organized it is!

Keeping to the pace we've laid out above may not seem natural. But that's why we're offering five practice sample arguments (coming up soon) for your use. Don't just skim them to see what kind of arguments you may be given! Actually use them to practice pacing. See how long 4–6 minutes really is. Learn how much you can type in 22 minutes. You'll adjust to the schedule more quickly than you think.

An Analysis of an Argument Example

At the beginning of the GMAT, when you get to the AWA, the computer will present you with an argument such as the one you'll see below. You are tasked with analyzing that argument. Keep in mind, these arguments are *deliberately flawed.* At some point in the argument, a leap in reasoning will be taken or a flaw in logic will occur. These arguments read well and make sense up to a point, but then … Your job is to find that point and exploit it.

Here's a sample argument, including the directions that will be on the GMAT:

The following is a transcript of a statement made by a television network executive at an industry gathering:

Network television is suffering economically because of streaming television. Viewership is down and advertisers are seeking other venues to promote their products. This fate was an inevitable result of the television industry's misguided attempt to switch from scripted shows to reality television. Reality television is cheaper to produce but less sustainable as a series over multiple years and takes less focused attention from viewers. They became more comfortable with switching to other forms of watching television, such as using streaming devices. If network television wants to recover its viewership, it needs to return to an all-scripted show format. Also, reality television is terrible for children to watch.

Discuss how well-reasoned you find this argument. In your discussion, be sure to analyze the line of reasoning and the use of evidence in the argument. For example, you may need to consider what questionable assumptions underlie the thinking and what alternative examples or counterexamples might weaken the conclusion. You can also discuss what sort of evidence would strengthen or refute the argument, what changes in the argument would make it more logically sound, and what, if anything, would help you better evaluate its conclusion.

All AWAs are followed by similar instructions, so go ahead and get familiar with them now.

Now that you understand the directions, it's time to practice the first step: reading the argument carefully. You want to figure out exactly what the argument is saying: What is its thesis statement or conclusion? What are the premises the argument is based on? What are the unstated assumptions?

Let's start with the premises. This argument has at least three:

1. Network television is suffering economically because of streaming television.
2. This fate was an inevitable result of the television industry's misguided attempt to switch from scripted shows to reality television.
3. If network television wants to recover its viewership, it needs to return to an all-scripted show format.

You'll notice that the third premise is also the conclusion. Notice, also, that the conclusion isn't the last sentence in the paragraph, but the next-to-last. The last sentence is a bit of a tangent. We'll talk about that in a moment.

Next, we need to figure out if the argument presented is persuasive. Remember not to bring in your own biases. You might really hate reality television and be eager to find a way to dismiss it. But don't let your bias guide your analysis of whether *this* argument does that work or not.

So, how do we figure out if an argument is persuasive? We have to check to see if the following are true:

1. The premises themselves are true.
2. The solution suggested actually would solve the problem reported.
3. The solution suggested wouldn't lead to other results that would (perhaps inadvertently) make the problem worse.

While you can find flaws in the argument you're given, you should be careful about questioning the facts. Stick to what you're sure is an arguable point.

Let's check on this argument's persuasiveness:

1. **The premises themselves are true.** The first one does seem to be true, yes.
2. **The solution suggested actually would solve the problem reported.** The second premise is flawed: you probably already thought of a few reasons why people have switched from network television to online streaming: convenience, privacy, and low cost all come to mind. Plus, the connection between streaming television and reality television probably seems a little nebulous, right? That's because it is.
3. **The solution suggested wouldn't lead to other results that would make the problem worse.** The third premise is also flawed. There's no guarantee that returning to all-scripted format will draw viewers back to network television. Plus, this premise asserts that there was once a time when network television was entirely scripted, which was never the case.

With those thoughts in mind, you can begin to sketch out an outline of what you're going to say. You have noticed several distinct flaws in the argument, so you know where it is vulnerable. All you have to do is decide what your central rebuttal will be.

We're presenting the essay writing process as if it takes distinct steps, but of course, you can combine your thought processes. For example, in reading the prompt for the first time, you can make notes about the premises. And while debating the validity of the premises, you can arrive at the argument you're going to make.

Time to outline! Your outline might look something like this:

Paragraph 1: The argument is flawed. Although the author correctly asserts that network television has lost viewership due to online streaming, the argument is not built logically and cannot hold.

Paragraphs 2–4: The premises are flawed. People have switched to television streaming for many reasons, none of which are mentioned. The author makes a connection between streaming and reality television that isn't supported. And the author brings up a point about how children shouldn't watch reality TV that isn't connected to the rest of the argument.

Paragraph 5: The conclusion the author puts forward doesn't make sense—getting rid of reality television won't necessarily bring people back to network television.

Paragraph 6: Your conclusion, which is a summary: the argument is not clearly made and the conclusion not properly drawn from a logical review of the situation. A better solution to dwindling network television audiences can be proposed.

This is a pretty clearly drawn outline, as you can see. You certainly don't have to be so detailed. But the great thing about an outline like this one is that your essay itself is just connecting all of the above together. You've done the hard work of thinking through the argument and finding its flaws. Your logical structure is in place. Of course, no matter whether you jot down the barest outline or go into even more detail than we have here, what's most important is that you have time to write a fully realized essay. So don't spend more than about 5 minutes on the outline.

Now, let's take a look at a high-scoring essay that's written in response to the argument presented above.

> The television industry executive argues that streaming television is hurting network television's economic stability, and that in order to revive network television, it needs to abandon reality shows and "return to an all-scripted show format." While the executive does address a significant current problem for the television industry, the logic of her argument and the conclusion she reaches are both fundamentally flawed. The premises of her argument fail to adequately support her conclusion, and, more worryingly, if the conclusion presented here was implemented, the television industry would face an even greater economic burden.
>
> First, the premises are flawed. It is inaccurate to correlate viewers' switch to streaming television as a direct result of the network's switch to reality TV. It is incorrect to state that networks abandoned scripted television—scripted shows have been shown frequently throughout the medium's history—and the point overlooks the fact that streaming television often features reality television as well. It's also a well-known fact that reality television scores extremely high ratings in viewership numbers; in fact, more people watch "Survivor" than any show that streams off-network.
>
> Further, the author fails to mention the many other motivations for audiences switching from cable and network television to streaming television, including the quality of programming, the ability to watch shows on multiple devices, and the lower price of doing so. All of these factors influence a person's decision to switch to streaming television, and the executive's proposed solution does nothing to address them.
>
> Also, along with failing to explain the entire landscape of the presented problem, the executive dilutes her argument with her final sentence, a vague statement about how children shouldn't watch reality television. This has nothing to do with her premises and lends the argument the air of being biased against reality television for hidden reasons.
>
> The executive's most fundamental error is the certain failure of her proposed solution, which does not address the problem. She suggests that networks "return" to scripted shows and reject reality television. This implies, incorrectly, that scripted television shows have vanished from network television. They haven't. It also implies that viewers

have turned to streaming television because there they can find the scripted shows they miss on network television. Again, this misunderstands the appeal of television streaming. However, the executive's biggest mistake is to fail to see that scripted television is extremely expensive to produce, far more so than reality television. Insisting on an all-scripted format will force networks to pour more money into production costs without any guarantee that viewers will return to their shows.

For the reasons stated above, the executive's argument simply doesn't hold up. If she were truly serious about addressing the problem of dwindling network television numbers, she would thoroughly research the reasons why so many viewers prefer streaming television and come up with ways for network television to speak to those needs.

Let's take a look at some of the techniques used in this essay that will be helpful to you. Notice how closely it hews to the outline; even if the writer thought of a new idea as she was writing, she worked it into the essay without derailing the careful outline.

The writer also began with a brief paraphrase of the argument she was given. Notice that she did not bring up every point the executive made, but she did give a brief summary of the entire idea, tip to tail. This technique is helpful in two ways—it allows the writer to recap the argument (and make sure she understands it) while allowing readers to see what her main interest in the argument is. Also, it provides a nice lead-in to the thesis: that this argument is flawed.

After showing that she understands the argument presented, the writer goes on to explain why she is not convinced by it. The second, third, and fourth paragraphs all point out flaws in the argument (with the second paragraph pointing out the biggest flaw, while the third and fourth are each less important than the prior flaw). It's important to note that the writer was particularly effective in showing that the flaws in the executive's premise will keep her solution from being effective: they're fatal flaws, not just little blips.

The conclusion of the essay is also strong. In the fifth paragraph, the writer points out why the executive's idea won't solve the problem she's trying to address. And the conclusion offers a brief recap, noting that there are some good ideas in the argument, but that the solution won't fix the problem. The essay closes with a suggestion for a better plan that will work toward that solution.

Notice that throughout the essay the structure is clear. It's very easy to read and to follow the logic the writer is employing. Everything after the first paragraph flows from the thesis; unlike the example argument, this one sticks to its main point throughout. The essay also makes good use of structural words that guide the reader: *First, Next, Finally*, and so on. These signal that the argument flows. And while the writing here isn't going to set the house afire, there are no major grammatical or spelling errors.

What this essay doesn't employ is much in the way of support. There's a reference to a specific TV show, and some outside knowledge of television seems evident, but there are no anecdotes or statistics. Maybe the writer couldn't think of anything. That's okay, but it might knock the essay's score down a bit. Its likely score is a 5 or 6.

Sample Arguments

Practicing the AWA is a must before taking the GMAT. You will be amazed at how much more confident and prepared you feel if you just take the time to read several sample arguments, and then outline and type an essay. Like any skill, writing improves with practice. The AWA is a specific kind of writing, and your skill at it will vastly improve with practice. So, make the most of these practice arguments: set up conditions so that you actually type an AWA essay under timed conditions. (Limit yourself to 30 minutes.) Here's a reminder of the instructions:

Discuss how well reasoned you find this argument. In your discussion, be sure to analyze the line of reasoning and the use of evidence in the argument. For example, you may need to consider what questionable assumptions underlie the thinking and what alternative examples or counterexamples might weaken the conclusion. You can also discuss what sort of evidence would strengthen or refute the argument, what changes in the argument would make it more logically sound, and what, if anything, would help you better evaluate its conclusion.

1. The following appeared as a part of an article in a daily newspaper:

> A legally required computerized on-board warning system will be installed in all new train engines beginning in 2018. This warning system will virtually eliminate the chance of train collisions, a surprisingly common problem. One train's warning system can receive an alert from another train's GPS system. This will alert train personnel of the possibility of a collision should they fail to change their path. The warning system can also recommend actions that the train personnel should take.

2. The following appeared in a report by a school board member to the school community:

> As many of you know, we recently received our school's scores from the latest standardized test, and they were very disappointing. When compared with the test scores of students at Boyer Middle School, our scores are even more disappointing, averaging 20 points lower than theirs. Improving our students' scores is not negotiable; there is no other criteria that more clearly shows our school's ability to educate well. Therefore, I have made a study of the curriculum at Boyer Middle School. The majority of the students there study one or more ancient languages, including Latin. Therefore, I suggest that students at our school immediately begin to study Latin, too.

3. The following appeared in a promotional e-mail sent by a local website, OurTown.org, encouraging area businesses to purchase advertising on the site:

> The best way to reach your potential customers is by advertising on OurTown.org! Any local business owner will tell you the same! Why, seven of our town's top ten doctors, three of our top five restaurants, and two of our top eight pet groomers advertise with us! One local handyman chose not to purchase advertising on OurTown.org, because he thought "no one reads websites for the ads." Well, after a disappointing year of business, he purchased an ad on OurTown.org and says that his business has doubled in that time! The truth of it is, you can't afford NOT to advertise on OurTown.org!

4. The following appeared in an article in a business magazine's opinion page:

> Most companies would agree that as the potential for emotional trauma to employees rises, so, too, should employees' wages. As a society, we consistently recognize that jobs that require more from workers are the best at financial compensation. But there's a better idea out there: that is, that companies make their jobs less emotionally taxing. That would lower the potential trauma for employees and thus the need for larger paychecks. Ultimately, companies would be fiscally more responsible if they reduce the potential for emotional trauma for their employees.

5. The following statement was made by a member of the Board of Supervisors of Atlantic University:

> When Atlantic University had only one campus, it was more profitable than it is today, with five branch campuses. I think it makes sense to close down those five branch campuses and move everyone to our main campus. This will improve our profitability by cutting costs, and it will allow students to identify with Atlantic University more strongly, since they'll all be in one location.

Sample High-Scoring Responses

Following are two sample high-scoring essays (they'd likely receive a 5 or 6) for your use in comparing your own essays in response to the first two sample arguments in this section.

1. The article states that a new on-board warning system, to be installed in new train engines beginning in 2018, will improve train safety by warning train personnel about potential collisions between trains. While it's undeniable that such a system could greatly improve train safety, the article's conclusion that the system will "virtually eliminate" train collisions is fundamentally flawed. The premise is flawed, because there is not enough evidence presented in the article to support this claim, and the conclusion drawn fails to consider many other potentialities that should be factored in.

To begin with, the article's premises are flawed. The new warning systems will not be installed until 2018 and then only on new engines. Unless all existing engines are removed from service and replaced by new engines at that time—an unlikely scenario—the warning system will not be comprehensive enough to be entirely effective. Further, there's not enough information presented about how the warning system will work. For example, how close will the trains be before the system is triggered? Will there even be enough time for a new route to be selected before a crash occurs?

However, the article's most fundamental flaw is to assume that train collisions occur only because train personnel are not aware of their proximity to other trains. This fails to recognize that there are many other factors in play that could lead to accidents. If the train personnel are not at their appointed stations, for example, they cannot see any information presented to them. The same is true if they are operating trains while inebriated or simply ignoring the information as it comes in. Also problematic is that the train's new system will simply provide options for avoiding a train collision for the operators to follow: what happens if the operators do not follow those instructions? The system continues to rely too heavily on flawed human operators.

Because this article leaves out several key issues and leaps to make an assumption about how train safety will improve, it is not sound. The author does make a reasonable case that the warning system will improve train safety, but the argument falls short of convincing readers that this improvement will solve the cause of many train crashes. If the author had investigated the cause of train collisions more thoroughly and presented the uncovered evidence in the essay, this argument would be much stronger.

2. The argument by a school board member describes how the school's students' standardized test scores are lower than the school board wanted, and asserts that low scores will put the school in a bad light. He then explains that another local school, Boyer Middle School, scored much higher, on average, than his school on the standardized tests. Noting that students at Boyer study Latin, he suggests that students at his school should study Latin as well. The conclusion that the writer draws is not based on the evidence he presents. It does not employ logical thinking and therefore is fundamentally flawed.

The argument is based on a set of premises that are not correct. Most important, the argument is based on the premise that what makes Boyer Middle School students excel is their study of Latin, and that if the other school's students merely begin to study

Latin their scores will automatically improve. But there's no direct correlation between the study of Latin and the standardized test scores. In fact, most standardized tests include questions involving a significant portion of math skills; why would studying Latin help students improve those skills? And why is the author so sure that Boyer's high scores are due to the study of Latin instead of the many other techniques the school might employ to help students score well on tests?

Further, the argument presumes that there are no criteria other than the scores on standardized tests that will show that his school can educate well. The wording is vague—what does it mean to "educate well"? No matter what the phrase means to the author, however, surely there are other criteria that would be considered, including graduation rate and college acceptance rate. The author doesn't even account for how the standardized test scores, which are not released directly to the public, would become well-known enough to affect his school's reputation.

Because the argument makes a giant leap to link the study of Latin with high standardized scores, it simply bends logic until it breaks. It cannot be considered sound. The author would be better off making a case for how the study of Latin can show improvements in many disciplines studied in middle school, and how improvement in those skills can, in turn, improve standardized testing scores. A more nuanced understanding of how schools' reputations are built would also be helpful in creating a persuasive argument.

Why Does the AWA Sample 1 Score Highly?

Notice that the essay opens with a clear restatement of facts from the article, indicating that the writer has familiarized himself with it. The end of the first paragraph contains a clear thesis—"The premise is flawed, because there is not enough evidence…"—which shows that the writer has considered the argument and intends to prove it is flawed by focusing on the lack of evidence and the weak conclusion.

This writer only includes two body paragraphs, but his writing is focused within them, making the total essay stronger than if he had written three weaker paragraphs. In the second paragraph, he repeats a key idea from his opening, even using the same words ("premises are flawed"). The rest of the paragraph shows the flaws and presents a few hypothetical questions, which is an effective argumentative technique. The third paragraph begins with a transition ("However"), which shows the writer will be thinking more deeply about the "fundamental flaw" in the essay. Here, too, he asks a question and uses information from the article. Notice that the paragraph has an opinion: the writer decided that this is the most fundamental flaw and states it boldly. He knows that even if a reader disagrees with him, the point of the essay is to craft a strong argument.

The conclusion is solid. The writer points out what's missing in the argument presented and shows how that means the argument is therefore flawed. He makes sure to show that the argument isn't without merit, just that it doesn't quite get the job done. That kind of fair tone is necessary in this essay—stridency is not the goal.

This essay isn't perfect, by any means. The author repeats the word *flaw* and its variations far too often and doesn't add much in the way of personality to the essay. But it gets the job done and therefore would score a 5 or 6 from AWA readers.

Why Does the AWA Sample 2 Score Highly?

The first paragraph in this essay is not as strong as the one in the prior sample essay, but it still would score well. Notice that the writer of this essay makes the assumption that the school board member quoted in the argument is a man. That's not clear in the question and indicates a tendency to make assumptions which might not please the grader. The writer here spends several sentences in the first paragraph summarizing the argument. That's not bad, exactly, so long as the rest of the essay is detailed, too. There is a clear thesis, which is great: "The conclusion that the writer draws is not based on the evidence he presents. It does not employ logical thinking and therefore is fundamentally flawed."

This writer has also produced two body paragraphs. In the first she approaches the first part of her thesis: that the argument is based on incorrect premises. It's a bit jarring to go from the first sentence to the transition "Most important…" because she has not explained what is of lesser importance. But the point that she's making—that there's no correlation between studying Latin and a rise in test scores—is clear and backs up her thesis. She strengthens this argument by bringing her own knowledge (that standardized tests include questions involving a significant portion of math skills) to it as well. She also effectively closes the paragraph with a few questions.

In the third paragraph, the author uses a transition ("Further…") and attacks the language of the argument, always an effective technique if the argument is vague at any point. After pointing out the vagueness, the essay writer digs deeper into the issue, showing how facile and vague the speaker's logic is. This is a very strong move and makes up for some of the opening paragraph's minor weaknesses.

And the conclusion is even stronger. The writer really sticks her landing here, with strong word choices like "giant leap" and "bends logic until it breaks." Anything more would be too harsh, but these phrases make it clear how facile she finds the argument to be. To conclude, she suggests how the argument could be made stronger, a good choice for showing openness to it. Although there are flaws that might, depending on the reader, bring down the score, it is most likely that this essay would score a 5 or a 6.

Common AWA Essay Writing Mistakes

- Starting without a plan. It's a rare writer who can organize an essay well without an outline before writing.
- Skipping the proofreading stage. There are mistakes in your first draft, and they will cost you points.
- Wandering off topic. The essay is about the argument as presented, and even if it evokes a strong personal response, you need to stay on that train of thought.
- Allowing common spelling errors (such as substituting "their" for "they're") and grammatical mistakes.
- Shifting through too many verb tenses and/or pronouns. (If you start the essay in the past tense, stay there, and make sure you're not writing the essay in "we" sometimes and "I" at other times.)
- Slipping into aphorisms or clichés. (Phrases like "You only live once" and "Just follow your dreams" indicate you've gone off topic and are struggling.)
- Changing your mind halfway through. (Even if you suddenly see the error in the argument you're making, it's best to see it through to the end instead of changing course. You are graded on the strength of your essay in presenting *an* argument, not presenting the *correct* argument.)

- Trying to have it both ways. It's best to settle on one line of thinking and see it through to the end.
- Focusing too narrowly. Make sure you understand the whole argument, not just a portion of it.
- Finding errors in the argument. (We don't mean errors of logic, of course, but rather finding what you think is a factual error. Your job is to accept the facts as presented and attack the logic and premises thereof.)
- Ending without concluding. We're not sure why this happens, but AWA essays all too often just end without a formal conclusion. Make sure you wrap up your thoughts. Check the sample essays in this chapter for ideas on how to do so if you're not sure.

The GMAT Integrated Reasoning Section

CHAPTER 5

Integrated Reasoning

Introduction

The Integrated Reasoning section tests your ability to synthesize math and verbal information to solve complex problems. This section may seem intimidating, but these questions simply test skills you've used in school and when taking other tests. The difference is that you must combine these skills to answer data-intensive questions correctly.

The Integrated Reasoning section is intended to provide business schools with additional information to help evaluate admissions candidates. The decision-making and analysis skills that candidates display in answering the questions can help schools identify which candidates are most likely to be successful within the classroom and in their careers.

The Integrated Reasoning section has a 30-minute time limit. The section includes 12 questions, some of which may have multiple parts.

A special online calculator is available to use for this section of the test only. You may NOT bring your own calculator, and you cannot use the online calculator for any other section of the test.

Integrated Reasoning questions test your ability to solve complicated problems using information from multiple sources that model real-world situations. They test your logic and reasoning abilities, your skills at analyzing and synthesizing information, and your math and computation skills. They also test your ability to convert between graphical and verbal representations of ideas. Several different skills may be tested by a single question. And, like real-world situations, extra information is often provided.

Integrated Reasoning questions do not test your business knowledge, but they do test the types of real-world skills you would use in the classroom or on the job. While you might never need to measure the hypotenuse of a right triangle over the course of your career, you will likely be required to read text, tables, and charts and to make decisions based on complex information.

There are four types of GMAT Integrated Reasoning (IR) questions:

1. Table Analysis
2. Graphics Interpretation
3. Multi-Source Reasoning
4. Two-Part Analysis

Each format requires you to solve complex problems using information from multiple sources. Understanding these formats will help you know what to expect and how to approach each question.

Be aware that IR questions not only differ in format from the other question types on the GMAT, but they also differ in content. The IR questions give you more information than is needed to arrive at correct answers. You must carefully go through the provided information to determine what information is relevant to the questions posed. A caveat: Even though you may have personal knowledge of the topic presented, always answer IR questions based only on the information given to you.

Table Analysis

Table Analysis (TA) questions require you to analyze data in sortable tables that look like spreadsheets. You may have to sort the data to determine the accuracy of given answer statements.

Each TA question is composed of a series of subquestions. You answer the subquestions, one by one, by selecting one of two opposite choices (e.g., "Yes/No," "True/False," "Would help explain/Would not help explain," etc.). You must answer all subquestions correctly to receive credit for the question.

Useful Tips for TA Questions

Keep the following points in mind when confronting TA questions.

- Inspect the table carefully. Make sure you know what information is provided.
- Tables are organized in *columns* and *rows*. The columns go up and down the table vertically from top to bottom, and the rows go across the table horizontally from left to right. Each unit of data is presented in a *cell*.
- The first row of a table is called the *header* row. The header row contains category names that identify the data in each column.
- To sort the information in a table, select the column's category name from the drop-down menu provided. The data in the entire table will be reorganized according to that column. Information can be sorted from lowest to highest (1–100 or A–Z) only.
- Use estimates where possible to calculate answers quickly. However, be prepared to do some arithmetic calculations (e.g., find a percentage, divide by a decimal, etc.). Use the online calculator as needed.
- Be sure to select an answer for all subquestions.

Example

The table below gives information on total deliveries (total delivery trips made to addresses on record) and total items delivered (packages and letters) in 2016 by a private company for a one-year period to 21 zip codes throughout the country. The 21 zip codes fall among the top 35 for this annual period in terms of both total deliveries and total items delivered by the company. In addition to providing the numbers of total deliveries and total items delivered for each route, the table also gives the percent of increase or decrease over the numbers for 2015 and the rank of the route for total deliveries and total items delivered.

On the real exam, you will be able to sort tables by any of their columns. (Columns can be sorted in ascending order only.) The table is shown with its data sorted in different ways to mirror the actual test.

Sorted by Percent Change in Deliveries (Column 5)

DELIVERY ROUTE			DELIVERIES			ITEMS DELIVERED		
CITY	STATE	ZIP CODE	NUMBER	% CHANGE	RANK	NUMBER	% CHANGE	RANK
Washington	DC	20011	73,997	−8.3	5	126,048	6.2	21
Bellevue	WA	98004	41,653	−1.9	22	125,297	4.1	22
Pensacola	FL	32506	69,472	−1.2	9	290,771	−1.7	1
Little Rock	AR	72203	76,247	−0.9	4	204,956	−0.6	10
Miami	FL	33124	69,804	−0.9	8	127,793	−7	20
Cambridge	MA	02138	47,181	−0.8	21	160,032	9.9	17
Baltimore	MD	21201	57,632	−0.3	16	210,955	−1.7	8
Tulsa	OK	74102	34,221	1.1	27	120,003	0.3	23
Milwaukee	WI	53201	38,274	1.2	25	157,961	−0.3	18
Springfield	IL	62701	61,041	1.5	14	136,249	−1.4	19
Hazard	KY	41701	58,334	1.9	15	263,842	3.5	2
Anchorage	AK	99524	77,105	2.7	2	230,219	9.4	3
Huntsville	AL	35801	77,289	2.7	1	184,359	−2.3	15
Phoenix	AZ	85054	76,493	3	3	175,504	−2.1	16
Washington	DC	20015	70,452	3.5	6	229,706	0.8	4
St. Louis	MO	63101	53,790	4.4	18	195,087	4.9	13
Camden	SC	29020	36,935	4.6	26	212,409	1.1	7
Atlanta	GA	30305	64,827	6	12	193,296	−0.5	14
Beverly Hills	CA	90209	70,360	6.1	7	196,923	1.1	11
Boston	MA	02136	52,885	6.7	19	217,632	−0.3	6
Atlanta	GA	30302	65,379	8.7	10	207,235	8.2	9

Sorted by Rank of Deliveries (Column 6)

DELIVERY ROUTE			DELIVERIES			ITEMS DELIVERED		
CITY	STATE	ZIP CODE	NUMBER	% CHANGE	RANK	NUMBER	% CHANGE	RANK
Huntsville	AL	35801	77,289	2.7	1	184,359	−2.3	15
Anchorage	AK	99524	77,105	2.7	2	230,219	9.4	3
Phoenix	AZ	85054	76,493	3	3	175,504	−2.1	16
Little Rock	AR	72203	76,247	−0.9	4	204,956	−0.6	10
Washington	DC	20011	73,997	−8.3	5	126,048	6.2	21
Washington	DC	20015	70,452	3.5	6	229,706	0.8	4
Beverly Hills	CA	90209	70,360	6.1	7	196,923	1.1	11
Miami	FL	33124	69,804	−0.9	8	127,793	−7	20
Pensacola	FL	32506	69,472	−1.2	9	290,771	−1.7	1
Atlanta	GA	30302	65,379	8.7	10	207,235	8.2	9
Atlanta	GA	30305	64,827	6	12	193,296	−0.5	14
Springfield	IL	62701	61,041	1.5	14	136,249	−1.4	19
Hazard	KY	41701	58,334	1.9	15	263,842	3.5	2
Baltimore	MD	21201	57,632	−0.3	16	210,955	−1.7	8
St. Louis	MO	63101	53,790	4.4	18	195,087	4.9	13
Boston	MA	02136	52,885	6.7	19	217,632	−0.3	6
Cambridge	MA	02138	47,181	−0.8	21	160,032	9.9	17
Bellevue	WA	98004	41,653	−1.9	22	125,297	4.1	22
Milwaukee	WI	53201	38,274	1.2	25	157,961	−0.3	18
Camden	SC	29020	36,935	4.6	26	212,409	1.1	7
Tulsa	OK	74102	34,221	1.1	27	120,003	0.3	23

Sorted by Percent Change in Items Delivered (Column 8)

DELIVERY ROUTE			DELIVERIES			ITEMS DELIVERED		
CITY	STATE	ZIP CODE	NUMBER	% CHANGE	RANK	NUMBER	% CHANGE	RANK
Miami	FL	33124	69,804	−0.9	8	127,793	−7	20
Huntsville	AL	35801	77,289	2.7	1	184,359	−2.3	15
Phoenix	AZ	85054	76,493	3	3	175,504	−2.1	16
Pensacola	FL	32506	69,472	−1.2	9	290,771	−1.7	1
Baltimore	MD	21201	57,632	−0.3	16	210,955	−1.7	8
Springfield	IL	62701	61,041	1.5	14	136,249	−1.4	19
Little Rock	AR	72203	76,247	−0.9	4	204,956	−0.6	10

Sorted by Percent Change in Items Delivered (Column 8) (*continued*)

DELIVERY ROUTE			DELIVERIES			ITEMS DELIVERED		
CITY	STATE	ZIP CODE	NUMBER	% CHANGE	RANK	NUMBER	% CHANGE	RANK
Atlanta	GA	30305	64,827	6	12	193,296	−0.5	14
Boston	MA	02136	52,885	6.7	19	217,632	−0.3	6
Milwaukee	WI	53201	38,274	1.2	25	157,961	−0.3	18
Tulsa	OK	74102	34,221	1.1	27	120,003	0.3	23
Washington	DC	20015	70,452	3.5	6	229,706	0.8	4
Beverly Hills	CA	90209	70,360	6.1	7	196,923	1.1	11
Camden	SC	29020	36,935	4.6	26	212,409	1.1	7
Hazard	KY	41701	58,334	1.9	15	263,842	3.5	2
Bellevue	WA	98004	41,653	−1.9	22	125,297	4.1	22
St. Louis	MO	63101	53,790	4.4	18	195,087	4.9	13
Washington	DC	20011	73,997	−8.3	5	126,048	6.2	21
Atlanta	GA	30302	65,379	8.7	10	207,235	8.2	9
Anchorage	AK	99524	77,105	2.7	2	230,219	9.4	3
Cambridge	MA	02138	47,181	−0.8	21	160,032	9.9	17

Sorted by Rank of Items Delivered (Column 9)

DELIVERY ROUTE			DELIVERIES			ITEMS DELIVERED		
CITY	STATE	ZIP CODE	NUMBER	% CHANGE	RANK	NUMBER	% CHANGE	RANK
Pensacola	FL	32506	69,472	−1.2	9	290,771	−1.7	1
Hazard	KY	41701	58,334	1.9	15	263,842	3.5	2
Anchorage	AK	99524	77,105	2.7	2	230,219	9.4	3
Washington	DC	20015	70,452	3.5	6	229,706	0.8	4
Boston	MA	02136	52,885	6.7	19	217,632	−0.3	6
Camden	SC	29020	36,935	4.6	26	212,409	1.1	7
Baltimore	MD	21201	57,632	−0.3	16	210,955	−1.7	8
Atlanta	GA	30302	65,379	8.7	10	207,235	8.2	9
Little Rock	AR	72203	76,247	−0.9	4	204,956	−0.6	10
Beverly Hills	CA	90209	70,360	6.1	7	196,923	1.1	11
St. Louis	MO	63101	53,790	4.4	18	195,087	4.9	13
Atlanta	GA	30305	64,827	6	12	193,296	−0.5	14
Huntsville	AL	35801	77,289	2.7	1	184,359	−2.3	15
Phoenix	AZ	85054	76,493	3	3	175,504	−2.1	16

(*continued*)

Sorted by Rank of Items Delivered (Column 9) (*continued*)

DELIVERY ROUTE			DELIVERIES			ITEMS DELIVERED		
CITY	STATE	ZIP CODE	NUMBER	% CHANGE	RANK	NUMBER	% CHANGE	RANK
Cambridge	MA	02138	47,181	−0.8	21	160,032	9.9	17
Milwaukee	WI	53201	38,274	1.2	25	157,961	−0.3	18
Springfield	IL	62701	61,041	1.5	14	136,249	−1.4	19
Miami	FL	33124	69,804	−0.9	8	127,793	−7	20
Washington	DC	20011	73,997	−8.3	5	126,048	6.2	21
Bellevue	WA	98004	41,653	−1.9	22	125,297	4.1	22
Tulsa	OK	74102	34,221	1.1	27	120,003	0.3	23

Review each of the following statements. Based on information provided in the table, indicate whether the statement is true or false.

True   False

○   ○   The delivery route with the median rank based on total number of deliveries is the same as the route with the median rank based on total number of items delivered.

○   ○   The total items delivered to Cambridge, MA, in 2015 was approximately 145,000.

○   ○   The delivery route experiencing the greatest percent increase in total deliveries from 2015 to 2016 is the same as the delivery route that saw the greatest increase in the percent of items delivered.

○   ○   For 2016, there were more delivery routes experiencing a percent decrease in the number of deliveries made than delivery routes experiencing a percent decrease in the number of items delivered.

Solution

True   False

○   ●   The delivery route with the median rank based on total number of deliveries is the same as the route with the median rank based on total number of items delivered.

●   ○   The total items delivered to Cambridge, MA, in 2015 was approximately 145,000.

○   ●   The delivery route experiencing the greatest percent increase in total deliveries from 2015 to 2016 is the same as the delivery route that saw the greatest increase in the percent of items delivered.

○   ●   For 2016, there were more delivery routes experiencing a percent decrease in the number of deliveries made than delivery routes experiencing a percent decrease in the number of items delivered.

The delivery route with the median rank based on total number of deliveries is Atlanta, GA (30305). The delivery route with the median rank based on total number of items delivered is St. Louis, MO (63101).

In 2016, there were approximately 160,000 items delivered in Cambridge. This represented an increase of about 10% over the previous year. In 2015, therefore, the number of items delivered was approximately 160,000/1.10, which is about 145,000.

The delivery route experiencing the greatest percent increase in total deliveries from 2015 to 2016 is Atlanta, GA (30302). The delivery route that saw the greatest increase in the percent of items delivered is Cambridge, MA (02138).

In 2016, 7 delivery routes experienced a percent decrease in the number of deliveries. There were 10 delivery routes that experienced a percent decrease in the number of items delivered.

Graphics Interpretation

Graphics Interpretation (GI) questions contain graphs, images, or other visual representation of data. You will be required to review the graphic and interpret it to answer a question. GI questions contain two fill-in-the-blank answer statements. For each statement, you must choose from several options on a drop-down menu. To receive credit for the question, both blanks must be filled in with the correct option.

Useful Tips for GI Questions

Here are some useful tips for GI questions.

- Inspect the graphical image carefully to make sure you understand what is being represented. Note any accompanying title and/or text.
- For graphs that show two variables plotted using horizontal and vertical axes (such as bar graphs, histograms, line graphs, and scatter plots), carefully examine the labels and scales on the axes.
- In line graphs, the slope of the line segments connecting the data points indicates how the variable on the vertical axis changed over time. A segment that slants upward from left to right has a positive slope, signaling an increase. A segment that slants downward from left to right has a negative slope, signaling a decrease. A horizontal segment means no change.
- In scatter plots of two variables, regression lines that have a positive slope suggest a positive correlation (relationship) between the two variables, and regression lines that have a negative slope suggest a negative correlation (relationship) between the two variables. When the data points are scattered without any discernible pattern or if the pattern is a horizontal line, the two variables have no relationship.
- Where possible, use estimation to answer questions. However, be prepared to do some arithmetic calculations (e.g., compute percentages, calculate an average, etc.). Use the online calculator as needed.
- Be sure to select options for both given statements.

Example

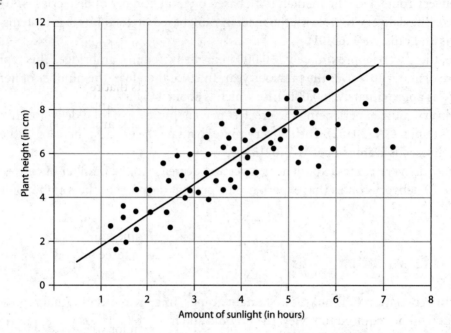

The graph above is a scatter plot with 60 points, each representing the amount of daily hours of sunlight to which 60 plants were exposed and the corresponding height, measured in centimeters, that each plant attained. The plant heights were measured after 6 weeks of consistent sun exposure. The solid line is the regression line, the line that best represents all the data points.

Select the best answer to fill in the blank for each of the statements below, based on the data shown in the graph.

The correlation between the amount of sun exposure and plant height is _____.

Ⓐ zero
Ⓑ negative
Ⓒ positive

The number of plants that received more than 6 hours of daily sun exposure is closest to _____ % of 60.

Ⓐ 0
Ⓑ 5
Ⓒ 10
Ⓓ 20
Ⓔ 40

Solutions

The answer to the first blank is **C**. The regression line has positive slope, therefore, the correlation between the amount of sun exposure and plant height is positive. As sun exposure increases, so does plant height.

The answer to the second blank is **B**. The number of plants that received more than 6 hours of daily sun exposure is closest to 5% of 60. Exactly 3 plants received more than 6 hours of daily sun exposure, so 5% of the plants received this amount because 3 divided by 60 is 0.05 or 5%.

Multi-Source Reasoning

Multi-Source Reasoning (MSR) questions require you to examine multiple sources and determine the correct answers to problems. Commonly, two to three sources of information will be provided: these may include text, graphs, charts, tables, or spreadsheets. You will have to consult more than one source to answer the question posed.

MSR questions may be presented as traditional multiple-choice questions (with five options) or as a set of subquestions each containing a statement for which you must select one of two opposite choices (e.g., "Yes/No," "True/False"). You must answer all subquestions correctly to receive credit for the question.

Useful Tips for MSR Questions

Keep the following points in mind when confronting MSR questions.

- MSR questions are presented in "tabbed" format. To view the different sources, click on the tabs at the top of the screen. Read each source carefully. Make sure you know what information is provided. You can view only one source at a time; however, you can refer back to a source as many times as necessary.
- If graphical information is provided, inspect the graphical image carefully to make sure you understand what is being represented. Note any accompanying title and/or text. If axes are shown, carefully examine the labels and scales.
- When determining whether an inference is supported, consider the source materials carefully. A topic might be mentioned in the sources without necessarily supporting an inference about it.

Example

E-mail #1—E-mail from *Division Director* to Donations Coordinator
August 10, 9:37 A.M.

Yesterday I spoke with the computer training lab administrator to update her on the status of donations for the school district's computer donations drive. She extended the donations deadline for another week, until next Tuesday. Are we on track to receive enough donations from students' families to meet our goal of 100 computer donations for the new training lab? Do we need to extend our request to local businesses too?

E-mail #2—E-mail from *Donations Coordinator* in Response to the Division Director's August 10, 9:37 A.M. message
August 10, 10:04 A.M.

To date, we have received 40 computers. We have requested help from all of the students' families, so we should invite local businesses as well. In all of our past drives, including this one so far, we have received donations from about 20 percent of those who receive requests. (Of course, we might always receive more or less than that average, so we should consider the possibilities of not meeting the goal or overspending the budget for the thank-you event.) Each individual or organization donating a computer will receive two invitations to our thank-you event to celebrate the opening of the lab. Refreshments and supplies for the event are expected to run $20 per person. What is the total budget for the thank-you event?

E-mail #3—E-mail from *Division Director* to Donations Coordinator in Response to the Donation Coordinator's August 10, 10:04 A.M. message
August 10, 10:35 A.M.

The budget for the thank-you event is fixed at $4,000. This would allow us to accommodate two attendees for each of the 100 computers donated. The budget is firm, so we should take care to ensure that the event costs stay within this amount. Although we do not have resources to extend the budget, if necessary we could determine ways to reduce the cost per person if we receive more donations than the original goal number.

Consider each of the following statements. Does the information in the three e-mails support each inference as stated?

Yes	No	
◉	○	The donations coordinator supports inviting local area businesses to contribute to the computer donation drive.
○	◉	The donations coordinator does not believe that the goal of the drive will be met even with the week's time extension.
○	◉	The division director is willing to determine methods for increasing the funds available for the thank-you event if the drive's donation goal is exceeded.
○	◉	The division director and the donations coordinator disagree regarding the amount to be budgeted per person for attendees at the thank-you event.

Solutions

Yes	No	
●	○	The donations coordinator supports inviting local area businesses to contribute to the computer donation drive.
○	●	The donations coordinator does not believe that the goal of the drive will be met even with the week's time extension.
○	●	The division director is willing to determine methods for increasing the funds available for the thank-you event if the drive's donation goal is exceeded.
○	●	The division director and the donations coordinator disagree regarding the amount to be budgeted per person for attendees at the thank-you event.

The donations coordinator states in E-mail #2 that local businesses should be invited to contribute to the drive.

The e-mails do not suggest that the donation coordinator does not believe the goal of the drive can be met. This inference is not supported by the information provided.

The division director states in E-mail #3 that the budget for the thank-you event is firm and cannot be extended.

The e-mails do not suggest a disagreement between the two over the per-person budget for the thank-you event. The donations coordinator mentions this amount in E-mail #2, and the division director proposes that attempts might be made to reduce the cost per person if necessary.

Two-Part Analysis

Two-Part Analysis (TPA) questions present a brief introductory prompt that asks you to answer two subquestions related to the information presented. The prompt is followed by a 3-column table. The third column contains a list of possible answer choices for the two subquestions. You choose an answer from the list for the first question by making a selection in the first column. You choose an answer from the list for the second question by making a selection in the second column. To answer the questions, you must consider different combinations of the possible answer choices, two at a time. You must answer both subquestions correctly to receive credit for the questions. Also, in some cases, both subquestions might have the same answer choice.

Useful Tips for TPA Questions

When answering TPA questions, remember these tips.

- Make two choices, one in each column. On the actual exam, you will not be able to select more than one answer in a column.
- Be prepared to perform arithmetic or simple algebra.
- Check your answers against the conditions given in the prompt.

Example

Acme Company currently produces 7,500 circuit board units per year. Brown Company currently produces 8,000 circuit board units. The numbers of units produced by both companies are increasing each year at a constant rate. If each of these companies continues to produce an increased number of units annually at its constant rate, in 10 years both companies will produce the same number of units for the first time. After the 10-year mark, Acme Company will produce more units per year than Brown Company.

In the table below, identify the rates of increase, in annual units produced, for each company that together meet the performance projections given above. Select only one option in each column.

ACME COMPANY	BROWN COMPANY	RATE OF INCREASE (UNITS PER YEAR)
○	○	15
○	○	25
○	○	50
○	○	100
○	○	125
○	○	140

Solution

The correct answer is 100 units per year for Acme Company and 50 units per year for Brown Company.

ACME COMPANY	BROWN COMPANY	RATE OF INCREASE (UNITS PER YEAR)
○	○	15
○	○	25
○	●	50
●	○	100
○	○	125
○	○	140

This problem can be solved by working backward. Start with a number in the middle for Acme—say, 50 units per year. If Acme increases its production by 50 units per year, in 10 years it will produce 8,000 units. If Brown increases its production by 50 units per year, in 10 years it will produce 8,500 units. The number of 50 for Acme is too small. Try the next larger number. If Acme increases its production by 100 units per year, in 10 years it will produce 8,500 units. This would match Brown's production at an increase of 50 units per year.

You can also use algebra to help find the answer. Set up an equation for the first outcome:

$$7{,}500 + 10x = 8{,}000 + 10y$$

Solve for x in terms of y:

$$7{,}500 + 10x = 8{,}000 + 10y$$
$$10x = 8{,}000 + 10y - 7{,}500$$
$$10x = 500 + 10y$$
$$\frac{10x}{10} = \frac{500 + 10y}{10}$$
$$x = 50 + y$$

This tells you that Acme's production (x) is 50 units more than Brown's production (y). The only options that fit from the table are 100 units for Acme and 50 units for Brown.

If Acme Company increases its production by 100 units per year, in 10 years it will produce 8,500 units per year. Brown Company would reach the 8,500-unit mark at the same time by producing 50 more units per year. Every year after the first 10, Acme will produce more units than Brown Company.

Integrated Reasoning Drill 1

Directions: **Select the best answer or answers for the questions below. You may use a calculator for this section of the test only.**

On the actual test, you will be provided with an online calculator. You will *not* be permitted to bring your own calculator to the test.

1. Saruna University currently enrolls 8,800 students per year. Luman College currently enrolls 15,100 students per year. The numbers of students enrolled by both schools are increasing each year at a constant rate. If each of these schools continues to enroll an increased number of students annually at its constant rate, in 7 years both schools will enroll the same number of students for the first time. Each year after 7 years, Saruna University will enroll more students per year than Luman College.

   In the table below, identify the rates of increase, in annual students enrolled, for each school that together meet the enrollment forecasts described above. Select only one option in each column.

SARUNA UNIVERSITY	LUMAN COLLEGE	RATE OF INCREASE (ENROLLMENTS PER YEAR)
○	○	100
○	○	250
○	○	400
○	◉	900
○	○	1,200
◉	○	1,800

2. The graph shown is a scatter plot with 48 points, each representing the average number of radio ads per hour run by a company each day over 48 months, and the corresponding monthly sales revenue that the company earned. The sales revenues, measured in thousands of dollars, were tallied on the last day of each month that the ads were run. The solid line is the regression line. Select the best answer to fill in the blanks in each of the statements below based on the data shown in the graph.

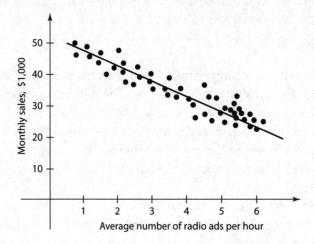

The number of months in which the company generated more than $50,000 of revenue is closest to _____ % of 48.

Ⓐ 0
Ⓑ 10
Ⓒ 15
Ⓓ 17
Ⓔ 25

The correlation between the radio ads run per hour and sales revenue is _____.

Ⓐ negative
Ⓑ zero
Ⓒ positive

3. The table below gives information on the total inventory in 2017 and the total items sold by an international furniture manufacturer over a three-year period, from 2015 through 2017. The 19 furniture items were included in the table because they fall among the top 25 items produced by the company in terms of both total inventory and total items sold. In addition to listing the total inventory and total number sold for each furniture type, the table also gives the percent increase or decrease over the 2016 inventory and 2012–2014 sales numbers and the rank of each furniture type for total inventory and total items sold.

On the actual exam, you will have the ability to sort the table by any of its columns. (Columns can be sorted in ascending order only.) The table is shown below sorted in different ways to mirror the test.

Sorted by Percent Change in Inventory (Column 5)

FURNITURE TYPE			INVENTORY			NUMBER SOLD		
ITEM	WOOD	COLOR	NUMBER	% CHANGE	RANK	NUMBER	% CHANGE	RANK
Desk	Pine	Natural	263,094	−8	9	1,295,076	−0.8	13
Nightstand	Cherry	Red Mahogany	287,610	−6.2	7	1,327,299	−0.1	9
Armoire	Cherry	Red Mahogany	300,515	−4.7	4	1,200,033	−6.1	18
Table	Cherry	Red Mahogany	200,407	−3.1	19	1,346,204	−2.3	5
Cabinet	Maple	Ebony	207,663	−2.9	17	1,252,046	−3.2	15
Chest	Oak	Natural	240,755	−0.3	13	1,332,100	−0.4	7
Chair	Cherry	Red Mahogany	199,328	0.4	20	1,201,189	−4	17
Chest	Cherry	Red Mahogany	187,612	0.7	21	1,357,999	−0.9	4
Chest	Pine	Natural	219,247	1.2	16	1,240,397	−2	16
Chair	Oak	Natural	327,145	1.2	1	1,192,847	−0.3	19
Table	Oak	White	299,628	1.3	5	1,296,821	−0.7	12
Bench	Oak	Natural	236,087	1.7	14	1,254,131	−8.1	14
Bookshelf	Pine	Natural	306,243	2	3	1,301,414	−6	11
Table	Oak	Natural	319,887	3.4	2	1,306,507	−2.5	10
Nightstand	Maple	Ebony	287,509	6	8	1,190,786	−2	20
Cabinet	Oak	Natural	258,713	7.8	11	1,189,031	−1.9	21
Chair	Maple	Natural	298,403	9.2	6	1,395,240	−2	1
Bench	Cherry	Red Mahogany	249,321	9.6	12	1,367,118	−3.5	2
Desk	Oak	Natural	201,325	9.7	18	1,360,203	−7	3

Sorted by Rank of Inventory (Column 6)

FURNITURE TYPE			INVENTORY			NUMBER SOLD		
ITEM	WOOD	COLOR	NUMBER	% CHANGE	RANK	NUMBER	% CHANGE	RANK
Chair	Oak	Natural	327,145	1.2	1	1,192,847	−0.3	19
Table	Oak	Natural	319,887	3.4	2	1,306,507	−2.5	10
Bookshelf	Pine	Natural	306,243	2	3	1,301,414	−6	11
Armoire	Cherry	Red Mahogany	300,515	−4.7	4	1,200,033	−6.1	18
Table	Oak	White	299,628	1.3	5	1,296,821	−0.7	12
Chair	Maple	Natural	298,403	9.2	6	1,395,240	−2	1
Nightstand	Cherry	Red Mahogany	287,610	−6.2	7	1,327,299	−0.1	9
Nightstand	Maple	Ebony	287,509	6	8	1,190,786	−2	20
Desk	Pine	Natural	263,094	−8	9	1,295,076	−0.8	13
Cabinet	Oak	Natural	258,713	7.8	11	1,189,031	−1.9	21
Bench	Cherry	Red Mahogany	249,321	9.6	12	1,367,118	−3.5	2
Chest	Oak	Natural	240,755	−0.3	13	1,332,100	−0.4	7
Bench	Oak	Natural	236,087	1.7	14	1,254,131	−8.1	14
Chest	Pine	Natural	219,247	1.2	16	1,240,397	−2	16
Cabinet	Maple	Ebony	207,663	−2.9	17	1,252,046	−3.2	15
Desk	Oak	Natural	201,325	9.7	18	1,360,203	−7	3
Table	Cherry	Red Mahogany	200,407	−3.1	19	1,346,204	−2.3	5
Chair	Cherry	Red Mahogany	199,328	0.4	20	1,201,189	−4	17
Chest	Cherry	Red Mahogany	187,612	0.7	21	1,357,999	−0.9	4

Sorted by Percent Change in Number Sold (Column 8)

FURNITURE TYPE			INVENTORY			NUMBER SOLD		
ITEM	WOOD	COLOR	NUMBER	% CHANGE	RANK	NUMBER	% CHANGE	RANK
Bench	Oak	Natural	236,087	1.7	14	1,254,131	−8.1	14
Desk	Oak	Natural	201,325	9.7	18	1,360,203	−7	3
Armoire	Cherry	Red Mahogany	300,515	−4.7	4	1,200,033	−6.1	18
Bookshelf	Pine	Natural	306,243	2	3	1,301,414	−6	11
Chair	Cherry	Red Mahogany	199,328	0.4	20	1,201,189	−4	17
Bench	Cherry	Red Mahogany	249,321	9.6	12	1,367,118	−3.5	2
Cabinet	Maple	Ebony	207,663	−2.9	17	1,252,046	−3.2	15
Table	Oak	Natural	319,887	3.4	2	1,306,507	−2.5	10
Table	Cherry	Red Mahogany	200,407	−3.1	19	1,346,204	−2.3	5

(continued)

Sorted by Percent Change in Number Sold (Column 8) (*continued*)

FURNITURE TYPE			INVENTORY			NUMBER SOLD		
ITEM	WOOD	COLOR	NUMBER	% CHANGE	RANK	NUMBER	% CHANGE	RANK
Chair	Maple	Natural	298,403	9.2	6	1,395,240	−2	1
Nightstand	Maple	Ebony	287,509	6	8	1,190,786	−2	20
Chest	Pine	Natural	219,247	1.2	16	1,240,397	−2	16
Cabinet	Oak	Natural	258,713	7.8	11	1,189,031	−1.9	21
Chest	Cherry	Red Mahogany	187,612	0.7	21	1,357,999	−0.9	4
Desk	Pine	Natural	263,094	−8	9	1,295,076	−0.8	13
Table	Oak	White	299,628	1.3	5	1,296,821	−0.7	12
Chest	Oak	Natural	240,755	−0.3	13	1,332,100	−0.4	7
Chair	Oak	Natural	327,145	1.2	1	1,192,847	−0.3	19
Nightstand	Cherry	Red Mahogany	287,610	−6.2	7	1,327,299	−0.1	9

Sorted by Rank of Number Sold (Column 9)

FURNITURE TYPE			INVENTORY			NUMBER SOLD		
ITEM	WOOD	COLOR	NUMBER	% CHANGE	RANK	NUMBER	% CHANGE	RANK
Chair	Maple	Natural	298,403	9.2	6	1,395,240	−2	1
Bench	Cherry	Red Mahogany	249,321	9.6	12	1,367,118	−3.5	2
Desk	Oak	Natural	201,325	9.7	18	1,360,203	−7	3
Chest	Cherry	Red Mahogany	187,612	0.7	21	1,357,999	−0.9	4
Table	Cherry	Red Mahogany	200,407	−3.1	19	1,346,204	−2.3	5
Chest	Oak	Natural	240,755	−0.3	13	1,332,100	−0.4	7
Nightstand	Cherry	Red Mahogany	287,610	−6.2	7	1,327,299	−0.1	9
Table	Oak	Natural	319,887	3.4	2	1,306,507	−2.5	10
Bookshelf	Pine	Natural	306,243	2	3	1,301,414	−6	11
Table	Oak	White	299,628	1.3	5	1,296,821	−0.7	12
Desk	Pine	Natural	263,094	−8	9	1,295,076	−0.8	13
Bench	Oak	Natural	236,087	1.7	14	1,254,131	−8.1	14
Cabinet	Maple	Ebony	207,663	−2.9	17	1,252,046	−3.2	15
Chest	Pine	Natural	219,247	1.2	16	1,240,397	−2	16
Chair	Cherry	Red Mahogany	199,328	0.4	20	1,201,189	−4	17
Armoire	Cherry	Red Mahogany	300,515	−4.7	4	1,200,033	−6.1	18
Chair	Oak	Natural	327,145	1.2	1	1,192,847	−0.3	19
Nightstand	Maple	Ebony	287,509	6	8	1,190,786	−2	20
Cabinet	Oak	Natural	258,713	7.8	11	1,189,031	−1.9	21

Review each of the statements below. Based on information provided in the table, indicate whether the statement is true or false.

True False

○ ⦿   Exactly 50% of the furniture items that experienced a decrease in both total inventory and total items sold are Red Mahogany.

○ ○   The furniture type experiencing the greatest percentage increase in total inventory from 2016 to 2017 also experienced the greatest percentage decrease in the total number of items sold.

○ ⦿   The furniture type with the highest rank based on total inventory is the same as the type with the highest rank based on total items sold.

⦿ ○   The total inventory of Cherry Red Mahogany Tables in 2016 was approximately 206,800.

4. Read the sources below before answering the question that follows.

E-mail #1 E-mail from *Division Director* to Donations Coordinator
August 10, 9:37 A.M.

Yesterday I spoke with the computer training lab administrator to update her on the status of donations for the school district's computer donations drive. She extended the donations deadline for another week, until next Tuesday. Are we on track to receive enough donations from students' families to meet our goal of 100 computer donations for the new training lab? Do we need to extend our request to local businesses too?

E-mail #2 E-mail from *Donations Coordinator* in Response to Division Director's August 10, 9:37 A.M. message
August 10, 10:04 A.M.

To date we have received 40 computers. We have requested help from all of the students' families, so we should invite local businesses as well. In all of our past drives, including this one so far, we have received donations from about 20 percent of those who received requests. (Of course, we might always receive more or less than that average, so we should consider the possibilities of not meeting the goal or overspending the budget for the thank-you event.) Each individual or organization donating a computer will receive 2 invitations to our thank-you event to celebrate the opening of the lab. Refreshments and supplies for the event are expected to run $20 per person. What is the total budget for the thank-you event?

E-mail #3 E-mail from _Division Director_ to Donations Coordinator in Response to Donation Coordinator's August 10, 10:04 a.m. Message
August 10, 10:35 A.M.

The budget for the thank-you event is fixed at $4,000. This would allow us to accommodate 2 attendees for each of the 100 computers donated. The budget is firm, so we should take care to ensure that the event costs stay within this amount. Although we do not have resources to extend the budget, if necessary we could determine ways to reduce the cost per person if we receive more donations than the original goal number.

Suppose that the donations coordinator requests computer donations from 400 local businesses. If all of the information in the three e-mails is accurate, the number of people that will be invited to participate in the thank-you event is closest to which of the following?

- ◯ 135
- ◯ 160
- ◯ 200
- ◉ 240
- ◯ 300

5. Company X currently owes $200,000 on a business loan. Company Y currently owes $410,000 on a business loan. Both companies repay their loans at a fixed dollar amount per year that includes both interest and principal. If each company repays its loan at its fixed dollar amount per year, in 3 years the companies will owe the same amount. After 3 years, Company Y will owe less than Company X until the loans are paid off.

In the table below, identify the fixed dollar annual repayment amounts for each company that together meet the repayment projections given above. Select only one option in each column.

COMPANY X	COMPANY Y	REPAYMENT AMOUNT (DOLLARS PER YEAR)
◯	◯	5,000
◯	◯	10,000
◯	◯	25,000
◯	◯	40,000
◯	◯	67,500
◯	◯	80,000

6.

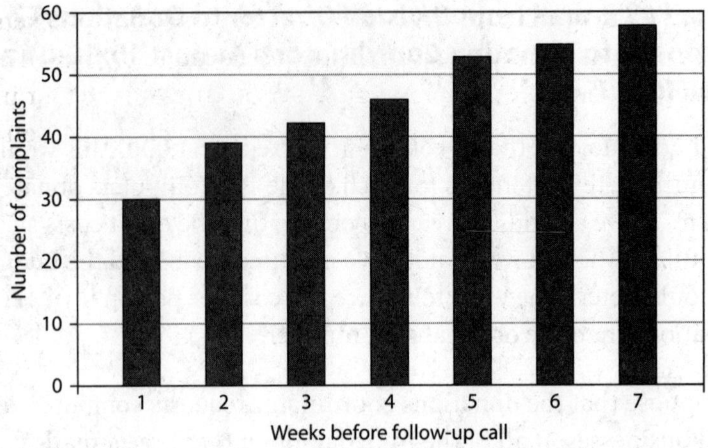

The graph above is a bar graph with 7 bars, each representing the number of complaints received by a cable company from its new customers. The customers received follow-up calls anywhere from 1 to 7 weeks after placing their orders. The customers were grouped by follow-up call timing, and the number of complaints was recorded for each group over a one-year period. Select the best answer to fill in the blanks in each of the statements below based on the data shown in the graph.

The number of complaints made by customers who received a follow-up call 1 week after placing their orders is closest to _____ % of the number of complaints made by customers who received a follow-up call 7 weeks after placing their orders.

Ⓐ 0
Ⓑ 15
Ⓒ 30
Ⓓ 50
Ⓔ 75

Based on the information shown in the graph, if the company wishes to limit its complaints to 40 or fewer per year, it should make follow-up calls no later than _____ weeks after customers place their orders.

Ⓐ 4
Ⓑ 3
Ⓒ 2
Ⓓ 1

7. The table below gives information on the total number of tickets sold and the total sales revenue earned by a touring performance act in 2017. The 19 tour cities included in the table were among the top 30 cities on the tour in terms of both total number of tickets sold and total sales revenue. In addition to listing the total tickets sold and total sales revenue for each tour city, the table also gives the percent increase or decrease over the 2016 numbers and the rank of each tour city for total tickets sold and total sales revenue.

On the actual exam, you will have the ability to sort the table by any of its columns. (Columns can be sorted in ascending order only.) The table is shown below sorted in different ways to mirror the test.

Sorted by Percent Change in Tickets Sold (Column 5)

TOUR CITIES			TICKETS SOLD			SALES REVENUE		
CITY	STATE	CODE	NUMBER	% CHANGE	RANK	AMOUNT	% CHANGE	RANK
Syracuse	NY	NE91	7,215	0.4	23	$230,880	4.1	30
Baltimore	MD	MA35	12,291	1.4	18	$417,894	6.5	12
Providence	RI	NE22	10,004	2.1	20	$320,128	1.7	24
Dallas	TX	ST16	17,625	2.4	10	$590,438	−1.3	4
Las Vegas	NV	SW33	15,015	2.5	13	$352,853	8.3	21
Houston	TX	ST29	16,433	3.7	11	$624,454	−0.7	2
Denver	CO	SW06	15,291	6.3	12	$688,095	9.2	1
Miami	FL	ST73	19,699	7.8	9	$315,184	6.9	25
Chicago	IL	MW27	19,735	8.7	7	$473,640	4.2	6
New York	NY	NE00	20,221	9	6	$444,862	4.1	9
Phoenix	AZ	SW29	14,876	9	16	$409,090	0.4	14
Los Angeles	CA	WC07	27,458	9.1	5	$439,328	7	10
Portland	OR	WC08	14,994	9.1	15	$404,838	0.2	15
Boston	MA	NE03	9,287	9.2	21	$510,785	2.9	5
San Francisco	CA	WC23	29,321	9.2	3	$388,503	6.9	19
Santa Fe	NM	SW72	15,003	9.2	14	$352,571	1.1	22
Washington	DC	MA01	30,432	9.3	1	$403,224	1.2	17
Atlanta	GA	ST00	9,562	9.9	22	$286,860	3.5	26
Seattle	WA	NW12	30,097	9.7	2	$361,164	0.3	20

Sorted by Rank of Tickets Sold (Column 6)

TOUR CITIES			TICKETS SOLD			SALES REVENUE		
CITY	STATE	CODE	NUMBER	% CHANGE	RANK	AMOUNT	% CHANGE	RANK
Washington	DC	MA01	30,432	9.3	1	$403,224	1.2	17
Seattle	WA	NW12	30,097	9.7	2	$361,164	0.3	20
San Francisco	CA	WC23	29,321	9.2	3	$388,503	6.9	19
Los Angeles	CA	WC07	27,458	9.1	5	$439,328	7	10
New York	NY	NE00	20,221	9	6	$444,862	4.1	9
Chicago	IL	MW27	19,735	8.7	7	$473,640	4.2	6
Miami	FL	ST73	19,699	7.8	9	$315,184	6.9	25
Dallas	TX	ST16	17,625	2.4	10	$590,438	−1.3	4
Houston	TX	ST29	16,433	3.7	11	$624,454	−0.7	2
Denver	CO	SW06	15,291	6.3	12	$688,095	9.2	1
Las Vegas	NV	SW33	15,015	2.5	13	$352,853	8.3	21
Santa Fe	NM	SW72	15,003	9.2	14	$352,571	1.1	22
Portland	OR	WC08	14,994	9.1	15	$404,838	0.2	15
Phoenix	AZ	SW29	14,876	9	16	$409,090	0.4	14
Baltimore	MD	MA35	12,291	1.4	18	$417,894	6.5	12
Providence	RI	NE22	10,004	2.1	20	$320,128	1.7	24
Boston	MA	NE03	9,287	9.2	21	$510,785	2.9	5
Atlanta	GA	ST00	9,562	9.9	22	$286,860	3.5	26
Syracuse	NY	NE91	7,215	0.4	23	$230,880	4.1	30

Sorted by Percent Change in Sales Revenue (Column 8)

TOUR CITIES			TICKETS SOLD			SALES REVENUE		
CITY	STATE	CODE	NUMBER	% CHANGE	RANK	AMOUNT	% CHANGE	RANK
Dallas	TX	ST16	17,625	2.4	10	$590,438	−1.3	4
Houston	TX	ST29	16,433	3.7	11	$624,454	−0.7	2
Portland	OR	WC08	14,994	9.1	15	$404,838	0.2	15
Seattle	WA	NW12	30,097	9.7	2	$361,164	0.3	20

(continued)

Sorted by Percent Change in Sales Revenue (Column 8) (*continued*)

TOUR CITIES			TICKETS SOLD			SALES REVENUE		
CITY	STATE	CODE	NUMBER	% CHANGE	RANK	AMOUNT	% CHANGE	RANK
Phoenix	AZ	SW29	14,876	9	16	$409,090	0.4	14
Santa Fe	NM	SW72	15,003	9.2	14	$352,571	1.1	22
Washington	DC	MA01	30,432	9.3	1	$403,224	1.2	17
Providence	RI	NE22	10,004	2.1	20	$320,128	1.7	24
Boston	MA	NE03	9,287	9.2	21	$510,785	2.9	5
Atlanta	GA	ST00	9,562	9.9	22	$286,860	3.5	26
New York	NY	NE00	20,221	9	6	$444,862	4.1	9
Syracuse	NY	NE91	7,215	0.4	23	$230,880	4.1	30
Chicago	IL	MW27	19,735	8.7	7	$473,640	4.2	6
Baltimore	MD	MA35	12,291	1.4	18	$417,894	6.5	12
San Francisco	CA	WC23	29,321	9.2	3	$388,503	6.9	19
Miami	FL	ST73	19,699	7.8	9	$315,184	6.9	25
Los Angeles	CA	WC07	27,458	9.1	5	$439,328	7	10
Las Vegas	NV	SW33	15,015	2.5	13	$352,853	8.3	21
Denver	CO	SW06	15,291	6.3	12	$688,095	9.2	1

Sorted by Rank of Sales Revenue (Column 9)

TOUR CITIES			TICKETS SOLD			SALES REVENUE		
CITY	STATE	CODE	NUMBER	% CHANGE	RANK	AMOUNT	% CHANGE	RANK
Denver	CO	SW06	15,291	6.3	12	$688,095	9.2	1
Houston	TX	ST29	16,433	3.7	11	$624,454	−0.7	2
Dallas	TX	ST16	17,625	2.4	10	$590,438	−1.3	4
Boston	MA	NE03	9,287	9.2	21	$510,785	2.9	5
Chicago	IL	MW27	19,735	8.7	7	$473,640	4.2	6
New York	NY	NE00	20,221	9	6	$444,862	4.1	9
Los Angeles	CA	WC07	27,458	9.1	5	$439,328	7	10
Baltimore	MD	MA35	12,291	1.4	18	$417,894	6.5	12
Phoenix	AZ	SW29	14,876	9	16	$409,090	0.4	14

(continued)

Sorted by Rank of Sales Revenue (Column 9) (*continued*)

TOUR CITIES			TICKETS SOLD			SALES REVENUE		
CITY	STATE	CODE	NUMBER	% CHANGE	RANK	AMOUNT	% CHANGE	RANK
Portland	OR	WC08	14,994	9.1	15	$404,838	0.2	15
Washington	DC	MA01	30,432	9.3	1	$403,224	1.2	17
San Francisco	CA	WC23	29,321	9.2	3	$388,503	6.9	19
Seattle	WA	NW12	30,097	9.7	2	$361,164	0.3	20
Las Vegas	NV	SW33	15,015	2.5	13	$352,853	8.3	21
Santa Fe	NM	SW72	15,003	9.2	14	$352,571	1.1	22
Providence	RI	NE22	10,004	2.1	20	$320,128	1.7	24
Miami	FL	ST73	19,699	7.8	9	$315,184	6.9	25
Atlanta	GA	ST00	9,562	9.9	22	$286,860	3.5	26
Syracuse	NY	NE91	7,215	0.4	23	$230,880	4.1	30

Review each of the statements below. Based on information provided in the table, indicate whether the statement is true or false.

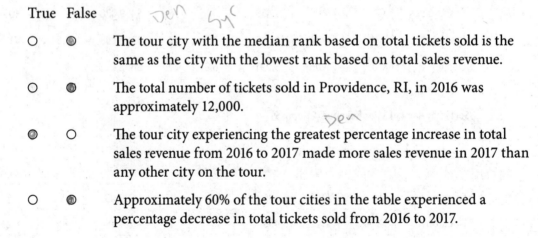

True False

○ ◉   The tour city with the median rank based on total tickets sold is the same as the city with the lowest rank based on total sales revenue.

○ ◉   The total number of tickets sold in Providence, RI, in 2016 was approximately 12,000.

◉ ○   The tour city experiencing the greatest percentage increase in total sales revenue from 2016 to 2017 made more sales revenue in 2017 than any other city on the tour.

○ ◉   Approximately 60% of the tour cities in the table experienced a percentage decrease in total tickets sold from 2016 to 2017.

The sources that follow accompany questions 8 and 9.

E-mail #1 E-mail from *Marketing Director* to Research Associate
November 12, 1:15 P.M.

What was our return on investment last year from ads placed in various media? I am developing our marketing budget for next year and would like to determine whether Internet advertising should be continued as extensively as we have in past years. Also, is there data to show how returns from various advertising campaigns differ from quarter to quarter?

E-mail #2 E-mail from *Research Associate* in Response to Marketing Director's November 12, 1:15 P.M. Message
November 12, 1:35 P.M.

Attached is a graph that shows the return on investment from last year's advertising campaigns. Typically we do not repeat campaigns in media that return less than 20% in any quarter. The return on investment for Internet ads was strong throughout the year, which supports continuing Internet advertising as we have in the past.

Graph #1 Attached to Research Associate's November 12, 1:35 P.M. Message

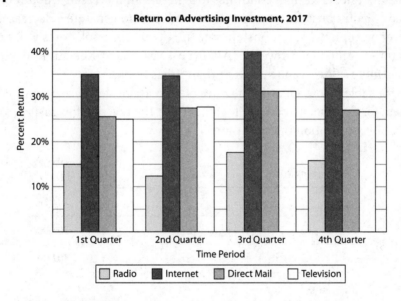

8. Consider each of the following statements. Does the information in the three sources support the inference as stated?

Yes	No	
○	◉	The research associate does not believe that the 2017 advertising campaign was successful as a whole.
○	◉	The marketing director plans to recommend against continuing Internet advertising as extensively as the company has in past years.
◉	○	To increase total advertising returns, the company's Internet campaign might be expanded during 3rd quarter 2018.
◉	○	Based on the company's typical practices, radio advertising should be discontinued in 2018.

9. Suppose that the 2018 returns from campaigns in all advertising media remain the same as those received in 2017. If all of the information in the three sources is accurate, and the company spends $100,000 on television advertising during the first quarter of 2018, the returns received from television advertising during this quarter will be closest to which of the following?

   ○ $10,000

   ○ $15,500

   ◉ $25,000

   ○ $30,000

   ○ $30,750

10. Keenan Booksellers currently generates $50,000 in annual sales revenue. Its competitor, Rivas Books, currently generates $490,000 in annual sales revenue. The sales revenue generated by Keenan Booksellers is increasing each year at a constant rate, while the sales revenue generated by Rivas Books is decreasing each year at a constant rate. If Keenan continues to generate an increased amount of revenue annually at its constant rate, and Rivas continues to generate a decreased amount of revenue annually at its constant rate, in 4 years the bookstores will earn the same amount of annual sales revenue. After the 4-year mark, Keenan Booksellers will receive more sales revenue per year than Rivas Books.

    In the table below, identify the rates of increase or decrease, in annual revenue earned, for each bookstore that together meet the revenue forecasts described above. Select only one option in each column.

KEENAN BOOKSELLERS	RIVAS BOOKS	RATE OF INCREASE OR DECREASE (DOLLARS PER YEAR)
○	○	10,000
○	◉	20,000
○	○	40,000
○	○	60,000
◉	○	90,000
○	○	170,000

11. The table below gives information from a gallery management database regarding the total number of exhibits and the total number of art pieces maintained for 18 artists from around the world. The artists in the table are among the top 30 artists internationally in terms of both total numbers of exhibits and total pieces in the company's collection. The table shows the cities in which the artists reside, the artists' codes, and their ranks according to their total exhibits and total pieces in the art collection.

On the actual exam, you will have the ability to sort the table by any of its columns. (Columns can be sorted in ascending order only.) The table is shown below sorted in different ways to mirror the test.

Sorted by Artist Code (Column 3)

ARTIST			EXHIBITS		PIECES IN COLLECTION	
CITY	COUNTRY	CODE	NUMBER	RANK	NUMBER	RANK
New York	USA	A219	190	13	97	2
Paris	France	A221	170	18	89	11
Florence	Italy	A223	185	16	67	20
London	England	A347	169	20	95	4
London	England	A629	191	11	94	6
Barcelona	Spain	A648	200	4	95	3
Lyons	France	A684	194	9	71	19
Athens	Greece	A724	200	6	92	7
Des Moines	USA	A743	191	12	103	1
Paris	France	A935	243	1	90	10
Boston	USA	A985	207	2	73	18
Montreal	Canada	B221	193	10	86	14
Chicago	USA	B253	200	7	78	17
Milan	Italy	B309	201	3	87	13
Berlin	Germany	B557	173	17	65	21
New York	USA	B607	186	15	82	15
Rome	Italy	B657	188	14	92	9
Seattle	USA	B681	196	8	59	27

Sorted by Rank of Exhibits (Column 5)

ARTIST			EXHIBITS		PIECES IN COLLECTION	
CITY	STATE	ZIP CODE	NUMBER	RANK	NUMBER	RANK
Paris	France	A935	243	1	90	10
Boston	USA	A985	207	2	73	18
Milan	Italy	B309	201	3	87	13
Barcelona	Spain	A648	200	4	95	3
Athens	Greece	A724	200	6	92	7
Chicago	USA	B253	200	7	78	17
Seattle	USA	B681	196	8	59	27
Lyons	France	A684	194	9	71	19
Montreal	Canada	B221	193	10	86	14
London	England	A629	191	11	94	6
Des Moines	USA	A743	191	12	103	1
New York	USA	A219	190	13	97	2
Rome	Italy	B657	188	14	92	9
New York	USA	B607	186	15	82	15
Florence	Italy	A223	185	16	67	20
Berlin	Germany	B557	173	17	65	21
Paris	France	A221	170	18	89	11
London	England	A347	169	20	95	4

Sorted by Rank of Pieces in the Collection (Column 7)

| ARTIST | | | EXHIBITS | | PIECES IN COLLECTION | |
CITY	STATE	ZIP CODE	NUMBER	RANK	NUMBER	RANK
Des Moines	USA	A743	191	12	103	1
New York	USA	A219	190	13	97	2
Barcelona	Spain	A648	200	4	95	3
London	England	A347	169	20	95	4
London	England	A629	191	11	94	6
Athens	Greece	A724	200	6	92	7
Rome	Italy	B657	188	14	92	9
Paris	France	A935	243	1	90	10
Paris	France	A221	170	18	89	11
Milan	Italy	B309	201	3	87	13
Montreal	Canada	B221	193	10	86	14
New York	USA	B607	186	15	82	15
Chicago	USA	B253	200	7	78	17
Boston	USA	A985	207	2	73	18
Lyons	France	A684	194	9	71	19
Florence	Italy	A223	185	16	67	20
Berlin	Germany	B557	173	17	65	21
Seattle	USA	B681	196	8	59	27

Review each of the statements below. Based on information provided in the table, indicate whether the statement is true or false.

True   False

○   ◉   The top ranking artists, in terms of both total exhibits and total number of pieces in the collection, live in the United States.

◉   ○   The lowest ranking artist, in terms of number of exhibits, participated in approximately 70% as many exhibits as did the top ranking artist in this category.

○   ◉   All of the codes for the top five ranking artists, in terms of both number of exhibits and pieces in the collection, begin with the letter A.

○   ◉   Exactly 15% of the 18 artists in the table participated in 200 exhibits.

12. The graph shown is a scatter plot with 60 points, each representing the average number per month of quality assurance inspections conducted on products manufactured at one of 60 different factories, and the corresponding average number per month of product recalls experienced by each factory during a one-year period. Select the best answer to fill in the blanks in each of the statements below based on the data shown in the graph.

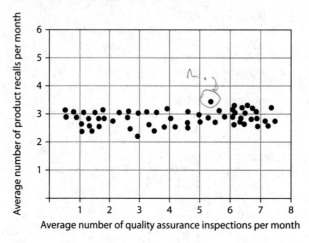

The number of factories that received a monthly average greater than 7 quality assurance inspections is _____ the number of factories that received a monthly average less than 1.

  Ⓐ less than
  Ⓑ equal to
  Ⓒ greater than

The greatest monthly average number of recalls occurred in a factory that had a monthly average number of quality assurance inspections between _____.

  Ⓐ 5 and 6
  Ⓑ 6 and 7
  Ⓒ 7 and 8

Answers

1. The correct answer is 1,800 enrollments per year for Saruna University and 900 enrollments per year for Luman College.

SARUNA UNIVERSITY	LUMAN COLLEGE	RATE OF INCREASE (ENROLLMENTS PER YEAR)
○	○	100
○	○	250
○	○	400
○	●	900
○	○	1,200
●	○	1,800

   If Saruna University increases its enrollment by 1,800 students per year, in 7 years it will enroll 21,400 students. If Luman College increases its enrollment by 900 students per year, in 7 years it will enroll 21,400 students as well. After the 7-year mark, Saruna University will enroll more students each year than Luman College.

2. The answer to the first blank is **A**. The number of months in which the company generated more than $50,000 of revenue is closest to 0% of 48. According to the graph, only one month generated $50,000 in revenue; no months generated more than $50,000.

   The answer to the second blank is **A**. The relationship between the radio ads run per hour and sales revenue is negative. As the number of ads per hour increases, the monthly revenue decreases.

3. The correct answers are shown below.

True	False	
○	●	Exactly 50% of the furniture items that experienced a decrease in both total inventory and total items sold are Red Mahogany.
●	○	The furniture type experiencing the greatest percentage increase in total inventory from 2016 to 2017 also experienced the greatest percentage decrease in the total number of items sold.
○	●	The furniture type with the highest rank based on total inventory is the same as the type with the highest rank based on total items sold.
●	○	The total inventory of Cherry Red Mahogany Tables in 2016 was approximately 206,400.

   There were 6 furniture items that experienced a decrease in total inventory. Of these, 3 (exactly 50%) are Red Mahogany. However, all 19 furniture items experienced a decrease in total items sold. Only 6 of these (32%) are Red Mahogany, so the statement is false.

Not correct

The furniture type experiencing the greatest percentage increase in total inventory from 2016 to 2017 is the Oak Natural Desk, at 9.7%. This same item also experienced the greatest percentage decrease in the total number of items sold (–8.1%).

The furniture type with the highest rank based on total inventory is the Oak Natural Chair. The furniture type with the highest rank based on total items sold is the Maple Natural Chair.

The total inventory of Cherry Red Mahogany Tables in 2017 was 200,407. This furniture type experienced a 3.1% decrease in total inventory. Its inventory in 2016 was therefore 200,407/(1 − 0.031) = 200,407/0.969, which is about 206,800.

4. The correct answer is **240**.

In E-mail #2, the donations coordinator states that donations are usually received from about 20 percent of those who receive requests. The computer drive had already received 40 donations, and each donor would receive 2 invitations to the thank-you event, for a total of 80 invitees. If requests were extended to 400 local businesses, and 20 percent of those made a donation, the drive would receive 80 computers from businesses. That would add 160 invitations to the thank-you event, for a total of 240 invitees.

5. The correct answer is $10,000 per year for Company X and $80,000 per year for Company Y.

COMPANY X	COMPANY Y	REPAYMENT AMOUNT (DOLLARS PER YEAR)
○	○	5,000
●	○	10,000
○	○	25,000
○	○	40,000
○	○	67,500
○	●	80,000

If Company X repays its loan at a rate of $10,000 per year, in 3 years it will owe $170,000. If Company Y repays its loan at a rate of $80,000 per year, in 3 years it will also owe $170,000. After the first 3 years, Company X will owe more on its loan than Company Y, until the loans are paid off.

6. The answer to the first blank is **D**. The number of complaints made by customers who received a follow-up call 1 week after placing their orders is closest to 50% of the number of complaints made by customers who received a follow-up call 7 weeks after placing their orders. Approximately 30 complaints were made by customers who received a follow-up call 1 week after placing their orders, and nearly 60 complaints were made by customers who received a call after 7 weeks.

The answer to the second blank is **C**. If the company wishes to limit its complaints to 40 or fewer per year, it should make follow-up calls no later than 2 weeks after customers place their orders. If the company waits 3 weeks or longer, it is likely to receive more than 40 complaints per year.

7. The correct answers are shown below.

True	False	
○	●	The tour city with the median rank based on total tickets sold is the same as the city with the lowest rank based on total sales revenue.
○	●	The total number of tickets sold in Providence, RI, in 2016 was approximately 12,000.
●	○	The tour city experiencing the greatest percentage increase in total sales revenue from 2016 to 2017 made more sales revenue in 2017 than any other city on the tour.
○	●	Approximately 60% of the tour cities in the table experienced a percentage decrease in total tickets sold from 2016 to 2017.

    The tour city with the median rank based on total tickets sold is Denver, CO. Denver has the highest rank based on total sales revenue, so the statement is false.

    The total number of tickets sold in Providence, RI, in 2017 was 10,004. Providence experienced a 2.1% *increase* in ticket sales from 2016 to 2017. So, the number of tickets sold in 2016 would be less than 10,000, not greater than 10,000.

    Denver, CO, experienced the greatest percentage increase in total sales revenue from 2016 to 2017, at 9.2%. It also made more sales revenue in 2015 than any other city on the tour, at $688,095.

    None of the tour cities in the table experienced a percentage decrease in total tickets sold from 2016 to 2017. All of the cities experienced a percentage increase in total tickets sold over this period.

8. The correct answers are shown below.

Yes	No	
○	●	The research associate does not believe that the 2017 advertising campaign was successful as a whole.
○	●	The marketing director plans to recommend against continuing Internet advertising as extensively as the company has in past years.
●	○	To increase total advertising returns, the company's Internet campaign might be expanded during 3rd quarter 2018.
●	○	Based on the company's typical practices, radio advertising should be discontinued in 2018.

    The first inference is not supported by the information in the three sources. The research associate does not evaluate the advertising campaign as a whole in E-mail #2.

    The marketing director does not imply an intent to recommend reducing Internet advertising. In E-mail #1, the director requests data to determine whether Internet advertising should be continued as extensively as it has been in past years.

    The graph shows that returns from Internet advertising were strongest during 3rd Quarter 2017. To increase total advertising returns, the company might expand its Internet advertising during this quarter, to capitalize on the potential for additional gains.

    In E-mail #2, the research associate explains that the company typically does not repeat campaigns in media that return less than 20% in any quarter. Radio advertising returned less than 20% in every quarter of 2017, so based on the company's practices, the radio campaign should be discontinued.

9. The correct answer is **$25,000**.

   The graph shows that television advertising returned 25% on funds invested in first quarter 2017. If the return remains the same for 2018, the $100,000 invested in television advertising would produce gains of 25%, or $25,000.

10. The correct answer is **$90,000** per year for Keenan Booksellers and **$20,000** per year for Rivas Books.

KEENAN BOOKSELLERS	RIVAS BOOKS	RATE OF INCREASE OR DECREASE (DOLLARS PER YEAR)
○	○	10,000
○	●	20,000
○	○	50,000
○	○	60,000
●	○	90,000
○	○	170,000

   If Keenan Booksellers increases its sales revenue by $90,000 per year, in 4 years it will earn $410,000 in annual revenue. If Rivas Books decreases its sales revenue by $20,000 per year, in 4 years it will also earn $410,000 in annual revenue. After the 4th year, Keenan Booksellers will generate more sales revenue each year than Rivas Books.

11. The correct answers are shown below.

True	False	
○	●	The top ranking artists, in terms of both total exhibits and total number of pieces in the collection, live in the United States.
●	○	The lowest ranking artist, in terms of number of exhibits, participated in approximately 70% as many exhibits as did the top ranking artist in this category.
○	●	All of the codes for the top five ranking artists, in terms of both number of exhibits and pieces in the collection, begin with the letter A.
○	●	Exactly 15% of the 18 artists in the table participated in 200 exhibits.

   The top ranking artist for total exhibits is from Paris, France.

   The lowest ranking artist, in terms of number of exhibits, participated in 169 exhibits. The highest ranking artist in this category participated in 243 exhibits. The lowest ranking artist participated in 69.5% as many exhibits as the top ranking artist, or approximately 70%.

   The third-ranking artist for exhibits is code B309, so the third statement is false.

   A total of 3 artists participated in 200 exhibits. There are 18 artists listed in the table, so 3 artists represents 16.67% of the total, not 15%.

12. The answer to the first blank is **B**. The graph shows that 4 factories received a monthly average greater than 7 quality assurance inspections and 4 factories received a monthly average less than 1.

The answer to the second blank is **A**. The greatest monthly average number of recalls occurred in a factory that had a monthly average number of quality assurance inspections between 5 and 6.

Integrated Reasoning Drill 2

Directions: **Select the best answer or answers for the questions below. You may use a calculator for this section of the test only.**

On the actual test, you will be provided with an online calculator. You will *not* be permitted to bring your own calculator to the test.

1. The graph below is a scatter plot with 20 points, each representing the average temperature in degrees Celsius of a major European city, measured against elevation in meters. Select the best answer to fill in the blanks in each of the statements below based on the data shown in the graph.

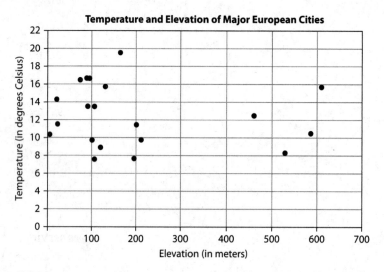

Of the two coldest cities, one is _____ percent higher above sea level than the other.

- Ⓐ 10
- Ⓑ 20
- Ⓒ 50
- Ⓓ 100
- Ⓔ 200

According to the graph, the correlation between average temperature and elevation is best described as _____.

- Ⓐ negative
- Ⓑ zero
- Ⓒ positive

2. Jamie is self-employed and pays her taxes quarterly. For the first quarter, she paid $1,700 dollars in taxes, based on her income. She expects her taxes to increase by 14 percent from the first quarter to the second quarter, by 17.5 percent from the second quarter to the third quarter, and by 21 percent from the third quarter to the fourth quarter.

   In the table below, identify the amount of taxes Jamie can expect to pay in the third quarter. Also, based on the information given, identify how much more in taxes Jamie will pay in the fourth quarter than in the second quarter. Select only one answer in each column.

3RD QUARTER TAXES	DIFFERENCE BETWEEN 2ND AND 4TH QUARTERS	AMOUNT (IN DOLLARS)
○	○	$238.00
○	●	$817.35
○	○	$1,938.00
●	○	$2,277.15
○	○	$2,755.35
○	○	$2,965.05

3. Read the sources below before answering the question that follows.

Services

Marysville Property Management Company provides services to owners of residential apartment complexes. Leasing, rental contracts, routine maintenance, and repairs are provided by MPMC, with some major repairs contracted to third parties. In-house staff members include a resident manager for each complex, an on-call maintenance crew based out of MPMC's office facilities, and a general operations manager. A minimum population for each complex is set at 180 residents or 135 units. Requests for maintenance from residents for plumbing, electrical, or heating and cooling problems performed by the MPMC maintenance crew are charged to the client at standard base rates, plus time and material exceeding the base.

Charges

- Maintenance staff labor rates are charged at $18/hour, or $23/hour for after-hours and holidays.
- Minor repairs during normal business hours are charged at $35/hour.
- Plumbing or electrical calls are $65 per call, with a surcharge of $50/call for after-hours or holiday calls.
- Annual heating and cooling checkups are $45 per unit.
- Carpet, roofing, and rehab contractors are charged on a case-by-case basis, plus a 10% premium to MPMC.

Costs

Annual staff labor costs for MPMC are calculated as follows:

1. The operations manager has a yearly salary of $52,780.
2. Resident managers receive free apartments as a portion of their salary: 4 apartment rentals valued at $9,360 to $10,700, with a total of $39,800.
3. Resident manager salaries are paid at a range of $28,600 to $37,300, with an average of $32,000; the total paid annually is $128,000.
4. The maintenance staff of three employees is paid a total of $112,000 annually.

Suppose that MPMC manages three apartment complexes that each meets the minimum population requirements exactly. The total charges for providing annual heating and cooling checkups for all units in each of the three apartment complexes is closest to:

- ○ $6,075
- ○ $8,100
- ○ $12,225
- ◉ $18,225
- ○ $24,300

4. This table displays data on band merchandise sold by a major record label in 2017.

Sorted by Item (Column 1)

ITEM	SALES REVENUE, NATIONAL SHARE (%)	SALES REVENUE, NATIONAL RANK	SALES VOLUME, NATIONAL SHARE (%)	SALES VOLUME, NATIONAL RANK
Hats	26	3	24	2
Decals	61	2	43	1
Buttons	74	1	35	1
Posters	50	2	62	3
Programs	7	5	12	5
T-shirts	36	3	16	4
Hoodies	59	2	35	2
Key rings	94	1	78	1
Bumper stickers	82	1	71	1

For each of the following statements, select *Yes* if the statement can be shown to be true based on information in the table. Otherwise select *No*.

Yes	No	
●	○	This record label's average revenue per button sold was higher than the average for other labels.
○	●	This label sold more posters than T-shirts in 2017.
○	●	In 2017, decals were more popular than hats among those who purchased this label's merchandise nationwide.

5. The way Americans in the U.S. have incorporated meat into their diets has changed significantly for a number of reasons, including cost, dietary discoveries, and more. The table below compares the number of pounds consumed annually, per meat type, by the average American in 1970 and 2005. Select the best answer to fill in the blanks in each of the statements below based on the data shown in the graph.

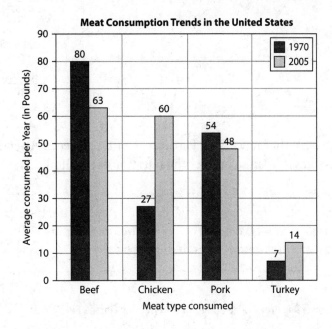

The total amount of all four types of meat consumed annually by the average American was _____ in 2005 compared to 1970.

Ⓐ greater
Ⓑ the same
Ⓒ less

The amount in pounds of beef consumed by the average American in 2005 is closest to _____ % of the amount in pounds consumed in 1970.

Ⓐ 60
Ⓑ 75
Ⓒ 85
Ⓓ 120
Ⓔ 130

6. A major manufacturer of MP3 players wants to produce both black and white plastic cases for its new 32 GB MP3 line. The manufacturer wants to spend a maximum of $200,000 on case production. White plastic cases cost $2 more per case to produce than do black plastic cases.

   Using W to represent the cost of producing each white case and B to represent the cost of producing each black case, select the expression that reflects the cost of producing one white case, and select the expression that reflects the maximum number of each type of case that can be produced within the company's $200,000 budget if the same number of black and white MP3 cases are made. Make only two selections, one in each column.

COST OF PRODUCING ONE WHITE CASE	MAXIMUM NUMBER OF EACH COLOR CASE	EXPRESSION
●	○	$B + \$2$
○	○	$2W + B$
○	●	$\dfrac{\$200{,}000}{2B + \$2}$
○	○	$\$200{,}000(W + B)$
○	○	$\dfrac{\$200{,}000B}{\$2W}$

7. Use the table that follows on Percentage of Dog Breeds Attending Selected Training Classes, Single Year, to answer the question that follows.

   On the actual exam, you will have the ability to sort the table by any of its columns. (Columns can be sorted in ascending order only.) The table is shown below sorted in different ways to mirror the test.

Percentage of Dog Breeds Attending Selected Training Classes, Single Year

Sorted by Breed (Column 1)

BREED	AGILITY	OBEDIENCE	SERVICE TRAINING	SEARCH & RESCUE
Australian shepherd	37	19	22	44
Boxer	18	25	36	8
Doberman pinscher	34	21	13	12
German shepherd	55	27	42	68
Husky	26	17	34	44
Rottweiler	20	25	17	32
Weimaraner	12	14	9	5

Sorted by Percentage Attending Obedience Classes (Column 3)

BREED	AGILITY	OBEDIENCE	SERVICE TRAINING	SEARCH & RESCUE
Weimaraner	12	14	9	5
Husky	26	17	34	44
Australian shepherd	37	19	22	44
Doberman pinscher	34	21	13	12
Boxer	18	25	36	8
Rottweiler	20	25	17	32
German shepherd	55	27	42	68

Sorted by Percentage Attending Search & Rescue Classes (Column 5)

BREED	AGILITY	OBEDIENCE	SERVICE TRAINING	SEARCH & RESCUE
Weimaraner	12	14	9	5
Boxer	18	25	36	8
Doberman pinscher	34	21	13	12
Rottweiler	20	25	17	32
Husky	26	17	34	44
Australian shepherd	37	19	22	44
German shepherd	55	27	42	68

For each of the following statements, select *Would help explain* if it would, if true, help explain some of the information in the table. Otherwise select *Would not help explain*.

Would help explain	Would not help explain	
○	◉	German shepherds as a breed are naturally obedient.
○	◉	Weimaraners are the most popular breed of service dog.
◉	○	Boxers lack the physical strength needed for search and rescue activities.

8. Read the sources below before answering the question that follows.

E-mail #1 *USFS Publications Director* to County Commissioners of Western Colorado
July 1, 9:12 A.M.

Due to the pine beetle infestation in the Rocky Mountain National Forest in Colorado, the U.S. Forest Service is required to provide estimates of the number of acres affected and the numbers of dead trees per acre. These numbers are based on USFS aerial photos and county field observation reports.

Each county in Colorado must submit its field reports to the USFS by October 1 of this year, for the publication of statewide maps of the affected areas. The Forest Service will compile the data from photos and county field observation reports for its annual report to Congress. Please see the attached list of counties that must comply with the reporting requirements. Counties with no Forest Service lands are not required to participate. Field observation reports must follow the designated format found in the document attached.

We rely on your cooperation to fulfill this reporting requirement and would remind you to take all necessary precautions to ensure the safety of your field observers in the infested areas.

E-mail #2 *County Commissioner of Summit County* in Response to USFS Publications Director's E-mail of July 1
July 5, 11:45 A.M.

Regarding field observation reports of pine beetle infestation: our county budget has been reduced by the recent economic downturn. Will there be funds available for hiring field observers, data entry workers, and report writers? We estimate that compliance with the reporting requirements will cost an estimated $286,000. Please advise.

E-mail #3 *USFS Publications Director* in Response to Summit County Commissioner's E-mail of July 5
July 8, 7:30 A.M.

Our understanding is that reporting costs will be reimbursed to you based on a percentage of the actual number of affected acres in your county. Keep in mind that the number of affected acres in your county is based on last year's estimates of total affected acreage. If you observe an increase, it must correlate with this year's aerial photos to qualify for increased reimbursement costs. Current reimbursement costs are calculated at 70% of total acreage, with a per-acre reimbursement of $6.00.

Suppose that Summit County completes the reporting required by the Forest Service, and its reporting costs total $286,000. If all of the information in the three e-mails is accurate, in order for Summit County to be reimbursed for its entire reporting costs, the number of acres affected by the pine beetle infestation in the county would have to be closest to which of the following?

○ 29,762

○ 33,092

○ 47,667

◉ 68,096

○ 72,132

9. Consider each of the following statements. Does the information in the three sources support the inference as stated?

Yes	No	
◉	○	The Summit County Commissioner plans to hire workers to provide reporting assistance to meet the Forest Service's requirements.
○	◉	The Forest Service is most likely to reimburse Summit County for 70% of its reporting costs.
○	◉	The Summit County Commissioner believes Summit County has experienced an increase over the previous year in the total number of forest acres affected by the pine beetle infestation.

10. The table below gives information on the total vehicles sold and the total sales revenue for a national Internet auto dealer over a four-year period, from 2013 through 2017. The 22 models were included in the table because they fall among the top 30 models sold by the company in terms of both the total number sold and total sales revenue. In addition to listing the total number sold and total sales revenue for each vehicle model, the table also gives the percent of increase or decrease over the 2008–2012 numbers sold and sales revenue and the rank of each vehicle model for total number sold and total sales revenue.

On the actual exam, you will have the ability to sort the table by any of its columns. (Columns can be sorted in ascending order only.) The table is shown below sorted in different ways to mirror the test.

Sorted by Make (Column 2)

VEHICLE			NUMBER SOLD			SALES REVENUE		
MODEL	MAKE	COLOR	NUMBER	% CHANGE	RANK	AMOUNT	% CHANGE	RANK
Focus	Ford	White	4,703	2	3	77,599,506	−6.0	8
Fusion	Ford	Black	4,337	−6.2	7	86,740,772	−0.1	5
Escape	Ford	Blue	4,326	6	8	90,846,301	−2.0	4
Fiesta	Ford	Red	3,584	−8.0	9	46,592,004	−0.8	19
Focus	Ford	Green	1,876	0.7	25	31,014,032	−0.9	25
Fit	Honda	Black	3,569	7.8	10	53,535,055	−1.9	16
Civic	Honda	White	2,984	1.7	13	44,760,490	−7.0	20
Accord	Honda	Blue	2,876	1.2	14	60,396,593	−2.0	11
Element	Honda	Red	2,875	−2.9	15	60,375,391	−3.2	12
Sportage	Kia	Silver	2,070	0.5	21	76,490,231	0.1	9
Forte	Kia	Blue	2,068	0.6	22	32,234,465	−0.3	23
Soul	Kia	Green	1,927	1.2	23	48,892,345	0.2	18
Optima	Kia	Red	1,907	0.9	24	43,678,210	−0.4	21
Outlander	Mitsubishi	White	4,573	−4.7	4	99,752,338	−6.1	1
Galant	Mitsubishi	White	2,493	9.7	16	55,646,253	−8.1	13
Eclipse	Mitsubishi	Green	2,076	0.4	19	42,547,620	−4.0	22
Forester	Subaru	Silver	4,721	3.4	2	98,811,903	−2.5	3
Outback	Subaru	Blue	4,513	1.3	5	98,812,913	−0.7	2
Impreza	Subaru	Red	4,349	9.2	6	73,933,449	−2.0	10
Legacy	Subaru	Black	2,996	−0.3	12	53,928,527	−0.4	14
Corolla	Toyota	Blue	4,937	1.2	1	78,995,520	−0.3	7
Tacoma	Toyota	Red	3,345	9.6	11	79,206,444	−3.5	6
Prius	Toyota	Black	2,192	−3.1	18	52,390,992	−2.3	17

Sorted by Color (Column 3)

VEHICLE			NUMBER SOLD			SALES REVENUE		
MODEL	MAKE	COLOR	NUMBER	% CHANGE	RANK	AMOUNT	% CHANGE	RANK
Fusion	Ford	Black	4,337	−6.2	7	86,740,772	−0.1	5
Fit	Honda	Black	3,569	7.8	10	53,535,055	−1.9	16
Legacy	Subaru	Black	2,996	−0.3	12	53,928,527	−0.4	14
Prius	Toyota	Black	2,192	−3.1	18	52,390,992	−2.3	17
Corolla	Toyota	Blue	4,937	1.2	1	78,995,520	−0.3	7
Outback	Subaru	Blue	4,513	1.3	5	98,812,913	−0.7	2
Escape	Ford	Blue	4,326	6	8	90,846,301	−2.0	4
Accord	Honda	Blue	2,876	1.2	14	60,396,593	−2.0	11
Forte	Kia	Blue	2,068	0.6	22	32,234,465	−0.3	23
Eclipse	Mitsubishi	Green	2,076	0.4	19	42,547,620	−4.0	22
Soul	Kia	Green	1,927	1.2	23	48,892,345	0.2	18
Focus	Ford	Green	1,876	0.7	25	31,014,032	−0.9	25
Impreza	Subaru	Red	4,349	9.2	6	73,933,449	−2.0	10
Fiesta	Ford	Red	3,584	−8.0	9	46,592,004	−0.8	19
Tacoma	Toyota	Red	3,345	9.6	11	79,206,444	−3.5	6
Element	Honda	Red	2,875	−2.9	15	60,375,391	−3.2	12
Optima	Kia	Red	1,907	0.9	24	43,678,210	−0.4	21
Forester	Subaru	Silver	4,721	3.4	2	98,811,903	−2.5	3
Sportage	Kia	Silver	2,070	0.5	21	76,490,231	0.1	9
Focus	Ford	White	4,703	2	3	77,599,506	−6.0	8
Outlander	Mitsubishi	White	4,573	−4.7	4	99,752,338	−6.1	1
Civic	Honda	White	2,984	1.7	13	44,760,490	−7.0	20
Galant	Mitsubishi	White	2,493	9.7	16	55,646,253	−8.1	13

Sorted by Rank in Number Sold (Column 6)

	VEHICLE		NUMBER SOLD			SALES REVENUE		
MODEL	MAKE	COLOR	NUMBER	% CHANGE	RANK	AMOUNT	% CHANGE	RANK
Corolla	Toyota	Blue	4,937	1.2	1	78,995,520	−0.3	7
Forester	Subaru	Silver	4,721	3.4	2	98,811,903	−2.5	3
Focus	Ford	White	4,703	2	3	77,599,506	−6.0	8
Outlander	Mitsubishi	White	4,573	−4.7	4	99,752,338	−6.1	1
Outback	Subaru	Blue	4,513	1.3	5	98,812,913	−0.7	2
Impreza	Subaru	Red	4,349	9.2	6	73,933,449	−2.0	10
Fusion	Ford	Black	4,337	−6.2	7	86,740,772	−0.1	5
Escape	Ford	Blue	4,326	6	8	90,846,301	−2.0	4
Fiesta	Ford	Red	3,584	−8.0	9	46,592,004	−0.8	19
Fit	Honda	Black	3,569	7.8	10	53,535,055	−1.9	16
Tacoma	Toyota	Red	3,345	9.6	11	79,206,444	−3.5	6
Legacy	Subaru	Black	2,996	−0.3	12	53,928,527	−0.4	14
Civic	Honda	White	2,984	1.7	13	44,760,490	−7.0	20
Accord	Honda	Blue	2,876	1.2	14	60,396,593	−2.0	11
Element	Honda	Red	2,875	−2.9	15	60,375,391	−3.2	12
Galant	Mitsubishi	White	2,493	9.7	16	55,646,253	−8.1	13
Prius	Toyota	Black	2,192	−3.1	18	52,390,992	−2.3	17
Eclipse	Mitsubishi	Green	2,076	0.4	19	42,547,620	−4.0	22
Sportage	Kia	Silver	2,070	0.5	21	76,490,231	0.1	9
Forte	Kia	Blue	2,068	0.6	22	32,234,465	−0.3	23
Soul	Kia	Green	1,927	1.2	23	48,892,345	0.2	18
Optima	Kia	Red	1,907	0.9	24	43,678,210	−0.4	21
Focus	Ford	Green	1,876	0.7	25	31,014,032	−0.9	25

Sorted by Rank in Sales Revenue (Column 9)

VEHICLE			NUMBER SOLD			SALES REVENUE		
MODEL	MAKE	COLOR	NUMBER	% CHANGE	RANK	AMOUNT	% CHANGE	RANK
Outlander	Mitsubishi	White	4,573	−4.7	4	99,752,338	−6.1	1
Outback	Subaru	Blue	4,513	1.3	5	98,812,913	−0.7	2
Forester	Subaru	Silver	4,721	3.4	2	98,811,903	−2.5	3
Escape	Ford	Blue	4,326	6	8	90,846,301	−2.0	4
Fusion	Ford	Black	4,337	−6.2	7	86,740,772	−0.1	5
Tacoma	Toyota	Red	3,345	9.6	11	79,206,444	−3.5	6
Corolla	Toyota	Blue	4,937	1.2	1	78,995,520	−0.3	7
Focus	Ford	White	4,703	2	3	77,599,506	−6.0	8
Sportage	Kia	Silver	2,070	0.5	21	76,490,231	0.1	9
Impreza	Subaru	Red	4,349	9.2	6	73,933,449	−2.0	10
Accord	Honda	Blue	2,876	1.2	14	60,396,593	−2.0	11
Element	Honda	Red	2,875	−2.9	15	60,375,391	−3.2	12
Galant	Mitsubishi	White	2,493	9.7	16	55,646,253	−8.1	13
Legacy	Subaru	Black	2,996	−0.3	12	53,928,527	−0.4	14
Fit	Honda	Black	3,569	7.8	10	53,535,055	−1.9	16
Prius	Toyota	Black	2,192	−3.1	18	52,390,992	−2.3	17
Soul	Kia	Green	1,927	1.2	23	48,892,345	0.2	18
Fiesta	Ford	Red	3,584	−8.0	9	46,592,004	−0.8	19
Civic	Honda	White	2,984	1.7	13	44,760,490	−7.0	20
Optima	Kia	Red	1,907	0.9	24	43,678,210	−0.4	21
Eclipse	Mitsubishi	Green	2,076	0.4	19	42,547,620	−4.0	22
Forte	Kia	Blue	2,068	0.6	22	32,234,465	−0.3	23
Focus	Ford	Green	1,876	0.7	25	31,014,032	−0.9	25

Review each of the statements below. Based on the information provided in the table, indicate whether the statement is true or false.

True   False

●   ○   More Ford Focuses than Toyota Corollas were sold by this retailer.

○   ●   The highest-selling blue model from each manufacturer was outsold by at least one other model from the same manufacturer.

○   ●   The Kia models all ranked lower than 20th in sales revenue.

●   ○   No green car was among the top ten cars by rank in either number sold or sales revenue.

11. The graph below models the 10-day trend of stock prices for two rival shoe companies trading on the NASDAQ. The 10-day trend was recorded between the 10th and the 20th of January in 2015. NKE stock is shown on the upper line, and AG stock is shown on the lower line. Select the best answer to fill in the blanks in each of the statements below based on the data shown in the graph.

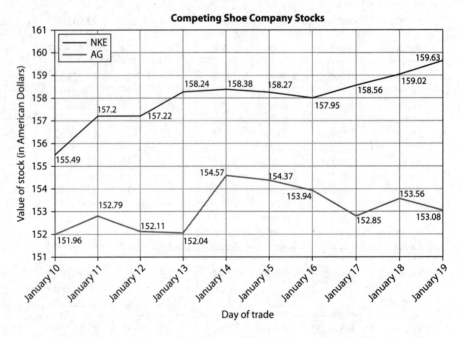

The percent change in the value of NKE stock over the entire ten days is about _____ the percent change in the value of AG stock over that same period.

(A) equal to
(B) 2 times
(C) 4 times

For the span between January 13th and January 16th, the average (arithmetic mean) value of AG stock falls approximately between _____ dollars.

(A) 151 and 153
(B) 153 and 155
(C) 155 and 157

12. Classic Whites runs two seasonal white sales, one in January and one in August. Each sale runs for 14 days. The January sale this year sold an average of 3,500 sheet sets per week during its two-week price cut. The August sale exceeded the January sale by an average of 130 sets per day during its two-week price cut, despite the fact that it sold only 1,200 sets during its first week. The event to be held next January is expected to sell a weekly average of 75% of the sheet sets sold during the second week of this year's August event.

In the table below, identify the number of sheet sets sold in the second week of this year's August white sale event, and identify the total number of sheet sets that are expected to be sold during the entire sale next January. Make only one selection in each column.

THIS AUGUST	NEXT JANUARY	SHEET SETS SOLD
SECOND WEEK	ENTIRE SALE	
○	○	3,500
○	⊙	5,715
●	○	7,620
○	○	8,820
○	●	11,430
○	○	13,335

J₂

Answers

1. The answer to the first blank is **D**. Of the two cities whose average temperature is below 8 degrees Celsius, one has an elevation of 100 meters and the other has an elevation of 200 meters, which is 100 percent higher.

   The answer to the second blank is **B**. In the graph, there is no consistent pattern of temperature rising as elevation rises (positive correlation) or temperature falling as elevation rises (negative correlation), so the correlation between temperature and elevation is best described as zero.

2. The correct answers are **$2,277.15** for the third quarter taxes and **$817.35** for the amount of additional taxes paid in the fourth quarter compared to the second quarter.

3RD QUARTER TAXES	DIFFERENCE BETWEEN 2ND AND 4TH QUARTERS	AMOUNT (IN DOLLARS)
○	○	$238.00
○	●	$817.35
○	○	$1,938.00
●	○	$2,277.15
○	○	$2,755.35
○	○	$2,965.05

   In the second quarter, Jamie pays 14% more taxes than she paid in the first quarter. She paid $1,700 in the first quarter, so her second quarter tax increase is $1,700 × 0.14, or $238. Her total second quarter taxes are $1,700 + $238, or $1,938.

   In the third quarter, Jamie pays 17.5% more than she pays in the second quarter—an increase of $1,938 × 0.175, or $339.15. Her total third quarter taxes are $1,938 + $339.15, or $2,277.15.

   In the fourth quarter, Jamie pays 21% more than she pays in the third quarter. This is an increase of $2,277.15 × 0.21, or $478.20. Her total fourth quarter taxes are $2,277.15 + $478.20, or $2,755.35. This amount exceeds her second quarter tax payment by $817.35.

3. The correct answer is **18,225**.

   Each of the three apartment complexes has 135 units. The cost for annual checkups is $45 per unit. The total cost for all three complexes is 135 × 3 × $45, or $18,225.

4. The correct answers are shown below.

   Yes No
   - ● ○ This record label's average revenue per button sold was higher than the average for other labels.
   - ○ ● This label sold more posters than T-shirts in 2017.
   - ○ ● In 2017, decals were more popular than hats among those who purchased this label's merchandise nationwide.

   For this label to have made three-quarters of the nation's revenue from button sales while making only one-third of the total volume of sales, the label must have earned more money per button than did its competitors.

The label sold more posters compared to other labels than it did T-shirts compared to other labels, but you can't know if it sold more posters than it did T-shirts without more information, such as how many total posters and T-shirts were sold by all the labels.

No information is available about the actual number of decals or hats sold by the label nationwide, so you cannot determine which was more popular.

5. The answer to the first blank is **A**. In 1970, the average American consumed an average total of 168 pounds of the four types of meat shown; in 2005, the average total was 185 pounds.

The answer to the second blank is **B**. The 63 pounds of beef consumed in 2005 is about 79 percent of the 80 pounds consumed in 1970.

6. The correct answers are **B + $2** for the cost of producing one white case, and $\frac{\$200,000}{2B+\$2}$ for the maximum number of each color case that can be produced.

COST OF PRODUCING ONE WHITE CASE	MAXIMUM NUMBER OF EACH COLOR CASE	EXPRESSION
●	○	$B + \$2$
○	○	$2W + B$
○	●	$\frac{\$200,000}{2B+\$2}$
○	○	$\$200,000(W+B)$
○	○	$\frac{\$200,000B}{\$2W}$

White cases cost $2 more to produce per case than black cases. The cost of producing one white case is represented by the expression $B + \$2$.

The company produces the same number of black and white cases. Let x represent the number of each color case that is produced. Set up an equation that shows the parameters given:

$$(\text{cost of white cases}) + (\text{cost of black cases}) \leq \$200,000$$

To find the cost of each type of case, multiply the number of cases by the cost per case:

$$(\text{number of white cases} \times \text{cost}) + (\text{number of black cases} \times \text{cost}) \leq \$200,000$$

Substitute x for the number of white and black cases. Substitute B for the cost of black cases and B + $2 for the cost of white cases:

$$x(B) + x(B+\$2) \leq \$200,000$$

Now solve for x, the number of each type of case:

$$x(B + B + \$2) \leq \$200,000$$
$$x(2B + \$2) \leq \$200,000$$
$$x \leq \frac{\$200,000}{2B + \$2}$$

7. The correct answers are shown below.

Would help explain	Would not help explain	
○	●	German shepherds as a breed are naturally obedient.
○	●	Weimaraners are the most popular breed of service dog.
●	○	Boxers lack the physical strength needed for search and rescue operations.

A more obedient breed of dog would not be more likely to be sent to obedience training classes; if anything, it might be less likely to need the training.

The most popular breed of service dog would probably not be the breed with the lowest percentage attending service training.

A breed that is poorly suited to search and rescue operations would be less likely to be trained for them.

8. The correct answer is **68,096**.

The third e-mail tells you that the reimbursement cost is $6 per acre. To cover its report costs completely, Summit County would have to be reimbursed for $286,000 ÷ $6, or about 47,667 affected acres.

The Forest Service only reimburses counties for 70% of their total affected acreage. To receive reimbursement for 47,667 acres, Summit County would have to have a total acreage larger than 47,667. To determine the amount, divide 47,667 by 70%, or 0.70. The answer is approximately 68,096. If Summit County had a total of 68,096 affected acres, it could be reimbursed for 68,096 × 0.70, or 47,667 acres.

9. The correct answers are shown below.

Yes	No	
●	○	The Summit County Commissioner plans to hire workers to provide reporting assistance to meet the Forest Service's requirements.
○	●	The Forest Service is most likely to reimburse Summit County for 70% of its reporting costs.
○	●	The Summit County Commissioner believes Summit County has experienced an increase over the previous year in the total number of forest acres affected by the pine beetle infestation.

The first inference is supported by the information in the three sources. The second e-mail indicates that the Summit County Commissioner has estimated costs for meeting the reporting requirements. A total of $286,000 will be spent to hire field observers, data entry workers, and report writers.

The second inference is not supported by the information in the three sources. The Forest Service instructs the County Commissioner on how reimbursements are calculated. No mention is made of the exact reporting costs for Summit County or the total number of affected acres. Therefore, the reimbursement percentage cannot be determined.

The third inference is not supported by the information in the three sources. This statement is not suggested in any of the three sources.

10. The correct answers are shown below.

True	False	
●	○	More Ford Focuses than Toyota Corollas were sold by this retailer.
○	●	The highest-selling blue model from each manufacturer was outsold by at least one other model from the same manufacturer.
○	●	The Kia models all ranked lower than 20th in sales revenue.
●	○	No green car was among the top ten cars by rank in either number sold or sales revenue.

Two colors of Focus are shown in the table; altogether, 6,579 of those were sold compared to only 4,937 Corollas.

The blue Forte, Escape, Accord, and Outback were outsold by other models of the same make, but the blue Toyota Corolla was not outsold by any other Toyota model.

The Kia models all ranked lower than 20th in number sold, two Kia models ranked higher than 20th in sales revenue.

Sorting the table by rank in number sold and then by rank in sales revenue, you can see that the top ten cars each time include no green cars.

11. The answer to the first blank is **C**. The value of AG stock increased by about 0.7 percent ([153.08 − 151.96]/151.96) over the ten days; meanwhile, the value of NKE stock increased by about 2.7 percent ([159.63 − 155.49]/155.49), or about four times as much.

The answer to the second blank is **B**. The average value of AG stock for the span between January 13th and January 16th is a little under 154 dollars.

12. The correct answers are **7,620** sheet sets sold in the second week this August, and **11,430** total sheet sets sold during the entire sale next January.

THIS AUGUST	NEXT JANUARY	SHEET SETS SOLD
SECOND WEEK	ENTIRE SALE	
○	○	3,500
○	○	5,715
●	○	7,620
○	○	8,820
○	●	11,430
○	○	13,335

An average of 3,500 sheet sets was sold per week last January. The sale is two weeks long, so 7,000 sheet sets were sold in last January's sale.

The August event exceeded last January's total by an average of 130 sheet sets per day. The event runs for 14 days, so August's sales exceeded January's sales by 130 × 14, or 1,820 sheet sets. The total for August was 7,000 + 1,820, or 8,820 sheet sets.

The first column asks for the number of sheets sold in the *second* week of the August event. In the first week, 1,200 sheets were sold, so in the second week this August, 7,620 sheets were sold.

The second column asks for the total number of sheet sets expected to be sold during the entire two-week sale next January. Next January's event is expected to have a weekly average of about 75% of sheet sets sold during the second week this August, or $0.75 \times 7,620 = 5,715$. The total sales are expected to be twice that number: $5,715 \times 2$, or 11,430 sheet sets.

Integrated Reasoning Drill 3

Directions: Select the best answer or answers for the questions below. You may use a calculator for this section of the test only.

On the actual test, you will be provided with an online calculator. You will *not* be permitted to bring your own calculator to the test.

The sources that follow accompany questions 1 and 2.

Source #1 Voice Mail from Real Estate Agent

I have excellent news. The owners have accepted your bid of $179,000! You close on your new home in 30 days. Call me back soon and we will work out the details.

Source #2 January 2016 Mortgage Statement

Payment Due	$978.79
Monthly Principal and Interest	$760.03
Escrow Payment	$218.76
If paid after January 24, 2016, please pay	$999.16

Source #3 Amortization Table

Loan Summary	
Monthly Principal and Interest	$760.03
Total of 360 Payments	$273,610.80
Total Interest Paid	$123,610.80
Maturity Date	February 2046

YEAR	INTEREST	PRINCIPAL	BALANCE
2016	$7,111.39	$2,008.95	$147,991.05
2017	$6,608.20	$2,512.13	$145,478.92
2018	$6,492.80	$2,627.54	$142,851.38
2019	$6,372.09	$2,748.25	$140,103.14
2020	$6,245.84	$2,874.50	$137,228.64
2021	$6,113.78	$3,006.55	$134,222.08
2022	$5,975.66	$3,144.67	$131,077.41
2023	$5,831.19	$3,289.14	$127,788.27
2024	$5,680.09	$3,440.24	$124,348.02
2025	$5,522.05	$3,598.29	$120,749.74
2026	$5,356.74	$3,763.59	$116,986.15
2027	$5,183.84	$3,936.49	$113,049.65

1. Consider each of the following statements. Does the information in the three sources support the inference as stated?

Yes   No

○   ○   The late payment fee assessed by the mortgage company is 2% of the total mortgage payment.

○   ○   The previous owners were asking more than $179,000 for their property.

○   ○   Making double payments on the principal in the first year would mean paying an extra $265 per month.

2. If the information contained in all three sources is correct and the first payment on the loan was made in January 2016, the down payment made on the purchase of the home was closest to which of the following?

   ○ $17,900
   ○ $21,600
   ○ $23,400
   ○ $29,000
   ○ $35,200

3. The graph below is a scatter plot with 35 points, each representing the teen birth rate in a major American city. The population of teenage females, age 15 to 19, was measured against the number of births within that population over a 12-month period. Select the best answer to fill in the blanks in each of the statements below based on the data shown in the graph.

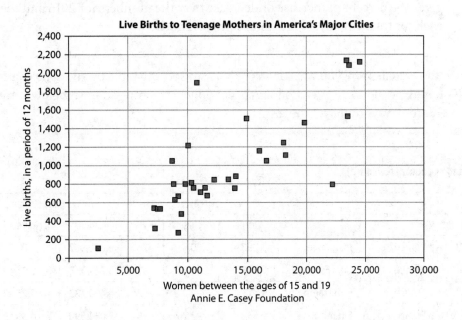

The city with the largest population of 15- to 19-year-old women had about _____ percent as many births in that age group as the city with the smallest population.

   Ⓐ 5
   Ⓑ 10
   Ⓒ 21
   Ⓓ 210
   Ⓔ 2,100

The relationship between the number of women between 15 and 19 and the number of births within that population is best described as _____.

   Ⓐ negative
   Ⓑ no relationship
   Ⓒ positive

4. The table below gives information on the total employees and total sales revenue in 2017 for divisions of an international conglomerate. The 24 company divisions included in the table fall among the top 30 divisions for this annual period in terms of both total employees and total sales revenue. In addition to providing the numbers of total employees and total sales revenue for each division, the table also gives the percent of increase or decrease over the numbers for 2016 and the rank of each for total employees and total sales revenue.

On the actual exam, you will have the ability to sort the table by any of its columns. (Columns can be sorted in ascending order only.) The table is shown below sorted in different ways to mirror the test.

Sorted by Country (Column 2)

DIVISION			EMPLOYEES			SALES REVENUE		
SYMBOL	COUNTRY	TYPE	NUMBER	% CHANGE	RANK	AMOUNT	% CHANGE	RANK
ZOT	France	Insurance	1,298	0.5	26	6,080,987	−9.0	4
HBP	France	Real Estate	9,608	−0.3	7	5,749,857	0.8	7
SCIC	France	Entertainment	9,813	−9.0	2	4,499,723	1.2	12
AGA	France	Financial	9,552	−3.2	8	2,034,590	0.3	20
ACL	France	Education	4,983	9.5	21	1,233,390	−4.0	23
LLT	Hong Kong	Entertainment	4,892	4.2	23	6,079,345	0.4	5
KRD	Hong Kong	Insurance	9,801	0.6	3	4,003,434	3.8	15
JBVX	Hong Kong	Real Estate	9,743	4.2	5	3,389,332	2.4	16
MCD	Hong Kong	Education	2,978	0.4	25	3,067,888	−5.0	18
VIP	Japan	Real Estate	9,490	3.2	10	6,234,232	0.7	2
DAI	Japan	Education	4,735	−9.0	24	2,107,892	−4.0	19
CORT	Mexico	Real Estate	4,907	2.5	22	6,197,750	0.4	3
JVSC	Mexico	Education	5,889	0.1	20	3,274,322	1.5	17
MBT	Mexico	Entertainment	9,254	3.4	13	1,199,876	6	24
FTTP	Mexico	Insurance	9,332	2.9	11	1,099,054	4.1	25
CME	UK	Entertainment	7,497	−4.3	18	5,427,904	0.5	9
ZPR	UK	Insurance	7,495	−3.1	19	4,059,458	2.1	14
LMBY	UK	Real Estate	9,145	3.2	15	1,033,967	3.8	26
GROG	UK	Financial	1,194	6.1	28	1,029,543	2.4	27
FTMR	US	Insurance	9,905	−1.2	1	6,239,533	3	1
ROVC	US	Real Estate	8,309	−4.9	16	5,650,041	−0.5	8
BRO	US	Financial	9,684	−5.6	6	5,140,327	0.7	10
MAIR	US	Entertainment	7,904	−4.0	17	1,894,390	4.3	21
GJG	US	Insurance	9,314	−3.5	12	1,363,901	1.3	22

Sorted by Type (Column 3)

	DIVISION		EMPLOYEES			SALES REVENUE		
SYMBOL	COUNTRY	TYPE	NUMBER	% CHANGE	RANK	AMOUNT	% CHANGE	RANK
JVSC	Mexico	Education	5,889	0.1	20	3,274,322	1.5	17
MCD	Hong Kong	Education	2,978	0.4	25	3,067,888	−5.0	18
DAI	Japan	Education	4,735	−9.0	24	2,107,892	−4.0	19
ACL	France	Education	4,983	9.5	21	1,233,390	−4.0	23
LLT	Hong Kong	Entertainment	4,892	4.2	23	6,079,345	0.4	5
CME	UK	Entertainment	7,497	−4.3	18	5,427,904	0.5	9
SCIC	France	Entertainment	9,813	−9.0	2	4,499,723	1.2	12
MAIR	US	Entertainment	7,904	−4.0	17	1,894,390	4.3	21
MBT	Mexico	Entertainment	9,254	3.4	13	1,199,876	6	24
BRO	US	Financial	9,684	−5.6	6	5,140,327	0.7	10
AGA	France	Financial	9,552	−3.2	8	2,034,590	0.3	20
GROG	UK	Financial	1,194	6.1	28	1,029,543	2.4	27
FTMR	US	Insurance	9,905	−1.2	1	6,239,533	3	1
ZOT	France	Insurance	1,298	0.5	26	6,080,987	−9.0	4
ZPR	UK	Insurance	7,495	−3.1	19	4,059,458	2.1	14
KRD	Hong Kong	Insurance	9,801	0.6	3	4,003,434	3.8	15
GJG	US	Insurance	9,314	−3.5	12	1,363,901	1.3	22
FTTP	Mexico	Insurance	9,332	2.9	11	1,099,054	4.1	25
VIP	Japan	Real Estate	9,490	3.2	10	6,234,232	0.7	2
CORT	Mexico	Real Estate	4,907	2.5	22	6,197,750	0.4	3
HBP	France	Real Estate	9,608	−0.3	7	5,749,857	0.8	7
ROVC	US	Real Estate	8,309	−4.9	16	5,650,041	−0.5	8
JBVX	Hong Kong	Real Estate	9,743	4.2	5	3,389,332	2.4	16
LMBY	UK	Real Estate	9,145	3.2	15	1,033,967	3.8	26

Sorted by Rank in Number of Employees (Column 6)

	DIVISION		EMPLOYEES			SALES REVENUE		
SYMBOL	COUNTRY	TYPE	NUMBER	% CHANGE	RANK	AMOUNT	% CHANGE	RANK
FTMR	US	Insurance	9,905	−1.2	1	6,239,533	3	1
SCIC	France	Entertainment	9,813	−9.0	2	4,499,723	1.2	12
KRD	Hong Kong	Insurance	9,801	0.6	3	4,003,434	3.8	15
JBVX	Hong Kong	Real Estate	9,743	4.2	5	3,389,332	2.4	16
BRO	US	Financial	9,684	−5.6	6	5,140,327	0.7	10
HBP	France	Real Estate	9,608	−0.3	7	5,749,857	0.8	7
AGA	France	Financial	9,552	−3.2	8	2,034,590	0.3	20
VIP	Japan	Real Estate	9,490	3.2	10	6,234,232	0.7	2
FTTP	Mexico	Insurance	9,332	2.9	11	1,099,054	4.1	25
GJG	US	Insurance	9,314	−3.5	12	1,363,901	1.3	22
MBT	Mexico	Entertainment	9,254	3.4	13	1,199,876	6	24
LMBY	UK	Real Estate	9,145	3.2	15	1,033,967	3.8	26
ROVC	US	Real Estate	8,309	−4.9	16	5,650,041	−0.5	8
MAIR	US	Entertainment	7,904	−4.0	17	1,894,390	4.3	21
CME	UK	Entertainment	7,497	−4.3	18	5,427,904	0.5	9
ZPR	UK	Insurance	7,495	−3.1	19	4,059,458	2.1	14
JVSC	Mexico	Education	5,889	0.1	20	3,274,322	1.5	17
ACL	France	Education	4,983	9.5	21	1,233,390	−4.0	23
CORT	Mexico	Real Estate	4,907	2.5	22	6,197,750	0.4	3
LLT	Hong Kong	Entertainment	4,892	4.2	23	6,079,345	0.4	5
DAI	Japan	Education	4,735	−9.0	24	2,107,892	−4.0	19
MCD	Hong Kong	Education	2,978	0.4	25	3,067,888	−5.0	18
ZOT	France	Insurance	1,298	0.5	26	6,080,987	−9.0	4
GROG	UK	Financial	1,194	6.1	28	1,029,543	2.4	27

Sorted by Rank in Sales (Column 9)

	DIVISION		EMPLOYEES			SALES REVENUE		
SYMBOL	COUNTRY	TYPE	NUMBER	% CHANGE	RANK	AMOUNT	% CHANGE	RANK
FTMR	US	Insurance	9,905	−1.2	1	6,239,533	3.0	1
VIP	Japan	Real Estate	9,490	3.2	10	6,234,232	0.7	2
CORT	Mexico	Real Estate	4,907	2.5	22	6,197,750	0.4	3
ZOT	France	Insurance	1,298	0.5	26	6,080,987	−9.0	4
LLT	Hong Kong	Entertainment	4,892	4.2	23	6,079,345	0.4	5
HBP	France	Real Estate	9,608	−0.3	7	5,749,857	0.8	7
ROVC	US	Real Estate	8,309	−4.9	16	5,650,041	−0.5	8
CME	UK	Entertainment	7,497	−4.3	18	5,427,904	0.5	9
BRO	US	Financial	9,684	−5.6	6	5,140,327	0.7	10
SCIC	France	Entertainment	9,813	−9.0	2	4,499,723	1.2	12
ZPR	UK	Insurance	7,495	−3.1	19	4,059,458	2.1	14
KRD	Hong Kong	Insurance	9,801	0.6	3	4,003,434	3.8	15
JBVX	Hong Kong	Real Estate	9,743	4.2	5	3,389,332	2.4	16
JVSC	Mexico	Education	5,889	0.1	20	3,274,322	1.5	17
MCD	Hong Kong	Education	2,978	0.4	25	3,067,888	−5.0	18
DAI	Japan	Education	4,735	−9.0	24	2,107,892	−4.0	19
AGA	France	Financial	9,552	−3.2	8	2,034,590	0.3	20
MAIR	US	Entertainment	7,904	−4.0	17	1,894,390	4.3	21
GJG	US	Insurance	9,314	−3.5	12	1,363,901	1.3	22
ACL	France	Education	4,983	9.5	21	1,233,390	−4.0	23
MBT	Mexico	Entertainment	9,254	3.4	13	1,199,876	6.0	24
FTTP	Mexico	Insurance	9,332	2.9	11	1,099,054	4.1	25
LMBY	UK	Real Estate	9,145	3.2	15	1,033,967	3.8	26
GROG	UK	Financial	1,194	6.1	28	1,029,543	2.4	27

Review each of the statements below. Based on the information provided in the table, indicate whether the statement is true or false.

True False

○ ○ No financial divisions ranked among the top five in sales revenue.

○ ○ No country had more than two divisions of the same type.

○ ○ The division with the most employees also had the highest sales revenue.

○ ○ The real estate division with the most employees was in France.

The sources that follow accompany question 5.

Memo #1 from *CEO* to Market Analyst

We are consistently seeing more growth in the Northwest sector than in the three other sectors of the United States. Although we are spending equal amounts on advertising and the same product is being marketed across the country, sales fail to meet our expectations in the Northeast, Southwest, and Southeast. We would like to determine how to convince potential customers in other regions that our product is a better buy than the competitors' products.

Memo #2 from *Market Analyst* to CEO

Our research suggests that potential customers do not fully understand the benefits of your product; in warmer regions the idea that it might keep the skin cool—rather than just insulating against the cold—is not well understood. In the Northeast, though advertising is as frequent, there are significantly fewer retailers of the product, which may make it less visible in some communities. I recommend developing separate lines of advertisement for each sector of the country that emphasize the specific benefits of the product for that particular area. Also, in regions of dense population, attempts should be made to increase the number of product retailers per capita.

5. In the marketing analyst's review of the company's advertising strategy, it is brought to light that a cause and effect relationship exists between the way advertising is handled and the company's product sales experiences. Choose the cause and subsequent effect in the table below, based on the market analyst's suggestions. Make only one selection in each column.

CAUSE	EFFECT	STATEMENTS
○	○	1. Customers do not fully understand all of the product's possible uses.
○	○	2. Separate lines of advertisement have been developed for each U.S. sector.
○	○	3. Product sales were down in the warmer regions.
○	○	4. The Northwest sector has had the best sales reports.
○	○	5. Sales locations are more numerous in dense areas of population.
○	○	6. Competitors are succeeding in sectors where this company is not performing well.

6. Life expectancy for both males and females regularly increases as medical science improves. The graph below models the life expectancy trends for both men and women from 1965 to the present. Select the best answer to fill in the blanks in each of the statements below based on the data shown in the graph.

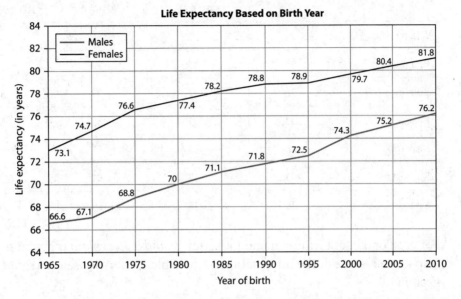

The percent difference in life expectancy for males born in 1995 as compared to those born in 1990 is approximately _____ the difference in life expectancy for females born in 1995 as compared to those born in 1990.

(A) equal to
(B) 5 times
(C) 10 times

The number of years by which the average female born in 2010 can expect to outlive the average male born the same year is closest to _____ percent of the number of years by which the average female born in 1975 can expect to outlive the average male born the same year.

(A) 50
(B) 60
(C) 70

7.

Percentage of Dance Studios Offering Instruction in Selected Styles, Single Year Sorted by City (Column 1)				
CITY	LATIN/SALSA	BALLROOM	BALLET	JAZZ & MODERN
Albany	21	25	50	13
Binghamton	13	16	20	4
Buffalo	28	17	29	36
Ithaca	33	21	38	53
New York	46	34	57	68
Rochester	21	32	41	30
Syracuse	15	14	29	30

For each of the following statements, select *Would help explain* if it would, if true, help explain some of the information in the table. Otherwise select *Would not help explain*.

Would help explain	Would not help explain	
○	○	Albany has more dance studios than Binghamton.
○	○	New York City has recently experienced a surge of interest in swing dancing.
○	○	In Rochester, jazz and modern dance are only taught at ballet studios, but not all ballet studios teach them.

8. Read the sources below before answering the question that follows.

Source #1 Candy Fun Company Price List

Chocolate Cost:	$3.58/lb	Dark Chocolate
	$3.24/lb	Milk Chocolate
	$2.94/lb	White Chocolate/Vanilla
	$3.78/lb	Specialty Colors

Colors Available Include:

Pink, Light Green, Dark Green, Yellow, Orange, Purple, Light Blue, Dark Blue, and Red

| | $5.85/lb | Sugar-Free Chocolates |

Flavors Available Include:

Dark Chocolate, Vanilla, and Milk Chocolate

	$2.95/lb	Coconut Shavings
	$5.20/lb	Caramel
	$1.40/oz	High-Quality Flavorings for Chocolate

Source #2 E-mailed Order

Hi Candy Fun Company,

I would like to place an order for chocolate mints for a retirement celebration on April 14, 2017. We will require 6 pounds of small mints in the midsize range. Please use at least three colors in your presentation, preferably including blue and green, since those are the primary colors in our company logo. The shape of the mints is unimportant as long as the appearance is professional; either basic round mints or flower-shaped mints are fine.

Thanks,

Betsy Carver

Source #3 Candy Fun Company Invoice

Invoice: #200515   Customer: Betsy Carver, Bandercom Inc.
Order: April 1, 2017   Delivery Date: April 14, 2017

Order #1

	2 pounds white mint discs	$7.89	$15.78
	2 pounds blue floral mints	$8.99	$17.98
	2 pounds green leaf mints	$8.99	$17.98
Delivery Charge (not taxed)		$10.00	
Subtotal		$61.74	
Tax (7.85%)		$ 4.06	
Total		**$65.80**	

Consider each of the following statements. Does the information in the three sources support the inference as stated?

Yes   No

○   ○   The average price per pound of the mints including tax and delivery is $10.29.

○   ○   Sugar-free chocolates cost about 80% more, on average, than regular varieties of chocolate.

○   ○   The Candy Fun Company charged $0.75 per pound for delivery services.

9. This table displays data on undeliverable mail received by a Philadelphia post office in 2010.

Sorted by Month (Column 1)				
MONTH	PACKAGES, CITY SHARE (%)	PACKAGES, CITY RANK	LETTERS, CITY SHARE (%)	LETTERS, CITY RANK
01—January	27	1	46	3
02—February	14	1	39	1
03—March	8	4	18	4
04—April	5	5	13	1
05—May	24	1	56	2
06—June	10	1	31	1
07—July	8	3	20	1
08—August	17	2	25	2
09—September	12	2	9	3

For each of the following statements, select *Yes* if the statement can be shown to be true based on information in the table.

Otherwise select *No*.

Yes   No

○   ○   More letters than packages were mailed in Philadelphia.

○   ○   There was an upward trend over the course of the year in the number of undeliverable packages.

○   ○   In September, more undeliverable packages than letters went through this post office.

10. The following excerpt is from a fictitious article in a journal of psychiatric medicine about a fictitious mental health condition called *diaemotiopluralism*.

For psychiatrists studying the behavior of those suffering from *diaemotiopluralism*, there is critical significance in observing the subject both when alone and when interacting with his or her peers. Such observations allow researchers to study not only the normal or "base" state of the affected person, including the effect that being alone has on an individual, but also the effects of *diaemotiopluralism* on social interactions, position in social order, and ability to participate in constructive workplace relationships. Individuals who suffer from *diaemotiopluralism* are often susceptible to overstimulation, particularly in situations involving high levels of interpersonal contact. Moreover, there are varying degrees of *diaemotiopluralism*, with different social situations affecting individuals in unique ways. It is interesting to observe not only the actual symptoms of the disorder but also the coping mechanisms that the individual develops in an attempt to compensate for, overcome, or manage his or her condition.

In the table below, identify the scenario that is likely to be the most difficult to manage for a person with *diaemotiopluralism* based on the definition given above, and then identify the scenario that a person suffering from *diaemotiopluralism* is likely to find least difficult to manage.

MOST DIFFICULT	LEAST DIFFICULT	SCENARIOS
○	○	Working in an office
○	○	Riding alone in a car
○	○	Having lunch at home with a spouse
○	○	Watching television with a friend
○	○	Sleeping

11. The graph below represents the results of a survey given to four focus groups labeled A, B, C, and D. Each group was shown a different image of the same person dressed for a professional interview. Each image pictured a different interview outfit containing more profession markers than the previous image, including a jacket, formal shoes, a briefcase, and other factors. After the group viewed the image, members were asked to respond yes or no to three questions: "Do you feel the candidate is dressed professionally?", "Do you feel the attire increases the candidate's hiring potential?", and "Do you feel the candidate will be hired for the position?"

The position of each circle on the graph reflects the perceived level of professionalism of the attire in a given photo, (based on the percentage of focus group members who indicated that the outfit was professional) versus the perceived hiring potential of the subject (based on the percentage of focus group members who deemed the subject hirable). The relative size of the circle is used as a device to show the degree to which focus group members agreed that the candidate would be hired (the larger the circle, the higher the agreement). Select the best answer to fill in the blank in each of the statements below based on the data shown in the graph.

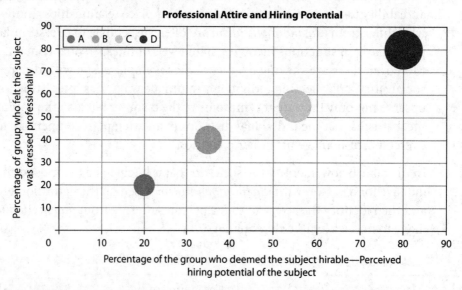

The relationship between the percentage of the group who felt the subject was dressed professionally and the percentage of the group who believed the subject would be hired is best described as _____.

Ⓐ negative
Ⓑ no relationship
Ⓒ positive

The percentage of people in group B who felt the candidate was dressed professionally is closest to _____ times the percentage of people in group A who felt the candidate was dressed professionally.

Ⓐ 1.5
Ⓑ 2
Ⓒ 2.5

12. Libby Ketchup purchases products from 25 tomato suppliers and 30 packaging suppliers.

In the table below, select two numbers among the numbers listed that are consistent with the information given. In the first column, select the largest number of suppliers that sell either tomatoes or packaging products to Libby, and in the second column, select the largest number of suppliers that could possibly sell both tomatoes and packaging products to Libby. Select only one option in each column.

EITHER TOMATOES OR PACKAGING PRODUCTS	BOTH TOMATOES AND PACKAGING PRODUCTS	NUMBER OF SUPPLIERS
○	○	10
○	○	20
○	○	30
○	○	40
○	○	50
○	○	60

Answers

1. The correct answers are shown below.

Yes   No

● ○   The late payment fee assessed by the mortgage company is 2% of the total mortgage payment.

○ ●   The previous owners were asking more than $179,000 for their property.

○ ●   Making double payments on the principal in the first year would mean paying an extra $265 per month.

The late payment fee is 2% of the total payment amount. The amount of the late payment can be determined by subtracting the regular payment from the late payment amount. This gives a difference of $20.37. Divide this difference by the regular payment to find the percentage charged.

In Source #1, the real estate agent states that the buyers' bid has been accepted. However, there is no information regarding the original asking price of the house.

There is no fixed amount that would result in double payments on the principal. The reason is that the amount paid toward the principal changes from month to month.

2. The correct answer is **$29,000**. At the end of the first year of the loan, the mortgage balance is $147,991.05. During this year, the total principal paid on the loan was $2,008.95. So, at the start of 2016, the amount owing on the loan was $150,000. The purchase price for the house was $179,000, so the buyers made a down payment of $29,000.

3. The answer to the first blank is **E**. The city with the largest population (the farthest right on the graph) had about 2,100 births; the smallest city (the farthest left) had about 100 births. So the largest city had about 21 times as many births as the smallest, or about 2,100 percent.

The answer to the second blank is **C**. Generally, the number of births is greater for cities with larger populations, so the relationship between those variables is positive.

4. The correct answers are shown below.

True   False

● ○   No financial divisions ranked among the top five in sales revenue.

○ ●   No country had more than two divisions of the same type.

● ○   The division with the most employees also had the highest sales revenue.

○ ●   The real estate division with the most employees was in France.

The top five divisions in sales revenue were all insurance, real estate, and entertainment divisions.

The U.S. had two different insurance divisions.

Division FTMR had the most employees and the highest sales revenue.

The real estate division in Hong Kong had more employees than the one in France.

5. The correct answers are **Statement #1** for the cause, and **Statement #2** for the effect.

CAUSE	EFFECT	STATEMENTS
●	○	1. Customers do not fully understand all of the product's possible uses.
○	○	2. Separate lines of advertisement have been developed for each U.S. sector.
○	●	3. Product sales were down in the warmer regions.
○	○	4. The Northwest sector has had the best sales reports.
○	○	5. Sales locations are more numerous in dense areas of population.
○	○	6. Competitors are succeeding in sectors where this company is not performing well.

The analyst determined that people in the warmer regions were not purchasing the product because they did not understand that its insulating properties could have a cooling effect. They believed the product was strictly for protection against the cold. As a result, they were not buying as much of the product as the company had hoped.

6. The answer to the first blank is **C**. Life expectancy for females born in 1995 is about 0.1 percent greater than for females born in 1990; life expectancy for males born in 1995 is about 1 percent greater than for males born in 1990, so the increase is about ten times as great.

The answer to the second blank is **C**. The average female born in 1975 can expect to outlive the average male born the same year by 7.8 years; the average female born in 2010 can expect to outlive the average male born the same year by 5.6 years, or about 72 percent of 7.8 years.

7. The correct answers are shown below.

Would help explain	Would not help explain	
○	●	Albany has more dance studios than Binghamton.
○	●	New York City has recently experienced a surge of interest in swing dancing.
●	○	In Rochester, jazz and modern dance are only taught at ballet studios, but not all ballet studios teach them.

The total number of dance studios in a city doesn't affect what percentage of them offer which styles.

It's not apparent what effect the popularity of swing dancing in New York City would have on the relative popularities of other styles.

If all studios in Rochester that teach jazz and modern teach ballet, but not all the studios that teach ballet teach jazz and modern, that explains why fewer studios in Rochester teach jazz and modern than teach ballet.

8. The correct answers are shown below.

Yes	No	
○	●	The price per pound of the chocolates after tax and delivery is $8.17.
●	○	Sugar-free chocolates cost about 80% more, on average, than regular varieties of chocolate.
○	●	The Candy Fun Company charges $0.75 per pound for delivery services.

The cost per pound is $10.97 after tax and delivery. This is calculated by dividing the total cost of the shipment, in this case $65.80, by the number of pounds of candy delivered: $65.80 ÷ 6 = $10.97.

Sugar-free chocolates cost $5.85 a pound, while regular chocolates cost an average of about $3.25 per pound. Sugar-free chocolates cost $2.60 more per pound than regular chocolates, on average. This is 80% more than the cost of regular chocolates.

The Candy Fun Company charged $10.00 to deliver Betsy Carver's order. The order consisted of 6 pounds of chocolate. That works out to $10.00 ÷ 6, or $1.67 per pound.

9. The correct answers are shown below.

Yes	No	
○	●	More letters than packages were mailed in Philadelphia.
○	●	There was an upward trend over the course of the year in the number of undeliverable packages.
○	●	In September, more undeliverable packages than letters went through this post office.

The table doesn't provide any information about how many total letters or packages were sent through this post office, let alone in the entire city.

No trend is visible over the course of the year.

A greater percentage of the city's undeliverable packages went through this post office than did undeliverable letters, but not necessarily a greater *number* of undeliverable packages compared to letters.

10. The correct answers are working in an office as most difficult to manage, and sleeping as least difficult to manage.

MOST DIFFICULT	LEAST DIFFICULT	SCENARIOS
●	○	Working in an office
○	○	Riding alone in a car
○	○	Having lunch at home with a spouse
○	○	Watching television with a friend
○	●	Sleeping

We know from the information given in the journal article that those with diaemotiopluralism have a problem with overstimulation from social interactions. Working in an office is the scenario in which there is likely to be the most social interaction to stimulate an individual. When sleeping, stimulation from outside sources would most likely not be an issue.

11. The answer to the first blank is **C**. As the percentage of the group who felt the subject was dressed professionally increased, so did the percentage of the group who believed the subject would be hired; the relationship between those percentages is positive.

The answer to the second blank is **B**. About 20 percent of group A felt the candidate was dressed professionally, and about 40 of group B did, which is twice as much.

12. The correct answers are at most **50** suppliers that sell either tomatoes or packaging products to Libby, and at most **20** suppliers that could possibly sell both tomatoes and packaging products to Libby.

EITHER TOMATOES OR PACKAGING PRODUCTS	BOTH TOMATOES AND PACKAGING PRODUCTS	NUMBER OF SUPPLIERS
○	○	10
○	●	20
○	○	30
○	○	40
●	○	50
○	○	60

Libby has 25 tomato suppliers and 30 packaging suppliers. The total number of tomato and packaging suppliers combined is 25 + 30, or 55. The largest number listed in the table is 60, which is too large, so there are at most 50 suppliers providing either tomatoes or packaging products.

If all of the tomato suppliers were also packaging suppliers, there would be 25 suppliers providing both items. This is the largest number of suppliers who could provide both tomatoes and packaging products. The number 25 is not listed in the table, however, and 30 is too large. So, of the numbers listed in the table, the largest number of suppliers who could be providing Libby with both tomatoes and packaging products is 20.

The GMAT Quantitative Section

CHAPTER 6

GMAT Problem-Solving Questions

About Problem-Solving Questions

The GMAT problem-solving questions are multiple-choice questions. Each question provides five answer choice options. Most of the questions present a problem situation that requires a single response. Some of the question stems will have Roman numeral options. The five answer options will include various combinations of the Roman numeral options. In either case, you must select the one best answer choice from the five answer choice options.

Strategies for Problem-Solving Questions

Start by reading the question stem. Determine what the question is asking. Skim through the answer choices. Decide on an optimum approach for answering the question. Here are some strategic ways to attack problem-solving questions.

Write and Solve an Equation

For many questions, writing and solving an equation is a straightforward method for determining the answer. Let the variable represent the unknown in the question. When you have more than one unknown in a problem question, you might be able to express one in terms of the other. For instance, if a first unknown is described in terms of a second unknown, it is usually easier to let the variable equal the second unknown. For such problems, you also can choose to assign a variable name to each unknown. Just remember that you will need as many equations as you have variables in order to determine specific values for the variables. Here is an example.

A rectangular swimming pool is twice as long as it is wide. If the perimeter of the pool is 180 feet, what is the length, in feet, of the pool?

- (A) 30
- (B) 60
- (C) 70
- (D) 80
- (E) 90

The perimeter, P, of a rectangle is $P = 2l + 2w = 2(l + w)$, where l is the rectangle's length and w is its width. (See Chapter 10 Geometry Review for formulas of geometric figures).

Method 1: Use one variable.

The length of the pool is described in terms of its width. Let w = the width, in feet, of the pool. Then $2w$ = the length, in feet, of the pool. Write an equation that represents the facts given in the question.

180 feet = $2(2w + w)$ or, equivalently, $2(2w + w) = 180$ feet

Solve the equation, omitting the units for convenience.

$$2(2w + w) = 180$$
$$2(3w) = 180$$
$$6w = 180$$
$$w = \frac{180}{6}$$
$$w = 30$$
$$2w = 60$$

The length of the pool is 60 feet. The correct response is B.

Tip: Make sure you answer the question asked. In this question, after you obtain w, you must calculate $2w$ to answer the question.

Method 2: Use two variables.

Let w = the width, in feet, of the pool and l = the length, in feet, of the pool. Write two equations that represent the facts given in the question.

- (1) $l = 2w$
- (2) $2(l + w) = 180$ feet

Simultaneously solve the two equations, omitting the units for convenience.

Using the substitution method, substitute $l = 2w$ from equation (1) into equation (2) to obtain

$$2(2w + w) = 180$$

Complete the solution as shown in Method 1.

Check the Answer Choices

When you are provided numerical answer choices, you might determine the correct choice by checking the answer choices. Here is an example.

> Henry must pay a 7% penalty tax on the portion of the total value of an item that exceeds $100. If Henry paid a penalty tax of $8.75, what was the total value of the item?
>
> (A) $185
> (B) $225
> (C) $240
> (D) $275
> (E) $300

Before you start checking the answer choices, write an equation to make sure you understand the question. Let x = the total value in dollars of the item. Then x − $100 is the portion of the item that is subject to the 7% penalty tax. Using the information in the question, set up an equation that represents the facts of the question.

$$7\%(x - \$100) = \$8.75$$
$$0.07(x - \$100) = \$8.75$$

Now check the answer choices in the equation. The answers are listed in ascending order, so start with choice C. If choice C is incorrect, you might be able to use logical reasoning to eliminate other answer choices as well. This will enable you to determine the correct answer sooner and save time. Check C:

$$0.07(x - \$100) = \$8.75$$
$$0.07(\$240 - \$100) \overset{?}{=} \$8.75$$
$$0.07(\$140) \overset{?}{=} \$8.75$$
$$\$9.80 > \$8.75$$

Choice C is too high, so eliminate choices D and E as too high as well. Check B:

$$0.07(x - \$100) = \$8.75$$
$$0.07(\$225 - \$100) \overset{?}{=} \$8.75$$
$$0.07(\$125) \overset{?}{=} \$8.75$$
$$\$8.75 \overset{\surd}{=} \$8.75$$

Choice B is the correct response.

Plug in 100 for an Unknown Base in Percentage Questions

When you have questions involving percentages in which the base is not given, you can usually plug in 100 for the base to make the problem easier to work out. Here is an example.

Marvin invested in a stock whose value had increased 5% by the end of 2012, decreased 2% by the end of 2013, and increased 10% by the end of 2014. What is the percent increase in the value of the stock from the end of 2012 to the end of 2014?

- (A) 7.80%
- (B) 8.19%
- (C) 12.50%
- (D) 13.00%
- (E) 17.00%

The percent increase in the stock is

$$\frac{\left|(\text{value of the stock at end of }2014) - (\text{value of the stock at end of }2012)\right|}{(\text{value of the stock at end of }2012)} \times 100\%$$

For convenience let $100 be the initial value of the stock. Then the value of the stock at the end of 2012 was 105%($100) = $105. By the end of 2013, the value of the stock was 98%($105) = $102.90. By the end of 2014, the value of the stock was 110%($102.90) = $113.19. The percent increase is

$$\frac{\left|(113.19) - (105.00)\right|}{(105.00)} \times 100\% = \frac{8.19}{105} \times 100\% = 0.078 \times 100\% = 7.8\%$$

The percent increase in the stock is 7.8%. Choice A is the correct response.

Evaluate Expressions Using Suitable Values for Variables

When the question stem and the answer choices both contain one or more variables, you might try evaluating the expressions given in the question stem and answer choices for suitable values of the variables. Make sure the values you select satisfy all the conditions presented in the question. Suitable values are small numbers such as 2, 3, and 4. Avoid using 0 or 1, because these numbers have special properties that might lead you to believe an incorrect answer choice is correct. Look for an answer choice that evaluates to the same value as the expression in the question stem. *Tip:* You must evaluate *all* the answer choices to make sure two choices (or possibly more) do not evaluate to the same value as the expression in the question stem. If this occurs, start over and choose different values for the variables. Here is an example.

Which expression is equivalent to $\dfrac{x}{x-y} - \dfrac{y}{x+y}$?

(A) $\dfrac{x-y}{x^2-y^2}$

(B) $\dfrac{x+y}{x^2-y^2}$

(C) $\dfrac{x^2-y^2}{x^2+y^2}$

(D) $\dfrac{x^2+y^2}{x^2-y^2}$

(E) $\dfrac{x^2+2xy+y^2}{x^2-y^2}$

Let $x=3$ and $y=2$. $\dfrac{x}{x-y} - \dfrac{y}{x+y} = \dfrac{3}{3-2} - \dfrac{2}{3+2} = \dfrac{3}{1} - \dfrac{2}{5} = \dfrac{15}{5} - \dfrac{2}{5} = \dfrac{13}{5}$

Check A: $\dfrac{x-y}{x^2-y^2} = \dfrac{3-2}{9-4} = \dfrac{1}{5} \neq \dfrac{13}{5}$

Check B: $\dfrac{x+y}{x^2-y^2} = \dfrac{3+2}{9-4} = \dfrac{5}{5} \neq \dfrac{13}{5}$

Check C: $\dfrac{x^2-y^2}{x^2+y^2} = \dfrac{9-4}{9+4} = \dfrac{5}{13} \neq \dfrac{13}{5}$

Check D: $\dfrac{x^2+y^2}{x^2-y^2} = \dfrac{9+4}{9-4} = \dfrac{13}{5} \checkmark$

Check E: $\dfrac{x^2+2xy+y^2}{x^2-y^2} = \dfrac{9+12+4}{9-4} = \dfrac{25}{5} \neq \dfrac{13}{5}$

Choice D is the correct response.

Do the Math

In many cases, the most efficient way to answer a problem-solving question is simply to do the math. Here is an example.

$$4x^2 - 8x - 5 = 0$$

What is the sum of the roots of the preceding quadratic equation?

(A) −8
(B) −2
(C) 2
(D) 4
(E) 8

Solve the quadratic equation by factoring.

$$4x^2 - 8x - 5 = 0$$
$$(2x - 5)(2x + 1) = 0$$
$$2x - 5 = 0 \text{ or } 2x + 1 = 0$$
$$x = \frac{5}{2} \text{ or } x = -\frac{1}{2}$$

Compute the sum $\frac{5}{2} - \frac{1}{2} = \frac{4}{2} = 2$.

Choice C is the correct response.

This question is an example of a way a test maker can compose a question to thwart the strategy of checking the answer choices.

Other Helpful Advice

- *Use logical reasoning to eliminate answer choices.* You can eliminate some answer choices from the outset based on logical reasoning. For instance, if you figure out the answer must be even, you can eliminate all odd answer choices.
- *Make rough sketches for geometry questions.* For geometry problems, sketches help you organize the question information. However, make quick rough sketches. Do not spend unnecessary time making them.
- *Know your math.* No matter which strategy you use in a problem-solving question, you will need to know and understand math. Most of the math concepts on the GMAT are ones you likely have encountered in the past. However, you might have forgotten some if not most of them. Study the math review in this book to refresh your knowledge and skills.

Directions for the Problem-Solving Questions

Select the *best* of the given answer choices.

Note: Unless otherwise stated, you can assume all of the following.

- All numbers used are real numbers.
- All figures lie in a plane.
- Lines shown as straight are straight lines, and straight lines might sometimes appear jagged.
- Figures are drawn accurately, but are NOT necessarily drawn to scale.
- All angle measures are greater than zero.
- The relative positions of points, angles, and regions are in the order shown.

Problem-Solving Questions Drill 1

1. A grocery store's electricity cost in January is $1,420. After installing a new energy-efficient heating and cooling system, the manager estimates that the electricity cost will decrease by 2.5% per month over the next six months. Based on this estimate, which expression represents the grocery store's electricity cost in March of the same year?

    (A) ($1,420)(0.975) + ($1,420)(0.950)
    (B) $1,420 − ($1,420)(0.025)(0.025)
    (C) $1,420 − ($1,420)(0.025)(0.025)(0.025)
    (D) ($1,420)(0.975)(0.975)
    (E) ($1,420)(0.975)(0.950)

2. Of the 4,800 residents of an apartment complex, $\frac{1}{4}$ are college students. Suppose the number of college students is reduced by $\frac{1}{3}$. If no other changes occur, what portion of the total remaining residents are college students?

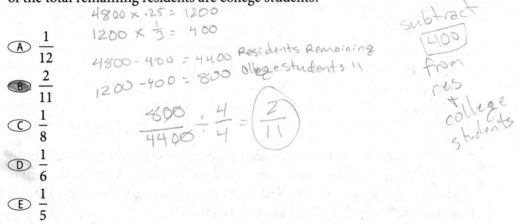

    (A) $\frac{1}{12}$
    (B) $\frac{2}{11}$
    (C) $\frac{1}{8}$
    (D) $\frac{1}{6}$
    (E) $\frac{1}{5}$

3. Fifty percent of a couple's retirement account is invested in stocks, 25% in a mutual fund, and 20% in Treasury bonds. The remaining $20,000 is in certificates of deposit. In the couple's retirement account, what is the total amount invested?

    (A) $200,000
    (B) $300,000
    (C) $400,000
    (D) $1,000,000
    (E) $4,000,000

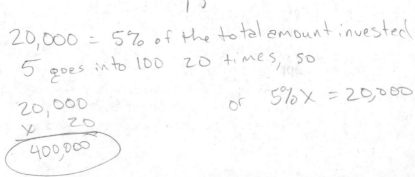

4. Which of the following expressions has $-\frac{2}{3}$ as a numerical value?

   ✓ I. $-2\frac{1}{2} \div 3\frac{3}{4}$ $-\frac{3}{2} \div \frac{15}{4} = \frac{\cancel{3}}{\cancel{2}} \times \frac{\cancel{4}^2}{\cancel{15}_3} = -\frac{2}{3}$

   ✓ II. $\left(-\frac{1}{2}\right)\left(1\frac{1}{3}\right)$ $-\frac{1}{\cancel{2}} \times \frac{\cancel{4}^2}{3} = -\frac{2}{3}$

   III. $-\frac{2}{7} + \frac{20}{21}$ has positive value so it can't be this one

   Ⓐ I only
   Ⓑ II only
   Ⓒ I and II only
   Ⓓ II and III only
   Ⓔ I, II, and III

5. The original price of a video game console was $400. The console was reduced by 25% for a sale. After the sale, the price increased to $375. What is the percent increase over the sale price?

   Ⓐ 0.2% $400 - 25\% = 300$, then ↑ 375
   Ⓑ 0.25% $4 = 25\%$
   Ⓒ 20% $\frac{75}{300}$
   Ⓓ 25%   dollar
   Ⓔ 30%   difference

   $\frac{\text{new sale price} - \text{old sale price}}{\text{sale price}}$

   $\frac{375 - 300}{300} = \frac{75}{300} = \frac{1}{4} = 25\%$

6. Tovia is a delivery person for a specialty frozen food company. Besides her base weekly pay of $350, she makes a 6% commission on all items that she sells to customers. Last week Tovia's weekly pay plus commissions totaled $920. What amount is the total of Tovia's sales for last week?

   items = 920

   Ⓐ $604.20 $\begin{array}{r}920\\-350\\\hline 570\end{array}$ base pay plus 6% of items = 920
   Ⓑ $1,105.80
   Ⓒ $9,000.00 $350 + .06x = 920$ asks for total amount of sales
   Ⓓ $9,500.00 $\frac{.06x}{.06} = \frac{570}{.06}$
   Ⓔ $15,333.33

   $x = 9,500$

   or check answer choices

7. If the sum of three consecutive integers is doubled, the result is 71 more than $\frac{5}{2}$ times the third integer. What is the value of the third integer?

   After you solve for x, make sure you know what the question is asking!

   Ⓐ 19
   Ⓑ 20
   Ⓒ 21
   Ⓓ 22
   Ⓔ 23

   $2(n + (n+1) + (n+2)) = 71 + \frac{5}{2}(n+2)$ go ahead & divide it out if you can

   $2(3n+3) = 71 + \frac{5}{2}n + 5$

   $\begin{array}{r}6n + 6 = 76 + 2.5n\\-2.5n - 6 \quad -6 -2.5n\end{array}$

   $\frac{3.5n}{3.5} = \frac{70}{3.5}$

   $n = 20$ HEY! LOOK AT THE QUESTION! What is the value of the third integer?

   $n + 2 = ?$

   $20 + 2 = \boxed{22}$

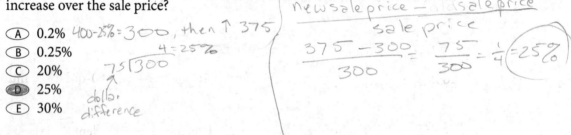

Do charts like this

8. Lucy is twice as old as Bret. In five years, the sum of their ages will be 52. How old will Lucy be 10 years from now?

when	Bret	Lucy	Sum
now	2x	2x	?
5 years	x+5	2x+5	52
10 years	x+10	(2x+10)	?

(A) 14
(B) 24
(C) 28
(D) 38
(E) 43

SOLVE FOR 2x+10

$x+5+2x+5=52$
$\frac{3x}{3}=\frac{42}{3}$
$x=14$
so
$2(14)+10=38$

9. If $x=\left(1+\left(2+3^{-1}\right)^{-1}\right)^{-1}$, then $10x=$

-1 exponent, make reciprocal of that #
$2\frac{1}{3}$ is same as $2+\frac{1}{3}$
mixed #s are sum of whole # + fraction

(A) $\dfrac{100}{3}$

(B) $\dfrac{100}{7}$

(C) $\dfrac{60}{7}$

(D) 7

(E) 3

$\left(1+\left(2+\frac{1}{3}\right)^{-1}\right)^{-1}$
$\left(1+\left(\frac{7}{3}\right)^{-1}\right)^{-1}$
$\left(1+\frac{3}{7}\right)^{-1}$
$\left(\frac{10}{7}\right)^{-1}$
$x=\frac{7}{10}$ THEN what does $10x=$?

$10\left(\frac{7}{10}\right)$
$\frac{10}{1}\cdot\frac{7}{10}=\frac{70}{10}=7$

10. To include a penalty for guessing, the scoring formula for a 60-question, multiple-choice test is $s=r-\dfrac{1}{4}w$, where s is the score on the test, r is the number of correct responses, and w is the number of incorrect responses. A student answers all 60 questions. Which of the following scores could be the student's score?

I. −15
II. 10
III. 32

(A) I only
(B) I and II only
(C) I and III only
(D) II and III only
(E) I, II, and III

$w=60-r$
wrong answers
60 Questions − right answers
so
$s=r-.25(60-r)$
$r-15+.25r$
$s=1.25r-15$

r has to be a whole #

so if student got 0 right, then
$s=1.25(0)-15$
$s=-15$

plug in answers

$10=1.25r-15$
$+15 \quad +15$
$\frac{25}{1.25}=\frac{1.25r}{1.25}$
$20=r$

$32=1.25r-15$
$+15$
$\frac{47}{1.25}=\frac{1.25r}{1.25}$
$37.6=r$

11. In triangle *ABC*, sides $\overline{AB}$ and $\overline{AC}$ are congruent. The measure of angle *C* is 36°. What is the measure of angle *A*?

    Ⓐ 28°
    Ⓑ 36°
    Ⓒ 72°
    Ⓓ 104°
    Ⓔ 108°

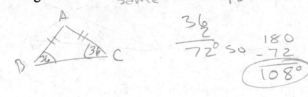

12. In the preceding figure, lines *m* and *n* are parallel and cut by the transversal *t*. What is the measure of angle *θ*?

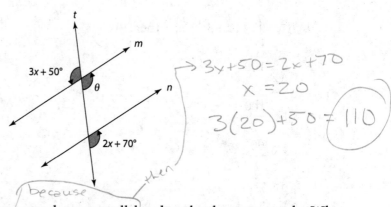

    Ⓐ 20°
    Ⓑ 40°
    Ⓒ 60°
    Ⓓ 110°
    Ⓔ 120°

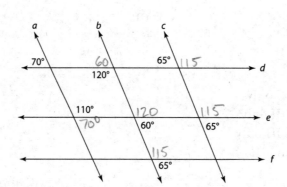

13. Based on the preceding figure, which statement is true?

    Ⓐ *a* ∥ *b*
    Ⓑ *a* ∥ *c*
    Ⓒ *b* ∥ *c*
    Ⓓ *d* ∥ *e*
    Ⓔ *d* ∥ *f*

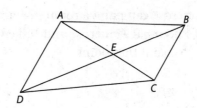

14. How many triangles are in the preceding figure?

  (A) 4
  (B) 7
  (C) 8
  (D) 9
  (E) 10

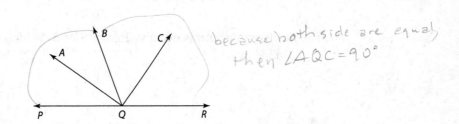

because both side are equal, then ∠AQC = 90°

15. In the preceding figure, ∠AQP ≅ ∠AQB and ∠BQC ≅ ∠CQR. What is the measure of ∠AQC?

  (A) 100°
  (B) 90°
  (C) 80°
  (D) 75°
  (E) 70°

16. A van leaves City A at 9 a.m., moving at an average speed of 50 miles per hour. Without making any stops, the van arrives at City B at 2 p.m. At approximately what time would the van have arrived if the driver had maintained an average speed of 65 miles per hour?

  (A) 12:24 p.m.
  (B) 12:51 p.m.
  (C) 1:24 p.m.
  (D) 1:51 p.m.
  (E) 2:24 p.m.

9am 50mph × 5hours = 250 miles 2pm
3.84 hours
65)250
9am + 3h 50min
d = rt
t = d/r

17. A candy store owner mixes candy that normally sells for $2.50 per pound and candy that normally sells for $3.75 per pound to make a 90-pound mixture to sell at $3.00 per pound. To make sure that $3.00 per pound is a fair price, how many pounds of the $2.50 candy should the owner use?

  (A) 54
  (B) 50
  (C) 42
  (D) 36
  (E) 30

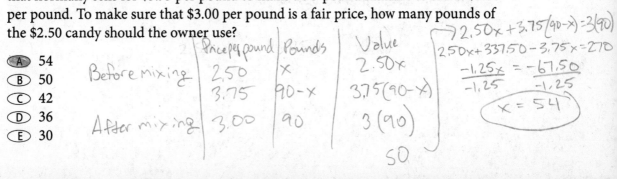

2.50x + 3.75(90-x) = 3(90)
250x + 337.50 - 3.75x = 270
−1.25x = −67.50
−1.25   −1.25
x = 54

	Price per pound	Pounds	Value
Before mixing	2.50	x	2.50x
	3.75	90-x	3.75(90-x)
After mixing	3.00	90	3(90)

18. Working alone, Annerose can paint a room in 6 hours. Mike working alone can do the same job in 4 hours. If Annerose and Mike work together, how many hours should it take them to paint the room?

    (A) 5

    (B) $3\frac{1}{2}$

    (C) 3

    (D) $2\frac{2}{5}$

    (E) $1\frac{4}{5}$

    $$\frac{6(4)}{6+4} = \frac{24}{10} = 2.4 \left(= 2\frac{2}{5}\right)$$

19. The positive integer n is not divisible by 2 or 3. Which could be the remainder when n is divided by 6?

    I.   1
    II. 3
    III. 5

    (A) I only
    (B) I and II only
    (C) I and III only
    (D) II and III only
    (E) I, II, and III

20. A teacher buys pencils and pens for her classroom. The pencils come 12 in a pack, and the pens come 8 in a pack. The teacher buys the same number of pens as she does pencils, with none left over. What is the least number of each she could buy?

    (A) 8
    (B) 12
    (C) 24
    (D) 48
    (E) 96

In the solutions for each group of drills, two different strategies might be illustrated for the same question. The two strategies will be designated Method 1 and Method 2. Please be aware that the numbering of the methods does not indicate that one method is preferred over the other. Use your own judgment to decide which method might work best for you.

Answers

1. **D** In February, the electricity cost is $\$1,420-0.025(\$1,420)=(\$1,420)(1-0.025)=$ $(\$1,420)(0.975)$. In March, the electricity cost is $(\$1,420)(0.975)(1-0.025)=$ $(\$1,420)(0.975)(0.975)$.

2. **B** Calculate the initial number of college students: $\frac{1}{4}\times4,800=1,200$. Calculate $\frac{1}{3}$ of this number: $\frac{1}{3}\times1,200=400$. Calculate the number of college students remaining: $1,200-400=800$. Calculate the number of total residents remaining: $4,800-400=4,400$. Calculate the portion of the total remaining who are college students: $\frac{800}{4,400}=\frac{2}{11}$.

3. **C** Let $x=$ The total amount in dollars invested. The percent invested in stocks, the mutual fund, and bonds is $50\%+25\%+20\%=95\%$. Thus, the percent invested in certificates of deposit is $100\%-95\%=5\%$. Write the following percent equation to represent the facts given in the question.

$$5\%x = \$20,000$$

Solve for x, the total amount invested.
   Method 1: Solve the equation using a conventional procedure, omitting the units for convenience.

$$5\%x = 20,000$$
$$0.05x = 20,000$$
$$x = \frac{20,000}{0.05}$$
$$x = 400,000$$

The total amount invested is $\$400,000$.
   Method 2: Solve the equation using logical reasoning and mental math. Given 5% of x is $\$20,000$. Then $\frac{1}{20}$ of x is $\$20,000$. So x is $\$20,000$ times 20, which is $\$400,000$. Or given 5% of x is $\$20,000$. Then 10% of x is $\$40,000$. So x is $\$40,000$ times 10, which is $\$400,000$.

Knowing the fractional equivalent of common percents such as $5\%=\frac{1}{20}$ and $10\%=\frac{1}{10}$ is helpful.

4. **C** Eliminate Roman III because, without doing any calculations, you know the sum is positive because $\dfrac{2}{7} < \dfrac{20}{21}$. Eliminate choices D and E because each contains Roman III. Now check Roman I and II.

Check Roman I: $-2\dfrac{1}{2} \div 3\dfrac{3}{4} = -\dfrac{5}{2} \div \dfrac{15}{4} = -\dfrac{\cancel{5}^{1}}{\cancel{2}_{1}} \times \dfrac{\cancel{4}^{2}}{\cancel{15}_{3}} = -\dfrac{2}{3}$ √

Check Roman II: $\left(-\dfrac{1}{2}\right)\left(1\dfrac{1}{3}\right) = \left(-\dfrac{1}{\cancel{2}_{1}}\right)\left(\dfrac{\cancel{4}^{2}}{3}\right) = -\dfrac{2}{3}$ √

Thus, choice C is correct.

5. **D** The sale price is $400 minus (25% of $400) =

$$\$400 - \left(\dfrac{1}{4} \times \$400\right) = \$400 - \$100 = \$300.$$

The percent increase is $\dfrac{\text{new price} - \text{sale price}}{\text{sale price}} = \dfrac{\$375 - \$300}{\$300} = \dfrac{\$75}{\$300} = \dfrac{1}{4} = 25\%.$

6. **D** Let $x =$ the amount in dollars of Tovia's total sales last week. Write an equation that represents the facts given in the question.

$$\$350 + 6\%x = \$920$$

Method 1: Solve for x using a conventional procedure, omitting the units for convenience.

$$350 + 6\%x = 920$$
$$350 + 0.06x = 920$$
$$350 + 0.06x - 350 = 920 - 350$$
$$0.06x = 570$$
$$x = \dfrac{570}{0.06}$$
$$x = 9,500$$

The amount of Tovia's total sales last week is $9,500.

Method 2: Check the answer choices. Check C:

$$\$350 + 6\%x = \$920$$
$$\$350 + 6\%(\$9,000) \overset{?}{=} \$920$$
$$\$350 + 0.06(\$9,000) \overset{?}{=} \$920$$
$$\$350 + \$540 \overset{?}{=} \$920$$
$$\$890 < \$920$$

Eliminate choice C as too low. Eliminate choices A and B as too low as well. Check D:

$$\$350 + 6\%x = \$920$$

$$\$350 + 6\%(\$9,500) \overset{?}{=} \$920$$

$$\$350 + 0.06(\$9,500) \overset{?}{=} \$920$$

$$\$350 + \$570 \overset{?}{=} \$920$$

$$\$920 \overset{\checkmark}{=} \$920$$

Choice D is the correct response.

7. **D** Let x, $x + 1$, and $x + 2$ represent the three consecutive integers. From the information in the question, set up an equation and solve for $x + 2$.

$$2\left[x + (x+1) + (x+2)\right] = 71 + \frac{5}{2}(x+2)$$

$$2(x + x + 1 + x + 2) = 71 + \frac{5}{2}(x+2)$$

$$2(3x + 3) = 71 + \frac{5}{2}x + 5$$

$$6x + 6 = 76 + 2.5x$$

$$6x + 6 - 2.5x = 76 + 2.5x - 2.5x$$

$$3.5x + 6 = 76$$

$$3.5x + 6 - 6 = 76 - 6$$

$$3.5x = 70$$

$$\frac{3.5x}{3.5} = \frac{70}{3.5}$$

$$x = 20$$

Thus, the third integer is $x + 2 = 22$.

Make sure you answer the question asked. In this question, after you obtain x, you must calculate $x + 2$ to answer the question.

---

8. **D** Let x = Bret's age now, in years. Then $2x$ = Lucy's age now, in years. Make a chart to organize the information in the question.

WHEN?	BRET'S AGE (IN YEARS)	LUCY'S AGE (IN YEARS)	SUM
Now	x	$2x$	Not given
5 years from now	$x + 5$ years	$2x + 5$ years	52 years
10 years from now	$x + 10$ years	$2x + 10$ years	Not given

Write an equation that represents the facts given.

$$(x + 5 \text{ years}) + (2x + 5 \text{ years}) = 52 \text{ years}$$

Solve the equation, omitting the units for convenience.

$$(x+5)+(2x+5)=52$$
$$x+5+2x+5=52$$
$$3x+10=52$$
$$3x+10-10=52-10$$
$$3x=42$$
$$x=\frac{42}{3}$$
$$x=14,\text{ Bret's age now}$$

$2x=28$, Lucy's age now

$28+10=38$, Lucy's age 10 years from now

Make sure you answer the question that is asked. In this question, after you obtain Bret's age now, you must calculate Lucy's age 10 years from now.

---

9. **D** Substitute the given value of x, and use your knowledge of exponents to solve for $10x$.

$$10x=10\left(1+\left(2+3^{-1}\right)^{-1}\right)^{-1}$$

$$=10\left(1+\left(2+\frac{1}{3}\right)^{-1}\right)^{-1}=10\left(1+\left(\frac{7}{3}\right)^{-1}\right)^{-1}=10\left(1+\frac{3}{7}\right)^{-1}=10\left(\frac{10}{7}\right)^{-1}=10\left(\frac{7}{10}\right)=7$$

10. **B** The number of wrong answers, w, is $60-r$ (the number of right answers). Therefore, $s=r-\frac{1}{4}w=r-0.25(60-r)=r-15+0.25r=1.25r-15$. You know that r is a whole number such that $0\le r\le 60$. When $r=0$, the least score is $s=1.25r-15=1.25(0)-15=-15$, Roman I. Eliminate choice D because it does not include Roman I. Solving $s=1.25r-15$ for r yields $r=\frac{s+15}{1.25}$. Now use $r=\frac{s+15}{1.25}$ to check the other Roman numeral options to see whether r computes to be a whole number between 0 and 60.

Check Roman II: $r=\frac{10+15}{1.25}=20\surd$; eliminate choices A and C because neither includes Roman II.

Check Roman III: $r=\frac{32+15}{1.25}=37.6$, not a whole number.

Eliminate choice E because it includes Roman III. Choice B is the correct response.

11. **E** Make a sketch, filling in the question information.

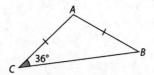

Angles C and B are base angles of an isosceles triangle, so their measures are equal, that is, $m\angle B = m\angle C = 36°$. The sum of the angles of a triangle is $180°$. Thus, $\angle A = 180° - 2(36°) = 180° - 72° = 108°$. *Note:* $m\angle X$ denotes the measure of angle X.

12. **D** θ and $3x + 50°$ are congruent because they are vertical angles; θ and $2x + 70°$ are congruent because they are corresponding angles of parallel lines. Thus, $\theta = 3x + 50° = 2x + 70°$, so $x = 20°$. Thus, $\theta = 3 \cdot 20° + 50° = 110°$.

13. **D** Check the answer choices. Check A: a ‖ b is false, because the corresponding angles [$70°$ and $(180° - 120°) = 60°$] are not congruent. Check B: a ‖ c is false, because the corresponding angles ($70°$ and $65°$) are not congruent. Check C: b ‖ c is false, because the corresponding angles ($60°$ and $65°$) are not congruent. Check D: d ‖ e is true, because the corresponding angles [$70°$ and $(180° - 110°) = 70°$] are congruent. Because choice D is correct, move on to the next question.

14. **C** List the triangles, proceeding systematically. You have triangles *ABC*, *ABD*, *ABE*, *ACD*, *ADE*, *BCD*, *BCE*, and *CDE*, for a total of 8 triangles.

15. **B** From the figure, you can see that $\angle AQC = \angle AQB + \angle BQC$ and that $m\angle AQP + m\angle AQB + m\angle BQC + m\angle CQR = 180°$. Given $\angle AQP \cong \angle AQB$ and $\angle BQC \cong \angle CQR$, then $2(m\angle AQB) + 2(m\angle BQC) = 180°$. Dividing both sides of the equation by 2, $m\angle AQB + m\angle BQC = 90° = m\angle AQC$.

16. **B** The distance formula is $d = rt$, where d is the distance traveled at a uniform rate of speed r for a length of time t. The van traveled 5 hours at 50 miles per hour (mph), so the distance, d, from City A to City B is $d = rt = (50 \text{ mph})(5 \text{ hr}) = 250$ miles. At 65 mph, the time would be

$$t = \frac{d}{r} = \frac{250 \text{ miles}}{65 \text{ mph}} \approx 3.846 \text{ hr} \approx 3 \text{ hr } 51 \text{ min}$$

The approximate time of arrival would be 9 a.m. plus 3 hours 51 minutes, which is 12:51 p.m.

17. **A** Let x = the number of pounds of the candy priced at $2.50 per pound needed. Then $90 - x$ = the number of pounds of the candy priced at $3.75 per pound needed. Make a chart to organize the information in the question.

WHEN	PRICE PER POUND	NUMBER OF POUNDS	VALUE
Before mixing	$2.50	x	2.50x$
	$3.75	$90 - x$	$3.75(90 - x)$
After mixing	$3.00	90	$3.00(90)$

The value of the candy before it is mixed should equal the value after it is mixed. Using the information in the chart, set up an equation that represents the facts given in the question (omitting "pounds" and "per pound" because these units cancel each other).

$$\$2.50x + \$3.75(90 - x) = \$3.00(90)$$

Solve for x.

Method 1: Solve the equation using a conventional procedure, omitting the units for convenience.

$$2.50x + 3.75(90 - x) = 3.00(90)$$
$$2.50x + 337.50 - 3.75x = 270.00$$
$$-1.25x + 337.50 - 337.50 = 270.00 - 337.50$$
$$-1.25x = -67.50$$
$$x = \frac{-67.50}{-1.25}$$
$$x = 54$$

The owner should use 54 pounds of the $2.50 candy.

Method 2: Solve the equation using logical reasoning and mental math. If the owner used half of each type of candy, then the price should be the average of $2.50 and $3.75, which is about $3.13. So, you know that to bring the price down to $3.00 per pound will require more than 45 pounds (half) of the lower-priced candy. Therefore, eliminate choices C, D, and E right away. Now check choice B in the equation:

$$\$2.50x + \$3.75(90 - x) = \$3.00(90)$$
$$\$2.50(50) + \$3.75(90 - 50) \overset{?}{=} \$270$$
$$\$125 + \$3.75(40) \overset{?}{=} \$270$$
$$\$125 + \$150 \overset{?}{=} \$270$$
$$\$275 > \$270$$

Choice B doesn't satisfy the equation. By elimination, choice A is the correct response.

18. **D** In a "work" problem, it is usually necessary to determine the rate at which someone or something does a task or job. The rate equals the amount of work done divided by the total time worked. Let t = the time (in hours) it will take Annerose and Mike, working together, to paint the room.

Method 1: When you have *only two* workers, a handy shortcut method for finding the time it will take the two of them to do a job, working together, is to divide the *product* of their times working alone by the *sum* of their times working alone. Using the shortcut method and omitting the units for convenience, the time it should take Annerose and Mike, working together, to paint the room is:

$$\frac{(\text{Annerose's time working alone})(\text{Mike's time working alone})}{(\text{Annerose's time working alone}) + (\text{Mike's time working alone})}$$
$$= \frac{(6)(4)}{6 + 4} = \frac{24}{10} = \frac{12}{5} = 2\frac{2}{5}$$

It should take Annerose and Mike, working together, $2\frac{2}{5}$ hours to paint the room.

Method 2: Make a chart to organize the information in the question.

WORKER	RATE	TIME (IN HOURS)	AMOUNT OF WORK (IN ROOMS)
Annerose	$\dfrac{1\text{ room}}{6\text{ hr}}=\dfrac{1}{6}$ room/hr	t	$\dfrac{1}{6}t$
Mike	$\dfrac{1\text{ room}}{4\text{ hr}}=\dfrac{1}{4}$ room/hr	t	$\dfrac{1}{4}t$
N/A	N/A	Total:	1

Using the information in the chart, set up an equation that represents the facts given in the question. Solve for t.

$$\frac{1}{6}t+\frac{1}{4}t=1$$

$$\frac{2}{12}t+\frac{3}{12}t=1$$

$$\frac{5}{12}t=1$$

$$\frac{\cancel{12}}{\cancel{5}}\cdot\frac{\cancel{5}}{\cancel{12}}t=\frac{12}{5}\cdot1$$

$$t=\frac{12}{5}=2\frac{2}{5}$$

It should take Annerose and Mike, working together, $2\frac{2}{5}$ hours to paint the room.

You should eliminate choice A at the outset because the time for Annerose and Mike working together should be less than either of their times working alone. Also, notice that the faster worker is the one who takes less time when working alone than does the other worker, and so completes more of the job when they work together.

---

19. **C** When you divide a positive number by 6, the remainder is 0, 1, 2, 3, 4, or 5. Thus, any nonnegative integer has the form $6k$, $6k+1$, $6k+2$, $6k+3$, $6k+4$, or $6k+5$ ($k=0$, 1, 2, …). Because n is not divisible by 2 or 3, n must have the form $6k+1$ or $6k+5$. Thus, the remainder when n is divided by 6 is either 1 (Roman I) or 5 (Roman III). Choice C is the correct response.

20. **C** Solve this problem by finding the least common multiple (LCM) of 12 and 8.

    Method 1: Start listing multiples of 12 until you reach one that is also a multiple of 8.
    Multiples of 12: 12, 24. Stop because $24=3\times8$, a multiple of 8. So, the LCM of 12 and 8 is 24. The teacher bought 24 pencils (2 packs of 12 in a pack) and 24 pens (3 packs of 8 in a pack).

    Method 2: The LCM of two numbers is their product divided by their greatest common factor (GCF). The GCF of 12 and 8 is 4. The LCM of 12 and 8 is:

$$\frac{(12)(8)}{4}=\frac{(\overset{3}{\cancel{12}})(8)}{\underset{1}{\cancel{4}}}=24.$$ The teacher bought 24 pencils (2 packs of 12 in a pack) and 24 pens (3 packs of 8 in a pack).

Problem-Solving Questions Drill 2

1. The ratio of zinc to copper in a certain alloy is 2 to 5. If 120 grams of copper are used, how many grams of zinc are needed to make this alloy?

   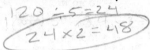

   - (A) 24
   - **(B) 48**
   - (C) 60
   - (D) 200
   - (E) 300

**DISTRIBUTION OF STUDENTS AT COMMUNITY COLLEGE X
BY AGE AND GENDER**

AGE (IN YEARS)	MALE	FEMALE
Under 20	475	425
20	700	750
21	500	540
Over 21	250	360

2. The preceding table shows the distribution of students attending Community College X by age and gender. Suppose a student is randomly selected. To the nearest hundredth, what is the probability that the student is male or 21 years or older?

   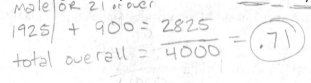

   - (A) 0.41
   - (B) 0.48
   - (C) 0.57
   - **(D) 0.71**
   - (E) 0.89

3. In a cooking contest, five judges score each contestant. To calculate a contestant's final score, the judges discard the highest number and lowest number, and then they take the arithmetic average of the remaining numbers. The five judges score a contestant as 6.3, 7.1, 6.4, 6.5, and 6.2. What is the contestant's final score?

   - (A) 6.7
   - (B) 6.6
   - (C) 6.5
   - **(D) 6.4**
   - (E) 6.3

4. The value of an investment triples every 10 years. By what factor does the value increase over a 30-year period?

   - (A) 3
   - (B) 6
   - (C) 9
   - **(D) 27**
   - (E) 30

(handwritten: Figure out pattern + go from there)

5. What is the units digit of 3^{102}?

(handwritten work: $3^0=1$ $3^1=3$ $3^2=9$ $3^3=27$ $3^4=81$ $3^5=243$)
$3^{4.25}=34.25_9$ $3^{4.25}=34.25_9$
$3^{102}=3^{100}\,3^2=3^2$

   (A) 1
   (B) 3
   (C) 6
   (D) 7
   (E) 9 *(circled)*

6. Quinn wants a trendy but expensive toy. It goes on sale at a local toy store for 15% less than the original price. Before Quinn can buy the toy, however, the toy store raises the price by 20%. If the 15%-off sale price was $119, the final price is what percent of the original price?

   (A) 95%
   (B) 98%
   (C) 102% *(circled)*
   (D) 105%
   (E) 120%

(handwritten work:
final price / orig price (sale)
$1x - .15x = 119$
$.85x = 119$
$\frac{.85x}{.85} = \frac{119}{.85}$
$x = 140$ sale price
$119 + (.2)119 =$
$119 + 23.8 = 142.80$
$\frac{142.80}{140} = 102\%$ (circled))*

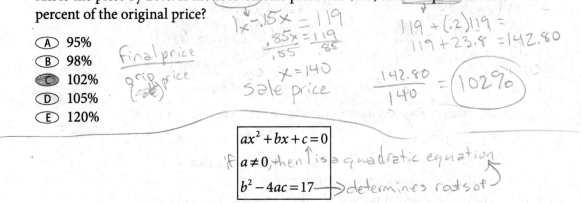

(boxed handwritten:
$ax^2 + bx + c = 0$
If $a \neq 0$, then ↑ is a quadratic equation
$b^2 - 4ac = 17$ → determines roots of)

7. From the preceding information given, which statement is true about the equation $ax^2 + bx + c = 0$?

(handwritten:
if $b^2 - 4ac < 0$, no real roots
if " $= 0$, then one real, rational root
if " > 0 then two real roots
rational if $b^2 - 4ac$ is perfect square
irrational if not)

   (A) It has no real roots.
   (B) It has exactly one real, rational root.
   (C) It has exactly one real, irrational root.
   (D) It has exactly two real, rational roots.
   (E) It has exactly two real, irrational roots. *(circled)*

8. The operation $\otimes$ is defined on the set of real numbers by $a \otimes b = 2a + ab$, where a and b are real numbers and the operations on the right side of the equal sign denote the standard operations for the real number system. What is $(3 \otimes 2) \otimes 5$?

   (A) 30
   (B) 60
   (C) 74
   (D) 84 *(circled)*
   (E) 96

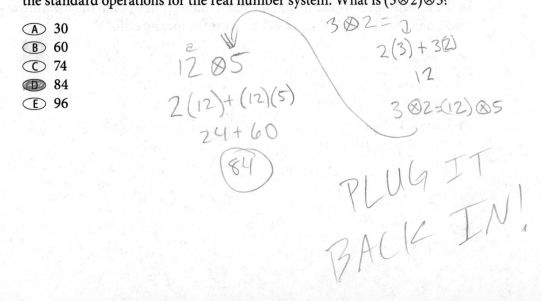

(handwritten work:
$3 \otimes 2 = 2$
$2(3) + 3(2)$
12
$3 \otimes 2 = (12) \otimes 5$
$12 \otimes 5$
$2(12) + (12)(5)$
$24 + 60$
84 (circled)
PLUG IT BACK IN!)

[handwritten: Plug in values or divide everything by y]

[handwritten: 2]

9. If $\dfrac{x}{y} = 20$ and $\dfrac{y}{z} = 10$, with $y \cdot z \neq 0$, what is the value of $\dfrac{x}{y+z}$?

[handwritten: x=400 y=20 z=2]

   (A) $\dfrac{11}{200}$

   (B) $\dfrac{11}{20}$

   (C) $\dfrac{20}{11}$

   (D) $\dfrac{200}{11}$

   (E) $\dfrac{100}{3}$

[handwritten work: $\dfrac{400}{20+2} = \dfrac{400}{22} \div 2 = \dfrac{200}{11}$]

[handwritten work: $\dfrac{\frac{x}{y}}{\frac{y}{y}+\frac{z}{y}} = \dfrac{20}{1+\frac{1}{10}} \cdot 10 = \dfrac{200}{10+1} = \dfrac{200}{11}$]

$$3(x+1)(x-1) + \dfrac{x(4x-6)}{2}$$

10. Which expression is equivalent to the preceding expression?

   (A) $5x^2 + 3x - 6$

   (B) $3x^2 + 3x - 6$

   (C) $-x^2 + 3x + 3$

   (D) $5x^2 - 3x + 3$

   (E) $5x^2 - 3x - 3$

[handwritten work: $(3x+3)(x-1)$]
[handwritten work: $3x^2 - 3x + 3x - 3$]
[handwritten work: $3x^2 - 3 + \dfrac{4x^2 - 6x}{2}$]
[handwritten work: $3x^2 - 3 + 2x^2 - 3x$]
[handwritten work: $5x^2 - 3x - 3$]

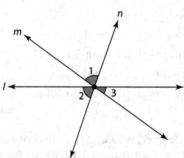

11. In the preceding figure the lines l, m, and n intersect in a point, the measure of $\angle 1$ is 65°, and the measure of $\angle 2$ is 85°. What is the measure of $\angle 3$?

   (A) 20°

   (B) 25°

   (C) 30°

   (D) 35°

   (E) 40°

[handwritten work: 65 + 85 = 150 - 180 = 30]

12. Angles a and b are complementary angles, and angles c and d are complementary angles. If angles a and d are congruent, which statement must be true?

    (A) Angles b and c are congruent.
    (B) Angles b and d are congruent.
    (C) Angles a and d are complementary.
    (D) Angles b and c are complementary.
    (E) Angles a and c are congruent.

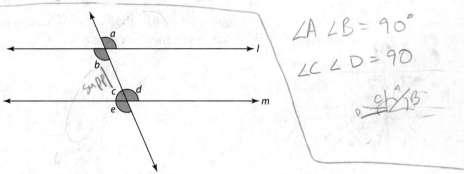

Handwritten notes: congruent = same angles; complementary = when 2 angles add to 90°; $\angle A \angle B = 90°$; $\angle C \angle D = 90$

13. In the preceding figure, angles b and c are supplementary. Which statement must be true?

    (A) $\angle a \cong \angle c$
    (B) $\angle a \cong \angle d$
    (C) $\angle b \cong \angle c$
    (D) $\angle c \cong \angle d$
    (E) $\angle c \cong \angle e$

Handwritten note: equals 180°

14. Points R, P, and S lie above line segment $\overline{MN}$ in the relative order given. Line segment $\overline{PQ}$ is perpendicular to line segment $\overline{MN}$ at the point Q. Hence, Point R lies to the left of $\overline{PQ}$ and point S lies to its right. The segment $\overline{PQ}$ bisects $\angle RPS$ and $\overline{RP} \cong \overline{PS}$. The measure of $\angle PQS = 35°$. What is the measure of $\angle RQM$?

    (A) 35°
    (B) 45°
    (C) 55°
    (D) 65°
    (E) 75°

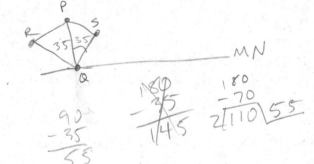

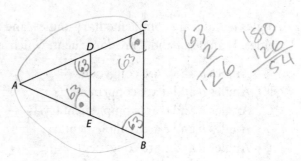

15. In the preceding figure, $\overline{AC} \cong \overline{AB}$, $\angle ABC \cong \angle ADE$, and $\angle ACB \cong \angle AED$. The measure of $\angle ADE$ is 63°. What is the measure of $\angle A$?

   (A) 27°

   (B) 37°

   (C) 44°

   (D) 54°

   (E) 63°

16. A truck leaves a location traveling due east at a constant speed of 50 miles per hour. One hour later a car leaves the same location traveling in the same direction at a constant speed of 70 miles. If both vehicles continue in the same direction at their same respective speeds, how many hours will it take the car to catch up to the truck?

   (A) 1

   (B) 1.5

   (C) 2

   (D) 2.5

   (E) 3

17. Rhys has $7.50 in dimes and quarters. The total number of coins is 48. How many more dimes than quarters does Rhys have?

   (A) 8

   (B) 12

   (C) 18

   (D) 22

   (E) 30

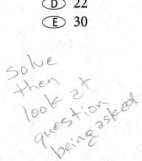

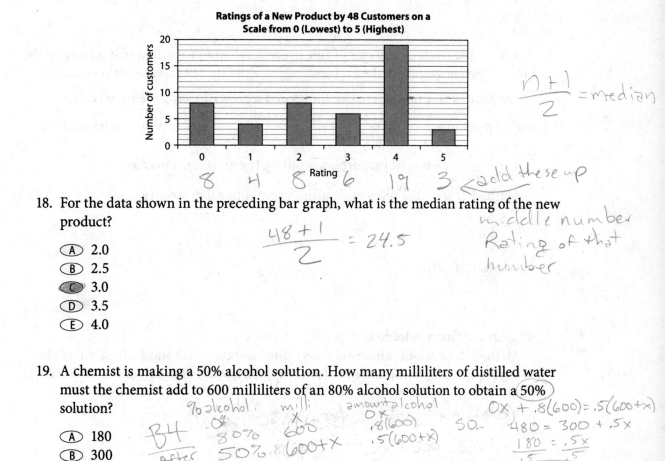

Ratings of a New Product by 48 Customers on a Scale from 0 (Lowest) to 5 (Highest)

[handwritten: $\frac{n+1}{2}$ = median]

[handwritten under graph: 8   4   8   6   19   3 ← add these up]

18. For the data shown in the preceding bar graph, what is the median rating of the new product?

[handwritten: $\frac{48+1}{2} = 24.5$]

[handwritten: middle number / Rating of that number]

  (A) 2.0
  (B) 2.5
  (C) 3.0
  (D) 3.5
  (E) 4.0

19. A chemist is making a 50% alcohol solution. How many milliliters of distilled water must the chemist add to 600 milliliters of an 80% alcohol solution to obtain a 50% solution?

[handwritten:
% alcohol   milli   amount alcohol
B4   0%   x   0x
80%   600   .8(600)
After   50%   600+x   .5(600+x)

0x + .8(600) = .5(600+x)
480 = 300 + .5x
180 = .5x
.5   .5
x = 360]

  (A) 180
  (B) 300
  (C) 360
  (D) 480
  (E) 600

20. An investor receives interest on two simple interest investments, one at 3%, annually, and the other at 2%, annually. The two investments together earn $900 annually. The amount invested at 3% is $20,000. How much money is invested at 2%?

  (A) $10,000
  (B) $12,000
  (C) $15,000
  (D) $20,000
  (E) $35,000

[handwritten:
600   20,000   3% ann } $900
300   15,000   2% ann]

Answers

1. **B** Let x = the number of grams of zinc needed. Set up a proportion that represents the facts of the question. Use the first sentence to write the left ratio of the proportion: $\frac{2}{5}$ (the ratio of zinc to copper). Use the second sentence to write the right ratio of the proportion: $\frac{\text{number of grams of zinc needed}}{120 \text{ grams of copper}} = \frac{x}{120 \text{ grams}}$. Write the proportion: $\frac{2}{5} = \frac{x}{120 \text{ grams}}$. Solve the proportion, omitting the units for convenience.

    Method 1: Solve the proportion using a conventional procedure.

    $$\frac{2}{5} = \frac{x}{120}$$
    $$x = \frac{(2)(120)}{5}$$
    $$x = 48$$

    48 grams of zinc are needed.

    Method 2: Check the answer choices. Eliminate choices D and E. The ratio of zinc to copper is 2 to 5, so the amount of zinc must be less than the amount of copper in the alloy.

    Check C:

    $$\frac{2}{5} = \frac{x}{120}$$
    $$\frac{2}{5} \overset{?}{=} \frac{(60)}{120}$$
    $$\frac{2}{5} < \frac{1}{2}$$

    Choice C gave a result that is too large.

    Check B:

    $$\frac{2}{5} = \frac{x}{120}$$
    $$\frac{2}{5} \overset{?}{=} \frac{(48)}{120}$$
    $$\frac{2}{5} \overset{\checkmark}{=} \frac{2}{5}$$

    Choice B is the correct response.

2. **D** Complete the chart by computing the totals in each category.

DISTRIBUTION OF STUDENTS AT COMMUNITY COLLEGE X BY AGE AND GENDER

AGE (IN YEARS)	MALE	FEMALE	TOTAL
Under 20	475	425	900
20	700	750	1450
21	500	540	1040
Over 21	250	360	610
Total	1,925	2,075	4,000

According to the chart, the total number of students is 4,000. There are 1,925 male students and 540 + 360 = 900 female students who are 21 years or older. Thus, of the 4,000 students, there are 1,925 + 900 = 2,825 students who are male or 21 years or older. *Tip*: Don't double count the 500 + 250 = 750 male students who are 21 years or older. These students are already counted as part of the 1,925 male students. Therefore, the probability that a randomly selected student is male or 21 years or older is

$$\frac{\text{number of favorable outcomes}}{\text{number of possible outcomes}} = \frac{2,825}{4,000} \approx 0.71.$$

The symbol "$\approx$" is read "is approximately equal to."

3. **D** Discarding the highest number (7.1) and the lowest number (6.2) leaves 6.3, 6.4, and 6.5. The arithmetic average of these three numbers, by inspection, is 6.4.

4. **D** For convenience, suppose the investment is $100. In 10 years, its value will be $300. In 20 years, its value will be $900. Finally, in 30 years, the value of the investment will be $2,700. Because $2,700 is 27 times $100, the investment increased by a factor of 27. *Tip*: Picking a convenient amount for the investment is a useful strategy in problems like this one.

5. **E** Looking for a pattern is the best strategy for this problem. Calculate powers of 3:

$$3^0 = 1, 3^1 = 3, 3^2 = 9, 3^3 = 27, 3^4 = 81, \text{ and } 3^5 = 243.$$

Because the units digit of 3^5 is 3, the next power, 3^6, will have units digit 9 (because $3 \times 3 = 9$), and 3^7 will have units digit 7 (because $9 \times 3 = 27$). Thus, the units digit for powers of 3 has the pattern 1, 3, 9, 7, 1, 3, 9, 7, and so on. Therefore, 3^{4n} has units digit 1. Hence,

$$3^{102} = 3^{100}3^2 = 3^{4\cdot25}3^2 = 3^{4\cdot25}\cdot9 \text{ has units digit 9.}$$

6. **C** After the toy store raises the sale price by 20%, the final price is $119 + 20\%($119$) = $119 + 0.20($119$) = $119 + $23.80 = 142.80. Let $x =$ original price of the toy in dollars. Set up an equation that represents the facts in the question.

$$x - 15\%x = \$119$$
$$100\%x - 15\%x = \$119$$
$$85\%x = \$119$$

Solve for x, omitting the units for convenience.

$$85\%x = 119$$

$$0.85x = 119$$

$$x = \frac{119}{0.85}$$

$$x = 140$$

The original price of the toy was \$140. Hence,

$$\frac{\text{Final price}}{\text{Original price}} = \frac{\$142.80}{\$140.00} = 1.02 = 102\%$$

Before you compute the percent, you know that it is greater than 100% because \$142.80 is greater than \$140. So eliminate choices A and B because these percents are less than 100%.

---

7. **E** When $a \neq 0$, $ax^2 + bx + c = 0$ is a quadratic equation. The quantity $b^2 - 4ac$ is its discriminant. The discriminant determines the nature of the roots of the equation. If $b^2 - 4ac < 0$, there are no real roots; if $b^2 - 4ac = 0$, there is exactly one real, rational root; and if $b^2 - 4ac > 0$ (as in this question), there are exactly two real roots. Both of these roots are rational if $b^2 - 4ac$ is a perfect square; otherwise, both are irrational. Because 17 is not a perfect square, the equation has exactly two real, irrational roots.

8. **D** $(3 \otimes 2) = 2 \cdot 3 + 3 \cdot 2 = 12$, so $(3 \otimes 2) \otimes 5 = 12 \otimes 5 = 2 \cdot 12 + 12 \cdot 5 = 24 + 60 = 84$.

9. **D** **Method 1:** To solve, divide every term of $\dfrac{x}{y+z}$ by y. Then substitute terms for which you know the value and simplify.

$$\frac{x}{y+z} = \frac{\dfrac{x}{y}}{\dfrac{y}{y} + \dfrac{z}{y}} = \frac{20}{1 + \dfrac{1}{10}} = \frac{10(20)}{10\left(1 + \dfrac{1}{10}\right)} = \frac{200}{10+1} = \frac{200}{11}$$

Method 2: Plug in suitable values for x, y, and z. Let $x = 400$, $y = 20$, and $z = 2$. *Tip:* Be sure to pick values for the variables that satisfy all conditions given in the question.

Check: $\dfrac{x}{y} = \dfrac{400}{20} = 20\,\checkmark\,;\, \dfrac{y}{z} = \dfrac{20}{2} = 10\,\checkmark\,;\, y \cdot z = 20 \cdot 2 = 40 \neq 0\,\checkmark$. Then substitute the values and simplify.

$$\frac{x}{y+z} = \frac{400}{20+2} = \frac{400}{22} = \frac{200}{11}$$

10. **E** **Method 1:** Simplify the given expression by performing the indicated operations.

$$3(x+1)(x-1) + \frac{x(4x-6)}{2}$$

$$= 3\left(x^2 - 1\right) + \frac{4x^2 - 6x}{2}$$

$$3\left(x^2-1\right)+\frac{4x^2}{2}-\frac{6x}{2}$$
$$= 3x^2-3+2x^2-3x = 5x^2-3x-3$$

Method 2: Evaluate the expression for a suitable value of x. Then check the answer choices using the same value for x. Let $x=2$.

$$3(x+1)(x-1)+\frac{x(4x-6)}{2} = 3(2+1)(2-1)+\frac{2(4\cdot2-6)}{2}$$
$$= 3(3)(1)+\frac{\cancel{2}(8-6)}{\cancel{2}}$$
$$= 9+2$$
$$= 11$$

Eliminate A and B because these expressions would evaluate to be even numbers when $x=2$. Therefore, neither will evaluate to be 11.

Check C: $-x^2+3x+3=-(2)^2+3(2)+3=-4+6+3=5\neq11$

Check D: $5x^2-3x+3=5(2)^2-3(2)+3=5(4)-6+3=20-3=17\neq11$

Check E: $5x^2-3x-3=5(2)^2-3(2)-3=5(4)-6-3=20-9=11\checkmark$

Choice E is the correct response.

11. **C** $\angle3$ is congruent to the vertical angle between $\angle1$ and $\angle2$. Therefore, $m\angle1+m\angle3+m\angle2=180°$. Substitute the measures and solve for $m\angle3$.

$$65°+m\angle3+85°=180°$$
$$m\angle3+150°=180°$$
$$m\angle3=30°$$

12. **A** $m\angle A+m\angle B=90°$, and $m\angle C+m\angle D=90°$, so $m\angle A+m\angle B=m\angle C+m\angle D$. If $\angle A\cong\angle D$, then their measures are equal, so $m\angle B=m\angle C$. Thus, $\angle B\cong\angle C$. None of the statements in the other answer choices must be true.

13. **B** Given angles b and c are supplementary, then lines l and m are parallel. Thus, $\angle a\cong\angle d$ because they are corresponding angles of parallel lines. None of the statements in the other answer choices must be true.

14. **C** Make a sketch, filling in the information given in the question.

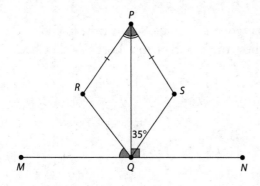

$\overline{RP} \cong \overline{PS}$, $\angle RPQ \cong \angle SPQ$, and $\overline{PQ} \cong \overline{PQ}$; Therefore, $\triangle PQR \cong \triangle PQS$ because two sides and the included angle of $\triangle PQR$ are congruent to the corresponding parts of $\triangle PQS$. Thus, $m\angle PQR = m\angle PQS = 35°$ (corresponding parts of congruent triangles are congruent). Given that $\overline{PQ}$ is perpendicular to $\overline{MN}$, $m\angle RQM = 90° - 35° = 55°$.

15. **D** Triangle ABC is isosceles, so $m\angle ABC = m\angle ACB$ (the base angles of an isosceles triangle are congruent). Given that $\angle ABC \cong ADE$ and $m\angle ADE = 63°$, you know that $m\angle ABC = m\angle ACB = 63°$. Thus, $m\angle A = 180° - 2(63°) = 54°$.

16. **D** The distance formula is $d = rt$, where d is the distance traveled at a uniform rate of speed r for a length of time t. Let t = the time in hours the car will travel before it catches up to the truck. Then $t + 1$ hour = the time in hours that the truck travels before the car catches up to it. Make a chart to organize the information in the question.

VEHICLE	RATE (IN MPH)	TIME (IN HOURS)	DISTANCE (IN MILES)
car	70	t	$70t$
truck	50	$t+1$	$50(t+1)$

Using the chart, write an equation to represent the facts given in the question. When the car catches up to the truck, both vehicles have traveled the same distance. Thus, $70t = 50(t+1)$.
Method 1: Solve for t using a conventional procedure.

$$70t = 50(t+1)$$
$$70t = 50t + 50$$
$$70t - 50t = 50t + 50 - 50t$$
$$20t = 50$$
$$t = \frac{50}{20}$$
$$t = 2.5$$

The car will catch up to the truck in 2.5 hours.
Method 2: Check the answer choices. Check C:

$$70t = 50(t+1)$$
$$70(2) \overset{?}{=} 50(2+1)$$
$$140 \overset{?}{=} 50(3)$$
$$140 < 150$$

The car has gone 140 miles, but the truck has gone 150 miles. So the time in choice C is too short. Eliminate choices A and B because these times will be too short as well. Check D:

$$70t = 50(t+1)$$
$$70(2.5) \overset{?}{=} 50(2.5+1)$$
$$175 \overset{?}{=} 50(3.5)$$
$$175 \overset{\checkmark}{=} 175$$

Choice D is the correct response.

17. **B** Let d = the number of dimes. Let q = the number of quarters. Make a chart to organize the question information.

DENOMINATION	DIMES	QUARTERS	TOTAL
Face value per coin	$0.10	$0.25	N/A
Number of coins	d	q	48
Value of coins	$0.10d	$0.25q	$7.50

Using the chart, write two equations that represent the facts of the question.

$$d + q = 48$$
$$\$0.10d + \$0.25q = \$7.50$$

When you have two variables, you must write two equations in order to determine a solution.

Solve the system, omitting the units for convenience. Using the method of substitution, solve $d + q = 48$ for q in terms of d.

$$d + q = 48$$
$$d + q - d = 48 - d$$
$$q = 48 - d$$

Substitute $q = 48 - d$ into the equation $0.10d + 0.25q = 7.50$ and solve for d.

$$0.10d + 0.25q = 7.50$$
$$0.10d + 0.25(48 - d) = 7.50$$
$$0.10d + 12 - 0.25d = 7.50$$
$$-0.15d + 12 - 12 = 7.50 - 12$$
$$-0.15d = -4.50$$
$$d = \frac{-4.50}{-0.15}$$
$$d = 30$$

Substitute $d = 30$ into the equation $d + q = 48$ and solve for q.

$$d + q = 48$$
$$(30) + q = 48$$
$$30 + q - 30 = 48 - 30$$
$$q = 18$$

Rhys has 30 dimes and 18 quarters. He has $30 - 18 = 12$ more dimes than quarters.

18. **C** According to the bar graph shown, the new product received eight ratings of 0, four ratings of 1, eight ratings of 2, six ratings of 3, nineteen ratings of 4, and three ratings

of 5. In an ordered set of n data values, the location of the median is the $\frac{n+1}{2}$ position. For these data, $\frac{n+1}{2} = \frac{48+1}{2} = 24.5$, so the median is halfway between the 24th and 25th data values. From the information in the graph, you can determine that the 24th data value equals the 25th data value, which equals 3, so the median is 3.

19. **C** Let x = number of milliliters of distilled water to be added. Make a chart to organize the information in the question.

WHEN?	PERCENT ALCOHOL STRENGTH	NUMBER OF MILLILITERS	AMOUNT OF ALCOHOL
Before mixing	0% (distilled water)	x	0%x
	80%	600	80%(600)
After mixing	50%	$x + 600$	50%($x + 600$)

The amount of alcohol before mixing equals the amount of alcohol after mixing. Using the information in the chart, set up an equation that represents the facts of the question.

$$0\%x + 80\%(600) = 50\%(x + 600)$$

Method 1: Solve for x using a conventional procedure.

$$0\%x + 80\%(600) = 50\%(x + 600)$$
$$0.8(600) = 0.5(x + 600)$$
$$480 = 0.5x + 300$$
$$480 - 300 = 0.5x + 300 - 300$$
$$180 = 0.5x$$
$$\frac{180}{0.5} = \frac{0.5x}{0.5}$$
$$360 = x$$

The chemist must add 360 milliliters of distilled water.

Method 2: Check the answer choices. Eliminate choice E because adding 600 milliliters to a 600-milliliter 80% alcohol solution would dilute it to a 40% alcohol solution. Check C:

$$0\%x + 80\%(600) = 50\%(x + 600)$$
$$0\%(360) + 80\%(600) \overset{?}{=} 50\%(360 + 600)$$
$$0.8(600) \overset{?}{=} 0.5(960)$$
$$480 \overset{\surd}{=} 480$$

Choice C is the correct response.

20. **C** The simple-interest formula is $I = PRT$, where I is the simple interest earned, P is the amount of the investment, R is the annual interest rate, and T is the time of the investment (in years). Let x = the amount invested at 2% annually. Make a chart to organize the information in the question.

P	R	T (IN YEARS)	I
x	2%	1	2%x
$20,000	3%	1	3%($20,000)
N/A	N/A	Total:	$900

Using the information in the chart, set up an equation that represents the facts in the question.

$$2\%x + 3\%(\$20,000) = \$900$$

Method 1: Solve for x using a conventional procedure, omitting the units for convenience.

$$2\%x + 3\%(\$20,000) = \$900$$
$$0.02x + 0.03(\$20,000) = \$900$$
$$0.02x + \$600 = \$900$$
$$0.02x = \$300$$
$$\frac{0.02x}{0.02} = \frac{\$300}{0.02}$$
$$x = \$15,000$$

$15,000 is invested at 2%.

Method 2: Check the answer choices. Check C:

$$2\%x + 3\%(\$20,000) = \$900$$

$$2\%(\$15,000) + 3\%(\$20,000) \overset{?}{=} \$900$$

$$\$300 + \$600 \overset{?}{=} \$900$$

$$\$900 \overset{\surd}{=} \$900$$

Choice C is the correct response.

Problem-Solving Questions Drill 3

1. Three daughters and two sons inherit land from their parents. The older son inherits $\frac{1}{4}$ of the land, and the oldest daughter inherits $\frac{1}{3}$. The three remaining children equally share the remaining land. What fraction of the land does the younger son inherit?

   (A) $\frac{1}{12}$

   (B) $\frac{5}{36}$

   (C) $\frac{5}{21}$

   (D) $\frac{7}{36}$

   (E) $\frac{7}{21}$

   handwritten: $3\frac{1}{4}+4\frac{1}{3}=\frac{3}{12}+\frac{4}{12}=\frac{7}{12}$ so $1-\frac{7}{12}=\frac{5}{12}\div 3$

   handwritten: $\frac{5}{12}\times\frac{1}{3}=\frac{5}{36}$

2. A science book has scale drawings of insects. The scale shows that 1 centimeter in the drawing represents 2.5 centimeters of actual length. What is the length (in centimeters) of the scale drawing of a grasshopper if the grasshopper is actually 9.0 centimeters long?

   handwritten: Plug in answers

   (A) 3.6

   (B) 4.0

   (C) 4.5

   (D) 18.0

   (E) 22.5

   handwritten: 1 cm = 2.5 cm (actual)   ? cm = 9

   OR $\frac{x}{9}=\frac{1}{2.5}$ $\frac{x2.5}{2.5}=\frac{9}{2.5}$ $x = 3.6$

   $\begin{array}{r}2.5\\ \times 3.6\\ \hline 150\\ 75\\ \hline 9.00\end{array}$

3. A farmer wants to partition a rectangular 24 feet by 30 feet garden into smaller square plots. What is the length, in feet, of the sides of the largest square plots into which the farmer can partition the garden so that no land is left over?

   handwritten: has to be a factor of 24 + 30

   1,2,3,4,6,8,12,24

   1,2,3,5,6,10,15,30

   so, 6 is the answer

   (A) 2

   (B) 3

   (C) 6

   (D) 8

   (E) 12

4. A college student recently worked four weeks in a new summer job. In the fourth week, the student worked 20% more hours than in the third week. In the third week, the student worked 25% more hours than in the second week. In the second week, the student worked 40% more hours than in the first week. The student worked 42 hours in the fourth week on the job. How many hours did the student work in the first week on the job?

   handwritten: Plug in answers + work forward

   1. 2
   2. 40%
   3. 20%
   4. 42

   (A) 15

   (B) 20

   (C) 25

   (D) 30

   (E) 35

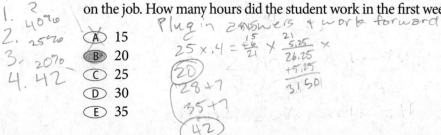

5. A fast-food restaurant gives a coupon for a free drink to customers who wait in line more than 15 minutes. The dot plot shows the number of minutes 20 customers waited in line one Monday morning at the restaurant.

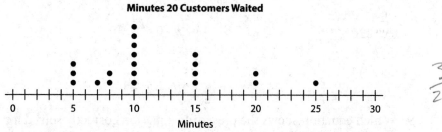

Minutes 20 Customers Waited

Minutes

What is the probability that a customer randomly selected from the 20 customers received a coupon for the free drink that Monday morning?

(A) $\dfrac{1}{20}$

(B) $\dfrac{1}{10}$

(C) $\dfrac{3}{20}$

(D) $\dfrac{1}{5}$

(E) $\dfrac{7}{20}$

6. Which number line illustrates the solution set of $-7 < 2x + 1 < 5$?

(A)
-5 -4 -3 -2 -1 0 1 2 3 4 5

(B)
-5 -4 -3 -2 -1 0 1 2 3 4 5

(C)
-5 -4 -3 -2 -1 0 1 2 3 4 5

(D)
-5 -4 -3 -2 -1 0 1 2 3 4 5

(E)
-5 -4 -3 -2 -1 0 1 2 3 4 5

7. If $f(x) = x^2 + x + 1$ and $g(x) = \sqrt{x}$, then what is the value of $\dfrac{f(1)}{g(4)}$?

(A) $\dfrac{3}{2}$

(B) $\dfrac{3}{16}$

(C) 3

(D) $\pm\dfrac{3}{2}$

(E) ± 3

$$(m+n)^2 - 2 + 2(m+n) + \frac{m+n}{3}$$

8. When $m + n = -6$, what is the value of the above expression?

   (A) −52

   (B) −28

   (C) 20

   (D) 28

   (E) 44

   $(-6)^2 - 2 + 2(-6) + \frac{-6}{3}$

   $36 - 2 - 12 - 2$

$$2t(t-2)=1$$

9. Which equation shows the preceding equation correctly solved for t?

   (A) $t = 1 \pm \sqrt{3}$

   (B) $t = 1 \pm \sqrt{6}$

   (C) $t = \dfrac{-2 \pm \sqrt{6}}{2}$

   (D) $t = \dfrac{2 \pm \sqrt{6}}{2}$

   (E) $t = \dfrac{1}{2}$ or 3

   solve it

   $2t^2 - 4t - 1 = 0$ Quadratic formula

   $\dfrac{-b \pm \sqrt{b^2 - 4ac}}{2a}$

   $\dfrac{4 \pm \sqrt{-4^2 - 4(2)(-1)}}{2(2)}$

   $\dfrac{4 \pm \sqrt{16 + 8}}{4}$

   $\dfrac{4 \pm \sqrt{24}}{4}$ $\sqrt{4 \cdot 6}$ $\dfrac{4 \pm 2\sqrt{6}}{4}$ $\dfrac{2 \pm \sqrt{6}}{2}$

10. For which of the following expressions is $x - y$ a factor?

    I. $y^3 - x^3$

    II. $\left(x^2 - y^2\right)^5$

    III. $x^3 - 3x^2y + 3xy^2 - y^3$

    (A) I and II only

    (B) I and III only

    (C) II only

    (D) II and III only

    (E) I, II, and III

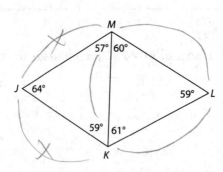

11. In the preceding figure with angle measures as shown, which segment is longest?

    (A) $\overline{JK}$

    (B) $\overline{KL}$

    (C) $\overline{LM}$

    (D) $\overline{JM}$

    (E) $\overline{KM}$

    largest angle = longer side   *largest angle = longer side*

12. Which of the following sets of numbers could NOT be the lengths of the sides of a triangle?

(handwritten: sum of any 2 sides must be greater than the third)

    I. 8, 14, 18

    II. 6, 16, 24

    III. 2, 3, 5

    (A) I only

    (B) I and II only

    (C) I and III only

    (D) II and III only

    (E) I, II, and III

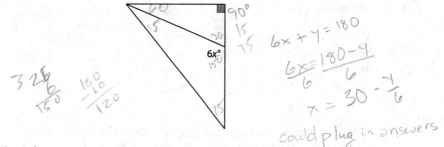

13. In the preceding figure, which of the following values could be a value of x?

    (A) 10

    (B) 15

    (C) 25

    (D) 30

    (E) 35

(handwritten work:
$6x + y = 180$
$\dfrac{6x}{6} = \dfrac{180 - y}{6}$
$x = 30 - \dfrac{y}{6}$
could plug in answers
$\dfrac{90}{6} < \dfrac{6x}{6} < \dfrac{180}{6}$
$15 < x < 30$
$x = 25$ *)*

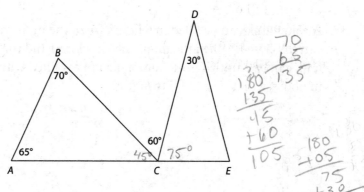

14. In the preceding figure with the measure of the angles as shown, what is the measure of $\angle E$?

    (A) 85°

    (B) 75°

    (C) 70°

    (D) 65°

    (E) 60°

(handwritten: lines = 180°   triangles = 180°)

15. If the perimeter of triangle *ABC* is 60 centimeters, what is the perimeter in centimeters of the triangle formed by connecting the midpoints of the sides of triangle *ABC*?

    (A) 10
    (B) 15
    (C) 20
    (D) 25
    (E) 30

16. The measures of the angles of a triangle are in the ratio 2:3:5. What is the measure of the smallest angle?

    (A) 9°
    (B) 18°
    (C) 36°
    (D) 54°
    (E) 90°

17. A 50-foot rope is cut into two pieces so that the longer piece is 50% longer than the shorter piece. What is the length, in feet, of the longer piece?

    (A) $16\frac{2}{3}$
    (B) 20
    (C) 25
    (D) 30
    (E) $33\frac{1}{3}$

18. A water tank can be filled in 6 hours when the input valve is open and the outlet valve is closed. When the input valve is closed and the outlet valve is open, the same tank can be emptied in 10 hours. If a tank is filled with both valves open, how long, in hours, will it take to fill the tank?

    (A) 4
    (B) 8
    (C) 12
    (D) 15
    (E) 16

19. The number of elements in the union of sets *A* and *B* is 160, and the number of elements in the intersection of sets *A* and *B* is 20. If the number of elements in set *A* is 50, what is the number of elements in set *B*?

    (A) 30
    (B) 60
    (C) 90
    (D) 110
    (E) 130

20. To estimate the number of turtles in a lake, a team of biologists captures and tags 20 turtles and then releases the turtles unharmed back into the lake. Two weeks later, the team returns to the lake and captures 30 turtles, 6 of which have tags indicating that they are recaptured turtles. Based on this capture-recapture method, what is the best estimate of the number of turtles in the lake?

- (A) 200
- (B) 100
- (C) 75
- (D) 50
- (E) 25

guessed

20T

30T 6 have tags

P = population

$$\frac{6}{30} = \frac{20}{P}$$

$$\frac{6P}{6} = \frac{30(20)}{6}$$

$$P = \frac{30(20)}{6}$$

$$P = 100$$

$$\frac{20}{?} = \frac{6}{30}$$

$$\frac{6P}{6} = 20(30) = \frac{600}{6}$$

$$\boxed{P = 100}$$

Answers

1. **B** The fraction of the land inherited by the older son and oldest daughter together is $\dfrac{1}{4}+\dfrac{1}{3}=\dfrac{3}{12}+\dfrac{4}{12}=\dfrac{7}{12}$. The fraction remaining is $1-\dfrac{7}{12}=\dfrac{5}{12}$. The fraction inherited by each of the three remaining children (including the younger son) is $\dfrac{5}{12}\div3=\dfrac{5}{12}\times\dfrac{1}{3}=\dfrac{5}{36}$.

2. **A** Let $x=$ the length (in centimeters) of the grasshopper scale drawing. Set up a proportion that represents the facts of the question. Use the first sentence to write the right-side ratio of the proportion: $\dfrac{1\text{ cm}}{2.5\text{ cm}}$. Use the second sentence to write the left-side ratio of the proportion: $\dfrac{x}{9\text{ cm}}$. Write the proportion: $\dfrac{x}{9\text{ cm}}=\dfrac{1\text{ cm}}{2.5\text{ cm}}$. Solve the proportion, omitting the units for convenience.

$$\frac{x}{9}=\frac{1}{2.5}$$
$$x=\frac{(9)(1)}{2.5}$$
$$x=3.6$$

The length of the scale drawing is 3.6 centimeters.

3. **C** The length of the sides of the square plots into which the farmer can partition the garden must be a factor of both 24 and 30. The largest such factor is the GCF of 24 and 30. Factors of 24 are 1, 2, 3, 4, ⟨6⟩, 8, 12, and 24; factors of 30 are 1, 2, 3, 5, ⟨6⟩, 10, 15, and 30; GCF is 6. So, 6 feet is the length of the sides of the largest square plots into which the farmer can partition the garden so that no land is left over.

4. **B** Working backward is the best strategy for this problem. In the fourth week, the student worked 20% more hours than in the third week, so write the following percent equation and solve for x, where x is the number of hours worked in the third week: $42=120\%x$. Thus, $\dfrac{42}{120\%}=x$. Change 120% to a fraction, and then divide:

$$x=42\div1\frac{1}{5}=\frac{42}{1}\div\frac{6}{5}=\frac{\overset{7}{\cancel{42}}}{1}\times\frac{5}{\cancel{6}_{1}}=35 \text{ hours worked in the third week}$$

In the third week, the student worked 25% more hours than in the second week, so write the following percent equation and solve for y, where y is the number of hours worked in the second week: $35=125\%y$. Thus, $\dfrac{35}{125\%}=y$. Change 125% to a fraction, and then divide:

$$x=35\div1\frac{1}{4}=\frac{35}{1}\div\frac{5}{4}=\frac{\overset{7}{\cancel{35}}}{1}\times\frac{4}{\cancel{5}_{1}}=28 \text{ hours worked in the second week}$$

In the second week, the student worked 40% more hours than in the first week, so write the following percent equation and solve for z, where z is the number of hours worked in the first week: $28=140\%z$. Thus, $\dfrac{28}{140\%}=z$. Change 140% to a fraction, and then divide:

$$x = 28 \div 1\frac{2}{5} = \frac{28}{1} \div \frac{7}{5} = \frac{\overset{4}{\cancel{28}}}{1} \times \frac{5}{\underset{1}{\cancel{7}}} = 20 \text{ hours worked in the first week}$$

Notice that changing percents to fractions in this problem simplified the calculations. You will find it helpful to memorize the fractional equivalents of common percentages, such as 20%, 25%, and 40%.

---

5. **C** The dot plot shows 1 customer waited 25 minutes and 2 customers waited 20 minutes for a total of 3 of the 20 customers who waited more than 15 minutes. The probability that a randomly selected customer received a coupon for the free drink is $\frac{\text{number of favorable outcomes}}{\text{number of possible outcomes}} = \frac{3}{20}$.

6. **C** Solve the double inequality.

$$-7 < 2x + 1 < 5$$
$$-7 - 1 < 2x + 1 - 1 < 5 - 1$$
$$-8 < 2x < 4$$
$$-4 < x < 2, \text{ which corresponds to choice C.}$$

Because the inequalities in the problem are strictly "less than," the interval will not include endpoints. Therefore, you can eliminate B and D right off, as these intervals include endpoints.

---

7. **A** Substitute and evaluate.

$$\frac{f(1)}{g(4)} = \frac{1^2 + 1 + 1}{\sqrt{4}} = \frac{3}{2}$$

8. **C** Substitute the value of $m + n$ into the given expression and evaluate.

$$(m+n)^2 - 2 + 2(m+n) + \frac{m+n}{3} = (-6)^2 - 2 + 2(-6) + \frac{-6}{3}$$
$$= 36 - 2 - 12 - 2$$
$$= 20$$

9. **D** Multiply factors and collect terms so you can use the quadratic formula.

$$2t(t-2) = 1$$
$$2t^2 - 4t - 1 = 0$$
$$a = 2, \ b = -4, \text{ and } c = -1$$
$$t = \frac{-b \pm \sqrt{b^2 - 4ac}}{2a}$$
$$= \frac{-(-4) \pm \sqrt{(-4)^2 - 4(2)(-1)}}{2(2)} = \frac{4 \pm \sqrt{16+8}}{4} = \frac{4 \pm \sqrt{24}}{4} = \frac{4 \pm \sqrt{4 \cdot 6}}{4} = \frac{4 \pm 2\sqrt{6}}{4} = \frac{2 \pm \sqrt{6}}{2}$$

10. **E** Check each of the given expressions. Check Roman I:

$$y^3 - x^3 = -\left(x^3 - y^3\right) = -(x-y)\left(x^2 + xy + y^2\right).$$

So $x - y$ is a factor. Eliminate choices C and D because these choices do not include Roman I. Check Roman II:

$$\left(x^2 - y^2\right)^5 = \left((x+y)(x-y)\right)^5.$$

So $x - y$ is a factor. Eliminate choice B because it does not include Roman II. Check Roman III:

$$x^3 - 3x^2 y + 3xy^2 - y^3 = (x-y)^3.$$

So $x - y$ is a factor. Choice E is the correct response.

11. **C** In triangle JKM, $\overline{KM}$ is opposite the largest angle, so it is longer than $\overline{JM}$ and $\overline{JK}$. In triangle KLM, $\overline{LM}$ is opposite the largest angle, so it is longer than $\overline{KM}$ and $\overline{KL}$, making it the longest segment in the figure.

12. **D** In a triangle, the sum of the lengths of any two sides must be greater than the length of the third side (triangle inequality). Only the lengths given in Roman I satisfy this criterion. The lengths given in Roman II and III could *not* be the lengths of the sides of a triangle. Choice D is the correct response.

13. **C** $6x° < 180°$ because it is an interior angle of a triangle and $6x° > 90°$ because the measure of an exterior angle of a triangle is greater than the measure of either nonadjacent interior angle. Thus, $90 < 6x < 180$, which implies $15 < x < 30$. Of the answer choices, only 25 (choice C) satisfies this inequality.

14. **B** Start with the angles for which you can find the measure by using the given information. As you determine the measure of each angle, you will gain enough information to find the solution.

$$m\angle ACB = 180° - 65° - 70° = 45°$$
$$m\angle DCA = 60° + 45° = 105°$$

The measure of an exterior angle of a triangle equals the sum of the measures of the remote interior angles. Thus, $m\angle DCA = 105° = 30° + m\angle E$. Hence, $m\angle E = 105° - 30° = 75°$.

15. **E** For any triangle, if P, Q, and R are the midpoints of the sides, the perimeter of triangle PQR is one-half the perimeter of the original triangle because the segment between the midpoints of any two sides of a triangle is half as long as the third side. Thus, the perimeter of the triangle formed by connecting the midpoints of the sides of triangle ABC is 30 centimeters.

16. **C** Let $2x =$ the measure of the smallest angle, in degrees. Then the measures of the other two angles are $3x$ and $5x$. Given that the angles of a triangle sum to $180°$, set up an equation and solve for $2x$.

$$2x + 3x + 5x = 180°$$
$$10x = 180°$$
$$x = 18°$$
$$2x = 36°$$

17. **D** Let x = the length in feet of the shorter piece. Then $x + 50\%x = 150\%x$ is the length in feet of the longer piece. Because there is a longer and a shorter piece, you know the rope was not cut in half. Therefore, the longer piece has to be longer than 25 feet (half of 50 feet). So, eliminate choices A, B, and C. Check D: If the longer piece is 30 feet, then the shorter piece is 20 feet. Because 30 is 150% of 20 = 1.5(20), choice D is the correct response.

18. **D** Analyze this problem as a "work problem." The key idea in a work problem is that the rate at which work is done equals the amount of work accomplished divided by the amount of time worked: rate = $\dfrac{\text{amount of work done}}{\text{time worked}}$. For the situation in this problem, the work to be done is to fill the tank. However, only the input valve works to fill the tank. The output valve works counter to the input valve because it works to empty the tank. Let t = the time, in hours, it will take to fill the tank with both valves open. To find t, first, determine the rate, r_{fill}, at which the tank can be filled when the input valve is open and the outlet valve is closed and the rate r_{empty}, at which the tank can be emptied when the input valve is closed and the outlet valve is open. Next, write an equation that represents the facts of the question.

$$\text{The rate for filling the tank is } r_{\text{fill}} = \frac{1 \text{ full tank}}{6 \text{ hr}} = \frac{1}{6} \text{ tank}/\text{hr}$$

$$\text{The rate for emptying the tank is } r_{\text{empty}} = \frac{1 \text{ full tank}}{10 \text{ hr}} = \frac{1}{10} \text{ tank}/\text{hr}$$

$$\text{Thus, 1 full tank} = \left(\frac{1}{6} \text{ tank}/\text{hr} \right)t - \left(\frac{1}{10} \text{ tank}/\text{hr} \right)t$$

Solve for t, omitting the units for convenience.

$$1 = \frac{1}{6}t - \frac{1}{10}t$$

$$1 = \frac{5}{30}t - \frac{3}{30}t$$

$$1 = \frac{2}{30}t$$

$$1 = \frac{1}{15}t$$

$$15 \cdot 1 = \cancel{15}\left(\frac{1}{\cancel{15}}t \right)$$

$$15 = t$$

It will take 15 hours to fill the tank.

19. E Sketch a Venn diagram, and add the problem information.

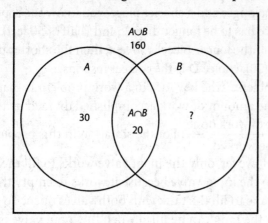

The number of elements that are only in set A is $50 - 20 = 30$. Let $x =$ the number of elements that are only in set B. Set up an equation to solve for the number of elements that are only in set B.

$$30 + 20 + x = 160$$
$$x = 160 - 50 = 110$$

Finally, determine the total number of elements in set B: $110 + 20 = 130$.

20. B If all the tagged turtles are still active in the lake when the second group of turtles is captured, the proportion of tagged turtles in the second group should equal the proportion of tagged turtles in the whole population, P, of turtles in the lake. Set up a proportion and solve for P.

$$\frac{6}{30} = \frac{20}{P}$$
$$P = \frac{(30)(20)}{6}$$
$$P = 100$$

The best estimate of the number of turtles in the lake is 100.

Problem-Solving Questions Drill 4

1. A mixture weighs 7.8 grams. It consists of ingredients X, Y, and Z in the ratio 2:5:6, respectively, by weight. How many less grams of ingredient X than ingredient Z are in the mixture?

   (A) 0.8
   (B) 1.2
   (C) 1.8
   (D) 2.4
   (E) 3.0

2. The government allocated $800 million for disaster relief in a hurricane-damaged region. This amount of money is about equal to spending $1 per second for how many years?

   (A) 5
   (B) 25
   (C) 50
   (D) 100
   (E) 150

3. What is the least positive integer that is *not* a factor of 20! and is *not* a prime?

   (A) 19
   (B) 23
   (C) 36
   (D) 46
   (E) 58

4. Which expression is equivalent to $12^x + 15^x$?

   (A) 27^{2x}
   (B) 27^x
   (C) $3^x \cdot 9^x$
   (D) $3(4^x + 5^x)$
   (E) $3^x(4^x + 5^x)$

5. The tokens in a game are distributed among five locations in the ratio 5:3:2:4:1. To win the game, a player must collect at least $\frac{1}{8}$ of the tokens in each of three or more of the five locations. This requirement represents what minimum percent of the total tokens?

   (A) 3%
   (B) 4%
   (C) 5%
   (D) 6%
   (E) 7%

*if you take √ from both sides
attach x*

$$z = \frac{1.2y}{x^2}, \ x \neq 0$$

6. Which equation shows the preceding equation correctly solved for x?

(A) $x = \frac{1.2y}{z}$

$Z = \frac{12y}{x^2}$

(B) $x = \pm \frac{1.2y}{z}$

(C) $x = \sqrt{\frac{1.2y}{z}}$

→ (D) $x = \pm \sqrt{\frac{1.2y}{z}}$

(E) $x = \pm \sqrt{1.2yz}$

$$4x + 5y = -2$$
$$-4x + 3y + 5z = 13$$
$$2 \cdot 2x + 5y - z = 5 \cdot 2$$

7. For the preceding system of equations, what is the value of y?

(A) −3

(B) −1

(C) 1

→ (D) 2

(E) 3

$4x + 10y - 2z = 10$

$4x + 5y = -2$
$-4x + 3y + 5z = 13$

$-4x + 3y + 5z = 13$
$5 \cdot 13y + 3z = 23 \cdot 5$

$-3 \cdot 8y + 5z = 11 \cdot -3$

$-24y - 15z = -33$
$65y + 15z = 115$
$41y = 82 \quad y = 2$

8. Which of the following sets of ordered pairs is a function?

I. $\{(-1,3),(1,2),(1,5),(3,8)\}$

II. $\{(4,4)\}$

III. $\{(1,5),(2,5),(3,5),(4,5)\}$

can't have same first elements

only 2+3

(A) I only

(B) I and II only

(C) I and III only

(D) II and III only

(E) I, II, and III

9. Which interval is the solution of $|2x - 1| > 7$?

(A) $x > -3$ and $x < 4$

(B) $x > -4$ and $x < 3$

(C) $x < -3$ or $x > 4$

(D) $x < -3$ or $x < 4$

(E) $x < -4$ or $x > 3$

$-7 > 2x - 1 > 7$

$\frac{-6}{2} > \frac{2x}{2} > \frac{8}{2}$

$-3 > x > 4$

(handwritten: plug in values & do the math   m=3 n=2)

$$\frac{m}{m^2-n^2}-\frac{n}{m^2+mn}$$

(handwritten: $\frac{3}{9-4}-\frac{2}{9+6}$ $\frac{3}{5}-\frac{2}{15}$ $\frac{9}{15}-\frac{2}{15}=\boxed{\frac{7}{15}}$)

10. Which expression is equivalent to the preceding expression?

(A) $\dfrac{m^2-mn-n^2}{m(m+n)}$ *(handwritten: $\frac{9-6-4}{9+6}$ $-\frac{7}{15}$)*

(B) $\dfrac{m^2-mn+n^2}{m(m+n)(m-n)}$ *(handwritten: $\frac{9-6+4}{(9+6)(3-2)}=\frac{9-2}{15(1)}=\boxed{\frac{7}{15}}$)*

(C) $\dfrac{m^2-mn-n^2}{m(m+n)(m-n)}$

(D) $\dfrac{m-n}{m(m+n)}$

(E) $\dfrac{m-n}{n(m+n)}$

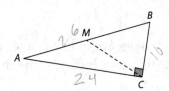

11. In the preceding right triangle ABC, $\overline{CM}$ is the median to the hypotenuse. If AC is 24 inches, BC is 10 inches, and AB is 26 inches, what is the measure, in inches, of $\overline{CM}$?

(handwritten: in a right triangle CM is always ½ of the hypotenuse)

(A) 12
(B) 13
(C) 14
(D) 15
(E) 16

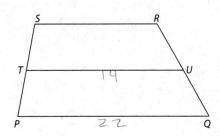

12. In the preceding trapezoid $PQRS$, $\overline{TU}$ is the line segment connecting the midpoints of the two nonparallel sides $\overline{SP}$ and $\overline{RQ}$. If $PQ = 22$ and $TU = 14$, what is the measure of $\overline{SR}$?

(handwritten: TU connects midpoints of a non parallel trapezoid & is ½ the sum of the length of its bases)

(A) 6
(B) 7
(C) 11
(D) 12
(E) 18

(handwritten: $14=\frac{1}{2}(SR+PQ)$ $14=\frac{1}{2}(SR+22)$ $=\frac{1}{2}SR+11$ $3=\frac{1}{2}SR$ $\boxed{6=SR}$)

13. How many 4-inch by 4-inch tiles are needed to cover a wall 8 feet by 6 feet?

   Ⓐ 6,912
   Ⓑ 1,728
   Ⓒ 864
   Ⓓ 432
   Ⓔ 216

   $$\frac{(8 \times 12)(6 \times 12)}{(4)(4)} = \frac{96(72)}{16} = \frac{6912}{16} = 432$$

14. A square and a rectangle have equal areas. The rectangle has dimensions 16 centimeters by 25 centimeters. What is the length, in centimeters, of a side of the square?

   16 × 25 = 400

   Ⓐ 9
   Ⓑ 18
   Ⓒ 20
   Ⓓ 29
   Ⓔ 40

15. If a rhombus has a side of length 16 inches and the measure of one interior angle is 150°, what is the area, in square inches, of the rhombus?

   Ⓐ 256
   Ⓑ 144
   Ⓒ 128
   Ⓓ 96
   Ⓔ 64

   A = bh
   A = 16 · ?

   so in a 30° 60° 90° triangle, the 30° side has a length ½ of hypotenuse. so ½ · 16 = 8
   so A = 16 · 8 = 128

   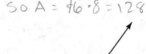

16. In the preceding figure, x and y are integers. Which of the following is a possible ratio of x to y?

   x + y = 180° so ratio must be a factor of 180

   I. 2:1   2 + 1 = 3 ✓
   II. 5:4   5 + 4 = 9 ✓
   III. 10:5   10 + 5 = 15 ✓

   Ⓐ I only
   Ⓑ II only
   Ⓒ I and III only
   Ⓓ II and III only
   Ⓔ I, II, and III

17. What is *n* if 12 is the greatest common factor of *n* and 84, and 756 is the least common multiple of *n* and 84?

(A) 52
(B) 108
(C) 168
(D) 324
(E) 378

the least common multiple of two positive integers is their product ÷ by their greatest common factor.

$(12) 756 = \dfrac{84n}{12}$ ×12 $\dfrac{9072}{84} = \dfrac{84n}{84}$ $n = 108$

18. Two vehicles leave the same location at exactly the same time, one traveling due north at *r* miles per hour and the other traveling due south at *r* + 10 miles per hour. In how many hours will the two vehicles be *d* miles apart?

(A) $\dfrac{d}{2r+10}$

(B) $\dfrac{d}{r^2+10}$

(C) $\dfrac{r(r+10)}{d}$

(D) $\dfrac{d}{r}+\dfrac{d}{r+10}$

(E) $\dfrac{0.5d}{r}+\dfrac{0.5d}{r+10}$

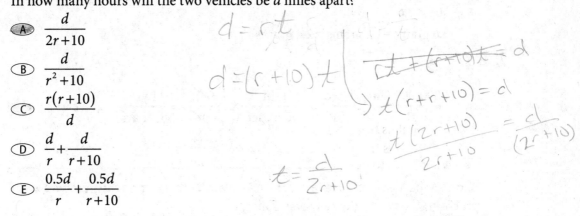

$d = rt$

$d = (r+10)t$ $rt + (r+10)t = d$

$t(r+r+10) = d$

$t(2r+10) = d$

$\dfrac{t(2r+10)}{2r+10} = \dfrac{d}{(2r+10)}$

$t = \dfrac{d}{2r+10}$

19. Two identical devices can complete a task in 10 hours. How many hours will it take five such devices to do the same task?

one device takes 20 hours
÷ 5 devices
4 hours

(A) 2
(B) 4
(C) 5
(D) 8
(E) 20

20. *doesn't say consecutive*

The sum of two integers is 168. If the larger integer is three times the smaller integer, what is the value of the larger integer?

(A) 42
(B) 56
(C) 84
(D) 126
(E) 252

$x + 3x = 168$
$4x = 168$
$\dfrac{4x}{4} = \dfrac{168}{4}$
$= 42$

$168 - 84 = 84$

$\begin{array}{r} 168 \\ 126 \\ \hline 42 \end{array}$

$\begin{array}{r} 42 \\ +3 \\ \hline 126 \end{array}$

$\begin{array}{r} 126 \\ 42 \\ +168 \end{array}$

Answers

1. **D** Let $2x$, $5x$, and $6x$ equal the weight (in grams) of ingredients X, Y, and Z, respectively, in the mixture. Then $2x + 5x + 6x = 7.8$ grams. Simplify and solve for the weights of ingredients X and Z, omitting the units for convenience.

$$13x = 7.8$$
$$x = \frac{7.8}{13}$$
$$x = 0.6$$
$$2x = 1.2$$
$$6x = 3.6$$
$$3.6 \text{ grams} - 1.2 \text{ grams} = 2.4 \text{ grams}$$

2. **B**

$$\frac{\$800,000,000}{1} \times \frac{1 \text{ sec}}{\$1} \times \frac{1 \text{ hr}}{3,600 \text{ sec}} \times \frac{1 \text{ day}}{24 \text{ hr}} \times \frac{1 \text{ yr}}{365 \text{ days}} \approx 25 \text{ years}$$

Because the answer choices are not close to each other, round the numbers in this problem to estimate the answer as follows:

$$\frac{800,000,000}{1} \times \frac{1}{1} \times \frac{1}{4,000} \times \frac{1}{20} \times \frac{1}{400} = \frac{\overset{200}{\cancel{800,000,000}}}{1} \times \frac{1}{\underset{1}{\cancel{4,000}}} \times \frac{1}{\underset{2}{\cancel{20}}} \times \frac{1}{\underset{4}{\cancel{400}}}$$

$$= \frac{\overset{100}{\cancel{200}}}{1} \times \frac{1}{\underset{1}{\cancel{2}}} \times \frac{1}{4}$$

$$= 25$$

---

3. **D** By definition,

$$20! = 20 \cdot 19 \cdot 18 \cdot 17 \cdot 16 \cdot 15 \cdot 14 \cdot 13 \cdot 12 \cdot 11 \cdot 10 \cdot 9 \cdot 8 \cdot 7 \cdot 6 \cdot 5 \cdot 4 \cdot 3 \cdot 2 \cdot 1$$

Hence, you can eliminate A because any positive integer ≤ 20 is a factor of 20!. Eliminate B because it is a prime. Any positive integer > 20 that can be expressed as the product of factors of 20! is a factor of 20!. For instance, $36 = 2 \cdot 18$ is a factor of 20!, so you can eliminate C. Choice D, 46, is not a prime *and* $46 = 2 \cdot 23$ is not a factor of 20!, because 23 is not a factor of 20!. Thus, choice D is the correct response. You do not have to check choice E, because $46 < 58$.

4. **E** Factor using your knowledge of exponents.

$$12^x + 15^x = (3 \cdot 4)^x + (3 \cdot 5)^x = 3^x \cdot 4^x + 3^x \cdot 5^x = 3^x \left(4^x + 5^x\right)$$

5. C For convenience, designate the locations A, B, C, D, and E with tokens in the ratio 5:3:2:4:1, respectively. Letting x be the number of tokens in location E, express the number of tokens in locations A, B, C, D, and E as $5x$, $3x$, $2x$, $4x$, and x tokens, respectively. The minimum number of tokens needed to win is $\frac{1}{8}$ of the tokens in locations B, C, and E (because these locations have the fewest tokens):

$$\frac{1}{8}(3x)+\frac{1}{8}(2x)+\frac{1}{8}x=\frac{6x}{8}=\frac{3}{4}x.$$

The total number of tokens is $5x+3x+2x+4x+x=15x$. The minimum percent needed to win is therefore:

$$\frac{\frac{3}{4}x}{15x}=\frac{3}{4}\div 15=\frac{\cancel{3}^{1}}{4}\times\frac{1}{\cancel{15}_{5}}=\frac{1}{20}=5\%$$

6. D Solve the given equation for x.

$$z=\frac{1.2y}{x^2}$$

$$zx^2=1.2y$$

$$x^2=\frac{1.2y}{z}$$

$$x=\pm\sqrt{\frac{1.2y}{z}}$$

When you take the square root of both sides, you must attach $\pm$ to the square root.

7. D For convenience, number the equations.

$$4x+5y=-2 \quad (1)$$
$$-4x+3y+5z=13 \quad (2)$$
$$2x+5y-z=5 \quad (3)$$

Proceed systematically to eliminate x and z from the equations so you can solve for y. First, to eliminate x from the first two equations, add equations (1) and (2).

$$4x+5y \qquad =-2 \quad (1)$$
$$\underline{-4x+3y+5z=13 \quad (2)}$$
$$8y+5z=11 \quad (4)$$

To eliminate x from the third equation, multiply both sides of it by 2 and then add the result to equation (2).

$$4x+10y-2z=10 \quad (3)$$
$$\underline{-4x+3y+5z=13 \quad (2)}$$
$$13y+3z=23 \quad (5)$$

Now eliminate z from equations (4) and (5). Multiply both sides of equation (4) by –3, and multiply both sides of equation (5) by 5. Add the results and then solve for y.

$$-24y-15z=-33 \quad (4)$$
$$65y+15z=115 \quad (5)$$
$$41y=82$$
$$y=2$$

8. **D** A function is a set of ordered pairs for which each first element is paired with *one and only one* second element. In other words, in a function, no two ordered pairs have the same first element but different second elements. Only the set of ordered pairs in Roman I fails to satisfy the definition of a function. The ordered pairs $(1, 2)$ and $(1, 5)$ have the same first element but different second elements. Eliminate choices A, B, C, and E. Choice D is the correct response.

9. **C** $|2x-1|>7$ if and only if $2x-1<-7$ or $2x-1>7$. Solve each condition to find the solution set.

$$2x-1<-7 \text{ or } 2x-1>7$$
$$2x-1+1<-7+1 \text{ or } 2x-1+1>7+1$$
$$2x<-6 \text{ or } 2x>8$$
$$x<-3 \text{ or } x>4$$

This solution corresponds to choice C.

10. **B Method 1:** Simplify the expression. To combine the terms, you will need a common denominator.

$$\frac{m}{m^2-n^2}-\frac{n}{m^2+mn}=\frac{m}{(m+n)(m-n)}-\frac{n}{m(m+n)}$$

The denominator has one common factor, $(m + n)$. The least common multiple is $m(m + n)(m - n)$.

$$\frac{m\cdot m}{m(m+n)(m-n)}-\frac{n(m-n)}{m(m+n)(m-n)}=\frac{m^2}{m(m+n)(m-n)}-\frac{nm-n^2}{m(m+n)(m-n)}$$
$$=\frac{m^2-mn+n^2}{m(m+n)(m-n)}$$

When you subtract fractions, apply a minus sign preceding a fraction to each term of the numerator.

Method 2: Evaluate the expression for suitable values for m and n. Then check *all* the answer choices using the same values for m and n. Let $m=2$ and $n=3$.

$$\frac{m}{m^2-n^2}-\frac{n}{m^2+mn}=\frac{2}{(2)^2-(3)^2}-\frac{3}{(2)^2+(2)(3)}$$

$$=\frac{2}{4-9}-\frac{3}{4+6}=-\frac{2}{5}-\frac{3}{10}=-\frac{4}{10}-\frac{3}{10}=-\frac{7}{10}$$

Check A: $\dfrac{m^2-mn-n^2}{m(m+n)}=\dfrac{(2)^2-(2)(3)-(3)^2}{2(2+3)}=\dfrac{4-6-9}{2(5)}=\dfrac{-11}{10}\neq-\dfrac{7}{10}$

Check B: $\dfrac{m^2-mn+n^2}{m(m+n)(m-n)}=\dfrac{(2)^2-(2)(3)+(3)^2}{2(2+3)(2-3)}=\dfrac{4-6+9}{2(5)(-1)}=\dfrac{7}{-10}=-\dfrac{7}{10}\ \checkmark$

Check C: This choice has the same numerator as choice A, so substitute in the

value. $\dfrac{m^2-mn-n^2}{m(m+n)(m-n)}=\dfrac{-11}{2(2+3)(2-3)}=\dfrac{-11}{2(5)(-1)}=\dfrac{-11}{-10}\neq-\dfrac{7}{10}$

Check D: $\dfrac{m-n}{m(m+n)}=\dfrac{2-3}{2(2+3)}=\dfrac{-1}{2(5)}\neq-\dfrac{7}{10}$

Check E: This choice has the same numerator as choice D, so substitute in the

value. $\dfrac{m-n}{n(m+n)}=\dfrac{-1}{3(2+3)}=\dfrac{-1}{3(5)}\neq-\dfrac{7}{10}$

Choice B is the correct response.

11. **B** In a right triangle, the median to the hypotenuse is one-half the length of the hypotenuse, so the length in inches of $\overline{CM}$ is 13.

12. **A** The length of the segment connecting the midpoints of two nonparallel sides of a trapezoid is one-half the sum of the lengths of its bases. Thus, $TU=14=\frac{1}{2}(SR+PQ)=\frac{1}{2}(SR+22)$. Solve $14=\frac{1}{2}(SR+22)$ for SR.

Method 1: Solve the equation using a conventional procedure.

$$14=\frac{1}{2}(SR+22)$$

$$14=\frac{1}{2}SR+11$$

$$14-11=\frac{1}{2}SR+11-11$$

$$3=\frac{1}{2}SR$$

$$6=SR$$

Method 2: Check the answer choices. Check A:

$$14 = \frac{1}{2}(SR + 22)$$

$$14 \overset{?}{=} \frac{1}{2}(6 + 22)$$

$$14 \overset{?}{=} \frac{1}{2}(28)$$

$$14 \overset{\surd}{=} 14$$

Choice A is the correct response.

13. **D** The area of the wall in square feet is (8)(6). The area of the wall in square inches is $(8 \times 12)(6 \times 12)$. The area of one tile in square inches is (4)(4). To find the number of tiles needed, divide the area of the wall in square inches by the area of 1 tile in square inches.

$$\frac{(8 \times 12)(6 \times 12)}{(4)(4)} = \frac{\left(8 \times \cancel{12}^{3}\right)\left(6 \times \cancel{12}^{3}\right)}{\left(\cancel{4}_1\right)\left(\cancel{4}_1\right)} = 8 \times 3 \times 6 \times 3 = 432$$

Expressing quantities in factored form, as demonstrated in this problem, can make computations easier.

---

14. **C** Let $x =$ the length in centimeters of a side of the square. Then $x^2 =$ the area of the square in square centimeters. The area of the rectangle in square centimeters = length × width = $16 \times 25 = 400$. The two areas are equal. Thus, $x^2 = 400$, so $x = \sqrt{400} = 20$.

15. **C** Make a sketch, filling in the information given in the question.

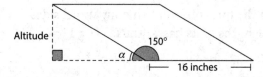

The area A, is $A = bh$, where b is the base and h is the height (the length of the altitude). The measure of angle $\alpha = 180° - 150° = 30°$. The indicated altitude is the side opposite the 30° angle in a 30°-60°-90° right triangle that has a hypotenuse of length 16 inches. The sides of a 30°-60°-90° right triangle are in the ratio $1 : \sqrt{3} : 2$. The side opposite the 30° angle is half the hypotenuse. Thus, the altitude's length in inches is $\frac{1}{2} \cdot 16 = 8$, and the area in square inches is $bh = 16 \times 8 = 128$.

16. **E** Check the Roman numeral choices. Check Roman I: If the ratio is 2:1, let $2m = x$ and $1m = y$. The sum of x and y is $x + y = 2m + 1m = 3m$. Thus, the sum must be a multiple of 3. From the figure, the two angles are supplementary, so their sum is 180°, a multiple of 3. Therefore, the ratio 2:1 is possible. Eliminate choices B and D because these choices do not contain Roman I. By inspection, the ratio in Roman III is equivalent to the ratio in Roman I, so it is a possible ratio of x to y. Eliminate choice A because it does not include Roman III. Check Roman II. If the ratio is 5:4, the sum of x and y must be a multiple of $5 + 4 = 9$. Therefore, the ratio 5:4 is possible because 180° is a multiple of 9. Eliminate choice C because it does not include Roman II. Choice E is the correct response.

17. **B** The least common multiple of two positive integers is their product divided by their greatest common factor. Thus,

$$756 = \frac{84n}{12}; \; n = \frac{(756)\left(\cancel{12}^{1}\right)}{\cancel{84}_{7}}; \; n = \frac{756}{7} = 108.$$

This question demonstrates the use of a well-known fact about the relationship between least common multiple and greatest common factor.

---

18. **A** The distance formula is $d = rt$, where d is the distance traveled at a uniform rate of speed r for a length of time t. Let $t =$ the time in hours that the two vehicles will be d miles apart. Make a chart to organize the information in the question.

VEHICLE	RATE (IN MPH)	TIME (IN HOURS)	DISTANCE
Vehicle 1	r	t	rt
Vehicle 2	$r + 10$	t	$(r + 10)t$
		Total:	d

Using the information in the chart, set up an equation and solve for t.

$$rt + (r + 10)t = d$$
$$t(r + r + 10) = d$$
$$t(2r + 10) = d$$
$$t = \frac{d}{2r + 10}$$

19. **B** Use logical reasoning to solve this problem. If two identical devices take 10 hours, then one such device will take twice as long, which is 20 hours. Five such devices would take one-fifth as long as one device. Therefore, five such devices will take $\frac{1}{5}$ of 20 hours, which is 4 hours.

It will take 4 hours for five such devices to do the same task.

You should eliminate choice E at the outset because it doesn't make sense that 5 devices would take longer than 2 devices to do the task.

---

20. **D** **Method 1:** Let $x =$ the smaller integer. Then $3x =$ the larger integer. Using the information in the question, set up an equation that represents the facts of the question.

$$x + 3x = 168$$

When you have two unknowns and a first unknown is described in terms of a second unknown, it is usually easier to let the variable equal the second unknown. In this question, the larger integer is described in terms of the smaller integer, so let x equal the smaller integer. But because the question asks for the value of the larger integer, remember to solve for the larger integer after you find x.

Solve the equation.

$$x + 3x = 168$$
$$4x = 168$$
$$x = \frac{168}{4}$$
$$x = 42$$
$$3x = 126, \text{ the larger integer}$$

Method 2: Check the answer choices using logical reasoning. Eliminate choice B because 56 is not divisible by 3.

Check C: If the larger integer is 84, the smaller integer is $\frac{1}{3}(84) = 28$. Their sum 28 + 84 = 112. So 84 is too small. Eliminate choice A as too small as well. Eliminate E because it is larger than 168.

Check D: If the larger integer is 126, the smaller integer is $\frac{1}{3}(126) = 42$. Their sum 42 + 128 = 168√. Choice D is the correct response.

Problem-Solving Questions Drill 5

1. What is the value of $\left(\sqrt{5+\sqrt{15}}-\sqrt{5-\sqrt{15}}\right)^2$? 2

   (A) −10
   (B) 0
   (C) $2\sqrt{15}$
   (D) $8\sqrt{10}$
   (E) $10-2\sqrt{10}$

2. Two hundred people will attend a university fund-raiser if tickets cost $30 per person. For each $15 increase in ticket price, 25 fewer people will attend. What ticket price will yield the maximum amount of money for the university?

   (A) $30 × 200 = 6,000
   (B) $45 × 175 7875
   (C) $60 × 150 9000
   (D) $75 × 125 9375
   (E) $90 × 100 9000

3. A solution of water and sugar is 20% sugar by weight. After several weeks, some of the water evaporates so that the solution is 60% sugar by weight. What is the ratio of the initial weight of water to the final weight of water in the mixture?

   (A) 1:6
   (B) 1:4
   (C) 1:3
   (D) 4:1
   → (E) 6:1

4. The football coach at a certain midsized university earns $\frac{1}{4}$ more in salary than does the university's basketball coach. The basketball coach's salary represents what percent of the football coach's salary?

   125 F
   100 B

   (A) 125%
   (B) 120%
   (C) 90%
   (D) 80%
   (E) 75%

5. Violet inherited a gold and diamond pendant from her grandmother in 2014. In 2015, the value of the pendant decreased by 10%. Its value increased by 20% in 2016 and then decreased by 10% in 2017. How does the 2017 value of the pendant compare with its value in 2014?

[handwritten: 2014 2015   2016   2017]
[handwritten: $100 -10% +20% -10%]

Ⓐ 2.8% decrease in value

Ⓑ 1.4% decrease in value   *[handwritten: $90 $108 $97.20]*

Ⓒ No change

Ⓓ 1.4% increase in value

Ⓔ 2.8% increase in value

6. If $\sqrt{3x+3} = \sqrt{3x} + 1$, what is the value of $3x$?

Ⓐ 0

Ⓑ $\dfrac{1}{3}$ *[handwritten: $\sqrt{3x+3} = \sqrt{3x} + 1$]*

[handwritten: $\sqrt{3+3} = \sqrt{3} + 1$]

Ⓒ $\pm\dfrac{1}{3}$ *[handwritten: $3 = \sqrt{3}$]*

Ⓓ 1

Ⓔ ± 1

$$\begin{cases} y = 3x - 5 \\ y = x^2 - x - 5 \end{cases}$$

7. Which values of x are in the solution set of the preceding system of equations?

Ⓐ 0, 4   *[handwritten: $3x - 5 = x^2 - x - 5$]*

Ⓑ −4, 0

Ⓒ −2, 5

Ⓓ −2, −5

Ⓔ 2, 5

x	$f(x)$	$g(x)$
1	5	3
2	4	1
3	3	4
4	2	2
5	1	5

8. The preceding table shows selected values of the functions f and g. What is the value of $g(f(4))$?

[handwritten: $f(4) = 2$ so $g(2) = 1$]

Ⓐ 1

Ⓑ 2

Ⓒ 3

Ⓓ 4

Ⓔ 5

$$|2n+1| \le 6$$

9. How many integers n satisfy the preceding absolute value inequality?

    (A) Seven
    (B) Six
    (C) Five
    (D) Four
    (E) None

    Handwritten work:
    $-6 \le 2n+1 \le 6$
    $-7 \le 2n \le 5$
    $\frac{-7}{2} \le n < 2.5$
    $-3, -2, -1, 0, 1, 2$
    $-3.5 \le n < 2.5$

10. If 5 is one solution of the equation $x^2 - 2x + k = 14$, where k is a constant, what is the other solution?

    (A) −5
    (B) −3
    (C) −1
    (D) 3
    (E) 5

    Handwritten work:
    $5^2 - 2(5) + k = 14$
    $25 - 10 + k = 14$
    $k = -1$ so plug in answers
    $-3^2 - 2(-3) - 1 = 14$
    $9 + 6 - 1 = 14$
    -3

11. Which of the following sets of numbers could be the lengths of the sides of a right triangle?

    I.   7, 10, 13
    II. 2, $2\sqrt{3}$, 4
    III. 1, $\frac{3}{4}$, $1\frac{1}{4}$

    (A) I only
    (B) I and II only
    (C) I and III only
    (D) II and III only
    (E) I, II, and III

    Handwritten work:
    the square of the length of hyp is = to square of the lengths of the legs
    $7^2 + 10^2 = 149$
    $13^2 = 169$
    $1^2 + .75^2 = 1.5625$
    $1.25^2 = 1.5625$

12. A bike rider leaves camp and travels 7 miles due north, then 3 miles due east, and then 3 miles due south. At this point, the rider stops to rest. What is the rider's true distance from camp in miles?

    (A) 13
    (B) 10
    (C) 7
    (D) 5
    (E) 4

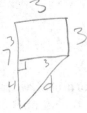

    Handwritten work:
    $4^2 + 3^2 = 25$
    $\sqrt{25} = 5$

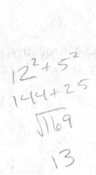

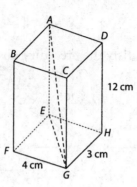

13. A rectangular prism has the dimensions 4 centimeters by 3 centimeters by 12 centimeters as shown in the preceding figure. What is the length, in centimeters, of the diagonal $\overline{AG}$?

    (A) 5
    (B) 11
    (C) 13
    (D) 15
    (E) 25

14. What is the area, in square inches, of an equilateral triangle that has altitude of length 12 inches?

    (A) $4\sqrt{3}$
    (B) $8\sqrt{3}$
    (C) $24\sqrt{3}$
    (D) $48\sqrt{3}$
    (E) $96\sqrt{3}$

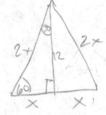

15. In a circle whose radius is 13 centimeters, a chord is 12 centimeters from the center of the circle. What is the chord's length in centimeters?

    (A) 12
    (B) 10
    (C) 8
    (D) 6
    (E) 5

16. A 30-ounce mixture contains cornmeal, wheat germ, and flaxseed by weight in the ratio 5:3:2, respectively. What is the number of ounces of flaxseed in the mixture?

    (A) 2
    (B) 3
    (C) 6
    (D) 9
    (E) 15

17. The shaded area of the preceding figure represents a triangular flower bed. A homeowner wants to put decorative bricks around the flower bed. One side of the flower bed is 10 feet long and makes a 45° angle with a walkway that runs east to west. A second side runs parallel to the east-west walkway, and the third side makes a 30° angle with the east-west walkway. What is the perimeter in feet of the flower bed?

Ⓐ $10\left(2+\sqrt{2}+\sqrt{6}\right)$

Ⓑ $10\left(2+\sqrt{2}+\sqrt{3}\right)$

Ⓒ $10\left(2+\sqrt{8}\right)$

Ⓓ $5\left(2+\sqrt{2}+\sqrt{6}\right)$

Ⓔ $5\left(2+\sqrt{2}+\sqrt{3}\right)$

18. Four people are to be seated in four identical chairs placed in a circle. How many different arrangements of the four people (relative to one another) in the four chairs are possible?

Ⓐ 256
Ⓑ 128
Ⓒ 48
Ⓓ 24
Ⓔ 6

19. Tess and Sunil join different fitness clubs. Tess joins a club that charges a one-time enrollment fee of $50 and $20 for each month of membership. Sunil joins a club that charges a one-time enrollment fee of $70 and $18 for each month of membership. After how many months of membership will Tess and Sunil have paid the same total amount?

Ⓐ 10
Ⓑ 15
Ⓒ 20
Ⓓ 25
Ⓔ 30

20. Two consecutive angles of a parallelogram have measures $x - 30°$ and $2x + 60°$.
What is the measure of the smaller angle?

- (A) 20°
- (B) 40°
- (C) 50°
- (D) 70°
- (E) 160°

$2(x - 30) + 2(2x + 60) = 360$

$2x - 60 + 4x + 120 = 360$

$6x + 60 = 360$

$\dfrac{6x}{6} = \dfrac{300}{6}$

$x = 50°$

$50 - 30 = \boxed{20}$

$2(50) + 60 = 160$

Answers

1. **E** Square the expression and simplify.

$$\left(\sqrt{5+\sqrt{15}}-\sqrt{5-\sqrt{15}}\right)^2=\left(\sqrt{5+\sqrt{15}}\right)^2-2\sqrt{5+\sqrt{15}}\sqrt{5-\sqrt{15}}+\left(\sqrt{5-\sqrt{15}}\right)^2$$

$$=5+\sqrt{15}-2\sqrt{25-\left(\sqrt{15}\right)^2}+5-\sqrt{15}$$

$$=10-2\sqrt{25-15}$$

$$=10-2\sqrt{10}$$

2. **D** Checking the answer choices is a logical strategy for figuring out the optimum ticket price. Checking A: At \$30 per ticket, 200 people will attend, yielding $200 \times \$30 = \$6{,}000$ in ticket sales. Checking B: At \$45 per ticket, 175 people will attend, yielding $175 \times \$45 = \$7{,}875$ in ticket sales. Checking C: At \$60 per ticket, 150 people will attend, yielding $150 \times \$60 = \$9{,}000$ in ticket sales. Checking D: At \$75 per ticket, 125 people will attend, yielding $125 \times \$75 = \$9{,}375$ in ticket sales. Checking E: At \$90 per ticket, 100 people will attend, yielding $100 \times \$90 = \$9{,}000$ in ticket sales. So, a \$75 ticket price (choice D) will yield the maximum amount of money for the university.

3. **E** The percent water by weight in the initial solution is $100\% - 20\% = 80\%$. For convenience, suppose initially the solution weighed 100 grams. Then it would contain 20 grams (20% of 100) of sugar and 80 grams (80% of 100) of water. After evaporation, the number of grams of sugar is still 20. This represents 60% of the evaporated solution by weight. Write the following percent equation and solve for x, the new weight of the solution (after evaporation).

$$60\%x = 20 \text{ g}$$

$$x = \frac{20 \text{ g}}{60\%} = \frac{20 \text{ g}}{1} \div \frac{3}{5} = \frac{20 \text{ g}}{1} \times \frac{5}{3} = \frac{100 \text{ g}}{3} = 33\frac{1}{3} \text{ g}$$

Subtract the weight of the sugar to find the final weight of water in the evaporated solution. $33\frac{1}{3} \text{ g} - 20 \text{ g} = 13\frac{1}{3} \text{ g} = \frac{40}{3} \text{ g}$. Use this value to find the ratio of the initial weight to the final weight of water in the solution, omitting the units for convenience.

$$\frac{80}{40/3} = \frac{80}{1} \div \frac{40}{3} = \frac{\overset{2}{\cancel{80}}}{1} \times \frac{3}{\underset{1}{\cancel{40}}} = \frac{6}{1}$$

The ratio of the initial weight of water to the final weight of water is 6:1.

Using logical reasoning, eliminate choices A, B, and C at the outset. These answer choices imply the final weight of water (after evaporation) is greater than the initial weight of water (before evaporation). It doesn't make sense that the amount of water would weigh more after some of it has evaporated.

---

4. **D** For convenience, let $100 = the basketball coach's salary. Then the football coach's salary is $100 + \frac{1}{4}(\$100) = \$125$. The percent is $\frac{100}{125} = \frac{4}{5} = 80\%$. *Tip*: Picking a value to work with (even if it is not realistic) can simplify a problem.

5. **A** For convenience, let the value of the pendant in 2014 equal $100. In 2015, the value of the pendant was $100 − 10%(100) = $90. In 2016, the value of the pendant was $90 + 20%(90) = $108. In 2017, the value of the pendant was $108 − 10%(108) = $97.20. The percent change is

$$\frac{|\text{New Value} - \text{Old Value}|}{\text{Old Value}} \times 100\% = \frac{|\$97.20 - \$100|}{\$100} \times 100\%$$

$$= \frac{|-\$2.80|}{\$100} \times 100\% = \frac{\$2.80}{\$100} \times 100\% = 2.8\% \text{ decrease}$$

6. **D** $\sqrt{3x+3} = \sqrt{3x} + 1$. Square both sides and simplify.

$$\left(\sqrt{3x+3}\right)^2 = \left(\sqrt{3x} + 1\right)^2$$

$$3x + 3 = \left(\sqrt{3x}\right)^2 + 2\sqrt{3x} + 1$$

$$3x + 3 = 3x + 2\sqrt{3x} + 1$$

$$2 = 2\sqrt{3x}$$

$$1 = \sqrt{3x}$$

Square both sides.

$$1^2 = \left(\sqrt{3x}\right)^2$$

$$1 = 3x$$

7. **A** Substitute $y = 3x - 5$ into the second equation, and solve for x.

$$3x - 5 = x^2 - x - 5$$

$$0 = x^2 - 4x$$

$$0 = x(x - 4)$$

$$x = 0 \text{ or } x = 4$$

8. **A** Using the table, $f(4) = 2$, so $g(f(4)) = g(2) = 1$.

9. **B** $|2n+1| \leq 6$ if and only if $-6 \leq 2n+1 \leq 6$. Solve this double inequality.

$$-6 \leq 2n + 1 \leq 6$$

$$-6 - 1 \leq 2n + 1 - 1 \leq 6 - 1$$

$$-7 \leq 2n \leq 5$$

$$-3.5 \leq n \leq 2.5$$

The integers that satisfy this double inequality are −3, −2, −1, 0, 1, and 2. Thus, there are six integers that satisfy $|2n+1| \leq 6$.

10. B First, substitute $x = 5$ into $x^2 - 2x + k = 14$ and solve for k.

$$5^2 - 2 \cdot 5 + k = 14$$
$$25 - 10 + k = 14$$
$$15 + k = 14$$
$$k = -1$$

Next, substitute $k = -1$ into $x^2 - 2x + k = 14$ and solve for x.

$$x^2 - 2x - 1 = 14$$
$$x^2 - 2x - 15 = 0$$
$$(x - 5)(x + 3) = 0$$
$$x = 5 \text{ or } x = -3$$

Once you know that the equation is $x^2 - 2x - 1 = 14$, you can substitute in the answer choices to determine that B is the correct response.

---

11. D In a right triangle, the square of the length of the hypotenuse is equal to the sum of the squares of the lengths of the legs. Only the set of numbers in Roman I fail to meet this requirement for a right triangle ($7^2 + 10^2 = 149 \neq 169 = 13^2$). Choice D is the correct response.

12. D Let $d =$ the true distance in miles from camp. Make a sketch, filling in the information given in the question.

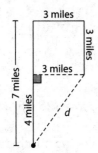

From the sketch, d is the length of the hypotenuse of a right triangle with legs of lengths 3 miles and 4 miles. Therefore, d is 5 miles. *Tip*: Knowing Pythagorean triples (such as 3, 4, 5) can be very helpful when working with right triangles.

13. C The diagonal $\overline{AG}$ is the hypotenuse of a right triangle with legs $\overline{AE}$ and $\overline{EG}$. $\overline{AE}$ is the height of the rectangular prism, and $\overline{EG}$ is the diagonal of its base. Omitting the units, $AE = 12$, and $EG = 5$ (because it is the hypotenuse of a 3-4-5 right triangle). Therefore, $AG = \sqrt{5^2 + 12^2} = \sqrt{25 + 144} = \sqrt{169} = 13$.

14. D Make a sketch, filling in the information given in the question.

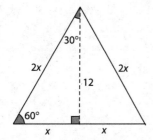

The angles in an equilateral triangle each measure 60°. Also, in an equilateral triangle, an altitude bisects the angle at the vertex from which it is drawn and the side to which it is drawn. The altitude shown is the leg opposite the 60° angle in a 30°-60°-90° right triangle. The sides of a 30°-60°-90° right triangle are in the ratio $1 : \sqrt{3} : 2$. Omitting the units for convenience, set up a proportion and solve for x and $2x$.

$$\frac{x}{12} = \frac{1}{\sqrt{3}}$$

$$x = \frac{12}{\sqrt{3}} = \frac{12\sqrt{3}}{3} = 4\sqrt{3}$$

$$2x = 8\sqrt{3}$$

Hence, the area is $\frac{1}{2}\left(8\sqrt{3}\right)(12) = 48\sqrt{3}$.

15. **B** In a circle, a radius that is perpendicular to a chord bisects the chord. Let x = one-half the length of the chord. Then $2x$ = the length of the chord. Make a sketch, filling in the question information.

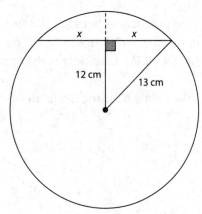

Using the Pythagorean theorem, $x^2 = 13^2 - 12^2 = 169 - 144 = 25$. So $x = \sqrt{25} = 5$, and $2x = 10$.

16. **C** Let $2x$ = the number of ounces of flaxseed in the mixture. Then $3x$ = the number of ounces of wheat germ in the mixture, and $5x$ = the number of ounces of cornmeal in the mixture. Using the information in the question, write an equation and solve for $2x$.

$$2x + 3x + 5x = 30$$
$$10x = 30$$
$$x = 3$$
$$2x = 6$$

The number of ounces of flaxseed in the mixture is 6 ounces.

17. D Make a quick sketch, and mark on the figure as shown below.

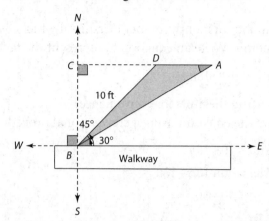

Constructing the perpendicular from A to C creates two right triangles, DCB and ACB. Angle CBD measures 45° (90° − 45°) because $\overline{BD}$ makes a 45° angle with the walkway. Given that $\overline{DA}$ is parallel to the walkway, angle CAB measures 30° because it is congruent with the 30° angle that $\overline{BA}$ makes with the walkway (alternate interior angles of parallel lines are congruent). Thus, triangle DCB is a 45°-45°-90° right triangle, and triangle ACB is a 30°-60°-90° right triangle.

The perimeter of the flower bed in feet equals $10 + BA + DA$. In triangle DCB, $\overline{CB}$ and $\overline{CD}$ are the legs of a 45°-45°-90° right triangle whose hypotenuse is 10. Because the sides of a 45°-45°-90° right triangle are in the ratio $\sqrt{2}:\sqrt{2}:2$, $CB = CD = \dfrac{10}{2}\sqrt{2} = 5\sqrt{2}$. In 30°-60°-90° right triangle ACB, $\overline{CB}$ is the side opposite the 30° angle, and $\overline{CA}$ is the side opposite the 60° angle. Because the sides of a 30°-60°-90° right triangle are in the ratio $1:\sqrt{3}:2$, $BA = 2(CB) = 2\left(5\sqrt{2}\right) = 10\sqrt{2}$ and $CA = \sqrt{3}(CB) = \sqrt{3}\left(5\sqrt{2}\right) = 5\sqrt{6}$. Thus, $DA = CA - CD = 5\sqrt{6} - 5\sqrt{2} = 5\left(\sqrt{6} - \sqrt{2}\right)$. Therefore, the perimeter is $10 + 10\sqrt{2} + 5\left(\sqrt{6} - \sqrt{2}\right) = 5\left(2 + 2\sqrt{2} + \sqrt{6} - \sqrt{2}\right) = 5\left(2 + \sqrt{2} + \sqrt{6}\right)$.

This question illustrates the value of making an astute construction on a figure. When you are given angle values of 30° and/or 45°, look for ways you can make 30°-60°-90° and/or 45°-45°-90° right triangles. Also, the explanation for this question is lengthy, but in reality, once you have created the two special right triangles, the computations are straightforward and can be done quickly—even mentally.

---

18. E The people are not assigned to particular seats but are arranged relative to one another only. For instance, the four arrangements shown in the following diagram are the same because the people (P1, P2, P3, and P4) are in the same order clockwise.

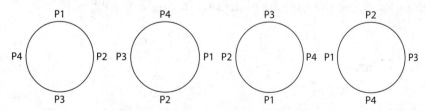

Hence, the position of P1 is immaterial. What counts are the positions of the other three people relative to P1. Therefore, keeping P1 fixed, there are $3 \cdot 2 \cdot 1 = 6$ different ways to arrange the other three people, so there are 6 different arrangements of the four people in a circle.

19. **A** Let n be the number of months of membership at which Tess and Sunil will have paid the same total amount. Write an equation to represent the facts.

$$\$50 + \$20n = \$70 + \$18n$$

Solve for n, omitting the units for convenience.

Method 1: Solve the equation using a conventional procedure.

$$50 + 20n = 70 + 18n$$
$$50 + 20n - 18n = 70 + 18n - 18n$$
$$2n + 50 - 50 = 70 - 50$$
$$2n = 20$$
$$n = 10$$

After 10 months, Tess and Sunil will have paid the same total amount.

Method 2: Check the answer choices. Check A:

$$50 + 20n = 70 + 18n$$
$$50 + 20(10) \overset{?}{=} 70 + 18(10)$$
$$50 + 200 \overset{?}{=} 70 + 180$$
$$250 \overset{\checkmark}{=} 250$$

After 10 months, Tess and Sunil will have paid the same total amount.

20. **A** Consecutive angles of a parallelogram are supplementary. Write an equation and solve for x.

$$(x - 30°) + (2x + 60°) = 180°$$
$$x - 30° + 2x + 60° = 180°$$
$$3x + 30° = 180°$$
$$3x + 30° - 30° = 180° - 30°$$
$$3x = 150°$$
$$\frac{3x}{3} = \frac{150°}{3}$$
$$x = 50°$$

Use the value of x to find the measure of the smaller angle: $x - 30° = 20°$.

CHAPTER 7

GMAT Data Sufficiency Questions

About Data Sufficiency Questions

Data sufficiency questions are unique to the GMAT. In these questions, you are presented with a problem question followed by two statements containing additional information. The problem question will be either one to which you can answer *yes* or *no* or one that asks for the *value* of a quantity. You do not actually have to answer the question posed. Instead, your task is to determine whether the data given are <u>sufficient</u> to answer the question. When the question is a yes or no question, the data are sufficient only when it is possible to answer with a definite yes or no. That is, you must be able to answer *always* yes or *always* no, not sometimes yes or no. When the question asks for the value of a quantity, the data are sufficient only when it is possible to determine *exactly one* numerical value for the quantity.

Strategies for Data Sufficiency Questions

All data sufficiency questions offer you the same five answer choices. Here is an example of a data sufficiency question.

Is $x > 3$?
   (1) $\sqrt{x^2} = 4$
   (2) $x > 0$

  Ⓐ   Statement (1) ALONE is sufficient, but statement (2) alone is not sufficient.
  Ⓑ   Statement (2) ALONE is sufficient, but statement (1) alone is not sufficient.
  Ⓒ   BOTH statements TOGETHER are sufficient, but NEITHER statement ALONE is sufficient.
  Ⓓ   EACH statement ALONE is sufficient.
  Ⓔ   Statements (1) and (2) TOGETHER are NOT sufficient.

Use a Systematic Approach

Start by reading the question stem. The problem question is asking for a yes or no answer. Next, read statement (1). Decide whether the information in statement (1) alone is sufficient to answer the problem question. If statement (1) alone is sufficient, then A or D are the only possible answers. You can cross off B, C, and E as possibilities. On the other hand, if statement (1) alone is not sufficient, then the correct answer *cannot* be A or D. Consider the question given. Is statement (1) alone sufficient?

$$(1) \ \sqrt{x^2} = 4$$

The information in (1) tells you that $\sqrt{x^2} = 4$. This statement is equivalent to the statement $|x| = 4$. Both −4 and 4 have absolute value equal to 4. Without further information, you do not know whether x is −4 or 4. Hence, you cannot decide whether $x > 3$; so, statement (1) alone is not sufficient. Therefore, the correct answer is either B, C, or E.

Go on to statement (2). As you make your decision about whether statement (2) alone is sufficient, avoid considering the information given in statement (1). If statement (2) alone is sufficient, then the answer cannot be C or E. Is statement (2) alone sufficient?

$$(2) \ x > 0$$

From the information in (2), you know that x is a positive number, but there is not enough information to determine whether $x > 3$. For instance, x could be a number between 0 and 3; so, statement (2) alone is not sufficient.

Now consider statements (1) and (2) together. Do they together provide sufficient information for you to answer the problem question? If they do, then the correct answer is C. If they do not, the correct answer is E.

Taking (1) and (2) together, you can determine from (1) that x is either −4 or 4, and then using (2), you can determine that x is 4. Thus, the problem answer is yes, $x > 3$. Therefore, BOTH statements together are sufficient, but NEITHER statement ALONE is sufficient. Choice C is the correct response.

You should approach every data sufficiency question with the same technique as illustrated in this example. Here is a summary of the process as a decision tree.

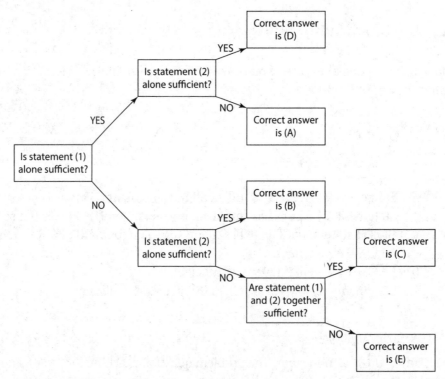

As the decision tree shows, if statement (1) alone is sufficient, you must go on to determine whether statement (2) alone is sufficient. Don't make the mistake of selecting A without checking statement (2).

Memorize the Answer Choices

The answer choices for data sufficiency questions do not change. The five options are always the same. Memorize them! You will save valuable time on the test by knowing them without hesitation.

Know Your Math

Having a good grasp of math will be of great help to you on data sufficiency questions. Some questions are easily answered when you have an understanding of the math concepts in the question. Also, you can avoid common pitfalls if you are knowledgeable about math concepts. For instance, as shown in the example question, knowing that $\sqrt{x^2} = 4$ is equivalent to $|x| = 4$ can keep you from making the error of assuming x is 4. Most of the math concepts on the GMAT are ones you likely have encountered in the past. However, you might have forgotten some if not most of them. Study the math review in this book to refresh your knowledge and skills.

Write Equations, But Don't Solve Them

In this chapter, even though the solutions to the practice drills include writing equations, most of the time you should *not* solve the equations. The equations help you organize your thinking and let you know quickly whether you have sufficient data to answer the question. When you have more than one unknown in a problem question, assign a variable name to each unknown. This strategy will help you decide whether you have sufficient information to answer the problem question. In most cases, you will need as many linear equations as you have variables in order to determine single values for variables. *Tip*: A **two-variable linear equation** is one that can be written as $ax + by = c$, where x and y are variables and a, b, and c are real numbers. Be careful though, when you have two variables and two linear equations. Make sure that the two equations are *distinct* equations. For instance, $x + y = 5$ and $2x + 2y = 10$ are different versions of the same equation. When your two-variable equations are not distinct, you will be unable to obtain a single value as an answer for a target variable. Usually, you can use visual inspection to check the two equations.

Use Your Time Wisely

Don't solve equations or work out computations unless doing so is necessary to help you make the correct answer choice. Stop working! Click your answer choice and move on to the next question. For geometry problems, sketches help you organize the question information. Make quick rough sketches. Do not spend unnecessary time making them.

Directions for the Data Sufficiency Questions

Each problem presents a question and two statements, labeled (1) and (2), in which certain data are given. Using your knowledge of mathematics and everyday facts (such as the number of minutes in an hour or the meaning of the word *perpendicular*), decide whether the given data are sufficient to answer the question. Then select one of the answer choices that follow.

Note: When a data sufficiency problem asks for the value of a quantity, the data given are sufficient only when it is possible to determine exactly one numerical value for the quantity.

Also, unless otherwise stated, you can assume all of the following.

- All numbers used are real numbers.
- All figures lie in a plane.
- Lines shown as straight are straight lines, and straight lines might sometimes appear jagged.
- Figures are drawn accurately, but are NOT necessarily drawn to scale.
- All angle measures are greater than zero.
- The relative position of points, angles, and regions are in the order shown.

Data Sufficiency Questions Drill 1

1. A grandson and two granddaughters inherit land from their grandparents. What fraction of the land does the younger granddaughter inherit?

   (1) The grandson inherits $\frac{1}{4}$ of the land.

   (2) The older daughter inherits 50 percent more land than does the younger daughter.

   Ⓐ Statement (1) ALONE is sufficient, but statement (2) alone is not sufficient.

   Ⓑ Statement (2) ALONE is sufficient, but statement (1) alone is not sufficient.

   Ⓒ BOTH statements TOGETHER are sufficient, but NEITHER statement ALONE is sufficient.

   Ⓓ EACH statement ALONE is sufficient.

   Ⓔ Statements (1) and (2) TOGETHER are NOT sufficient.

2. What is the value of the integer n?

   (1) LCM$(n, 50) = 100$

   (2) GCF$(n, 50) = 50$

   Ⓐ Statement (1) ALONE is sufficient, but statement (2) alone is not sufficient.

   Ⓑ Statement (2) ALONE is sufficient, but statement (1) alone is not sufficient.

   Ⓒ BOTH statements TOGETHER are sufficient, but NEITHER statement ALONE is sufficient.

   Ⓓ EACH statement ALONE is sufficient.

   Ⓔ Statements (1) and (2) TOGETHER are NOT sufficient.

3. On a shelf are 55 fiction and nonfiction books. What is the ratio of fiction to nonfiction books on the shelf?

   (1) The number of nonfiction books is 10 more than twice the number of fiction books.

   (2) The total number of books on the shelf is 10 more than three times the number of fiction books.

   Ⓐ Statement (1) ALONE is sufficient, but statement (2) alone is not sufficient.

   Ⓑ Statement (2) ALONE is sufficient, but statement (1) alone is not sufficient.

   Ⓒ BOTH statements TOGETHER are sufficient, but NEITHER statement ALONE is sufficient.

   Ⓓ EACH statement ALONE is sufficient.

   Ⓔ Statements (1) and (2) TOGETHER are NOT sufficient.

4. Among a group of university students, all are either science majors or art majors. How many are art majors?

   (1) The number of science majors is half the number of art majors.
   (2) The number of art majors is $\frac{2}{3}$ the total number of students in the group.

   Ⓐ Statement (1) ALONE is sufficient, but statement (2) alone is not sufficient.
   Ⓑ Statement (2) ALONE is sufficient, but statement (1) alone is not sufficient.
   Ⓒ BOTH statements TOGETHER are sufficient, but NEITHER statement ALONE is sufficient.
   Ⓓ EACH statement ALONE is sufficient.
   Ⓔ Statements (1) and (2) TOGETHER are NOT sufficient.

5. The funds in a retirement account include $300,000 allocated to municipal bonds and oil stocks. What is the amount invested in municipal bonds?

   300,000 - x = 150% x

   (1) The amount invested in oil stocks is 150 percent of the amount invested in municipal bonds.
   (2) The amount invested in municipal bonds is 24% of the total amount in the retirement account.

   Ⓐ Statement (1) ALONE is sufficient, but statement (2) alone is not sufficient.
   Ⓑ Statement (2) ALONE is sufficient, but statement (1) alone is not sufficient.
   Ⓒ BOTH statements TOGETHER are sufficient, but NEITHER statement ALONE is sufficient.
   Ⓓ EACH statement ALONE is sufficient.
   Ⓔ Statements (1) and (2) TOGETHER are NOT sufficient.

6. A thrift shop has a used-book bin in which paperbacks sell for $2 each and hardcover books sell for $5 each. How many paperback books from the used-book bin did the thrift shop sell last week?

   42

   (1) Last week, the number of paperback books sold from the used-book bin was 42 more than twice the number of hardcover books sold from the bin.
   (2) Last week, the thrift shop's sales of paperback books and hardcover books from the used-book bin totaled $309.

   Ⓐ Statement (1) ALONE is sufficient, but statement (2) alone is not sufficient.
   Ⓑ Statement (2) ALONE is sufficient, but statement (1) alone is not sufficient.
   Ⓒ BOTH statements TOGETHER are sufficient, but NEITHER statement ALONE is sufficient.
   Ⓓ EACH statement ALONE is sufficient.
   Ⓔ Statements (1) and (2) TOGETHER are NOT sufficient.

7. If a, b, and c are three consecutive integers (in the order given), what is the value of c?

   (1) $2(a+b+c)=6(a+1)$

   (2) $\dfrac{1}{2}(a+b+c)=a+23$

   Ⓐ Statement (1) ALONE is sufficient, but statement (2) alone is not sufficient.

   Ⓑ Statement (2) ALONE is sufficient, but statement (1) alone is not sufficient.

   Ⓒ BOTH statements TOGETHER are sufficient, but NEITHER statement ALONE is sufficient.

   Ⓓ EACH statement ALONE is sufficient.

   Ⓔ Statements (1) and (2) TOGETHER are NOT sufficient.

8. Gina is twice as old as Oliver. How old will Gina be five years from now? $2x = x$

   (1) Five years ago, Gina was the same age as Oliver will be in five years. $2x+5 = x+5$

   (2) The sum of Gina and Oliver's ages is 30.

   Ⓐ Statement (1) ALONE is sufficient, but statement (2) alone is not sufficient.

   Ⓑ Statement (2) ALONE is sufficient, but statement (1) alone is not sufficient.

   Ⓒ BOTH statements TOGETHER are sufficient, but NEITHER statement ALONE is sufficient.

   Ⓓ EACH statement ALONE is sufficient.

   Ⓔ Statements (1) and (2) TOGETHER are NOT sufficient.

9. What is the value of $|x-2|$?

               $x^2-4(x-12$ $x=-2$

               $(x-6)(x+2)$ $x=+6$

               $x^2\ 2x-6x-12$

   (1) $x^2-4x=12$

   (2) $x<2$

   Ⓐ Statement (1) ALONE is sufficient, but statement (2) alone is not sufficient.

   Ⓑ Statement (2) ALONE is sufficient, but statement (1) alone is not sufficient.

   Ⓒ BOTH statements TOGETHER are sufficient, but NEITHER statement ALONE is sufficient.

   Ⓓ EACH statement ALONE is sufficient.

   Ⓔ Statements (1) and (2) TOGETHER are NOT sufficient.

10. What percent of students at a small community college are male on-campus residents?

   (1) Of the male students at the community college, 10 percent are on-campus residents.

   (2) Of the female students at the community college, 15 percent are on-campus residents.

   Ⓐ Statement (1) ALONE is sufficient, but statement (2) alone is not sufficient.

   Ⓑ Statement (2) ALONE is sufficient, but statement (1) alone is not sufficient.

   Ⓒ BOTH statements TOGETHER are sufficient, but NEITHER statement ALONE is sufficient.

   Ⓓ EACH statement ALONE is sufficient.

   Ⓔ Statements (1) and (2) TOGETHER are NOT sufficient.

11. In triangle *ABC*, what is the measure of angle *A*?

    (1)   Sides $\overline{AB}$ and $\overline{AC}$ are congruent.

    (2)   The measure of angle *C* is 65°.

    (A) Statement (1) ALONE is sufficient, but statement (2) alone is not sufficient.

    (B) Statement (2) ALONE is sufficient, but statement (1) alone is not sufficient.

    (C) BOTH statements TOGETHER are sufficient, but NEITHER statement ALONE is sufficient.

    (D) EACH statement ALONE is sufficient.

    (E) Statements (1) and (2) TOGETHER are NOT sufficient.

12. What is the perimeter of the preceding right triangle with the measure shown?

    (1) $AB = 3.5$

    (2) $AC = 2.8$

    (A) Statement (1) ALONE is sufficient, but statement (2) alone is not sufficient.

    (B) Statement (2) ALONE is sufficient, but statement (1) alone is not sufficient.

    (C) BOTH statements TOGETHER are sufficient, but NEITHER statement ALONE is sufficient.

    (D) EACH statement ALONE is sufficient.

    (E) Statements (1) and (2) TOGETHER are NOT sufficient.

13. Based on the preceding figure, is $XZ > 2(YZ)$?

    (1) $\overline{XY} \cong \overline{YZ}$

    (2) $XZ = 7$

    (A) Statement (1) ALONE is sufficient, but statement (2) alone is not sufficient.

    (B) Statement (2) ALONE is sufficient, but statement (1) alone is not sufficient.

    (C) BOTH statements TOGETHER are sufficient, but NEITHER statement ALONE is sufficient.

    (D) EACH statement ALONE is sufficient.

    (E) Statements (1) and (2) TOGETHER are NOT sufficient.

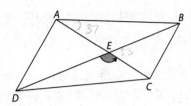

14. In the preceding figure, what is the measure of angle *DEC*?

   (1) $m\angle BAC = 37°$
   (2) $m\angle BEC = 53°$
   Ⓐ Statement (1) ALONE is sufficient, but statement (2) alone is not sufficient.
   Ⓑ Statement (2) ALONE is sufficient, but statement (1) alone is not sufficient.
   Ⓒ BOTH statements TOGETHER are sufficient, but NEITHER statement ALONE is sufficient.
   Ⓓ EACH statement ALONE is sufficient.
   Ⓔ Statements (1) and (2) TOGETHER are NOT sufficient.

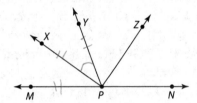

15. In the preceding figure, what is the measure of $\angle XPY$?

   (1) $\overline{PM} \cong \overline{PX}$
   (2) $\overline{PX} \cong \overline{PY}$
   Ⓐ Statement (1) ALONE is sufficient, but statement (2) alone is not sufficient.
   Ⓑ Statement (2) ALONE is sufficient, but statement (1) alone is not sufficient.
   Ⓒ BOTH statements TOGETHER are sufficient, but NEITHER statement ALONE is sufficient.
   Ⓓ EACH statement ALONE is sufficient.
   Ⓔ Statements (1) and (2) TOGETHER are NOT sufficient.

16. On the preceding number line, a point between points *A* and *B* is randomly selected. What is the probability that the point selected is within 2 units of point *P*?

   (1) $AP = 14$
   (2) $PB = 6$
   Ⓐ Statement (1) ALONE is sufficient, but statement (2) alone is not sufficient.
   Ⓑ Statement (2) ALONE is sufficient, but statement (1) alone is not sufficient.
   Ⓒ BOTH statements TOGETHER are sufficient, but NEITHER statement ALONE is sufficient.
   Ⓓ EACH statement ALONE is sufficient.
   Ⓔ Statements (1) and (2) TOGETHER are NOT sufficient.

17. If $x = 6m^2 + 4n^2$, what is the greatest even number that must be a factor of x?

    (1) m and n are even.

    (2)   GCF $(m,n) = 2$

    Ⓐ Statement (1) ALONE is sufficient, but statement (2) alone is not sufficient.

    Ⓑ Statement (2) ALONE is sufficient, but statement (1) alone is not sufficient.

    Ⓒ BOTH statements TOGETHER are sufficient, but NEITHER statement ALONE is sufficient.

    Ⓓ EACH statement ALONE is sufficient.

    Ⓔ Statements (1) and (2) TOGETHER are NOT sufficient.

18. Of the 3,600 full-time and part-time positions at a company, $\frac{1}{x}$ $(x > 0)$ are part-time. If the company reduces the number of part-time positions by $\frac{1}{x}$, how many part-time positions will it eliminate?

    (1) $x^2 = 9$

    (2)   The number of full-time positions at the company is 2,400.

    Ⓐ Statement (1) ALONE is sufficient, but statement (2) alone is not sufficient.

    Ⓑ Statement (2) ALONE is sufficient, but statement (1) alone is not sufficient.

    Ⓒ BOTH statements TOGETHER are sufficient, but NEITHER statement ALONE is sufficient.

    Ⓓ EACH statement ALONE is sufficient.

    Ⓔ Statements (1) and (2) TOGETHER are NOT sufficient.

19. Yael is making a vegan sandwich consisting of one bread type and one bean-based sandwich filling. If she has a choice of x types of bread and y kinds of fillings, how many different sandwich combinations are possible?

    (1) $x + y = 13$

    (2) $xy > x^2$

    Ⓐ Statement (1) ALONE is sufficient, but statement (2) alone is not sufficient.

    Ⓑ Statement (2) ALONE is sufficient, but statement (1) alone is not sufficient.

    Ⓒ BOTH statements TOGETHER are sufficient, but NEITHER statement ALONE is sufficient.

    Ⓓ EACH statement ALONE is sufficient.

    Ⓔ Statements (1) and (2) TOGETHER are NOT sufficient.

20. In a league of x teams, each team plays each of the other teams two times during the season. How many total games are played during the season?

    (1) $x! = 120$

    (2)   There are 10 pairings of the x teams in the league.

    Ⓐ Statement (1) ALONE is sufficient, but statement (2) alone is not sufficient.

    Ⓑ Statement (2) ALONE is sufficient, but statement (1) alone is not sufficient.

    Ⓒ BOTH statements TOGETHER are sufficient, but NEITHER statement ALONE is sufficient.

    Ⓓ EACH statement ALONE is sufficient.

    Ⓔ Statements (1) and (2) TOGETHER are NOT sufficient.

Answers

1. **C** Let x = the portion inherited by the younger granddaughter. From the information in (1), you can determine that the two granddaughters inherit $\frac{3}{4}$ of the land, but further information is needed to determine x, the specific fractional portion inherited by the younger granddaughter; so (1) is NOT sufficient. From the information in (2), you know that $x+(x+50\%x)$ is the portion of the land inherited by the two granddaughters together, but further information is needed to determine x, so (2) alone is NOT sufficient. Taking (1) and (2) together, you can determine from (1) that the two granddaughters inherit $\frac{3}{4}$ of the land, and then using (2), you can write and solve the equation $x+(x+50\%x)=\frac{3}{4}$ for a single value of x. Therefore, BOTH statements together are sufficient, but NEITHER statement ALONE is sufficient.

2. **A** The information in (1) implies that n cannot be 25 or 50, because $\text{LCM}(25, 50)=50$ and $\text{LCM}(50, 50)=50$. Therefore, $n \geq 100$. The multiples of 100 are 100, 200, and so on. The multiples of 50 are 50, 100, 150, and so on. Thus, $n = 100$, because $\text{LCM}(100, 50)=100$. Thus, (1) is sufficient. The information in (2) implies that n could be 50, 150, 200, or some other multiple of 50; however, there is no further way to distinguish n, so (2) is NOT sufficient. Therefore, statement (1) ALONE is sufficient, but statement (2) alone is not sufficient.

3. **D** Let x = the number of fiction books; then $55-x$ = the number of nonfiction books. Then the ratio of fiction books to nonfiction books is $\frac{x}{55-x}$. From the information in (1), you can write the equation $55-x=2x+10$, which you can solve for a single value of x and then compute $\frac{x}{55-x}$. Therefore, (1) is sufficient. From the information in (2), you can write the equation $55=3x+10$, which you can solve for a single value of x and then compute $\frac{x}{55-x}$. Therefore, (2) is sufficient, so EACH statement ALONE is sufficient.

4. **E** Let a = the number of art majors and s = the number of science majors, then $a + s$ = the total number of students in the group. From the information in (1), you can write the equation $s=\frac{1}{2}a$, which (because you have two variables and only one equation) does not yield a single value for a. Therefore, (1) alone is NOT sufficient. From the information in (2), you can write the equation $a=\frac{2}{3}(a+s)$, which (because you have two variables and only one equation) does not yield a single value for a. Therefore, (2) alone is NOT sufficient. Taking (1) and (2) together, you have two equations both of which are equivalent to $s=\frac{1}{2}a$, so you cannot determine a single value for a. Therefore, statements (1) and (2) TOGETHER are NOT sufficient.

5. **A** Let x = the amount, in dollars, invested in municipal bonds; then $\$300,000-x$ = the amount invested in oil stocks. From the information in (1), you can write the equation $\$300,000-x=150\%x$, which you can solve for a single value of x. Therefore, (1) alone is sufficient. Let R = the total amount, in dollars, in the retirement account. From the information in (2), you can write the equation $24\%R=x$, which (because you have two variables and only one equation) does not yield one single value for x. Therefore, (2) alone is NOT sufficient. Statement (1) ALONE is sufficient, but statement (2) alone is not sufficient.

6. **C** Let x = the number of paperback books sold from the used-book bin last week and y = the number of hardcover books sold from the used-book bin last week. From the information in (1), you have the equation $x = 2y + 42$, which (because you have two variables and only one equation) does not yield a single value for x, so (1) is NOT sufficient. From the information in (2), you have the equation $2x + 5y = 309$, which (because you have two variables and only one equation) does not yield a single value for x, so (2) also is NOT sufficient. Taking (1) and (2) together, you have two linear equations and two variables. You can solve the two equations simultaneously for a single value of x. Therefore, BOTH statements TOGETHER are sufficient, but NEITHER statement ALONE is sufficient.

   Tip: Use your time wisely, especially the way that is shown in this question. Don't solve equations or work out computations unless doing so is necessary to help you make the correct answer choice. Stop working! Click your answer choice and move on to the next question.

7. **B** From the question information, you have $b = a + 1$, and $c = a + 2$. You can simplify the information in (1) as $(a + b + c) = 3(a + 1)$, which says the sum of the three integers equals three times the middle integer. This statement is true for any three consecutive integers, so further information is needed, and (1) is NOT sufficient. From the information in (2), you have the equation $\frac{1}{2}[a + (a + 1) + (a + 2)] = a + 23$. You can solve this equation for a single value of a and use that value to obtain $c = a + 2$, so (2) is sufficient. Therefore, statement (2) ALONE is sufficient, but statement (1) alone is not sufficient.

8. **D** Let x = Oliver's age now, $2x$ = Gina's age now, and $2x + 5$ = Gina's age 5 years from now. From the information in (1), you have $2x - 5 = x + 5$. You can solve this equation for a single value of x and use that value to obtain $2x + 5$, Gina's age 5 years from now. Therefore, (1) is sufficient. From the information in (2), you have $x + 2x = 30$. You can solve this equation for a single value of x and use that value to obtain $2x + 5$, Gina's age 5 years from now, so (2) also is sufficient. Therefore, EACH statement ALONE is sufficient.

9. **A** You can rewrite the information in (1) as follows:

$$x^2 - 4x = 12$$
$$x^2 - 4x + 4 = 12 + 4$$
$$(x - 2)^2 = 16$$

This implies that $(x - 2)$ is either 4 or -4, each of which gives the value 4 for $|x - 2|$, so (1) is sufficient. From the information in (2), $x - 2 < 0$, so $|x - 2| = -(x - 2) = -x + 2$, but further information is needed to determine the value of this expression. Therefore, (2) is NOT sufficient. Statement (1) ALONE is sufficient, but statement (2) alone is not sufficient.

10. **E** The information in (1) indicates that 10% of the male students are on-campus residents, but neither the total of male students nor the number of students at the college is known. Thus, further information is needed, and (1) is NOT sufficient. The information in (2) is not helpful. It does not give information as to the total number of students at the college or the number of male on-campus residents, so (2) is NOT sufficient. Taking (1) and (2) together, the percent of men who are on-campus residents and the percent of women who are on-campus residents are known, but further

information (such as the total number of students at the college and the number of male on-campus residents) is needed to determine the percent of students at the college who are male on-campus residents. Therefore, statements (1) and (2) TOGETHER are NOT sufficient.

11. **C** Sketch a figure.

Sketches help you organize the question information, but do not spend unnecessary time making them. They should be quick and rough.

From the question information, $m\angle A + m\angle B + m\angle C = 180°$. From the information in (1), $m\angle C = m\angle B$ (base angles of an isosceles triangle are congruent), but further information is needed to determine the measure of angle A, so (1) is NOT sufficient. From the information in (2), $m\angle A + m\angle B + 65° = 180°$, which (because you have two unknowns and one equation) does not yield a single value for $m\angle A$, so (2) also is NOT sufficient. Taking (1) and (2) together, you can substitute the equation from (1) into the equation from (2) to obtain $m\angle A + 65° + 65° = 180°$, which you can solve for a single value of $m\angle A$. Therefore, BOTH statements TOGETHER are sufficient, but NEITHER statement ALONE is sufficient.

12. **D** From the figure, $BC = 2.1$, and triangle ABC is a right triangle with $\angle C = 90°$. The perimeter, P, of triangle ABC is $P = AB + BC + AC$. From the information in (1), since $\overline{AB}$ is the hypotenuse of right triangle ABC and you know that $BC = 2.1$, you can use the Pythagorean theorem to compute AC and thereafter determine a single value for P. Therefore, (1) is SUFFICIENT. From the information in (2), since $\overline{AC}$ is a leg of right triangle ABC and you know the measure of the other leg ($BC = 2.1$), you can use the Pythagorean theorem to compute AB and thereafter determine a single value for P. Therefore, (2) also is SUFFICIENT. EACH statement ALONE is sufficient.

13. **A** Sketch triangle XZY.

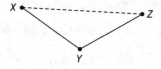

Then by the triangle inequality, $XZ < XY + YZ$. From the information in (1), $XY = YZ$, so substitute YZ for XY in the equation: $XZ < YZ + YZ$, which implies $XZ < 2(YZ)$. Thus, (1) is SUFFICIENT. From the information in (2), $7 < XY + YZ$, but further information is needed to answer the question, so (2) is NOT sufficient. Therefore, statement (1) ALONE is sufficient, but statement (2) alone is not sufficient.

14. **B** From the information in (1), in triangle ABE, $37° + m\angle AEB + m\angle ABE = 180°$. Because $\angle AEB$ and $\angle DEC$ are vertical angles, you can substitute and rearrange to obtain $m\angle DEC = 180° - 37° - m\angle ABE$, which (because you have two unknowns and one equation) does not yield a single value for $m\angle DEC$. Therefore, (1) is NOT sufficient. To

apply the information in (2), notice in the figure that $\angle BEC$ and $\angle DEC$ are supplementary angles. Thus, $m\angle DEC = 180° - 53°$, a single value, and (2) is SUFFICIENT. Therefore, statement (2) ALONE is sufficient, but statement (1) alone is not sufficient.

15. **E** The information in (1) concerns segment lengths of the sides of $\angle MPX$, so by itself it is not useful in finding $m\angle XPY$. Further information about angle measures is needed, and (1) is NOT sufficient. The information in (2) concerns segment lengths of the sides of $\angle XPY$. You can deduce that if you construct triangle PXY, then $m\angle PXY = m\angle PYX$, but without further information about angle measures, you cannot determine $m\angle XPY$. Thus, (2) is NOT sufficient. Taking (1) and (2) together, you have only information about segment lengths. Further information about angle measures is needed to determine $m\angle XPY$. Therefore, statements (1) and (2) TOGETHER are NOT sufficient.

16. **C** (1) Let $x =$ the coordinate of point P and $y =$ the coordinate of point B. Then the probability that the point selected is within 2 units of point P is expressed as follows:

$$\frac{(x+2)-(x-2)}{AB} = \frac{4}{y-(-6)} = \frac{4}{y+6}$$

From the information in (1), you can write the equation $x-(-6) = x+6 = 14$, from which you can determine $x = 8$, but you need further information to determine $AB = y+6$. From the information in (2), you can write the equation $y-x = 6$, which implies $y = x+6$. Substituting into $AB = y+6$ gives $AB = x+6+6 = x+12$, but you need further information to determine $AB = y+6 = x+12$. Taking (1) and (2) together, substitute $x = 8$ into $AB = x+12$. This gives $AB = 8+12 = 20$. Now you have the information to solve the expression for probability: $\frac{4}{AB} = \frac{4}{20} = \frac{1}{5}$. Therefore, BOTH statements together are sufficient, but NEITHER statement ALONE is sufficient.

17. **D** From the information in (1), you know that both m and n have at least one factor of 2, so you can write $m = 2y$ and $n = 2z$. Substitute those terms into the given equation: $x = 6m^2 + 4n^2 = 6(2y)^2 + 4(2z)^2 = 6\cdot 2^2 y^2 + 4\cdot 2^2 z^2 = 2\cdot 3\cdot 2^2 y^2 + 2^2 \cdot 2^2 z^2$. From this expression, you can determine that the greatest even number that must be a factor of x is $2^3 = 8$, so (1) is sufficient. From the information in (2), you know that both m and n have at least one factor of 2, so you can again write $m = 2y$ and $n = 2z$ and find the solution in the same way. Therefore, (2) also is sufficient, and EACH statement ALONE is sufficient.

18. **A** From the information in (1), because the number of part-time positions that are lost is $(3,600)\left(\frac{1}{x}\right)\left(\frac{1}{x}\right) = \frac{3,600}{x^2}$, you have $\frac{3,600}{x^2} = \frac{3,600}{9} = 400$. Therefore, (1) is sufficient. From the information in (2), the number of part-time positions is $3,600 - 2,400 = 1,200$. Thus, the number of part-time positions that are lost is $\left(\frac{1}{x}\right)(1,200)$. Without further information, $\left(\frac{1}{x}\right)(1,200)$ cannot be determined. Therefore, statement (1) ALONE is sufficient, but statement (2) alone is NOT sufficient.

19. **E** The number of possible combinations is xy. The information in (1) tells you that the pair, x and y, is one of a pair of integers that sum to 13. For instance, $x = 1$ and $y = 12$ is such a pair whose product is 12, and $x = 8$ and $y = 5$ is such a pair whose product is 40. Thus, further information is needed to determine a single value of xy, and (1) is NOT sufficient. From the information in (2), you can assume—based on the question information—that x is positive, so you can determine that $y > x$, but you need further

information to determine xy. Therefore, (2) is NOT sufficient. Taking (1) and (2) together, you know from (1) that the pair, x and y, is one of a pair of integers that sum to 13, and from (2) you can narrow the list of those pairs to ones in which $y > x$. For instance, $x = 1$ and $y = 12$ is such a pair whose product is 12, and $x = 2$ and $y = 11$ is such a pair whose product is 22. However, you are unable to determine a single value for xy. Therefore, statements (1) and (2) TOGETHER are NOT sufficient.

20. D To apply (1), recall that $n! = n(n-1)(n-2)\cdots(2)(1)$. Because $5! = 5\cdot4\cdot3\cdot2\cdot1 = 120$, you can determine that $x = 5$. The number of ways to pair 5 teams is five things taken two at a time, which equals $\dbinom{5}{2} = \dfrac{5!}{2!3!} = \dfrac{5\cdot4\cdot\cancel{3!}}{2\cdot1\cdot\cancel{3!}} = 10$. Thus, the total number of games played during the season is $2\cdot10 = 20$. The information in (1) is sufficient. *Tip*: You also can figure out the number of ways to pair 5 teams by designating the teams as A, B, C, D, and E. Then systematically list all of the 10 ways to match the teams two at a time: AB, AC, AD, AE, BC, BD, BE, CD, CE, and DE. From the information in (2), you can determine that the total number of games played during the season is $2\cdot10 = 20$. Therefore, (2) is sufficient, and EACH statement ALONE is sufficient.

Data Sufficiency Questions Drill 2

1. An urn contains 15 marbles, all identical except for color. Each marble is either black, green, or red. What is the probability of drawing a black or red marble when a single marble is drawn at random from the urn?

    (1) The number of red marbles is 2.
    (2) The number of green marbles is 5.
    Ⓐ Statement (1) ALONE is sufficient, but statement (2) alone is not sufficient.
    Ⓑ Statement (2) ALONE is sufficient, but statement (1) alone is not sufficient.
    Ⓒ BOTH statements TOGETHER are sufficient, but NEITHER statement ALONE is sufficient.
    Ⓓ EACH statement ALONE is sufficient.
    Ⓔ Statements (1) and (2) TOGETHER are NOT sufficient.

2. At an appliance store's going-out-of-business sale, 152 customers bought a washer only, a dryer only, or both a washer and a dryer. If 22 customers bought both a washer and a dryer, how many customers bought only a washer?

    (1) Ninety-four customers bought a washer.
    (2) Eighty customers bought a dryer.
    Ⓐ Statement (1) ALONE is sufficient, but statement (2) alone is not sufficient.
    Ⓑ Statement (2) ALONE is sufficient, but statement (1) alone is not sufficient.
    Ⓒ BOTH statements TOGETHER are sufficient, but NEITHER statement ALONE is sufficient.
    Ⓓ EACH statement ALONE is sufficient.
    Ⓔ Statements (1) and (2) TOGETHER are NOT sufficient.

3. In October, the amount Jaime spent on food was $\frac{2}{5}$ of the amount she spent on rent.

    The amount Jaime spent on rent was how many times the average (arithmetic mean) of the total amounts she spent on food and clothing?

    (1) The amount she spent on clothing was $\frac{1}{4}$ of the amount she spent on food.

    (2) The amount she spent on rent was 250% of the amount she spent on food.
    Ⓐ Statement (1) ALONE is sufficient, but statement (2) alone is not sufficient.
    Ⓑ Statement (2) ALONE is sufficient, but statement (1) alone is not sufficient.
    Ⓒ BOTH statements TOGETHER are sufficient, but NEITHER statement ALONE is sufficient.
    Ⓓ EACH statement ALONE is sufficient.
    Ⓔ Statements (1) and (2) TOGETHER are NOT sufficient.

4. The square of integer m is 20 more than the square of integer n. What is the value of $m - n$?
   (1) $n^2 = 16$
   (2) $m^2 = 36$

   (A) Statement (1) ALONE is sufficient, but statement (2) alone is not sufficient.
   (B) Statement (2) ALONE is sufficient, but statement (1) alone is not sufficient.
   (C) BOTH statements TOGETHER are sufficient, but NEITHER statement ALONE is sufficient.
   (D) EACH statement ALONE is sufficient.
   (E) Statements (1) and (2) TOGETHER are NOT sufficient.

5. The sale price of a jacket was $125. After the sale, the price increased. What is the percent increase over the sale price?
   (1) The original price was $156.25.
   (2) The sale price increased by $25.

   (A) Statement (1) ALONE is sufficient, but statement (2) alone is not sufficient.
   (B) Statement (2) ALONE is sufficient, but statement (1) alone is not sufficient.
   (C) BOTH statements TOGETHER are sufficient, but NEITHER statement ALONE is sufficient.
   (D) EACH statement ALONE is sufficient.
   (E) Statements (1) and (2) TOGETHER are NOT sufficient.

6. The sum of two numbers is 20. What is the value of the larger number?
   (1) The product of the two numbers is 96.
   (2) The larger number is 20 minus the smaller number.

   (A) Statement (1) ALONE is sufficient, but statement (2) alone is not sufficient.
   (B) Statement (2) ALONE is sufficient, but statement (1) alone is not sufficient.
   (C) BOTH statements TOGETHER are sufficient, but NEITHER statement ALONE is sufficient.
   (D) EACH statement ALONE is sufficient.
   (E) Statements (1) and (2) TOGETHER are NOT sufficient.

7. Myla has only dimes and quarters in a coin bank. How many dimes are in the coin bank?
   (1) There are 33 coins altogether.
   (2) The face value of the coins is $4.35.

   (A) Statement (1) ALONE is sufficient, but statement (2) alone is not sufficient.
   (B) Statement (2) ALONE is sufficient, but statement (1) alone is not sufficient.
   (C) BOTH statements TOGETHER are sufficient, but NEITHER statement ALONE is sufficient.
   (D) EACH statement ALONE is sufficient.
   (E) Statements (1) and (2) TOGETHER are NOT sufficient.

8. If b, c, and h are constants and $x^2 + bx + c = (x + h)^2$, what is the value of c?

    (1) $h = 5$

    (2) $b = 10$

    Ⓐ Statement (1) ALONE is sufficient, but statement (2) alone is not sufficient.

    Ⓑ Statement (2) ALONE is sufficient, but statement (1) alone is not sufficient.

    Ⓒ BOTH statements TOGETHER are sufficient, but NEITHER statement ALONE is sufficient.

    Ⓓ EACH statement ALONE is sufficient.

    Ⓔ Statements (1) and (2) TOGETHER are NOT sufficient.

9. Working alone, Dylan can paint a room in 3 hours. How many hours does Drake, working alone, take to paint the room?

    (1)   The time needed for Drake painting alone is 48 minutes longer than for Dylan and Drake painting the room together.

    (2)   Working together, Dylan and Drake can paint the room in 1 hour 12 minutes.

    Ⓐ Statement (1) ALONE is sufficient, but statement (2) alone is not sufficient.

    Ⓑ Statement (2) ALONE is sufficient, but statement (1) alone is not sufficient.

    Ⓒ BOTH statements TOGETHER are sufficient, but NEITHER statement ALONE is sufficient.

    Ⓓ EACH statement ALONE is sufficient.

    Ⓔ Statements (1) and (2) TOGETHER are NOT sufficient.

10. The majority of the science majors at a small college are freshmen and sophomores, while the remainder are juniors and seniors. What fraction of the science majors are seniors?

    (1)   Seven-twelfths of the science majors are freshmen and sophomores.

    (2)   The total number of junior and senior science majors is 150.

    Ⓐ Statement (1) ALONE is sufficient, but statement (2) alone is not sufficient.

    Ⓑ Statement (2) ALONE is sufficient, but statement (1) alone is not sufficient.

    Ⓒ BOTH statements TOGETHER are sufficient, but NEITHER statement ALONE is sufficient.

    Ⓓ EACH statement ALONE is sufficient.

    Ⓔ Statements (1) and (2) TOGETHER are NOT sufficient.

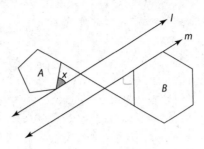
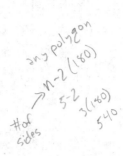

11. In the preceding figure, what is the measure of ∠x?

    (1)   Lines *l* and *m* are parallel.

    (2)   *A* and *B* are regular polygons.

    Ⓐ Statement (1) ALONE is sufficient, but statement (2) alone is not sufficient.

    Ⓑ Statement (2) ALONE is sufficient, but statement (1) alone is not sufficient.

    Ⓒ BOTH statements TOGETHER are sufficient, but NEITHER statement ALONE is sufficient.

    Ⓓ EACH statement ALONE is sufficient.

    Ⓔ Statements (1) and (2) TOGETHER are NOT sufficient.

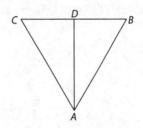

12. In the preceding figure, is △*ABD* ≅ △*ACD*?

    (1) $\overline{AC} \cong \overline{AB}$

    (2)   ∠*C* ≅ ∠*B*

    Ⓐ Statement (1) ALONE is sufficient, but statement (2) alone is not sufficient.

    Ⓑ Statement (2) ALONE is sufficient, but statement (1) alone is not sufficient.

    Ⓒ BOTH statements TOGETHER are sufficient, but NEITHER statement ALONE is sufficient.

    Ⓓ EACH statement ALONE is sufficient.

    Ⓔ Statements (1) and (2) TOGETHER are NOT sufficient.

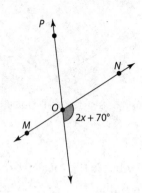

13. In the preceding figure, what is the degree measure of *x*?

(1) $m\angle PON = 65°$
(2) $m\angle POM = 115°$

Ⓐ Statement (1) ALONE is sufficient, but statement (2) alone is not sufficient.
Ⓑ Statement (2) ALONE is sufficient, but statement (1) alone is not sufficient.
Ⓒ BOTH statements TOGETHER are sufficient, but NEITHER statement ALONE is sufficient.
Ⓓ EACH statement ALONE is sufficient.
Ⓔ Statements (1) and (2) TOGETHER are NOT sufficient.

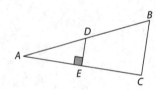

14. In the preceding figure, is triangle *ABC* similar to triangle *ADE*?

(1) Angle *C* is a right angle.
(2) *D* is the midpoint of $\overline{AB}$.

Ⓐ Statement (1) ALONE is sufficient, but statement (2) alone is not sufficient.
Ⓑ Statement (2) ALONE is sufficient, but statement (1) alone is not sufficient.
Ⓒ BOTH statements TOGETHER are sufficient, but NEITHER statement ALONE is sufficient.
Ⓓ EACH statement ALONE is sufficient.
Ⓔ Statements (1) and (2) TOGETHER are NOT sufficient.

15. Given triangle *PQR* and triangle *XYZ* such that $\dfrac{PQ}{XY} = \dfrac{QR}{YZ}$, are triangles *PQR* and *XYZ* similar?

(1) $\angle R \cong \angle Z$
(2) $\angle Q \cong \angle Y$

Ⓐ Statement (1) ALONE is sufficient, but statement (2) alone is not sufficient.
Ⓑ Statement (2) ALONE is sufficient, but statement (1) alone is not sufficient.
Ⓒ BOTH statements TOGETHER are sufficient, but NEITHER statement ALONE is sufficient.
Ⓓ EACH statement ALONE is sufficient.
Ⓔ Statements (1) and (2) TOGETHER are NOT sufficient.

16. If $g(x)$ is in the domain of f, what is the value of $f(g(-1))$?
    (1) $f = \{(-1, 2), (1, 5), (3, -4)\}$
    (2) $g = \{(-4, 2), (-1, 3), (4, -4)\}$
    (A) Statement (1) ALONE is sufficient, but statement (2) alone is not sufficient.
    (B) Statement (2) ALONE is sufficient, but statement (1) alone is not sufficient.
    (C) BOTH statements TOGETHER are sufficient, but NEITHER statement ALONE is sufficient.
    (D) EACH statement ALONE is sufficient.
    (E) Statements (1) and (2) TOGETHER are NOT sufficient.

17. A **vertical asymptote** is a vertical line that corresponds to a value for the variable that produces zero in the denominator of a simplified rational function. At what value of x does the graph of the function $y = \dfrac{(x-a)^2(x+b)}{(x-a)^3(x+b)}$ have a vertical asymptote?
    (1) $a = 2$
    (2) $b = -3$
    (A) Statement (1) ALONE is sufficient, but statement (2) alone is not sufficient.
    (B) Statement (2) ALONE is sufficient, but statement (1) alone is not sufficient.
    (C) BOTH statements TOGETHER are sufficient, but NEITHER statement ALONE is sufficient.
    (D) EACH statement ALONE is sufficient.
    (E) Statements (1) and (2) TOGETHER are NOT sufficient.

18. What is the value of $f(3)$?
    (1) $f(n) = 2f(n-1) + f(n-2)$, for $n \geq 3$
    (2) $f(2) = 2$
    (A) Statement (1) ALONE is sufficient, but statement (2) alone is not sufficient.
    (B) Statement (2) ALONE is sufficient, but statement (1) alone is not sufficient.
    (C) BOTH statements TOGETHER are sufficient, but NEITHER statement ALONE is sufficient.
    (D) EACH statement ALONE is sufficient.
    (E) Statements (1) and (2) TOGETHER are NOT sufficient.

19. For a and b, both positive numbers, what is the value of x if $\sqrt{x^2 + b} = x + a$?
    (1) $a = \sqrt{b}$
    (2) $\dfrac{b}{a} = a$
    (A) Statement (1) ALONE is sufficient, but statement (2) alone is not sufficient.
    (B) Statement (2) ALONE is sufficient, but statement (1) alone is not sufficient.
    (C) BOTH statements TOGETHER are sufficient, but NEITHER statement ALONE is sufficient.
    (D) EACH statement ALONE is sufficient.
    (E) Statements (1) and (2) TOGETHER are NOT sufficient.

20. If all of the fans at the game are either home-team fans or visiting-team fans, how many of the 6,000 fans at the game are home-team fans?

    (1)   Twenty percent of the fans at the game are from out of town.

    (2)   The home-team fans outnumber the visiting-team fans by 540.

    Ⓐ Statement (1) ALONE is sufficient, but statement (2) alone is not sufficient.

    Ⓑ Statement (2) ALONE is sufficient, but statement (1) alone is not sufficient.

    Ⓒ BOTH statements TOGETHER are sufficient, but NEITHER statement ALONE is sufficient.

    Ⓓ EACH statement ALONE is sufficient.

    Ⓔ Statements (1) and (2) TOGETHER are NOT sufficient.

Answers

1. **B** Let x = the number of black marbles, y = the number of green marbles, and z = the number of red marbles. The probability of drawing a black or red marble is $\frac{x+z}{15}$. *Tip*: Notice that to determine the solution, you do not need the specific values of x and z, only their sum, $x+z$. From the information in (1), $\frac{x+z}{15} = \frac{x+2}{15}$, but you cannot compute the probability without knowing x. Therefore, (1) is NOT sufficient. From the information in (2), $15 = x+y+z = x+5+z$, from which you can reason that $x+z = 15-5 = 10$. Then you can substitute $x+z = 10$ into $\frac{x+z}{15}$ to obtain $\frac{10}{15} = \frac{2}{3}$. Therefore, (2) is sufficient. Statement (2) ALONE is sufficient, but statement (1) alone is not sufficient.

2. **D** Let x = the number of customers who bought only a washer. Draw a Venn diagram, using the question information.

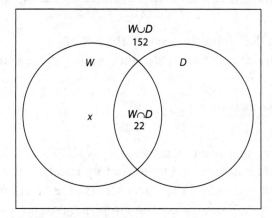

From the information in (1), you can write the equation $94 = x+22$, which you can solve for a single value of x. Therefore, (1) is sufficient. From the information in (2), you can write the equation $x+80 = 152$, which you can solve for a single value of x. Therefore, (2) also is sufficient. EACH statement ALONE is sufficient.

3. **A** Let r = the amount spent on rent, f = the amount spent on food $= \frac{2}{5}r$, and c = the amount spent on clothing. Then the average of the total amounts spent on food and clothing is $\frac{f+c}{2}$. From the question information and the information in

(1), $c = \frac{1}{4}f = \frac{1}{4} \cdot \frac{2}{5}r = \frac{1}{10}r$. Then, $\frac{f+c}{2} = \frac{1}{2}(f+c) = \frac{1}{2}\left(\frac{2}{5}r + \frac{1}{10}r\right) = \frac{1}{2}\left(\frac{4}{10}r + \frac{1}{10}r\right) = \frac{1}{2}\left(\frac{5}{10}r\right) = \frac{1}{2}\left(\frac{1}{2}r\right) = \frac{1}{4}r$. This result implies that r equals 4 times $\frac{f+c}{2}$, the average of the

amounts spent on food and clothing. Therefore, (1) is sufficient. From the information in (2), you can write the equation $r = 250\% f = \dfrac{5}{2} f$, which is equivalent to $f = \dfrac{2}{5} r$, information provided in the question, so (2) is not helpful. In other words, (2) is not sufficient. Therefore, statement (1) ALONE is sufficient, but statement (2) alone is not sufficient.

4. **E** From the question information, $m^2 = n^2 + 20$. From the information in (1), you can determine that $n = \pm 4$ and $m = \pm 6$ (because $m^2 = 16 + 20 = 36$). Thus, the difference $m - n$ could be $-10, -2, 2,$ or 10, *not* one single value; (1) is NOT sufficient. The information in (2) implies that $m = \pm 6$ and $n = \pm 4$ (because $36 = n^2 + 20$, $n^2 = 16$). Thus, the difference $m - n$ could be $-10, -2, 2,$ or 10, *not* one single value; (2) is NOT sufficient. Taking (1) and (2) together, you still know only that $n = \pm 4$ and $m = \pm 6$, so again the difference could be $-10, -2, 2,$ or 10, not one single value. Therefore, statements (1) and (2) TOGETHER are NOT sufficient.

5. **B** To determine the percent increase over the sale price, you need to compute the following expression:

$$\frac{\text{Amount the sale price increased}}{\text{Sale price}} \cdot 100\% = \frac{\text{Amount the sale price increased}}{\$125} \cdot 100\%$$

From the information in (1), you cannot determine the amount the sale price increased, so (1) is NOT sufficient. With the information in (2), you are given the amount the sale price increased:

$$\frac{\text{Amount the sale price increased}}{\$125} \cdot 100\% = \frac{\$25}{\$125} \cdot 100\%$$

From this information, you can compute the percent increase, so (2) is SUFFICIENT. Thus, statement (2) ALONE is sufficient, but statement (1) alone is not sufficient.

6. **A** Let $x =$ the larger number and $y =$ the other number. Then, according to the question, $x + y = 20$. From the information in (1), $xy = 96$. From the question information, you can determine that $y = 20 - x$. Substituting from this equation into $xy = 96$ gives $x(20 - x) = 96$, which you can solve as follows:

$$x(20 - x) = 96$$
$$20x - x^2 = 96$$
$$x^2 - 20x + 96 = 0$$
$$(x - 8)(x - 12) = 0$$

Thus, $x = 8$ with $y = 12$ (reject because x is the larger number) or $x = 12$ with $y = 8$. Thus, 12 is the larger number, and (1) is sufficient. From the information in (2), $x = 20 - y$, which is equivalent to $x + y = 20$. Thus, additional information is needed, and (2) is NOT sufficient. Therefore, statement (1) ALONE is sufficient, but statement (2) alone is not sufficient.

When you have two variables and two linear equations, make sure that the two equations are distinct equations; otherwise, you will be unable to obtain a single value as an answer. Usually, you can use visual inspection to check the two equations.

7. **C** Let d = the number of dimes in the coin bank and q = the number of quarters in the coin bank. From the information in (1), $d + q = 33$, which (because you have two variables and only one equation) does not yield a single value for d. Therefore, (1) is NOT sufficient. From the information in (2), $\$0.10d + \$0.25q = \$4.35$, which (because you have two variables and only one equation) does not yield a single value for d. Therefore, (2) also is NOT sufficient. Taking (1) and (2) together, you have two linear equations and two variables. You can solve the two equations simultaneously for a single value of d. Therefore, BOTH statements TOGETHER are sufficient, but NEITHER statement ALONE is sufficient.

8. **D** First, $x^2 + bx + c = (x+h)^2$ implies that $x^2 + bx + c = x^2 + 2hx + h^2$, and hence $b = 2h$ and $c = h^2$ (because corresponding coefficients are equal). From the information in (1), $c = h^2 = 5^2$, so (1) is sufficient. From the information in (2), because $b = 2h$, $10 = 2h$, which implies that $h = 5$ and $c = h^2 = 5^2$. Thus, (2) is sufficient. Therefore, EACH statement ALONE is sufficient.

9. **D** Let x = the time, in hours, it takes Drake to paint the room working alone and t = the time, in hours, it takes Dylan and Drake to paint the room together. From the information in (1), and given that 48 minutes = 0.8 hour, $x = t + 0.8$ hour, which implies $t = x - 0.8$ hour. According to the question information, Dylan's room-painting rate is $\frac{1}{3}$ of the room per hour. Drake's room-painting rate is $\frac{1}{x}$ of the room per hour. Thus, you can write the equation $\frac{1}{x}(x - 0.8) + \frac{1}{3}(x - 0.8) = 1$ room. This equation is equivalent to the quadratic equation $x^2 - 0.8x - 2.4 = 0$. Because x must be positive, you can solve this equation for a single value of x. Thus, (1) is SUFFICIENT. From the information in (2), given that 12 minutes = 0.2 hour, $t = 1.2$ hours. According to the question information, Dylan's room-painting rate is $\frac{1}{3}$ of the room per hour. Drake's room-painting rate is $\frac{1}{x}$ of the room per hour. Thus, you can write the equation $\frac{1}{x}(1.2) + \frac{1}{3}(1.2) = 1$ room, which you can solve for a single value of x. So, statement (2) is sufficient. Therefore, EACH statement ALONE is sufficient.

10. **E** From the information in (1), you can determine that $\frac{5}{12}$ of the science majors are juniors and seniors, but neither the total number of science majors nor the total number of senior science majors is known. Therefore, (1) is NOT sufficient. The information in (2) gives you the total number of junior and senior science majors, but neither the total number of science majors nor the total number of senior science majors is known. Therefore, (2) is NOT sufficient. Taking (1) and (2) together and letting x = the total number of science majors, you have $\frac{5}{12}x = 150$, from which you can determine x, the total number of science majors. However, the number of seniors who are science majors is still unknown. Therefore, statements (1) and (2) TOGETHER are NOT sufficient.

11. **C** From the figure, polygon A is a pentagon, and polygon B is a hexagon. You can compute the sum of the measures of the interior angles of each of these polygons by using the formula $(n-2)180°$, where n is the number of sides. Thus, the sum of the measures of the interior angles of polygon A is $(5-2)180° = 3 \cdot 180° = 540°$, and of polygon B is $(6-2)180° = 4 \cdot 180 = 720°$. To organize the angle information in this question, label relevant angles in the figure.

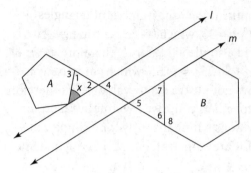

To use the information in (1), knowing that lines *l* and *m* are parallel will allow you to identify congruent angles of parallel lines cut by a transversal, but without information about the measures of individual angles in the figure, you cannot determine $m\angle x$. Therefore, (1) is NOT sufficient. To apply the information in (2), remember that in a regular polygon, all interior angles are congruent. Thus, $m\angle 3 = \dfrac{540°}{5} = 108°$, and $m\angle 8 = \dfrac{720°}{6} = 120°$. From the figure, $\angle 1$ and $\angle 3$ are supplementary, so $m\angle 1 = 180° - 108° = 72°$. Also, $m\angle x + m\angle 1 + m\angle 2 = 180°$, which implies that $m\angle x + 72° + m\angle 2 = 180°$, but without knowing $m\angle 2$, you cannot determine $m\angle x$, so (2) also is NOT sufficient. Taking (1) and (2) together, $\angle 6$ and $\angle 7$ are each supplementary with an interior angle of polygon *B*. Thus, $m\angle 6 = m\angle 7 = 180° - 120° = 60°$. Hence, $m\angle 5 = 180° - 2 \cdot 60° = 60°$ (because the sum of the angles of a triangle is $180°$). Then $m\angle 4 = m\angle 5 = 60°$ (corresponding angles of parallel lines are congruent). Also, $m\angle 4 = m\angle 2 = 60°$ (vertical angles are congruent), from which you can determine a single value of $m\angle x$ with the following equation: $m\angle x + 72° + m\angle 2 = m\angle x + 72° + 60° = 180°$. Therefore, BOTH statements TOGETHER are sufficient, but NEITHER statement ALONE is sufficient.

12. **E** As you work through this question, recall Side-Side-Side (SSS), Side-Angle-Side (SAS), Angle-Side-Angle (ASA), and Angle-Angle-Side (AAS) as the four ways to show that two triangles are congruent. From the figure, you can see that $\overline{AD}$ is a common side in the two triangles. From the information in (1), and the common side, $\overline{AD}$, you have two pairs of corresponding sides congruent to each other. Without further information confirming congruency between the included angles or between the other pair of corresponding sides, you cannot establish congruence, so (1) is NOT sufficient. From the information in (2), you have a pair of corresponding angles congruent to each other. Without further information, you cannot establish congruence, so (2) also is NOT sufficient. Taking (1) and (2) together, two pairs of corresponding sides are congruent and the pair of corresponding nonincluded angles are congruent. You need further information that either the pair of included angles are congruent (SAS) or that the third pair of corresponding sides are congruent (SSS). Therefore, statements (1) and (2) TOGETHER are NOT sufficient. *Tip*: Side-Side-Angle (SSA) does not guarantee congruence.

13. **D** From the information in (1), and the figure showing $\angle PON$ and angle $(2x + 70°)$ are supplementary, $m\angle PON + (2x + 70°) = 65° + (2x + 70°) = 180°$. You can solve this equation to determine a single value of *x*, so (1) is SUFFICIENT. From the information in (2), and the figure showing $\angle POM$ and angle $(2x + 70°)$ are vertical angles, $m\angle POM = 115° = (2x + 70°)$. You can solve this equation to determine a single value of *x*, so (2) also is SUFFICIENT. Therefore, EACH statement ALONE is sufficient.

14. **A** From the information in (1), $\angle A$ is a common angle in the two right triangles *ABC* and *ADE*. Thus, the two triangles are similar (because corresponding angles are congruent), so (1) is SUFFICIENT. From the information in (2), a pair of corresponding sides, $\overline{AB}$ and $\overline{AD}$, are proportional in the ratio 2:1. Also, $\angle A$ is common to both triangles. The two triangles would be similar if $\overline{AC}$ and $\overline{AE}$ could be shown to be proportional in the ratio 2:1, but further information is needed to establish that relationship, so (2) is NOT sufficient. Therefore, statement (1) ALONE is sufficient, but statement (2) alone is not sufficient.

15. **B** Sketch a figure.

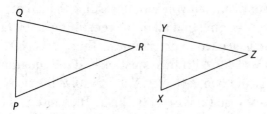

From the question information, in triangles *PQR* and *XYZ*, two pairs of corresponding sides are proportional. From the information in (1), $\angle R \cong \angle Z$, but $\angle R$ and $\angle Z$ are not the included angles between the two pairs of corresponding proportional sides. Further information is needed to establish similarity, so (1) is NOT sufficient. From the information in (2), you have that two pairs of corresponding sides are proportional, and the included angles are congruent, so triangles *PQR* and *XYZ* are similar, and (2) is SUFFICIENT. Statement (2) ALONE is sufficient, but statement (1) alone is not sufficient.

16. **C** From the information in (1), the possible values for $f\left(g(-1)\right)$ are -4, 2, or 5. This solution is not a single value, so (1) is NOT sufficient. From the information in (2), $f\left(g(-1)\right) = f(3)$, but further information is needed to determine $f(3)$. Therefore, (2) is NOT sufficient. Taking (1) and (2) together, from (2), you can determine that $f\left(g(-1)\right) = f(3)$, and from (1), you can determine that $f(3) = -4$. Therefore, BOTH statements TOGETHER are sufficient, but NEITHER statement ALONE is sufficient.

17. **A** Observe that in simplified form, $y = \dfrac{(x-a)^2(x+b)}{(x-a)^3(x+b)} = \dfrac{1}{x-a}$, which will have a vertical asymptote when $x - a = 0$, that is, when $x = a$. From the information in (1), $y = \dfrac{(x-a)^2(x+b)}{(x-a)^3(x+b)} = \dfrac{1}{x-a}$ will have a vertical asymptote at $x = 2$, so (1) is SUFFICIENT. The information in (2) is irrelevant to the determination of vertical asymptotes of $y = \dfrac{(x-a)^2(x+b)}{(x-a)^3(x+b)} = \dfrac{1}{x-a}$, so it is NOT sufficient. Therefore, statement (1) ALONE is sufficient, but statement (2) alone is not sufficient.

18. **E** From the information in (1), $f(3) = 2f(2) + f(1)$. However, without knowing the values of $f(2)$ and $f(1)$, you cannot determine the value of $f(3)$, so (1) is NOT sufficient. From the information in (2) and without further information, the value of $f(3)$ cannot be determined, so (2) is NOT sufficient. Taking (1) and (2) together, $f(3) = 2f(2) + f(1) = f(3) = 2 \cdot 2 + f(1) = 4 + f(1)$. However, without knowing the value of $f(1)$, you cannot determine the value of $f(3)$. Therefore, statements (1) and (2) TOGETHER are NOT sufficient.

19. **D** From the information in (1), $\sqrt{x^2+b}=x+\sqrt{b}$. Squaring both sides of this equation yields $x^2+b=x^2+2x\sqrt{b}+b$, from which you can obtain $0=2x\sqrt{b}$. Because $b>0$, this equation implies that $x=0$. Therefore, (1) is <u>SUFFICIENT</u>. From the information in (2), $b=a^2$, so after substituting, you have $\sqrt{x^2+a^2}=x+a$. Squaring both sides of this equation yields $x^2+a^2=x^2+2ax+a^2$, from which you can obtain $0=2ax$. Because $a>0$, this equation implies that $x=0$. Therefore, (2) also is SUFFICIENT. EACH statement ALONE is sufficient.

20. **B** Let $x=$ the number of home-team fans and $y=$ the number of visiting-team fans. Then from the question information, $x+y=6{,}000$. From the information in (1), you know that $20\%\,(6{,}000)=1{,}200$ fans are from out of town, but you cannot assume that all of these fans are visiting-team fans, nor can you assume that all of the remaining 4,800 fans are home-team fans, so further information is needed to determine x. Thus, (1) is NOT sufficient. From the information in (2), $x=y+540$. With this equation and the equation $x+y=6{,}000$, you have two linear equations and two variables. You can solve the two equations simultaneously for a single value of x, so (2) is SUFFICIENT. Therefore, statement (2) ALONE is sufficient, but statement (1) alone is not sufficient.

Data Sufficiency Questions Drill 3

1. Given m and n are positive integers such that $\dfrac{m}{n} = x$, then is 5 the remainder when m is divided by n?

   (1) $m = 85$
   (2) $x = 4.25$
   Ⓐ Statement (1) ALONE is sufficient, but statement (2) alone is not sufficient.
   Ⓑ Statement (2) ALONE is sufficient, but statement (1) alone is not sufficient.
   Ⓒ BOTH statements TOGETHER are sufficient, but NEITHER statement ALONE is sufficient.
   Ⓓ EACH statement ALONE is sufficient.
   Ⓔ Statements (1) and (2) TOGETHER are NOT sufficient.

2. A chemist is making an alloy of tin and copper. How many total grams are in the alloy?

   (1) The ratio of tin to copper in the alloy is 1 to 4.
   (2) The number of grams of copper in the alloy is 36.
   Ⓐ Statement (1) ALONE is sufficient, but statement (2) alone is not sufficient.
   Ⓑ Statement (2) ALONE is sufficient, but statement (1) alone is not sufficient.
   Ⓒ BOTH statements TOGETHER are sufficient, but NEITHER statement ALONE is sufficient.
   Ⓓ EACH statement ALONE is sufficient.
   Ⓔ Statements (1) and (2) TOGETHER are NOT sufficient.

3. A pet store specializes in selling Scottish terrier dogs. Does the pet store have a greater number of male Scottish terriers?

   (1) The number of male Scottish terriers is less than 2 times the number of female Scottish terriers.
   (2) One-fourth of the number of female Scottish terriers is less than the number of male Scottish terriers.
   Ⓐ Statement (1) ALONE is sufficient, but statement (2) alone is not sufficient.
   Ⓑ Statement (2) ALONE is sufficient, but statement (1) alone is not sufficient.
   Ⓒ BOTH statements TOGETHER are sufficient, but NEITHER statement ALONE is sufficient.
   Ⓓ EACH statement ALONE is sufficient.
   Ⓔ Statements (1) and (2) TOGETHER are NOT sufficient.

4. If $x = \sqrt{\dfrac{m^2}{81}}$, what is the value of $\sqrt{x}$?

   (1) $m = -4$

   (2) m is an even integer such that $|m| < 5$.

   Ⓐ Statement (1) ALONE is sufficient, but statement (2) alone is not sufficient.

   Ⓑ Statement (2) ALONE is sufficient, but statement (1) alone is not sufficient.

   Ⓒ BOTH statements TOGETHER are sufficient, but NEITHER statement ALONE is sufficient.

   Ⓓ EACH statement ALONE is sufficient.

   Ⓔ Statements (1) and (2) TOGETHER are NOT sufficient.

5. The parents of a newborn child allocated $20,000 of their savings to an investment that earns annual interest, compounded monthly. If there were no other transactions in the investment account, what is the amount of money (to the nearest cent) in the account 6 months after the account is opened? The compound-interest formula is $A = P\left(1 + \dfrac{r}{n}\right)^{nt}$, where A is the amount accumulated, P is the initial investment, r is the annual rate, n is the number of times interest is compounded per year, and nt is the total number of compounding periods.

   (1) The monthly rate on the investment is 0.0625%.

   (2) The annual rate, compounded monthly, on the investment is 0.75%.

   Ⓐ Statement (1) ALONE is sufficient, but statement (2) alone is not sufficient.

   Ⓑ Statement (2) ALONE is sufficient, but statement (1) alone is not sufficient.

   Ⓒ BOTH statements TOGETHER are sufficient, but NEITHER statement ALONE is sufficient.

   Ⓓ EACH statement ALONE is sufficient.

   Ⓔ Statements (1) and (2) TOGETHER are NOT sufficient.

6. If x and y are integers, is $\sqrt[5]{x + y^3}$ an integer?

   (1) $x = 24$

   (2) $x = y^3\left(y^2 - 1\right)$

   Ⓐ Statement (1) ALONE is sufficient, but statement (2) alone is not sufficient.

   Ⓑ Statement (2) ALONE is sufficient, but statement (1) alone is not sufficient.

   Ⓒ BOTH statements TOGETHER are sufficient, but NEITHER statement ALONE is sufficient.

   Ⓓ EACH statement ALONE is sufficient.

   Ⓔ Statements (1) and (2) TOGETHER are NOT sufficient.

7. A sales clerk in a computer store earns a 1% commission on all computer and accessory sales that the clerk makes. Last week, what were the clerk's total sales?

   (1) Last week, the clerk sold two $399 laptop computers and one $249 notebook computer. The clerk also sold suitable accessories to go along with these sales.
   (2) Last week, the clerk earned $13.72 in commission.
   (A) Statement (1) ALONE is sufficient, but statement (2) alone is not sufficient.
   (B) Statement (2) ALONE is sufficient, but statement (1) alone is not sufficient.
   (C) BOTH statements TOGETHER are sufficient, but NEITHER statement ALONE is sufficient.
   (D) EACH statement ALONE is sufficient.
   (E) Statements (1) and (2) TOGETHER are NOT sufficient.

8. Is $x < 0$?

   (1) $-\left(\dfrac{1}{2}x+1\right) > 0$

   (2) $x^5 + 3 < 0$
   (A) Statement (1) ALONE is sufficient, but statement (2) alone is not sufficient.
   (B) Statement (2) ALONE is sufficient, but statement (1) alone is not sufficient.
   (C) BOTH statements TOGETHER are sufficient, but NEITHER statement ALONE is sufficient.
   (D) EACH statement ALONE is sufficient.
   (E) Statements (1) and (2) TOGETHER are NOT sufficient.

9. Does $5x - 2y = 0$?

   (1) $\dfrac{x}{y} = 0.4$
   (2) $x - y < 0$
   (A) Statement (1) ALONE is sufficient, but statement (2) alone is not sufficient.
   (B) Statement (2) ALONE is sufficient, but statement (1) alone is not sufficient.
   (C) BOTH statements TOGETHER are sufficient, but NEITHER statement ALONE is sufficient.
   (D) EACH statement ALONE is sufficient.
   (E) Statements (1) and (2) TOGETHER are NOT sufficient.

10. What is the perimeter of the rectangle?

    (1) The length of the rectangle is 3 meters more than its width.
    (2) The perimeter of the rectangle is 6 meters less than 4 times its length.
    (A) Statement (1) ALONE is sufficient, but statement (2) alone is not sufficient.
    (B) Statement (2) ALONE is sufficient, but statement (1) alone is not sufficient.
    (C) BOTH statements TOGETHER are sufficient, but NEITHER statement ALONE is sufficient.
    (D) EACH statement ALONE is sufficient.
    (E) Statements (1) and (2) TOGETHER are NOT sufficient.

$2(3x) + 2(x)$

$6x + 2x$

$8x$

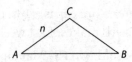

11. In △*ABC*, is *n* less than 7?

   (1)   ∠*A* ≅ ∠*B*
   (2)   *AB* = 15
   Ⓐ Statement (1) ALONE is sufficient, but statement (2) alone is not sufficient.
   Ⓑ Statement (2) ALONE is sufficient, but statement (1) alone is not sufficient.
   Ⓒ BOTH statements TOGETHER are sufficient, but NEITHER statement ALONE is sufficient.
   Ⓓ EACH statement ALONE is sufficient.
   Ⓔ Statements (1) and (2) TOGETHER are NOT sufficient.

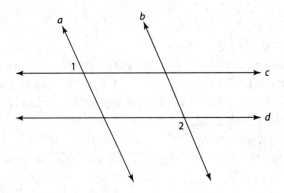

12. In the preceding figure, what is the measure of ∠2?

   (1) $c \parallel d$
   (2) $m\angle 1 = 70°$
   Ⓐ Statement (1) ALONE is sufficient, but statement (2) alone is not sufficient.
   Ⓑ Statement (2) ALONE is sufficient, but statement (1) alone is not sufficient.
   Ⓒ BOTH statements TOGETHER are sufficient, but NEITHER statement ALONE is sufficient.
   Ⓓ EACH statement ALONE is sufficient.
   Ⓔ Statements (1) and (2) TOGETHER are NOT sufficient.

13. How many centimeters will a cylindrical barrel roll in 10 revolutions along a smooth surface?

   (1)   The diameter of the barrel is 56 centimeters.
   (2)   The radius of the barrel is 28 centimeters.
   Ⓐ Statement (1) ALONE is sufficient, but statement (2) alone is not sufficient.
   Ⓑ Statement (2) ALONE is sufficient, but statement (1) alone is not sufficient.
   Ⓒ BOTH statements TOGETHER are sufficient, but NEITHER statement ALONE is sufficient.
   Ⓓ EACH statement ALONE is sufficient.
   Ⓔ Statements (1) and (2) TOGETHER are NOT sufficient.

14. What is the area (in square inches) of the circle created by the minute hand of a clock as it sweeps an hour?

    (1)   The minute hand of the clock is 6 inches long.

    (2)   The hour hand of the clock is 4 inches long.

    Ⓐ Statement (1) ALONE is sufficient, but statement (2) alone is not sufficient.

    Ⓑ Statement (2) ALONE is sufficient, but statement (1) alone is not sufficient.

    Ⓒ BOTH statements TOGETHER are sufficient, but NEITHER statement ALONE is sufficient.

    Ⓓ EACH statement ALONE is sufficient.

    Ⓔ Statements (1) and (2) TOGETHER are NOT sufficient.

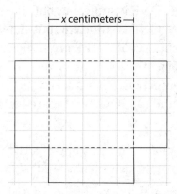

15. The figure shown on the grid consists of five rectangles. If the four outer rectangles are folded up and taped to make an open box, what is the box's volume in cubic centimeters?

    (1)   The base of the box is a square.

    (2) $x = 5$

    Ⓐ Statement (1) ALONE is sufficient, but statement (2) alone is not sufficient.

    Ⓑ Statement (2) ALONE is sufficient, but statement (1) alone is not sufficient.

    Ⓒ BOTH statements TOGETHER are sufficient, but NEITHER statement ALONE is sufficient.

    Ⓓ EACH statement ALONE is sufficient.

    Ⓔ Statements (1) and (2) TOGETHER are NOT sufficient.

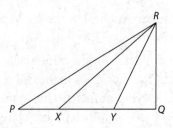

16. In triangle *PQR*, triangles *RPY* and *RYQ* have areas 90 and 45, respectively. What is the length of $\overline{XY}$?

    (1)   Angle *Q* is a right angle.
    (2) $PY = XQ = 10$
    (A)   Statement (1) ALONE is sufficient, but statement (2) alone is not sufficient.
    (B)   Statement (2) ALONE is sufficient, but statement (1) alone is not sufficient.
→ (C)   BOTH statements TOGETHER are sufficient, but NEITHER statement ALONE is sufficient.
    (D)   EACH statement ALONE is sufficient.
    (E)   Statements (1) and (2) TOGETHER are NOT sufficient.

17. A tank for holding water is in the shape of a right circular cylinder. What is the diameter of the base of the cylinder?

    (1)   When the tank is at full capacity, the volume of water in the tank is 128π cubic feet.
    (2)   When the tank is $\dfrac{3}{4}$ full, the volume of water in the tank is 96π cubic feet.
    (A)   Statement (1) ALONE is sufficient, but statement (2) alone is not sufficient.
    (B)   Statement (2) ALONE is sufficient, but statement (1) alone is not sufficient.
    (C)   BOTH statements TOGETHER are sufficient, but NEITHER statement ALONE is sufficient.
    (D)   EACH statement ALONE is sufficient.
    (E)   Statements (1) and (2) TOGETHER are NOT sufficient.

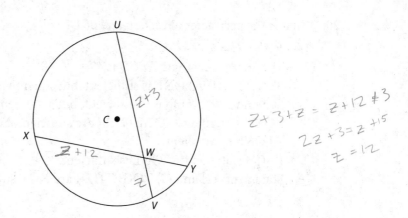

18. In the preceding diagram of circle C, chord $\overline{XY}$ intersects chord $\overline{UV}$ at W. If $XW = z + 12$, $UW = z + 3$, and $WV = z$, what is the length of $\overline{XY}$?

   (1) $XW = 6WY$
   (2) $WY = 3$
   Ⓐ Statement (1) ALONE is sufficient, but statement (2) alone is not sufficient.
   Ⓑ Statement (2) ALONE is sufficient, but statement (1) alone is not sufficient.
   Ⓒ BOTH statements TOGETHER are sufficient, but NEITHER statement ALONE is sufficient.
   Ⓓ EACH statement ALONE is sufficient.
   Ⓔ Statements (1) and (2) TOGETHER are NOT sufficient.

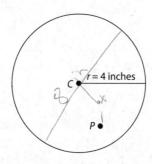

19. If X and P are points in the plane of the preceding circle C, does X lie within circle C?

   (1) $CX = 3$ inches
   (2) $PX = 2$ inches
   Ⓐ Statement (1) ALONE is sufficient, but statement (2) alone is not sufficient.
   Ⓑ Statement (2) ALONE is sufficient, but statement (1) alone is not sufficient.
   Ⓒ BOTH statements TOGETHER are sufficient, but NEITHER statement ALONE is sufficient.
   Ⓓ EACH statement ALONE is sufficient.
   Ⓔ Statements (1) and (2) TOGETHER are NOT sufficient.

20. What is the perimeter of rectangle *ABCD*?

   (1) $BD = AC = 5$

   (2)   The area of rectangle *ABCD* is 12.

   Ⓐ Statement (1) ALONE is sufficient, but statement (2) alone is not sufficient.

   Ⓑ Statement (2) ALONE is sufficient, but statement (1) alone is not sufficient.

   Ⓒ BOTH statements TOGETHER are sufficient, but NEITHER statement ALONE is sufficient.

   Ⓓ EACH statement ALONE is sufficient.

   Ⓔ Statements (1) and (2) TOGETHER are NOT sufficient.

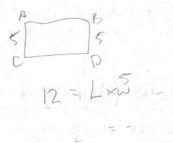

Answers

1. **C** From the information in (1), you have $\frac{85}{n} = x$, but without knowing either n or x, you cannot answer the question. Therefore, (1) is NOT sufficient. From the information in (2), you have $\frac{m}{n} = 4.25$, so $m = 4.25n$, which means $0.25n$ is the remainder when m is divided by n. But, without knowing n, you cannot determine whether $0.25n$ is 5. Therefore, (2) is NOT sufficient. Taking (1) and (2) together, you have $\frac{85}{n} = 4.25$, which you can solve for n to obtain $n = 20$ and $0.25n = 5$ (remainder). This latter equation verifies that 5 is the remainder when m is divided by n. Therefore, BOTH statements together are sufficient, but NEITHER statement ALONE is sufficient.

2. **C** Let $x =$ the number of grams of tin in the alloy and $y =$ the number of grams of copper in the alloy. To answer the question, you must determine $x + y$. From the information in (1), you can write the equation $\frac{x}{y} = \frac{1}{4}$, but you cannot determine the value of $x + y$ from this relationship. Therefore, (1) is NOT sufficient. From the information in (2), $y = 36$, so $x + y = x + 36$, but this does not result in a single value for $x + y$. Therefore, (2) is NOT sufficient. Taking (1) and (2) together, you can determine from (1) that $y = 4x$ and then substitute this value of y into the equation $y = 36$ from (2) to obtain $4x = 36$. From this equation, you can find x, and thereafter $x + y = x + 36$. Therefore, BOTH statements together are sufficient, but NEITHER statement ALONE is sufficient.

3. **E** Let $x =$ the number of male Scottish terriers and $y =$ the number of female Scottish terriers. From the information in (1), you can write the inequality $x < 2y$, but this does not tell you whether x or y is greater. For instance, $x = 4$ and $y = 3$ satisfies this inequality, and so does $x = 2$ and $y = 3$. Therefore, (1) is NOT sufficient. From the information in (2), you can write the inequality $\frac{1}{4}y < x$, but this does not tell you whether x or y is greater. For instance, $x = 5$ and $y = 4$ satisfies this inequality, and so does $x = 2$ and $y = 4$. Therefore, (2) is NOT sufficient. Taking (1) and (2) together, you can restate the inequalities in terms of y: $\frac{1}{2}x < y$ and $y < 4x$. Combining these two inequalities gives $\frac{1}{2}x < y < 4x$, but this does not tell you whether x or y is greater. For instance, $x = 4$ and $y = 3$ satisfies this inequality, and so does $x = 2$ and $y = 4$. Therefore, statements (1) and (2) TOGETHER are NOT sufficient.

4. **A** The square root symbol $\sqrt{}$ always denotes the principal (nonnegative) square root. From the information in (1), substitute the given value to find the square root:

$$x = \sqrt{\frac{m^2}{81}} = \sqrt{\frac{(-4)^2}{81}} = \sqrt{\frac{16}{81}} = \frac{4}{9}$$

$$\sqrt{x} = \sqrt{\frac{4}{9}} = \frac{2}{3}$$

You can find the answer, so (1) is sufficient. From the information in (2), m has a range of values, so $x = \sqrt{\frac{m^2}{81}}$ and, consequently, $\sqrt{x}$, have a range of values, not a single value. Therefore, (2) is NOT sufficient. Statement (1) ALONE is sufficient, but statement (2) alone is not sufficient.

5. **D** From the question information, you have $A = \$20,000\left(1+\dfrac{r}{12}\right)^6$, so you need either r,

the annual rate compounded monthly, or $\dfrac{r}{12}$, the monthly rate, to determine A. The

information in (1) gives you the monthly rate, $\dfrac{r}{12} = 0.0625\%$, so you can compute A.

Therefore, (1) is sufficient. The information in (2) gives you the annual rate, $r = 0.75\%$, so you can compute A. Therefore, (2) also is sufficient. EACH statement ALONE is sufficient.

6. **B** From the information in (1), $\sqrt[5]{x+y^3} = \sqrt[5]{24+y^3}$. Without knowing y, you cannot decide whether this expression equals an integer. For instance, if $y=2$, $\sqrt[5]{24+y^3} = \sqrt[5]{24+8} = \sqrt[5]{32} = 2$, which is an integer, but if $y=1$, $\sqrt[5]{24+y^3} = \sqrt[5]{24+1} = \sqrt[5]{25}$, which is not an integer. Therefore, (1) is NOT sufficient. From the information in (2), $\sqrt[5]{x+y^3} = \sqrt[5]{y^3(y^2-1)+y^3} = \sqrt[5]{y^5-y^3+y^3} = \sqrt[5]{y^5} = y$, an integer. Therefore, statement (2) ALONE is sufficient, but statement (1) alone is not sufficient.

7. **B** Let $x =$ the clerk's total sales last week. Then $1\%x = 0.01x =$ the clerk's commission last week. The information in (1) tells you that the clerk's computer sales were $\$1,047$, but the amount from the accessory sales is not given, so further information is needed. Therefore, (1) is NOT sufficient. From the information in (2), you have $0.01x = \$13.72$, which you can solve for a single value of x. Therefore, statement (2) ALONE is sufficient, but statement (1) alone is not sufficient.

8. **D** Solve the expression in (1) for x.

$$-\left(\frac{1}{2}x+1\right)>0$$

$$\left(\frac{1}{2}x+1\right)<0$$

$$\frac{1}{2}x<-1$$

$x<-2$, so the information in (1) is SUFFICIENT. *Tip*: Remember to reverse the direction of an inequality when you multiply (or divide) both sides of an inequality by a negative number.

Solve the expression in (2) for x.

$$x^5+3<0$$

$$x^5<-3$$

$x<\sqrt[5]{-3}<0$, so (2) is SUFFICIENT. *Tip*: If the index is odd and the radicand is negative, the principal root is negative. (See "Roots and Radicals" in Chapter 8 for a discussion of this topic.)

Therefore, EACH statement ALONE is sufficient.

9. **A** Solve the equation in (1) for x: $\dfrac{x}{y}=0.4$ is equivalent to $x=0.4y=\dfrac{2}{5}y$. Substituting

this result into $5x-2y=0$ yields $5x-2y=0=5\left(\dfrac{2}{5}y\right)-2y=2y-2y=0$, so (1) is

SUFFICIENT. From the information in (2), you can determine that $x<y$, but further information is needed to determine whether $5x-2y=0$. For instance, for $x=1$ and $y=2$,

$5x - 2y = 1 \neq 0$; but for $x = 2$ and $y = 5$, $5x - 2y = 0$. Thus, (2) is NOT sufficient. Therefore, statement (1) ALONE is sufficient, but statement (2) alone is not sufficient.

10. **E** Let l = the length of the rectangle and w = the width of the rectangle. Then the perimeter $P = 2l + 2w$. From the information in (1), $l = w + 3$, which (because you have two variables and only one equation) does not yield a single value for l or w, so you cannot compute P; (1) is NOT sufficient. From the information in (2), $P = 2l + 2w = 4l - 6$, which (because you have two variables and only one equation) does not yield a single value for l or w, so you cannot compute P; (2) also is NOT sufficient. Taking (1) and (2) together, you have two linear equations and two variables, but the equation, $2l + 2w = 4l - 6$, in (2) simplifies to $w = l - 3$, which (by inspection) is equivalent to the equation $l = w + 3$ in (1). Thus, further information is needed to determine P. Therefore, statements (1) and (2) TOGETHER are NOT sufficient.

11. **C** From the information in (1), the triangle is isosceles with base angles A and B. So, $AC = BC = n$, but further information is needed to determine whether $n < 7$, so (1) is NOT sufficient. From the information in (2) and the triangle inequality (the sum of any two sides of a triangle is greater than the third side), $n + BC > 15$, $n + 15 > BC$, and $15 + BC > n$, but further information is needed to determine whether $n < 7$, so (2) also is NOT sufficient. Taking (1) and (2) together, you can use $BC = n$ from (1) and substitute it into $n + BC > 15$, so $n + n > 15$ or, equivalently, $2n > 15$, and $n > 7.5$. Therefore, BOTH statements TOGETHER are sufficient, but NEITHER statement ALONE is sufficient.

12. **E** From the information in (1), knowing that lines c and d are parallel will allow you to identify congruent angles of parallel lines cut by a transversal, but without information about the measures of angles in the figure, you cannot determine $m\angle 2$, so (1) is NOT sufficient. The information in (2) is not helpful, because you cannot establish a relationship between $\angle 1$ and $\angle 2$ without further information, so (2) also is NOT sufficient. Taking (1) and (2) together, you still cannot establish a relationship between $\angle 1$ and $\angle 2$ without further information. Therefore, statements (1) and (2) TOGETHER are NOT sufficient.

13. **D** From the question information, you know that in one revolution, the cylindrical barrel will roll a distance equal to its circumference, $\pi d = 2\pi r$. Thus, in 10 revolutions, the barrel will roll a distance of $10\pi d = 20\pi r$. From the information in (1), you can substitute $d = 56$ centimeters into $10\pi d$ and then compute a single value for the distance rolled, so (1) is SUFFICIENT. From the information in (2), you can substitute $r = 28$ centimeters into $20\pi r$ and then compute a single value for the distance rolled, so (2) also is SUFFICIENT. Therefore, EACH statement ALONE is sufficient.

14. **A** From the question information, the area equals πr^2, where r is the length of the minute hand. From the information in (1), you can substitute $r = 6$ inches into πr^2 and then compute a single value for the area, so (1) is SUFFICIENT. With the information from (2), you need the length of the minute hand to answer the question, so this information is not useful, and (2) is NOT sufficient. Therefore, statement (1) ALONE is sufficient, but statement (2) alone is not sufficient.

15. **B** From the question information, the volume of the box is $V = lwh$, where l = length, w = width, and h = height of the box. The information in (1) tells you about the shape of the base of the box, but you need further information about the dimensions to determine V, so (1) is NOT sufficient. The information in (2) tells you that, by referring to the figure, the length l of the box is 5 centimeters, and it also tells you that each square of the grid has sides of 1 centimeter. Thus, from the figure, $l = w = 5$ centimeters, and $h = 2$

centimeters. Now that you have these dimensions, you can determine a single value of V, so (2) is SUFFICIENT. Therefore, statement (2) ALONE is sufficient, but statement (1) alone is not sufficient.

16. **C** From the information in (1), the area of right triangle $RYQ = 45 = \frac{1}{2}(RQ)(YQ)$, which implies that $(RQ)(YQ) = 90$. Also, the area of right triangle $RPY = 90 = \frac{1}{2}(RQ)(PY)$, which implies that $(RQ)(PY) = 180$. Thus, $(RQ)(YQ) = \frac{1}{2}(RQ)(PY)$, which implies that $(YQ) = \frac{1}{2}(PY)$. Thus, from the figure, $PY = PX + XY$, so $(YQ) = \frac{1}{2}(PX + XY)$, but further information is needed to determine a single value for XY, so (1) is NOT sufficient.

From the information in (2), $PX + XY = XY + YQ = 10$, which implies that $PX = YQ$. However, further information is needed to determine a single value for XY, so (2) also is NOT sufficient. Taking (1) and (2) together, you can substitute $PY = 10$ from (2) into $(YQ) = \frac{1}{2}(PY)$ from (1) to determine that $(YQ) = \frac{1}{2}(10) = 5$. Then you can substitute $YQ = 5$ into $XY + YQ = 10$ to obtain $XY + 5 = 10$, which you can solve for a single value of XY. Therefore, BOTH statements TOGETHER are sufficient, but NEITHER statement ALONE is sufficient.

17. **E** Glancing at (1) and (2), you can see that both mention the volume of the tank. From the question information, the tank is cylindrical. Thus, its volume, V, equals $Bh = \pi r^2 h$, where B is the area of the cylinder's base, r is the base's radius, and h is the cylinder's height. The diameter, d, of the base of the cylinder is $2r$. From the information in (1), you know that $V = \pi r^2 h = 128\pi$ cubic feet. This equation implies that $r^2 h = 128$ cubic feet, which (because you have two variables and only one equation) does not yield a single value for r, so you are unable to determine $d = 2r$, and (1) is NOT sufficient.

From the information in (2), $\frac{3}{4}V = \frac{3}{4}\pi r^2 h = 96\pi$ cubic feet. This equation implies that $r^2 h = 96 \cdot \frac{4}{3} = 128$ cubic feet, which (because you have two variables and only one equation) does not yield a single value for r, so you are unable to determine $d = 2r$, and (2) also is NOT sufficient. Taking (1) and (2) together, you still end up with $r^2 h = 128$ cubic feet, from which you are unable to determine d. Therefore, statements (1) and (2) TOGETHER are NOT sufficient.

18. **D** From the question information, the length of $\overline{XY} = XY = XW + WY = (z + 12) + WY$. Also, because $\overline{XY}$ and $\overline{UV}$ are two chords in C intersecting at W, then $UW \cdot WV = XW \cdot WY$. Substituting the known information into this equation yields $(z + 3)(z) = (z + 12)WY$.

From the question information and the information in (1), $WY = \frac{XW}{6} = \frac{z + 12}{6}$. Set up the equation $XY = XW + WY = 7WY = 7\left(\frac{z + 12}{6}\right)$. Thus, you can determine a single value for XY if you can determine a single value for z. Now, substitute what you know into $UW \cdot WV = XW \cdot WY$, to obtain $(z + 3)(z) = (z + 12)\left(\frac{z + 12}{6}\right)$. This equation is equivalent to the quadratic equation $5z^2 - 6z - 144 = 0$. Because z must be positive, you can solve this equation for a single value of z. Thus, (1) is SUFFICIENT.

From the information in (2), you can set up the equation $XY = (z+12)+3$. Furthermore, $(z+3)(z) = (z+12)(3)$, which simplifies to $z^2 = 36$. Because you can assume that, as a measurement of length, z is positive, this equation yields $z = 6$, from which you can compute $XY = (z+12)+3$. Thus, (2) is SUFFICIENT. Therefore, EACH statement ALONE is sufficient.

19. **A** From the figure, the radius, r, of the circle is 4 inches. A point will lie within circle C if its distance from the center C is less than 4 inches. From the information in (1), X lies within circle C because $CX = 3$ inches < 4 inches, so (1) is SUFFICIENT. From the information in (2), you know only that X is 2 inches from P. You need further information to determine whether $CX < 4$ inches. For instance, suppose that C, P, and X are collinear (in this order) such that $CP = 3$ inches and $PX = 2$ inches; then X would lie outside circle C. Thus, (2) is NOT sufficient. Statement (1) ALONE is sufficient, but statement (2) alone is not sufficient.

20. **C** Sketch a figure.

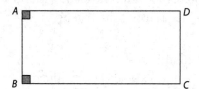

From the figure, the perimeter, P, is $P = 2l + 2w$, where the rectangle's length, l, is $AD = BC$, and its width, w, is $AB = DC$. The information in (1) gives you the lengths of the rectangle's diagonals. Each diagonal forms a right triangle in the rectangle that has legs of lengths l and w and a hypotenuse of length 5. Thus, by the Pythagorean theorem, $5^2 = l^2 + w^2$, which (because you have two variables and only one equation) does not yield single values for l and w, so you are unable to determine $P = 2l + 2w$; (1) is NOT sufficient. From the information in (2), you know that $lw = 12$, which (because you have two variables and only one equation) does not yield single values for l and w, so you are unable to determine $P = 2l + 2w$; (2) also is NOT sufficient. Taking (1) and (2) together, assume that, because they are measurements of distance, l and w are both positive. You can simultaneously solve $5^2 = l^2 + w^2$ from (1) and $lw = 12$ from (2), as shown here:

Solve $5^2 = l^2 + w^2$ for w to obtain $w = \sqrt{25 - l^2}$.

Substitute into $lw = 12$ to obtain $l\sqrt{25 - l^2} = 12$.

Square both sides to obtain $l^2(25 - l^2) = 144$.

Simplify to obtain $l^4 - 25l^2 + 144 = 0$.

Factor as you would a quadratic to obtain $(l^2 - 9)(l^2 - 16)$.

Keeping in mind that l is positive, then from these two equations, $l = 3$ with $w = 4$, or $l = 4$ with $w = 3$. Either way, $P = 2l + 2w = 14$. Therefore, BOTH statements TOGETHER are sufficient, but NEITHER statement ALONE is sufficient.

Data Sufficiency Questions Drill 4

1. If x and y are positive integers, is xy a multiple of 18?
   - (1) x is a multiple of 6.
   - (2) y is a multiple of 15.
   - (A) Statement (1) ALONE is sufficient, but statement (2) alone is not sufficient.
   - (B) Statement (2) ALONE is sufficient, but statement (1) alone is not sufficient.
   - (C) BOTH statements TOGETHER are sufficient, but NEITHER statement ALONE is sufficient.
   - (D) EACH statement ALONE is sufficient.
   - (E) Statements (1) and (2) TOGETHER are NOT sufficient.

2. Two friends rented a light-duty moving truck. The rental store charges $19.99 per hour or portion thereof for the truck rental plus $0.55 per mile traveled, with no charge for gasoline. How much did the friends pay for renting the truck?
   - (1) The total round-trip mileage was 100 miles.
   - (2) The friends returned the truck after 3 hours 20 minutes.
   - (A) Statement (1) ALONE is sufficient, but statement (2) alone is not sufficient.
   - (B) Statement (2) ALONE is sufficient, but statement (1) alone is not sufficient.
   - (C) BOTH statements TOGETHER are sufficient, but NEITHER statement ALONE is sufficient.
   - (D) EACH statement ALONE is sufficient.
   - (E) Statements (1) and (2) TOGETHER are NOT sufficient.

3. In a survey of students at a small private college, what percent are taking a foreign language?
   - (1) Twenty percent of the female students surveyed are taking a foreign language.
   - (2) Fifteen percent of the male students surveyed are taking a foreign language.
   - (A) Statement (1) ALONE is sufficient, but statement (2) alone is not sufficient.
   - (B) Statement (2) ALONE is sufficient, but statement (1) alone is not sufficient.
   - (C) BOTH statements TOGETHER are sufficient, but NEITHER statement ALONE is sufficient.
   - (D) EACH statement ALONE is sufficient.
   - (E) Statements (1) and (2) TOGETHER are NOT sufficient.

4. Is the variance of the population set of data values $x_1, x_2, \ldots, x_{100}$ equal to 9?
   - (1) For each data value x_i, $|x_i - \mu| = 3$, where μ is the mean of the population.
   - (2) The standard deviation is 3.
   - (A) Statement (1) ALONE is sufficient, but statement (2) alone is not sufficient.
   - (B) Statement (2) ALONE is sufficient, but statement (1) alone is not sufficient.
   - (C) BOTH statements TOGETHER are sufficient, but NEITHER statement ALONE is sufficient.
   - (D) EACH statement ALONE is sufficient.
   - (E) Statements (1) and (2) TOGETHER are NOT sufficient.

5. A driver makes a trip of *d* miles. The driver's average speed is 63 miles per hour for the first part of the trip and 70 miles per hour for the second part of the trip. Was the distance traveled for the second part of the trip longer than the distance traveled for the first part of the trip?

   (1) The time for the first part of the trip is 2 hours.
   (2) The total time for the entire trip is 3 hours 48 minutes.
   Ⓐ Statement (1) ALONE is sufficient, but statement (2) alone is NOT sufficient.
   Ⓑ Statement (2) ALONE is sufficient, but statement (1) alone is not sufficient.
   Ⓒ BOTH statements TOGETHER are sufficient, but NEITHER statement ALONE is sufficient.
   Ⓓ EACH statement ALONE is sufficient.
   Ⓔ Statements (1) and (2) TOGETHER are NOT sufficient.

6. To make a 20% alcohol solution, a scientist adds *x* liters of a 60% alcohol solution to *y* liters of a 10% solution. What is the value of *x*?

   (1) $x + y = 37.5$
   (2) $y = 30$
   Ⓐ Statement (1) ALONE is sufficient, but statement (2) alone is not sufficient.
   Ⓑ Statement (2) ALONE is sufficient, but statement (1) alone is not sufficient.
   Ⓒ BOTH statements TOGETHER are sufficient, but NEITHER statement ALONE is sufficient.
   Ⓓ EACH statement ALONE is sufficient.
   Ⓔ Statements (1) and (2) TOGETHER are NOT sufficient.

7. If $\dfrac{4}{3a} + \dfrac{x}{2a} = 1$, where $a \neq 0$, what is the value of *x*?

   (1) $3x = 6a - 8$
   (2) $\dfrac{x}{a} = \dfrac{2}{3}$
   Ⓐ Statement (1) ALONE is sufficient, but statement (2) alone is not sufficient.
   Ⓑ Statement (2) ALONE is sufficient, but statement (1) alone is not sufficient.
   Ⓒ BOTH statements TOGETHER are sufficient, but NEITHER statement ALONE is sufficient.
   Ⓓ EACH statement ALONE is sufficient.
   Ⓔ Statements (1) and (2) TOGETHER are NOT sufficient.

8. The sum of the reciprocals of two nonzero numbers is $\dfrac{3}{5}$. What is the value of the larger number?

   (1) The larger number is 5 times the smaller number.
   (2) Five times the sum of the reciprocals of the two numbers is 3.
   Ⓐ Statement (1) ALONE is sufficient, but statement (2) alone is not sufficient.
   Ⓑ Statement (2) ALONE is sufficient, but statement (1) alone is not sufficient.
   Ⓒ BOTH statements TOGETHER are sufficient, but NEITHER statement ALONE is sufficient.
   Ⓓ EACH statement ALONE is sufficient.
   Ⓔ Statements (1) and (2) TOGETHER are NOT sufficient.

9. An auditorium has only balcony seats and orchestra seats. Tickets for the first performance of a concert at the auditorium are $80 for orchestra seats and $50 for balcony seats. How many balcony seats were sold for the first performance?

    (1)   The auditorium sold 800 tickets.
    (2)   Total receipts for tickets for the first performance were $49,000.
    Ⓐ   Statement (1) ALONE is sufficient, but statement (2) alone is not sufficient.
    Ⓑ   Statement (2) ALONE is sufficient, but statement (1) alone is not sufficient.
    Ⓒ   BOTH statements TOGETHER are sufficient, but NEITHER statement ALONE is sufficient.
    Ⓓ   EACH statement ALONE is sufficient.
    Ⓔ   Statements (1) and (2) TOGETHER are NOT sufficient.

10. A box contains a collection of marbles, all identical except for color. Each marble is either black, red, or white. If a marble is randomly drawn from the box, what is the probability that the marble is white?

    (1)   The box contains 120 marbles.
    (2)   There are twice as many black marbles as white marbles in the box.
    Ⓐ   Statement (1) ALONE is sufficient, but statement (2) alone is not sufficient.
    Ⓑ   Statement (2) ALONE is sufficient, but statement (1) alone is not sufficient.
    Ⓒ   BOTH statements TOGETHER are sufficient, but NEITHER statement ALONE is sufficient.
    Ⓓ   EACH statement ALONE is sufficient.
    Ⓔ   Statements (1) and (2) TOGETHER are NOT sufficient.

11. A quilted shawl is made up of 9-inch by 9-inch squares. What is its perimeter?

    (1)   The shawl has four rows and six columns.
    (2)   The shawl consists of 24 squares.
    Ⓐ   Statement (1) ALONE is sufficient, but statement (2) alone is not sufficient.
    Ⓑ   Statement (2) ALONE is sufficient, but statement (1) alone is not sufficient.
    Ⓒ   BOTH statements TOGETHER are sufficient, but NEITHER statement ALONE is sufficient.
    Ⓓ   EACH statement ALONE is sufficient.
    Ⓔ   Statements (1) and (2) TOGETHER are NOT sufficient.

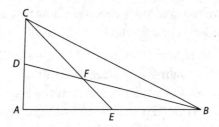

12. In the preceding figure, what is the length of $\overline{FB}$?

    (1) $\overline{DB}$ and $\overline{CE}$ are medians.
    (2) $DF = 15$
    Ⓐ Statement (1) ALONE is sufficient, but statement (2) alone is not sufficient.
    Ⓑ Statement (2) ALONE is sufficient, but statement (1) alone is not sufficient.
    Ⓒ BOTH statements TOGETHER are sufficient, but NEITHER statement ALONE is sufficient.
    Ⓓ EACH statement ALONE is sufficient.
    Ⓔ Statements (1) and (2) TOGETHER are NOT sufficient.

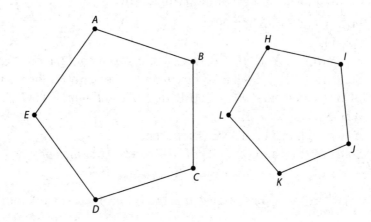

13. In the preceding figure, $ABCDE \sim HIJKL$. What is the ratio of the area of $ABCDE$ to the area of $HIJKL$?

    (1) $\dfrac{AB}{HI} = \dfrac{4}{3}$

    (2) $\dfrac{LK}{ED} = \dfrac{3}{4}$
    Ⓐ Statement (1) ALONE is sufficient, but statement (2) alone is not sufficient.
    Ⓑ Statement (2) ALONE is sufficient, but statement (1) alone is not sufficient.
    Ⓒ BOTH statements TOGETHER are sufficient, but NEITHER statement ALONE is sufficient.
    Ⓓ EACH statement ALONE is sufficient.
    Ⓔ Statements (1) and (2) TOGETHER are NOT sufficient.

14. If a bicycle is traveling at 5 miles per hour, how fast is the bicycle's front wheel turning in revolutions per minute?

   (1)   The front wheel has a diameter of 25 inches.

   (2)   The bicycle is traveling at 440 feet per minute.

   Ⓐ Statement (1) ALONE is sufficient, but statement (2) alone is not sufficient.

   Ⓑ Statement (2) ALONE is sufficient, but statement (1) alone is not sufficient.

   Ⓒ BOTH statements TOGETHER are sufficient, but NEITHER statement ALONE is sufficient.

   Ⓓ EACH statement ALONE is sufficient.

   Ⓔ Statements (1) and (2) TOGETHER are NOT sufficient.

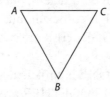

15. What is the area of the preceding triangle *ABC*?

   (1) $m\angle A = m\angle B = m\angle C = 60°$

   (2) $AB = 12$

   Ⓐ Statement (1) ALONE is sufficient, but statement (2) alone is not sufficient.

   Ⓑ Statement (2) ALONE is sufficient, but statement (1) alone is not sufficient.

   Ⓒ BOTH statements TOGETHER are sufficient, but NEITHER statement ALONE is sufficient.

   Ⓓ EACH statement ALONE is sufficient.

   Ⓔ Statements (1) and (2) TOGETHER are NOT sufficient.

16. If $y = \dfrac{k}{x}$, where *k* is a constant, what is the value of *y* when *x* = 360?

   (1) $y = \dfrac{2}{9}$ when *x* = 540

   (2) $xy = k$

   Ⓐ Statement (1) ALONE is sufficient, but statement (2) alone is not sufficient.

   Ⓑ Statement (2) ALONE is sufficient, but statement (1) alone is not sufficient.

   Ⓒ BOTH statements TOGETHER are sufficient, but NEITHER statement ALONE is sufficient.

   Ⓓ EACH statement ALONE is sufficient.

   Ⓔ Statements (1) and (2) TOGETHER are NOT sufficient.

17. A dress that usually sells for \$85.00 is marked down for an end-of-season clearance sale. If the sales tax rate is 8%, how much does a customer pay for the dress at the marked-down price including tax?

    (1)   Including tax, the customer saves a total of \$18.36.
    (2)   The sales tax on the marked-down price is \$5.44.
    Ⓐ   Statement (1) ALONE is sufficient, but statement (2) alone is not sufficient.
    Ⓑ   Statement (2) ALONE is sufficient, but statement (1) alone is not sufficient.
    Ⓒ   BOTH statements TOGETHER are sufficient, but NEITHER statement ALONE is sufficient.
    Ⓓ   EACH statement ALONE is sufficient.
    Ⓔ   Statements (1) and (2) TOGETHER are NOT sufficient.

18. What is the value of a_{20} if $a_n = a_1 + (n-1)d$?

    (1) $a_4 = 17$
    (2) $a_{10} = 47$
    Ⓐ   Statement (1) ALONE is sufficient, but statement (2) alone is not sufficient.
    Ⓑ   Statement (2) ALONE is sufficient, but statement (1) alone is not sufficient.
    Ⓒ   BOTH statements TOGETHER are sufficient, but NEITHER statement ALONE is sufficient.
    Ⓓ   EACH statement ALONE is sufficient.
    Ⓔ   Statements (1) and (2) TOGETHER are NOT sufficient.

19. If x and y are positive integers such that $x + y = 10$, what is the value of y?

    (1) $37 < 5x + 2y < 41$
    (2) $x > 5$
    Ⓐ   Statement (1) ALONE is sufficient, but statement (2) alone is not sufficient.
    Ⓑ   Statement (2) ALONE is sufficient, but statement (1) alone is not sufficient.
    Ⓒ   BOTH statements TOGETHER are sufficient, but NEITHER statement ALONE is sufficient.
    Ⓓ   EACH statement ALONE is sufficient.
    Ⓔ   Statements (1) and (2) TOGETHER are NOT sufficient.

20. If the area of a square having sides of length x is equal to the area of a parallelogram having base b, what is the height, h, of the parallelogram to that base?

    (1) $x = 10$
    (2) $b = 20$
    Ⓐ   Statement (1) ALONE is sufficient, but statement (2) alone is not sufficient.
    Ⓑ   Statement (2) ALONE is sufficient, but statement (1) alone is not sufficient.
    Ⓒ   BOTH statements TOGETHER are sufficient, but NEITHER statement ALONE is sufficient.
    Ⓓ   EACH statement ALONE is sufficient.
    Ⓔ   Statements (1) and (2) TOGETHER are NOT sufficient.

Answers

1. **C** From the information in (1), $x = 6m$, for a value of m that is a counting number, but there is no way to determine an exact value for m. Therefore, (1) is NOT sufficient. From the information in (2), $y = 15n$, for a value of n that is a counting number, but there is no way to determine an exact value for n. Therefore, (2) also is NOT sufficient. Taking (1) and (2) together, combine the two equations by multiplying $x = 6m$ by $y = 15n$: $xy = (6m)(15n) = (6m)(3 \cdot 5n) = (6 \cdot 3)(5mn) = 18(5mn)$. Because 5, m, and n are counting numbers, their product $5mn$ is a counting number. Thus, xy is a multiple of 18. Therefore, BOTH statements together are sufficient, but NEITHER statement ALONE is sufficient.

2. **C** Let $t =$ the number of hours the friends will be charged at \$19.99 per hour and $d =$ the total mileage the friends will be charged at \$0.55 per mile. Then the cost, C, for the rental is \$19.99t + \$0.55d. From the information in (1), $d = 100$ miles, but without knowing t, you cannot compute the cost. Therefore, (1) is NOT sufficient. From the information in (2), $t = 4$ hours (because they are charged a full hour for a portion of an hour), but without knowing d, you cannot compute the cost. Therefore, (2) also is NOT sufficient. Taking (1) and (2) together, you can substitute the values of t and d into the equation: $C = \$19.99t + \$0.55d = \$19.99(4) + \$0.55(100)$, which you can compute to obtain the cost. Therefore, BOTH statements together are sufficient, but NEITHER statement ALONE is sufficient.

3. **E** Let $x =$ the number of female students surveyed and $y =$ the number of male students surveyed. Then $x + y =$ the number of students surveyed. The information in (1) tells you that 20%x is the number of female students who are taking a foreign language, but you need further information to determine how many students surveyed are taking a foreign language. Therefore, (1) is NOT sufficient. From the information in (2), you know that 15%y is the number of male students who are taking a foreign language, but you need further information to determine how many students surveyed are taking a foreign language; so (2) also is NOT sufficient. From (1) and (2) taken together, $\dfrac{20\%x + 15\%y}{x + y}$

is the percent of students surveyed who are taking a foreign language. Without further information, this expression cannot be simplified to a single value. Therefore, statements (1) and (2) TOGETHER are NOT sufficient.

4. **D** From the subscripts on the data values, you know there are 100 data values. The variance is a measure of how much these values are spread out relative to the mean, μ, of these numbers. You compute this population variance by subtracting the mean from each data value, squaring each difference, and then summing up the 100 squared differences and dividing by 100. From the information in (1), the variance is $\dfrac{100 \cdot 3^2}{100} = 9$. Therefore, (1) is sufficient. From the information in (2), the variance equals the square of the standard deviation, so the variance $= 3^2 = 9$. Thus, (2) is sufficient. In sum, EACH statement ALONE is sufficient.

5. **C** The entire distance traveled is d. Let $t =$ the time for the second part of the trip. From the information in (1), the distance traveled for the first two hours of the trip is (63 mph)(2 hr) = 126 miles. The distance traveled for the second part of the trip is $d - 126 = 70$ mph(t). However, without knowing d or t, you cannot compute the distance traveled for the second part of the trip, so (1) is NOT sufficient. From the information in (2), the time for the first part of the trip is = 3.8 hours − t (*Note:* 48 minutes is 0.8 hour).

Then, omitting the units, the distance traveled for the first part of the trip is $63(3.8 - t)$ and the distance traveled for the second part of the trip is $70t$. But without knowing t, you cannot compare the two distances. Therefore, (2) is NOT sufficient. Taking (1) and (2) together, from (1) the distance traveled for the first two hours of the trip is (63 mph)(2 hr) = 126 miles. From (1) and (2) the time for the second part of the trip equals 3.8 hr. − 2 hr. = 1.8 hr, so the distance traveled for the second part of the trip is (70 mph)(1.8 hr) = 126 miles. Now that you know the two distances are equal, you can answer "No" to the question posed. Therefore, BOTH statements together are sufficient, but NEITHER statement ALONE is sufficient.

6. **D** From the information in the question, after mixing, the 20% alcohol solution contains $(x + y)$ liters. From the information in (1), $y = 37.5 - x$. The amount of alcohol before mixing equals the amount of alcohol after mixing, so $60\%x + 10\%(37.5 - x) = 20\%(37.5)$, which you can solve to determine a single value of x. Therefore, (1) is SUFFICIENT. From the information in (2), $x + y = x + 30$. The amount of alcohol before mixing equals the amount of alcohol after mixing. Therefore, $60\%x + 10\%(30) = 20\%(x + 30)$, which you can solve to determine a single value of x. Therefore, (2) also is SUFFICIENT. EACH statement ALONE is sufficient.

7. **B** First, simplify the given equation as follows:

$$\frac{4}{3a} + \frac{x}{2a} = 1$$

$$6a\left(\frac{4}{3a}\right) + 6a\left(\frac{x}{2a}\right) = 6a(1)$$

$$8 + 3x = 6a$$

By inspection, you can see that the equation in (1), $3x = 6a - 8$, is equivalent to $8 + 3x = 6a$, so further information is needed. Therefore, (1) is NOT sufficient. With the equation in (2), that is, $\frac{x}{a} = \frac{2}{3}$ (which is equivalent to $3x = 2a$), and $8 + 3x = 6a$, you have two linear equations and two variables. You can solve the two equations simultaneously for a single value of x. Therefore, (2) is SUFFICIENT. Statement (2) ALONE is sufficient, but statement (1) alone is not sufficient.

8. **A** Let x = the smaller number and y = the larger number. Then, according to the question, $\frac{1}{x} + \frac{1}{y} = \frac{3}{5}$. From the information in (1), $y = 5x$. You can substitute from this equation into $\frac{1}{x} + \frac{1}{y} = \frac{3}{5}$ to obtain $\frac{1}{x} + \frac{1}{5x} = \frac{3}{5}$. Multiply both sides of this equation by $5x$ to obtain $6 = 3x$, which you can solve for a single value of x. You can substitute your answer into the equation $y = 5x$ to obtain the value of the larger number. Therefore, (1) is SUFFICIENT. From the information in (2), $5\left(\frac{1}{x} + \frac{1}{y}\right) = 3$, which you can see by inspection is equivalent to $\frac{1}{x} + \frac{1}{y} = \frac{3}{5}$, so further information is needed, meaning (2) is NOT sufficient. Therefore, statement (1) ALONE is sufficient, but statement (2) alone is not sufficient.

9. **C** Let x = the number of balcony seats sold and y = the number of orchestra seats sold. From the information in (1), $x + y = 800$, which (because you have two variables and only

one equation) does not yield a single value for x. Therefore, (1) is NOT sufficient. From the information in (2), $\$50x + \$80y = \$49{,}000$, which (because you have two variables and only one equation) does not yield a single value for x. Therefore, (2) also is NOT sufficient. Taking (1) and (2) together, you have two linear equations and two variables. You can solve the two equations simultaneously for a single value of x. Therefore, BOTH statements TOGETHER are sufficient, but NEITHER statement ALONE is sufficient.

10. **E** Let $b =$ the number of black marbles in the box, $r =$ the number of red marbles in the box, and $w =$ the number of white marbles in the box. Then the probability P of randomly drawing a white marble from the box is $P = \dfrac{w}{b+r+w}$. From the information in (1), $b + r + w = 120$, so $P = \dfrac{w}{b+r+w} = \dfrac{w}{120}$, but without knowing w, you cannot determine the probability. Therefore, (1) is NOT sufficient. From the information in (2), $b = 2w$, so $P = \dfrac{w}{b+r+w} = \dfrac{w}{2w+r+w} = \dfrac{w}{3w+r}$, but without knowing r and w, you cannot determine the probability. Therefore, (2) also is NOT sufficient. Taking (1) and (2) together, you can set the two expressions for P equal to each other, giving $\dfrac{w}{120} = \dfrac{w}{3w+r}$. If you divide both sides by w and simplify, you obtain $3w + r = 120$, which (because you have two variables and only one equation) does not yield a single value for w, from which you could calculate P. Therefore, statements (1) and (2) TOGETHER are NOT sufficient.

  Tip: It was permissible to divide both sides of $\dfrac{w}{120} = \dfrac{w}{3w+r}$ by w because, in the context of this question, $w \neq 0$. Always be careful when you divide by a variable—you need to be confident that the variable has a nonzero value.

11. **A** From the question information, the perimeter, P, of the shawl is $P = 2l + 2w$, where $l =$ length and $w =$ width of the shawl. From the information in (1), you can compute $l = 6 \cdot 9$ inches and $w = 4 \cdot 9$ inches, and with these, you can determine a single value of $P = 2(6 \cdot 9 \text{ inches}) + 2(4 \cdot 9 \text{ inches})$. Thus, (1) is SUFFICIENT. From the information in (2), you cannot determine the exact dimensions of the shawl and thereby a single value of P. For instance, if the shawl has four rows and six columns (24 squares), $P = 108$ inches + 72 inches = 180 inches, but if the shawl has three rows and eight columns (24 squares), $P = 144$ inches + 54 inches = 198 inches. Thus, (2) is NOT sufficient. Therefore, statement (1) ALONE is sufficient, but statement (2) alone is not sufficient.

12. **C** Applying the information in (1), the medians in a triangle intersect at a point that is two-thirds of the distance from each vertex to the midpoint of the opposite side, so $FB = \dfrac{2}{3}DB$. However, further information is needed to determine a single value for FB, so (1) is NOT sufficient. From the figure, $DB = DF + FB$, and applying the information in (2), $DB = 15 + FB$, but further is needed to determine a single value for FB. Thus, (2) also is NOT sufficient.

  Taking (1) and (2) together, because $FB = \dfrac{2}{3}DB$ and $DB = DF + FB$, it follows that $DF = \dfrac{1}{3}DB$. Substituting $DF = 15$ into this equation, you can determine DB and use that value to calculate $FB = \dfrac{2}{3}DB$. Therefore, BOTH statements TOGETHER are sufficient, but NEITHER statement ALONE is sufficient.

13. **D** From the information in (1), the ratio of the area of *ABCDE* to the area of *HIJKL* is $\left(\dfrac{4}{3}\right)^2 = \dfrac{16}{9}$ or 16 to 9, so (1) is SUFFICIENT. From the information in (2), $\dfrac{ED}{LK} = \dfrac{4}{3}$. Thus, the ratio of the area of *ABCDE* to the area of *HIJKL* is $\left(\dfrac{4}{3}\right)^2 = \dfrac{16}{9}$ or 16 to 9, and (2) also is SUFFICIENT. Therefore, EACH statement ALONE is sufficient.

14. **A** From the information in (1), in one revolution, the wheel will travel a distance equal to its circumference, $\pi d = \pi(25 \text{ inches})$. Convert $5 \dfrac{\text{miles}}{\text{hour}}$ into revolutions per minute:

$$5 \, \frac{\cancel{\text{mi}}}{\cancel{\text{hr}}} \cdot \frac{5{,}280 \, \cancel{\text{ft}}}{1 \, \cancel{\text{mi}}} \cdot \frac{12 \, \cancel{\text{in}}}{1 \, \cancel{\text{ft}}} \cdot \frac{1 \, \cancel{\text{hr}}}{60 \, \text{min}} \cdot \frac{1 \text{ revolution}}{\pi\left(25 \, \cancel{\text{in}}\right)}$$

You can use this to compute a single value for the answer in revolutions per minute, so (1) is SUFFICIENT. The information in (2) is not helpful, because the speed 440 feet per minute is equivalent to 5 miles per hour, so no additional information is gained; thus, (2) is NOT sufficient. Statement (1) ALONE is sufficient, but statement (2) alone is not sufficient.

15. **C** From the information in (1), you know that triangle *ABC* is an equilateral triangle. The formula for the area, *A*, of an equilateral triangle is $A = \dfrac{s^2\sqrt{3}}{4}$. Thus, further information is needed to find *A*, and (1) is NOT sufficient. *Tip:* If you do not recall that the area of an equilateral triangle is $\dfrac{s^2\sqrt{3}}{4}$, you can construct an altitude of the triangle. The altitude divides the equilateral triangle into two 30°-60°-90° right triangles. You can use one of these right triangles to determine that the length of the altitude is $\dfrac{s\sqrt{3}}{2}$, so:

$$A = \frac{1}{2}bh = \frac{1}{2}sh = \frac{1}{2}s\left(\frac{s\sqrt{3}}{2}\right) = \frac{s^2\sqrt{3}}{4}.$$

From the information in (2), you can write the area of triangle *ABC* as $\dfrac{1}{2}(\text{base})(\text{height}) = \dfrac{1}{2}(12)h$, but without knowing the height *h*, you cannot compute a single value for the area, so (2) also is NOT sufficient. Taking (1) and (2) together, you can substitute the length of side *AB* from (2) into the formula $A = \dfrac{s^2\sqrt{3}}{4}$ based on the information from (1) and then compute a single value for *A*. Therefore, BOTH statements TOGETHER are sufficient, but NEITHER statement ALONE is sufficient.

16. **A** To answer the question, you need to determine $y = \dfrac{k}{360}$. From the information in (1), $\dfrac{2}{9} = \dfrac{k}{540}$, from which you can determine *k* and thereafter, $y = \dfrac{k}{360}$. Thus, (1) is sufficient. From the information in (2), $y = \dfrac{k}{x}$, which you know already, so further information is needed, and (2) is NOT sufficient. Therefore, statement (1) ALONE is sufficient, but statement (2) alone is not sufficient.

17. **D** Let x = the marked-down price. Then $x + 8\%x$ = the amount the customer pays for the dress at the marked-down price including tax. From the information in (1), you can write the equation $(\$85 + 8\% \cdot \$85) - (x + 8\%x) = \$91.80 - 1.08x = \$18.36$, which you can solve for a single value of x. Thereafter, you can compute $x + 8\%x$. Therefore, (1) is sufficient. From the information in (2), you can write the equation $0.08x = \$5.44$, which you can solve for a single value of x. Thereafter, you can compute $x + 8\%x$. Therefore, (2) also is sufficient, and EACH statement ALONE is sufficient.

18. **C** From the question information, $a_{20} = a_1 + (20 - 1)d = a_1 + (19)d$, so you need the values of a_1 and d to determine a_{20}. From the information in (1), $a_4 = 17 = a_1 + 3d$, which (because you have two variables and only one equation) does not yield single values for a_1 and d, so (1) is NOT sufficient. From the information in (2), $a_{10} = 47 = a_1 + 9d$, which (because you have two variables and only one equation) does not yield single values for a_1 and d, so (2) also is NOT sufficient. Taking (1) and (2) together, you have two linear equations and two variables. You can solve the two equations simultaneously to determine values for a_1 and d, and you can use that solution to determine a_{20}. Therefore, BOTH statements TOGETHER are sufficient, but NEITHER statement ALONE is sufficient.

19. **A** From the question information, you can make a table of possible paired values for x and y:

x	1	2	3	4	5	6	7	8	9
y	9	8	7	6	5	4	3	2	1

    Using the information in (1) and checking through the possible paired values for x and y, only one pair ($x = 6$ and $y = 4$) satisfies the double inequality, $37 < 5x + 2y < 41$. Thus, (1) is SUFFICIENT. The information in (2) limits the possible paired values for x and y to the four pairs for which $x > 5$, but further information is needed to determine a single value for y. Thus, (2) is NOT sufficient. Statement (1) ALONE is sufficient, but statement (2) alone is not sufficient.

20. **C** From the question information, x^2 (the area of the square) $= bh$ (the area of the parallelogram). From the information in (1), $x^2 = (10)^2 = 100 = bh$, which (because you have two variables and only one equation) does not yield a single value for h, so (1) is NOT sufficient. From the information in (2), $x^2 = bh = 20h$, which (because you have two variables and only one equation) does not yield a single value for h, so (2) also is NOT sufficient. Taking (1) and (2) together, you have $100 = 20h$, which you can solve to determine a single value of h. Therefore, BOTH statements TOGETHER are sufficient, but NEITHER statement ALONE is sufficient.

Data Sufficiens Questions Drill 5

1. If m and p are integers, is $m^p < 0$?

   (1) $m < 0$
   (2) p is even.
   Ⓐ Statement (1) ALONE is sufficient, but statement (2) alone is not sufficient.
   Ⓑ Statement (2) ALONE is sufficient, but statement (1) alone is not sufficient.
   Ⓒ BOTH statements TOGETHER are sufficient, but NEITHER statement
   ALONE is sufficient.
   Ⓓ EACH statement ALONE is sufficient.
   Ⓔ Statements (1) and (2) TOGETHER are NOT sufficient.

2. In a survey asking 25 students in a classroom about their juice preferences (apple,
   orange, grape, and/or none), 15 said they like orange juice, and 10 said they like
   apple juice. How many students like both orange and apple juice?

   (1) One student said she did not like any kind of juice.
   (2) Three students said they like grape juice but not orange or apple juice.
   Ⓐ Statement (1) ALONE is sufficient, but statement (2) alone is not sufficient.
   Ⓑ Statement (2) ALONE is sufficient, but statement (1) alone is not sufficient.
   Ⓒ BOTH statements TOGETHER are sufficient, but NEITHER statement
   ALONE is sufficient.
   Ⓓ EACH statement ALONE is sufficient.
   Ⓔ Statements (1) and (2) TOGETHER are NOT sufficient.

3. What is the smallest of three consecutive odd integers?

   (1) The sum of the three integers is 147.
   (2) The largest integer is 4 more than the smallest integer.
   Ⓐ Statement (1) ALONE is sufficient, but statement (2) alone is not sufficient.
   Ⓑ Statement (2) ALONE is sufficient, but statement (1) alone is not sufficient.
   Ⓒ BOTH statements TOGETHER are sufficient, but NEITHER statement
   ALONE is sufficient.
   Ⓓ EACH statement ALONE is sufficient.
   Ⓔ Statements (1) and (2) TOGETHER are NOT sufficient.

4. If the temperature is 20° at 5 a.m. and rises at the rate of $y°$ per hour, what is the
   value of y?

   (1) At 6 a.m., the temperature is $20° + y°$.
   (2) The temperature at noon is 41°.
   Ⓐ Statement (1) ALONE is sufficient, but statement (2) alone is not sufficient.
   Ⓑ Statement (2) ALONE is sufficient, but statement (1) alone is not sufficient.
   Ⓒ BOTH statements TOGETHER are sufficient, but NEITHER statement
   ALONE is sufficient.
   Ⓓ EACH statement ALONE is sufficient.
   Ⓔ Statements (1) and (2) TOGETHER are NOT sufficient.

5. A customer makes a deposit of $x and withdrawals of $y and $z from a checking account. If the initial balance was $195 and no other transactions have taken place, what is the customer's new balance?

  (1) $x - (\$y + \$z) = \$135$
  (2) The difference between $x and $y is $135 more than $z.
  Ⓐ Statement (1) ALONE is sufficient, but statement (2) alone is not sufficient.
  Ⓑ Statement (2) ALONE is sufficient, but statement (1) alone is not sufficient.
  Ⓒ BOTH statements TOGETHER are sufficient, but NEITHER statement ALONE is sufficient.
  Ⓓ EACH statement ALONE is sufficient.
  Ⓔ Statements (1) and (2) TOGETHER are NOT sufficient.

6. What is the value of the larger of two consecutive integers?

  (1) The greater integer is odd.
  (2) The product of the two integers is 182.
  Ⓐ Statement (1) ALONE is sufficient, but statement (2) alone is not sufficient.
  Ⓑ Statement (2) ALONE is sufficient, but statement (1) alone is not sufficient.
  Ⓒ BOTH statements TOGETHER are sufficient, but NEITHER statement ALONE is sufficient.
  Ⓓ EACH statement ALONE is sufficient.
  Ⓔ Statements (1) and (2) TOGETHER are NOT sufficient.

7. What is the value of $\left(x\sqrt{3} + y\sqrt{3} \right)^2$?

  (1) $2x + 2y = 20$
  (2) $x^2 + xy = 100 - y^2 - xy$
  Ⓐ Statement (1) ALONE is sufficient, but statement (2) alone is not sufficient.
  Ⓑ Statement (2) ALONE is sufficient, but statement (1) alone is not sufficient.
  Ⓒ BOTH statements TOGETHER are sufficient, but NEITHER statement ALONE is sufficient.
  Ⓓ EACH statement ALONE is sufficient.
  Ⓔ Statements (1) and (2) TOGETHER are NOT sufficient.

8. What is the value of $a^{-0.6}$?

  (1) $\sqrt[5]{a} = 2$
  (2) $a^2 = 32a$
  Ⓐ Statement (1) ALONE is sufficient, but statement (2) alone is not sufficient.
  Ⓑ Statement (2) ALONE is sufficient, but statement (1) alone is not sufficient.
  Ⓒ BOTH statements TOGETHER are sufficient, but NEITHER statement ALONE is sufficient.
  Ⓓ EACH statement ALONE is sufficient.
  Ⓔ Statements (1) and (2) TOGETHER are NOT sufficient.

9. To the nearest dollar, what is the value of the money in a rectangular box filled to capacity with twenty-dollar bills?

   (1) The box measures 24 by 16 by 8 inches.
   (2) A stack of 100 twenty-dollar bills is 0.43 inch tall.
   (A) Statement (1) ALONE is sufficient, but statement (2) alone is not sufficient.
   (B) Statement (2) ALONE is sufficient, but statement (1) alone is not sufficient.
   (C) BOTH statements TOGETHER are sufficient, but NEITHER statement ALONE is sufficient.
   (D) EACH statement ALONE is sufficient.
   (E) Statements (1) and (2) TOGETHER are NOT sufficient.

10. How many days will it take four identical machines working together to do a job?

    (1) Each machine does $\frac{1}{4}$ of the job.
    (2) Two such machines can do the job in 8 days.
    (A) Statement (1) ALONE is sufficient, but statement (2) alone is not sufficient.
    (B) Statement (2) ALONE is sufficient, but statement (1) alone is not sufficient.
    (C) BOTH statements TOGETHER are sufficient, but NEITHER statement ALONE is sufficient.
    (D) EACH statement ALONE is sufficient.
    (E) Statements (1) and (2) TOGETHER are NOT sufficient.

11. Can $130°$ be the measure of an exterior angle of triangle ABC?

    (1) $m\angle B = 55°$
    (2) $m\angle C = 65°$
    (A) Statement (1) ALONE is sufficient, but statement (2) alone is not sufficient.
    (B) Statement (2) ALONE is sufficient, but statement (1) alone is not sufficient.
    (C) BOTH statements TOGETHER are sufficient, but NEITHER statement ALONE is sufficient.
    (D) EACH statement ALONE is sufficient.
    (E) Statements (1) and (2) TOGETHER are NOT sufficient.

12. How many sides does the regular convex polygon have?

    (1) The measure of each exterior angle is $45°$.
    (2) The measure of each interior angle is $135°$.
    (A) Statement (1) ALONE is sufficient, but statement (2) alone is not sufficient.
    (B) Statement (2) ALONE is sufficient, but statement (1) alone is not sufficient.
    (C) BOTH statements TOGETHER are sufficient, but NEITHER statement ALONE is sufficient.
    (D) EACH statement ALONE is sufficient.
    (E) Statements (1) and (2) TOGETHER are NOT sufficient.

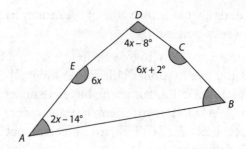

13. In the preceding pentagon *ABCDE*, what is the measure, in degrees, of the largest angle?

   (1)   ∠*C* is the largest angle.
   (2) $m\angle B = 2x$
   (A) Statement (1) ALONE is sufficient, but statement (2) alone is not sufficient.
   (B) Statement (2) ALONE is sufficient, but statement (1) alone is not sufficient.
   (C) BOTH statements TOGETHER are sufficient, but NEITHER statement ALONE is sufficient.
   (D) EACH statement ALONE is sufficient.
   (E) Statements (1) and (2) TOGETHER are NOT sufficient.

14. *P* and *Q* are points in a coordinate plane. What is the distance between *P* and *Q*?

   (1)   *P* has coordinates $(-3, 2)$, and *Q* has coordinates $(3, 4)$.
   (2)   The midpoint between *P* and *Q* is $(0, 3)$.
   (A) Statement (1) ALONE is sufficient, but statement (2) alone is not sufficient.
   (B) Statement (2) ALONE is sufficient, but statement (1) alone is not sufficient.
   (C) BOTH statements TOGETHER are sufficient, but NEITHER statement ALONE is sufficient.
   (D) EACH statement ALONE is sufficient.
   (E) Statements (1) and (2) TOGETHER are NOT sufficient.

15. A translation from $P(x, y)$ to $P'(x', y')$ is described as "8 units right and 5 units down." What is the value of x'?

   (1) $y' = -1$
   (2) $y = 4$
   (A) Statement (1) ALONE is sufficient, but statement (2) alone is not sufficient.
   (B) Statement (2) ALONE is sufficient, but statement (1) alone is not sufficient.
   (C) BOTH statements TOGETHER are sufficient, but NEITHER statement ALONE is sufficient.
   (D) EACH statement ALONE is sufficient.
   (E) Statements (1) and (2) TOGETHER are NOT sufficient.

16. A box contains cards with the names of boys and girls in a classroom written on them. Only one name is written on each card, and the cards are identical in size and shape. Two cards are randomly drawn from the box, one after the other. What is the probability that the students whose names are drawn are both boys?

    (1) The first card drawn is not replaced before the second card is drawn.
    (2) The box contains the names of 8 boys and 12 girls.
    Ⓐ Statement (1) ALONE is sufficient, but statement (2) alone is not sufficient.
    Ⓑ Statement (2) ALONE is sufficient, but statement (1) alone is not sufficient.
    Ⓒ BOTH statements TOGETHER are sufficient, but NEITHER statement ALONE is sufficient.
    Ⓓ EACH statement ALONE is sufficient.
    Ⓔ Statements (1) and (2) TOGETHER are NOT sufficient.

17. Is $\dfrac{4^{x+3}}{64}>1$?

    (1) $4^{x+3}>0$
    (2) $4^{x}>1$
    Ⓐ Statement (1) ALONE is sufficient, but statement (2) alone is not sufficient.
    Ⓑ Statement (2) ALONE is sufficient, but statement (1) alone is not sufficient.
    Ⓒ BOTH statements TOGETHER are sufficient, but NEITHER statement ALONE is sufficient.
    Ⓓ EACH statement ALONE is sufficient.
    Ⓔ Statements (1) and (2) TOGETHER are NOT sufficient.

18. A collection of coins consists of only nickels, dimes, and quarters. How many quarters are in the collection?

    (1) The face value of the coins is $5.
    (2) There are 58 coins in all.
    Ⓐ Statement (1) ALONE is sufficient, but statement (2) alone is not sufficient.
    Ⓑ Statement (2) ALONE is sufficient, but statement (1) alone is not sufficient.
    Ⓒ BOTH statements TOGETHER are sufficient, but NEITHER statement ALONE is sufficient.
    Ⓓ EACH statement ALONE is sufficient.
    Ⓔ Statements (1) and (2) TOGETHER are NOT sufficient.

19. Triangle *ABC* is isosceles. What is its perimeter?

    (1) $AB=15$
    (2) $BC=20$
    Ⓐ Statement (1) ALONE is sufficient, but statement (2) alone is not sufficient.
    Ⓑ Statement (2) ALONE is sufficient, but statement (1) alone is not sufficient.
    Ⓒ BOTH statements TOGETHER are sufficient, but NEITHER statement ALONE is sufficient.
    Ⓓ EACH statement ALONE is sufficient.
    Ⓔ Statements (1) and (2) TOGETHER are NOT sufficient.

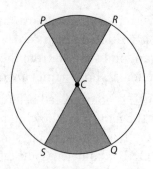

20. What fraction of circle C is shaded?

  (1) $m\angle PCS = 120°$
  (2)   length of $\overset{\frown}{PR}$ = length of $\overset{\frown}{SQ}$

  (A) Statement (1) ALONE is sufficient, but statement (2) alone is not sufficient.
  (B) Statement (2) ALONE is sufficient, but statement (1) alone is not sufficient.
  (C) BOTH statements TOGETHER are sufficient, but NEITHER statement ALONE is sufficient.
  (D) EACH statement ALONE is sufficient.
  (E) Statements (1) and (2) TOGETHER are NOT sufficient.

Answers

1. **B** If, according to (1), m is negative, then m^p is positive if p is even and negative if p is odd. For instance, if $m = -1$ and $p = 2$, then $m^p = (-1)^2 = 1 > 0$, and if $m = -1$ and $p = 1$, then $m^p = (-1)^1 = -1 < 0$. Thus, further information is needed, and (1) is NOT sufficient. If, according to (2), p is even, then m^p is positive whether m is positive or negative. For instance, if $m = -1$ and $p = 2$, $m^p = (-1)^2 = 1 > 0$, and if $m = 1$ and $p = 2$, $m^p = (1)^2 = 1 > 0$. Therefore, statement (2) ALONE is sufficient, but statement (1) alone is not sufficient.

2. **C** From the information in (1), you know that 24 students like some kind of juice, but without further information about the students who like grape juice, you cannot determine how many students like both orange and apple juice. Therefore, (1) is NOT sufficient. From the information in (2), you know that three students like only grape juice, but without further information about the students who do not like any of the three kinds of juices, you cannot determine how many students like both orange and apple juice. Therefore, (2) is NOT sufficient.

   Taking (1) and (2) together, let x = the number of students who like both orange and apple juice, o = the number of students who like only orange juice, a = the number of students who like only apple juice, and g = the number of students who like only grape juice. Draw a Venn diagram, using the question information and statements (1) and (2).

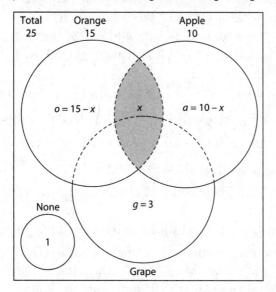

   From the Venn diagram, you can write the equation $(15 - x) + x + (10 - x) + 3 + 1 = 25$, which you can solve for a single value of x, the number of students who like both orange and apple juice. Therefore, BOTH statements TOGETHER are sufficient, but NEITHER statement ALONE is sufficient.

3. **A** Let n, $n + 2$, and $n + 4$ be the three consecutive odd integers. From the information in (1), you can write the equation $n + (n + 2) + (n + 4) = 147$, which you can solve for a single value of n. Therefore, (1) is sufficient. From the information in (2), you can write the equation $n + 4 = n + 4$, which has an infinite number of solutions, so it is NOT sufficient. Therefore, statement (1) ALONE is sufficient, but statement (2) alone is not sufficient.

4. **B** From the information in (1), you can determine that the temperature rises y degrees in 1 hour, but additional information is needed to determine y; so (1) is NOT sufficient. From the information in (2), given that noon is 7 hours past 5 a.m., you can write the

equation $20° + 7y° = 41°$, which you can solve for a single value of y. Therefore, statement (2) ALONE is sufficient, but statement (1) alone is not sufficient.

5. **D** The customer's new balance is the initial balance plus deposits minus withdrawals, or $\$195 + \$x - \$y - \$z$. From the information in (1), $\$195 + \$x - \$y - \$z = 195 + \$x - (\$y + \$z) = \$195 + \$135 = \$330$. Therefore, (1) is sufficient. From the information in (2), you can write the equation $\$x - \$y = \$z + \$135$, from which you can obtain the equation $\$x - \$y - \$z = \$135$. Substituting this value of $\$x - \$y - \$z$ into the equation for the new balance, you have $\$195 + \$x - \$y - \$z = \$195 + \$135 = \$330$. Therefore, (2) is sufficient, and EACH statement ALONE is sufficient.

6. **C** Let $n =$ the smaller integer and $n + 1 =$ the greater integer. From the information in (1), you know that n is even and $n + 1$ is odd, but further information is needed to determine $n + 1$, so (1) is NOT sufficient. From the information in (2), $n(n+1) = 182$, which can be solved as follows:

$$n(n+1) = 182$$

$$n^2 + n - 182 = 0$$

$$(n+14)(n-13) = 0$$

Thus, $n = -14$ with $n+1 = -13$, or $n = 13$ with $n+1 = 14$, so further information is needed, meaning (2) also is NOT sufficient. Taking (1) and (2) together, use (1) to pick the solution in (2) where n is even and $n + 1$ is odd: $n = -14$ with $n+1 = -13$. Therefore, BOTH statements TOGETHER are sufficient, but NEITHER statement ALONE is sufficient.

7. **D** First, observe that $\left(x\sqrt{3} + y\sqrt{3}\right)^2 = \left(\sqrt{3}(x+y)\right)^2 = \left(\sqrt{3}\right)^2 (x+y)^2 = 3(x+y)^2$. From the information in (1), $2x + 2y = 20$ is equivalent to $x + y = 10$, so $\left(x\sqrt{3} + y\sqrt{3}\right)^2 = 3(x+y)^2 = 3(10)^2$, and (1) is SUFFICIENT. From the information in (2), $x^2 + xy = 100 - y^2 - xy$ is equivalent to $x^2 + 2xy + y^2 = 100$, which can be written as $(x+y)^2 = 100$, so $\left(x\sqrt{3} + y\sqrt{3}\right)^2 = 3(x+y)^2 = 3(100)$, and (2) also is SUFFICIENT. Therefore, EACH statement ALONE is sufficient.

8. **A** From the information in (1), $a = 2^5$, which you can substitute into the equation given in the problem: $a^{-0.6} = \left(2^5\right)^{-0.6}$. You can compute the answer as a single value, so (1) is SUFFICIENT. From the information in (2), $a^2 - 32a = a(a-32) = 0$, which implies that $a = 0$ or $a = 32$. The solution is not a single value, so (2) is NOT sufficient. *Tip:* You must NOT divide both sides of $a^2 = 32a$ by a, because you have no way of determining whether $a = 0$. Therefore, statement (1) ALONE is sufficient, but statement (2) alone is not sufficient.

9. **E** From the information in (1), the box's capacity (volume) measures $24 \times 16 \times 8$ cubic inches, but further information is needed to determine how many $20 bills will fit inside of it, so (1) is NOT sufficient. The information in (2) gives you the height of a stack of a hundred $20 bills, but further information is needed to determine how many stacks will fit inside the box, so (2) also is NOT sufficient. Taking (1) and (2) together, you can determine the capacity of the box from (1), but without knowing the length and width of a stack of a hundred $20 bills, in addition to the stack's height of 0.43 inch from (2), you cannot determine how many stacks will fit inside the box. Therefore, statements (1) and (2) TOGETHER are NOT sufficient.

10. **B** Let d = the number of days it will take four machines to do the job. The question information implies that, over the period of d days, each machine does $\frac{1}{4}$ of the job (because the machines are identical), so the information in (1) is not helpful. Thus, further information is needed to determine d. Therefore, (1) is NOT sufficient. From the information in (2), if 2 machines take 8 days, then 4 machines will take half as long, which implies that d = 4 days. Therefore, (2) is SUFFICIENT. Therefore, statement (2) ALONE is sufficient, but statement (1) alone is not sufficient.

11. **C** From the information in (1), you know that the measure of the exterior angle that is adjacent to $\angle B$ equals $180° - 55° = 125° \neq 130°$, but you need additional information to determine the measures of the exterior angles at A and C, so (1) is NOT sufficient. From the information in (2), you know that the measure of the exterior angle that is adjacent to $\angle C$ equals $180° - 65° = 115° \neq 130°$, but you need additional information to determine the measures of the exterior angles at A and B, so (2) also is NOT sufficient. Taking (1) and (2) together, neither of the exterior angles at B or C can measure 130°. Furthermore, the measure of the exterior angle at A equals the sum of the measures of the two nonadjacent interior angles. Thus, the measure of the exterior angle at $A = 55° + 65° = 120° \neq 130°$. So none of the exterior angles of triangle ABC can measure 130°. Therefore, BOTH statements TOGETHER are sufficient, but NEITHER statement ALONE is sufficient.

12. **D** From the information in (1), $\frac{360°}{n} = 45°$ (because the measure of each exterior angle of a regular convex polygon is $\frac{360°}{n}$). You can solve this equation for a single value of n, so (1) is SUFFICIENT. From the information in (2), $\frac{(n-2)180°}{n} = 135°$ (because the measure of each interior angle of a regular convex polygon is $\frac{(n-2)180°}{n}$). You can solve this equation for a single value of n, so (2) also is SUFFICIENT. Therefore, EACH statement ALONE is sufficient.

13. **B** From the question information, the sum of the measures of the angles of pentagon $ABCDE$ is $(n-2)180° = (5-2)180° = (3)180° = 540°$. Thus, $(2x-14) + m\angle B + (6x+2) + (4x-8) + 6x = 540°$. From the information in (1), you know that $6x + 2$ is the greatest of the measures of the angles, but further information is needed to determine a single value for $6x + 2$, so (1) is NOT sufficient. From the information in (2), you can set up the equation $(2x-14) + (2x) + (6x+2) + (4x-8) + 6x = 540°$, which you can solve for a single value of x. You can use that value to compute $6x + 2$, the measure of the largest angle, so (2) is SUFFICIENT. Therefore, statement (2) ALONE is sufficient, but statement (1) alone is not sufficient.

14. **A** To apply the information in (1), recall that the distance d between two points (x_1, y_1) and (x_2, y_2) in a coordinate plane is $d = \sqrt{(x_2 - x_1)^2 + (y_2 - y_1)^2}$. Thus, you can substitute the coordinates of P and Q into this formula and determine a single value of d, so (1) is SUFFICIENT. To apply the information in (2), recall that the midpoint between two points (x_1, y_1) and (x_2, y_2) in a coordinate plane is the point with coordinates $\left(\frac{x_1 + x_2}{2}, \frac{y_1 + y_2}{2} \right)$. Thus, $\left(\frac{x_1 + x_2}{2}, \frac{y_1 + y_2}{2} \right) = (0, 3)$, but you need further information to determine the values of x_1, y_1, x_2, and y_2, which you can use to determine the distance between P and Q. Thus, (2) is NOT sufficient. Statement (1) ALONE is sufficient, but statement (2) alone is not sufficient.

15. **E** From the question information, $(x', y') = (x+8, y-5)$. From the information in (1), you can determine y but not x', so (1) is NOT sufficient. From the information in (2), you can determine y' but not x', so (2) also is NOT sufficient. Taking (1) and (2) together, without having information about x, you cannot determine x'. Therefore, statements (1) and (2) TOGETHER are NOT sufficient.

16. **C** The probability, P, that the students whose names are drawn are both boys is the probability that a boy's name is drawn first times the *conditional* probability that a boy's name is drawn second *given that a boy's name was drawn first*. The information in (1) tells you that because the card is not replaced, the outcome of the first draw influences the outcome of the second draw. But, you are unable to determine the desired probability, so (1) is NOT sufficient. From the information in (2), the probability that a boy's name is drawn first is $\dfrac{8}{8+12} = \dfrac{8}{20}$. However, without knowing whether the first card is replaced, the *conditional* probability that a boy's name is drawn second cannot be determined; so (2) is NOT sufficient. Taking (1) and (2) together, $P = \left(\dfrac{8}{20}\right)\left(\dfrac{7}{19}\right)$, which you can compute. Therefore, BOTH statements together are sufficient, but NEITHER statement ALONE is sufficient.

17. **B** Observe that $\dfrac{4^{x+3}}{64} = \dfrac{4^x \cdot 4^3}{4^3} = 4^x$. The information in (1) is irrelevant because 4 raised to any power is greater than 0, so (1) is NOT sufficient. Applying the information in (2), $\dfrac{4^{x+3}}{64} = 4^x$, and as given, $4^x > 1$. Therefore, statement (2) ALONE is sufficient, but statement (1) alone is not sufficient.

18. **E** Let n = the number of nickels, d = the number of dimes, and q = the number of quarters. From the information in (1), $\$0.05n + \$0.10d + \$0.25q = \$5.00$, which (because you have three variables and one equation) does not yield a single value for q, so (1) is NOT sufficient. From the information in (2), $n + d + q = 58$, which (because you have three variables and one equation) does not yield a single value for q, so (2) also is NOT sufficient. Taking (1) and (2) together, you have you have two equations and three variables, so further information is needed to determine a single value for q. Therefore, statements (1) and (2) TOGETHER are NOT sufficient.

19. **E** From the question information, let x = the length of one of the two congruent sides of triangle ABC and y = the length of the noncongruent side. Then the perimeter, P, of the triangle is $P = 2x + y$. From the information in (1), you cannot determine whether AB equals x or y. If $AB = x$, then $P = 2 \cdot 15 + y = 30 + y$, but without knowing the value of y, you cannot determine P. Similarly, if $AB = y$, then $P = 2x + 15$, but without knowing the value of x, you cannot determine P. Thus, either way, further information is needed, and (1) is NOT sufficient. From the information in (2), you cannot determine whether BC equals x or y. If $BC = x$, then $P = 2 \cdot 20 + y = 40 + y$, but without knowing the value of y, you cannot determine P. Similarly, if $BC = y$, then $P = 2x + 20$, but without knowing the value of x, you cannot determine P. Thus, either way, further information is needed, and (2) is NOT sufficient. Taking (1) and (2) together, if $AB = x$ and $BC = y$, then $P = 2 \cdot 15 + 20 = 50$. But if $AB = y$ and $BC = x$, then $P = 2 \cdot 20 + 15 = 55$. Thus, you cannot determine a single value for P. Therefore, statements (1) and (2) TOGETHER are NOT sufficient.

20. **A** From the information in (1), $m\angle PCR = m\angle PCS = 120°$ (vertical angles are equal). Thus, $\dfrac{2\cdot 120°}{360°} = \dfrac{240°}{360°} = \dfrac{2}{3}$ of the circle is not shaded. Hence, $\dfrac{1}{3}$ of the circle is shaded, so (1) is SUFFICIENT. Knowing from the information in (2) that these two arcs have equal lengths does not provide enough information for you to determine what fractional part of the circle they represent, so (2) is NOT sufficient. Therefore, statement (1) ALONE is sufficient, but statement (2) alone is not sufficient.

PART 6

GMAT Math Review

CHAPTER 8

Arithmetic Review

- Numbers and operations
- Roots and radicals
- Exponents
- Order of operations
- Scientific notation
- Sets
- Counting techniques
- Basic probability
- Graphical representation of data
- Descriptive measures of data
- Simple Linear Regression

Numbers and Operations

Counting Numbers, Whole Numbers, and Integers

The **counting** numbers (or **natural numbers**) are the numbers 1, 2, 3, and so on. The **whole numbers** are the numbers 0, 1, 2, 3, and so on. Whole numbers that are greater than 1 are either *prime* or *composite*. A **prime number** is a whole number greater than 1 that has exactly two distinct whole number factors: itself and 1. The first 10 prime numbers are 2, 3, 5, 7, 11, 13, 17, 19, 23, and 29. The whole numbers greater than 1 that are *not* prime are the **composite numbers**. They are the numbers that have more than two distinct whole number factors. The number 1 is neither prime nor composite.

The **integers** are either **positive** (1, 2, 3, . . .) or **negative** (. . . –3, –2, –1) or **zero**. Note: The three dots indicate that the pattern continues without end. On the number line, positive numbers are located to the right of zero and negative numbers are to the left of zero. Zero is neither positive nor negative:

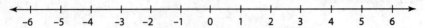

Integers that divide evenly by 2 are **even**. The even integers are ...−6, −4, −2, 0, 2, 4, 6, ... Integers that do *not* divide evenly by 2 are **odd**. The odd integers are . . . −5, −3, −1, 1, 3, 5, ... *Tip*: Notice that 0 is an even integer.

Decimals

Decimals are written using a **base-10 place-value system**. The value of a decimal number is determined by the placement of the decimal point in the number. A place-value diagram for some of the positional values of the decimal system is shown here.

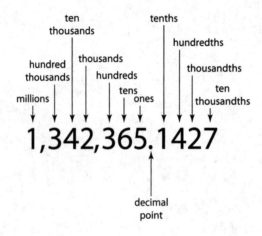

In a whole number, the decimal point is understood to be to the immediate right of the rightmost digit.

Fractions

The **fraction** $\frac{n}{d}$ is composed of three parts. The line between n and d is the **fraction bar**. The number above the fraction bar is the **numerator**, and the number below the fraction bar is the **denominator**. The fraction $\frac{n}{d}$ means $n \div d$. *Tip*: The denominator of a fraction can never be zero, because division by zero is undefined. The **reciprocal** of the fraction $\frac{a}{b}$ is the fraction $\frac{b}{a}$, provided $a \neq 0$ and $b \neq 0$.

In **proper fractions** (such as $\frac{5}{12}$), the numerator is less than the denominator. In **improper fractions** (such as $\frac{8}{5}$ and $\frac{4}{4}$), the numerator is greater than or equal to the denominator. The value of an improper fraction is greater than or equal to one. A **mixed number** (such as $1\frac{3}{5}$) is the sum of a whole number and a fraction. Change an improper fraction to a mixed number or a whole number by performing the indicated division. If there is a remainder, write it as the numerator of a fraction that has the divisor as the denominator, for example:

$$\frac{8}{5} = 5\overline{)\begin{array}{l} 1 \\ 8 \\ -5 \\ \hline 3 \end{array}} = 1\frac{3}{5}$$

Change a mixed number to an improper fraction by multiplying the whole number part by the denominator of the fractional part. Then add the numerator of the fractional part to the resulting product. Place the resulting sum over the denominator of the fractional part, for example:

$$1\frac{3}{5} = \frac{1\times5+3}{5} = \frac{5+3}{5} = \frac{8}{5}$$

If both the numerator and denominator of a fraction are multiplied or divided by the same nonzero number, the value of the fraction is unchanged. The resulting fraction is **equivalent** to the original fraction. For example, $\frac{2}{3}$ and $\frac{2\times2}{3\times2} = \frac{4}{6}$ are equivalent fractions. Similarly, $\frac{12}{15}$ and $\frac{12\div3}{15\div3} = \frac{4}{5}$ are equivalent fractions.

To write two fractions as equivalent fractions with the same denominator, use the least common multiple as the common denominator. A **multiple** of a number is the product of the number and any counting number. The **least common multiple** (or **LCM**) of two numbers is the least counting number that is a multiple of both numbers. List multiples of the greater number, in order. Stop when you first list a multiple that is also a multiple of the other number. This multiple will be the LCM of the two numbers. For instance, to write $\frac{3}{20}$ and $\frac{2}{15}$ as fractions with the same denominator, find the LCM (20, 15). List the multiples of 20, in order: 20, 40, 60. Stop. The number 60 is the first multiple of 20 that is also a multiple of 15, so 60 is the LCM (20, 15). Thus,

$$\frac{3}{20} = \frac{3\times3}{20\times3} = \frac{9}{60} \text{ and } \frac{2}{15} = \frac{2\times4}{15\times4} = \frac{8}{60}.$$

When the only common factor between the numerator and denominator of a fraction is one, the fraction is in **lowest terms**. **Reduce** a fraction to lowest terms by dividing the numerator and denominator by their greatest common factor. The **greatest common factor** (or **GCF**) of two numbers is the largest factor common to the two numbers. *Tip*: The GCF is always positive. For example, reduce $\frac{60}{84}$ by dividing its numerator and denominator by the GCF of 60 and 84. List the positive factors of 60 in pairs:

1	2	3	4	5	6
60	30	20	15	12	10

List the positive factors of 84 in pairs:

1	2	3	4	6	7
84	42	28	21	14	12

To read the factors of a number from least to greatest: Start at the top left of the factor table, move left to right across the top row, and then right to left across the bottom row.

Examination of the two lists shows GCF (60, 84) is 12. Thus,

$$\frac{60}{84} = \frac{60 \div 12}{84 \div 12} = \frac{5}{7} \text{ in lowest terms.}$$

To obtain the equivalent decimal representation of a fraction, such as $\frac{4}{5}$, perform the indicated division. Divide the numerator by the denominator. Insert a decimal point in the numerator and one or more zeros (as needed) to the right of the decimal point to complete the division:

$$\frac{4}{5} = 5\overline{)\begin{array}{l} 0.8 \\ 4.0 \\ \underline{-40} \\ 0 \end{array}} = 0.8$$

Percents

Percent means "per hundred." The % sign means "times $\frac{1}{100}$" or "times 0.01." To change a percent to an equivalent fraction, substitute multiplying by $\frac{1}{100}$ for the percent sign. For example, $25\% = 25\left(\frac{1}{100}\right) = \frac{25}{100} = \frac{25 \div 25}{100 \div 25} = \frac{1}{4}$. To change a percent to an equivalent decimal, substitute multiplying by 0.01 for the percent sign. For example, $25\% = 25(0.01) = 0.25$.

Rational and Irrational Numbers

All of the counting numbers, whole numbers, integers, fractions, decimals, and percents are rational numbers. The **rational numbers** are numbers that can be expressed as $\frac{p}{q}$, where p and q are integers ($q \neq 0$). In other words, a rational number is a number that can be expressed as a quotient of an integer divided by an integer other than zero. *Tip:* Zero is excluded as a denominator for $\frac{p}{q}$ because division by zero is undefined, so $\frac{p}{0}$ has no meaning no matter what number you put in the place of p.

The decimal representations of rational numbers terminate or repeat a block of digits. For instance, $\frac{1}{4} = 0.25$ is a rational number whose decimal representation terminates, and $\frac{2}{11} = 0.1818\ldots$ is a rational number whose decimal representation repeats the block of digits "18." In most problems, you can round repeating decimals to a certain number of decimal places. For instance, rounded to two decimal places, $\frac{2}{11}$ is approximately 0.18.

The **irrational numbers** are numbers whose decimal representations neither terminate nor repeat. These numbers cannot be expressed as the quotient of two integers. For instance, the positive number that multiplies by itself to give 2 is an irrational number called "the positive square root of 2." You use the square root symbol $\left(\sqrt{}\right)$ to show the positive square root of 2 like this: $\sqrt{2}$. You cannot express $\sqrt{2}$ as the quotient of two integers, nor can you express it precisely in decimal form. Its decimal equivalent continues on and on without a pattern of any kind. No matter how far you go with decimal places, you can only approximate $\sqrt{2}$. For instance, rounded to three decimal places, $\sqrt{2}$ is approximately 1.414. There are infinitely many square roots and other roots as well that are irrational.

Real Numbers

The **real numbers** are all the rational and irrational numbers put together. All numbers used on the GMAT are real numbers. The relationship of the various sets of numbers included in the real numbers is shown here.

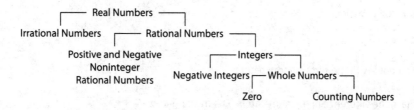

Real numbers are sometimes called **signed numbers** because they are positive, negative, or zero. Positive numbers lie to the right of zero on the number line and negative numbers lie to the left of zero. Zero is neither positive nor negative. It has no sign.

The **absolute value** of a real number is its distance from zero on the number line. The absolute value of a nonzero real number is positive. The absolute value of zero is zero. For example, the absolute value of −3.4 is 3.4, written as $|{-3.4}| = 3.4$.

Every real number has an **opposite**. If a real number is positive, its opposite is negative. If a real number is negative, its opposite is positive. For example, the numbers $\frac{3}{5}$ and $-\frac{3}{5}$ are opposites. Zero is its own opposite. A number and its opposite have the same absolute value. For instance,

$$\left|\frac{3}{5}\right| = \frac{3}{5} \text{ and } \left|-\frac{3}{5}\right| = \frac{3}{5}.$$

Operations with Real Numbers

Addition, subtraction, multiplication, and division are the four basic arithmetic operations. Following are rules that you will find useful for completing basic operations:

Adding Fractions

RULE	EXAMPLE
1. Fractions with the same denominators:	$\dfrac{5}{14}+\dfrac{3}{14}=$
Place the sum of the numerators over the common denominator.	$\dfrac{5+3}{14}=\dfrac{8}{14}$
Reduce to lowest terms, if possible.	$=\dfrac{8\div 2}{14\div 2}=\dfrac{4}{7}$
2. Fractions with different denominators:	$\dfrac{3}{20}+\dfrac{2}{15}=$
Find a common denominator by determining the least common multiple (LCM) of the denominators.	LCM (20, 15) = 60
Write each fraction as an equivalent fraction having the common denominator as a denominator.	$\dfrac{3}{20}=\dfrac{3\times 3}{20\times 3}=\dfrac{9}{60}$
	$\dfrac{2}{15}=\dfrac{2\times 4}{15\times 4}=\dfrac{8}{60}$
Add the transformed fractions using Rule 1.	$\dfrac{3}{20}+\dfrac{2}{15}=\dfrac{9}{60}+\dfrac{8}{60}=\dfrac{17}{60}$
Reduce to lowest terms, if needed.	Not needed.

Subtracting Fractions

RULE	EXAMPLE
1. Fractions with the same denominators:	$\dfrac{7}{12}-\dfrac{5}{12}=$
Place the difference of the numerators over the common denominator.	$\dfrac{7-5}{12}=\dfrac{2}{12}$
Reduce to lowest terms, if needed.	$=\dfrac{2\div 2}{12\div 2}=\dfrac{1}{6}$
2. Fractions with different denominators:	$\dfrac{7}{8}-\dfrac{5}{12}=$
Find a common denominator.	LCM (8, 12) = 24
Write each fraction as an equivalent fraction having the common denominator as a denominator.	$\dfrac{7}{8}=\dfrac{7\times 3}{8\times 3}=\dfrac{21}{24}$
	$\dfrac{5}{12}=\dfrac{5\times 2}{12\times 2}=\dfrac{10}{24}$
Subtract the transformed fractions using Rule 1.	$\dfrac{7}{8}-\dfrac{5}{12}=\dfrac{21}{24}-\dfrac{10}{24}=\dfrac{11}{24}$
Reduce to lowest terms, if needed.	Not needed.

Multiplying Fractions

RULE	EXAMPLE
1. Two proper fractions, two improper fractions, or a proper fraction and an improper fraction:	$\dfrac{2}{3} \times \dfrac{3}{4} =$
Place the product of the numerators over the product of the denominators.	$\dfrac{2}{3} \times \dfrac{3}{4} = \dfrac{6}{12}$
Reduce to lowest terms, if needed.	$= \dfrac{6 \div 6}{12 \div 6} = \dfrac{1}{2}$
2. A fraction and a whole number:	$\dfrac{3}{8} \times 12 =$
Write the whole number as a fraction with 1 as the denominator, and then multiply using Rule 1.	$\dfrac{3}{8} \times \dfrac{12}{1} = \dfrac{36}{8} = \dfrac{36 \div 4}{8 \div 4} = \dfrac{9}{2} \text{ or } 4\dfrac{1}{2}$
3. Two mixed numbers or a fraction and a mixed number:	$1\dfrac{3}{5} \times 2\dfrac{1}{2} =$
Change the mixed numbers to improper fractions and then multiply using Rule 1.	$1\dfrac{3}{5} \times 2\dfrac{1}{2} = \dfrac{8}{5} \times \dfrac{5}{2} = \dfrac{40}{10} = 4$

The process of multiplying fractions can be simplified by dividing out common factors, if any, before doing any multiplication. For example, $\dfrac{2}{3} \times \dfrac{3}{4} = \dfrac{\cancel{2}^{1}}{\cancel{3}_{1}} \times \dfrac{\cancel{3}^{1}}{\cancel{4}_{2}} = \dfrac{1}{2}$.

Also, remember you do *not* have to find a common denominator when multiplying fractions.

Dividing Fractions

RULE	EXAMPLE
1. Two proper fractions, two improper fractions, or a proper fraction and an improper fraction:	$\dfrac{3}{4} \div \dfrac{5}{8} =$
Multiply the first fraction by the reciprocal of the second fraction using multiplication Rule 1.	$\dfrac{3}{4} \div \dfrac{5}{8} = \dfrac{3}{\cancel{4}_{1}} \times \dfrac{\cancel{8}^{2}}{5} = \dfrac{6}{5} \text{ or } 1\dfrac{1}{5}$
2. A fraction divided by a whole number:	$\dfrac{9}{10} \div 3 =$
Write the whole number as a fraction with 1 as the denominator, and then divide using division Rule 1.	$\dfrac{9}{10} \div \dfrac{3}{1} = \dfrac{\cancel{9}^{3}}{10} \times \dfrac{1}{\cancel{3}_{1}} = \dfrac{3}{10}$
3. Two mixed numbers or a fraction and a mixed number:	$1\dfrac{3}{4} \div 2\dfrac{1}{3} =$
Change the mixed numbers to improper fractions, and then divide using division Rule 1.	$1\dfrac{3}{4} \div 2\dfrac{1}{3} = \dfrac{7}{4} \div \dfrac{7}{3} = \dfrac{\cancel{7}^{1}}{4} \times \dfrac{3}{\cancel{7}_{1}} = \dfrac{3}{4}$

Adding Decimals

RULE	EXAMPLE
Two or more decimals: Write the decimals one above the other, being careful to line up the decimal points vertically. *Tip*: Put zeros in empty decimal places to avoid adding incorrectly. Add as you would with whole numbers, ignoring the decimal points. Place the decimal point in the answer directly under the decimal points in the problem.	$75.2 + 0.54 + 3 + 8.001 =$ 75.200 0.540 3.000 + 8.001 86.741

Subtracting Decimals

Two decimals: Write the first decimal above the second one, being careful to line up the decimal points vertically. Put zeros in empty decimal places, when needed. Subtract as you would with whole numbers. Place the decimal point in the answer directly under the decimal points in the problem.	$7.3 - 5.257 =$ 7.300 − 5.257 2.043

Multiplying Decimals

RULE	EXAMPLE
Two decimals: Multiply the numbers as whole numbers, ignoring the decimal points. Correctly place the decimal point in the product. There are as many decimal places in the product as the total of decimal places in all the factors. If there are not enough places in the product, insert one or more zeros as needed to the left of the leftmost nonzero digit.	$35.8 \times 2.25 =$ 35.8　　(1 place) × 2.25　(+ 2 places) 80.550　(3 places)

Dividing Decimals

RULE	EXAMPLE
1. A decimal by a whole number: Divide as you would with whole numbers. Place the decimal point in the quotient directly above the decimal point in the dividend. *Tip*: Recall that in a division problem, the labels of the numbers are $\dfrac{\text{quotient}}{\text{"divisor)dividend"}}$	$2.84 \div 4 =$ $\dfrac{0.71}{4)2.84}$
2. A decimal by a decimal: Multiply both the dividend and divisor by the power of 10 (10, 100, 1,000, and so forth) to make the divisor a whole number. Do this multiplication mentally. *Tip*: To multiply any number by 10, 100, 1,000, and so forth, move its decimal point to the right as many places as there are zeros in the multiplier. If necessary, attach additional zeros after the dividend's rightmost digit. Divide using Rule 1.	$2.3415 \div 0.005 =$ $0.005)2.3415 = 5)\overset{468.3}{2341.5}$

Adding and Subtracting Real Numbers

RULE	EXAMPLE(S)
1. The sum of 0 and any number is the number.	$0 + 2.54 = 2.54 + 0 = 2.54$
2. The sum of a number and its opposite is 0.	$\dfrac{3}{5} + \left(-\dfrac{3}{5}\right) = -\dfrac{3}{5} + \dfrac{3}{5} = 0$
3. To add two numbers that have the same sign, add their absolute values and give the sum their common sign.	$15 + 10 = 25$ $-20 + -14 = -34$
4. To add two numbers that have opposite signs, subtract the lesser absolute value from the greater absolute value and give the result the same sign as the number with the greater absolute value.	$15 + -10 = 5$ $-45 + 30 = -15$
5. To subtract a number, add its opposite.	$15 - 10 = 15 + -10 = 5$ $-35 - 20 = -35 + -20 = -55$ $16 - -12 = 16 + 12 = 28$ $-45 - -30 = -45 + 30 = -15$

Multiplying and Dividing Real Numbers

RULE	EXAMPLE(S)
1. Zero times any number is 0.	$0 \cdot 1235 = 1235 \cdot 0 = 0$
2. The product of two numbers with the same sign is positive.	$(-4)(-3) = 12$ $(5)(6) = 30$
3. The product of two numbers with opposite signs is negative.	$(-4)(3) = -12$ $(5)(-6) = -30$
4. When 0 is one of the factors, the product is always 0; otherwise, products with an even number of negative factors are positive, whereas those with an odd number of negative factors are negative.	$(120)\left(-\dfrac{13}{30}\right)(0)(7.876) = 0$ $(-1)\left(\dfrac{1}{2}\right)(-2)(5)(-5)\left(-\dfrac{1}{5}\right) = 5$ $(-1)\left(\dfrac{1}{2}\right)(-2)(5)(-5)\left(\dfrac{1}{5}\right) = -5$
5. To divide by a nonzero number, follow the same rules for the sign of the quotient as those for multiplication.	$(-100) \div (-2) = 50$ $\dfrac{100}{2} = 50$ $(-100) \div (2) = -50$ $\dfrac{100}{-2} = -50$
6. The quotient is 0 when the dividend is 0 and the divisor is a nonzero number.	$0 \div 25 = 0$ $0 \div (-25) = 0$
7. The quotient is undefined when the divisor is 0.	$\dfrac{-150}{0}$ is undefined $\dfrac{4.6}{0}$ is undefined $\dfrac{0}{0}$ is undefined

Properties of Operations with Real Numbers

The following 11 properties hold for the operations of addition and multiplication for all real numbers *a*, *b*, and *c*:

- **Closure Property of Addition:** $(a + b)$ is a real number. This property guarantees that the sum of any two real numbers is always a real number.
- **Closure Property of Multiplication:** $(a \cdot b)$ is a real number. This property guarantees that the product of any two real numbers is always a real number.
- **Commutative Property of Addition:** $a + b = b + a$. This property allows you to reverse the order of the numbers when you add, without changing the sum.
- **Commutative Property of Multiplication:** $a \cdot b = b \cdot a$. This property allows you to reverse the order of the numbers when you multiply, without changing the product.
- **Associative Property of Addition:** $(a + b) + c = a + (b + c)$. This property says that when you have three numbers to add together, the final sum will be the same regardless of the way you group the numbers (two at a time) to perform the addition.
- **Associative Property of Multiplication:** $(ab)c = a(bc)$. This property says that when you have three numbers to multiply together, the final product will be the same regardless of the way you group the numbers (two at a time) to perform the multiplication.

The associative property is needed when you have to add or multiply more than two numbers because you can do addition or multiplication on only two numbers at a time. Thus, when you have three numbers, you must decide which two numbers you want to start with—the first two or the last two (assuming you keep the same order). Either way, your final answer is the same.

- **Additive Identity Property:** There exists a real number 0, called the additive identity, such that $a + 0 = a$ and $0 + a = a$. This property guarantees that you have a real number, namely 0, for which its sum with any real number is the number itself.
- **Multiplicative Identity Property:** There exists a real number 1, called the multiplicative identity, such that $a \cdot 1 = a$ and $1 \cdot a = a$. This property guarantees that you have a real number, namely 1, for which its product with any real number is the number itself.
- **Additive Inverse Property:** For every real number *a*, there is a real number called its additive inverse, denoted $-a$, such that $a + -a = 0$ and $-a + a = 0$. This property guarantees that every real number has an additive inverse (its opposite) that is a real number whose sum with the number is 0.
- **Multiplicative Inverse Property:** For every *nonzero* real number *a*, there is a real number called its multiplicative inverse, denoted a^{-1} or $\frac{1}{a}$, such that $a \cdot a^{-1} = a \cdot \frac{1}{a} = 1$ and $a^{-1} \cdot a = \frac{1}{a} \cdot a = 1$. This property guarantees that every real number, *except zero*, has a multiplicative inverse (its reciprocal) whose product with the number is 1.

Notice that when you add the additive inverse to a number, you get the additive identity (0) as an answer, and when you multiply a number by its multiplicative inverse, you get the multiplicative identity (1) as an answer.

- **Distributive Property:** $a(b+c)=a \cdot b + a \cdot c$ and $(b+c)a = b \cdot a + c \cdot a$. This property says that when you have a number times a sum (or a sum times a number), you can either add first and then multiply, or multiply first and then add. Either way, the final answer is the same.

Notice that the distributive property involves both addition and multiplication at the same time. Another way to express the distributive property is to say that *multiplication distributes over addition*.

Roots and Radicals

Square Roots

Every positive number has two square roots that are equal in absolute value, but opposite in sign. Zero has only one square root, namely 0. For instance, 4 and −4 are the two square roots of 16. The positive square root is the **principal square root**. The square root **radical** $\left(\sqrt{}\right)$ always denotes the principal square root. Thus, $\sqrt{(4)(4)} = \sqrt{16} = 4$ and $\sqrt{(-4)(-4)} = \sqrt{16} = 4$. *Tip*: $\sqrt{16} = 4$, not −4 or ±4. You indicate the negative square root of 16 as $-\sqrt{16}$. Thus, $-\sqrt{16} = -4$. To be well-prepared for the GMAT, you should memorize the following 19 principal square roots:

$$\sqrt{1}=1 \qquad \sqrt{4}=2 \qquad \sqrt{9}=3 \qquad \sqrt{16}=4 \qquad \sqrt{25}=5$$

$$\sqrt{36}=6 \qquad \sqrt{49}=7 \qquad \sqrt{64}=8 \qquad \sqrt{81}=9 \qquad \sqrt{100}=10$$

$$\sqrt{121}=11 \qquad \sqrt{144}=12 \qquad \sqrt{169}=13 \qquad \sqrt{196}=14 \qquad \sqrt{225}=15$$

$$\sqrt{256}=16 \qquad \sqrt{289}=17 \qquad \sqrt{400}=20 \qquad \sqrt{625}=25$$

On the GMAT, don't try to find square roots of negative numbers, because no real number will multiply by itself to give a negative number.

Cube Roots

Every real number has one real cube root, called its **principal cube root**. For example, because $4 \times 4 \times 4 = 64$, 4 is the principal cube root of 64. Likewise, because $(-4)(-4)(-4) = -64$, −4 is the principal cube root of −64. As you can see, the principal cube root of a positive number is positive, and the principal cube root of a negative number is negative. You use the cube root radical $\left(\sqrt[3]{}\right)$ to designate the principal cube root. The small number 3 in the radical indicates that the cube root is desired. This number is the **index** of the radical. Thus, $\sqrt[3]{64} = 4$ and $\sqrt[3]{-64} = -4$.

Here is a list of principal cube roots of some positive **perfect cubes**.

$$\sqrt[3]{0}=0 \quad \sqrt[3]{1}=1 \quad \sqrt[3]{8}=2 \quad \sqrt[3]{27}=3 \quad \sqrt[3]{64}=4 \quad \sqrt[3]{125}=5 \quad \sqrt[3]{1,000}=10$$

For the GMAT, it would be a good idea for you to know these roots.

Higher Roots

In general, the index of the radical tells you which root to find. *Tip*: The index for the square root radical is understood to be 2. Here are examples of higher roots.

$$\sqrt[4]{16}=2 \quad \sqrt[4]{625}=5 \quad \sqrt[5]{243}=3 \quad \sqrt[5]{-32}=-2 \quad \sqrt[6]{64}=2$$

The number under the radical is the **radicand**. Here are some points to keep in mind:

- If the index is even and the radicand is positive, the principal root is positive.
- If the index is even and the radicand is negative, there is no real root.
- If the index is odd and the radicand is positive, the principal root is positive.
- If the index is odd and the radicand is negative, the principal root is negative.

Exponents

Terminology

An **exponent** is a small raised number written to the upper right of a quantity, which is called the **base** for the exponent. In the **exponential expression** b^n, b is the base and n is the exponent: $b^n \underset{\leftarrow \text{ Base}}{\leftarrow \text{Exponent}}$. The act of doing what the exponent indicates is **exponentiation**.

Types of Exponents

Let m and n be positive integers. Here are types of exponents and their meanings.

TYPE OF EXPONENT	MEANING	EXAMPLE
Positive Integer	$b^n = \underbrace{(b)(b)(b)\cdots(b)}_{n \text{ factors}}$	$3^5 = 3\cdot3\cdot3\cdot3\cdot3 = 243$ *Tip*: When you evaluate 3^5, you are raising 3 to the fifth power.
Zero	$b^0 = 1$, provided $b \neq 0$	$(1,267)^0 = 1$ *Caution*: The expression 0^0 is undefined.
Negative Integer	$b^{-n} = \dfrac{1}{b^n}$, provided $b \neq 0$	$3^{-5} = \dfrac{1}{3^5} = \dfrac{1}{243}$
Unit Fraction	$b^{\frac{1}{n}} = \sqrt[n]{b}$, provided $b \geq 0$, when n is even.	$(-32)^{\frac{1}{5}} = \sqrt[5]{-32} = -2$
Positive Rational	$b^{\frac{m}{n}} = \left(\sqrt[n]{b}\right)^m$ or $b^{\frac{m}{n}} = \sqrt[n]{b^m}$ provided $b \geq 0$, when n is even.	$64^{\frac{2}{3}} = \left(\sqrt[3]{64}\right)^2 = 4^2 = 16$ or $64^{\frac{2}{3}} = \sqrt[3]{64^2} = \sqrt[3]{4,096} = 16$ *Tip*: As this example illustrates, for most numerical situations, it usually is easier to find the root first and then raise to the power.

Rules of Exponents

The following rules for exponents hold.

RULE	EXAMPLE
$b^m b^n = b^{m+n}$	$2^3 2^4 = 2^{3+4} = 2^7$
$\dfrac{b^m}{b^n} = b^{m-n},\ b \neq 0$	$\dfrac{5^6}{5^2} = 5^{6-2} = 5^4$
$\left(b^m\right)^p = b^{mp}$	$\left(4^3\right)^2 = 4^{3 \cdot 2} = 4^6$
$(ab)^p = a^p b^p$	$(3 \cdot 2)^4 = 3^4 2^4$
$\left(\dfrac{a}{b}\right)^p = \dfrac{a^p}{b^p},\ b \neq 0$	$\left(\dfrac{6}{2}\right)^3 = \dfrac{6^3}{2^3}$
$\left(\dfrac{a}{b}\right)^{-p} = \left(\dfrac{b}{a}\right)^p = \dfrac{b^p}{a^p},\ a \neq 0, b \neq 0$	$\left(\dfrac{2}{5}\right)^{-2} = \left(\dfrac{5}{2}\right)^2 = \dfrac{5^2}{2^2}$

Clarifications About Exponents

- An exponent applies only to the base to which it is attached:

$$(-5)^2 = (-5)(-5) = 25, \text{ but } -5^2 = -(5 \cdot 5) = -25$$

To avoid errors, enclose negative numbers, fractions, and decimals in parentheses when an exponent is to be applied.

- Which number is the exponent and which is the base makes a difference in the value of an exponential expression:

$$2^5 \neq 5^2;\ 2^5 = 2 \times 2 \times 2 \times 2 \times 2 = 32, \text{ but } 5^2 = 5 \times 5 = 25.$$

- Exponentiation does not distribute over addition (or subtraction):

$$(4 + 1)^3 \neq 4^3 + 1^3;\ (4 + 1)^3 = (5)^3 = 125, \text{ but } 4^3 + 1^3 = 64 + 1 = 65.$$

- A negative number raised to an even power yields a positive product:

$$(-3)^4 = (-3)(-3)(-3)(-3) = 81.$$

- A negative number raised to an odd power yields a negative product:

$$(-3)^5 = (-3)(-3)(-3)(-3)(-3) = -243.$$

- A negative exponent tells you to write a reciprocal; it does not tell you to make your answer negative:

$$2^{-3} = \frac{1}{2^3} = \frac{1}{8} \text{ not } -\frac{1}{8}.$$

Order of Operations

Grouping Symbols

Grouping symbols such as parentheses ( ), brackets [ ], and curly braces { } are used to keep things together that belong together. Fraction bars, absolute value bars, and radicals also are grouping symbols. When you are performing computations, perform operations in grouping symbols *first*. It is *very important* that you do so when you have addition or subtraction inside the grouping symbol. For instance, $(5-3)^3 \neq 5^3 - 3^3$; $(5-3)^3 = 2^3 = 8$, but $5^3 - 3^3 = 125 - 27 = 98$. When you no longer need the grouping symbol, omit it.

PEMDAS

Follow the order of operations when you evaluate numerical expressions:

1. Do computations inside **P**arentheses (or other grouping symbols). If there is more than one operation inside the grouping symbol, follow the order of operations given here to do the computations inside the parentheses. If there are grouping symbols within grouping symbols, start with the innermost grouping symbols.
2. Evaluate **E**xponential expressions (also, evaluate absolute value, square root, and other root expressions).
3. **M**ultiply and **D**ivide in the order in which they occur from left to right.
4. **A**dd and **S**ubtract in the order in which they occur from left to right.

Try the mnemonic "**P**lease **E**xcuse **M**y **D**ear **A**unt **S**ally"—abbreviated as PEMDAS—to help you remember the order of operations. The first letters stand for "**P**arentheses, **E**xponentiation, **M**ultiplication, **D**ivision, **A**ddition, and **S**ubtraction." Example:

Evaluate $90 - 5 \cdot 3^2 + \dfrac{(40+2)}{\sqrt{100-64}}$.

$90 - 5 \cdot 3^2 + \dfrac{(40+2)}{\sqrt{100-64}}$ First, compute inside grouping symbols.

$= 90 - 5 \cdot 3^2 + \dfrac{42}{\sqrt{36}}$ Next, evaluate exponents and roots.

$= 90 - 5 \cdot 9 + \dfrac{42}{6}$ Then, multiply and divide from left to right.

$= 90 - 45 + 7$ Finally, add and subtract from left to right.

$= 52$

Scientific Notation

A number expressed in scientific notation is written as a product of two factors. The first factor is a decimal number greater than or equal to 1, but less than 10. The second factor is a power of 10. The product of the two factors equals the original number. Any decimal number can be expressed in scientific notation:

$$45,000 = 4.5 \times 10^4$$
$$3.6 = 3.6 \times 10^0$$
$$5,285,000 = 5.285 \times 10^6$$
$$0.000978 = 9.78 \times 10^{-4}$$
$$0.00000001243 = 1.243 \times 10^{-8}$$

Sets

Terminology

A **set** is a collection of objects. Sets are usually named with uppercase letters, such as A and B. The set's objects are its **elements** or **members**. In the **roster notation** for sets, the set's elements, separated by commas, are listed between curly braces. For instance, the set P, consisting of the first ten prime numbers, is $P = \{2, 3, 5, 7, 11, 13, 17, 19, 23, 29\}$. You write $11 \in P$ to mean 11 is an element of P. The set that contains no elements is the **empty set**, denoted $\emptyset$. The number of elements in set A is its **cardinality**, denoted $|A|$ (also, #A). For instance, if $A = \{2, 3, 5\}$, $|A| = 3$.

Set Relationships

Two sets are **equal** if and only if they contain *exactly* the same elements, without regard to the order in which the elements are listed in the two sets or whether elements are repeated. For instance, $\{2, 3, 5\} = \{2, 5, 3\} = \{2, 2, 3, 3, 5, 5\}$.

Set A is a **subset** of set B, written $\boldsymbol{A \subseteq B}$, if every element of A is an element of B. For example, $\{2, 5\} \subseteq \{2, 3, 5\}$. In a discussion, the **universal set** (often denoted U) contains all the sets under consideration as subsets.

The **union** of two sets A and B, denoted $\boldsymbol{A \cup B}$, is the set of all elements that are in A or in B or in both. *Tip*: The word *or* in this definition is *inclusive*; that is, *or* means "one or the other, or possibly both at the same time." For example, if $A = \{2, 3, 5\}$ and $B = \{3, 5, 7, 11\}$, then $A \cup B = \{2, 3, 5, 7, 11\}$. *Tip*: When you form the union of two sets, do not list an element more than once, because it is unnecessary to do so.

The **intersection** of two sets A and B, denoted $\boldsymbol{A \cap B}$, is the set of all elements that are common to both sets. For instance, if $A = \{2, 3, 5\}$ and $B = \{3, 5, 7, 11\}$, then $A \cap B = \{3, 5\}$. **Disjoint** sets have no elements in common. Their intersection is the empty set. For instance, if $A = \{2, 3, 5\}$ and $C = \{7, 11, 13, 17\}$, then $A \cap C = \emptyset$ and A and C are disjoint.

The **complement** of set A, denoted A^C (also, $\overline{A}$ or ~A), is the set of all elements in the universal set U that are *not* in A. For instance, if $U = \{1, 2, 3, 4, 5, 6, 7, 8, 9\}$ and $A = \{2, 3, 5\}$, then $A^C = \{1, 4, 6, 7, 8, 9\}$.

Venn diagrams visually depict set relationships. In a Venn diagram, circles represent sets—with the exception that the universal set is represented by a rectangular region, enclosing everything else in the diagram. Shading depicts the results of relationships. Here are examples.

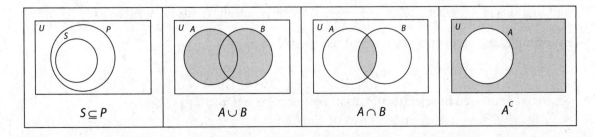

Counting Techniques

The **product rule** for counting: For a sequence of k tasks, if a first task can be done in any one of n_1 different ways, and for each of these ways, a subsequent second task can be done in any one of n_2 different ways, and for each of these ways, a subsequent third task can be done in any one of n_3 different ways, and so on to the kth task, which can be done in any one of n_k different ways, then the total number of different ways the sequence of k tasks can be done is $n_1 \times n_2 \times n_3 \times \cdots \times n_k$. Here are examples:

- The number of 3-digit codes that are possible using the digits 1 through 5, if repetitions of digits are allowed, is $5 \times 5 \times 5 = 125$ (because you have 5 ways to pick each of the 3 digits).
- The number of 3-digit codes that are possible using the digits 1 through 5, if repetitions of digits are *not* allowed, is $5 \times 4 \times 3 = 60$ (because once a particular digit is selected, it is no longer available to be picked).
- The number of different ways to arrange the three letters in the word *cat*, if repetitions of letters is not allowed, is $3 \times 2 \times 1 = 6$.

A **permutation** is an ordered arrangement of distinct objects in which repetition of objects is not allowed and different orderings of the same objects are counted as different outcomes. For instance, *cat, cta, act, atc, tca,* and *tac* are the six permutations of the letters in the word *cat*. For instance, *cat* and *act* are different permutations. Through a direct application of the product rule for counting, the number of permutations of n distinct objects is $n!$, where $n! = (n)(n-1)(n-2) \cdots (3)(2)(1)$. Read $n!$ as "n factorial."

A factorial is the product of all positive integers less than or equal to a given positive integer. Exception: By definition $0! = 1$. For example, the number of different ways to arrange the three letters in the word *cat*, if repetition of letters is not allowed, is $3!$, which is $3 \times 2 \times 1 = 6$.

A **combination** is an arrangement of distinct objects in which repetition of objects is not allowed and different orderings of the same items are considered to be the same arrangement. That is, when the order in which you make a selection for an arrangement of objects does *not* determine different outcomes, the arrangement is a combination of the objects. There is only one combination of n distinct objects because all the different ways you can arrange the n objects are not counted as different combinations. For example, there is only one combination of the three letters in the word *cat*. The six arrangements, *cat, cta, act, atc, tca,* and *tac,* are considered to be the same.

When you select r objects from n distinct objects without repetition, the number of combinations is ${_nC_r}$, where ${_nC_r} = \dfrac{n!}{r!(n-r)!}$. *Tip:* The notation ${_nC_r}$ also is written as $\dbinom{n}{r}$.

For example, the number of ways to put five people in pairs is

$$_5C_2 = \frac{5!}{2!(5-2)!} = \frac{5!}{2!(3)!} = \frac{5 \cdot \cancel{4}^{2} \cdot \cancel{3} \cdot \cancel{2} \cdot \cancel{1}}{(\cancel{2} \cdot 1)(\cancel{3} \cdot \cancel{2} \cdot \cancel{1})} = 10$$

For combinations involving relatively small numbers like those given in this example, you might prefer to figure out the answer by listing the different combinations. Designate the people as *A*, *B*, *C*, *D*, and *E*. Then systematically list all of the 10 ways to match them two at a time: *AB*, *AC*, *AD*, *AE*, *BC*, *BD*, *BE*, *CD*, *CE*, and *DE*. Be careful when listing the combinations. You might overcount or undercount. Remember, *AB* and *BA*, *AC* and *CA*, and so forth are *not* different combinations. In general, using the combination formula saves time and is an accurate way to obtain the answer.

Basic Probability

Basic Concepts

A **random experiment** is a chance process that gives a single result that cannot be determined beforehand. For example, tossing a standard six-sided die and observing the up face is a random experiment. *Tip*: A standard six-sided die is a balanced cube for which each of the six faces has one, two, three, four, five, or six dots on it.

An **outcome** is a single result from a random experiment. When you toss a standard six-sided die, the six possible outcomes are 1, 2, 3, 4, 5, or 6, where "1" means "one dot on the up face," "2" means "two dots on the up face," and so forth.

An **event** is a collection of one or more outcomes. For instance, when you toss a standard die, the event *E* that the die shows a number less than 3 consists of the outcomes 1 and 2. *Tip*: Uppercase letters represent events. The **probability** of an event is the likelihood the event will occur. Outcomes are **equally likely** if each outcome is as likely to occur as any other outcome. When you toss a standard die, 1, 2, 3, 4, 5, and 6 are equally likely outcomes.

An event is **certain** to occur if and only if the probability of the event is 1. For example, when you toss a standard six-sided die, the probability a whole number of dots will show on the up face is 1. An event is **impossible** if and only if the probability of the event is 0. For example, the probability the die will show seven dots on the up face is 0. The probability of any event is a number between 0 and 1, inclusive. Thus, the lowest probability you can have is 0, and the highest probability you can have is 1. All other probabilities fall between 0 and 1. The closer the probability of an event is to 1, the more likely the event is to occur; and the closer the probability of an event is to zero, the less likely the event is to occur.

Compound Events

A **compound event** is a combination of two or more events. The event $A \cap B$ (read as "**A intersection B**") is the event consisting of all outcomes that *A* and *B* have in common. The event $A \cup B$ (read as "**A union B**") is the event consisting of all outcomes that are in *A* only, *B* only, or in their intersection. Specifically, if an outcome is in $A \cup B$, it is in at least one of the events *A* or *B*. The event $\overline{E}$ (read as "**complement of E**") is the set of outcomes that are not in *E*. It is the event that *E* does *not* occur. *Tip*: $\overline{E}$ is also known as the **opposite** of the event *E*. For example, suppose the possible outcomes for a random experiment are 1, 2, 3, 4, 5, 6, 7, 8, 9, and 10. Let event *A* consist of outcomes 2, 3, 5, and 7, and event *B* consist of outcomes 3, 5, 7, 9. Then event $A \cap B$ consists of outcomes 3, 5, and 7; event $A \cup B$ consists of outcomes 2, 3, 5, 7, and 9; and event $\overline{A}$ consists of outcomes 1, 4, 6, 8, 9, 10.

Mutually Exclusive Events

Two events are **mutually exclusive** if they have no outcomes in common, meaning the two events are **disjoint**. They cannot occur at the same time. The occurrence of one prevents the occurrence of the other. For instance, when you toss a standard die, the event M that the die shows an even number (2, 4, or 6) and the event N that the die shows an odd number (1, 3, or 5) are mutually exclusive.

Probability Formula

If all outcomes are equally likely, the probability of an event E, denoted $P(E)$, is

$$P(E) = \frac{\text{Number of outcomes favorable to } E}{\text{Total number of possible outcomes}}.$$

For example, for the die-tossing experiment, and the event E that the die shows a number less than 3,

$$P(E) = \frac{\text{Number of outcomes favorable to } E}{\text{Total number of possible outcomes}} = \frac{2}{6} = \frac{1}{3}.$$

The denominator for the probability of an event is always *larger than* or *equal to* the numerator. Check for this requirement when you calculate probabilities.

Probability of the Complement of an Event

The probability of the complement of an event E is $P(\overline{E}) = 1 - P(E)$; and, conversely, $P(E) = 1 - P(\overline{E})$. For example, if $P(E) = \frac{1}{3}$, then $P(\overline{E}) = 1 - \frac{1}{3} = \frac{2}{3}$.

If the probability of an event is difficult to compute, try to find the probability of the opposite of the event, then subtract from 1.

The Addition Rule

For two events A and B, the event $A \cup B$ is the event that A occurs or B occurs or that both occur simultaneously on one trial of an experiment.

The **Addition Rule** states that $P(A \cup B) = P(A) + P(B) - P(A \cap B)$. *Tip:* Keep in mind that this rule applies to *one* trial of an experiment. For example, given the following probabilities for tomorrow's weather: $P(\text{rain}) = 0.7$, $P(\text{temperature below } 32°F) = 0.3$, and $P(\text{rain and temperature below } 32°F) = 0.15$, then $P(\text{rain or temperature below } 32°F) = 0.7 + 0.3 - 0.15 = 0.85$.

In many situations, you must calculate the probabilities used in the addition rule. For example, you toss a standard six-sided die one time. Let event A be the outcome is even, and event B be the outcome is greater than 4. Then:

P(outcome is even or greater than 4) = P(outcome is even) +
$\quad$ P(outcome is greater than 4) − P(outcome is even and greater than 4)

$$= P(A \cup B) = P(A) + P(B) - P(A \cap B) = \frac{3}{6} + \frac{2}{6} - \frac{1}{6} = \frac{4}{6} = \frac{2}{3}$$

When you can determine the possible outcomes, an efficient way to find $P(A \cup B)$ is to sum the number of outcomes favorable to A and the number of outcomes favorable to B, *being sure to add in such a way that no outcome is counted twice*, and then divide by the total number of possible outcomes. Applying this strategy to the previous example, there are 3 outcomes that are even (namely, 2, 4, and 6) and 1 outcome greater than 4 that is *not* even (namely, 5). So, there are 3 + 1 = 4 distinct outcomes favorable to the event "outcome is even or greater than 4," Thus, P(outcome is even or greater than 4) = $\frac{4}{6} = \frac{2}{3}$.

When two events A and B are mutually exclusive, $P(A \cap B) = 0$. So, for mutually exclusive events, $P(A \cup B) = P(A) + P(B)$. If you toss a standard six-sided die:

P(outcome is less than 2 or greater than 4) = P(outcome is less than 2)
$\quad$ + P(outcome is greater than 4)

$$= \frac{1}{6} + \frac{2}{6} = \frac{3}{6} = \frac{1}{2}$$

When you want to find the chance that *at least one* of two events happens, use the addition rule.

Conditional Probability and Independent Events

$P(B|A)$ (read as "Probability B given A") is the **conditional probability** of event B, given that event A has already occurred. For $P(B|A)$, you must compute the probability of event B by taking into account that the event A has already occurred. For example, suppose that you randomly draw two marbles, one after the other, from a box containing 10 red marbles and 5 blue marbles. Then the probability of drawing a blue marble on the second draw given that a red marble was drawn *without replacement* on the first draw is $\frac{5}{14}$ (because after the red marble is drawn without replacement, there are 9 red marbles and 5 blue marbles in the box.) *Tip:* **Without replacement** means an object is NOT put back before the next object is selected. On the other hand, the probability of drawing a blue marble on the second draw given that a red marble was drawn *with replacement* on the first draw is $\frac{5}{15}$ (because after the red marble is drawn and then replaced, there are 10 red marbles and 5 blue marbles in the box.) *Tip:* **With replacement** means an object is put back before the next object is selected.

Two events *A* and *B* are **independent** if $P(B) = P(B|A)$ and $P(A) = P(A|B)$. In other words, *A* and *B* are independent if the occurrence of one does not affect the probability of the occurrence of the other. For instance, if you randomly draw two marbles, one after the other, from a box containing 10 red marbles and 5 blue marbles, the event of drawing a red marble *with replacement* on the first draw and the event of drawing a blue marble on the second draw are independent events. If events *A* and *B* are not independent, they are **dependent**. For example, if you randomly draw two marbles, one after the other, from a box containing 10 red marbles and 5 blue marbles, the event of drawing a red marble *without replacement* on the first draw and the event of drawing a blue marble on the second draw are dependent.

> When you draw at random *with replacement*, the draws are independent. When you draw at random *without replacement*, the draws are dependent.

The Multiplication Rule

The **multiplication rule** says that for two events *A* and *B*, the probability that event *A* occurs on the first trial and event *B* occurs on the second trial of an experiment is $P(A)P(B|A)$. This rule is used to find the probability of two events that *occur in sequence*. *Tip*: Keep in mind that this rule applies to *two* trials of an experiment. An efficient way to find the probability that event *A* occurs on the first trial and event *B* occurs on the second trial is to multiply the probability of event *A* times the probability of event *B*, where you have determined the probability of *B* by *taking into account that the event A has already occurred*. For example, suppose you draw two marbles, one after the other, without looking, from a box containing 10 red marbles and 5 blue marbles. *Tip*: A draw "without looking" is a random selection. The probability of drawing a red marble on the first draw without replacement and a blue marble on the second draw is

$$P(\text{red on first draw}) \cdot P(\text{blue on second draw}|\text{red on first draw without replacement})$$
$$= \frac{10}{15} \cdot \frac{5}{14} = \frac{5}{21}$$

When two events *A* and *B* are independent, the probability that event *A* occurs on the first trial and event *B* occurs on the second trial of an experiment is $P(A) P(B)$. For example, the probability of getting two heads on two flips of a coin is $P(H)P(H) = \frac{1}{2} \cdot \frac{1}{2} = \frac{1}{4}$ (because each flip of the coin is independent of the other).

> When you want to find the probability that both of two events will happen, use the multiplication rule.

Graphical Representation of Data

For the GMAT, be prepared to read and interpret information from frequency or relative frequency tables, pictographs, circle graphs, dot plots, stem-and-leaf plots, line graphs, bar graphs, and histograms.

Frequency Tables

A **frequency table** shows the frequency of each value in the data set. A **relative frequency table** shows the frequency as a proportion or percentage of the whole data set. Here is an example.

Exam 1 Grade Distribution of 20 Students		
GRADE	FREQUENCY	RELATIVE FREQUENCY
A	3	0.15
B	6	0.30
C	8	0.40
D	2	0.10
F	1	0.05
Total	**20**	**1.00**

According to the table, $0.40 + 0.30 + 0.15 = 0.85$ or 85% of the students made a C or better on Exam 1.

Pictographs

A **pictograph** represents data with symbols (or images). Each symbol, its meaning, and the quantity it represents are given on the graph. To read a pictograph, multiply the number of symbols in a row by the quantity it represents. If a fraction of a symbol is shown, approximate the fraction and use it accordingly. Here is an example.

Responses of 200 Women to the Question "Do You Have a Sibling?"

Yes

No

[= 10 women]

According to the graph, $15 \times 10 = 150$ women responded "Yes" to the survey question.

Circle Graphs

A circle graph (or **pie chart**) displays the relationships of different categories of data as portions of a whole, represented by a circle. The portions are labeled to show the categories for the graph. Percentages show the amount of the graph that corresponds to each category. Here is an example.

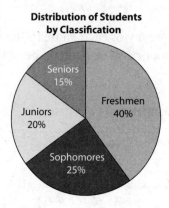

Distribution of Students by Classification

According to the graph 40% + 25% = 65% of the students are freshmen or sophomores.

Dot Plots

A **dot plot** (or **line plot**) shows the frequency of data values on a number line. Dots (or other similar symbols) are placed above each value corresponding to the number of times that particular value occurs in the data set. *Tip*: A useful feature of dot plots is that they show all the data values. Here is an example.

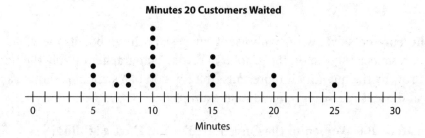

Minutes 20 Customers Waited

Minutes

The dot plot shows three customers waited more than 15 minutes.

Stem-and-Leaf Plots

A **stem-and-leaf plot** visually displays data values, separated into two parts: a stem and a leaf. For a particular data value, the leaf is usually the last digit, and the stem is the remaining digits. A **legend** explains what is represented by the stem and leaf so that the reader can interpret the information in the plot; for example, 5|7 = 57. *Tip*: A feature of a stem-and-leaf plot is that the original data are retained and displayed in the plot. Here is an example.

Ages in Years of 44 U.S. Presidents at Inauguration	
STEM	LEAVES
4	2 3 6 6 7 7 8 9 9
5	0 0 1 1 1 1 2 2 4 4 4 4 4 5 5 5 5 5 6 6 6 7 7 7 7 8
6	0 1 1 1 2 4 4 5 8 9

Legend: 5|7 = 57

According to the graph, five presidents were 54 years of age at the time of their inauguration.

Line Graphs

A **line graph** shows plotted points that represent data. Consecutive points are connected with line segments to facilitate identifying trends in the data. A line that slants upward from left to right indicates an increase. A line that slants downward from left to right indicates a decrease. A horizontal line (no slant) means the data remain constant. Line graphs are commonly used to show change over time. Here is an example.

The line graph shows an upward trend in average monthly sales from February to May.

Bar Graphs

A **bar graph** uses rectangular bars to represent frequencies, percentages, or amounts. The bars represent different categories that are labeled at the base of the bars. To read a bar graph, examine the scale to determine the units and the amount corresponding to each category. Here is an example.

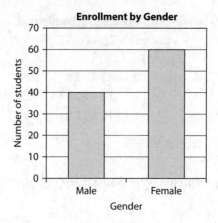

According to the graph, 40 males and 60 females are enrolled.

Histograms

A **histogram** summarizes data by displaying frequencies or relative frequencies of the data within intervals. The intervals are of equal length and cover from the lowest to the highest data value. The left and right endpoints for the intervals are selected so that each data value clearly falls within one and only one interval. The frequency or relative frequency of occurrence of the data values within an interval is represented by a rectangular (or vertical) column. The bars in a histogram are side by side (usually) with no space in between. Here is an example.

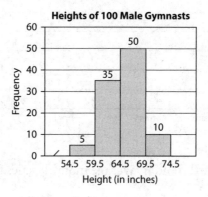

Descriptive Measures of Data

Mean

The **mean** of a data set is the arithmetic average of the data values:

$$\text{mean} = \frac{\text{sum of data values}}{\text{number of data values}}$$

For example, the mean of 25, 43, 40, 60, and 12 is $\dfrac{25+43+40+60+12}{5} = \dfrac{180}{5} = 36.$

Median

The **median** is the middle value or the arithmetic average of the two middle values in an *ordered* set of data. Fifty percent of the data values fall at or below the median and 50% fall at or above the median. To find the median, put the data values in order from least to greatest (or greatest to least), and then locate the middle value. If there is no single middle value, compute the average of the two middle values. For example, after putting the data values in order, the median of 12, 25, 40, 43, 60 is 40. For –7, –7, 1, 8, 16, 22, the median is $\frac{1+8}{2} = \frac{9}{2} = 4.5$. *Tip*: When finding a median, remember to put the numbers in order first.

In an ordered data set of n values, the median is in the $\frac{n+1}{2}$ position. For example, in the dot plot shown, the median is in the $\frac{20+1}{2} = \frac{21}{2} = 10.5$ position, meaning it is halfway between the 10th and 11th data values.

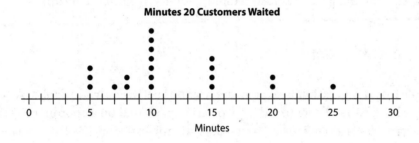

Minutes 20 Customers Waited

Minutes

The 10th and 11th data values are both 10 minutes, so the median for the data shown in the dot plot is 10 minutes.

Mode

The **mode** is the data value (or values) that occurs with the greatest frequency in a data set. For example, the mode of 30, 40, 50, 50, 60, and 70 is 50. *Tip*: A data set in which each data value occurs the same number of times has no mode.

Range

The **range** gives the spread between the greatest and least values of the data set. It is the difference between the maximum value and the minimum value in the data set. Thus, range = maximum value – minimum value. For example, the range of 6.7, 7.6, 7.5, 6.9, 9.3, 6.7, 7.6, and 8.5 is $9.3 - 6.7 = 2.6$.

Mean Absolute Deviation

The **mean absolute deviation** (**MAD**) quantifies the degree to which the data values vary from their mean. It is the average distance between each data value and the mean of the data values. The MAD for 30, 40, 50, 60, and 70 (which has a mean of 50) is

$$\frac{|30-50|+|40-50|+|50-50|+|60-50|+|70-50|}{5} = \frac{20+10+0+10+20}{5} = \frac{60}{5} = 12$$

Variance and Standard Deviation

Like the MAD, the **variance** and **standard deviation** are measures of the variability of a set of data values about the mean. If there is no variability in a data set, each data value equals the mean, so both the variance and standard deviation for the data set are zero. The more the data values vary from the mean, the greater are the variance and standard deviation.

You compute the variance by subtracting the mean from each data value, squaring each difference, and then summing up the squared differences and dividing by the number, n, of data values. The standard deviation is the square root of the variance. Note: When the data set is a sample from a population, you divide by $n - 1$ instead of n. Questions about variance or standard deviation on the GMAT might require you to examine two (or more) data sets with equal means and decide which has the greater (or lesser) variance or standard deviation. For example, the data set 30, 40, 50, 60, and 70 (which has a mean of 50) has a greater variance and standard deviation than does the data set 35, 47, 50, 53, 65 (which also has a mean of 50). The data in the second data set are clustered more tightly around the mean.

Simple Linear Regression

You use **simple linear regression** to explore associations between two variables. A **scatter plot** is a graph of ordered pairs of data from the two variables plotted on a coordinate grid. The scale for one of the variables is along the horizontal axis and the scale for the other variable is along the vertical axis. The ordered pairs have the form (horizontal coordinate, vertical coordinate). If the two variables are X and Y, then (x, y) is a **data point** in the scatter plot, where y is the value from the variable Y that is paired with x, a value from the variable X.

The scatter plot's pattern provides visual cues about whether there is a relationship between the two variables. If there is a relationship, often the nature of that relationship is revealed in the scatter plot. Tip: The data points in a scatter plot are not connected by line segments. The points are often described as forming a "cloud." When the points appear to cluster around a **trend line** passing through the cloud, the scatter plot suggests that a **linear relationship** (or **correlation**) exists between the two variables. When the data points are scattered without any discernible pattern or if the pattern is a horizontal line, the two variables have **no relationship**.

The trend line, called a **regression line**, is a straight line that best represents the data. Regression lines that have a positive slope (slant upward from left to right) suggest a **positive relationship** between the two variables, and regression lines that have a negative slope (slant downward from left to right) suggest a **negative relationship** between the two variables. In positive relationships, whenever one of the variables increases, the other variable increases, and when one of the variables decreases, the other variable decreases as well. In negative relationships, whenever one of the two variables increases, the other variable decreases, and conversely.

Arithmetic Drill

Directions: **Select the best answer choice.**

1. Which expression is equivalent to $\sqrt{400}$?

   (A) $\sqrt{200} + \sqrt{200}$

   (B) $100\sqrt{4}$

   (C) $\sqrt{(-20)^2}$

   (D) $4\sqrt{100}$

   (E) 200

$$\left(\frac{2}{9} + \frac{1}{2}\right)$$

2. Which fraction, when added to the previous sum, yields a sum of 0?

   (A) $\dfrac{1 - 9 - 2^2}{(9)(2)}$ $-\dfrac{12}{18}$

   (B) $\dfrac{-2^2 - 9}{(-2)(9)}$ $\dfrac{13}{18}$

   $\dfrac{2}{2} \cdot \dfrac{2}{9} + \dfrac{1}{2} \cdot \dfrac{9}{9}$

   $\dfrac{4}{18} + \dfrac{9}{18} = \dfrac{13}{18}$

   (C) $-\dfrac{(2)(9)}{2^2 + 9}$ $-\dfrac{18}{13}$

   (D) $\dfrac{-(9 + 2^2)}{(-2)(-9)}$ $-\dfrac{13}{18}$

   (E) $\dfrac{(2)(9)}{2^2 + 9}$ $\dfrac{18}{13}$

$$\begin{array}{r} 7 \\ 35\overline{)2?5} \,\text{Remainder}\, 20 \end{array}$$

3. What is the tens digit in the dividend of the problem shown?

   (A) 3

   (B) 4

   (C) 5

   (D) 6

   (E) 7

   $35\overline{)265}$ with quotient 7, 245, remainder 20

4. Given that *x* is a positive integer such that 19 divided by *x* has a remainder of 3, what is the sum of all the possible values of *x*?

(A) 12
(B) 20
(C) 24
(D) 28
(E) 32

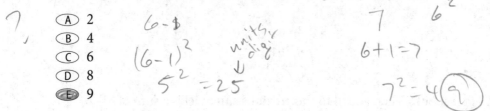

5. Suppose *n* is an integer such that $2 < n^2 < 100$. If the units digit of n^2 is 6 and the units digit of $(n-1)^2$ is 5, what is the units digit of $(n+1)^2$?

(A) 2
(B) 4
(C) 6
(D) 8
(E) 9

6. If the square root of the product of two positive integers is 15, which number CANNOT be the sum of the two integers?

(A) 34
(B) 42
(C) 50
(D) 78
(E) 226

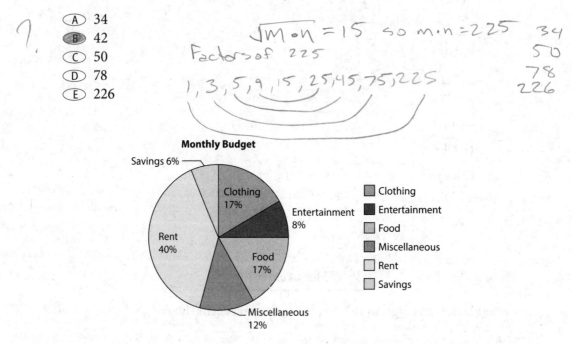

Monthly Budget

Savings 6%
Clothing 17%
Entertainment 8%
Rent 40%
Food 17%
Miscellaneous 12%

Clothing
Entertainment
Food
Miscellaneous
Rent
Savings

7. The preceding circle graph displays a budget for a monthly income of $3,500 (after taxes). According to the graph, how much more money is budgeted for rent than for food and clothing combined?

(A) $60
(B) $210
(C) $595
(D) $1,190
(E) $1,400

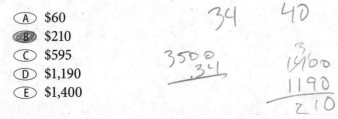

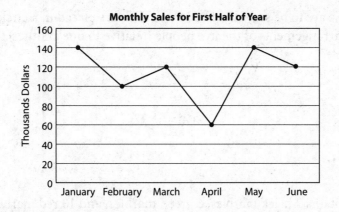

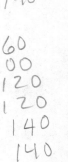

8. The preceding line graph depicts the monthly sales from January to June for a small business. What is the greatest amount that the monthly sales in January could increase without changing the median?

(A) $20,000 increase
(B) $40,000 increase
(C) $100,000 increase
(D) Any amount increase
(E) January sales cannot increase without changing the median.

9. How many different meal combinations consisting of one sandwich, one drink, and one type of chips are possible from a selection of eight types of sandwiches, five types of drinks, and seven types of chips?

(A) 280
(B) 140
(C) 40
(D) 35
(E) 20

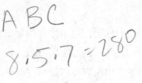

10. In a video game, a player is faced with the task of moving from point *A* to point *B* to point *C*, and then returning from point *C* to point *A* through point *B* without retracing any path. There are 5 paths from point *A* to point *B*, and 8 paths from point *B* to point *C*. In how many different ways can the player accomplish the task?

(A) 2,240
(B) 1,600
(C) 1,120
(D) 68
(E) 24

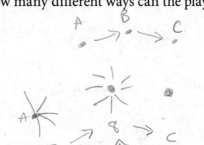

11. Five people are to be seated in five identical chairs placed in a circle. How many different arrangements of the five people (relative to one another) in the five chairs are possible?

    Ⓐ 256
    Ⓑ 128
    Ⓒ 48
    Ⓓ 24
    Ⓔ 6

12. A box contains 7 black marbles, 6 green marbles, and 10 red marbles, all identical except for color. What is the probability of drawing a black or red marble when a single marble is drawn at random from the box?

    Ⓐ $\dfrac{7}{23}$

    Ⓑ $\dfrac{10}{23}$

    Ⓒ $\dfrac{13}{23}$

    Ⓓ $\dfrac{16}{23}$

    Ⓔ $\dfrac{17}{23}$

13. A quiz consists of 5 multiple-choice questions, each of which has 4 possible answer choices (A, B, C, and D), one of which is correct. Suppose that an unprepared student does not read the questions but simply makes a random guess for each question. What is the probability that the student will guess correctly on at least one question?

    Ⓐ $\dfrac{1}{1,024}$

    Ⓑ $\dfrac{20}{1,024}$

    Ⓒ $\dfrac{243}{1,024}$

    Ⓓ $\dfrac{781}{1,024}$

    Ⓔ $\dfrac{1,023}{1,024}$

14. Suppose you randomly draw two marbles, successively without replacement, from a box containing 8 red marbles and 6 blue marbles. What is the probability of drawing a blue marble on the second draw, given that you drew a red marble on the first draw? (Assume the marbles are identical except for color.)

(A) $\dfrac{12}{49}$

(B) $\dfrac{3}{7}$

(C) $\dfrac{3}{13}$

(D) $\dfrac{6}{13}$

(E) $\dfrac{24}{91}$

8 R
6 B
_____
14

$\dfrac{6}{13}$ *dep*

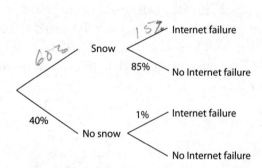

15. The preceding probability diagram represents the incidence of Internet failure during weather in which snow might occur. What is the probability that it snows and an Internet failure occurs?

(A) 0.4%

(B) 9%

(C) 39.6%

(D) 51%

(E) 60%

.60 ⟨ *.15*
      .6
.090

$\dfrac{15}{60}$

RIGHT!
Fill in probabilities

(60%)(15%) = 9%

Residence Status of Senior Students ($n = 250$)

	ON CAMPUS	OFF CAMPUS
Female	52	86
Male	38	74

16. The residence status, by sex, of 250 senior students at a community college is shown in the preceding table. If one of the 250 students is randomly selected, what is the probability that the student resides on campus, given that the student selected is a male student? Express your answer as a decimal rounded to two places.

    (A) 0.15
    (B) 0.34
    (C) 0.42
    (D) 0.51
    (E) 0.66

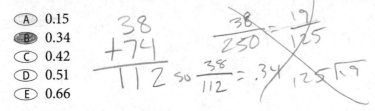

17. A real estate agent has determined probabilities for two neighboring houses, one of which is a model home. The probability that the model home will be sold is 0.60; the probability that the house next door will be sold is 0.50; and the probability that both houses will be sold is 0.40. Find the probability that at least one of the two houses will be sold.

    (A) 30%
    (B) 40%
    (C) 50%
    (D) 60%
    (E) 70%

Questions 18 to 25 each presents a question and two statements, labeled (1) and (2), in which certain data are given. Using your knowledge of mathematics and everyday facts (such as the number of minutes in an hour or the meaning of the word *perpendicular*), decide whether the given data are sufficient to answer the question. Then select one of the answer choices that follow.

18. Suppose m is an integer such that $2 < m < 10$. What is the units digit of m^2?
    (1) The units digit of $(m+1)^2$ is 4.
    (2) The units digit of $(m-1)^2$ is 6.

    (A) Statement (1) ALONE is sufficient, but statement (2) alone is not sufficient.
    (B) Statement (2) ALONE is sufficient, but statement (1) alone is not sufficient.
    (C) BOTH statements TOGETHER are sufficient, but NEITHER statement ALONE is sufficient.
    (D) EACH statement ALONE is sufficient.
    (E) Statements (1) and (2) TOGETHER are NOT sufficient.

19. On the shelf of a flower shop are *n* vases, some of which contain 8 flowers and some of which contain 10 flowers. How many vases contain 10 flowers?

    (1) The total number of flowers is 136.
    (2) *n* = 15

    Ⓐ Statement (1) ALONE is sufficient, but statement (2) alone is not sufficient.
    Ⓑ Statement (2) ALONE is sufficient, but statement (1) alone is not sufficient.
    Ⓒ BOTH statements TOGETHER are sufficient, but NEITHER statement ALONE is sufficient.
    Ⓓ EACH statement ALONE is sufficient.
    Ⓔ Statements (1) and (2) TOGETHER are NOT sufficient.

20. Is x^p a negative number?

    (1) $x < 0$
    (2) $p < 0$

    Ⓐ Statement (1) ALONE is sufficient, but statement (2) alone is not sufficient.
    Ⓑ Statement (2) ALONE is sufficient, but statement (1) alone is not sufficient.
    Ⓒ BOTH statements TOGETHER are sufficient, but NEITHER statement ALONE is sufficient.
    Ⓓ EACH statement ALONE is sufficient.
    Ⓔ Statements (1) and (2) TOGETHER are NOT sufficient.

21. Seth is studying for his fourth 100-point test in an economics class. What score must he earn on this test to have an average (mean) of 90 for the four tests?

    (1) Seth has the following scores on the first three tests: 77, 91, and 94.
    (2) The average of Seth's scores on the first and third tests is 85.5.

    Ⓐ Statement (1) ALONE is sufficient, but statement (2) alone is not sufficient.
    Ⓑ Statement (2) ALONE is sufficient, but statement (1) alone is not sufficient.
    Ⓒ BOTH statements TOGETHER are sufficient, but NEITHER statement ALONE is sufficient.
    Ⓓ EACH statement ALONE is sufficient.
    Ⓔ Statements (1) and (2) TOGETHER are NOT sufficient.

22. Set *A* consists of 20 numbers ranging from 1 to 10. Set *B* consists of 20 numbers ranging from 11 to 20. What is the average (arithmetic mean) of the 40 numbers in sets *A* and *B* combined?

    (1) The average of the numbers in Set *A* is 6.7.
    (2) The average of the numbers in Set *B* is 17.3.

    Ⓐ Statement (1) ALONE is sufficient, but statement (2) alone is not sufficient.
    Ⓑ Statement (2) ALONE is sufficient, but statement (1) alone is not sufficient.
    Ⓒ BOTH statements TOGETHER are sufficient, but NEITHER statement ALONE is sufficient.
    Ⓓ EACH statement ALONE is sufficient.
    Ⓔ Statements (1) and (2) TOGETHER are NOT sufficient.

23. Is $a > 5^8$?

    (1) $5^7 < a < 5^9$

    (2) $a = \dfrac{5^{10} - 5^8}{24}$

    Ⓐ Statement (1) ALONE is sufficient, but statement (2) alone is not sufficient.

    Ⓑ Statement (2) ALONE is sufficient, but statement (1) alone is not sufficient.

    Ⓒ BOTH statements TOGETHER are sufficient, but NEITHER statement ALONE is sufficient.

    Ⓓ EACH statement ALONE is sufficient.

    Ⓔ Statements (1) and (2) TOGETHER are NOT sufficient.

24. If a is an element of the set $\{12, 13, 15, 16, 18, 19, 21, 22\}$, what is the value of a?

    (1) a is a multiple of 3.

    (2) a is even.

    Ⓐ Statement (1) ALONE is sufficient, but statement (2) alone is not sufficient.

    Ⓑ Statement (2) ALONE is sufficient, but statement (1) alone is not sufficient.

    Ⓒ BOTH statements TOGETHER are sufficient, but NEITHER statement ALONE is sufficient.

    Ⓓ EACH statement ALONE is sufficient.

    Ⓔ Statements (1) and (2) TOGETHER are NOT sufficient.

25. What is the average of a, b, and c?

    (1) $2a + 3b + 5c = 42$

    (2) $4a + 3b + c = 30$

    Ⓐ Statement (1) ALONE is sufficient, but statement (2) alone is not sufficient.

    Ⓑ Statement (2) ALONE is sufficient, but statement (1) alone is not sufficient.

    Ⓒ BOTH statements TOGETHER are sufficient, but NEITHER statement ALONE is sufficient.

    Ⓓ EACH statement ALONE is sufficient.

    Ⓔ Statements (1) and (2) TOGETHER are NOT sufficient.

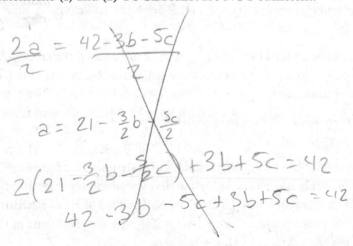

Answers

1. **C** Choice C is the correct response because $\sqrt{(-20)^2} = \sqrt{400}$.

2. **D** $\dfrac{2}{9} + \dfrac{1}{2} = \dfrac{4}{18} + \dfrac{9}{18} = \dfrac{13}{18}$, so look for an answer choice that equals $-\dfrac{13}{18}$. You can eliminate B and E because the quantities in these choices are positive. Check the remaining choices. For choice A, $\dfrac{1-9-2^2}{(9)(2)} = -\dfrac{12}{18} \neq -\dfrac{13}{18}$, so eliminate A. For C, $-\dfrac{(2)(9)}{2^2+9} = -\dfrac{18}{13} \neq -\dfrac{13}{18}$, so eliminate C. Choice D is correct because $\dfrac{-(9+2^2)}{(-2)(-9)} = \dfrac{-13}{18} = -\dfrac{13}{18}$.

3. **D** $35 \times 7 = 245$, and $245 + 20 = 265$, so the tens digit of the dividend is 6.

4. **D** You must find all the positive integers that leave a remainder of 3 when you divide 19 by the integer. These integers are 4, 8, and 16, the sum of which is 28.

5. **E** The squares between 2 and 100 that have units digit 6 are 16 and 36, so n is either 4 or 6. Suppose n is 4; then 9 is the units digit of $(n-1)^2 = 3^2 = 9$. Thus, n is not 4. If n is 6, 5 is the units digit of $(n-1)^2 = 5^2 = 25$. The units digit of $(n+1)^2 = 7^2 = 49$ is 9.

6. **B** Let m and n be the two positive integers. Then $\sqrt{m \cdot n} = 15$, so $m \cdot n = 225$. The positive factors of 225 are 1, 3, 5, 9, 15, 25, 45, 75, and 225. The possible two-factor combinations for m and n are 1 and 225, 3 and 75, 5 and 45, 9 and 25, and 15 and 15. The possible sums for the two-factor combinations are 226, 78, 50, 34, and 30, which makes choice B the correct response.

7. **B** The percent budgeted for rent is 40%. The percent budgeted for food and clothing combined is 17% + 17% = 34%. The percentage difference is 40% − 34% = 6%. Apply this percentage to find the difference in dollars: 6% of $3,500 = 0.06($3,500) = $210 more budgeted for rent than for food and clothing combined. *Tip*: Rather than working with the percentages first, you can obtain the same answer by computing the money amounts for each category first and then subtracting the amounts budgeted for food and clothing from the amount budgeted for rent.

8. **D** According to the line graph, monthly sales were $140,000 in January, $100,000 in February, $120,000 in March, $60,000 in April, $140,000 in May, and $120,000 in June. No computations are necessary for answering this question. The monthly revenues in January and May are the highest values shown on the graph. The median is the middle value, so it is not affected when one of these data values increases. In other words, the monthly revenue in January could increase by any amount without changing the median.

9. **A** The number of possible different meals is $8 \cdot 5 \cdot 7 = 280$.

10. **C** There are 5 ways to go from A to B, 8 ways to go from B to C, 7 ways to go from C to B without retracing a path, and 4 ways to go from B to A without retracing a path. Therefore, the task can be accomplished in a total of $5 \cdot 8 \cdot 7 \cdot 4 = 1{,}120$ ways.

11. **D** For convenience, label the five people as P1, P2, P3, P4, and P5. The people are not assigned to particular seats but are only arranged relative to one another. Hence, the position of P1 is immaterial. What counts are the positions of the other four people relative to P1. Therefore, keeping P1 fixed, there are $4 \times 3 \times 2 \times 1 = 24$ different ways to arrange the other four people, so there are 24 different arrangements of the five people in a circle.

12. **E** There are 17 favorable outcomes (7 black marbles plus 10 red marbles) out of 23 total outcomes. Thus, $P(\text{black or red}) = \dfrac{17}{23}$.

13. **D** For any one question, there are 3 wrong answer choices out of 4 total answer choices, so the probability of guessing wrong on a particular question is $\dfrac{3}{4}$. Because the student is randomly guessing, each guess on a question is independent of the guesses on the other questions, so the probability of getting all five questions wrong is the product of the probabilities for each question: $P(\text{none correct}) = \dfrac{3}{4} \cdot \dfrac{3}{4} \cdot \dfrac{3}{4} \cdot \dfrac{3}{4} \cdot \dfrac{3}{4} = \dfrac{243}{1{,}024}$. Therefore, the probability of at least one correct is $1 - P(\text{none correct}) = 1 - \dfrac{243}{1{,}024} = \dfrac{781}{1{,}024}$.

14. **D** After a red marble is drawn and not replaced, 7 red marbles and 6 blue marbles are left in the box. Thus, the probability of drawing blue on the second draw is $\dfrac{6}{13}$.

15. **B** Fill in the missing probabilities.

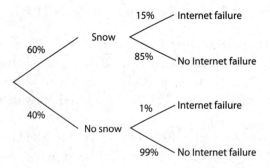

The probability that it snows and an Internet failure occurs is $(60\%)(15\%) = 9\%$.

16. **B** Complete the table by filling in the row and column totals.

Residence Status of Senior Students ($n = 250$)			
	ON-CAMPUS	OFF-CAMPUS	TOTAL
Female	52	86	138
Male	38	74	112
Total	90	160	250

It's given the student is male. The table shows that 38 of the 112 male students reside on campus. Thus, the probability that a randomly selected student resides on campus, given the student is male, is $\dfrac{38}{112} \approx 0.34$.

17. **E** Let A = the event that the model home will be sold, and let B = the event that the house next door will be sold. Then $P(A) = 0.60$, $P(B) = 0.50$, and $P(A \cap B) = 0.40$. The probability that at least one of the two houses will be sold is $P(A \cup B) = P(A) + P(B) - P(A \cap B) = 0.60 + 0.50 - 0.40 = 0.70$.

18. **A** From the question, you know that m is 3, 4, 5, 6, 7, 8, or 9. From the information in (1), m is 7 because the units digit of $(7+1)^2$ is 4 (because $8^2 = 64$). None of the other possible values for m have this property, so (1) is sufficient. From the information in (2), m is either 5 or 7, not a single value, so (2) is NOT sufficient. Therefore, statement (1) ALONE is sufficient, but statement (2) alone is not sufficient.

19. **C** Let $x =$ the number of vases with 10 flowers and $n - x =$ the number of vases with 8 flowers. Thus, the total number of flowers is $10x + 8(n - x) = 10x + 8n - 8x = 2x + 8n$. With this equation, if you know the total number of flowers and the value of n, you can find the value of x. From the information in (1), $2x + 8n = 136$, but the value of n is needed to determine x, so (1) is NOT sufficient. From the information in (2), $n = 15$, but the total number of flowers is needed to determine x, so (2) is NOT sufficient. Taking (1) and (2) together, $2x + 8(15) = 136$, which you can solve for a single value of x. Therefore, BOTH statements together are sufficient, but NEITHER statement ALONE is sufficient.

20. **E** If, as given in statement (1), $x < 0$, then x^p is positive if p is even and negative if p is odd. For instance, if $x = -1$ and $p = 2$, $x^p = (-1)^2 = 1 > 0$, and if $x = -1$ and $p = 1$, $x^p = (-1)^1 = -1 < 0$. Thus, further information is needed, and (1) is NOT sufficient. If, as given in (2), $p < 0$, then the sign of x^p cannot be determined without knowing whether x is positive or negative and whether p is odd or even. For instance, if $x = -1$ and $p = -2$, then $x^p = (-1)^{-2} = \dfrac{1}{(-1)^2} = 1$, but if $x = -1$ and $p = -3$, then $x^p = (-1)^{-3} = \dfrac{1}{(-1)^3} = -1$. Therefore, (2) is NOT sufficient. Taking (1) and (2) together with $x < 0$ and $p < 0$, the sign of x^p cannot be determined without knowing whether p is odd or even. Therefore, statements (1) and (2) TOGETHER are NOT sufficient.

21. **A** Let $x =$ the required score for the fourth test. From the information in (1), you can write the equation $\dfrac{77 + 91 + 94 + x}{4} = 90$ and solve for a single value of x. Therefore, (1) is sufficient. From the information in (2), you can determine that the sum of the first and third tests is $2(85.5) = 171$, but without knowing the score on the second test, you cannot determine x, so (2) is NOT sufficient. Therefore, statement (1) ALONE is sufficient, but statement (2) alone is not sufficient.

22. **C** From the information in (1), you know the average of the 20 numbers in set A, but without further information about set B, the combined average cannot be determined, so (1) is NOT sufficient. From the information in (2), you know the average of the 20 numbers in set B, but without further information about set A, the combined average cannot be determined, so (2) is NOT sufficient. Taking (1) and (2) together, because there are equal numbers in each set, the average of the 40 numbers combined is the sum of the two averages divided by 2, which you can compute. Therefore, BOTH statements together are sufficient, but NEITHER statement ALONE is sufficient.

23. **B** From the information in (1), a is any number between 5^7 and 5^9, but without further information, you cannot determine whether $a > 5^8$. So, statement (1) is NOT sufficient. From (2) $a = \dfrac{5^{10} - 5^8}{24} = \dfrac{5^8(5^2 - 1)}{24} = \dfrac{5^8(24)}{24} = 5^8$. So (2) is sufficient to give a definite "No" to the question posed. Therefore, statement (2) ALONE is sufficient, but statement (1) alone is not sufficient.

24. **E** From the information in (1), a is 12, 15, 18, or 21. From the information in (2), a is 12, 16, 18, or 22. Neither provides a single value, so neither is sufficient. Taking (1) and (2) together, a is 12 or 18, again not a single value. Therefore, statements (1) and (2) TOGETHER are NOT sufficient.

25. **C** The average is $\dfrac{a+b+c}{3}$. *Tip*: Notice that to answer the question, you do not need the specific values of a, b, and c. You need only the value of their sum, $a+b+c$. You cannot determine $\dfrac{a+b+c}{3}$ from the equation in (1), because you cannot solve for the three variables or their sum, so (1) is NOT sufficient. You also cannot determine $\dfrac{a+b+c}{3}$ from the equation in (2). Therefore, (2) also is NOT sufficient. Taking (1) and (2) together and adding the two equations yields the equation $6a+6b+6c=72$, which simplifies to $a+b+c=12$. Then $\dfrac{a+b+c}{3} = \dfrac{12}{3} = 4$. Therefore, BOTH statements together are sufficient, but NEITHER statement ALONE is sufficient.

Algebra Review

Algebraic Expressions

Basic Concepts

A **variable** holds a place open for a number (or numbers, in some cases) whose value may vary. Upper or lowercase letters (e.g., x, y, z, A, B, or C) represent variables. For simplicity, the letter is the "name" of the variable. In problem solving, you use variables to represent unknown quantities. Although a variable may represent any number, in many problems, the variables represent specific numbers, but the values are unknown.

A **constant** is a quantity that has a fixed, definite value that does not change in a problem situation. For example, all the real numbers are constants, including real numbers whose units are units of measure such as 5 feet, 60 degrees, 100 pounds, and so forth.

The result of multiplying 5 and x is $5x$. Thus, $5 \cdot x = x \cdot 5 = (5)(x) = (5)x = x(5) = 5x$. A constant factor times a variable is the variable's **numerical coefficient**. For example, 5 is the numerical coefficient of x in the expression $5x + 3$. A variable for which a numerical factor is not shown has the numerical coefficient of 1. For example, the numerical coefficient of x in the expression $x + 3$ is 1. The numerical coefficient of a variable that is multiplied by several factors is their product. For example, the numerical coefficient of x in the expression $(5)(4)x + 10$ is $(5)(4) = 20$.

An **algebraic expression** is a symbolic representation of a number. It can contain constants, variables, and computation symbols. Multiplication is shown by writing variables and coefficients or two or more variables (with or without constants) side by side with no multiplication symbol. Thus, $-5x$ means -5 times x, and $2xyz$ means 2 times x times y times z. Also, a number or variable written immediately next to a grouping symbol indicates multiplication. For instance, $6(x+1)$ means 6 times the quantity $(x+1)$, $7\sqrt{x}$ means 7 times $\sqrt{x}$, and $-1|-8|$ means -1 times $|-8|$.

Evaluating Algebraic Expressions

If you are given numerical values for the variables in an algebraic expression, you can evaluate the expression by substituting the given numerical value for each variable and then simplifying by performing the indicated operations, being sure to follow the order of operations as you proceed. For instance, when $x = 4$, $y = -8$, and $z = -5$:

$$\frac{2xyz+5(x-y)}{z+1} = \frac{2(4)(-8)(-5)+5(4-(-8))}{(-5)+1} = \frac{320+5(12)}{-4} = \frac{320+60}{-4} = \frac{380}{-4} = -95$$

When you substitute negative values into an algebraic expression, enclose them in parentheses to avoid careless errors.

Polynomials

Basic Concepts

In an algebraic expression, **terms** are the parts of the expression that are connected to the other parts by plus or minus signs. For example, the expression $-8x^2 - \frac{5x}{6} + 27$ has three terms: $-8x^2$, $\frac{5x}{6}$, and 27. If the algebraic expression has no plus or minus signs, then the algebraic expression itself is a term.

A **monomial** is a term that when simplified is a constant or a product of one or more variables raised to positive integer powers, with or without an explicit coefficient.

In monomials, no variable divisors, negative exponents, or fractional exponents are allowed. For example, 20, $5x$, $-54x$, $\frac{1}{2}xy$, $6x^2$, and $-100x^2y^2$ are monomials; but $\frac{2}{x}$, $-7x^{-3}$, and $-8x^{\frac{1}{3}}$ are not monomials.

Constants like 20 are monomials because you can write 20 as $20(1) = 20x^0$.

A **polynomial** is a single monomial or a sum of monomials. A polynomial that has exactly one term is a **monomial**. A polynomial that has exactly two terms is a **binomial**. A polynomial that has exactly three terms is a **trinomial**. A polynomial that has more than three terms is just a general polynomial.

Monomials that are constants or that have exactly the same variable factors (that is, the same letters with the same corresponding exponents) are **like terms**. Like terms are the same except, perhaps, for their coefficients. For example, $-10x$ and $25x$ are like terms; $4xy^2$ and $5xy^2$ are like terms; but $4xy^2$ and $5x^2y$ are *not* like terms. Monomials that are not like terms are **unlike terms**.

Addition and Subtraction of Monomials

- **Adding Monomials That Are Like Terms:** Add their numerical coefficients and use the sum as the coefficient of their common variable component. For example, $-10x + 25x = 15x$.
- **Subtracting Monomials That Are Like Terms:** Subtract their numerical coefficients and use the difference as the coefficient of their common variable component. For example, $4xy^2 - 9xy^2 = -5xy^2$.
- **Adding or Subtracting Unlike Terms:** Simply indicate the addition or subtraction. For example, $4xy^2 + 5x^2y$ is $4xy^2 + 5x^2y$. (These two terms cannot be combined into a single monomial term.)

Simplifying Polynomials

Polynomials are in **simplest form** when they contain no uncombined like terms. To organize the process of **simplifying a polynomial**, use the properties of real numbers to rearrange the expression so that matching like terms are together (later, you might choose to do this step mentally). If the expression includes unlike terms, just indicate the sums or differences of such terms. *Tip:* To avoid sign errors, change instances of $- -$ to $+$ and change instances of $- +$ or $+ -$ to $-$. Thereafter, keep a $-$ sign with the number that follows it. Here is an example.

$$4x^3 - -5x^2 - 10x + 25 + 2x^3 + -7x^2 - 5 = 4x^3 + 5x^2 - 10x + 25 + 2x^3 - 7x^2 - 5$$
$$= 4x^3 + 2x^3 + 5x^2 - 7x^2 - 10x + 25 - 5$$
$$= 6x^3 - 2x^2 - 10x + 20$$

As shown in this example, polynomials in one variable are usually written in descending order of the variable's exponents.

Dealing with Parentheses

If no sign or if a plus (+) sign immediately precedes parentheses that enclose an algebraic expression, remove the parentheses and rewrite the algebraic expression without changing any signs. Here is an example.

$$\left(9x^2 - 6x + 2\right) + \left(-7x^2 - 5x + 3\right) = 9x^2 - 6x + 2 - 7x^2 - 5x + 3$$
$$= 9x^2 - 7x^2 - 6x - 5x + 2 + 3$$
$$= 2x^2 - 11x + 5$$

If a negative (–) sign immediately precedes parentheses that enclose an algebraic expression, remove the parentheses and the negative sign and rewrite the algebraic expression but with all the signs changed. *Tip:* Change *all* the signs, not just the first one. Here is an example.

$$-\left(-7x^2-5x+3\right)=7x^2+5x-3$$

If a minus (–) sign immediately precedes parentheses that enclose an algebraic expression, remove the parentheses and the minus sign and rewrite the algebraic expression but with all the signs changed. Here is an example.

$$\left(9x^2-6x+2\right)-\left(-7x^2-5x+3\right)=9x^2-6x+2+7x^2+5x-3$$
$$=9x^2+7x^2-6x+5x+2-3$$
$$=16x^2-x-1$$

As you can see, negative and minus signs produce similar results. However, keep in mind that a negative sign is used to indicate the *opposite* of a number, but a minus sign is used to indicate *subtraction*.

If a number immediately precedes parentheses that enclose an algebraic expression, multiply the coefficient of each term inside the parentheses by the number. *Tip:* Multiply *each* coefficient, not just the first one. Here are examples.

$$2\left(4x^3-5x^2-x+3\right)=8x^3-10x^2-2x+6 \text{ and } -2\left(4x^3-5x^2-x+3\right)=-8x^3+10x^2+2x-6$$

Multiplying Polynomials

▪ **To Multiply Monomials:** Multiply the numerical coefficients, multiply the variable factors using rules for exponents, and then use the product of the numerical coefficients as the coefficient of the product of the variable factors to obtain the answer. Here are examples.

$$(5x)(-2x)=-10x^2,\,(-5x^3)(-2x^4)=10x^7,\text{ and }\left(x^3y^4\right)\left(xy^2\right)=x^4y^6$$

Remember, $x=x^1$.

▪ **To Multiply a Polynomial by a Monomial:** Multiply each term of the polynomial by the monomial. Here are examples.

$$x(3x-2)=3x^2-2x,\,5x(2x+4)=10x^2+20x,\text{ and}$$

$$-8x^3y^4\left(2x^2-7xy^2-3\right)=-16x^5y^4+56x^4y^6+24x^3y^4.$$

- **To Multiply Two Binomials:** Multiply all the terms of the second binomial by each term of the first binomial and then simplify. The **FOIL** method is a quick way to perform the multiplication. The word *FOIL* is an acronym for *first, outer, inner,* and *last.* Here is an example.

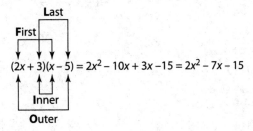

The inner and outer products are the *middle terms.*

- **To Multiply Two General Polynomials:** Multiply all the terms of the second polynomial by each term of the first polynomial and then simplify. Here is an example.

$$(2x-1)(3x^2-5x+4)=6x^3-10x^2+8x-3x^2+5x-4$$

$$=6x^3-13x^2+13x-4$$

Special Products

Here is a list of the forms of special products of polynomials that are helpful to know.

- **Perfect Squares**

$$(x+y)^2=x^2+2xy+y^2; \text{ for example, } (x+3)^2=x^2+6x+9$$

$$(x-y)^2=x^2-2xy+y^2; \text{ for example, } (x-3)^2=x^2-6x+9$$

- **Difference of Two Squares**

$$(x+y)(x-y)=x^2-y^2; \text{ for example, } (x+3)(x-3)=x^2-9$$

Notice that the two middle terms sum to zero.

■ **Perfect Cubes**

$$(x+y)^3 = x^3 + 3x^2y + 3xy^2 + y^3 ; \text{ for example, } (x+2)^3 = x^3 + 6x^2 + 12x + 8$$

$$(x-y)^3 = x^3 - 3x^2y + 3xy^2 - y^3 ; \text{ for example, } (x-2)^3 = x^3 - 6x^2 + 12x - 8$$

■ **Sum of Two Cubes**

$$(x+y)(x^2 - xy + y^2) = x^3 + y^3 ; \text{ for example, } (x+1)(x^2 - x + 1) = x^3 + 1$$

■ **Difference of Two Cubes**

$$(x-y)(x^2 + xy + y^2) = x^3 - y^3 ; \text{ for example, } (x-1)(x^2 + x + 1) = x^3 - 1$$

You can substitute any value or variable expression for x and y in the above forms. Here are examples.

$$(2x^5 - 3)(2x^5 + 3) = 4x^{10} - 9$$

$$(\sqrt{5x} + 1)^2 = (\sqrt{5x})^2 + 2\sqrt{5x} + 1 = 5x + 2\sqrt{5x} + 1$$

$$(\sqrt{3x} + \sqrt{5})(\sqrt{3x} - \sqrt{5}) = (\sqrt{3x})^2 - (\sqrt{5})^2 = 3x - 5$$

Factoring Polynomials

Factoring is the process of undoing multiplication. Here are some general guidelines for factoring polynomials.

■ **If the expression has a greatest common factor (GCF), factor out the GCF.** The GCF is the product of the greatest common numerical factor and a second component made up of the common variable factors, each with the highest power common to each term. Here is an example.

$$15x^3y^4 - 3x^2y^3 + 12xy^2 = 3xy^2(5x^2y^2 - xy + 4)$$

■ **If there are two terms, check for a special binomial product.**
  ■ Difference of two squares: $(4x^2 - 9) = (2x + 3)(2x - 3)$

Expressions that have the form $(x^2 + y^2)$ are not factorable on the GMAT. For example, $(4x^2 + 9)$ is not factorable.

  ■ Difference of two cubes: $8x^3 - 27 = (2x - 3)(4x^2 + 6x + 9)$
  ■ Sum of two cubes: $64x^3 + 125 = (4x + 5)(16x^2 - 20x + 25)$
■ **If there are three terms, check for a quadratic trinomial.** A quadratic trinomial has the form $ax^2 + bx + c$, where a, b, and c are nonzero constants. You can use *trial and error* to factor simple quadratic trinomials. As you proceed, call to mind the FOIL method for multiplying two binomials. When you use FOIL to multiply $(x + k)(x + h)$,

where k and h are constants, you get $x^2 + (k + h)x + kh$. If the coefficient of the middle term, $(k + h)$, is not zero, the product is a quadratic trinomial. If k and h have the same sign, the last term of the trinomial is their product, which is positive, and the coefficient of the middle term is their algebraic sum, with the same sign. If k and h have different signs, the last term of the trinomial is their product, which is negative, and the coefficient of the middle term is their algebraic sum, with the sign of whichever one has the greater absolute value. Here are examples.

$$(x+3)(x+5)= x^2 +8x +15$$
$$(x-3)(x-5)= x^2 -8x +15$$
$$(x+3)(x-5)= x^2 -2x -15$$
$$(x-3)(x+5)= x^2 +2x -15$$

Your task when factoring is to reverse the above process. Here are examples.
- To factor $x^2 - 9x + 14$, observe that the last term is positive and the middle term is negative. So, you want to find two negative numbers whose product is 14 and whose sum is −9. Thus, $x^2 -9x +14 = (x-7)(x-2)$.
- To factor $x^2 - 5x - 14$, observe that the last term is negative and the middle term is negative. So, you want to find two numbers with different signs whose product is −14 and whose sum is −5. Thus, $x^2 -5x -14 = (x-7)(x+2)$.

Always check whether any previously obtained factor can be factored further. For example,

$$25x^4 - 25$$
$$\downarrow$$
$$25(x^4 - 1)$$
$$\downarrow$$
$$25(x^2 + 1)(x^2 - 1)$$
$$\downarrow$$
$$25(x^2 + 1)(x + 1)(x - 1)$$

Rational Expressions

A **rational expression** is an **algebraic fraction** that has a polynomial for its numerator and a polynomial for its denominator. For instance, $\dfrac{x^2 -1}{x^2 +2x +1}$ is a rational expression. Because division by 0 is undefined, you must exclude values for the variable or variables that would make the denominator polynomial sum to 0. For convenience, you can assume such values are excluded as you work through the problems in this section.

Reducing Algebraic Fractions to Lowest Terms

Fundamental Principle of Rational Expressions: If P, Q, and R are polynomials, then:

$$\frac{PR}{QR} = \frac{RP}{RQ} = \frac{P}{Q}, \text{ provided neither } Q \text{ nor } R \text{ has a zero value.}$$

This principle allows you to reduce algebraic fractions to lowest terms by dividing the numerator and denominator by the greatest common factor (GCF).

Before applying the fundamental principle of rational expressions, *always* make sure that the numerator and denominator contain only *factored* polynomials as shown in the following examples.

$$\frac{15x^5y^2z}{30x^4y^3} = \frac{\left(15x^4y^2\right)(xz)}{\left(15x^4y^2\right)(2y)} = \frac{\left(\cancel{15x^4y^2}\right)(xz)}{\left(\cancel{15x^4y^2}\right)(2y)} = \frac{xz}{2y}$$

$$\frac{x-3}{3-x} = \frac{(x-3)}{-1(x-3)} = \frac{\cancel{(x-3)}^1}{-1\cancel{(x-3)}} = -1$$

$$\frac{x^2-1}{x^2+2x+1} = \frac{(x+1)(x-1)}{(x+1)(x+1)} = \frac{\cancel{(x+1)}(x-1)}{\cancel{(x+1)}(x+1)} = \frac{x-1}{x+1}$$

$$\frac{2x+6}{x^2+5x+6} = \frac{2(x+3)}{(x+3)(x+2)} = \frac{2\cancel{(x+3)}}{\cancel{(x+3)}(x+2)} = \frac{2}{x+2}$$

Multiplying Algebraic Fractions

To multiply algebraic fractions: (1) factor all numerators and denominators completely, (2) divide numerators and denominators by their common factors (as in reducing), and (3) multiply the remaining numerator factors to get the numerator of the answer and multiply the remaining denominator factors to get the denominator of the answer.

You can leave your answer in factored form as long as it is completely reduced.

Here is an example.

$$\frac{x^2-2x+1}{x^2-4} \cdot \frac{3x-6}{x-1} = \frac{(x-1)(x-1)}{(x+2)(x-2)} \cdot \frac{3(x-2)}{(x-1)}$$

$$= \frac{\cancel{(x-1)}(x-1)}{(x+2)\cancel{(x-2)}} \cdot \frac{3\cancel{(x-2)}}{\cancel{(x-1)}}$$

$$= \frac{3(x-1)}{(x+2)}$$

Be careful! Divide out *factors* only. If a numerator or denominator does not factor, enclose it in parentheses. Forgetting the parentheses can lead to a mistake.

Dividing Algebraic Fractions

To divide algebraic fractions: Multiply the first algebraic fraction (the dividend) by the reciprocal of the second algebraic fraction (the divisor). Here is an example.

$$\frac{x^2-2x+1}{x^2-x-6} \div \frac{x^2-3x+2}{x^2-4} = \frac{x^2-2x+1}{x^2-x-6} \cdot \frac{x^2-4}{x^2-3x+2}$$

$$= \frac{(x-1)(x-1)}{(x-3)(x+2)} \cdot \frac{(x+2)(x-2)}{(x-1)(x-2)}$$

$$= \frac{\cancel{(x-1)}(x-1)}{(x-3)\cancel{(x+2)}} \cdot \frac{\cancel{(x+2)}\cancel{(x-2)}}{\cancel{(x-1)}\cancel{(x-2)}}$$

$$= \frac{(x-1)}{(x-3)}$$

Adding (or Subtracting) Algebraic Fractions, Like Denominators

To add (or subtract) algebraic fractions that have like denominators: Place the sum (or difference) over the common denominator. Simplify and reduce to lowest terms, as needed. Here are examples.

$$\frac{x+2}{x-3} + \frac{2x-11}{x-3} = \frac{x+2+2x-11}{x-3} = \frac{3x-9}{x-3} = \frac{3\cancel{(x-3)}}{\cancel{(x-3)}} = \frac{3}{1} = 3$$

$$\frac{5x^2}{4(x+1)} - \frac{4x^2+1}{4(x+1)} = \frac{(5x^2)-(4x^2+1)}{4(x+1)} = \frac{5x^2-4x^2-1}{4(x+1)} = \frac{x^2-1}{4(x+1)} = \frac{(x+1)(x-1)}{4\cancel{(x+1)}} = \frac{(x-1)}{4}$$

change signs

When subtracting algebraic fractions, enclose the numerator of the second fraction in parentheses because you want to subtract the *entire numerator*, not just the first term.

Adding (or Subtracting) Algebraic Fractions, Unlike Denominators

To add (or subtract) algebraic fractions that have unlike denominators: (1) factor each denominator completely; (2) find the least common denominator (LCD), which is the product of each prime factor the *highest* number of times it is a factor in any one denominator; (3) using the fundamental principle, write each algebraic fraction as an equivalent fraction having the common denominator as a denominator; and (4) add (or subtract) as for like denominators. *Tip*: The LCD is the LCM of the denominators. Here are examples.

$$\frac{3x}{x^2-4}+\frac{x}{x-2}=\frac{3x}{(x+2)(x-2)}+\frac{x(x+2)}{(x-2)(x+2)}$$

$$=\frac{3x+x^2+2x}{(x+2)(x-2)}$$

$$=\frac{x^2+5x}{(x+2)(x-2)}$$

$$=\frac{x(x+5)}{(x+2)(x-2)}$$

$$\frac{2x-1}{x-3}-\frac{x}{2x+2}=\frac{2x-1}{(x-3)}-\frac{x}{2(x+1)}$$

$$=\frac{2(2x-1)(x+1)}{2(x-3)(x+1)}-\frac{x(x-3)}{2(x+1)(x-3)}$$

$$=\frac{4x^2+2x-2}{2(x-3)(x+1)}-\frac{x^2-3x}{2(x-3)(x+1)}$$

$$=\frac{4x^2+2x-2-x^2+3x}{2(x-3)(x+1)}$$

$$=\frac{3x^2+5x-2}{2(x-3)(x+1)}$$

$$=\frac{(3x-1)(x+2)}{2(x-3)(x+1)}$$

A **prime factor** is one that cannot be factored further.

Simplifying Complex Fractions

A **complex fraction** is a fraction that has fractions in its numerator, denominator, or both.

To simplify a complex fraction: Multiply its numerator and denominator by the least common multiple (LCM) of all the fractions in its numerator and denominator:

$$\frac{\frac{1}{x}+\frac{1}{y}}{\frac{1}{x}-\frac{1}{y}}=\frac{xy\left(\frac{1}{x}+\frac{1}{y}\right)}{xy\left(\frac{1}{x}-\frac{1}{y}\right)}=\frac{y+x}{y-x}$$

One-Variable Linear Equations and Inequalities

Solving One-Variable Linear Equations

To solve a one-variable linear equation, follow these steps.

Step 1. Remove parentheses, if any, using the distributive property.

Step 2. Combine like terms, if any, on each side of the equation.

Step 3. If variable terms are on both sides of the equation, add a variable term to both sides of the equation or subtract a variable term from both sides so that all variable terms are on only one side of the equation. Then simplify.

Step 4. Isolate the variable term. If a number is added to the variable term, subtract that number from both sides of the equation. If a number is subtracted from the variable term, add that number to both sides of the equation. Then simplify.

Step 5. Make the coefficient of the variable 1 by dividing both sides of the equation by the variable's coefficient. *Tip*: If the coefficient is a fraction, do the division by multiplying both sides of the equation by the fraction's reciprocal. Then simplify.

You can check the solution by substituting it into the original equation.

Here are examples.

Solve $-2(1-x)+4x=3x-14$.

$$-2(1-x)+4x=3x-14$$

$$-2+2x+4x=3x-14 \qquad \text{Remove parentheses.}$$

$$6x-2=3x-14 \qquad \text{Simplify.}$$

$$6x-2-3x=3x-14-3x \qquad \text{Subtract } 3x \text{ from both sides.}$$

$$3x-2=-14 \qquad \text{Simplify.}$$

$$3x-2+2=-14+2 \qquad \text{Add 2 to both sides.}$$

$$3x=-12 \qquad \text{Simplify.}$$

$$\frac{3x}{3}=\frac{-12}{3} \qquad \text{Divide both sides by 3.}$$

$$x=-4 \qquad \text{Simplify.}$$

$$-2(1-(-4))+4(4) = 3(-4)-14$$
$$(5)$$
$$-10-16 = -12-14$$
$$-26 = -26$$

Solve $\dfrac{2}{3}x - 45 = 12.5 - x$.

$$\dfrac{2}{3}x - 45 = 12.5 - x$$

$\dfrac{2}{3}x - 45 + x = 12.5 - x + x$ \qquad Add x to both sides.

$\dfrac{5}{3}x - 45 = 12.5$ \qquad Simplify.

$\dfrac{5}{3}x - 45 + 45 = 12.5 + 45$ \qquad Add 45 to both sides.

$\dfrac{5}{3}x = 57.5$ \qquad Simplify.

$\dfrac{3}{5} \cdot \dfrac{5}{3}x = \dfrac{3}{5}(57.5)$ \qquad Multiply both sides by $\dfrac{3}{5}$, the reciprocal of x's coefficient.

$x = 34.5$ \qquad Simplify.

Skip steps that are not needed for the particular equation you are solving.

Solving Two-Variable Linear Equations for One of the Variables

Use the procedure for solving a linear equation in one variable to solve a two-variable linear equation, such as $3x + 2y = -4$, for one of the variables in terms of the other variable. As you solve for the variable of interest, you simply treat the other variable as you would a constant. For instance, to solve $3x + 2y = -4$ for y, do as follows:

$$3x - 2y = -4$$

$3x - 2y - 3x = -4 - 3x$ \qquad Subtract $3x$ from both sides.

$-2y = -3x - 4$ \qquad Simplify.

$\dfrac{-2y}{-2} = \dfrac{-3x - 4}{-2}$ \qquad Divide both sides by -2.

$y = \dfrac{3}{2}x + 2$ \qquad Simplify.

$\dfrac{-3x - 4}{-2} \neq \dfrac{3}{2}x - 4$. You must divide both terms of the numerator by -2.

Solving Linear Inequalities

You solve linear inequalities in much the same way you solve linear equations. There is just one very important difference. When you multiply or divide both sides of an inequality by a negative number, you must *reverse* the direction of the inequality symbol. Here is an example.

Solve $-3x - 6 > 15$.

$$-3x - 6 > 15$$

$-3x - 6 + 6 > 15 + 6$ Add 6 to both sides.

$\quad\quad -3x > 21$ Simplify.

$\dfrac{-3x}{-3} < \dfrac{21}{-3}$ Divide both sides by -3, being sure to reverse the inequality symbol.

$\quad\quad x < -7$ Simplify.

You can write the two inequalities, $-12 < 5x + 2$ and $5x + 2 < 12$, as the **double inequality** $-12 < 5x + 2 < 12$. To solve a double inequality, undo what has been done to the variable expression. Perform the "undoing" operations on all three of the expressions that make up the double inequality. For example, to solve $-12 < 5x + 2$ and $5x + 2 < 12$, proceed as follows:

$$-12 < 5x + 2 < 12$$

$-12 - 2 < 5x + 2 - 2 < 12 - 2$ Subtract 2 from each of the three expressions.

$\quad\quad -14 < 5x < 10$ Simplify.

$\dfrac{-14}{5} < \dfrac{5x}{5} < \dfrac{10}{5}$ Divide each of the three expressions by 5.

$\quad\quad -2.8 < x < 2$ Simplify.

Quadratic Equations

A **quadratic equation** is an equation that can be expressed in standard form as $ax^2 + bx + c = 0$, where a, b, and c are real numbers and $a \neq 0$. The **roots** are the values for the variable that make the quadratic equation true. When you are restricted to real numbers (as is the case for the GMAT), a quadratic equation has two distinct real roots, one real root, or no real roots in its solution set.

Solving Quadratic Equations of the Form $x^2 = k$, $(k \geq 0)$

The equation $x^2 = k$, $(k \geq 0)$, has solution $x = \sqrt{k}$ or $x = -\sqrt{k}$. Commonly, you write this solution as $x = \pm\sqrt{k}$. Here are examples.

$$\text{If } x^2 = 16, \text{ then } x = \pm 4.$$

$$\text{If } x^2 = 7, \text{ then } x = \pm\sqrt{7}.$$

Solving Quadratic Equations by Factoring

When you solve quadratic equations by factoring, you use the following **zero factor property**: If the product of two numbers is 0, then at least one of the numbers is 0.

To solve a quadratic equation by factoring: Put the equation in standard form, factor the nonzero side of the equation, set each factor equal to zero, and then solve the resulting linear equations for the variable. Here is an example.

Solve $x^2 + x = 6$.

$$x^2 + x = 6$$
$$x^2 + x - 6 = 0 \qquad \text{Put the equation in standard form.}$$
$$(x+3)(x-2) = 0 \qquad \text{Factor.}$$
$$x + 3 = 0 \text{ or } x - 2 = 0 \qquad \text{Set each factor equal to zero.}$$
$$x = -3 \text{ or } x = 2 \qquad \text{Solve the resulting linear equations.}$$

Solve $x^2 + 5x = 0$.

$$x^2 + 5x = 0$$
$$x(x+5) = 0 \qquad \text{Factor.}$$
$$x = 0 \text{ or } x + 5 = 0 \qquad \text{Set each factor equal to zero.}$$
$$x = 0 \text{ or } x = -5 \qquad \text{Solve.}$$

Basic Function Concepts

Terminology

A **function** is a set of ordered pairs (x, y) such that no two different ordered pairs have the same *first* coordinate. The **domain** of a function is the set of all first coordinates of the ordered pairs in the function. The **range** of a function is the set of all second coordinates of the ordered pairs in the function. For example, the set of ordered pairs $f = \{(2, 5), (3, 7), (4, 1), (5, 5)\}$ is a function. The domain of f is $D = \{2, 3, 4, 5\}$ and its range is $R = \{1, 5, 7\}$. The set of ordered pairs $s = \{(4, 2), (4, 3), (5, 1), (6, 3)\}$ is *not* a function, because $(4, 2)$ and $(4, 3)$ have the same first coordinate.

It is common to use an equation to define a function. For example, the equation $y = 3x + 7$ specifies how to obtain the ordered pairs (x, y) for a function. As you substitute values for x into $y = 3x + 7$, you obtain corresponding values for y. Thus, for instance, $(-2, 1)$, $(1, 10)$, $(2, 13)$, $(3, 16)$, and $(4, 19)$ are ordered pairs in the function. You can refer to x as the **independent** variable and to y as the **dependent** variable.

A common notation for functions is to use the symbol $f(x)$ to denote the value of the function f at a given value for x. *Tip*: The notation $f(x)$ does not mean f times x. In this setting, it is convenient to designate x as the **input** value and $f(x)$ as the **output** value. In terms of ordered pairs, if $f = \{(2, 5), (3, 7), (4, 1), (5, 5)\}$ then $f(2) = 5$, $f(3) = 7$, $f(4) = 1$, and $f(5) = 5$.

You can express $y = 3x + 7$ as $f(x) = 3x + 7$, where $y = f(x)$. *Tip*: Even though a function f is a set of ordered pairs, it has become commonplace to refer to an equation that defines a function as the function; that is, to speak of "the function $y = 3x + 7$" or "the function $f(x) = 3x + 7$." Notice that you can use y and $f(x)$ interchangeably.

Evaluating Functions

To evaluate a function, replace the function's variable with the indicated number or expression. Here are examples.

When $f(x) = 3x + 7$, then $f(-2) = 3(-2) + 7 = -6 + 7 = 1$.

When $g(x) = \sqrt{5x+1}$, then $g(3) = \sqrt{5(3)+1} = \sqrt{15+1} = \sqrt{16} = 4$.

When $h(x) = 2x + 1$, then $h(a+10) = 2(a+10) + 1 = 2a + 20 + 1 = 2a + 21$.

Some Common Functions

Here are some common functions you might see on the GMAT.

FUNCTION NAME	GENERAL FORM	EXAMPLE
Linear function	$y = f(x) = ax + b$	$f(x) = 3x + 7$
Quadratic function	$y = f(x) = ax^2 + bx + c$, $a \neq 0$	$f(x) = x^2 - 5x + 6$
Absolute value function	$y = f(x) = |x|$	$f(x) = |x+2|$
Square root function	$y = f(x) = \sqrt{x}$, $x \geq 0$	$f(x) = \sqrt{5x+1}$, $5x + 1 \geq 0$
Polynomial function	$f(x) = P(x)$, where $P(x)$ is a polynomial	$f(x) = 2x^3 + x^2 - 13x + 6$
Rational function	$f(x) = \dfrac{P(x)}{Q(x)}$, where $P(x)$ and $Q(x)$ are polynomials, $Q(x) \neq 0$	$f(x) = \dfrac{x^2 - 9}{x+2}$, $x \neq -2$

Tip: The graph of a rational function might have vertical asympotes. A **vertical asymptote** is a vertical line that corresponds to a value for the variable that produces zero in the denominator of a simplified rational function.

Systems of Linear Equations

A pair of two linear equations, each with the same two variables, is a **system** when the two equations are considered simultaneously.

Solving a System of Equations by Substitution

To solve a system of two equations by **substitution**: Solve one of the equations for one of the variables in terms of the other variable and then use substitution to solve for the other variable. Plug the obtained value into one of the original equations, and solve for the unknown variable. Here is an example.

Solve the system.

$$-x + y = -7$$
$$3x + 2y = -4$$

Begin by solving the first equation, $-x + y = -7$, for y in terms of x.

$$-x + y = -7$$
$$y = x - 7$$

Substitute into the second equation and solve for x. *Tip*: Enclose substituted expressions in parentheses to avoid errors.

$$3x + 2y = -4$$
$$3x + 2(x - 7) = -4$$
$$3x + 2x - 14 = -4$$
$$5x - 14 = -4$$
$$5x - 14 + 14 = -4 + 14$$
$$5x = 10$$
$$x = 2$$

Substitute 2 for x in the first equation and solve for y. *Tip*: You can substitute the value for x in either equation. Just pick the one you think would be easier to work with.

$$-x + y = -7$$
$$-2 + y = -7$$
$$y = -5$$

The ordered pair $(2, -5)$ satisfies the system. *Tip*: Check the solution in the original equations.

Solving a System of Equations by Elimination

To solve a system of two equations by **elimination**: Multiply one or both equations by constants to produce opposite coefficients of one variable so that it can be eliminated by adding the two equations. Solve the resulting equation for the remaining variable. Plug the obtained value into one of the original equations, and solve for the unknown variable.

Here is an example.

Solve the system.

$$-x + y = -7$$
$$3x + 2y = -4$$

First, to eliminate x, multiply the first equation by 3.

$$-3x + 3y = -21$$
$$3x + 2y = -4$$

Add the resulting two equations, and then solve for y.

$$-3x + 3y = -21$$
$$\underline{3x + 2y = -4}$$
$$0 + 5y = -25$$
$$5y = -25$$
$$y = -5$$

Substitute −5 for y in the first equation and solve for x. *Tip*: You can substitute the value for x in either equation. Just pick the one you think would be easier to work with.

$$-x + y = -7$$
$$-x - 5 = -7$$
$$-x = -2$$
$$x = 2$$

The ordered pair (2, −5) satisfies the system. *Tip*: Check the solution in the original equations.

Important Considerations About Linear Equations

Generally, when solving linear equations, you need as many equations as you have variables in order to determine specific values for the variables. However, you need to make sure (1) the equations are not equivalent or (2) the equations do not contradict one another. If the equations are equivalent, there are infinitely many solutions to the system. For example, the system $2x - 3y = 5$ and $4x - 6y = 10$ has infinitely many solutions because the two equations are equivalent. If the equations contradict one another, the system does not have a solution. For example, the system $2x - 3y = 5$ and $2x - 3y = 8$ does not have a solution because the two equations contradict one another.

Finding Positive Integer Solutions to a Linear Equation in Two Variables

As indicated previously, if you have two variables in a linear equation, in most cases, you need a second equation to determine specific values for the variables. An exception to this rule occurs when the variable values are restricted to positive integers that have constraints attached. For example, let x and y be positive integers such that $x + 2y = 4$ and $y < 5$. Because under the constraint $y < 5$, the possible values for y are 1, 2, 3, or 4. Only $y = 1$ yields a positive integer value for x when substituted into the equation $x + 2y = 4$. This value is $x = 2$. The other possible values for y result in $x = 0$ or < 0. Therefore, the only solution is $x = 2$ and $y = 1$.

Algebra Drill

Directions: **Select the best answer choice.**

1. If $(2^x)(2^{2y}) = 64$, then what is x when y is 3?

   Ⓐ −2
   Ⓑ 0
   Ⓒ 1
   Ⓓ 2
   Ⓔ 3

   [handwritten: $2^6 = 64$]
   [handwritten: $x = 0$ so $2^x = 0$]

2. Which expression is equivalent to $(c^2 + 9)^{-\frac{1}{2}}$?

   Ⓐ $\dfrac{1}{c+3}$

   Ⓑ $-\dfrac{c^2+9}{2}$

   Ⓒ $\dfrac{1}{\sqrt{c^2+9}}$

   Ⓓ $-\sqrt{c^2+9}$

   Ⓔ $-\dfrac{1}{c+3}$

   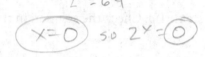
   [handwritten: − exponent take the reciprocal of the equation]
   [handwritten: ? $\dfrac{1}{c^2+9\frac{1}{2}} = \dfrac{1}{\sqrt{c^2+9}}$]
   [handwritten: negative reciprocal turns positive then $\frac{1}{2}$ exponent]
   [handwritten: $b^{\frac{1}{n}} = \sqrt[n]{b}$ $b^{\frac{a}{n}} (\sqrt[n]{\ })^m$]

3. Fifteen less than four times a number is the number increased by nine and one-half. If x denotes the number, which equation is equivalent to the numerical relationship expressed in the preceding statement?

   Ⓐ $4x - 15 = x + 9.5$

   Ⓑ $15 - 4x = 9x + \dfrac{1}{2}$

   Ⓒ $15 - 4x = x + 9\dfrac{1}{2}$

   Ⓓ $4x - 15 = x + 9\dfrac{1}{2}(x)$

   Ⓔ $\dfrac{1}{4}x - 15 = x + 9\dfrac{1}{2}$

   [handwritten: $4x - 15 = x + 9.5$]

4. A national health organization estimates that 45% of the U.S. population age 50 or older will get flu shots this year. According to a recent study, an estimated 1% of people who get flu shots will have some sort of adverse reaction. If N represents the number of people in the United States who are age 50 or older, about how many of these individuals will have an adverse reaction after getting a flu shot?

   (A) $0.46N$
   (B) $0.45N$
   (C) $0.01N$
   (D) $0.0045N$
   (E) $0.0046N$

5. Solve $x^2 - 16 = 20$.

   (A) $x = 6$
   (B) $x = 16$
   (C) $x = 24$
   (D) $x = -6$ or $x = 6$
   (E) $x = 16$ or $x = 24$

6. Which expression is equivalent to $18^x + 12^x$?

   (A) 30^{2x}
   (B) 30^x
   (C) $3^x \cdot 10^x$
   (D) $6(3^x + 2^x)$
   (E) $6^x(3^x + 2^x)$

   $$\left(\sqrt{\sqrt{\sqrt{x}}}\right)^6$$

7. Assuming $x \geq 0$, which expression is equivalent to the preceding expression?

   (A) x^3
   (B) x^2
   (C) $x^{\frac{3}{2}}$
   (D) $x^{\frac{3}{4}}$
   (E) $x^{\frac{1}{24}}$

x	f(x)	g(x)
1	4	5
2	5	1
3	3	4
4	1	2
5	2	3

8. The preceding table shows selected values of the functions f and g. What is the value of $g\big(f(4)\big)$?

   - (A) 1
   - (B) 2
   - (C) 3
   - (D) 4
   - (E) 5

$$|3n - 4| \leq 5$$

9. How many integers n satisfy the preceding absolute-value inequality?

   - (A) Seven
   - (B) Six
   - (C) Five
   - (D) Four
   - (E) Three

10. Which expression is equivalent to $\left(\dfrac{x^{-5}}{x^{-9}}\right)^{\frac{1}{2}}$?

    - (A) x^{-2}
    - (B) x^{-7}
    - (C) x^{2}
    - (D) x^{4}
    - (E) x^{7}

11. If $x = -8$, which statement is true?

    - (A) $x - 10 > x + 10$
    - (B) $5x < 2x$
    - (C) $-2x < 0$
    - (D) $\dfrac{1}{x} > -x$
    - (E) $-|-x| > -x$

12. If $\sqrt{5x+7} = \sqrt{5x}+1$, then what is the value of $5x$?

(A) 0

(B) $\dfrac{9}{5}$

(C) $\pm\dfrac{9}{5}$

(D) 9

(E) ±9

Handwritten work:

$5x+7 = 5x + 2\sqrt{5x}+1$

$7 = 2\sqrt{5x}+1$

$6 = 2\sqrt{5x}$

$3^2 = (\sqrt{5x})^2$

$9 = 5x$

$(\sqrt{5x+7})^2 = (\sqrt{5x}+1)^2 (\sqrt{5x}+1)$

$5x+7 = 5x + 2\sqrt{5x}+1$

$7 = 2\sqrt{5x}+1$

$\dfrac{6}{2} = \dfrac{2\sqrt{5x}}{2}$

$(3)^2 = (\sqrt{5x})^2$

$9 = 5x$

13. Given $16x^2 = 81$ and $x > 0$, solve for $\sqrt{x}$.

(A) $\dfrac{9}{2}$

(B) $\dfrac{3}{2}$

(C) $\pm\dfrac{3}{2}$

(D) $\dfrac{9}{4}$

(E) $\pm\dfrac{9}{4}$

Handwritten work:

$\dfrac{16x^2}{16} = \dfrac{81}{16}$

$\sqrt{x^2} = \sqrt{\dfrac{81}{16}}$

$x = \sqrt{\dfrac{9}{4}}$

$\sqrt{x} = \pm\dfrac{3}{2}$

14. If 4 is one solution of the equation $x^2 - x + k = 15$, where k is a constant, what is the other solution?

(A) -4

(B) -3

(C) 3

(D) 4

(E) 5

Handwritten work:

$4^2 - 4 + k = 15$

$16 - 4 = 12 + k = 15$

$k = 3$

$-3^2 - (-3) + 3 = 15$

$9 + 3 + 3 = 15$

$x^2 - x + 3 = 15$

$x^2 - x - 12$

$(x+3)(x-4)$

$x = -3$ or $x = 4$

PLUG IN

15. If the sum of two numbers is 35 and their product is 300, what is the value of the greater number?

(A) 10 $-3x$

(B) 15 $\cdot 20$

(C) 20

(D) 25

(E) 30

$$2(2x - 3y = 16)$$
$$3x + 6y = 10$$
$$4x - 6y = 32$$

16. What is the x value of the ordered pair that is a solution to the preceding system of equations?

- (A) -6
- (B) -4
- (C) $-\dfrac{4}{3}$
- (D) $\dfrac{4}{3}$
- (E) 6

$$y = 3x - 5$$
$$y = x^2 - x - 5$$

17. Which values of x are in the solution set of the preceding system of equations?

- (A) $0, 4$
- (B) $-4, 0$
- (C) $-2, 5$
- (D) $-2, -5$
- (E) $2, 5$

Questions 18 to 25 each presents a question and two statements, labeled (1) and (2), in which certain data are given. Using your knowledge of mathematics and everyday facts (such as the number of minutes in an hour or the meaning of the word *perpendicular*), decide whether the given data are sufficient to answer the question. Then select one of the answer choices that follow.

$$2, a_2, \ldots, 247$$

18. The preceding list of terms is an arithmetic sequence. How many terms are included in the list?

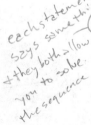

(1) $a_n = 5n - 3$
(2) $a_2 = 7$

- (A) Statement (1) ALONE is sufficient, but statement (2) alone is not sufficient.
- (B) Statement (2) ALONE is sufficient, but statement (1) alone is not sufficient.
- (C) BOTH statements TOGETHER are sufficient, but NEITHER statement ALONE is sufficient.
- (D) EACH statement ALONE is sufficient.
- (E) Statements (1) and (2) TOGETHER are NOT sufficient.

19. What is the value of *ab*?

    (1) $a+b=13$ ← *can't tell from this alone. could be several diff #s*

    (2) $\left(\sqrt{4ab}\right)=12$ $\dfrac{4ab}{4}=\dfrac{144}{4}$ $ab=36$

    (A) Statement (1) ALONE is sufficient, but statement (2) alone is not sufficient.
    (B) Statement (2) ALONE is sufficient, but statement (1) alone is not sufficient.
    (C) BOTH statements TOGETHER are sufficient, but NEITHER statement ALONE is sufficient.
    (D) EACH statement ALONE is sufficient.
    (E) Statements (1) and (2) TOGETHER are NOT sufficient.

20. Is $x < y$?

    (1) $y = x^2$
    (2) $x + y = 2$

    (A) Statement (1) ALONE is sufficient, but statement (2) alone is not sufficient.
    (B) Statement (2) ALONE is sufficient, but statement (1) alone is not sufficient.
    (C) BOTH statements TOGETHER are sufficient, but NEITHER statement ALONE is sufficient.
    (D) EACH statement ALONE is sufficient.
    (E) Statements (1) and (2) TOGETHER are NOT sufficient.

21. What is the value of $\dfrac{x+z}{x-z}$? $\dfrac{\frac{1}{2}}{-\frac{1}{2}}$ ∩ $\dfrac{1}{2}$ = $\dfrac{\frac{x}{z}+1}{\frac{x}{z}-1}$ $\dfrac{6}{4}=\dfrac{3}{2}$

    (1) $\dfrac{x}{z}=5$ *multiply by*

    (2) $x + z < 0$

    (A) Statement (1) ALONE is sufficient, but statement (2) alone is not sufficient.
    (B) Statement (2) ALONE is sufficient, but statement (1) alone is not sufficient.
    (C) BOTH statements TOGETHER are sufficient, but NEITHER statement ALONE is sufficient.
    (D) EACH statement ALONE is sufficient.
    (E) Statements (1) and (2) TOGETHER are NOT sufficient.

22. A team of biologists introduces a herd of deer onto an uninhabited island. The biologists model the expected growth of the deer population on the island with the function $P(t)=P_0 \cdot 2^{0.25t}$, where P_0 is the initial population and t is the elapsed time in years. What is the expected deer population in 20 years?

    (1)   In 4 years, the expected deer population is 50.
    (2)   In 12 years, the expected deer population is 200.

    (A) Statement (1) ALONE is sufficient, but statement (2) alone is not sufficient.
    (B) Statement (2) ALONE is sufficient, but statement (1) alone is not sufficient.
    (C) BOTH statements TOGETHER are sufficient, but NEITHER statement ALONE is sufficient.
    (D) EACH statement ALONE is sufficient.
    (E) Statements (1) and (2) TOGETHER are NOT sufficient.

23. What is the value of p?

Remember $\sqrt{}$ *can be* $(-)$ *or* $(+)$

(1) $4^p = 16$

(2) $\left(3^p\right)^p = 81$

Ⓐ Statement (1) ALONE is sufficient, but statement (2) alone is not sufficient.

Ⓑ Statement (2) ALONE is sufficient, but statement (1) alone is not sufficient.

Ⓒ BOTH statements TOGETHER are sufficient, but NEITHER statement ALONE is sufficient.

Ⓓ EACH statement ALONE is sufficient.

Ⓔ Statements (1) and (2) TOGETHER are NOT sufficient.

24. If w, x, y, and z are positive numbers, is $\dfrac{x}{y} > \dfrac{w}{z}$?

(1) $x > w$

(2) $y < z$

Ⓐ Statement (1) ALONE is sufficient, but statement (2) alone is not sufficient.

Ⓑ Statement (2) ALONE is sufficient, but statement (1) alone is not sufficient.

Ⓒ BOTH statements TOGETHER are sufficient, but NEITHER statement ALONE is sufficient.

Ⓓ EACH statement ALONE is sufficient.

Ⓔ Statements (1) and (2) TOGETHER are NOT sufficient.

25. If $3.5x + 1.5y + 1 = -0.5y - 2.5x$, what is the value of x?

(1) $y^2 = 4$ -2 or 2

(2) $y = \sqrt[3]{-8}$

Ⓐ Statement (1) ALONE is sufficient, but statement (2) alone is not sufficient.

Ⓑ Statement (2) ALONE is sufficient, but statement (1) alone is not sufficient.

Ⓒ BOTH statements TOGETHER are sufficient, but NEITHER statement ALONE is sufficient.

Ⓓ EACH statement ALONE is sufficient.

Ⓔ Statements (1) and (2) TOGETHER are NOT sufficient.

Answers

1. **B** Let $y = 3$, then the left side of the equation is $\left(2^x\right)\left(2^{2y}\right) = \left(2^x\right)\left(2^{2\cdot3}\right) = \left(2^x\right)(64)$. Thus, $\left(2^x\right)(64) = 64$, from which you have $\left(2^x\right) = 1$, which implies that $x = 0$.

2. **C** A negative exponent means to write the reciprocal of the expression, but with the exponent as positive; and an exponent of $\dfrac{1}{2}$ means to take the square root. Hence,

$$\left(c^2 + 9\right)^{-\frac{1}{2}} = \frac{1}{\left(c^2 + 9\right)^{\frac{1}{2}}} = \frac{1}{\sqrt{c^2 + 9}}$$

3. **A** Noting that $9\dfrac{1}{2} = 9.5$, only choice A is equivalent to the statement. Eliminate B and C because "Fifteen less than four times a number" x is $4x - 15$, not $15 - 4x$. Thus, the left sides of both equations are incorrect (the right side of B is also incorrect). Eliminate D because x "increased by $9\dfrac{1}{2}$" is $x + 9\dfrac{1}{2}$ (or, equivalently, $x + 9.5$), not $x + 9\dfrac{1}{2}(x)$. Eliminate E because "four times a number" x is $4x$, not $\dfrac{1}{4}x$.

4. **D** The number of people age 50 or older who get a flu shot is $45\%N = 0.45N$. Of this number, 1% will have an adverse reaction. Thus, the estimated number of people age 50 or older who will have an adverse reaction after getting flu shots is $(0.01)(0.45)N = 0.0045N$.

5. **D** Put the equation in the form $x^2 = k$ and then solve.

$$x^2 - 16 = 20$$
$$x^2 - 16 + 16 = 20 + 16$$
$$x^2 = 36$$
$$x = \sqrt{36} \text{ or } -\sqrt{36}$$
$$x = 6 \text{ or } -6$$

6. **E** Factor the two bases, and then use properties of exponents to obtain a common factor of 6^x: $18^x + 12^x = (6 \cdot 3)^x + (6 \cdot 2)^x = 6^x \cdot 3^x + 6^x \cdot 2^x = 6^x\left(3^x + 2^x\right)$

7. **D** A square root is equivalent to raising a number to the $\dfrac{1}{2}$ power. To raise an exponential expression to a power, multiply the exponents. Thus,

$$\left(\sqrt{\sqrt{\sqrt{x}}}\right)^6 = \left(\left(\left((x)^{\frac{1}{2}}\right)^{\frac{1}{2}}\right)^{\frac{1}{2}}\right)^6 = x^{\frac{1}{2}\frac{1}{2}\frac{1}{2}\frac{6}{1}} = x^{\frac{6}{8}} = x^{\frac{3}{4}}$$

8. **E** Using the table, $f(4) = 1$, then $g\left(f(4)\right) = g(1) = 5$.

9. **D** $|3n - 4| \leq 5$ if and only if $-5 \leq 3n - 4 \leq 5$. Solve this double inequality.

$$-5 \leq 3n - 4 \leq 5$$
$$-5 + 4 \leq 3n - 4 + 4 \leq 5 + 4$$
$$-1 \leq 3n \leq 9$$
$$-\frac{1}{3} \leq n \leq 3$$

The integers that satisfy this double inequality are 0, 1, 2, and 3. Thus, there are four integers that satisfy $|3n - 4| \leq 5$.

10. **C** First, simplify the expression within parentheses, and then multiply exponents.

$$\left(\frac{x^{-5}}{x^{-9}}\right)^{\frac{1}{2}} = \left(x^{-5+9}\right)^{\frac{1}{2}} = \left(x^4\right)^{\frac{1}{2}} = x^2$$

11. **B** Check the answer choices by substituting -8 for x in the statement.

Check A: $-18 > 2$, so this choice is false.

Check B: $-40 < -16$, which is true.

Choice B is correct, so move on to the next question. To verify this, however, choice C says $16 < 0$, D says $-\frac{1}{8} > 8$, and E says $-8 > 8$; clearly, all of these are false.

12. **D** Solve $\sqrt{5x+7} = \sqrt{5x} + 1$ for $5x$.

$$\sqrt{5x+7} = \sqrt{5x} + 1$$

$5x + 7 = 5x + 2\sqrt{5x} + 1$	Square both sides of the equation.
$7 = 2\sqrt{5x} + 1$	Subtract $5x$ from both sides.
$6 = 2\sqrt{5x}$	Subtract 1 from both sides.
$3 = \sqrt{5x}$	Divide both sides by 2.
$9 = 5x$	Square both sides.

Note that the question asks for the value of $5x$, not the value of x.

---

13. **C** Begin by solving for x^2, and then take the square root of both sides. Although the square root can be positive or negative, the problem specifies that $x > 0$, so you will not use the negative root. Therefore, take the square root of both sides once again.

$$16x^2 = 81$$
$$x^2 = \frac{81}{16}$$
$$x = \frac{9}{4}$$

$$\sqrt{x} = \pm\frac{3}{2} \quad \textit{Tip: } x > 0; \text{ it has two square roots: one positive and one negative.}$$

14. B First, let $x = 4$ and solve for k.

$$x^2 - x + k = 15$$
$$4^2 - 4 + k = 15$$
$$16 - 4 + k = 15$$
$$12 + k = 15$$
$$k = 3$$

Next, let $k = 3$ and solve for x.

$$x^2 - x + k = 15$$
$$x^2 - x + 3 = 15$$
$$x^2 - x - 12 = 0$$
$$(x - 4)(x + 3) = 0$$
$$(x - 4) = 0 \text{ or } (x + 3) = 0$$
$$x = 4 \text{ or } x = -3$$

Once you know that the equation is $x^2 - x + 3 = 15$, you can substitute in the answer choices to determine that B is the correct response.

---

15. C Let $x =$ the greater number. Then $35 - x =$ the lesser number. Using the information in the question, write an equation and solve for x.

$$x(35 - x) = 300$$
$$35x - x^2 = 300$$
$$x^2 - 35x = -300$$
$$x^2 - 35x + 300 = 0$$
$$(x - 20)(x - 15) = 0$$
$$(x - 20) = 0 \text{ or } (x - 15) = 0$$
$$x = 20 \text{ or } x = 15$$

Choose $x = 20$ because the problem asks for the greater number.

16. E For convenience, number the equations.

$$2x - 3y = 16 \quad (1)$$
$$3x + 6y = 10 \quad (2)$$

Eliminate y. Multiply equation (1) by 2, and then add the result to equation (2).

$$4x - 6y = 32 \quad (1)$$
$$\underline{3x + 6y = 10 \quad (2)}$$
$$7x + 0 = 42$$
$$7x = 42$$
$$x = 6$$

17. **A** Substitute $y = 3x - 5$ into the second equation, and solve for x.

$$y = x^2 - x - 5$$
$$3x - 5 = x^2 - x - 5$$
$$0 = x^2 - 4x$$
$$x^2 - 4x = 0$$
$$x(x-4) = 0$$
$$x = 0 \text{ or } x = 4$$

18. **D** Recall that the nth term of an arithmetic sequence can be written as $a_n = a_1 + (n-1)d$. From the information in (1), $247 = 5n - 3$, which you can solve for n, the number of terms in the list, so (1) is SUFFICIENT. From the information in (2), $7 = 2 + (2-1)d = 2 + d$, which you can solve to find $d = 5$. Thereafter, you can solve $247 = 2 + (n-1) \cdot 5$ for n, the number of terms in the list. Therefore, EACH statement ALONE is sufficient.

19. **B** The information in (1) gives you the sum of a and b, but further information is needed to determine their product, ab, so (1) is NOT sufficient. From the information in (2), $4ab = 12^2$, from which you can determine the value of ab, so (2) is SUFFICIENT. Therefore, statement (2) ALONE is sufficient, but statement (1) alone is not sufficient.

20. **E** The information in (1) is not sufficient to determine whether $x < y$. For instance, if $x = 2$, then $y = (2)^2 = 4$, in which case $x < y$. But if $x = \frac{1}{2}$, then $y = \left(\frac{1}{2}\right)^2 = \frac{1}{4}$, in which case $x > y$. The information in (2) is not sufficient to determine whether $x < y$. For instance, if $x = \frac{1}{2}$ and $y = 1\frac{1}{2}$, then $x < y$. But if $x = 1\frac{1}{2}$ and $y = \frac{1}{2}$, then $x > y$. Taking the information in (1) and (2) together yields $x + x^2 = 2$, which is equivalent to $x^2 + x - 2 = 0$. Factoring the left side of this equation yields $(x+2)(x-1) = 0$, from which you have $x = -2$ or $x = 1$. If $x = -2$, then $y = (-2)^2 = 4$, in which case $x < y$. If $x = 1$, then $y = (1)^2 = 1$, in which case $x = y$. Therefore, statements (1) and (2) TOGETHER are NOT sufficient.

21. **A** To apply the information in (1), rewrite the given expression to include the term $\frac{x}{z}$.

$$\frac{x+z}{x-z} = \frac{\frac{1}{z}(x+z)}{\frac{1}{z}(x-z)} = \frac{\frac{x}{z}+1}{\frac{x}{z}-1}$$

Next, substitute $\frac{x}{z} = 5$.

$$\frac{x+z}{x-z} = \frac{\frac{x}{z}+1}{\frac{x}{z}-1} = \frac{5+1}{5-1} = \frac{6}{4}$$

You can find a single solution, so (1) is SUFFICIENT. The information in (2) tells you that the numerator of $\frac{x+z}{x-z}$ is negative but nothing else about its value, so it is NOT sufficient. Therefore, statement (1) ALONE is sufficient, but statement (2) alone is not sufficient.

22. **D** From the question information, the expected deer population in 20 years is $P(20) = P_0 \cdot 2^{0.25(20)} = P_0 \cdot 2^5$. From the information in (1), $P(4) = 50 = P_0 \cdot 2^{0.25(4)} = P_0 \cdot 2^1$, from which you can obtain P_0. You can use that value to find $P(20) = P_0 \cdot 2^5$, so (1) is SUFFICIENT.

From the information in (2), $P(12) = 200 = P_0 \cdot 2^{0.25(12)} = P_0 \cdot 2^3$, from which you can obtain P_0. You can use that value to find $P(20) = P_0 \cdot 2^5$, so (2) also is SUFFICIENT. Therefore, EACH statement ALONE is sufficient.

23. **A** Using the equation in (1), $4^p = 16$ implies that $4^p = 4^2$, so $p = 2$, and (1) is SUFFICIENT. Using the equation in (2), $\left(3^p\right)^p = 81$ implies that $3^{p^2} = 3^4$, so $p^2 = 4$. Thus, p is −2 or 2, not one single value, so it is NOT sufficient. Therefore, statement (1) ALONE is sufficient, but statement (2) alone is not sufficient.

24. **C** From the information in (1), even if $x > w$, you cannot say for certain whether $\frac{x}{y} > \frac{w}{z}$.

For instance, suppose $x = 100$, $w = 50$, $y = 5$, and $z = 2$; then $\frac{x}{y} = \frac{100}{5} = 20 < \frac{w}{z} = \frac{50}{2} = 25$,

but for $x = 100$, $w = 50$, $y = 2$, and $z = 5$, $\frac{x}{y} = \frac{100}{2} = 50 > \frac{w}{z} = \frac{50}{5} = 10$. Thus, (1) is NOT sufficient.

From the information in (2), even if $y < z$, you cannot say for certain whether $\frac{x}{y} > \frac{w}{z}$.

For instance, suppose $x = 20$, $w = 100$, $y = 2$, and $z = 5$; then $\frac{x}{y} = \frac{20}{2} = 10 < \frac{w}{z} = \frac{100}{5} = 20$,

but for $x = 100$, $w = 20$, $y = 2$, and $z = 5$, $\frac{x}{y} = \frac{100}{2} = 50 > \frac{w}{z} = \frac{20}{5} = 4$. Thus, (2) also is NOT

sufficient. Taking (1) and (2) together, you know from (2) that $\frac{1}{y} > \frac{1}{z}$, which implies that

$\frac{x}{y} > \frac{x}{z}$, and from (1) you know that $\frac{x}{z} > \frac{w}{z}$. Combining $\frac{x}{y} > \frac{x}{z}$ and $\frac{x}{z} > \frac{w}{z}$ gives $\frac{x}{y} > \frac{w}{z}$.

Therefore, BOTH statements TOGETHER are sufficient, but NEITHER statement ALONE is sufficient.

25. **B** From the information in (1), y is 2 or −2, so x is one of two possible values, depending on which value of y is substituted into $3.5x + 1.5y + 1 = -0.5y - 2.5x$. Because there are two possible values when you solve for x, (1) is NOT sufficient. From the information in (2), y is −2, which you can substitute into $3.5x + 1.5y + 1 = -0.5y - 2.5x$. You can then solve to obtain a single value for x, so (2) is SUFFICIENT. Therefore, statement (2) ALONE is sufficient, but statement (1) alone is not sufficient.

CHAPTER 10

Geometry Review

This geometry review includes the following topics:

- Congruence and similarity
- Angles
- Lines
- Polygons
- Triangles
- Quadrilaterals
- Circles
- Geometric solids
- Perimeter, area, surface area, and volume
- Pythagorean theorem
- Coordinate geometry

Congruence and Similarity

Congruence

Congruent geometric figures have the same size and same shape. They will fit exactly on top of each other. The symbol ≅ denotes congruence.

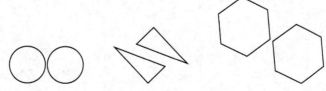

Corresponding parts of congruent figures are congruent.

Congruent parts (for example, angles and sides) of congruent figures have the same measure.

Congruent triangles are triangles for which corresponding sides and corresponding angles are congruent. In the figure shown, triangles *ABC* and *DEF* are congruent. Hash marks identify the congruent parts.

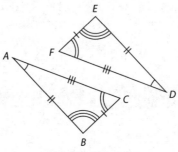

Congruent Triangles

Two triangles are congruent in the following situations.

- **Side-Side-Side (SSS):** If three sides of one triangle are congruent, correspondingly, to three sides of the other triangle.
- **Side-Angle-Side (SAS):** If two sides and the included angle of one triangle are congruent, correspondingly, to two sides and the included angle of the other triangle.
- **Angle-Side-Angle (ASA):** If two angles and the included side of one triangle are congruent, correspondingly, to two angles and the included side of the other triangle.
- **Angle-Angle-Side (AAS):** If two angles and the nonincluded side of one triangle are congruent, correspondingly, to two angles and the nonincluded side of the other triangle.

Two situations that do NOT guarantee congruence are **AAA** (three corresponding angles congruent) and **SSA** (two corresponding sides and the *nonincluded* angle congruent).

Similarity

Similar geometric figures have the same shape, but not necessarily the same size. The symbol ~ denotes similarity.

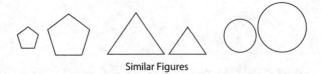

Similar Figures

Corresponding angles of similar shapes are congruent. Corresponding lengths of similar shapes are proportional. That is, the ratios of the lengths are equal.

The ratio of the areas of two similar figures is the square of the ratio of the lengths of any two corresponding sides. For instance, if corresponding sides of two squares are in the ratio 4 to 1, then the ratio of the area of the larger square to the area of the smaller square is 4^2 to 1^2, or 16 to 1.

Angles

Angles are measured in degrees. One degree (°) is $\frac{1}{360}$ of a complete rotation around a circle.

- A **right angle** measures exactly 90°.

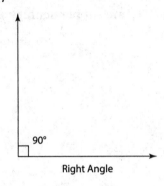

Right Angle

The box in the corner denotes a right angle.

- An **acute angle** measures greater than 0°, but less than 90°.

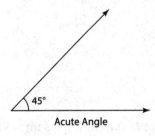

Acute Angle

- An **obtuse angle** measures greater than 90°, but less than 180°.

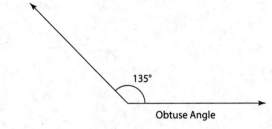

Obtuse Angle

- A **straight angle** measures exactly 180°.

Straight Angle

- Two angles whose sum is 90° are **complementary angles**. Each is the other's **complement**.

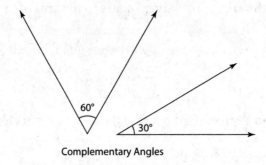

Complementary Angles

- Two angles whose sum is 180° are **supplementary angles**. Each is the other's **supplement**.

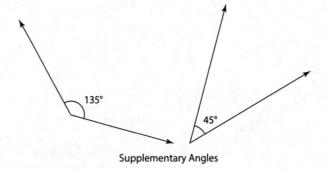

Supplementary Angles

- **Adjacent angles** are two angles that have a common vertex and a common side, with no overlap.

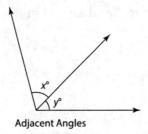

Adjacent Angles

- **Vertical angles** are two *nonadjacent* angles formed by two intersecting lines. *Tip*: Two intersecting lines form four angles.

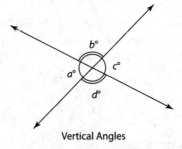

Vertical Angles

Vertical angles formed by two intersecting lines are congruent and thus have the same measure. In the figure shown, $a° = c°$ and $b° = d°$.

Lines

Descriptions of Lines

Lines in the same plane can be intersecting, parallel, or coincident. In geometry, *plane* is an undefined term. Intuitively, a plane is a two-dimensional, infinite surface. **Intersecting lines** cross at a point in the plane. **Parallel lines** never intersect. **Coincident lines** have all points in common. **Perpendicular lines** intersect at right angles. Here are examples.

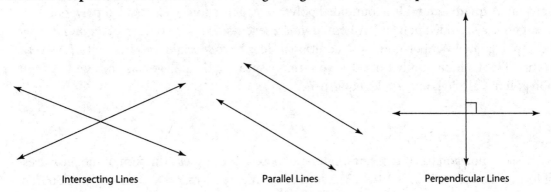

Intersecting Lines   Parallel Lines   Perpendicular Lines

A **tangent line** to a circle intersects the circle in exactly one point.

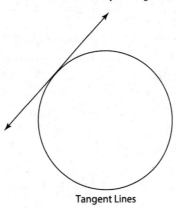

Tangent Lines

Notation

The notation $\overleftrightarrow{AB}$ stands for the line containing the points A and B and extending infinitely in both directions. To indicate $\overleftrightarrow{AB}$ is parallel to $\overleftrightarrow{CD}$, write $\overleftrightarrow{AB} \parallel \overleftrightarrow{CD}$. To indicate $\overleftrightarrow{AB}$ is perpendicular to $\overleftrightarrow{EF}$, write $\overleftrightarrow{AB} \perp \overleftrightarrow{EF}$.

The **line segment** $\overline{AB}$ is a part of a line connecting the points A and B and includes A and B. The points A and B are its **endpoints**. Its length is AB. Congruent segments have equal lengths.

Useful Information About Lines in a Plane

- The shortest distance from a point to a line is the perpendicular distance from the point to the line.
- Two (distinct) lines that are perpendicular to the same line are parallel.
- A line that is perpendicular to one of two parallel lines is perpendicular to the other one too.
- A radius drawn to the point where a tangent line meets a circle is perpendicular to the tangent at that exact point.

Polygons

Descriptions of Polygons

A **polygon** is a simple, closed plane figure composed of **sides** that are straight line segments that meet only at their endpoints. The point at which the two sides of a polygon intersect is a **vertex**. A **diagonal** is a line segment that connects two nonconsecutive vertices.

Polygons are named by the number of sides they have. A **triangle** is a three-sided polygon. A **quadrilateral** is a four-sided polygon. A **pentagon** is a five-sided polygon. A **hexagon** is a six-sided polygon. A **heptagon** is a seven-sided polygon. An **octagon** is an eight-sided polygon. Other polygons with additional sides have special names as well. However, eventually, at a high number of sides, you simply speak of the polygon as an ***n*-gon**. A **regular polygon** has all sides and angles congruent.

Interior and Exterior Angles

An *n*-sided polygon has *n* **interior angles** and *n* **exterior angles**. The sum of the measures of its interior angles is $(n - 2)180°$. The sum of the measures of its exterior angles is $360°$, no matter how many sides the polygon has.

An exterior angle of a polygon is the angle between one side of the polygon and the extension of the side adjacent to it. Here is an example of the interior and exterior angles of a triangle.

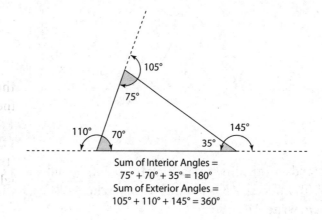

Sum of Interior Angles =
75° + 70° + 35° = 180°
Sum of Exterior Angles =
105° + 110° + 145° = 360°

There are two congruent exterior angles at each vertex. Either one is considered the exterior angle at that vertex.

Triangles

Descriptions of Triangles

- An **equilateral triangle** has three congruent sides. An **isosceles triangle** has at least two congruent sides. A **scalene triangle** has no congruent sides.

All equilateral triangles are isosceles triangles. However, not all isosceles triangles are equilateral triangles.

- An **acute triangle** has three acute angles. A **right triangle** has exactly one right angle.
- An **obtuse triangle** has exactly one obtuse angle.

Useful Information About Triangles

- The **triangle inequality** holds that the sum of the lengths of any two sides of a triangle must be greater than the length of the third side. Basically, for a triangle to exist, the longest side must be shorter than the sum of the other two sides. For example, 3, 8, and 10 can be the lengths of the sides of a triangle because $3 + 8 = 11$, which is greater than 10, the longest side. But 2, 5, and 8 cannot be the lengths of the sides of a triangle, because $2 + 5 = 7$, which is less than 8, the longest side.
- If two sides of a triangle are congruent, then the angles opposite those sides are congruent (that is, base angles of an isosceles triangle are congruent); and, conversely, if two angles of a triangle are congruent, then the sides opposite those angles are congruent. In the figure shown, $\overline{AB} \cong \overline{AC}$ implies $\angle C \cong \angle B$; and $\angle B \cong \angle C$ implies $\overline{AC} \cong \overline{AB}$.

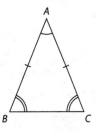

- If two sides of a triangle are unequal in length, the measures of the angles opposite the two sides are unequal and the angle opposite the greater side is the greater angle.
- If two angles of a triangle are unequal in measure, the lengths of the sides opposite the two angles are unequal and the side opposite the greater angle is the greater side.
- The measure of an exterior angle of a triangle equals the sum of the measures of the remote (nonadjacent) interior angles. For example, in the triangle shown below, $x° = 75° + 35° = 110°$, $y° = 70° + 35° = 105°$, and $z° = 70° + 75° = 145°$.

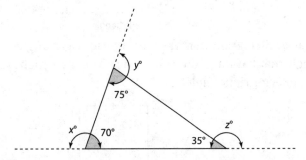

- A **median** of a triangle is a line segment from a vertex of the triangle to the midpoint of the opposite side.
- The medians of a triangle meet in a point that is $\frac{2}{3}$ of the way along each median, from the vertex to the opposite side.

- In a right triangle, the median to the hypotenuse is one-half the length of the hypotenuse.
- The line segment between the midpoints of two sides of a triangle is parallel to the third side and half as long.

Quadrilaterals

Descriptions of Quadrilaterals

- A **trapezoid** is a quadrilateral that has at least one pair of parallel sides.

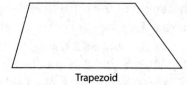

Trapezoid

Some authors define a trapezoid as a quadrilateral that has only one pair of parallel sides.

- A **parallelogram** is a quadrilateral whose opposite sides are parallel and congruent.

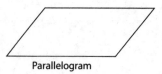

Parallelogram

- A **rhombus** is a parallelogram that has four congruent sides.

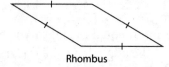

Rhombus

- A **rectangle** is a parallelogram that has four interior right angles.

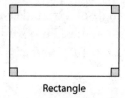

Rectangle

- A **square** is a parallelogram that has four interior right angles and four congruent sides. It is a rectangle that has four congruent sides. You also might say that it is a rhombus that has four interior right angles.

Square

Useful Information About Quadrilaterals

- If a quadrilateral's diagonals bisect each other, the quadrilateral is a parallelogram.
- If a quadrilateral has two sides that are parallel and congruent, the quadrilateral is a parallelogram.
- The diagonals of a rectangle or square are congruent.
- The diagonals of a rhombus or square are perpendicular to each other.
- If a quadrilateral's diagonals are perpendicular bisectors of each other, the quadrilateral is a rhombus.
- A parallelogram that has one interior right angle has four interior right angles and is a rectangle.
- Consecutive angles of a parallelogram are supplementary.

Circles

Parts of a Circle

- A **circle** is a closed plane figure for which all points are the same distance from the **center** within the circle.
- A circle's **radius** is a line segment joining the center of the circle to any point on the circle.
- A circle's **diameter** is a line segment through the center of the circle with endpoints on the circle. The diameter of a circle is twice the radius. Equivalently, the radius of a circle is half the diameter.
- A **chord** of a circle is a line segment whose endpoints lie on the circle.

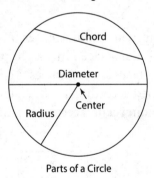

Parts of a Circle

Useful Information About Circles

- If a radius is drawn so that it is perpendicular to a chord, it bisects the chord.

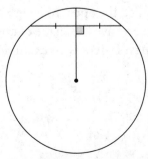

Radius Perpendicular to a Chord

- An angle inscribed in a semicircle is a right angle.

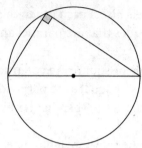

Angle Inscribed in a Semicircle

- If two chords intersect within a circle, the product of the lengths of the segments formed for one chord equals the product of the lengths of the segments formed for the other chord.

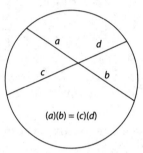

Two Intersecting Chords

Geometric Solids

Prisms and Pyramids

A **prism** is a solid with two congruent, parallel **bases**. A prism's **lateral faces** are parallelograms. (A *lateral* face is a *side* face.) In a **right prism**, the two bases are directly above each other and the lateral faces are rectangles. The bases of a prism can have the shape of any polygon. Prisms are named according to the shape of their bases. A **cube** is a right rectangular prism that has six congruent faces, all of which are squares. Here is an example.

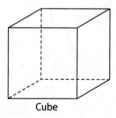

Cube

A **pyramid** is a solid with exactly one polygon-shaped base. A pyramid's lateral faces are triangles that meet at a point, called the **apex**. In a **right pyramid**, the apex is directly above the center of the base. The base can have the shape of any polygon. Pyramids are named according to the shape of their bases. Here is an example.

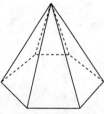

Hexagonal Pyramid

Cylinders and Cones

A **cylinder** has two parallel congruent bases, which are circles. In a **right cylinder**, the two bases are directly above each other. A rectangular side wraps around and connects the two bases.

Cylinder

A **cone** is a three-dimensional solid that has one circular base and a single apex. In a **right cone**, the apex is directly above the center of the base. A curved side wraps around to form the cone.

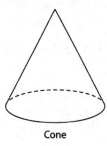

Cone

Spheres

A **sphere** is a three-dimensional solid that is shaped like a ball. Every point on its surface is the same distance from the **center** within the sphere. The sphere's **radius** is a line segment from the center of the sphere to any point on the sphere. The sphere's **diameter** is a line segment joining two points of the sphere and passing through its center. The radius of the sphere is half the diameter. Equivalently, the diameter is twice the radius.

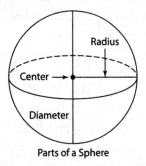

Parts of a Sphere

Perimeter, Area, Surface Area, and Volume

Perimeter

The **perimeter** of a simple, closed plane figure is the distance around it. Perimeter is measured in units of length such as inches (in), feet (ft), miles (mi), centimeters (cm), or meters (m).

- The perimeter of a triangle is the sum of its three sides.

The perimeter, P, of a triangle that has sides of lengths 6 inches, 8 inches, and 10 inches is $P = 6$ in $+ 8$ in $+ 10$ in $= 24$ inches.

- The perimeter of a quadrilateral is the sum of its four sides.

The perimeter, P, of a trapezoid that has sides of lengths 4 meters, 8 meters, 5 meters, and 10 meters is $P = 4$ m $+ 8$ m $+ 5$ m $+ 10$ m $= 27$ meters.

- The perimeter of a parallelogram is $P = 2a + 2b = 2(a + b)$, where a is the length of one of the congruent sides and b is the length of one of the congruent bases.

The perimeter of a parallelogram that has congruent sides of length 14 feet and congruent bases of length 23 feet is $P = 2(14$ ft $+ 23$ ft$) = 74$ feet.

- The perimeter of a rectangle is $P = 2l + 2w = 2(l + w)$, where l is its length and w is its width.

The perimeter of a rectangle that has length of 8 meters and width of 5 meters is $P = 2(8$ m $+ 5$ m$) = 26$ meters.

- The perimeter of a square is $P = 4s$, where s is the length of one of its sides.

The perimeter of a square whose sides are 12 centimeters is $P = 4(12$ cm$) = 48$ centimeters.

- The perimeter of a circle is **circumference**. The circumference of a circle is $C = \pi d = 2\pi r$, where d and r are the circle's diameter and radius, respectively.

To the nearest inch, the circumference of a circle that has diameter 16 inches is $C = \pi(16$ in$) \approx (3.14)(16$ in$) \approx 50$ inches.

For the GMAT, use $\pi \approx 3.14$. The symbol $\approx$ is read "is approximately equal to."

Area

The **area** of a closed plane figure is the amount of surface enclosed by the boundary of the figure. Area is measured in square units such as square inches (in²), square feet (ft²), square miles (mi²), square centimeters (cm²), and square meters (m²).

Regardless of the shape of the figure, the area units are always square units.

- The area of a triangle is $A = \frac{1}{2}bh$, where b is the length of a base of the triangle, and h is the height for that base.

The area of a triangle that has a base of 8 inches and a height of 6 inches is
$A = \frac{1}{2}(8 \text{ in})(6 \text{ in}) = 24 \text{ in}^2$.

Pick any convenient side of the triangle to serve as the base. The height for the base is the perpendicular distance from the opposite vertex to that base (or an extension of it).

- The area of an equilateral triangle is $A = \frac{\sqrt{3}}{4}a^2$, where a is the length of a side.

  The area of an equilateral triangle that has sides of length 20 centimeters is
  $A = \frac{\sqrt{3}}{4}(20 \text{ cm})^2 = \frac{\sqrt{3}}{4}(400 \text{ cm}^2) = 100\sqrt{3} \text{ cm}^2$.

- The area of a trapezoid is $A = \frac{1}{2}(b_1 + b_2)h$, where b_1 and b_2 are the lengths of its bases and h is the perpendicular distance between the two bases.

  The area of a trapezoid that has bases of 7 meters and 12 meters and a height of 4 meters is $A = \frac{1}{2}(7 \text{ m} + 12 \text{ m})(4 \text{ m}) = \frac{1}{2}(19 \text{ m})(4 \text{ m}) = 38 \text{ m}^2$.

- The area of a parallelogram is $A = bh$, where b is a base of the parallelogram and h is the perpendicular distance between the two bases.

  The area of a parallelogram that has a base of 15 feet and a height of 8 feet is $A = (15 \text{ ft}) \times (8 \text{ ft}) = 120 \text{ ft}^2$.

- The area of a rectangle is $A = lw$, where l is its length and w is its width.

  The area of a rectangle that has length of 25 meters and width of 7 meters is $A = (25 \text{ m}) \times (7 \text{ m}) = 175 \text{ m}^2$.

- The area of a square is $A = s^2$, where s is the length of one of its sides.

  The area of a square whose sides are 12 centimeters is $A = (12 \text{ cm})^2 = 144 \text{ cm}^2$.

- The area of a circle is $A = \pi r^2$, where r is the circle's radius.

  To the nearest square inch, the area of a circle that has a radius of 8 inches is $A = \pi(8 \text{ in})^2 = \pi(64 \text{ in}^2) \approx (3.14)(64 \text{ in}^2) \approx 201 \text{ in}^2$.

Surface Area

The **surface area** (SA) of a three-dimensional closed figure is the total area of its surface.

- The surface area of a prism or pyramid is the sum of the areas of all faces of the figure.

The surface area of the right rectangular prism (box) shown below is $SA = 2(10 \text{ in})(8 \text{ in}) + 2(10 \text{ in})(6 \text{ in}) + 2(8 \text{ in})(6 \text{ in}) = 160 \text{ in}^2 + 120 \text{ in}^2 + 96 \text{ in}^2 = 376 \text{ in}^2.$

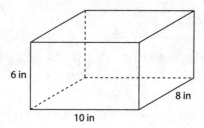

- The surface area of a right cylinder is $SA = 2(\pi r^2) + (2\pi r)h$, where r is the radius of one of the cylinder's congruent bases and h is the perpendicular distance between the two bases.

   The approximate surface area of a right cylinder in which the radius is 5 feet and the height is 14 feet is $SA = 2[\pi(5 \text{ ft})^2] + [2\pi(5 \text{ ft})](14 \text{ ft}) = 2[\pi(25 \text{ ft}^2)] + [2\pi(5 \text{ ft})](14 \text{ ft}) \approx 2[(3.14)(25 \text{ ft}^2)] + [2(3.14)(5 \text{ ft})(14 \text{ ft}) \approx 597 \text{ ft}^2.$

- The surface area of a sphere is $SA = 4\pi r^2$, where r is the radius of the sphere.

   The approximate surface area of a sphere with radius of 7 feet is $SA = 4\pi r^2 = 4\pi(7 \text{ ft})^2 = 4\pi(49 \text{ ft}^2) \approx 4(3.14)(49 \text{ ft}^2) \approx 615 \text{ ft}^2.$

Volume

Volume is a measure of the space or capacity inside a three-dimensional closed figure. Volume of geometric solids is measured in cubic units such as cubic inches (in^3), cubic feet (ft^3), cubic miles (mi^3), cubic centimeters (cm^3), and cubic meters (m^3).

- The volume of a prism or cylinder is $V = Bh$, where B is the area of one of the prism's or cylinder's congruent bases and h is the perpendicular distance between the two bases.

   The volume of the right rectangular prism (box) shown below is $V = Bh = [(l)(w)](h) = [(10 \text{ in})(8 \text{ in})](6 \text{ in}) = 480 \text{ in}^3.$

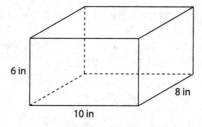

   The approximate volume of a cylinder in which the radius, r, is 5 feet and the height, h, is 14 feet is $V = Bh = [(\pi r^2)](h) = [\pi(5 \text{ ft})^2](14 \text{ ft}) \approx [(3.14)(25 \text{ ft}^2)](14 \text{ ft}) = 1,099 \text{ ft}^3.$

- The volume of a pyramid or cone is $V = \dfrac{1}{3}Bh$, where B is the area of the pyramid's or cone's base and h is the perpendicular distance from the apex to the base.

The volume of a square pyramid that has a 6-centimeter by 6-centimeter base and a height of 4 centimeters is $V = \frac{1}{3}Bh = \frac{1}{3}[(l)(w)](h) = \frac{1}{3}[(6 \text{ cm})(6 \text{ cm})](4 \text{ cm}) = 48 \text{ cm}^3$.

The volume of a cone that has a radius, r, of 10 inches and a height, h, of 9 inches is
$V = \frac{1}{3}Bh = \frac{1}{3}[\pi r^2](h) = \frac{1}{3}[\pi(10 \text{ in})^2](9 \text{ in}) \approx \frac{1}{3}[(3.14)(100 \text{ in}^2)](9 \text{ in}) = 942 \text{ in}^3$.

■ The volume of a sphere is $V = \frac{4}{3}\pi r^3$, where r is the radius of the sphere.

The approximate volume of a sphere with radius of 7 feet is
$V = \frac{4}{3}\pi(7 \text{ ft})^3 = \frac{4}{3}\pi(343 \text{ ft}^3) \approx \frac{4}{3}(3.14)(343 \text{ ft}^3) \approx 1,436 \text{ ft}^3$.

Pythagorean Theorem

In a right triangle, the **hypotenuse** is the side opposite the 90° angle. *Tip*: The hypotenuse is *always* the longest side of the right triangle. The other two sides are the **legs**.

The **Pythagorean theorem** tells us that, in a right triangle, $c^2 = a^2 + b^2$, where c is the length of the hypotenuse and a and b are the lengths of the legs of the right triangle. For example, use the Pythagorean theorem to find the length, c, of the hypotenuse of the right triangle shown below.

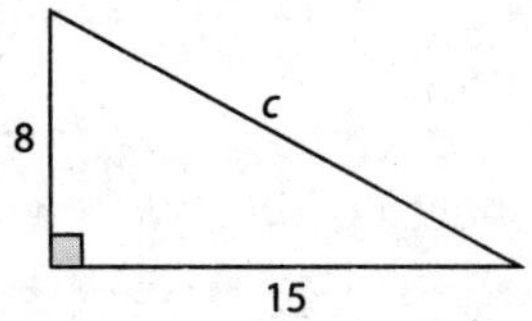

$$c^2 = a^2 + b^2$$
$$c^2 = 8^2 + 15^2$$
$$c^2 = 64 + 225$$
$$c^2 = 289$$
$$c = \sqrt{289}$$
$$c = 17$$

The number 289 has two square roots, 17 and −17. The negative value is discarded because the length of the hypotenuse (or any side) cannot be negative.

Coordinate Geometry

Basic Concepts

The **coordinate plane** is defined by two real number lines, one horizontal and one vertical, intersecting at right angles at their zero points. The two real number lines are the **coordinate axes**. Commonly, the **horizontal axis** with positive direction to the right is the **x-axis**, and the **vertical axis** with positive direction upward is the **y-axis**. The two axes determine a plane. Their point of intersection is the **origin**.

The axes divide the coordinate plane into four **quadrants**. The quadrants are numbered with Roman numerals—I, II, III, and IV—beginning in the upper right and going around counterclockwise.

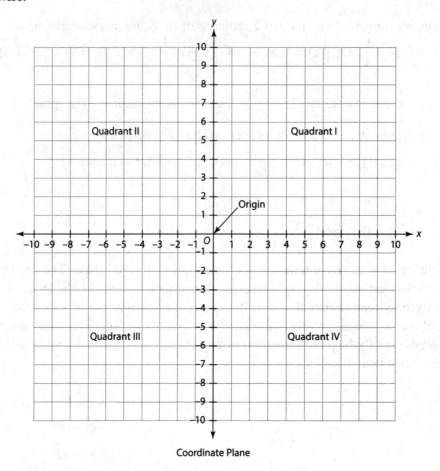

Coordinate Plane

Remember, the quadrants are numbered *counterclockwise*.

In the coordinate plane, each point P is identified by its **coordinates**, an **ordered pair** (x, y) of real numbers x and y. The ordered pair $(0, 0)$ is the origin. The order in the ordered pair (x, y) that corresponds to a point P is important. The absolute value of the first coordinate, x, is the perpendicular horizontal distance (right or left) of the point P from the y-axis. If x is positive, P is to the right of the y-axis; if x is negative, it is to the left of the y-axis. The absolute value of the second coordinate, y, is the perpendicular vertical distance (up or down) of the point P from the x-axis. If y is positive, P is above the x-axis; if y is negative, it is below the x-axis. For instance, in the coordinate plane shown below, the point P has coordinates $(-6, 9)$, the point Q has coordinates $(2, 4)$, the point R has coordinates $(0, -3)$, the point S has coordinates $(-4, -7)$, and the point T has coordinates $(5, -8)$.

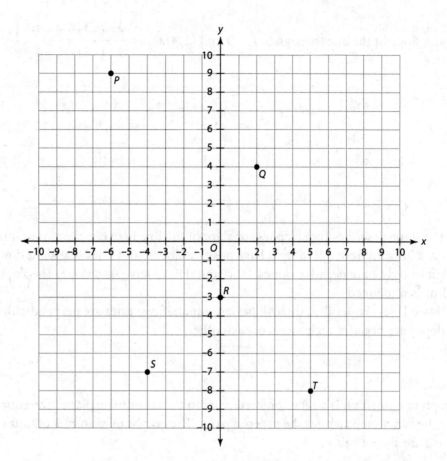

■ **Distance Between Two Points**   The distance between two points (x_1, y_1) and (x_2, y_2) in a coordinate plane is $d = \sqrt{(x_2 - x_1)^2 + (y_2 - y_1)^2}$. Here is an example.

The distance between (–6, 9) and (–4, –7) is $\sqrt{(-4-(-6))^2 + (-7-9)^2} =$ $\sqrt{(-4+6)^2 + (-7-9)^2} = \sqrt{(2)^2 + (-16)^2} = \sqrt{4+256} = \sqrt{260}$

To avoid careless errors when using the distance formula, enclose substituted negative values in parentheses.

■ **Midpoint Between Two Points:** The midpoint between two points (x_1, y_1) and (x_2, y_2) in a coordinate plane is the point with coordinates $\left(\dfrac{x_1 + x_2}{2}, \dfrac{y_1 + y_2}{2} \right)$. Here is an example.

The midpoint between (2, 4), and (0, –3) is $\left(\dfrac{2+0}{2}, \dfrac{4+(-3)}{2} \right) = \left(1, \dfrac{1}{2} \right)$.

■ **Slope of a Line Through Two Points**   The slope m of a line through two distinct points, (x_1, y_1) and (x_2, y_2), is $m = \dfrac{y_2 - y_1}{x_2 - x_1}$, provided $x_1 \neq x_2$. Here is an example.

The slope of the line through (−4, −7) and (2, 4) is $m = \dfrac{4-(-7)}{2-(-4)} = \dfrac{4+7}{2+4} = \dfrac{11}{6}$.

When you use the slope formula, be sure to subtract the coordinates in the same order in both the numerator and the denominator. That is, if x_2 is the first term in the numerator, then y_2 must be the first term in the denominator. Also, it a good idea to enclose substituted negative values in parentheses to guard against careless errors.

- The slope describes the steepness or slant of the line between the two points. Lines that slant upward from left to right have positive slopes, and lines that slant downward from left to right have negative slopes. Horizontal lines have zero slope. The slope of a vertical line is undefined.
- If two lines are parallel, their slopes are equal; if two lines are perpendicular, their slopes are negative reciprocals of each other.

Graphs of Functions

The graph of a function is a set of ordered pairs in the coordinate plane. The equation that defines the function generates the ordered pairs. The graphs of examples of four common functions are shown below.

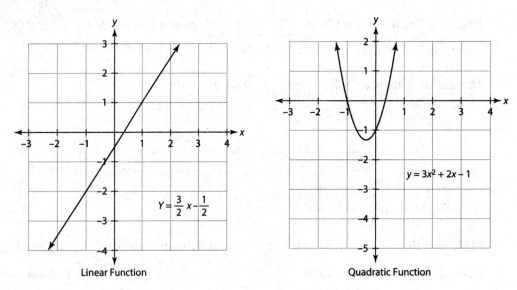

Linear Function   Quadratic Function

In the graph of a quadratic function that has real roots, the graph will intersect the x-axis at the roots.

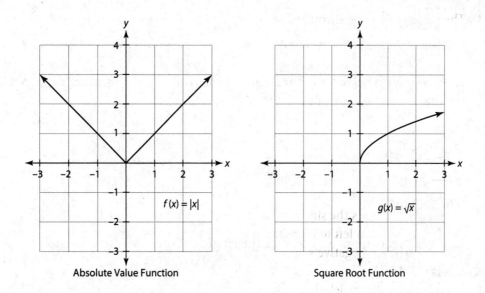

Absolute Value Function   Square Root Function

You can visually determine whether a graph is the graph of a function by using the **vertical line test:** A graph is the graph of a function if and only if no vertical line crosses the graph in more than one point. This test is the graphical equivalent of saying that no two different ordered pairs have the same first coordinate.

Distance from a Point to a Line

The distance from point (x_1, y_1) to the line whose equation is $Ax + By + C = 0$ is

$$d = \frac{\left| Ax_1 + By_1 + C \right|}{\sqrt{A^2 + B^2}}$$

For example, the distance from the point $(-1, 2)$ to the line whose equation is $4x - 3y - 1 = 0$ is

$$\frac{\left| 4(-1) - 3(2) - 1 \right|}{\sqrt{4^2 + (-3)^2}} = \frac{\left| -4 - 6 - 1 \right|}{\sqrt{16 + 9}} = \frac{\left| -11 \right|}{\sqrt{25}} = \frac{11}{5} = 2.2$$

Geometry Drill

Directions: **Select the best answer choice.**

1. In triangle ABC, sides $\overline{AB}$ and $\overline{AC}$ are congruent. If the measure of angle C is 40°, what is the measure of angle A?

  Ⓐ 38°
  Ⓑ 40°
  Ⓒ 80°
  Ⓓ 100°
  Ⓔ 120°

2. Which set of numbers could be the lengths of the sides of a triangle?

  Ⓐ 7, 13, 17
  Ⓑ 5, 15, 20
  Ⓒ 5, 14, 6
  Ⓓ 1, 3, 5
  Ⓔ 13, 8, 5

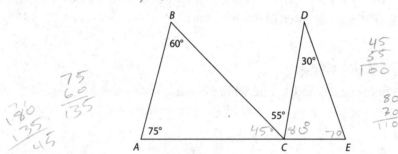

3. In the preceding figure with the measures of the angles as shown, what is the measure of $\angle E$?

  Ⓐ 85°
  Ⓑ 75°
  Ⓒ 70°
  Ⓓ 65°
  Ⓔ 60°

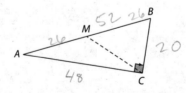

4. In the preceding right triangle ABC, $\overline{CM}$ is the median to the hypotenuse. If AC is 48 inches, BC is 20 inches, and AB is 52 inches, what is the measure in inches of $\overline{CM}$?

  Ⓐ 24
  Ⓑ 26
  Ⓒ 28
  Ⓓ 30
  Ⓔ 32

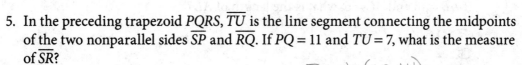

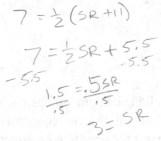

5. In the preceding trapezoid *PQRS*, $\overline{TU}$ is the line segment connecting the midpoints of the two nonparallel sides $\overline{SP}$ and $\overline{RQ}$. If $PQ = 11$ and $TU = 7$, what is the measure of $\overline{SR}$?

   (A) 3
   (B) 4
   (C) 5
   (D) 6
   (E) 7

6. In a circle whose radius is 17 centimeters, a chord is 8 centimeters from the center of the circle. What is the chord's length in centimeters?

   (A) 15
   (B) 16
   (C) 23
   (D) 30
   (E) 34

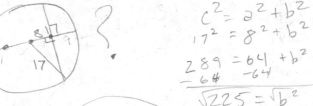

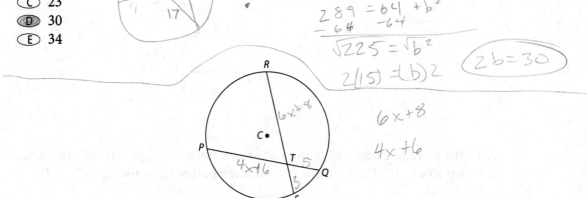

7. In the preceding diagram of circle *C*, chord $\overline{PQ}$ intersects chord $\overline{RS}$ at *T*. If $PQ = 4x + 6$, $TQ = 5$, $RS = 6x + 8$, and $TS = 3$, what is the value of *x*?

   (A) 3
   (B) 5
   (C) 10
   (D) 21
   (E) 35

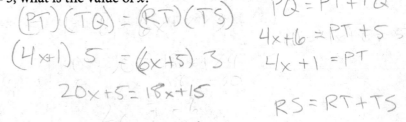

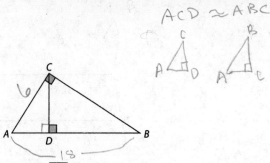

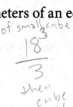

8. In the preceding right triangle ABC, $\overline{CD}$ is the altitude drawn to the hypotenuse $\overline{AB}$. If $AB = 18$ and $AC = 6$, what is the length of $\overline{AD}$?

Ⓐ 1.5
Ⓑ 2
Ⓒ 3
Ⓓ 12
Ⓔ 16

$$\frac{AD}{AC} = \frac{AC}{AB}$$

$$\frac{AD}{6} = \frac{6}{18}$$

$$AD = \frac{36}{18} \qquad AD = 2$$

9. A solid cube of metal has sides 18 centimeters long. A jeweler melts down the cube and uses all the molten metal to make three smaller cubes of exactly the same size. What is the length in centimeters of an edge of one of these smaller cubes?

Ⓐ $6\sqrt[3]{3}$
Ⓑ $6\sqrt[3]{9}$
Ⓒ $3\sqrt[3]{3}$
Ⓓ $3\sqrt[3]{9}$
Ⓔ 6

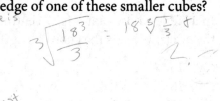

V of small cube is
$$\frac{18^3}{3}$$
then cube that

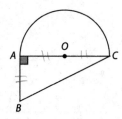

10. The preceding diagram shows a figure composed of right triangle ABC adjacent to semicircle $\overarc{AC}$. If $AB = OC = x$, what is the perimeter of the figure?

Ⓐ $x + x\sqrt{5} + \pi x$
Ⓑ $x + x\sqrt{5} + 2\pi x$
Ⓒ $x + x\sqrt{3} + \pi x$
Ⓓ $3x + x\sqrt{5} + \pi x$
Ⓔ $x + x\sqrt{5} + \dfrac{\pi x^2}{2}$

$AB + BC + \text{length } AC$

$AB = x$
$AC = 2x$
$BC^2 = \sqrt{x^2 + 2x^2}$

$\sqrt{5x^2}$
$x\sqrt{5}$

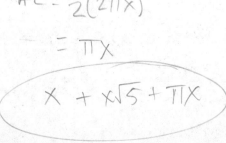

$AC = \frac{1}{2}(2\pi x)$

$= \pi x$

$X + x\sqrt{5} + \pi x$

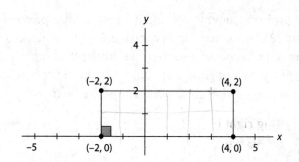

11. The preceding diagram shows the rectangle with vertices $(-2, 0), (-2, 2), (4, 0)$, and $(4, 2)$. What is the probability the x-coordinate of a randomly selected point in the rectangle is negative?

    (A) 1

    (B) $\dfrac{1}{3}$

    (C) $\dfrac{1}{6}$

    (D) $\dfrac{1}{12}$

    (E) 0

12. The grain storage bin shown in the preceding diagram has a right cylindrical top and a right conical base. The bin's overall height is 25 feet. If the bin's cylindrical top has radius 7 feet and its conical base has height 12 feet, what is the storage bin's approximate capacity in cubic feet?

    (A) 748

    (B) 1,100

    (C) 1,188

    (D) 2,616

    (E) 10,468

13. Disregarding units, if a sphere's surface area equals its volume, what is the sphere's diameter?

    (A) 3π

    (B) 6π

    (C) 6

    (D) 3

    (E) $\dfrac{1}{3}$

Volume box
$V = L \cdot W \cdot H$

14. For a craft project, students will form a rectangular piece of cardboard with dimensions 20 centimeters by 18 centimeters into a gift box by cutting congruent squares out of each corner and then folding up and taping together the remaining flaps. If each congruent square that is cut from the corners has sides of length s, which expression represents the volume of the box?

   (A) $4s^3 - 76s^2 + 360s$
   (B) $4s^3 + 76s^2 + 360s$
   (C) $s^3 - 38s^2 + 360s$
   (D) $s^2 - 38s + 360$
   (E) $4s^2 - 76s + 360$

$L \cdot W \cdot H$
$(20-2s)(18-2s)(s)$
$(360 - 40s - 36s + 4s^2)s$
$4s^3 - 76s^2 + 360s$

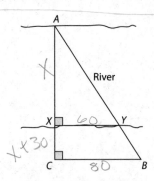

15. The preceding diagram shows the method that a park ranger is using to estimate the width of a river. If $XC = 30$ yards, $BC = 80$ yards, and $XY = 60$ yards, what is the river's width in yards?

   (A) $22\frac{1}{2}$
   (B) 45
   (C) 90
   (D) 120
   (E) 160

$AX = x = width$

$\frac{x}{x+30} = \frac{60}{80} = \frac{3}{4}$
$4x = 3(x+30)$
$4x = 3x + 90$
$x = 90$

16. If the line through the points $(-8, k)$ and $(2, 1)$ is parallel to the line through the points $(11, -1)$ and $(7, k+1)$, what is the value of k?

   (A) -4
   (B) $-\frac{1}{4}$
   (C) $-\frac{2}{7}$
   (D) 2
   (E) 4

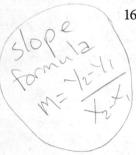

slope formula
$m = \frac{y_2 - y_1}{x_2 - x_1}$

$m = \frac{y_2 - y_1}{x_2 - x_1} = \frac{1-k}{2+8} = \frac{(k+1)+1}{7-11}$

$\frac{1-k}{10} = \frac{k+2}{-4}$

$-4(1-k) = 10(k+2)$
$-4 + 4k = 10k + 20$
$\frac{-24}{6} = \frac{6k}{6}$
$-4 = k$

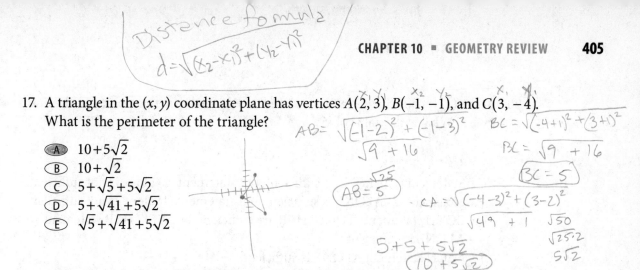

17. A triangle in the (x, y) coordinate plane has vertices $A(2, 3)$, $B(-1, -1)$, and $C(3, -4)$. What is the perimeter of the triangle?

  Ⓐ $10 + 5\sqrt{2}$
  Ⓑ $10 + \sqrt{2}$
  Ⓒ $5 + \sqrt{5} + 5\sqrt{2}$
  Ⓓ $5 + \sqrt{41} + 5\sqrt{2}$
  Ⓔ $\sqrt{5} + \sqrt{41} + 5\sqrt{2}$

Questions 18 to 25 each presents a question and two statements, labeled (1) and (2), in which certain data are given. Using your knowledge of mathematics and everyday facts (such as the number of minutes in an hour or the meaning of the word *perpendicular*), decide whether the given data are sufficient to answer the question. Then select one of the answer choices that follow.

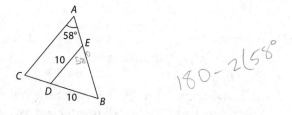

18. Is the measure of $\angle C$ greater than the measure of $\angle A$?

  (1) $\overline{AC} \parallel \overline{ED}$
  (2) $m\angle DEB = 58°$
  Ⓐ Statement (1) ALONE is sufficient, but statement (2) alone is not sufficient.
  Ⓑ Statement (2) ALONE is sufficient, but statement (1) alone is not sufficient.
  Ⓒ BOTH statements TOGETHER are sufficient, but NEITHER statement ALONE is sufficient.
  Ⓓ EACH statement ALONE is sufficient.
  Ⓔ Statements (1) and (2) TOGETHER are NOT sufficient.

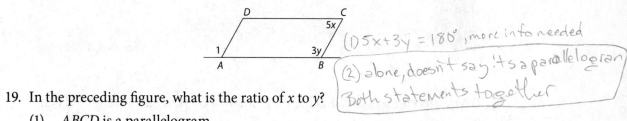

19. In the preceding figure, what is the ratio of x to y?

  (1) $ABCD$ is a parallelogram.
  (2) $m\angle 1 = 120°$
  Ⓐ Statement (1) ALONE is sufficient, but statement (2) alone is not sufficient.
  Ⓑ Statement (2) ALONE is sufficient, but statement (1) alone is not sufficient.
  Ⓒ BOTH statements TOGETHER are sufficient, but NEITHER statement ALONE is sufficient.
  Ⓓ EACH statement ALONE is sufficient.
  Ⓔ Statements (1) and (2) TOGETHER are NOT sufficient.

All the same
keep substituting

v = 2u+5

y = 2x+5
v+k = 2(u+h)+5
v+k = 2u+6+5
v+k = 2u+6+5
2u+5+k = 2u+6+5
k = 6

20. In the (x, y) coordinate plane, (u, v) and $(u + h, v + k)$ are two points on the line $y = 2x + 5$. What is the value of k?

    $y = 2x+5$ $2u+6+5 = 2u+5+k$
    $v+k = 2(u+3)+5$ $6 = k$
    $v+k = 2u+6+5$

    (1) $h = 3$
    (2) $k = 2h$
    Ⓐ Statement (1) ALONE is sufficient, but statement (2) alone is not sufficient.
    Ⓑ Statement (2) ALONE is sufficient, but statement (1) alone is not sufficient.
    Ⓒ BOTH statements TOGETHER are sufficient, but NEITHER statement ALONE is sufficient.
    Ⓓ EACH statement ALONE is sufficient.
    Ⓔ Statements (1) and (2) TOGETHER are NOT sufficient.

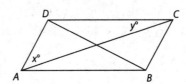

21. Is $x > y$?
    (1) $ABCD$ is a parallelogram.
    (2) $m\angle DAB = 50°$
    Ⓐ Statement (1) ALONE is sufficient, but statement (2) alone is not sufficient.
    Ⓑ Statement (2) ALONE is sufficient, but statement (1) alone is not sufficient.
    Ⓒ BOTH statements TOGETHER are sufficient, but NEITHER statement ALONE is sufficient.
    Ⓓ EACH statement ALONE is sufficient.
    Ⓔ Statements (1) and (2) TOGETHER are NOT sufficient.

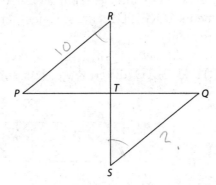

22. In the preceding figure, T is the midpoint of $\overline{PQ}$. What is the length of $\overline{QS}$?
    (1) $\angle R \cong \angle S$
    (2) $PR = 10$
    Ⓐ Statement (1) ALONE is sufficient, but statement (2) alone is not sufficient.
    Ⓑ Statement (2) ALONE is sufficient, but statement (1) alone is not sufficient.
    Ⓒ BOTH statements TOGETHER are sufficient, but NEITHER statement ALONE is sufficient.
    Ⓓ EACH statement ALONE is sufficient.
    Ⓔ Statements (1) and (2) TOGETHER are NOT sufficient.

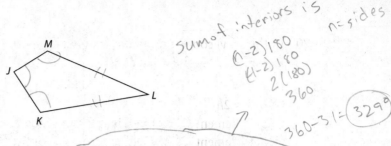

Handwritten notes:
sum of interiors is
(n-2)180   n=sides
(n-2)180
(4-2)180
2(180)
360
360-31 = (329)

23. For the preceding quadrilateral, what is $m\angle J + m\angle K + m\angle M$ in degrees?

Handwritten notes: not individually, but together ... that's why (1) works

(1) $m\angle L = 31°$
(2) $\overline{LK} \cong \overline{LM}$

Ⓐ Statement (1) ALONE is sufficient, but statement (2) alone is not sufficient.
Ⓑ Statement (2) ALONE is sufficient, but statement (1) alone is not sufficient.
Ⓒ BOTH statements TOGETHER are sufficient, but NEITHER statement ALONE is sufficient.
Ⓓ EACH statement ALONE is sufficient.
Ⓔ Statements (1) and (2) TOGETHER are NOT sufficient.

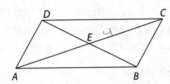

24. The preceding quadrilateral *ABCD* is a parallelogram. What is the length of $\overline{AC}$?

(1) $EC = 4$
(2) $AB = 6$

Ⓐ Statement (1) ALONE is sufficient, but statement (2) alone is not sufficient.
Ⓑ Statement (2) ALONE is sufficient, but statement (1) alone is not sufficient.
Ⓒ BOTH statements TOGETHER are sufficient, but NEITHER statement ALONE is sufficient.
Ⓓ EACH statement ALONE is sufficient.
Ⓔ Statements (1) and (2) TOGETHER are NOT sufficient.

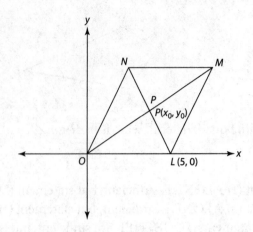

25. In the preceding parallelogram *LMNO*, *P* is the point of intersection of the diagonals. What is the value of x_0?

    (1)   Point *M* has coordinates (9, 10).
    (2)   Point *N* has coordinates (4, 10).
    (A) Statement (1) ALONE is sufficient, but statement (2) alone is not sufficient.
    (B) Statement (2) ALONE is sufficient, but statement (1) alone is NOT sufficient.
    (C) BOTH statements TOGETHER are sufficient, but NEITHER statement ALONE is sufficient.
    (D) EACH statement ALONE is sufficient.
    (E) Statements (1) and (2) TOGETHER are NOT sufficient.

Answers

1. **D** Make a sketch, filling in the question information.

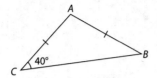

Angles C and B are base angles of an isosceles triangle, so their measures are equal, that is, $m\angle B = m\angle C = 40°$. The sum of the angles of a triangle is 180°. Thus, $\angle A = 180° - 2(40°) = 180° - 80° = 100°$. Note: $m\angle X$ denotes "the measure of angle X."

2. **A** In a triangle, the sum of the lengths of any two sides must be greater than the length of the third side (triangle inequality). The lengths given in choice A satisfy this criterion. The lengths given in the other answer choices do not.

3. **C** Start with the angles for which you can find the measure by using the given information. As you determine the measure of each angle, you will gain enough information to find the solution.

$$m\angle ACB = 180° - 75° - 60° = 45°$$
$$m\angle DCA = 45° + 55° = 100°$$

The measure of an exterior angle of a triangle equals the sum of the measures of the remote (nonadjacent) interior angles. Thus, $m\angle DCA = 100° = 30° + m\angle E$. Hence, $m\angle E = 100° - 30° = 70°$.

4. **B** In a right triangle, the median to the hypotenuse is one-half the length of the hypotenuse, so the length in inches of $\overline{CM}$ is 26.

5. **A** The length of the segment connecting the midpoints of two nonparallel sides of a trapezoid is one-half the sum of the lengths of its bases. Thus, $TU = 7 = \frac{1}{2}(SR + PQ) = \frac{1}{2}(SR + 11)$. Solve $7 = \frac{1}{2}(SR + 11)$ for SR.

$$7 = \frac{1}{2}(SR + 11)$$
$$7 = \frac{1}{2}SR + 5.5$$
$$1.5 = \frac{1}{2}SR$$
$$3 = SR$$

6. **D** In a circle, a radius that is perpendicular to a chord bisects the chord. Let x = one-half the length of the chord. Then $2x$ = the length of the chord. Make a sketch, filling in the question information.

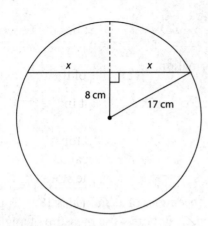

Using the Pythagorean theorem (omitting the units for convenience), $x^2 = 17^2 - 8^2 = 289 - 64 = 225$, so $x = 15$, and $2x = 30$.

7. **B** When two chords intersect within a circle, the products of their segments are equal. $\overline{PQ}$ and $\overline{RS}$ are two chords in C intersecting at T, so $(PT)(TQ) = (RT)(TS)$. $PQ = PT + TQ$, so $4x + 6 = PT + 5$, and $PT = 4x + 1$. $RS = RT + TS$, so $6x + 8 = RT + 3$, and $RT = 6x + 5$. Substitute into $(PT)(TQ) = (RT)(TS)$, and solve for x.

$$(4x+1)(5) = (6x+5)(3)$$
$$20x + 5 = 18x + 15$$
$$2x = 10$$
$$x = 5$$

8. **B** In a right triangle, the altitude to the hypotenuse separates the triangle into two triangles that are similar to each other and to the original triangle. Therefore, $\triangle ACD \sim \triangle ABC$. Set up a proportion based on corresponding sides of similar triangles, and solve for AD.

$$\frac{AD}{AC} = \frac{AC}{AB}$$
$$\frac{AD}{6} = \frac{6}{18}$$
$$AD = \frac{6 \cdot 6}{18} = \frac{36}{18} = 2$$

9. **B** The volume of the molten metal in one of the three smaller cubes is $\dfrac{18^3}{3}$. To find the length of an edge of one of the cubes, take the cube root of the volume.

$$\sqrt[3]{\frac{18^3}{3}} = 18\sqrt[3]{\frac{1}{3}} = 18\sqrt[3]{\frac{1 \cdot 3^2}{3 \cdot 3^2}} = 18\sqrt[3]{\frac{9}{3^3}} = \frac{18}{3}\sqrt[3]{9} = 6\sqrt[3]{9}$$

10. **A** The perimeter of the figure $= AB + BC + \text{length } \overparen{AC}$. $\overline{BC}$ is the hypotenuse of a right triangle with legs of lengths x and $2x$. Use the Pythagorean theorem to find the length of BC in terms of x. $BC = \sqrt{x^2 + (2x)^2} = \sqrt{5x^2} = x\sqrt{5}$.
The length of $\overparen{AC}$ is half the circumference of a circle with radius x. In terms of x, length $\overparen{AC} = \frac{1}{2}(2\pi x) = \pi x$. Thus, the perimeter $AB + BC + \text{length } \overparen{AC} = x + x\sqrt{5} + \pi x$.

11. **B** The probability will be the area of the rectangular portion that lies in the second quadrant divided by the area of the entire rectangle. By inspection, you can see that the rectangular portion that lies in the second quadrant is $\frac{1}{3}$ the size of the rectangle. So the probability is $\frac{1}{3}$ that the x-coordinate of a randomly selected point in the rectangle is negative.

12. **D** The capacity of the storage bin is the volume of the cylindrical top, with radius 7 feet and height 13 feet (25 feet − 12 feet), plus the volume of the conical base, with radius 7 feet and height 12 feet. Therefore, the capacity in cubic feet of the storage bin equals $\pi(7^2)(13)+\frac{1}{3}\pi(7^2)(12)=\pi(49)(13)+\frac{1}{3}\pi(49)(12)=\pi(49)(13)+\pi(49)(4)$. Rather than performing the calculations, to save time, get an approximate answer by rounding first: $\pi(49)(13)+\pi(49)(4)\approx 3(50)(10)+3(50)(4)=2{,}100$. Compare this result to the answer choices; only choice D is close, so pick choice D.

13. **C** Let d = the sphere's diameter; then $d=2r$, where r is its radius. Set up the following equality and solve for r.

Because r is a radius, you can assume $r > 0$.

$$4\pi r^2 = \frac{4}{3}\pi r^3$$

$$\frac{4\pi r^2}{4\pi r^2} = \frac{\frac{4}{3}\pi r^3}{4\pi r^2}$$

$$1 = \frac{1}{3}r$$

$$3 = r$$

$$d = 2r = 6$$

14. **A** Make a sketch, filling in the question information.

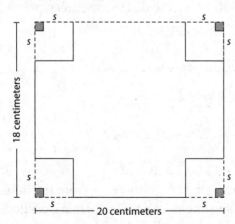

The volume of the box in cubic centimeters $= l \cdot w \cdot h = (20-2s)(18-2s)s = (360-76s+4s^2)s = 4s^3-76s^2+360s$.

15. **C** Let $AX = x =$ the width of the river. Right triangles AXY and ACB are similar because they have common angle A. Set up a proportion based on corresponding sides, and solve for x (omitting the units for convenience):

$$\frac{x}{x+30} = \frac{60}{80} = \frac{3}{4}$$
$$4x = 3(x+30)$$
$$4x = 3x + 90$$
$$x = 90$$

Simplifying $\dfrac{60}{80}$ to lowest terms $\left(\dfrac{3}{4}\right)$ makes the calculations easier to do in this problem.

---

16. **A** Parallel lines have equal slopes. The slope of the line through points (x_1, y_1) and (x_2, y_2) is $m = \dfrac{y_2 - y_1}{x_2 - x_1}$. Set up an equation and solve for k.

slope through $(-8, k)$ and $(2, 1)$ = slope through $(11, -1)$ and $(7, k+1)$

$$\frac{1-k}{2-(-8)} = \frac{(k+1)-(-1)}{7-11}$$
$$\frac{1-k}{2+8} = \frac{k+1+1}{-4}$$
$$\frac{1-k}{10} = \frac{k+2}{-4}$$
$$-4(1-k) = 10(k+2)$$
$$-4+4k = 10k+20$$
$$-6k = 24$$
$$k = -4$$

17. **A** The perimeter of the triangle is $AB + BC + CA$. The distance between points (x_1, y_1) and (x_2, y_2) is $d = \sqrt{(x_2 - x_1)^2 + (y_2 - y_1)^2}$. Therefore:

$$AB = \sqrt{(-1-2)^2 + (-1-3)^2} = \sqrt{9+16} = \sqrt{25} = 5$$
$$BC = \sqrt{(3+1)^2 + (-4+1)^2} = \sqrt{16+9} = \sqrt{25} = 5$$
$$CA = \sqrt{(2-3)^2 + (3+4)^2} = \sqrt{1+49} = \sqrt{50} = \sqrt{25 \cdot 2} = 5\sqrt{2}$$

Thus, the perimeter is $AB + BC + CA = 5 + 5 + 5\sqrt{2} = 10 + 5\sqrt{2}$.

18. **D** From the figure, because $ED = DB$, triangle EDB is isosceles. From the information in (1), $m\angle A = m\angle DEB = 58°$ (corresponding angles of parallel lines are congruent). Also, $m\angle B = m\angle DEB = 58°$ (base angles of an isosceles triangle are congruent). Thus, $m\angle C = 180° - 2(58°)$, so (1) is SUFFICIENT. From the information in (2), $m\angle B = m\angle DEB = 58°$ (base angles of an isosceles triangle are congruent). Thus, $m\angle C = 180° - 2(58°)$, so (2) also is SUFFICIENT. Therefore, EACH statement ALONE is sufficient.

19. **C** From the information in (1), $5x + 3y = 180°$ (any two consecutive angles of a parallelogram are supplementary), but further information is needed to determine $\dfrac{x}{y}$, so (1) is NOT sufficient. From the information in (2), $m\angle 1 = 120°$ but without further information, you cannot determine a relationship between $m\angle 1$ and $5x$ or $3y$, so (2) is NOT sufficient. Taking (1) and (2) together, $3y = m\angle 1 = 120°$ (corresponding angles of parallel lines are congruent), which you can solve to obtain $y = 40°$. Then substituting into $5x + 3y = 180°$ gives $5x + 120° = 180°$, which you can solve for x. Then using the value of x obtained and $y = 40°$, compute $\dfrac{x}{y}$. Therefore, BOTH statements TOGETHER are sufficient, but NEITHER statement ALONE is sufficient.

20. **A** From the question information, you can substitute the given coordinates into $y = 2x + 5$ to obtain the following system.

$$v = 2u + 5$$
$$(v + k) = 2(u + h) + 5$$

With the information in (1), the system is as follows:

$$v = 2u + 5$$
$$(v + k) = 2(u + 3) + 5$$

Substitute $v = 2u + 5$ into the second equation, and solve for k.

$$2u + 5 + k = 2u + 6 + 5$$
$$k = 6$$

Therefore, (1) is SUFFICIENT. With the information in (2), the system is as follows:

$$v = 2u + 5$$
$$(v + 2h) = 2(u + h) + 5$$

When simplified, the second equation is $v = 2u + 5$, which is the same as the first equation. Thus, you need further information to determine k, so (2) is NOT sufficient. Therefore, statement (1) ALONE is sufficient, but statement (2) alone is not sufficient.

21. **E** From the information in (1), $m\angle CAB = y°$ (alternate interior angles of parallel lines are congruent). If $ABCD$ is a rhombus, then $x° = y°$ (the diagonals of a rhombus bisect the vertex angles). Otherwise, $x° \neq y°$. Thus, (1) does not provide sufficient information to answer definitely whether $x > y$. From the information in (2) you know only $m\angle DAB$, which is not sufficient information to determine the relationship between x and y. Taking (1) and (2) together, you can establish that $x° + y° = 50°$, but there is not sufficient information to determine whether $x > y$. Therefore, statements (1) and (2) TOGETHER are NOT sufficient.

22. **C** From the question information, $\overline{PT} \cong \overline{QT}$. From the information in (1), $\angle R \cong \angle S$, $\angle PTR \cong \angle QTS$ (vertical angles are congruent), and $\overline{PT} \cong \overline{QT}$, so $\triangle PTR \cong \triangle QTS$, by Angle-Angle-Side (AAS). Thus, $\overline{PR} \cong \overline{QS}$ (corresponding parts of congruent triangles are congruent), but without further information, the length of $\overline{QS}$ cannot be determined, so (1) is NOT sufficient. From the information in (2) $PR = 10$, but further information is needed to establish a relationship between this information and QS. Thus, (2) also is NOT sufficient. Taking (1) and (2) together, from (1) you know that $\overline{PR} \cong \overline{QS}$, and from

(2) you know that $PR = 10$, so $QS = 10$. Therefore, BOTH statements TOGETHER are sufficient, but NEITHER statement ALONE is sufficient.

23. **A** $JKLM$ is a convex quadrilateral, so the sum of its interior angles is $(n-2)180° = (4-2)180° = 360°$. From the information in (1), $m\angle J + m\angle K + m\angle M = 360° - 31° = 329°$, so (1) is SUFFICIENT. The information in (2), $\overline{LK} \cong \overline{LM}$, cannot help you determine angle measures in the figure. Further information is needed, so (2) is NOT sufficient. Therefore, statement (1) ALONE is sufficient, but statement (2) alone is not sufficient.

24. **A** Using the information in (1), the diagonals of a parallelogram bisect each other, so if $EC = 4$, then $AC = 8$; thus, (1) is SUFFICIENT. Using the information in (2), $\overline{AC}$ and $\overline{AB}$ are sides in triangle ABC, but further information is needed to establish a relationship between their lengths, so (2) is NOT sufficient. Therefore, statement (1) ALONE is sufficient, but statement (2) alone is not sufficient.

25. **D** From the question information, the diagonals of a parallelogram bisect each other, so (x_0, y_0) is the midpoint of $\overline{OM}$ as well as the midpoint of $\overline{NL}$. From the information in (1), (x_0, y_0) is the midpoint between $(0, 0)$ and $(9, 10)$, so $x_0 = \dfrac{0+9}{2} = 4.5$, and (1) is SUFFICIENT. From the information in (2), (x_0, y_0) is the midpoint between $(4, 10)$ and $(5, 0)$, so $x_0 = \dfrac{4+5}{2} = 4.5$, and (2) also is SUFFICIENT. Therefore, EACH statement ALONE is sufficient.

CHAPTER 11

Word Problems

This review of word problems includes the following topics:

- Problem-solving process
- Representing verbal phrases and statements
- Consecutive numbers
- Ratios and proportions
- Percentage
- Simple interest
- Ages
- Mixtures
- Coins
- Distance-rate-time
- Work
- Right triangles
- Divisors and factors
- Greatest common factor and least common multiple
- Permutations and combinations
- Sequences

Problem-Solving Process

Here is a general process for problem solving on the GMAT.

1. **Understand the problem.** Ask yourself: What content area (arithmetic, algebra, or geometry) is the question's primary focus? Is the problem a familiar type (for example, a mixture problem)? Determine what you need to find. Look for words like *find*, *determine*, *what is*, *how many*, *how far*, *how much*, and the like. Decide how many unknowns are in the problem.

2. **Make a plan.** Decide how you should go about determining a solution. Identify the information in the problem. Is there a formula that you need? If measurement units are given, determine what units the answer should have. Decide whether making a chart or sketching a diagram would be helpful. Try to relate the current problem to practice problems you have worked out. Make sure your plan will result in a solution that answers the question.

3. **Carry out the plan.** Using the plan you decided upon, work out the solution on the erasable notepad provided at the testing center. Make sure you copy all information accurately. Write neatly so that you can check over your work. If the answer should have units, check whether your calculations will result in the proper units for the answer. *Tip*: If you are using an equation to find the solution, you might find it convenient to omit the units while solving the equation, given that you have already checked that the answer will have the proper units.

4. **Look back.** Verbalize your answer. Did you answer the question that was asked? Check your solution in the context of the problem. Does it make sense? Is it reasonable? Are units needed?

Representing Verbal Phrases and Statements

For many questions, writing and solving an equation is a straightforward method for determining the answer. When you use equations, you must represent verbal phrases and statements using mathematical symbolism. Here are some general guidelines.

SYMBOL	TYPICAL SIGNAL WORDS	EXAMPLE
addition	*add, plus, sum, more than, exceeded by, increased by*	$x + 5$
subtraction	*minus, difference, subtracted from, less than, decreased by, diminished by, reduced by*	$x - 3$
multiplication	*times, multiplied by, product, double, twice, triple, fraction or percent of*	$2x, 2 \cdot x, (2)(x), 2(x),$ or $(2)x$
division	*divided by, quotient, ratio, for each, for every, per*	$\dfrac{x}{4}$
equal sign	*equals, is, are, will be, results in, gives, yields*	$\dfrac{1}{2}x + 20 = 2x + 5$

Note: The variable *x* represents a real number.

Example: Ten less than three times a number is five more than twice the number. What is the number?

Let n = the number. Write an equation that represents the facts.

$$3n - 10 = 2n + 5$$

(Keep in mind that "Ten less than three times a number" is not $10 - 3n$.)
Solve the equation.

$$3n - 10 = 2n + 5$$
$$3n - 10 - 2n = 2n + 5 - 2n$$
$$n - 10 = 5$$
$$n - 10 + 10 = 5 + 10$$
$$n = 15$$

The number is 15.

Sometimes you have two or more unknowns in a problem. For this situation you can use a different variable name for each unknown. On the other hand, you might assign a variable name to one unknown and express the other unknowns in terms of that variable. For instance, if a first unknown is described in terms of a second unknown, let the variable equal the second unknown. In most cases, you will need as many equations as you have variables in order to determine specific values for the variables. No matter whether you go with one variable or two or more variables, ultimately, the process will culminate in a one-variable linear equation (or its equivalent).

The length of a lawn is 6 feet longer than its width. The lawn's perimeter is 68 feet. What is the lawn's length, in feet?

Method 1: Use one variable.

The lawn's length is described in terms of its width. Let w = the lawn's width, in feet. Then $w + 6$ feet = the lawn's length, in feet. Write an equation that represents the facts given in the question.

$$2[(w + 6 \text{ feet}) + w] = 68 \text{ feet}$$

Solve the equation, omitting the units for convenience.

$$2[(w + 6) + w] = 68$$
$$2[w + 6 + w] = 68$$
$$2[2w + 6] = 68$$
$$4w + 12 = 68$$
$$4w + 12 - 12 = 68 - 12$$
$$4w = 56$$
$$w = 14$$
$$w + 6 = 20$$

The lawn's length is 20 feet.

Make sure you answer the question that was asked. In this question, after you obtain w, you must calculate $(w + 6)$ to answer the question.

Method 2: Use two variables.

Let w = the lawn's width, in feet, and l = the lawn's length, in feet. Write two equations that represent the facts given in the question.

$$(1)\ l = w + 6 \text{ feet}$$
$$(2)\ 2(l + w) = 68 \text{ feet}$$

Simultaneously solve the two equations, omitting the units for convenience.

$$(1)\ l = w + 6$$
$$(2)\ 2(l + w) = 68$$

Using the substitution method, substitute $l = w + 6$ from equation (1) into equation (2) to obtain

$$2[(w + 6) + w] = 68$$

Complete the solution as shown in Method 1.

Consecutive Numbers

Consecutive integers differ by 1. For these problems, let n = the first integer (the least one), $n + 1$ = the second integer, $n + 2$ = the third integer, and so on.

Example: The greatest of three consecutive integers is 10 more than twice the second integer. What is the value of the greatest integer?

$$n + 2 = 2(n+1) + 10$$

Let n = the first integer, $n + 1$ = the second integer, and $n + 2$ = the third integer (the greatest one). Write an equation that represents the facts given in the question.

$$(n + 2) = 2(n + 1) + 10$$

Solve the equation.

Pay attention to what the question is asking

$$(n+2) = 2(n+1) + 10$$
$$n + 2 = 2n + 2 + 10$$
$$n - 2n = 10$$
$$-n = 10$$
$$n = -10$$
$$n + 2 = -8$$

The greatest integer is −8.

Consecutive even integers and **consecutive odd integers** differ by 2. For these problems, let n = the first even or odd integer, $n + 2$ = the second even or odd integer, and $n + 4$ = the third even or odd integer, and so on.

If you know the sum of three integers, the middle integer is their sum divided by 3. For example, if three consecutive even integers have a sum of 42, the middle even integer is $42 \div 3 = 14$, which makes the other two even integers 12 and 16.

Ratios and Proportions

Ratios

A ratio is a multiplicative comparison of two quantities. If two quantities are in the ratio a to b and you know their sum is c, solve $ax + bx = c$ for x, then compute ax or bx, whichever one is needed.

> **Example:** The ratio of boys to girls in a classroom of 21 students is 3 to 4. How many girls are in the classroom?

Solve $3x + 4x = 21$.

$$3x + 4x = 21$$
$$7x = 21$$
$$x = 3$$
$$4x = 12$$

There are 12 girls in the classroom.

You can extend this strategy to three or more quantities.

Proportions

A **proportion** is a mathematical statement that two ratios are equal. The statement $\dfrac{a}{b} = \dfrac{c}{d}$ is a proportion and is read "a is to b as c is to d." The fundamental property of proportions is that $\dfrac{a}{b} = \dfrac{c}{d}$ if and only if $ad = bc$. The numbers a, b, c, and d are the **terms** of the proportion. The products ad and bc are the **cross products** (illustrated below).

$$\frac{a}{b} \diagtimes \frac{c}{d}$$

If the values of three of the four terms of a proportion are known, the value of the fourth term can be determined by using the fundamental property of proportions. Find a cross product that results in a numerical value, and then divide by the numerical term you didn't use. For example,

$$\text{if } \frac{n}{60} = \frac{7}{15}, \text{ then } n = \frac{(60)(7)}{15} = \frac{(\overset{4}{\cancel{60}})(7)}{\underset{1}{\cancel{15}}} = 28.$$

When you have a word problem involving proportions, look for a sentence or phrase in the problem that provides the information you need for the left ratio of the proportion, and then look for another sentence or phrase that gives you the information you need for the right ratio of the proportion.

> **Example:** On a map, the distance between two cities is 13.5 inches. The scale on the map shows that 0.5 inch represents 20 miles. What is the distance, in miles, between the two cities?

Let $d =$ the distance, in miles between the two cities.

Information for the left ratio of the proportion is in the first sentence of the problem (13.5 inches represents d miles on the map), and information for the right ratio of the proportion is in the second sentence (0.5 inch represents 20 miles on the map).
Write the proportion.

$$\frac{d}{13.5 \text{ in}} = \frac{20 \text{ miles}}{0.5 \text{ in}}$$

Notice that the units in the left ratio match up with the units in the right ratio. You have miles in the numerator and inches in the denominator on the left, and you have miles in the numerator and inches in the denominator on the right. If the units in the left and right ratios don't match up, your proportion is incorrect.

Solve the proportion, omitting the units for convenience.

$$d = \frac{(13.5)(20)}{0.5} = 540$$

The distance between the two cities is 540 miles.

Percentage

Formula and Terminology

In simple percentage problems use the formula $P = RB$, where P is the **percentage** (the "part of the whole"), R is the **rate** (the quantity with a % sign or the word *percent* attached), and B is the **base** (the "whole amount").

In word problems, a percent without a base is usually meaningless. Be sure to identify the base associated with each percent mentioned in a problem.

Finding the Percentage

If the percentage is missing, multiply the base by the rate. Here is an example.

Devra works at a sports store that pays sales personnel a commission rate of 2% on total sales. Last week, Devra's sales totaled $2,428. What commission did Devra earn last week?

In this problem, Devra's commission is P, which is unknown; R is 2%; and B is $2,428. So, $P = RB = (2\%)(\$2,428) = (0.02)(\$2,428) = \$48.56$.

Devra earned $48.56 in commission last week.

Change percents to decimals or fractions to perform calculations.

Finding the Base

If the base is missing, divide the percentage by the rate. Here is an example.

An online store offered a 25% discount on all clothing items during a two-day sale. Laura got $74.75 off the price of a coat she purchased during the sale. What was the original price of the coat?

In this problem, the original price of the coat is B, which is unknown; R is 25%; and P is $74.75. So,

$$B = \frac{P}{R} = \frac{\$74.75}{25\%} = \frac{\$74.75}{0.25} = \$299 \text{ or } \frac{\$74.75}{\frac{1}{4}} = \$74.75 \times 4 = \$299.$$

Notice that using an equivalent fraction for the percent in this problem can simplify the calculations. For the GMAT, you will find it helpful to memorize the following fractional and decimal equivalents of common percentages.

if base is missing $B = \dfrac{P}{R}$

$100\% = 1.00 = 1$	$90\% = 0.90 = 0.9 = \dfrac{9}{10}$	$87\dfrac{1}{2}\% = 87.5\% = 0.875 = \dfrac{7}{8}$	$66\dfrac{2}{3}\% = 0.66\dfrac{2}{3} = \dfrac{2}{3}$
$75\% = 0.75 = \dfrac{3}{4}$	$80\% = 0.80 = 0.8 = \dfrac{4}{5}$	$62\dfrac{1}{2}\% = 62.5\% = 0.625 = \dfrac{5}{8}$	$33\dfrac{1}{3}\% = 0.33\dfrac{1}{3} = \dfrac{1}{3}$
$50\% = 0.50 = 0.5 = \dfrac{1}{2}$	$70\% = 0.70 = 0.7 = \dfrac{7}{10}$	$37\dfrac{1}{2}\% = 37.5\% = 0.375 = \dfrac{3}{8}$	$5\% = 0.05 = \dfrac{1}{20}$
$25\% = 0.25 = \dfrac{1}{4}$	$60\% = 0.60 = 0.6 = \dfrac{3}{5}$	$12\dfrac{1}{2}\% = 12.5\% = 0.125 = \dfrac{1}{8}$	$4\% = 0.04 = \dfrac{1}{25}$
	$40\% = 0.40 = 0.4 = \dfrac{2}{5}$		$1\% = 0.01 = \dfrac{1}{100}$
	$30\% = 0.30 = 0.3 = \dfrac{3}{10}$		
	$20\% = 0.20 = 0.2 = \dfrac{1}{5}$		
	$10\% = 0.10 = 0.1 = \dfrac{1}{10}$		

Finding the Rate

If the rate is missing, divide the percentage by the base. Express your answer as a percent.

> **Example:** Aaron paid a sales tax of $9.90 on a camera that cost $120. What was the sales tax rate for the purchase?

In this problem, the sales tax rate is R, which is unknown; P is $9.90, and B is $120. So,

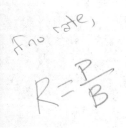

$$R = \frac{P}{B} = \frac{\$9.90}{\$120} = 0.0825 = 8.25\%$$

The sales tax rate was 8.25%.

Do not expect the rate to be less than 100% or the percentage to be less than the base in every problem. When the rate is greater than 100%, the percentage will be greater than the base. For example,

P		R		B
500	is	125%	of	400

because $(125\%)(400) = (1.25)(400) = 500$.

See the section "Numbers and Operations" in Chapter 8 for additional discussion about percents.

Percentage Increase or Decrease

The **percent change** (increase or decrease) in the value of an item is

$$\frac{\left|\text{New Value}-\text{Old Value}\right|}{\text{Old Value}}\times100\%$$

Always divide by the value that occurred first in time.

For example, suppose a necklace increased in value from $345.00 to $396.75. Then (omitting the units), the percent increase is

$$\frac{\left|\text{New Value}-\text{Old Value}\right|}{\text{Old Value}}\times100\%=\frac{\left|396.75-345.00\right|}{345.00}\times100\%$$

$$=\frac{\left|51.75\right|}{345}\times100\%=\frac{51.75}{345}\times100\%=0.15\times100\%=15\%\text{ increase.}$$

Similarly, suppose a book decreased in value from $25.90 to $23.31. Then (omitting the units), the percent decrease is

$$\frac{\left|\text{New Value}-\text{Old Value}\right|}{\text{Old Value}}\times100\%=\frac{\left|23.31-25.90\right|}{25.90}\times100\%$$

$$=\frac{\left|-2.59\right|}{25.90}\times100\%=\frac{2.59}{25.90}\times100\%=0.10\times100\%=10\%\text{ decrease}$$

Percent change, whether it is an increase or a decrease, is *always* positive.

Simple Interest

Simple interest is $I = Prt$, where I is the simple interest accumulated on a principal, P, at a simple interest rate, r, per time period for t time periods. For example, the simple interest earned on an investment of $10,000 at a 2% annual simple interest rate for 5 years is

$$I=Prt=(\$10,000)(2\%\text{ per year})(5\text{ years})=(\$10,000)\left(\frac{0.02}{\text{year}}\right)(5\text{ years})=\$1,000$$

[handwritten: I = PRT, interest, principal, rate, time period]

Put units that follow the word *per* in a denominator.

Ages

In age problems, comparisons are usually made in specified time periods (present, future, or past). Make a table to organize the age information to help you understand the question.

Example: Jaylon is twice as old as Kyle. Five years from now the sum of their ages will be 46. How old will Jaylon be in 10 years?

Let K = Kyle's age, in years, now. Then $2K$ = Jaylon's age, in years, now.

Make a table to organize the age information.

WHEN?	JAYLON'S AGE (IN YEARS)	KYLE'S AGE (IN YEARS)	SUM (IN YEARS)
Now	$2K$	K	Not given
In 5 years	$2K + 5$ years	$K + 5$ years	46 years
In 10 years	$2K + 10$ years	$K + 10$ years	Not given

Write an equation that represents the facts shown in the table.

$$(2K + 5 \text{ years}) + (K + 5 \text{ years}) = 46 \text{ years}$$

Solve the equation, omitting the units for convenience.

$$(2K + 5) + (K + 5) = 46$$
$$2K + 5 + K + 5 = 46$$
$$3K + 10 = 46$$
$$3K + 10 - 10 = 46 - 10$$
$$3K = 36$$
$$K = 12$$
$$2K + 10 = 2(12) + 10 = 24 + 10 = 34$$

Jaylon will be 34 years old in 10 years.

Mixtures

In a mixture problem, the amount (or value) of a substance before mixing equals the amount (or value) of that substance after mixing. Make a table to organize the mixture information to help you understand the question.

Example: How many milliliters of a 30% alcohol solution must be added to 500 milliliters of a 70% alcohol solution to yield a 40% alcohol solution?

Let x = the number of milliliters of the 30% solution to be added.

Make a table to organize the information in the question.

WHEN?	PERCENT ALCOHOL STRENGTH	NUMBER OF MILLILITERS	AMOUNT OF ALCOHOL
Before mixing	30%	x	30%x
	70%	500	70%(500)
After mixing	40%	$x + 500$	40%($x + 500$)

The amount of alcohol before mixing equals the amount of alcohol after mixing. Write an equation that represents the facts shown in the table.

$$30\%x + 70\%(500) = 40\%(x + 500)$$

Solve the equation.

$$30\%x + 70\%(500) = 40\%(x + 500)$$
$$0.30x + 0.70(500) = 0.40(x + 500)$$
$$0.30x + 350 = 0.40x + 200$$
$$0.30x + 350 - 0.40x = 0.40x + 200 - 0.40x$$
$$-0.10x + 350 - 350 = 200 - 350$$
$$-0.10x = -150$$
$$x = 1{,}500$$

1,500 milliliters of the 30% alcohol solution must be added.

Coins

In a coin problem, the value of a collection of coins equals the sum of the values of the coins in the collection. (Of course, you must assume there are no rare coins in the collection that would be worth more than their face values.) Make a table to organize the coin information to help you understand the question.

Example: Andre has a jar containing 759 U.S. nickels and dimes that have a total value of $53.30. How many nickels are in the jar?

Let n = the number of nickels. Let d = the number of dimes. Make a table to organize the coin information in the question.

DENOMINATION	NICKELS	DIMES	TOTAL
Face Value per Coin	$0.05	$0.10	N/A
Number of Coins	n	d	759
Value of Coins	$0.05n$	$0.10d$	$53.30

Using the table, write two equations that represent the facts.

$$n + d = 759$$

$$\$0.05n + \$0.10d = \$53.30$$

Remember, when you have two variables, you will need two equations in order to determine a solution.

Solve the system, omitting the units for convenience.

$$n + d = 759$$

$$0.05n + 0.10d = 53.30$$

Using the method of substitution, solve the first equation, $n + d = 759$, for d in terms of n.

$$d = 759 - n$$

Substitute the result into the second equation and solve for n.

$$0.05n + 0.10d = 53.30$$

$$0.05n + 0.10(759 - n) = 53.30$$

$$0.05n + 75.90 - 0.10n = 53.30$$

$$-0.05n + 75.90 - 75.90 = 53.30 - 75.90$$

$$-0.05n = -22.60$$

$$n = 452$$

There are 452 nickels in the jar.

Distance-Rate-Time

The distance formula is $d = rt$, where d is the distance a vehicle travels at a uniform rate of speed, r, for a given length of time, t. Make a table to organize the vehicle information and maybe sketch a rough diagram, if needed, to help you understand the question.

Example: At 8 p.m., a car and a van leave the same location. The car travels due east at 70 miles per hour. The van travels due west at 60 miles per hour. At what clock time will the two vehicles be 325 miles apart?

Let t = the time in hours the two vehicles will be 325 miles apart. Then 8 p.m. plus t is the clock time the two vehicles will be 325 miles apart. Make a chart to organize the information in the question.

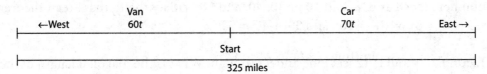

VEHICLE	RATE (IN MPH)	TIME (IN HOURS)	DISTANCE (IN MILES)
car	70	t	$70t$
van	60	t	$60t$

Sketch a diagram.

```
                    Van                        Car
     ←West          60t                        70t            East →
     ├──────────────┼────────────┬─────────────┼───────────────┤
                              Start
     ├───────────────────────────────────────────────────────┤
                              325 miles
```

Using the diagram, write an equation that represents the facts.

$$60t + 70t = 325 \text{ miles}$$

Solve the equation, omitting the units for convenience.

$$60t + 70t = 325$$
$$130t = 325$$
$$t = \frac{325}{130}$$
$$t = 2.5$$

The clock time the two vehicles will be 325 miles apart is 8 p.m. plus 2.5 hours = 10:30 p.m.

Work

In a typical work problem, you are given the time, call it x, that it will take one person (or device) to do a task, working alone, and the time, call it y, that it will take another person (or device) to do the same task, working alone. Then the time it will take both of them, working together, is

$$\frac{xy}{x+y}$$

Example: Working alone, Dylan can paint the walls of a long hallway in 4 hours. Jeremy can paint the walls of the hallway in 3 hours, working alone. How long will it take them, working together, to paint the hallway?

Omitting the units, calculate $\frac{(4)(3)}{4+3} = \frac{12}{7} = 1\frac{5}{7}$. The time it will take Dylan and Jeremy, working together, to paint the hallway is $1\frac{5}{7}$ hours.

Right Triangles

3-4-5 Right Triangles

You will likely see right triangles on the GMAT that have sides of lengths 3, 4, and 5 or of lengths that are multiples of 3, 4, and 5. The reason is that 3, 4, and 5 and any multiple of these numbers (such as 6, 8, and 10 or 30, 40, and 50) satisfy the Pythagorean theorem. That is, $3^2 + 4^2 = 5^2$, $6^2 + 8^2 = 10^2$, and $30^2 + 40^2 = 50^2$.

> **Example:** A wall is 12 feet long and 9 feet high. What is the diagonal length of the wall?

> The diagonal is the hypotenuse of a right triangle that has legs of 12 feet and 9 feet. The numbers 12 and 9 are multiples of 4 and 3 by a factor of 3, respectively. Therefore, the hypotenuse is a multiple of 5 by a factor of 3. Thus, the diagonal length of the garden is (3)(5 feet) = 15 feet.

30°-60°-90° Right Triangles

In a right triangle that has acute angles of 30° and 60°, the lengths of the triangle's three sides are in the ratio $\dfrac{1}{2} : \dfrac{\sqrt{3}}{2} : 1$ or, equivalently, $1 : \sqrt{3} : 2$.

> **Example:** Find BC in the right triangle shown below.

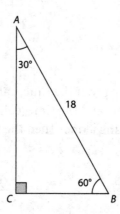

> The triangle is a 30°-60°-90° right triangle. $\overline{BC}$ is opposite the 30° angle. Therefore, $BC = \dfrac{1}{2}(18) = 9$.

45°-45°-90° Right Triangles

In an isosceles right triangle that has congruent acute angles of 45°, the lengths of the triangle's three sides are in the ratio $\dfrac{\sqrt{2}}{2} : \dfrac{\sqrt{2}}{2} : 1$ or, equivalently, $1 : 1 : \sqrt{2}$.

Example: Find the length of the hypotenuse in the right triangle shown below.

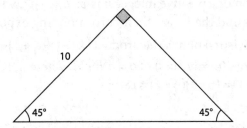

The triangle is a 45°-45°-90° right triangle. The three sides are in the ratio $1:1:\sqrt{2}$. Therefore, the length of the hypotenuse is $10\sqrt{2}$.

Divisors and Factors

Divisibility Rules

Here are some useful divisibility rules to know for the GMAT.

DIVISIBLE BY	RULE	EXAMPLE
2	The last digit is even.	9,357,834 is divisible by 2 because 4 (the last digit) is even.
3	The sum of the digits is divisible by 3.	252,414 is divisible by 3 because $2+5+2+4+1+4 = 18$ (the sum of the digits) is divisible by 3.
4	The last 2 digits form a number that is divisible by 4.	47,816 is divisible by 4 because 16 (the number formed by the last two digits) is divisible by 4.
5	The last digit is 0 or 5.	92,105 is divisible by 5 because the last digit is 5.
6	The number is divisible by both 2 and 3.	252,414 is divisible by 6 because it is divisible by both 2 and 3.
8	The last 3 digits form a number that is divisible by 8.	35,824 is divisible by 8 because 824 (the number formed by the last three digits) is divisible by 8.
9	The sum of the digits is divisible by 9.	252,414 is divisible by 9 because $2+5+2+4+1+4 = 18$ (the sum of the digits) is divisible by 9.
10	The last digit is 0.	68,460 is divisible by 10 because the last digit is 0.

- If an integer divides evenly into n, then it divides evenly into any multiple of n. For instance, 3 divides 594, so it also divides $(10)(594) = 5{,}940$.
- If an integer divides evenly into both m and n, then it divides evenly into $am + bn$, for any integers a and b. For instance, 3 divides evenly into 27, and 3 divides evenly into 60; so 3 divides evenly into $(5)(27) + 4(60) = 375$.

> A number's factors divide evenly into the number. Therefore, the results in this section concerning divisors and divisibility apply to factors as well.

Factors

If the prime factorization of a positive integer n is $p_1^{k_1} p_2^{k_2} \cdots p_n^{k_n}$, where the p's are distinct positive prime numbers and the k's are their corresponding exponents, then the number of positive factors (or divisors) of n is the product $(k_1+1)(k_2+1)\cdots(k_n+1)$. For example, the number of positive factors (or divisors) of $n = a^4 b^2 c^5 d$, where a, b, c, and d are prime numbers, is $(4+1)(2+1)(5+1)(1+1)=(5)(3)(6)(2)=180$.

Remember, if no exponent is written on a variable or number, the exponent is understood to be 1 (for instance, $d = d^1$).

On a smaller scale, the number of positive factors of 24, which equals $(2^3)(3)$, is $(3 + 1)(1 + 1) = (4)(2) = 8$. Because integers can have negative factors, the number of factors (positive and negative) of 24 is $2(8) = 16$.

Knowing simple tricks about integers such as how to quickly determine the number of positive factors (or divisors) of a positive integer can turn what looks like a difficult question into an easy computation exercise.

See "Numbers and Operations" in Chapter 8 for additional discussion of prime numbers and factors.

Greatest Common Factor and Least Common Multiple

Greatest Common Factor

The **greatest common factor** (or **GCF**) of two numbers is the greatest factor common to both numbers. In other words, it is the largest number that evenly divides into each of the two numbers. In GCF word problems you are seeking the greatest common number, the greatest common size, the greatest common measure, and so forth that can be used to evenly divide or distribute the objects or things from two unequal-size sets so that none are left over.

> **Example:** A civic club has 24 boys and 36 girls as members. For a community project, the club's faculty sponsor wants to evenly divide the boys and girls into groups, so that no one is left out. What is the greatest number of groups the faculty sponsor can make?
>
> The greatest number of groups is the GCF (24, 36) = 12. Each of the 12 groups will have 2 boys and 3 girls in it. *Tip*: Notice that $5 \times 12 = 60$, which is the total number of members ($24 + 36 = 60$).

Least Common Multiple

The **least common multiple** (or **LCM**) of two numbers is the least number that is a multiple of both numbers. In other words, it is the minimum number both numbers evenly divide into.

In LCM word problems you are seeking the minimum common number, the minimum common time, the minimum common measure, and so forth between two multiple events or items.

Example: At the entrance to an amusement park every 50th person gets a ticket for a free drink and every 75th person gets a ticket for a free ride. What is the minimum number of people who must enter for a person to receive both tickets?

The minimum number of people is the LCM (50, 75) = 150. The 150th person will be the first person to receive both tickets.

A quick way to compute the LCM of two numbers is to divide their product by their GCF. For example,

$$\text{LCM}(50,75) = \frac{(50)(75)}{\text{GCF}(50,75)} = \frac{(50)(75)}{25} = \frac{\left(\overset{2}{\cancel{50}}\right)(75)}{\underset{1}{\cancel{25}}} = 150.$$

See "Numbers and Operations" in Chapter 8 for additional discussion of greatest common factor and least common multiple.

Permutations and Combinations

Permutations

A permutation is a selection in which order is important. That is, different orderings of the same elements are counted separately. For example, two different permutations of the numbers from one to five are 12345 and 53142.

On the GMAT, use the product rule for counting to work permutation problems. Make sure that:

- The items from which you select are *mutually different* items (that is, no two are alike).
- You select *without replacement*.
- Different orderings of the same items are counted *separately*.

See "Counting Techniques" in Chapter 8 for an explanation of the product rule for counting.

Some situations that indicate you might have a permutation problem are the following: creating codes, passwords, or license plates; making words; assigning roles; filling positions; making ordered arrangements of things (people, objects, colors, and so on), selecting persons or things as first, second, third, and so on; distributing items among several objects or people; and similar scenarios.

For example, the number of different ways a club of 20 members can select a president, vice-president, and secretary from its membership if no person holds more than one office and all members are eligible for any one of the three positions is $20 \times 19 \times 18 = 6,840$. (There are 20 members from which to select a president. After that position is filled, there are 19 members from which to select a vice-president. After the first two positions are filled, there are 18 members from which to select a secretary.)

Combinations

A combination is a selection in which order is not important. For example, the set of vowels *a*, *e*, *i*, *o*, and *u* is the same combination as the set *i*, *a*, *u*, *o*, and *e*. However, two different combinations consisting of four vowels are the set *a*, *e*, *i*, and *o* and the set *a*, *e*, *i*, and *u*.

On the GMAT, to work combination problems use the combination formula

$$_nC_r = \frac{n!}{r!(n-r)!}$$

Make sure that:

▪ The items from which you select are *mutually different* items (that is, no two are alike).
▪ You select *without replacement*.
▪ Different orderings of the same items are not distinguished as being different from each other.

See "Counting Techniques" in Chapter 8 for an explanation of the combination formula.

Some situations that indicate you might have a combination problem are the following: making a collection of things (books, coins, and so on); selecting a committee; choosing questions from a test; counting the number of subsets of a given size from a set; dealing hands from a deck of cards; selecting pizza toppings; listing the combinations from a set of items; choosing students for groups; and similar scenarios.

Example: The number of different ways a club of 20 members can select a 3-member officer-nominating committee from its membership if all members are eligible to serve on the committee is

$$_{20}C_3 = \frac{20!}{3!17!} = \frac{20\cdot19\cdot18\cdot17!}{3\cdot2\cdot1\cdot17!} = \frac{\overset{10}{20}\cdot19\cdot\overset{6}{18}\cdot\cancel{17!}}{\cancel{3}\cdot\cancel{2}\cdot1\cdot\cancel{17!}} = 1,140$$

See "Counting Techniques" in Chapter 8 for additional discussion of permutations and combinations.

Sequences

A **sequence** is a list of **terms** written in a particular order.

In an **arithmetic sequence**, consecutive terms have a common difference. The sequence has the form $a_1, a_1 + d, a_1 + 2d, \ldots, a_1 + (n-1)d, \ldots$, where a_1 is the first term and d is the common difference between terms. The general term for an arithmetic sequence is $a_n = a_1 + (n-1)d$. For example, the first five terms of the arithmetic sequence that has first term $a_1 = 3$ and common difference $d = 5$ are 3, 8, 13, 18, and 23. The 20th term is $a_{20} = 3 + (20 - 1)(5) = 3 + (19)(5) = 98$.

In a **geometric sequence**, consecutive terms have a common ratio. The sequence has the form $a_1, a_1r, a_1r^2, \ldots, a_1r^{n-1}, \ldots$, where a_1 is the first term and r is the common ratio. The general term for a geometric sequence is $a_n = a_1r^{n-1}$. For example, the first five terms of the geometric sequence that has first term $a_1 = 10$ and common ratio $r = 2$ are 10, 20, 40, 80, and 160. The 10th term is $a_{10} = (10)(2^{10-1}) = (10)(2^9) = (10)(512) = 5{,}120$.

A **recursive definition** for a sequence includes the value of one or more initial terms and a formula for finding each term from previous terms. The **Fibonacci sequence** has the following recursive definition: $a_1 = 1$, $a_2 = 1$, and $a_n = a_{n-1} + a_{n-2}$, for $n \geq 3$. The first five terms of the sequence are 1, 1, 2, 3, and 5.

If you encounter sequences on the GMAT, look for a recognizable pattern. Is there a common difference? Is there a common ratio? Are the terms sequential perfect squares or cubes? Are the terms obtained by adding or subtracting the previous terms in some way?

> **Example:** The first five terms of a sequence are 2, 5, 8, 11, and 14. If the sequence continues in the same manner, what is its 50th term?

> The terms shown have a common difference of 3 with first term $a_1 = 2$. If this pattern continues in the same manner, the general term is $a_1 + (n-1)d = 2 + (n-1)(3)$. Thus, the 50th term is $a_{50} = 2 + (50 - 1)(3) = 2 + (49)(3) = 149$.

Word Problem Drill

Directions: **Select the best answer choice.**

$15x + 22.50(90-x) = 1620$
$15x + 2025 - 22.50x = 1620$
$\dfrac{-7.5x}{-7.5} = \dfrac{-405}{-7.5}$
$\boxed{x = 54}$

1. A candy store owner mixes candy that normally sells for $15.00 per pound and candy that normally sells for $22.50 per pound to make a 90-pound mixture to sell at $18.00 per pound. To make sure that $18.00 per pound is a fair price, how much (in pounds) of the $15.00 candy should the owner use?

   (A) 30
   (B) 36
   (C) 42
   (D) 50
   (E) 54

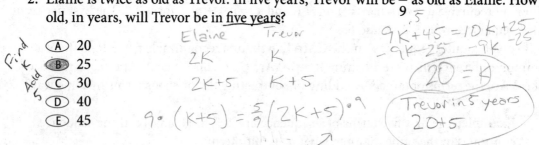

POUNDS $
$x + y = 90$ 15 x
$y = 90 - x$ 22.50 y
                18   90
$15x + 22.50y = 18(90)$

2. Elaine is twice as old as Trevor. In five years, Trevor will be $\dfrac{5}{9}$ as old as Elaine. How old, in years, will Trevor be in <u>five years</u>?

   (A) 20
   (B) 25
   (C) 30
   (D) 40
   (E) 45

Find K
Add 5

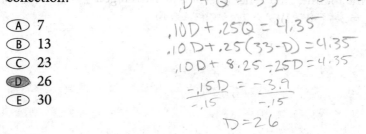

Elaine   Trevor
$2K$ K
$2K+5$ $K+5$
$9 \cdot (K+5) = \dfrac{5}{9}(2K+5) \cdot 9$

$9K+45 = 10K + 25$
$-9K - 25 \quad -9K - 25$
$\boxed{20 = K}$
Trevor in 5 years
$20 + 5$

3. A collection of 33 U.S. coins amounts to $4.35. If the collection consists of only dimes and quarters and contains no rare coins, how many dimes are in the collection?

   (A) 7
   (B) 13
   (C) 23
   (D) 26
   (E) 30

$D + Q = 33 \quad D = 33 - Q \quad Q = 33 - D$
$.10D + .25Q = 4.35$
$.10D + .25(33-D) = 4.35$
$.10D + 8.25 - .25D = 4.35$
$\dfrac{-.15D}{-.15} = \dfrac{-3.9}{-.15}$
$D = 26$

4. A chemist is making a 50% alcohol solution. How many milliliters of distilled water must the chemist add to 1,000 milliliters of a 70% alcohol solution to obtain a 50% solution?

   (A) 200
   (B) 400
   (C) 600
   (D) 800
   (E) 1,000

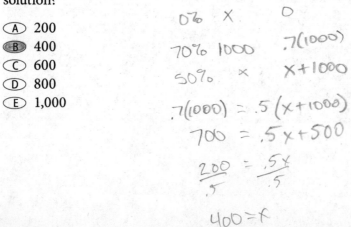

0% X 0
70%   1000   .7(1000)
50% x $X + 1000$

$.7(1000) = .5(x + 1000)$
$700 = .5x + 500$
$\dfrac{200}{.5} = \dfrac{.5x}{.5}$
$400 = x$

5. An investor receives interest on two simple-interest investments, one at 2.5% annually, and the other at 1.5% annually. The two investments together earn $460 annually. If the amount invested at 2.5% is $10,000, how much money is invested at 1.5%?

Ⓐ $10,000
Ⓑ $12,000
Ⓒ $14,000
Ⓓ $16,000
Ⓔ $18,000

(handwritten notes)
250   2.5 ⟩ 460
       1.5
250
210
10,000(.025)=250
14,000(.015)=210
460
or
.015X+ .025(10000)=460
X=14,000

6. Two vehicles leave the same location at exactly the same time, one traveling due west at r miles per hour and the other traveling due east at $r + 20$ miles per hour. In terms of r and d, what is t, the number of hours for the two vehicles to be d miles apart?

Ⓐ $\dfrac{d}{2r+20}$

Ⓑ $\dfrac{d}{r^2+20}$

Ⓒ $\dfrac{r(r+20)}{d}$

Ⓓ $\dfrac{d}{r}+\dfrac{d}{r+20}$

Ⓔ $\dfrac{0.5d}{r}+\dfrac{0.5d}{r+20}$

(handwritten notes)
$\frac{D}{r}=\frac{rt}{r}$
$t=\frac{D}{R}$

r   t
r+20   t
$rt + t(r+20) = d$
$rt + rt + 20t$
$2rt + 20t$
$t(2r+20)=d$
$\frac{}{2r+20}$
$t=\frac{d}{2r+20}$

7. Working alone, Angus can paint two rooms in 5 hours. Dimitri working alone can do the same job in 3 hours. If Angus and Dimitri work together, how much time, in hours, should it take them to paint the two rooms?

Ⓐ $1\dfrac{1}{2}$

Ⓑ $1\dfrac{7}{8}$

Ⓒ $2\dfrac{1}{2}$

Ⓓ $2\dfrac{3}{5}$

Ⓔ $5\dfrac{1}{2}$

(handwritten notes)
$\dfrac{\text{multiply hours}}{\text{add hours}}$ $\dfrac{(5)(3)}{5+3} = \dfrac{15}{8} = 1.875 = 1\frac{7}{8}$

8. Twice the sum of three consecutive integers is 42 more than twice the sum of the first and third integers. Find the value of the second integer.

   (A) 19
   (B) 20
   (C) 21
   (D) 22
   (E) 23

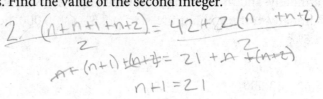

$$2 \cdot \frac{(n+n+1+n+2)}{2} = 42 + 2\left(n + n+2\right)$$

$$n + (n+1) + (n+2) = 21 + n + (n+2)$$

$$n+1 = 21$$

9. If the sum of two numbers is 30 and their product is 224, what is the greater number?

   (A) 12
   (B) 14
   (C) 16
   (D) 18
   (E) 20

   $x + y = 30$

   $xy = 224$

   $14 + 16$

10. A 24-pound mixture of nuts contains peanuts, pecans, and almonds by weight in the ratio 5:2:1, respectively. What is the amount, in pounds, of pecans in the mixture?

    (A) 2
    (B) 3
    (C) 6
    (D) 9
    (E) 12

    $\frac{24}{8} = 3$ $x + 2x + 5x = 24$

    or

    $5:2:1$ $\frac{8x}{8} = \frac{24}{8}$

    $15:6:3$ $x = 3$

    PN PE AL

11. Helene and Yannick both swam in the indoor pool at the YOLO Fitness Gym today. Helene swims at YOLO Fitness Gym every 12 days. Yannick swims there every 15 days. If both continue with their regular swimming schedule at YOLO Fitness Gym, the next time both will swim there on the same day is in how many days?

    (A) 15
    (B) 30
    (C) 60
    (D) 120
    (E) 180

    what does (12,15) factor into?

12. In triangle ABC, the measure of $\angle A$ is 25 degrees more than the measure of $\angle B$, and the measure of $\angle C$ is 9 degrees less than twice the measure of $\angle B$. What is the measure of the largest angle?

    (A) 36°
    (B) 41°
    (C) 66°
    (D) 73°
    (E) 82°

    $A = B + 25$

    $C = 2(B) - 9$

    $B = 41$

    $A = 41 + 25 = 66$

    $C = 2(41) - 9 = 82$

    $B + B + 25 + 2B - 9 = 180$

    $4B + 16 = 180$

    $\frac{4B}{4} = \frac{164}{4}$ $B = 41$

13. A rhombus has sides of length 20 inches, and the measure of one interior angle is 150°. What is the area of the rhombus in square inches?

   - (A) 400
   - (B) 200
   - (C) 100
   - (D) 80
   - (E) 60

   handwritten: in a 30° 60° 90° triangle, across from 30° side is $\frac{1}{2}$ of hyp

   handwritten: 20, 150, 30

   $\frac{1}{2}(20) = 10$

   $A = BH = 20(10) = 200$

14. Two jars of the same brand of blueberry jam have cylindrical shapes. One jar is twice the height of the other jar, but its diameter is one-half the diameter of the shorter jar. What is the ratio of the volume of the taller jar to the volume of the shorter jar?

   - (A) 1:1
   - (B) 1:2
   - (C) 1:4
   - (D) 2:1
   - (E) 4:1

   handwritten: $\pi r^2 h$ cylinder

   $\dfrac{\pi r^2\, 2h}{\pi (2r)^2 (h)} = \dfrac{\pi\, 2r^2\, h}{\pi\, 4r^2\, h} = \dfrac{1}{2} = 1:2$

15. A bank offers its business customers two different plans for monthly charges on checking accounts. With Plan A, the account holder pays a fee of $0.15 per check processed during the month with no monthly service charge on the account. With Plan B, the account holder pays a $10.00 monthly service charge with a fee of $0.05 per check processed during the month. Find the *break-even point* for the two plans. That is, find the number of checks processed per month for which the costs of the two plans are equal.

   - (A) 40
   - (B) 50
   - (C) 60
   - (D) 80
   - (E) 100

   handwritten:
   $.15x = 10 + .05x$
   $-.05x \qquad -.05x$
   $\dfrac{.10x}{.10} = \dfrac{10}{.10}$
   $x = 100$

$$a = 3^4 \cdot 5^2 \cdot 7$$
$$b = 2 \cdot 3^5 \cdot 5 \cdot 7^3$$

16. For *a* and *b* shown above, which of the following expressions represents the greatest common factor of *a* and *b*?

   - (A) $5 \cdot 7$
   - (B) $2 \cdot 3 \cdot 5 \cdot 7$
   - (C) $3^4 \cdot 5 \cdot 7$
   - (D) $2 \cdot 3^4 \cdot 5^2 \cdot 7^3$
   - (E) $2 \cdot 3^9 \cdot 5^3 \cdot 7^4$

17. For which of the following numbers would division by 8 result in a remainder of 0?

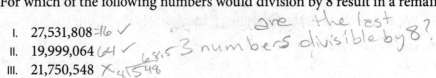

    I.   27,531,808 =16 ✓

    II. 19,999,064 64 ✓ 68.5 3 numbers divisible by 8?

    III. 21,750,548 ✗ 4√548

    Ⓐ I only

    Ⓑ I and II only

    Ⓒ I and III only

    Ⓓ II and III only

    Ⓔ I, II, and III

Questions 18 to 25 each presents a question and two statements, labeled (1) and (2), in which certain data are given. Using your knowledge of mathematics and everyday facts (such as the number of minutes in an hour or the meaning of the word *perpendicular*), decide whether the given data are sufficient to answer the question. Then select one of the answer choices that follow.

18. What is the value of a_{100} if $a_n = a_1 + (n-1)d$? $a + 4d$

    (1) $a_5 = 30$ $a_1 + (100-1)d$

    (2) $a_{20} = 105$ $a_1 + 99d$

    Ⓐ Statement (1) ALONE is sufficient, but statement (2) alone is not sufficient.

    Ⓑ Statement (2) ALONE is sufficient, but statement (1) alone is not sufficient.

    Ⓒ BOTH statements TOGETHER are sufficient, but NEITHER statement ALONE is sufficient.

    Ⓓ EACH statement ALONE is sufficient.

    Ⓔ Statements (1) and (2) TOGETHER are NOT sufficient.

19. Members of a club are electing a president, a vice-president, and a treasurer. If each club member is eligible for each position and no one can hold two positions, is the number of possible different outcomes greater than 900?

    (1)   The number of members in the club is greater than 10.

    (2)   After a president is elected, there are 11 members left from which to choose the other two positions.

    Ⓐ Statement (1) ALONE is sufficient, but statement (2) alone is not sufficient.

    Ⓑ Statement (2) ALONE is sufficient, but statement (1) alone is not sufficient.

    Ⓒ BOTH statements TOGETHER are sufficient, but NEITHER statement ALONE is sufficient.

    Ⓓ EACH statement ALONE is sufficient.

    Ⓔ Statements (1) and (2) TOGETHER are NOT sufficient.

$n(n-1)(n-2)$

$11(10)(9) = 990$ ✓ yes (1)

✓ yes (2)

20. Two vehicles leave the same location at exactly the same time, the first traveling due west and the second traveling due east. In how many hours will the two vehicles be 390 miles apart?

(1) The average speed of the first vehicle is 10 miles per hour faster than the average speed of the second vehicle.

(2) When the two vehicles are 390 miles apart, the second vehicle has gone a distance of 180 miles.

Ⓐ Statement (1) ALONE is sufficient, but statement (2) alone is not sufficient.

Ⓑ Statement (2) ALONE is sufficient, but statement (1) alone is not sufficient.

Ⓒ BOTH statements TOGETHER are sufficient, but NEITHER statement ALONE is sufficient.

Ⓓ EACH statement ALONE is sufficient.

Ⓔ Statements (1) and (2) TOGETHER are NOT sufficient.

21. A sporting goods store marks up the price of an exercise bike from its original cost. What percent of the selling price is the markup?

(1) The selling price of the exercise bike is $450.

(2) The markup on the exercise bike is 25% of the original cost.

Ⓐ Statement (1) ALONE is sufficient, but statement (2) alone is not sufficient.

Ⓑ Statement (2) ALONE is sufficient, but statement (1) alone is not sufficient.

Ⓒ BOTH statements TOGETHER are sufficient, but NEITHER statement ALONE is sufficient.

Ⓓ EACH statement ALONE is sufficient.

Ⓔ Statements (1) and (2) TOGETHER are NOT sufficient.

22. Given consecutive integers a, b, and c, is $c > 40$? $n(n+1)(n+2)$

(1) $a + b + c = 126$

(2) $a < b < c$

Ⓐ Statement (1) ALONE is sufficient, but statement (2) alone is not sufficient.

Ⓑ Statement (2) ALONE is sufficient, but statement (1) alone is not sufficient.

Ⓒ BOTH statements TOGETHER are sufficient, but NEITHER statement ALONE is sufficient.

Ⓓ EACH statement ALONE is sufficient.

Ⓔ Statements (1) and (2) TOGETHER are NOT sufficient.

23. Is the prime number x a factor of 48?

(1) x is a factor of 10.

(2) x is a factor of 28.

Ⓐ Statement (1) ALONE is sufficient, but statement (2) alone is not sufficient.

Ⓑ Statement (2) ALONE is sufficient, but statement (1) alone is not sufficient.

Ⓒ BOTH statements TOGETHER are sufficient, but NEITHER statement ALONE is sufficient.

Ⓓ EACH statement ALONE is sufficient.

Ⓔ Statements (1) and (2) TOGETHER are NOT sufficient.

24. How high up the wall will the wire reach?

    (1) The wire is anchored on the ground 9 feet from the base of the wall.
    (2) The wire is 15 feet long.
    (A) Statement (1) ALONE is sufficient, but statement (2) alone is not sufficient.
    (B) Statement (2) ALONE is sufficient, but statement (1) alone is not sufficient.
    (C) BOTH statements TOGETHER are sufficient, but NEITHER statement ALONE is sufficient.
    (D) EACH statement ALONE is sufficient.
    (E) Statements (1) and (2) TOGETHER are NOT sufficient.

25. In a social club, the number of members is 56. How many female members are in the club?

    (1) The ratio of male members to female members in the club is 3 to 5.
    (2) If four additional male members are recruited to the club while the number of female members remains unchanged, the ratio of male members to the number of members in the club will be 5 to 12.
    (A) Statement (1) ALONE is sufficient, but statement (2) alone is not sufficient.
    (B) Statement (2) ALONE is sufficient, but statement (1) alone is not sufficient.
    (C) BOTH statements TOGETHER are sufficient, but NEITHER statement ALONE is sufficient.
    (D) EACH statement ALONE is sufficient.
    (E) Statements (1) and (2) TOGETHER are NOT sufficient.

Answers

1. **E** Let x = the amount (in pounds) of the candy priced at \$15.00 per pound needed. Then $90 - x$ = the amount (in pounds) of the candy priced at \$22.50 per pound needed. Make a table to organize the candy information in the question.

WHEN?	PRICE PER POUND	AMOUNT IN POUNDS	VALUE
Before mixing	\$15.00	x	\$15.00x
	\$22.50	y	\$22.50y
After mixing	\$18.00	90	\$18(90)

The total amount (in pounds) is 90. The value of the candy before it is mixed should equal the value after it is mixed. Using the table, write two equations that represent the facts (omitting "pounds" and "per pound" because these units cancel each other).

$$x + y = 90$$
$$\$15.00x + \$22.50y = \$18.00(90)$$

Remember, when you have two variables, you must write two equations in order to determine a solution.

Solve the system, omitting the units for convenience.

$$x + y = 90$$
$$15.00x + 22.50y = 18.00(90)$$

Using the method of substitution, solve the first equation, $x + y = 90$, for y in terms of x.

$$y = 90 - x$$

Substitute the result into the second equation and solve for x.

$$15.00x + 22.50y = 18.00(90)$$
$$15.00x + 22.50(90 - x) = 18.00(90)$$
$$15.00x + 2{,}025 - 22.50x = 1{,}620$$
$$-7.5x + 2{,}025 - 2{,}025 = 1{,}620 - 2{,}025$$
$$-7.5x = -405$$
$$\frac{-7.5x}{-7.5} = \frac{-405}{-7.5}$$
$$x = 54$$

The candy store owner should use 54 pounds of the \$15.00 candy.

2. **B** Let T = Trevor's age now, in years. Then $2T$ = Elaine's age now, in years. Make a table to organize the age information.

WHEN?	ELAINE'S AGE (IN YEARS)	TREVOR'S AGE (IN YEARS)
Now	$2T$	T
In 5 years	$2T + 5$ years	$T + 5$ years

Write an equation that represents the facts given.

$$\left(T + 5 \text{ years}\right) = \frac{5}{9}\left(2T + 5 \text{ years}\right)$$

Solve the equation, omitting the units for convenience.

$$\left(T + 5\right) = \frac{5}{9}\left(2T + 5\right)$$

$$\left(T + 5\right) = \frac{5(2T + 5)}{9}$$

$$9(T + 5) = 5(2T + 5)$$

$$9T + 45 = 10T + 25$$

$$9T + 45 - 9T = 10T + 25 - 9T$$

$$45 = T + 25$$

$$45 - 25 = T + 25 - 25$$

$$20 = T$$

$$T + 5 = 20 + 5 = 25$$

Trevor will be 25 years old in 5 years.

3. **D** Let d = the number of dimes. Let q = the number of quarters. Make a table to organize the coin information in the question.

DENOMINATION	DIMES	QUARTERS	TOTAL
Face Value per Coin	$0.10	$0.25	N/A
Number of Coins	d	q	33
Value of Coins	$0.10d	$0.25q	$4.35

Using the table, write two equations that represent the facts.

$$d + q = 33$$

$$\$0.10d + \$0.25q = \$4.35$$

Solve the system, omitting the units for convenience.

$$d + q = 33$$

$$0.10d + 0.25q = 4.35$$

Using the method of substitution, solve the first equation, $d + q = 33$, for q in terms of d.

$$q = 33 - d$$

Substitute the result into the second equation and solve for d.

$$0.10d + 0.25q = 4.35$$
$$0.10d + 0.25(33 - d) = 4.35$$
$$0.10d + 8.25 - 0.25d = 4.35$$
$$-0.15d + 8.25 - 8.25 = 4.35 - 8.25$$
$$-0.15d = -3.90$$
$$\frac{-0.15d}{-0.15} = \frac{-3.90}{-0.15}$$
$$d = 26$$

There are 26 dimes in the collection.

4. **B** Let $x =$ the number of milliliters of distilled water to be added. Make a table to organize the information in the question.

WHEN?	PERCENT ALCOHOL STRENGTH	NUMBER OF MILLILITERS	AMOUNT OF ALCOHOL
Before mixing	0%	x	0
	70%	1,000	70%(1,000)
After mixing	50%	$x + 1,000$	50%($x + 1,000$)

The amount of alcohol before mixing equals the amount of alcohol after mixing. Write an equation that represents the facts shown in the table.

$$70\%(1,000) = 50\%(x + 1,000)$$

Solve the equation.

$$70\%(1,000) = 50\%(x + 1,000)$$
$$0.7(1,000) = 0.5(x + 1,000)$$
$$700 = 0.5x + 500$$
$$700 - 500 = 0.5x + 500 - 500$$
$$200 = 0.5x$$
$$\frac{200}{0.5} = \frac{0.5x}{0.5}$$
$$x = 400$$

The chemist must add 400 milliliters of distilled water.

You should eliminate choice E at the outset because adding 1,000 milliliters to a 1,000-milliliter 70% alcohol solution would dilute it to a 35% alcohol solution.

---

5. C Let x = the amount invested at 1.5% annually. Make a table to organize the investment information.

PRINCIPAL	RATE	TIME (IN YEARS)	INTEREST
x	1.5%	1	1.5%x
$10,000	2.5%	1	2.5%($10,000)
		Total:	$460

Using the information in the table, write an equation to represent the facts.

$$1.5\%x + 2.5\%(\$10,000) = \$460$$

Solve the equation, omitting the units for convenience.

$$1.5\%x + 2.5\%(10,000) = 460$$
$$0.015x + 0.025(10,000) = 460$$
$$0.015x + 250 = 460$$
$$0.015x + 250 - 250 = 460 - 250$$
$$0.015x = 210$$
$$\frac{0.015x}{0.015} = \frac{210}{0.015}$$
$$x = 14,000$$

The amount invested at 1.5% is $14,000.

6. A Make a table to organize the vehicle information in the question.

VEHICLE	RATE (IN MPH)	TIME (IN HOURS)	DISTANCE
Vehicle 1	r	t	rt
Vehicle 2	$r + 20$	t	$(r + 20)t$
		Total:	d

Using the information in the table, set up an equation and solve for t.

$$rt + (r + 20)t = d$$
$$rt + rt + 20t = d$$
$$2rt + 20t = d$$
$$t(2r + 20) = d$$
$$t = \frac{d}{2r + 20}$$

7. B Omitting the units, calculate $\dfrac{(5)(3)}{5+3} = \dfrac{15}{8} = 1\dfrac{7}{8}$. The time it will take Angus and Dimitri, working together, to paint the two rooms is $1\dfrac{7}{8}$ hours. You should eliminate choice E at the outset because the time for Angus and Dimitri working together should be less than either of their times working alone.

8. C Let n = the first integer, $n + 1$ = the second integer, and $n + 2$ = the third integer. Write an equation that represents the facts given in the question.

$$2[n + (n + 1) + (n + 2)] = 2[n + (n + 2)] + 42$$

Solve the equation. (*Hint*: For a quick solution, first, divide both sides by 2, and then remove terms that are the same from both sides.)

$$2\left[n+(n+1)+(n+2)\right]=2\left[n+(n+2)\right]+42$$
$$\left[n+(n+1)+(n+2)\right]=\left[n+(n+2)\right]+21$$
$$n+(n+1)+(n+2)=n+(n+2)+21$$
$$n+1=21$$

The second integer is 21.

9. **C** Let x = the greater number and y = the lesser number. Write two equations that represent the facts given in the question.

$$x+y=30$$
$$xy=224$$

Check the answer choices to solve.

Check C. If x is 16, then $x + y = 16 + y = 30$. So y is $30 - 16 = 14$; and xy is $(16)(14) = 224$. Thus, C is correct.

10. **C** Let x = the amount, in pounds, of almonds in the mixture, $2x$ = the amount, in pounds, of pecans in the mixture, and $5x$ = the amount, in pounds, of peanuts in the mixture. Using the information in the question, write an equation and solve.

$$x+2x+5x=24$$
$$8x=24$$
$$x=3$$
$$2x=6$$

The amount of pecans in the mixture is 6 pounds.

11. **C** The number of days until the next time is LCM (12, 15) = 60. It will be 60 days before Helene and Yannick both will swim at YOLO Fitness Gym on the same day.

12. **D** Let $x = m\angle B$. Then $x+25° = m\angle A$, and $2x-9° = m\angle C$. Given that the angles of a triangle sum to 180°, write an equation and solve, omitting the units for convenience.

$$x+(x+25)+(2x-9)=180$$
$$x+x+25+2x-9=180$$
$$4x+16=180$$
$$4x=164$$
$$x=41$$
$$x+25=66$$
$$2x-9=2(41)-9=82-9=73$$

The largest angle has measure 73°.

13. **B** Make a sketch, filling in the information given in the question.

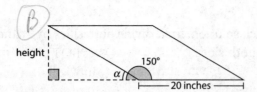

height

150°

α

20 inches

The area is base times height. Angle $\alpha = 180° - 150° = 30°$. The indicated height is the side opposite the 30° angle in a 30°-60°-90° right triangle. Thus, the height, in inches, is $\frac{1}{2}(20) = 10$, and the area in square inches is $(20)(10) = 200$.

14. **B** Let h = height of the shorter jar; then $2h$ = height of the taller jar. Let r = radius of the taller jar; then $2r$ = radius of the shorter jar. (The relationship between the radii is the same as that between the diameters.) Find the ratio of V_{taller}, the volume of the taller jar, to $V_{shorter}$, the volume of the shorter jar:

$$\text{Ratio} = \frac{V_{taller}}{V_{shorter}} = \frac{\pi r^2 (2h)}{\pi (2r)^2 (h)} = \frac{\pi (2r^2)(h)}{\pi (4r^2)(h)} = \frac{\cancel{\pi} (\overset{1}{\cancel{2}} r^2)(\cancel{h})}{\cancel{\pi} (\underset{2}{\cancel{4}} r^2)(\cancel{h})} = \frac{1}{2} \text{ or } 1:2$$

15. **E** Let x = the number of checks processed per month. For Plan A, the monthly cost is $0.15x$. For Plan B, the monthly cost is $0.05x + \$10$. To find the break-even point, set the costs of the two plans equal to each other and solve for x, omitting the units for convenience.

$$0.15x = 0.05x + 10$$
$$0.15x - 0.05x = 0.05x + 10 - 0.05x$$
$$0.10x = 10$$
$$x = \frac{10}{0.1}$$
$$x = 100$$

The break-even point for the two plans occurs when the number of checks processed per month is 100 checks.

$$a = 3^4 \cdot 5^2 \cdot 7$$
$$b = 2 \cdot 3^5 \cdot 5 \cdot 7^3$$

16. **C** Because a and b have common factors of 3^4, 5, and 7, the GCF of a and b is $3^4 \cdot 5 \cdot 7$.

17. **B** A number is divisible by 8 if the last three digits form a number that is divisible by 8. The numbers in (I) and (II) are divisible by 8 because 808 and 064 are divisible by 8. The number in (III) is not divisible by 8, because 548 is not divisible by 8. Thus, choice B is correct.

18. **C** From the question information, $a_{100} = a_1 + (100 - 1)d = a_1 + (99)d$, so you need the values of a_1 and d to determine a_{100}. From the information in (1), $a_5 = 30 = a_1 + 4d$, which (because you have two variables and only one equation) does not yield single values for a_1 and d, so (1) is NOT sufficient. From the information in (2), $a_{20} = 105 = a_1 + 19d$, which (because you have two variables and only one equation) does not yield single values for a_1 and d, so (2) also is NOT sufficient. Taking (1) and (2) together, you have two linear

equations and two variables, which you can solve simultaneously to determine values for a_1 and d, and you can use that solution to determine a_{100}. Therefore, BOTH statements TOGETHER are sufficient, but NEITHER statement ALONE is sufficient.

19. **D** Let n = the number of members in the club. From the question information, the number of possible outcomes is $n(n - 1)(n - 2)$. From the information in (1), you can determine that $n > 10$. Therefore, you know that n is at least 11, and the number of possible outcomes is at least $11(10)(9) = 990$. Thus, (1) is SUFFICIENT. From the information in (2), you can determine that n is 12, which you can substitute into $n(n - 1) \times (n - 2)$ to obtain $12(11)(10) = 1320$. Thus, (2) also is sufficient. Therefore, EACH statement ALONE is sufficient.

20. **C** Let t = the number of hours in which the two vehicles will be 390 miles apart, x = the speed of the first vehicle, and y = the speed of the second vehicle. Omitting the units, the equation $xt + yt = 390$ expresses the conditions given in the question, so $t = \dfrac{390}{x+y}$. From the information in (1), $x = 10 + y$, so $t = \dfrac{390}{x+y} = \dfrac{390}{(10+y)+y} = \dfrac{390}{10+2y}$, but without knowing the value of y, you cannot determine the value of $t = \dfrac{390}{10+2y}$. Therefore, (1) is NOT sufficient. From the information in (2), $yt = 180$, which implies that $t = \dfrac{180}{y}$, but without knowing the value of y, you cannot determine the value of $t = \dfrac{180}{y}$, so (2) is NOT sufficient. Taking (1) and (2) together, you can set the two expressions for t equal to each other, giving $\dfrac{390}{10+2y} = \dfrac{180}{y}$, which you can solve for y. Then you can determine the value of t, using either $t = \dfrac{390}{10+2y}$ or $t = \dfrac{180}{y}$. Therefore, BOTH statements TOGETHER are sufficient, but NEITHER statement ALONE is sufficient.

21. **B** Let c = the original cost of the exercise bike, m = the markup, and $s = c + m$ = the selling price. Then the markup is $\dfrac{m}{s} \cdot 100\%$ of the selling price. From the information in (1), $\dfrac{m}{s} \cdot 100\% = \dfrac{m}{450} \cdot 100\%$, but without knowing m, you cannot compute the percent, so (1) is NOT sufficient. From the information in (2), $m = 25\%c = 0.25c$ and $s = c + m = c + 0.25c = 1.25c$. Then $\dfrac{m}{s} \cdot 100\% = \dfrac{0.25}{1.25} \cdot 100\%$, which you can compute, so (2) is SUFFICIENT. Therefore, statement (2) ALONE is sufficient, but statement (1) alone is not sufficient.

22. **A** Using the information in (1), you can divide the sum by 3 to obtain the value of the middle integer. Using that value, you can obtain the values of the other two integers. Therefore, you have sufficient information to answer definitely "yes" or "no" as to whether $c > 40$, so (1) is SUFFICIENT. *Tip*: Notice that it is not necessary to perform calculations to answer the question posed. You should avoid taking time to do unnecessary calculations. However, just for your information, the three integers are 41, 42, and 43, all of which are greater than 40. The information in (2) lets you know the order of the three integers, but it does not provide sufficient information for you to

determine whether $c > 40$. So, (2) is NOT sufficient. Therefore, statement (1) ALONE is sufficient, but statement (2) alone is not sufficient.

23. **C** From the information in (1), you can determine that x is 2 or 5, the prime factors of 10. If x is 2, then the answer to the question posed is yes, but if x is 5, the answer is no. Thus, (1) is NOT sufficient. From the information in (2), you can determine that x is 2 or 7, the prime factors of 28. If x is 2, then the answer to the question posed is yes, but if x is 7, the answer is no. Thus, (2) is NOT sufficient. Taking (1) and (2) together, x is 2, which is also a factor of $2(10) + 1(28) = 20 + 28 = 48$. Therefore, BOTH statements together are sufficient, but NEITHER statement ALONE is sufficient.

24. **C** Make a rough sketch.

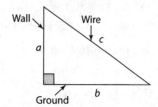

The wire makes a right triangle with portions a and b of the wall and ground, respectively. From the information in (1), you can determine that b is 9 feet, but without further information you cannot determine a, the distance up the wall. Thus, (1) is NOT sufficient. From the information in (2), you can determine that c is 15 feet, but without further information you cannot determine a, the distance up the wall. Thus, (2) is NOT sufficient. Taking (1) and (2) together, you have $b = 9$ feet and $c = 15$ feet. Because $9 = 3(3)$ and $15 = 3(5)$, you can use your knowledge of 3-4-5 triangles to determine a (or you can determine a using the Pythagorean theorem). Therefore, BOTH statements together are sufficient, but NEITHER statement ALONE is sufficient.

25. **D** Let $f =$ the number of female members in the club and $m =$ the number of male members in the club. Then from the question information, $f + m = 56$. From the information in (1), $\dfrac{m}{f} = \dfrac{3}{5}$, which is equivalent to $5m = 3f$. This equation and the equation $f + m = 56$ give you two linear equations with two variables, which you can solve simultaneously for a single value of f, so (1) is SUFFICIENT. From the information in (2), $\dfrac{m+4}{56+4} = \dfrac{5}{12}$, which you can solve for m. Then you can substitute the value of m into $f + m = 56$ to find f, so (2) also is SUFFICIENT. Therefore, EACH statement ALONE is sufficient.

PART 7

The GMAT Verbal Section

CHAPTER 12

GMAT Reading Comprehension Questions

Introduction

Like the rest of the GMAT's Verbal skills section, the Reading Comprehension section uses multiple-choice questions to measure your ability to read and comprehend the material presented. You'll be given a passage that can range from two paragraphs to five or more. The topic of the passage will be something of general interest—perhaps about the social sciences or the humanities—and you're not expected to bring any prior knowledge about it to the test. You're asked to read it carefully . . . but quickly, because you'll then need to read, contemplate, and answer three or four multiple-choice questions based on each passage. The computer you're taking the GMAT on will go to a split screen when you're in this section. The passage you need to read and use will stay on the left side, while the question you need to answer will be on the right. This is helpful, but remember, you'll still see only one question at a time, and once you confirm your answer, you can't go back.

You can expect to read quite a few passages on subjects taken from science, history, and the arts. You can also expect to see multicultural topics and for women to be well represented.

You can expect that about 15 of the Verbal skills' 50 or so questions will be Reading Comprehension. Some of the questions you'll be asked merely involve careful reading, as the answer will be contained within the passage. But some questions will ask you to infer—that is, to make assumptions based on the information presented in the reading. While you do get about a minute and three-quarters to answer each question, that timing doesn't include reading the passages, so, really, you have very little time to do all of that reading, thinking, and inferring (Sorry!).

There's one important note you need to know before you move on to the types of questions. Many standardized test prep books will advise you to read the questions in a Reading Comprehension section first and then save time by scanning the passage for the answers instead of reading it carefully first. Here, you don't have that option, we're sad to say. The questions appear one at a time, so all you can really do is pull up the first question and have it on the screen while you read the passage. Not much of a time saver!

We keep mentioning this, but it bears repeating: this is not a test you can skip around on. There's no way to skip over the Reading Comprehension section and come back to it after you've answered the other questions. That's one of the most difficult things about the test, because it goes against our instincts from other standardized tests.

The Different Kinds of Reading Comprehension Questions

Let's take a look at the types of questions you'll see in this section. First, you should know the directions that you'll see on the GMAT:

The questions in this group are based on the content of a passage. After reading the passage, choose the best answer to each question. Answer all questions following the passage on the basis of what is *stated or implied in the passage.*

That last part is important. Let's say you're an expert on penguins, and the passage you've been given to read is about penguins. Well, you can only answer the questions given based on what you read in the passage. No matter how much more you could add or how your additional knowledge might change the answer, please only use the reading passage's information!

Main Idea Questions

You've taken standardized tests before, so you know the drill. These questions test your ability to capture the thesis of a passage. Main idea questions (up next) are the most common of the Reading Comprehension questions, usually appearing right after the passage. Main idea questions might be worded like this:

- Which of the following statements most accurately captures the main point of the passage?
- Which of the following statements most accurately captures the central idea of the passage?
- The passage can best be described as which of the following?
- Of the following titles, which would be the most appropriate for the contents of this passage?

While you occasionally will come across a reading passage that explicitly states what its main idea is, it's more likely that you'll be required to use those inferring skills we mentioned earlier. The best place to look for the main idea are the first two sentences in the first paragraph, although it does sometimes appear at the end of the first paragraph, in the final paragraph, or—very rarely—in a middle paragraph.

If you can't find a clear thesis statement, it's helpful to ask yourself, "What is being discussed in this passage, and why?" The answer should point you to one of the choices given to the question. No matter what, since you know that you will likely be asked this question about nearly every passage, we think it's worthwhile to try to sum up the thesis before you read the questions. Then you can look for the answer that best matches what you've already arrived at. Inevitably, one of the answer choices will be a point from the passage—but not the *main* point. It's hard to not be tricked into choosing that answer, unless you've already determined the main idea.

Supporting Idea Questions

The second most common type of question is the supporting idea question. The test is seeking to measure how well you understand how an argument is built and supported. Being able to locate supporting ideas clearly helps show your skills. This type of question focuses on specific ideas or pieces of information presented in the passage. Sometimes you have to read the passage quite closely in order to find the answer. Questions of this type often look something like:

- According to the passage, Hong Kong regulators believe what about the stock market?
- According to the passage, HIV+ prevention programs have done what in Namibia?
- Which of the following statements best expresses the Confederates' outrage at Stewart's maneuvering?

The answers are almost always directly in the text, so no inferring is needed here. You should find the main nouns in the questions ("Hong Kong regulators" and "stock market," for example) by skimming the reading passage to locate them. The answer you're looking for should be within a couple of lines of their location. Sometimes the answer will be in a sentence that's been slightly paraphrased in an answer choice. At other times, you'll need to combine information from two or even three sentences to arrive at your answer. But, trust us, it is in there!

Inference Questions

Inference questions are just the opposite of supporting idea questions. Now you'll have to put together information to find an answer that's not there in black and white on your screen. This type of question deals with ideas that aren't in the passage, asking you to make a hop from the statements in the passage to a conclusion based on them. You have to *infer*, but to keep that inference relatively small: don't make a leap, remember, but a hop! Don't use any knowledge except that which is presented in the passage, and treat the information in the passage as if it is true even if you feel sure it isn't.

Inference questions often look something like this:

- Based on the information given in this passage, it can be reasonably inferred that Jefferson would approve of which amendment?
- The author of this passage would most likely agree with which of the following statements?
- Based on the contents of the passage, it can be inferred that an astrophysicist would be LEAST likely to observe a comet through which of the following methods?

Another kind of inference question is less about the logical conclusions that could be drawn from the passage and more about the author's purpose in writing the passage. For some people, these questions can be frustrating because logic tells them that we have no way of knowing why an author wrote a passage. Test-takers who feel that way must make a particular effort to push that conundrum out of their minds. Focus instead on the narrow view: what can we say the agenda or goal of the author might reasonably be deduced to be?

Inference questions are devious because they work on your instincts. You may feel sure that you know one of the answer choices is true, but if it's a leap and there's a hop available, don't get sucked in!

Usually, questions about the author's purpose focus on the main idea of the passage (aren't you glad you put that into words already?), but they may also look at the structure or tone of the passage. Some ask you to find the answer that best articulates what one could reasonably assume the next paragraph of the passage would say, had it been included. No matter what, make sure that your inference has clear support in the text. This sort of question might read like these:

- The author most likely mentions the opera *Otello* for what purpose?
- From the information presented in the final paragraph, it can be reasonably inferred that the author believes which of the following is true about Occam's theory?

Applying Information Questions

This type of question also asks you to do something more than find the answer in the passage and note it. You'll have to take the information given in the passage and apply it logically to a context outside of the passage. Again, you'll need to take a logical hop, since you'll need to be able to recognize the argument or idea from the text in a different context. These questions can be quite tricky; remember to stick to the passage and make the most logical choice you can. A few examples:

- Which of the following situations is most similar to the environmental situation described in the second paragraph?
- The medical test in the passage would most likely be helpful for which of the following groups?
- Johnson's reasoning, as presented in the passage, is most similar to which of the following lines of reasoning?

Logical Structure Questions

Exactly as they sound, these questions ask you to analyze the structure of the reading passage and to determine how the passage combines individual pieces into a cohesive whole. They usually require a blend of broad reading (the kind that helps you find the main idea) and focused reading (to identify those smaller parts). Questions that are about logical structure might look like this:

- The third paragraph plays what role in this passage?
- The author incorporates a quote from Shakespeare's *The Tempest* in lines 3–4 for what purpose?
- Which of the following most accurately describes the structure of the passage?

It might be helpful to approach a logical structure question as if you were going to write an Analytical Writing Assessment about the passage. What would you identify as the thesis? How about the premises?

Style and Tone Questions

This is the least common type of question you might encounter in the Reading Comprehension portion of the GMAT. In fact, you could take the entire test without bumping into a style and tone question. But, just in case, know that this type of question asks you to draw a conclusion about the author or the passage based on the author's use of language. The truth of the matter is that most of the reading passages on the test are far too dry to have any real tone or style; if you read a passage that has a little more zing to it, you can expect that you'll be asked a style and tone question.

The key to answering these questions is to find the words in the passage that point to a tone— look for those with both positive and negative connotations. A positive tone might appear in a phrase like "an auspicious beginning" or "a brilliant innovation," whereas a negative tone is clear from phrases like "an utter failure" and "a complete debacle." Don't worry too much about being asked to give a name to a very subtle or literary tone; the test sticks to broad styles in the answer choices, and in general the passages are fairly moderate in opinion. You're more likely to read something along the lines of "The author is guardedly enthusiastic about the innovation" than "The author raves with near-zeal about the innovation." If you can't find tone words, look for the overall feel of the article and trust your instinct: if you think the author is taking a dim view of the topic, he or she probably is. Style and tone questions will resemble these examples:

- The author's attitude toward international malaria prevention efforts could best be characterized as which of the following?
- Which of the following best describes the author's tone in the passage?
- Based on the statements in lines 30–35, which of the following could be inferred about the author's attitude toward Highland Cattle?

Be careful not to confuse your own opinion with the tone of a passage. If you detest going to the beach, and the passage is about the dangers of sun exposure, you might leap to the conclusion that the author is against going to the beach. But does the passage's tone really justify that opinion?

Problem-Solving Strategies

There are a few specific strategies you can use to approach the Reading Comprehension questions on the GMAT. We'll review them here, and you can attempt them in the problem-solving drills that close the chapter.

Strategic Reading

Now that you have an idea of what kind of questions you'll be asked in the Reading Comprehension section, we'll suggest a method you can follow to be successful in this section. First, skim/read the passage in one to two minutes. Focus on the main idea of the passage, and jot it down on scrap paper when you think you've found it. Also, ask yourself what the basic structure of the passage is, and think about what each paragraph does as part of that structure. You can also think in terms of keywords: if someone tapped you on the shoulder and asked you what the passage is about, what would you say?

> As tempting as it is to use a pen or pencil to mark up the passage when using our practice questions, we suggest you try to use a separate piece of paper instead. The GMAT will be on a computer screen, and you won't be able to write on that.

Remember that you are not being tested on anything but the three or four questions about the passage. At no point will you be asked to explain every idea in it or recall the entirety of the passage. Don't waste your time trying to master the entire thing. Just try to get a clear idea of what the passage is about. If you get to the end and feel lost, go back and try again.

Take a few notes as you read. Jot down that main idea if you find it. If you don't, try to put it into your own words at the end of your read-through. You should also number your paper to match the number of paragraphs (1–5 for a five-paragraph passage) and jot down a few words that capture each of the supporting paragraphs. If you see any words that point to the tone, you should jot those down too. And if there are any words that indicate a reversal in thinking (such as "However," or "On the other hand,"), you can make note of them, as well.

Focused Reading

Once you have a good grip on the passage, it's time to put that knowledge to work. You'll need to get more focused to answer the questions. Slow down and read the questions, their answer choices, and the relevant parts of the passage carefully. Make sure you understand the question, and reread the relevant parts of the passage until you're sure you have the right answer. The correct answer is always in the text!

The test-makers put a lot of time and energy into creating answer choices that look like they might be correct but, in fact, are wrong. After all, if it were easy to spot the wrong choices, the test would be pretty . . . easy. And it's not. Keep in mind that they also aren't above little tricks like using words that look similar but mean something different, or giving you a couple of choices that are *probably* true, plus one that is *definitely* true. The last one is the only one you want to click on, of course, but you're going to have to eliminate those near-misses first.

Look for the type of question being asked, because that will help you know what kind of answer to choose. If you recognize a question as being a main idea question, look back at your notes. What did you jot down for the main idea? Which answer choice most closely matches your note? There's your answer.

Supporting idea questions are almost always rooted in the text. When you run into one, find the specific place in the text that it's referring to and choose the answer choice that best matches. These questions have to be indisputable, so the answer is in the text somewhere. Find it and move on.

Inference and applying information questions require you to take a step back and think about the passage. The question should give you a specific subject matter; take a moment to think about what the passage has to say about it and to infer the larger message. Once you have that in mind, find the answer choice that best matches what you think. To put it simply: find the answer choice that has to be true if the statements in the passage are true.

If you hit a style and tone question—remember that these are only asked about passages that have a tone!—you probably jotted down a few telling words from the passage. Choose the answer that best matches, remembering that the moderate choice is usually the best.

Be Aware of How the GMAT Wants to Trick You

The Reading Comprehension section can drive you absolutely batty if you let it, because there's just so much room for subjectivity. How you read a passage will probably be quite different from how the person next to you in the testing center reads it. And neither of you are wrong, of course: it's just that reading is subjective. In order to create questions that have correct answers, the test-makers go out of their way to make sure that the other answers are definitely wrong (and not just a matter of opinion or reading). Here are two of the techniques that they might use:

- **Leaping Instead of Hopping.** You might recall that we encouraged you to take a hop when inferring, since the correct answer will not be found in the passage. The test-makers like to make a leap in one of the answer choices, hoping you'll choose it because it seems like it could be true (but isn't quite proven by the passage). Remember, stick as close as you can to the text. Choose the little jump instead of the big one. And never add in your outside knowledge!
- **Catching You Skimming.** Another popular trick is to offer you an answer that's clearly taken directly from the text, in the hope that you will recognize, choose it, and move on. The only problem is that you've chosen the correct answer to a different question! For example, the test might offer the thesis of the passage as an answer choice . . . but the question is about the supporting idea. Whoops! Don't get tricked: read carefully!

Reading Comprehension Drills

Now that you've been thoroughly indoctrinated into the Reading Comprehension section's ways, let's put that knowledge into practice. You'll find three sets of Reading Comprehension questions ahead, with 20 to 22 questions each. Use them to practice, and make sure you time yourself. It's a good idea to cover the questions so that you can only look at one at a time, just like on the test. After you complete each drill, check out the answers in the following section. Learn from your mistakes, and you'll be even better prepared for the GMAT!

Reading Comprehension Drill 1

Directions: Each of the reading comprehension questions is based on the content of a passage. After reading the passage, answer all questions pertaining to it on the basis of what is stated or implied in the passage. For each question, select the best answer of the choices given.

Among common errors still persisting in the minds of educated people, one which dies very hard is the theory that a dialect is an arbitrary distortion of the mother tongue, a willful mispronunciation of the sounds, and disregard of the syntax of a standard language. This comes of reading dialect stories by authors who have no personal knowledge of any dialect whatever, and who have never studied any language scientifically. All they have done, perhaps, is to have purchased the Dialect Glossary of some district, or maybe they have asked a friend to supply a little local coloring. Authors of this type put into the mouths of their dialect-speaking characters a kind of doggerel which their readers then run away with, believing it is a real, living, English dialect.

As a matter of fact, our English dialects exemplify the sound-laws of living speech and the historical development of an originally inflected language. But the field of English dialects offers other allurements besides those which attract the philologist and the grammarian. The language-specialist merely digs and quarries, as it were, in the bare soil and rock, where he finds rich ores amply sufficient to repay his pains and toil, but there remains plenty of room for the rest of us who are less laboriously inclined, and at every turn are enticing paths. The real charm lies in the fact that it is a "faire felde ful of folke," natural, homely, witty folk. The study of our English dialects may not only contribute to the advancement of knowledge, but also give us a clearer insight into the life and character of the British peasant and artisan, and so it will have achieved the aim and object of its existence.

Questions 1–3 refer to the passage above.

1. According to the passage, what does the author feel may have contributed to the misunderstanding of dialects?

   Ⓐ That plenty of room remains for the rest of us who are less laboriously inclined toward the study of dialects
   Ⓑ The willful mispronunciation of sounds by speakers of dialects
   Ⓒ Insufficient research and understanding on the part of authors who employ dialects for their characters' speech
   Ⓓ That educated people do not speak in dialect
   Ⓔ That a dialect is not a real, living language

2. The author is primarily concerned with

   (A) discussing different types of dialects
   (B) refuting a socioeconomic bias against dialects
   (C) making a case for the study of dialects in order to increase our understanding of them
   (D) berating authors who write in dialect
   (E) revealing new evidence

3. According to the passage, authors who put doggerel into the voices of their characters cause which of the following?

   (A) A belief that use of a dialect indicates low intelligence
   (B) A belief that real people do speak in doggerel
   (C) A belief that dialects offer allurements
   (D) A belief that dialects aren't worth studying
   (E) A belief that England's educational system is in decline

The Rev. Rose Fuller Whistler, in his *Annals of an English Family* (1887), writes that John le Wistler de Westhannye (1272–1307) was the founder of the family. Most of the Whistlers lived in Goring, Whitchurch, or Oxford, England, and are buried in many a church and churchyard of the Thames Valley.

The men were mostly soldiers and parsons. A few made names for themselves. The shield of Gabriel Whistler, of Combe, Sussex, is one of six in King's College Chapel, Cambridge. Anthony Whistler, poet, friend of Shenstone, belonged to the Whitchurch family. Dr. Daniel Whistler (1619–1684), of the Essex branch, was a Fellow of Merton, an original Fellow of the Royal Society, and a member and afterwards President of the College of Physicians. He fell under a cloud with the officials of the College of Physicians, and his portrait has been consigned to a back stairway of the Hall in Pall Mall. In the seventeenth century Francis Whistler was a settler of Virginia.

The American Whistlers are descended from John Whistler of the Irish branch. In his youth he ran away and enlisted. He received his discharge, eloped with Anna, daughter of Sir Edward Bishop or Bischopp, and, returning to America, settled at Hagerstown, Maryland. He again enlisted, this time in the United States army. He rose to the brevet rank of major and served in the war of 1812 against Great Britain. In 1815, upon the reduction of the army, Major John Whistler was retired. He died in 1817, at Bellefontaine, Missouri. Of his fifteen children, three sons are remembered as soldiers, and three daughters married army officers. George Washington, the most distinguished son, was the father of James Abbott McNeill Whistler.

Questions 4–7 refer to the passage above.

4. The primary purpose of the passage is to

   (A) give an overview of the forces that shaped the artist James Abbott McNeill Whistler

   (B) explain why James Abbott McNeill Whistler was proud of his eccentric family

   (C) lead into the proposal that James Abbott McNeill Whistler should be better known than he is

   (D) provide an overview of the interesting familial background of James Abbott McNeill Whistler

   (E) explain why the Whistler family came to be established in America

5. According to the passage, the James Abbott McNeill Whistler's family originally hails from what area of Britain?

   (A) Combe, Sussex

   (B) Goring, Whitchurch, and Oxford

   (C) Cambridge

   (D) Hagerstown

   (E) Shenstone

6. The purpose of the second paragraph of the passage is to

   (A) make it clear that Whistler came from good stock

   (B) include a few interesting anecdotes

   (C) prove that Whistler came by his artistic impulses from his genetic lineage

   (D) help readers understand that Whistler's ancestors were mostly soldiers and parsons with a few exceptions

   (E) show how exceptional Whistler was in comparison with his ancestry

7. What can be inferred from the passage regarding Whistler's ancestry?

   (A) Whistler was extremely proud of his family.

   (B) Whistler turned out to be the most remarkable of an already remarkable family.

   (C) If the Whistlers had not immigrated to America, his artistic talent wouldn't have been discovered.

   (D) Whistler's often painted his family and ancestors into his work.

   (E) Whistler's family is well documented.

Since the early 1800s, *neurasthenia* has referred to a mechanical weakness of the nerves, denoting a medical condition with the symptoms of anxiety, headaches, and depression. Because Americans were said to be particularly prone to neurasthenia—also called *nervosism*—it was sometimes called *Americanitis*, as well.

The exhaustion of the central nervous system's energy was said to be the cause of neurasthenia. And the cause of the exhaustion of that energy? "Civilization," one doctor explained succinctly. Others explained that urbanization and the increasingly competitive business environment were also to blame. Unsurprisingly, the condition was associated with the upper class and business professionals.

Freud blamed an "insufficient libidinal drive" as the cause of the condition, saying that neurasthenia had a toxic, even poisonous effect on people who had it. He drew a line between neurasthenia and neurotic anxiety, and while his findings on the latter are far better known, he was deeply interested in the treatment, through psychoanalysis, of both.

Questions 8–10 refer to the passage above.

8. A good title for this passage would be

    (A) Understanding Mental Health
    (B) The Uniquely American Mental Illness
    (C) Freud's Secondary Interest
    (D) Neurasthenia: Anxiety's Less-Known Twin
    (E) Neurasthenia and How to Treat It

9. According to the passage, another name for neurasthenia implies which of the following?

    (A) That the stresses that caused it were particularly prevalent in Americans
    (B) That Americans sought help for neurasthenia more often than any other nationality
    (C) That Americans had an "insufficient libidinal" drive
    (D) That American culture was far too stressful for most people
    (E) That America was more civilized than other countries at the time

10. According to the passage, for what illness is Freud's treatment better known?

    (A) Neurasthenia
    (B) Americanitis
    (C) Nervosism
    (D) Neurotic Anxiety
    (E) Depression

Who has not heard of the Vikings—the dauntless sea-rovers, who in the days of long ago were the dread of Northern Europe? These fierce fighting men came in their ships across the North Sea from Norway on more than one occasion to invade England. But they came once too often, and were thoroughly defeated at the Battle of Stamford Bridge, when, as will be remembered, Harald the Hard, King of Norway, was killed in attempting to turn his namesake, King Harold of England, off his throne.

Norwegian historians, however, do not say very much about this particular invasion. They prefer to dwell on the great deeds of another King Harald, who was called "Fairhair," and who began his reign some two hundred years earlier. This Harald the Fairhair was only a boy of ten years of age when he came to the throne, but he determined to increase the size of his kingdom, which was then but a small one, so he trained his men to fight, built grand new ships, and then began his conquests. Norway was at that time divided up into a number of districts or small kingdoms, each of which was ruled over by an Earl or petty King, and it was these rulers whom Harald set to work to subdue. He intended to make one united kingdom of all Norway, and he eventually succeeded in doing so. But he had many a hard fight; and if the Sagas, as the historical records of the North are called, speak truly, he fought almost continuously during twelve long years before he had accomplished his task, and even then he was only just twenty-one years of age.

Questions 11–14 refer to the passage above.

11. According to the passage, Harald the Fairhair's desire was to do what?

   (A) Train his men to fight
   (B) Overthrow King Harold of England
   (C) Fight continuously over twelve years
   (D) Get revenge on the English for their victory at the Battle of Stamford Bridge
   (E) Make one united kingdom of Norway

12. It can be inferred from the passage that Harald the Fairhair achieved his goal because

   (A) there is a united Norway still today
   (B) everyone had heard of the Vikings
   (C) every king that came after him took the name "the Fairhair" too
   (D) England and Norway are no longer at war
   (E) no one remembers the Battle of Stamford Bridge

13. The passage provides what information in support of the idea that Norwegian historians prize certain aspects of the country's history above others?

   (A) The story of King Harald the Fairhair is of more interest than the Battle of Stamford Bridge.
   (B) Vikings were called "sea-rovers."
   (C) Norway was divided into a number of districts.
   (D) English troops defeated Harald the Hard.
   (E) The sagas might not be historically accurate.

14. What can be concluded about the factual nature of the story of Harald the Fairhair?

   Ⓐ He was most likely mythical.
   Ⓑ He was probably a combination of several historical figures.
   Ⓒ Because the Sagas of Norway are most likely false, we cannot be sure he existed.
   Ⓓ If the Sagas are true, he was a Norwegian king of renown.
   Ⓔ In order to believe that Harald the Fairhair existed, one must believe that the stories of his near-miraculous exploits are true.

When Ada Lovelace was born in 1815, her birth was noted because of her famous father: Lord Byron. Her father separated from her mother, Anne Isabella Byron, just a month after Ada was born. He died when Ada was 8 years old. In order to guard against the mental illness Anne worried that Ada would inherit from her father, the mother encouraged the daughter to study mathematics and logic. This turned out to be the key to Ada's life: She would go on to achieve far more than was expected by a well-born lady of her time.

Chief among Ada's successes were her work on Charles Babbage's early mechanical general-purpose computer, which they called the "Analytical Engine." Notes that Ada made in developing the machine reveal what is widely believed to be an algorithm intended to be performed by the engine. As the algorithm became known by mathematicians, its existence has given rise to the belief that Ada was the world's first computer programmer.

Questions 15–17 refer to the passage above.

15. Which of the following can reasonably be said to be an accurate depiction of the author's attitude toward Ada Lovelace?

   Ⓐ Grateful amazement
   Ⓑ Awe at her unexpected accomplishments
   Ⓒ Pride in her accomplishments
   Ⓓ Surprise at the course her life took
   Ⓔ Respect at her achievements

16. According to the passage, Ada Lovelace's mother encouraged her interest in mathematics for which of the following reasons?

   Ⓐ Ada already showed a knack for developing algorithms.
   Ⓑ Anne hoped to keep Ada from developing the mental illness that plagued her father.
   Ⓒ She wanted to keep Ada distracted from mourning her father.
   Ⓓ Ada showed signs of becoming a poet.
   Ⓔ Ada showed signs of mental illness.

17. A good title for this passage would be

   (A) Poets' Surprising Progeny
   (B) She Could Have Been a Poet
   (C) Greatness Is in the Blood
   (D) Ada Lovelace: Inventor of the Computer
   (E) She Wrote the Algorithm That Changed the World

We have been used to considering early Christian history and primitive Christian art as matters of secondary importance, and hardly worthy the attention of the classical student. Thus, none of the four or five hundred volumes on the topography of ancient Rome speaks of the basilicas raised by Constantine; of the church of S. Maria Antiqua, built side by side with the Temple of Vesta, the two houses of worship dwelling together as it were, for nearly a century; of the Christian burial-grounds; of the imperial mausoleum near S. Peter's; of the porticoes, several miles in length, which led from the center of the city to the churches of S. Peter, S. Paul, and S. Lorenzo; of the palace of the Caesars transformed into the residence of the Popes. Why should these constructions of monumental and historical character be expelled from the list of classical buildings? And why should we overlook the fact that many great names in the annals of the empire are those of members of the Church, especially when the knowledge of their conversion enables us to explain events that had been, up to the latest discoveries, shrouded in mystery?

It is a remarkable fact that the record of some of these events should be found, not in church annals, calendars, or itineraries, but in passages in the writings of pagan annalists and historians. It seems that when the official *feriale*, or calendar, was resumed, after the end of the Christian persecutions, preference was given to names of those confessors and martyrs whose deeds were still fresh in the memory of the living, and of necessity little attention was paid to those of the first and second centuries, whose acts either had not been written down, or had been lost during the persecutions.

Questions 18–20 refer to the passage above.

18. The passage is primarily concerned with

   (A) contrasting the lives of Roman Christians with that of Roman pagans
   (B) questioning why history has not better captured the lives of early Christians in Rome
   (C) explaining what a *feriale* was and how it was inclusive of Pagans
   (D) showing that there were many early Christians in Rome
   (E) accusing Roman historians as biased against Christians

19. According to the passage, what happened to the Palace of the Caesars?

    - (A) It became the residence of the Popes.
    - (B) The Vatican took it over.
    - (C) It was destroyed and the Vatican City was built in its place.
    - (D) The people of Rome gave it to the Pope.
    - (E) It is directly across the street from the Church of S. Lorenzo.

20. According to the passage, each of the following is proof of the presence of early Christians in Rome, EXCEPT:

    - (A) The basilicas raised by Constantine
    - (B) The imperial mausoleum near St. Peter's
    - (C) The foundation of the Vatican City
    - (D) The church of S. Maria Antiqua
    - (E) Christian burial grounds

Answers

1. **C** This question is a supporting idea question. You need to scan the passage for where a supporting idea is found. Several of the provided answers directly quote from the passage, making this a tricky question! However, the correct answer, C, is not a direct quote. Yet it is the only answer choice that refers directly to a supporting idea of the passage.

2. **C** This question asks you to infer the author's purpose, and it is also a variation on the main idea question. A can be immediately eliminated, as types of dialects are not discussed. D is the opposite of what the author intends. While B could be inferred to be part of the author's agenda, and E could be a broad statement about her goals, neither is as satisfactory as C, which best fits the end of the passage.

3. **B** This question asks you to look back into the passage to find a supporting idea. B is the answer clearly indicated in the passage. The answer choices provided slow you down by offering the same opening ("A belief that . . ."). Answers D and E are too broad in their inferring (remember, a hop, not a leap!). C merely takes a quote from the passage and presents it in the hope that you'll leap upon it as correct since it is a quote. And A alludes to other arguments presented in the passage but is not the best answer.

4. **D** This is the only answer that is fully supported by the passage provided. A and C might turn out to be true, should more of the passage be available, but there's not enough information provided to justify the leap that inferring those answers would require. Conversely, E is too narrow: while several of the sentences explain why the Whistlers came to live in America, the rest of the passage covers much more information than that. And B is unsupported by the passage, which doesn't consider Whistler's view at all.

5. **B** All of the places mentioned in the answer choices are taken from the passage, so you simply have to read it carefully to ascertain that B is the correct answer. By the way, notice that D isn't even in Britain!

6. **D** This is the only answer fully supported by the passage. B is potentially correct, except that one-line descriptions of a few ancestors don't quite meet the criteria for an "anecdote." A, C, and E might be what the author is up to, but it's a leap too far to justify these based on the passage given. D is the best (and safest) answer.

7. **E** Alas, the least-interesting conclusion is the only one that can truly be justified. The extent of the information provided by the author shows that Whistler's family tree was well documented. The other answers all require a leap of logic, or for the reader to bring outside knowledge to bear (which, of course, you know never to do). It's possible that B is true, but E is more likely to be true.

8. **D** is the best answer (although one could argue it isn't a great title!). Notice that this is a way of asking a main idea question. A is far too broad, and both B and C take a small element of the passage and blow it up to be the main point. E seems like it could be right, but a careful reader will have noted that there's nothing in the passage about treatment. D is left.

9. **A** is the best answer for this inferring question. It is reasonable to infer that the stresses that were believed to have caused the disorder were particularly prevalent in Americans. C, D, and E all employ flawed logic, applying other facts that are true about the disorder as though they must be true for Americans. B might be true but is not justified by the passage, which does not provide any other facts about the nationality of patients seeking treatment.

10. **D** This is a supporting idea question. You must read through the passage to find the answer, D, that is supplied there. The other answer choices are mentioned in the passage but are incorrect as an answer to this question.

11. **E** This is a main idea question (although it looks a bit like a supporting idea question since it asks about a fact). The answer choices provided all come from the passage, so it's up to you to read it carefully enough to be able to tell that E is the only answer that fits the question.

12. **A** This is an inference question. C isn't addressed at all in the passage, and E calls for the kind of speculation that cannot be inferred. While D is true, it seems a bit of a stretch to attribute this to Harald. B can be tempting—after all, it refers to the opening of the passage—but it doesn't connect to Harald's stated goal. A is the best choice. By the way, you might be thinking that this question pretty much gives away the answer to the prior question (11). Yes, it does, but remember, you can't go back on the test!

13. **A** This is another hybrid inference/supporting idea question, in which you are asked to find the best support for an inference. B, C, and D are easy to eliminate. They are correct facts from the passage but have little to do with how Norwegian historians are said to present the country's history. E is an inference taken from the text, but it requires too big a leap into asserting that the historians willfully pretend the sagas are historically correct. That isn't justified by the passage.

14. **D** This is a question of logic so you must find the most logical answer. A and B are not justified by the passage, which treats Harald the Fairhair as a real person. You'd only choose those if you had not read carefully or if your outside experiences cause you to question the source of the stories. C supposes the exact opposite of the assumption the author makes in the passage. E sounds logical, so it's tempting, but it sets up an "if . . . then" statement that isn't justified by the passage.

15. **E** This is a question about tone. Hopefully, while reading the passage you noticed that there are a few words that gesture toward the author's tone, such as the closing phrase, "an idea that's difficult to dispute." If you're thinking that phrase seems rather tame, yes, indeed. Remember that tone is often very subtle, although the answer choices may seem to want you to infer something far more passionate. Notice the use of "amazement" in A, "awe" in B, and "pride" in C. It is possible that the author feels this way about Ada Lovelace, but there's nothing in the passage that justifies the use of those extreme words. That leaves D, which could be correct. Tone questions can feel very subjective, and it's possible that the author feels surprise (as you might) when reading about Lovelace's accomplishments. However, this would be very difficult to prove. Only E is justified, as the passage is suffused with the respectful tone the author uses when discussing the subject.

16. **B** It's a straight-up supporting idea question. We simply don't know enough about Ada to choose D or E. While A and C might be true, you'd have to make a leap in order to choose them, which isn't necessary since B is obviously true and proven in the text.

17. **E** is the best answer. A could be true if the passage was longer, but since we read about only one poet's child, it seems to be a stretch. (By the way, notice the grammar of that title—it indicates more than one poet.) B seems limiting (yes, she could have been a poet, but there's no indication in the passage that she wanted to, nor had any aptitude for it). C could work but seems quite broad. And D is simply incorrect. So that leaves E as the best answer.

18. **B** is the best answer. This is a main idea question, so you must decide what you think the author's purpose in this passage is. A is not sustained by the passage, which contains no such comparison, whereas C refers directly to the passage, but to a small portion of it. D doesn't go far enough—the author does show that there were many early Christians in Rome, but goes further than that. And E is too extreme; the tone is much more restrained than "accusing."

19. **A** This is a factual question. You need to read the passage carefully to find the answer. E can be eliminated (although S. Lorenzo is mentioned in the passage, so don't be fooled). B, C, and D all make assumptions about what happened when the Palace became the Pope's residence. B, in particular, sounds very likely. But only A actually expresses what's in the passage.

20. **C** Vatican City is never mentioned in the passage. This is a fact-finding question that requires you to read the passage and answer choices carefully. Notice that the question capitalizes "EXCEPT." Don't skim past this helpful clue!

Reading Comprehension Drill 2

Directions: Each of the reading comprehension questions is based on the content of a passage. After reading the passage, answer all questions pertaining to it on the basis of what is stated or implied in the passage. For each question, select the best answer of the choices given.

Benjamin Banneker was born in Maryland in 1731, the son of a woman who was a freed slave, and a free-born father. Largely self-taught, he did formally study with a Quaker friend until he was old enough to work on his family's farm. By 1788, again with the help of neighboring Quakers, Banneker had begun to study astronomy. The next year, he calculated a solar eclipse. Soon, Banneker found work with a surveyor, who was marking the territory that would eventually become the original District of Columbia. He used his astronomical observations to mark a starting location for the surveyors, and maintained a clock that related the positions of the stars to points on the ground.

Poor health and a long delay in the surveying kept Banneker from staying with the project. Instead he turned his attention to further astronomical calculations, eventually publishing a series of almanacs which were hugely popular. These accurately predicted both coming solar and lunar eclipses. That Banneker was an African-American scientist in a time period that routinely attributed low intelligence and potential to his race only makes his achievements more remarkable.

Questions 1–4 refer to the passage above.

1. The passage suggests that in order for Benjamin Banneker to achieve his success as an astronomer, the following was likely true:

   (A) The Quakers must have given him a great deal of help in calculations.
   (B) He most likely did not have many demands on his time while working for the surveyors.
   (C) Because of prejudice against his race, he had to have shown great determination.
   (D) He started studying stars from a very early age.
   (E) The surveyors must have taught him how to use the tools of their trade.

2. The passage suggests what about Banneker's study of astronomy?

   (A) He had been interested in the stars since he was a child.
   (B) He was well into adulthood before he began.
   (C) He was a young man when he began.
   (D) His parents sparked his interest in astronomy.
   (E) He learned astronomy because he needed a job with the surveyors.

3. In the context of the passage as a whole, the second paragraph serves primarily to

    Ⓐ explain why Banneker turned away from surveying as an occupation
    Ⓑ elaborate on Banneker's great success as a published author
    Ⓒ show how Banneker outgrew his homespun beginnings
    Ⓓ discuss how Banneker transformed his knowledge of astronomy into a new
       pursuit
    Ⓔ point out that Banneker's success was solely the result of luck

4. The passage LEAST supports the inference that

    Ⓐ it was unusual for a free black man to be a scientist in the 1700s
    Ⓑ Quakers were taught scientific reasoning in their schools
    Ⓒ surveyors needed good astronomers on their payroll
    Ⓓ Washington DC was a planned city
    Ⓔ astronomy was of little interest to the general reading public

As for what to wear on a camping trip, a good deal of nonsense has been written about
"strong, coarse woolen clothes." You do not want coarse woolen clothes. Fine woolen
cassimere of medium thickness for coat, vest and pantaloons, with no cotton lining.
Color: slate gray or dead-leaf (either is good). Two soft, thick woolen shirts; two pairs of
fine, but substantial, woolen pants; two pairs of strong woolen socks or stockings; these
are what you need, and all you need in the way of clothing for the woods, excepting hat
and boots.

Boots are best—providing you do not let yourself be inveigled into wearing a pair
of long-legged heavy boots with thick soles, as has been often advised by writers who
knew no better. Heavy, long-legged boots are a weary, tiresome encumbrance on a
hard tramp through rough woods. Even moccasins are better. Light boots are best.
They will weigh considerably less than half as much as the clumsy, costly boots usually
recommended for the woods; and the added comfort must be tested to be understood.

The proper covering for head and feet is no slight affair, and will be found worth
some attention. Be careful that the boots are not too tight, or the hat too loose. The
above rig will give the hiker one shirt, one pair of drawers and a pair of socks to carry
as extra clothing. A soft, warm sleeping bag, open at the ends, and just long enough to
cover the sleeper, with an oblong square of water-proofed cotton cloth 6 × 8 feet, will
give warmth and shelter by night and will weigh together five or six pounds. This, with
the extra clothing, will make about eight pounds of dry goods to pack over carries,
which is enough. Probably, also, it will be found little enough for comfort.

Questions 5–7 refer to the passage above.

5. A good title for the passage might be

    Ⓐ A Hat Is Important
    Ⓑ Careful Outfitting Will Improve Your Hike
    Ⓒ Sleeping Bags Are Optional
    Ⓓ Skiing Takes Preparation
    Ⓔ A Guide to the Appalachian Trail

6. In the context of the passage as a whole, the second paragraph serves primarily to

    Ⓐ reiterate the points made in the first paragraph
    Ⓑ alert the reader to information that may save his or her life
    Ⓒ make clear the importance of proper footwear
    Ⓓ introduce the evidence that hiking can be very dangerous
    Ⓔ anticipate possible arguments readers might make against proper footwear

7. The passage suggests which of the following?

    Ⓐ Clothing of slate gray or brown is appropriate.
    Ⓑ The reader should purchase the heaviest boots available.
    Ⓒ A whistle is a good accessory to carry at all times.
    Ⓓ A 12-foot square of cotton should be carried.
    Ⓔ Word should be left about one's plans before departing.

The Siege of Godesberg kicked off the Cologne War in 1583. Godesberg was an important fortress, dating from the early 13th century. The Bavarians began the siege in hopes of controlling Godesberg, and thus the roads leading to and from Bonn, Cologne's capital city, as well as the Rhine valley. It seemed to be an impossible task, as the fortress was believed to be impenetrable.

The Bavarians shot cannonball after cannonball into the fortress to no effect. Finally, they were able to tunnel through the basalt core of the mountain on which Godesberg sat, and blew up part of the fortress. Casualties were heavy on the defenders' side, but the resulting rubble blocked a clear path for the Bavarians' further assault. The siege wore on for nearly a month, until the attackers were able to enter the fortress through the latrine system. The commander in Godesberg negotiated a safe passage for himself, his wife, and his lieutenant, leaving the other defenders to their fate. Most were killed. Bonn fell to the Bavarians soon after.

Questions 8–11 refer to the passage above.

8. The passage suggests that the people of Godesberg were

   (A) unaware that their fortress was under attack
   (B) surprised by the arrival of the Bavarians
   (C) complacent about the fortress's supposed impenetrability
   (D) awaiting reinforcements from Bonn
   (E) unable to rouse a substantial defense after their fortress was partially blown up

9. The primary purpose of the passage is to

   (A) explain why there is still animosity between the Bavarians and Germans to this day
   (B) give an overview of the Siege of Godesberg
   (C) connect the Siege of Godesberg to the other events of the Cologne War
   (D) point out that one man's lack of valor can affect hundreds of lives
   (E) reveal a major turning point in the history of Bonn

10. Which of the following, if true, would most weaken the explanation of the Siege of Godesberg?

   (A) The entirety of the passage is based on historical documents.
   (B) Historians disagree about whether the attackers arrived through the latrine system.
   (C) Bonn never produced significant economic help to the Bavarians.
   (D) Newly discovered records from Godesberg indicate that the residents began to negotiate a peaceful takeover shortly after the Bavarians arrived.
   (E) Dental records indicate that a number of people living in the fortress died from scurvy.

11. According to the passage, Godesberg was built when?

   (A) In the 1200s
   (B) In the 1300s
   (C) Before Bonn
   (D) After 1800
   (E) By 1000

Helium, the most abundant element after hydrogen, is also the most stable element, with the lowest melting and boiling points. It exists as a gas except under the most extreme conditions; when temperatures near absolute zero, helium is a liquid.

Many people do not realize that helium is a non-renewable resource. For those who think that the most critical use of helium is for balloons, helium's fixed amount may not be a concern. However, helium is used for much more than children's birthday parties. It is used in essential medical diagnostic equipment such as MRIs. National defense applications include rocket engine testing and surveillance craft. Helium is used to cool thermographic cameras and equipment used by search and rescue teams. Various industries use helium to detect gas leaks in their products, including manufacturers of aerosol products, tires, refrigerators, fire extinguishers, and air conditioners. Also, cutting-edge space science and research requires helium. NASA uses helium to keep hot gases and ultra-cold liquid fuel separated during lift off of rockets.

Given the many uses of helium, it's not surprising that the U.S. government has taken an interest in preserving the element. The Federal Helium Reserve is a self-sustaining and profit-making branch of the U.S. Department of Interior's Bureau of Land Management. Last year, it returned over $400,000 per day to the U.S. Treasury.

Questions 12–15 refer to the passage above.

12. The passage mentions each of the following industries that use helium EXCEPT:

     (A) manufacturers of aerosol products
     (B) manufacturers of tires
     (C) manufacturers of balloons
     (D) manufacturers of fire extinguishers
     (E) manufacturers of air conditioners

13. The second paragraph plays what role in the passage?

     (A) It presents the strongest argument for why helium use should be carefully monitored.
     (B) It expands the hypothesis that helium is a little-understood element.
     (C) It refutes readers' belief that helium is a dangerous chemical compound.
     (D) It reveals helium's secret use in the NASA rocket program.
     (E) It provides background information relevant to the argument that use of helium should be severely curtailed.

14. The author's attitude toward the use of helium can best be described as

     (A) angry and concerned
     (B) factual and illuminating
     (C) concerned and uneasy
     (D) ambivalent and questioning
     (E) engaged and active

15. Which branch of the federal government oversees the sale and use of helium in the United States?

    (A) The U.S. Treasury
    (B) NASA
    (C) The Department of Science
    (D) The Bureau of Land Management
    (E) The federal government

In the hopes of helping employees arrive at brilliant, innovative ideas, many companies have embraced the technique of brainstorming. "Say anything!" is the mantra in these meetings, in which everyone from the CEO to the intern gathers to blurt out ideas for the next innovation. Surely, the thinking goes, if we throw enough spaghetti at the wall, something will stick?

Well, no, as it turns out. Research shows that such measures may not work—regularly, or at all. Instead, scientists are increasingly convinced that what does work is a clear understanding of how thoughts link up. Knowing that A leads to B leads to C may seem rather simple, sure, but it's a better reflection of how our brains work than the brainstorming model. Creativity is a series of small steps: one thought leads to another, linked thought. Little by little, this inching forward might eventually lead to an innovative idea.

Thus, instead of starting a meeting by asking everyone to throw out any idea that comes to mind, it's probably more beneficial to give people a starting point. Where's the next logical step from there? Or, work backwards: if this is where you want to end up, what would be the step before, and the step before that? The process may be less exciting, but there will be less spaghetti on the floor when you're done!

Questions 16–19 refer to the passage above.

16. Which of the following statements best summarizes the main idea of the passage?

    (A) Brainstorming doesn't work.
    (B) Understanding how thoughts link up can lead to better ways of developing new ideas.
    (C) Innovative ideas take time.
    (D) Only shoddy managers would ask their staff to brainstorm.
    (E) More research is needed to understand how thinking works.

17. The relationship between linked thoughts and innovation is most similar to which of the following?

    (A) The relationship between research and a doctoral thesis
    (B) The relationship between a driver and a car
    (C) The relationship between bread and a bakery
    (D) The relationship between a wild turkey and a domesticated chicken
    (E) The relationship between scientific research and scientific experimentation

18. The author's attitude toward brainstorming can best be described as which of the following?

    Ⓐ Utterly dismissive
    Ⓑ Supportive
    Ⓒ Abusive
    Ⓓ Skeptical
    Ⓔ Uninterested

19. The comparison of brainstorming to throwing spaghetti at a wall is meant to emphasize which of the following?

    Ⓐ The messiness of brainstorming
    Ⓑ That pasta must be cooked correctly to taste good
    Ⓒ That disorder sometimes yields results
    Ⓓ That brainstorming can involve a lot of failure to yield success that sticks
    Ⓔ That, as with cooking, brainstorming improves the more one does it

The Eiffel Tower, completed in 1889, makes the rest of Paris look like a toy landscape. It stands alone in the center of the city, commanding all viewers to look and marvel at it. What's truly remarkable is that the tower—now widely hailed as the symbol of Paris—was first greeted with skepticism.

    It was designed to serve as the entrance to the World's Fair that marked the 100th anniversary of the French Revolution. Over 100 artists competed for the right to build the monument, but the architect Alexandre-Gustave Eiffel won. His design used an innovative metal armature which employed more than 18,000 pieces of iron and 2.5 million rivets. Building it took over 2 years, and when they were finished, the Tower was the tallest structure in the world, an honor it held until 1930 when the Chrysler Building opened in New York.

Questions 20–22 refer to the passage above.

20. The last sentence of the first paragraph reveals a flaw in the passage. Which of the following best describes that flaw?

    Ⓐ It presents unsubstantiated facts.
    Ⓑ It confuses the flow of the paragraph.
    Ⓒ It presents the author's personal opinion.
    Ⓓ It misunderstands a quoted text.
    Ⓔ It presents a key idea that is not explored.

21. According to the passage, what was the Eiffel Tower originally designed to do?

   Ⓐ Serve as the entrance to the World's Fair
   Ⓑ Celebrate the 100th Anniversary of the French Revolution
   Ⓒ Represent Alexandre-Gustave Eiffel's skills
   Ⓓ Represent Paris in the imagination of the world
   Ⓔ Draw tourists to Paris

22. A good title for this passage might be

   Ⓐ Controversial Beauty
   Ⓑ The Many Amazing Creations of Eiffel
   Ⓒ The Beginnings of a Legend: The Eiffel Tower
   Ⓓ Paris Looks Tiny from Here
   Ⓔ Innovation Should Be Rewarded

Answers

1. **C** is the best answer to this inferring question. The only answer that finds support is the one that refers to the last sentence in the passage. In fact, C restates that sentence. A seems a bit condescending, never a good choice. And B, D, and E might be true, but there's no reason to be sure that they are. A good hint is that if several answers seem equally likely to be possibly correct, none of them are the right choice.

2. **B** If you reread the passage, you'll note that it states that "by 1788" Banneker had begun to study the stars. There's no other indication about when in his life he became interested or began his study, nor about who or what prompted him to do so. So, while this seems like it is an inferring question, it's actually factual. You just have to read carefully to find the fact that answers the question. A, C, D, and E are not supported by the passage (and A, again, has a hint of condescension to it).

3. **D** is the best answer to this structural question. A and B refer to information presented in the passage, but neither is the main purpose of the paragraph. C and E make leaps in logic that are not supported by the passage.

4. **E** This is a question of logic, and a tricky one. Notice how the question is worded so that you must think of the LEAST likely answer. When this is the case, you must consider all of the answers and choose the one that has the least support from the passage. A, C, and D can be eliminated since they contradict the inferences one makes by reading the passage. B seems a little more tempting, but a read-through of the passage would remind you that there's no indication that Quakers avoided science in their schools. Remember, don't bring outside knowledge or suspicions to the GMAT. That leaves E, which is directly contradicted by the phrase "hugely popular." If the almanacs were hugely popular, then the general public was likely quite interested in astronomy.

5. **B** is the best answer. The passage doesn't really explain what activity is being prepared for, but the way it reads makes it clear that it involves being outside. Since you don't know if it's for skiing (D) or hiking the Appalachian Trail (E), you can eliminate those answers. A and C are supported by the text, but they refer to minor points whereas a title should be more general. Given the choices, then, B is the best.

6. **C** This is another structural question. You must consider what purpose the second paragraph serves in the passage. It is not making the same point as in the first paragraph (A), nor anticipating arguments that readers might make against footwear (E). B and D seem to be saying the same thing, which is always a good indication that neither can be right. That leaves C as the best answer.

7. **A** is the best answer for this fact-finding question. C and E sound like good advice for hikers but are not mentioned in the passage. B directly contradicts the passage's advice, while D misstates the size of the cloth suggested. All that is required for success here is a careful rereading of the passage!

8. **E** is the best choice. You must infer the most likely answer, being careful to stick to the facts. You know from the passage that heavy casualties affected the defenders after the explosion, so it's a small hop to assume that they were severely affected in being able to defend the fortress. The other answers are either unsupported by the text (A, B, and D) or require a leap (C) that cannot be proven by the text.

9. **B** The passage is a quick overview of the Siege. It does not connect to the rest of Bonn's history (E) or explain how it connects to the rest of the war, as in C. While you might derive a lesson about valor, D, the rest of the passage does not help to prove this point. As for A, there's not enough here to know what the purpose of the passage was in a larger piece.

10. **D** This is a question of logic, which requires you to speculate on which answer choice, if true, would provide the most logical reason to find the explanation of the siege weak. A would only strengthen the explanation, while B and E affect only a small part of the explanation, not the entire passage. That leaves C and D. Go ahead and try them out—which, if true, affects the passage the most? D is the only answer.

11. **A** This is a fact-finding question, and a tricky one to boot. The test-makers are hoping that you'll be eager to move on to the next passage, and thus will select B based on remembering a "13" in your reading. But, of course, the 13th century is the 1200s. The other answers are equally wrong except for A.

12. **C** While children's party balloons are mentioned in the passage, and you surely associated helium with balloons, there's no mention that balloon manufacturers use helium (and, if you think about it, why would they?). A, B, D, and E are directly referred to in the text. Basically, this supporting idea question just wants to make you work hard to arrive at a simple answer.

13. **A** is the best answer to this logical structure question. You must decide what the second paragraph is doing in the essay. A makes the most sense, because while E seems correct at first, it misstates the passage's goal. B describes the first paragraph, while C is, again, incorrect about the purpose of the passage. As for D, the word "secret"—so dramatic!—gives away the unlikelihood of that being the answer. There's no "secret" in this passage.

14. **B** This is a question of tone. Always try to err on the side of reasonableness. The GMAT doesn't like extreme emotions. That makes B the best answer, especially since the passage isn't really presenting an argument or a call to action. That eliminates A and C. D is a more moderate choice, but there doesn't seem to be much ambivalence in the passage. E is closer, since the writer does seem to be engaged—but what does "active" even mean? B is the better choice.

15. **D** The first two answers, A and B, refer to other organizations mentioned in the passage, but which do not oversee the use and sale of helium. C is a made-up department (perhaps the test-makers are hoping you'll guess it in desperation) whereas E repeats a portion of the question. Obviously, this factual question could fool you if you don't take the time to reread and guess, incorrectly, at the right answer.

16. **B** is the best answer. It is a little unusual in its wording, but a moment's consideration should tell you that this question is a main idea, or thesis, question. E seems likely to be true but is not addressed by the passage (don't bring outside knowledge in!). A and C are reasonable inferences from the passage (although A is a little strong in wording) but neither is the main idea. That leaves D, which is far too bold for the GMAT.

17. **A** This is a kind of logic question that asks you to see the relationship given in another set of examples. The best way to solve this sort of question is to put the given relationship in words. In this case, innovation is derived from linked thoughts. Now, test all of the answer choices. B can't be right, since a car isn't derived from a driver. A bakery isn't derived from bread (C) nor is a domesticated chicken derived from a wild turkey as in D. It's possible that scientific experimentation is derived from scientific research as E offers, but the relationship doesn't have to run that way. Give it a maybe. That leaves A, and we can definitely say that a doctoral thesis is derived from research. It's the better answer, so drop E and go with A.

18. **D** This is another question of tone. Again, it's always best to drop the most extreme answers. That eliminates A and C. This passage questions brainstorming, so B (*supportive*) doesn't seem right. E, *uninterested*, also seems off, since the passage's author is, by default, interested in brainstorming. That leaves D as the best answer. The author is indeed *skeptical* about brainstorming's validity.

19. **D** is the best answer, here. B can be eliminated as silly. A, C, and E are relatively positive views of brainstorming, whereas you know that the author's purpose is, at least somewhat, to suggest that there are better ways to think than brainstorming. That leaves D, which shows that brainstorming is inefficient and, at least at times, unproductive.

20. **E** The last sentence in the first paragraph indicates that the Tower was controversial, and its placement indicates that this idea will be explored, but the rest of the passage does not refer to that idea again. Thus, in this logic question, E is the best answer. A is the second-best choice, but whether this could be considered an "unsubstantiated fact" is debatable. B is wrong; there's no break in the flow of the text. C cannot be correct either, as there's no reason why the author cannot present his or her opinion. That leaves D, and there's no quoted material in the text at all.

21. **A** This is a straightforward supporting idea question, asking only that you read carefully enough (or, if needed, reread!) to be able to point to the purpose of the tower, which was to serve as the entrance to the World's Fair. B refers to what the Fair itself commemorated, while C, D, and E are possibly other ideas the builders had about the Tower but are not referenced in the passage.

22. **C** is the best answer. A refers to the controversy briefly mentioned in the passage. However, if you recollect the prior question (which, of course, you wouldn't be able to go back to reread), you'll know that a flaw in the passage is that this controversy isn't explained. E sounds like an argument that isn't made in this passage, and B is too broad: the passage only details Eiffel's tower, without the rest of his creations. D has potential, but it's a little whimsical, even literary. Remember, you're taking the GMAT, so straightforward is always the best bet.

Reading Comprehension Drill 3

Upon reaching the charming home of a friend in Massachusetts last June, almost the first thing I saw was a pair of purple crow blackbirds in trouble. First arose a medley of odd husky tones, clamorous baby cries, and excited oriole voices, with violent agitation of the leaves of a tall elm, ending with the sudden exit of a blackbird, closely followed by a pair of Baltimore orioles. The pursued flew leisurely across the lawn, plainly in no haste, and not at all with the air of the thief and nest robber he is popularly supposed to be. Clearly the elm belonged by bird custom to the orioles.

The blackbird has no secrets in his life; the whole world is welcome to know his affairs, and in fact he proclaims them loudly himself. It was easy to see that he had anxiety enough of his own just then, without thinking of disturbing his neighbors, for he was engaged in the task of introducing his young family to the world.

If the young blackbirds escape the dangers peculiar to the nest, the devouring jaws of squirrel or owl, the hands of the egg thief, being shaken out by the wind, smothered by an intrusive cow-bunting, or orphaned by the gun of a "collector"; if, neither stolen, eaten, thrown out, nor starved, he arrives at the age that his wings begin to stir and force him out of the leafy green tent of his birth, a new set of dangers meet him at the door. He may entangle himself in a hair of the nest-lining, and hang himself at the very threshold of life—a not uncommon occurrence; or he may safely reach the nearest twig and from there fall and break his neck—not a rare accident; he may be attacked by a bird who questions his right to be on the tree; he may fly, and, not reaching his goal, come to the ground, an easy prey to any prowler.

Questions 1–4 refer to the passage above.

1. The author of the passage is primarily concerned with

   (A) painting a vivid image of nature
   (B) giving readers insight into why the life of a baby blackbird is treacherous
   (C) explaining why orioles pose a threat to other birds
   (D) relating the particulars of her visit to a friend's home
   (E) sounding the alarm about the danger of global warming

2. What is the purpose of the second paragraph in the passage?

   (A) To explain why the orioles acted in such an aggressive way
   (B) To reveal what the author learned by observing the birds
   (C) To turn the passage to the consideration of the blackbirds' difficulty in raising their babies
   (D) To move the passage from a micro to a macro view
   (E) To begin to put forth an argument toward managed tree planting

3. The author provides several facts that explain why the life of a baby blackbird is precarious. All of the following are mentioned EXCEPT:

   (A) Blackbirds who hatch too early may freeze during cold spring nights.
   (B) Collectors may kill a blackbird's parent, leaving it with no source of food.
   (C) A blackbird may fall out of the nest and break its neck.
   (D) Blackbird eggs may be stolen before they can hatch.
   (E) Predators may attack baby blackbirds or eat their eggs.

4. The characterization of the blackbird in the second paragraph is meant to

   (A) make the blackbird seem more real to readers
   (B) contrast the blackbird's personality with that of other birds
   (C) add a note of humor to an otherwise grim passage
   (D) help the reader care about the orioles' plight
   (E) allow the reader insight into the depth of the problem faced by blackbirds in their attempt to help their babies' survival

As the social and religious objections appeared against the demand for women's political rights, the discussion became many-sided, contradictory, and as varied as the idiosyncrasies of individual character. Some said, "Man is woman's natural protector, and she can safely trust him to make laws for her." She might with fairness reply, as he uniformly robbed her of all property rights to 1848, he cannot safely be trusted with her personal rights in 1880, though the fact that he did make some restitution at last, might modify her distrust in the future. However, the calendars of our courts still show that fathers deal unjustly with daughters, husbands with wives, brothers with sisters, and sons with their own mothers. Though woman needs the protection of one man against his whole sex, in pioneer life, in threading her way through a lonely forest, on the highway, or in the streets of the metropolis on a dark night, she sometimes needs, too, the protection of all men against this one. But even if she could be sure, as she is not, of the ever-present, all-protecting power of one strong arm, that would be weak indeed compared with the subtle, all-pervading influence of just and equal laws for all women. Hence woman's need of the ballot, that she may hold in her own right hand the weapon of self-protection and self-defense.

Questions 5–7 refer to the passage above.

5. The first sentence of the paragraph serves what purpose?

   (A) To explain that the idea that the need for women's political rights was not universally shared among women

   (B) To make clear the prejudices against women's political rights held by mainstream religious leaders

   (C) To change the course of the author's argument in order to include an outsider's perspective

   (D) To introduce and argue against one of the key objections that were made to women having political rights

   (E) To cast judgment on those who disagreed on the need for women's political rights

6. Based on the passage, the author would agree with which of the following statements?

   (A) The arguments made against women's political rights were all illogical.

   (B) The debate over women's political rights did not generate much interest.

   (C) Women's political rights are necessary for her ability to protect and defend herself.

   (D) Women do not need men in any way.

   (E) The loss of women's property rights is not connected to the proposed loss of women's political rights.

7. The main purpose of this passage is to

   (A) make a logical argument for why women need political rights based on their ill-treatment by men in the past

   (B) trace the historical progression of women's political rights to the time of the writing

   (C) provide an anecdotal look at the beginning of the women's rights movement

   (D) highlight some of the important ideas that support the idea of women's property rights

   (E) argue against the notion of women's political rights

Among the many concerns that gardeners must address is to decide whether the land they wish to cultivate is suitable for the types of plants they wish to grow. This means checking the soil's pH, a measure of how acid or alkaline a substance is. Soil's pH is important because it explains how difficult it will be for plants to take nutrients from the soil. Plant roots absorb the nutrients they need—such as iron and nitrogen—when those nutrients are dissolved in water. If the soil solution (the mixture of water and nutrients in the soil) is too acid or alkaline, some nutrients won't dissolve easily, so they won't be available for uptake by roots.

While seed manufacturers will often suggest a good pH range for their plants, the truth is that most plants will tolerate a far wider range in pH than what is suggested. Most nutrients that plants need can dissolve easily when the pH of the soil solution ranges from 6.0 to 7.5. Below pH 6.0, some nutrients, such as nitrogen, phosphorus, and potassium, are less available. When pH exceeds 7.5, iron, manganese, and phosphorus are less available.

Soil pH is affected by many factors, including the amount of local rainfall and the temperature range in the area. In the Pacific Northwest and the Eastern United States, where rainfall is heavy, the soil tends to be moderately acidic. In the Midwest, soil tends to be neutral. In the western United States, especially in areas of frequent drought, soil tends to be alkaline. Of course, soils that have been cultivated are often quite different than the naturally occurring soil in any region. During construction of homes and other buildings, topsoil is frequently removed and may be replaced by a different type of soil.

Questions 8–11 refer to the passage above.

8. The first sentence in the third paragraph is meant to

  (A) provide a comparison of soil pH levels for readers to use based on their location
  (B) give a general overview of the range of soil pH levels in the United States
  (C) present soil pH as a fixed measurement that can be learned
  (D) introduce the idea of soil pH
  (E) explain that the rest of the paragraph will give advice on what kind of plants to grow in various areas

9. Based on the passage, the author would agree with all of the following statements EXCEPT:

  (A) Soil pH is a shifting and unpredictable quality.
  (B) Understanding the soil pH of his garden will help the gardener grow more robust plants.
  (C) Soil pH levels vary widely within the United States.
  (D) Seed manufacturers are careful to give clear instructions on the best soil pH for their plants, and their directives must be followed.
  (E) Soil pH helps explain why plants can or cannot take in nutrients.

10. The author's main purpose in this passage is to

   (A) provide growing advice for gardeners based on where in the United States they live
   (B) give an overview of soil pH levels and make a case for how understanding them can improve a gardener's yield
   (C) review best gardening practices
   (D) demonstrate how to calculate soil pH
   (E) explain how to test for soil pH

11. According to the passage, what factors might affect a soil's pH?

   (A) Wind and temperature
   (B) Rainfall and temperature
   (C) Rainfall and wind
   (D) Topsoil and alkalinity
   (E) Alkalinity and acidity

The Romans, having conquered almost the whole of Britain in the first century, retained possession of the southern parts for nearly four hundred years; and during their occupancy they not only instructed the natives in the arts of civilization, but also with their aid, as we learn from Tacitus, began at an early period to erect temples and public edifices, though doubtless much inferior to those at Rome, in their municipal towns and cities. The Christian religion was also early introduced, but for a time its progress was slow; nor was it till the conversion of Constantine, in the fourth century, that it was openly tolerated by the state, and churches were publicly constructed for its worshippers; though even before that event, as we are led to infer from the testimony of Gildas, the most ancient of our native historians, particular structures were appropriated for the performance of its divine mysteries: for that historian alludes to the British Christians as reconstructing the churches which had, in the Dioclesian persecution, been leveled to the ground. But in the fifth century Rome, oppressed on every side by enemies, and distracted with the vastness of her conquests, which she was no longer able to maintain, recalled her legions from Britain; and the Romanized Britons being left without protection, and having, during their subjection to the Romans, lost their ancient valor and love of liberty, in a short time fell a prey to the Northern Barbarians; in their extremity they called over the Saxons to assist them, when the latter perceiving their defenseless condition, turned round upon them, and made an easy conquest of this country. In the struggle which then took place, the churches were again destroyed, the priests were slain at the very altars, and though the British Church was never annihilated, Paganism for a while became triumphant.

Questions 12–14 refer to the passage above.

12. Based on the passage, the author would be most likely to agree with which of the following statements about Roman Britain?

   (A) The Romans' abandonment contributed to a decline in the quality of life in Britain in the fifth and sixth centuries.
   (B) Britons preferred rule by Rome to self-rule.
   (C) Christianity did not take a firm hold in Britain until the fifth century.
   (D) Rome left Britain because of the rise of Paganism in the area.
   (E) The Northern Barbarians took advantage of Rome's exit from Britain in order to conquer the region.

13. The last sentence of the passage serves what purpose in the structure of the passage?

   (A) Reveals the importance of Roman rule to Britain
   (B) Presents an opposing viewpoint on the importance of Roman rule in Britain
   (C) Turns the reader's attention to fluidity of religious identity in early Britain
   (D) Emphasizes that while Paganism took hold in early Britain, the Christian church wasn't eliminated
   (E) Contradicts earlier statements regarding the presence of Christianity in early Roman Britain

14. What is the best example given in the passage that reveals the way early Christian Britons made use of what Rome had left in their region?

   (A) That temples built in Roman Britain were inferior to those built in Rome
   (B) That Paganism soon took hold in Britain after the Romans left
   (C) That Constantine converted to Christianity
   (D) That the Britons called on the Saxons to help them
   (E) That the British used the existent foundations from otherwise-destroyed Roman churches in the region for their new Christian churches

When looking at the sky, each of us is apt to make patterns from the stars which appear to us to form shapes. Once we are familiar with the constellations as named, we tend to see those shapes more clearly. Modern astronomy recognizes 88 constellations, which are technically not patterns of the stars, but areas of the sky. The 88 constellations depict 42 animals, 29 inanimate objects, and 17 human or mythical characters.

Most of the constellations we recognize today were first plotted and named by the Sumerians, and then by the Greeks. These are principally found in the northern sky. Constellations in the southern sky were first mapped out by explorers and voyagers who journeyed through the oceans of the southern hemisphere.

Many people would be quick to name the Big Dipper or Orion's Belt as the most famous constellation. In fact, they aren't constellations at all, but asterisms, patterns of stars recognized in the night sky. Some asterisms, such as Orion's Belt, are smaller parts of larger patterns recognized as constellations. While this may seem like a small concern, a carelessness about understanding the night sky and its denizens is an unfortunate trend in our 21st century world. The 88 constellations are but a small portion of the wonders in the night sky that can be explored.

Questions 15–18 refer to the passage above.

15. The main purpose of this passage is to

  A trace the historical and cultural changes that have lead the myriad of constellations as accepted by different cultures
  B explain what the 88 different constellations represent
  C provide details as to why some popular patterns in the night sky are not constellations
  D argue against astronomical illiteracy by using the constellations as examples of the wonders of the night sky
  E press readers into political action to protect the night sky

16. Which of the following inferences can be drawn from the third paragraph?

  A Asterisms may be better known than constellations.
  B All constellations contain asterisms.
  C All asterisms appear in one of the 88 constellations.
  D Someday, asterisms will become constellations.
  E Asterisms are not called constellations, because they do not have the level of permanency expected in a constellation.

17. The author's attitude toward the study of astronomy can best be described as which of the following?

  A Apathetic objectivity
  B Passionate engagement
  C Overzealous subjectivity
  D Curious optimism
  E Hostile defensiveness

18. All of the following are true, according to the passage, EXCEPT:

    (A) Sumerians named many of the existent constellations.
    (B) There are 17 constellations named after human or mythical characters.
    (C) The southern sky constellations are more complex than those in the northern sky.
    (D) Orion's Belt is not a constellation.
    (E) An asterism may be part of a constellation.

Although many readers will associate the song "Respect" with Aretha Franklin's definitive version, the song was written and first recorded by Otis Redding in 1965. Franklin's version became a hit upon release in 1967. Although the song is recognizably the same in both versions, each artist gave it a unique flavor.

Redding's song is a plea that his woman return to him—he'll give her anything she wants, so long as she respects him. He sings in the voice of a hard-working man who wants to come home to the comforts he expects. The song returns repeatedly to the idea of respect, even in the verses, and has the feel of a blues song.

Franklin turned the song into a feminist declaration, demanding the respect she knows she deserves. It's more up-tempo, jazzed to life by the back-up singers'—Franklin's sisters Erma and Carolyn—repetition of "Sock it to me." Franklin's version also includes the iconic spelling of R-E-S-P-E-C-T as part of the bridge, an improvisation that propels the song to a new level.

Redding admitted that Franklin had made the song better. In 1967, he joked that she'd "stolen" it but was said to be delighted with her version. Redding must have recognized what was already becoming clear, that Franklin had taken a good song and turned it into a classic.

Questions 19–21 refer to the passage above.

19. Which of the following statements best summarizes the main idea of the passage?

    (A) Aretha Franklin stole Otis Redding's song "Respect."
    (B) Otis Redding was a canny producer and gave "Respect" to another artist who could improve it.
    (C) Franklin's recording of "Respect" shows how feminism was on the rise in America in the 1960s.
    (D) Franklin's harmonies with her sisters elevate the record.
    (E) Many readers may not know that Aretha Franklin was not the first R & B legend to record the song "Respect," although her version is definitive.

20. The author characterizes Redding's response to Franklin's recording as which of the following?

   (A) Hostile
   (B) Appreciative
   (C) Dismissive
   (D) Mercenary
   (E) Optimistic

21. According to the passage, all of the following are contributions Aretha Franklin made to the song's success EXCEPT:

   (A) adding a bridge to the song
   (B) making it a feminist manifesto
   (C) changing the lyrics
   (D) including back-up singers
   (E) dropping the song into a minor key

Answers

1. **B** is the best answer. This is a main idea question, and requires a bit of inferring and tone consideration as well. While A and D are somewhat accomplished by the passage, these cannot be considered the author's main intent. E is too broad and not justified by the passage. C is the opposite—too narrow to be the full purpose. That leaves B. It's worth noting that B is the only answer that contains the words "baby blackbirds," which are clearly the main topic. That makes it a good guess even for someone who is skimming.

2. **C** A cannot be correct, as that is accomplished in the first paragraph. B is correct, except that the entire passage reveals what the author observed, making it too broad to attribute to the second paragraph. D does not reflect the tone of the piece, which never moves to a wider view. And E is not supported by the passage, which never mentions managed tree planting.

3. **A** This is a supporting idea question that asks you to reread the passage to find the correct facts. All of the listed threats to baby blackbirds are included in the passage except for A, making it the only choice.

4. **E** This is an inference question, and one that requires you to think about the author's purpose. Knowing that the main idea of this passage is to explain the precarious circumstances facing baby blackbirds should help you choose E as the best choice. A and C are possible results but cannot be the author's *main* purpose. B is somewhat accomplished but seems less specific than E, whereas D makes the orioles the main subject of the passage, which is incorrect. Again, knowing what the main idea of the passage is helps answer this question correctly.

5. **D** The passage is quite short but the language within it is dense. Read it carefully. The sentence seems to be a structural question about the first sentence, but it soon becomes clear that understanding the entire passage is necessary to be able to point out the work that its introduction is doing. Answer choices A and B seem correct only if the entire passage has not been carefully read. However, it is clear that A is incorrect—the passage does not go in to detail concerning women in particular—as is B, because the passage is not about mainstream religious leaders' objections. We don't see enough of the passage to know if C could be correct (what was the author's original argument that he or she might be changing course from?), and E misstates the tone of the piece, which does not seem to be judgmental. That leaves D as the best choice. The passage does go on to explain a key objection that was raised, and to argue against it.

6. **C** is the best answer to this logic question. Take note of answer choices that use words like "all" and "always"; they are usually wrong. That takes out A, which overstates the author's idea. B is disproved by the passage itself, which refers to myriad responses regarding the debate over women's political rights. D again overstates, and E cannot be right since the connection is very clearly made within the passage.

7. **A** is the best answer to this main idea question. It correctly refers to the overall purpose of the passage. B doesn't refer to this passage, because it is not a historical documentation. C also doesn't fit the style of the passage, which is not anecdotal. D seems like it could be the right answer, but the insertion of the word "property" in the answer makes it incorrect. And E is simply wrong, a complete misstatement of the purpose of the passage. Only those who haven't read the passage in its entirety would choose it, which is not you, right?

8. **B** is the best answer for this supporting idea question (that also refers to structure). The sentence in question is introductory in tone, alerting readers that more information on the variety of soil pH levels in the country is to come. A sounds similar, but the information given isn't supposed to be very detailed, so B is still better. C is also off; the passage is clearly speaking in general terms, breaking thousands of square miles into three regions. D can't be right because this is the second paragraph—the topic of soil pH levels has been under discussion for a paragraph already. And E is disproven by the remainder of the passage, which does not advise on specific plants.

9. **D** is the best answer. Questions set up like this are exasperating, since you must read through all of the answer choices, compare them to the passage, and find the one that cannot be true. In this case, A, B, C, and E are all broad statements whose wording is not found directly in the passage—but they are correct statements. It's helpful that D is clearly incorrect, contradicting the author's advice. So, even if you're not entirely sure that A, B, C, and E are supported by the passage, D remains the best choice.

10. **B** Often, the longest answer in a main idea question is the correct answer, but be sure to read to the very end. A seems like it could be correct, especially if you haven't read the entire passage, but it's soon clear that no advice is given. C is too broad, implying far more information is covered than soil pH. D and E say practically the same thing, but are both incorrect: there's no such information in the passage.

11. **B** It takes a close reading of the text, but this is a fact-finding question: not too hard. The passage refers to rainfall and temperature as the two major factors in soil pH. The information is found at the beginning of the third paragraph.

12. **A** is the best answer. This question requires some inferring as well as close rereading. C, D, and E are all answer choices that take some element of the passage and present it in hopes that you'll remember the phrase it contains and choose it. But all present the information from the text incorrectly, which is why it's important to double-check. B is a bit trickier, as it makes a broader statement that can't be checked by looking at the passage's facts. However, it is quite broad and you know that the GMAT rewards careful choices, not broad inferences. That makes A the best choice.

13. **D** is the best answer. This question asks the test-taker to understand the last sentence's purpose structurally, not just restate the information of the sentence. Nothing in the sentence contradicts the rest of the paragraph, so B and E can be eliminated. A and C both speak to the entire passage's purpose, not just this sentence. While they are tempting choices, D is more focused, making it the better choice. Remember, the GMAT almost always wants you to go micro, not macro.

14. **E** is the best answer. This is a fact-finding question, and one that requires careful rereading. The other answer choices all present facts that we know to be true from the passage. However, only E presents a fact that speaks to the question of how the Britons appropriated Roman remains for their own use.

15. **D** Remember that the main idea is often the first or last sentence in the passage. Here, the main idea is found in the last couple of sentences, as the passage builds to the argument. A and B imply the kind of detail about particular aspects of the topic that is not dealt with in this passage. C is a supporting idea in the passage, but not the main idea. And E overstates the author's purpose; he or she does not call for political action but makes a plea for better understanding of the wonders of astronomy.

16. **A** is the best answer. This is an inference question. You must use the information in the passage to infer the best correct answer about asterisms. B and C are essentially saying the same thing, so you can eliminate them even if you didn't read the passage again to see that there's no statement about whether all constellations contain asterisms or all asterisms appear in constellations. Similarly, D and E both ask to take leaps in inferring that simply are too broad to find support in the passage. If you hop, rather than leap, you'll agree that A is the best answer.

17. **B** This set of answers hopes to slow you down with a parade of big words. But it's actually not very difficult to eliminate answers if you think through each choice. Remember the tone of the passage (rereading if you need to), especially at the end. It certainly wasn't apathetic (A), overzealous (C), or hostile (E). That leaves B or D, but D seems wrong. Would an expert be "curious"? And how is the passage "optimistic"? That makes B the best choice.

18. **C** This is a fact-finding question, made more complex because four of the answer choices are correct but you want to find the one that is wrong. So long as you don't rush, you'll be fine. A, B, D, and E are all factual, found in the passage. C sounds good but is not mentioned in the passage. Even if you're sure that the facts stated in C are correct, you can't prove it using the passage, so it must be the right choice.

19. **E** is the best choice in this main idea question. A and B present opinions that are not justified by the neutral tone of the text. C may be true, but again, is not justified by the text, which only makes a brief connection to feminism. That leaves D and E, but D is just a fact pulled from the passage, not a thesis. Note that E is also the longest answer, and you know that often serves as an alert that it's the best choice.

20. **B** This question asks you to characterize the author's tone through how he or she had described one of the characters in the passage viewpoint. Redding is depicted, in this passage anyway, as appreciative, not hostile (A) or dismissive (C). "Optimistic" (E) doesn't make much sense here, and while we might suspect that any songwriter would feel mercenary (D) if his or her song became a hit, there's nothing in the passage to justify that answer.

21. **E** is the best answer. This is a fact-finding question. You'll have to reread the passage to make sure you've chosen the facts as presented. E is the only answer choice that isn't in the passage, so while it may be true, it cannot be correct here.

CHAPTER 13

GMAT Critical Reasoning Questions

Introduction

The Critical Reasoning questions appear in the Verbal section of the GMAT. Along with the Reading Comprehension questions, Critical Reasoning questions will be included with Sentence Correction questions (which we'll cover in Chapter 14). Generally, there are about 40 questions in the Verbal section, which means you'll be asked to complete 12 or so Critical Reasoning questions. As before, you'll be shown the passage and the question on a split screen, and once you confirm your answer, the question and passage will disappear. Remember, you'll get 75 minutes for the entire Verbal section.

Consider yourself warned: *Critical Reasoning questions are unusual.* You won't have seen anything similar to them on the SAT or GRE. They're designed to test your skills in evaluating the strengths and weaknesses of arguments. The good news is that you actually do this all the time, whether you're comparison shopping for a new washer and dryer or deciding whether someone's story could be the truth! You have to evaluate the arguments being made to decide what's the best next thing to do. The Critical Reasoning section asks you to do the same thing.

Instructions

The instructions for this section read like this:

Each of the Critical Reasoning questions is based on a short argument, a set of statements, or a plan of action. For each question, select the best answer of the choices given.

Not wildly helpful, right? Here's what the instructions don't tell you: you'll be presented with a brief passage (much shorter than the Reading Comprehension passages) that will present some kind of argument. Immediately after the passage will be a short question that asks you to examine some aspect of the reasoning in the passage. There will be five answer choices, and only one of those will be correct.

Much like the Reading Comprehension questions, the passages in this section will cover many different topics. However, in the Reading Comprehension section you were able to answer between three and five questions based on one passage before moving on. Here, each question will refer to a different passage, which can be disorienting. The passages are shorter, about 100 words, but as you can tell, that doesn't make for less work.

Also, you'll be asked to work through different kinds of convoluted logic, switching back and forth between reasoning techniques as you move through this section. As always, the GMAT test-makers will try to trip you up or mislead you.

It bears repeating as a reminder: you have to work through the questions in order on the GMAT. So, even if you'd like to go through and answer all of the Reading Comprehension questions first, you can't. You'll have to answer Critical Reasoning questions as they appear.

The good news is that this section will show you many examples of the types of questions you'll be asked (along with 60 practice questions at the end of the chapter) as well as the strategies you need to employ to do well on this section. You'll be in good shape by the time you finish this chapter.

Types of Critical Reasoning Questions

What Do We Mean by "Argument"?

Critical Reasoning passages are concerned with "arguments", but that turn of phrase can seem confusing. We don't mean the type of arguments one has about who left the milk out. In other words, this kind of argument is not a disagreement but rather the way a premise is presented to support a conclusion. Most of the questions in the Critical Reasoning section will detail a premise or two and present a conclusion that is supposedly drawn from the premise(s). However, the conclusion is not only based on the premise, but also on unstated assumptions that are being made to help support it. These unstated assumptions—the secret traps of logic—are what most Critical Reasoning questions are concerned with.

For example, let's look at an argument:

Floods often destroy athletic fields that are not built at least 100 feet above the flood plain. The Richland Rams' football field was built 120 feet above the flood plain, so it will survive the next flood.

In this argument, there are two premises:

- That floods often destroy athletic fields that are not built at least 100 feet above the flood plain.
- That the Richland Rams' football field was built 120 feet above the flood plain.

These premises lead to one conclusion:

Therefore, the Rams' football field will survive the next flood.

In this case, the premises presented are not enough to prove the conclusion correct. Stating that fields built below the flood plain are often destroyed by flooding does not prove that a field built above the flood plain will always survive flooding. Therefore, the argument includes (but does not state) several assumptions, including:

- Fields that are built above the flood plain will survive any flood.
- The next flood will not rise above the flood plain.
- The next flood will not cause any other related disasters (including mudslides or downed trees) that will affect the field's survival.

There are other assumptions at work, but these serve to show how the argument is built upon more than the premises stated. While this argument is simpler than most that you'll find in the GMAT's Critical Reasoning section, it aptly demonstrates how you can look for flaws in the logic presented, and thus the argument's stability. You'll be asked to either take out one of the assumptions to weaken the argument or to prop up the argument with an additional assumption or premise.

Assumption Questions

Most of the Critical Reasoning questions you'll face are assumption questions, which ask you to identify the assumption of the argument presented. Questions of this type will read something like these examples:

- Which of the following is an assumption that enables the conclusion presented to be properly drawn?
- Which of the following is an assumption made in drawing the conclusion above?
- The conclusion of the argument as stated above cannot be true unless which of the following is true?
- Any of the following, if introduced into the argument above as an additional premise, makes the argument above logically correct EXCEPT

As you can see, the wording is not concise, but clear: These questions ask you to look at the premises and the conclusion of the argument and see what's not being said. You'll need to determine the other conditions that must be necessary for the argument to work. In the example above, you need to figure out the assumption that gets you from the premise that the Rams' field was built 120 feet above the flood plain to the conclusion that the Rams' field will survive the next flood. The assumption there—and therefore your answer—will be something along the lines of:

Fields that are built 120 feet or higher off the flood plain will survive the next flood.

Weaken the Argument Questions

Another very common type of Critical Reasoning question is weaken-the-argument questions, which ask you to do exactly what the name implies: weaken the presented argument. They often have wording similar to the following examples:

- Which of the following, if true, most clearly points to a flaw in the manufacturer's plan?
- Which of the following, if true, would most weaken the conclusion above?
- Which of the following, if true, most severely undermines the argument presented above?

To answer this type of question, you'll have to think in a way that's very similar to how you needed to work through an assumption question. However, here, you'll need to take it a step further, determining which assumptions have to be true for the argument to work, and then find the answer that challenges one of those assumptions. With our example argument, a correct answer might look something like one of the following:

- When the last major flood occurred in the area, several athletic fields that were built more than 100 feet above the flood plain were destroyed by flooding.
- Scientists predict that the next major flood to hit the area will be at least five times as severe as the worst prior flood.

Clearly, both of the answers take away the sturdiness of the argument by attacking one of the unspoken assumptions. The first answer choice eliminates the assumption that floods never rise higher than 100 feet, while the second takes away the assumption that floods are likely to remain at the same level of severity.

Another way to think of this type of question is to recognize that you need to look for flaws in the argument. That's likely to be something you do every day, whether you're evaluating someone's excuse or figuring out why someone's logic doesn't convince you. But do be careful not to choose the answer choice that actually strengthens the argument. There will probably be one, and it's easy to get confused when you're trying to move quickly through the questions.

Strengthen the Argument

As you might guess, another form of Critical Reasoning questions is to ask you to strengthen the argument presented. This is not nearly as popular as weaken-the-argument questions, but you'll see at least a few of them on your GMAT. They often have wording like the following examples:

- Which of the following, if true, offers the strongest support for the manager's conclusion that the windows were not at fault?
- Which of the following, if true, provides the strongest evidence in favor of the treasurer's hypothesis?
- Which of the following, if true, would most significantly strengthen the conclusion drawn in the passage?

If you look at our example, you'll see that in a strengthen-the-argument question, you'd need to find a statement that confirms one of the assumptions on which the argument is based. If you knew it was true, the argument would be stronger. For example, any of the following would help:

- In the last flood, no fields that were at least 100 feet above the flood plain were damaged, although fields below that level were ruined.
- Scientists predict that the next flood in the region will be smaller in scale than any prior floods.

Each of the above statements addresses flaws in the argument. It's not that the statement proves the argument, by the way. Rather, the correct statement will eliminate a potential flaw in logic in the argument.

You'll notice that those flaws are exactly the same ones a weaken-the-argument question would try to exploit! That's the thing about the arguments on the GMAT's Critical Reasoning section: they're designed to be flexible, able to be weakened or strengthened by additional statements. As with weaken-the-argument questions, the strengthen-the-argument questions will often include an answer choice that does exactly the opposite (that is, weaken when you want to strengthen), so be sure to read and choose carefully, as always.

Inference Questions

You might have hoped to leave inferring behind with Critical Reading, but, alas, it's still a major part of the GMAT. There will be at least one inference question in most Critical Reasoning sections. These questions ask you to make a logical inference based on the information presented in the passage. Basically, this type of question asks: if the statements in the passage are true, what else has to be true?

You might be thinking that assumption questions, which we've already covered, asked you to infer. Yep, that's correct! Assumption questions are a specific kind of inference question. By asking if the argument is valid, you can infer that which of the following assumptions must be true in order to logically connect the premise and the conclusion?

While the same type of logic is at work in other inference questions (If _____ is true, what else must be true?), what is being inferred is a bit different. You might not be asked to infer something that is a vital component of the argument, but rather a logical extension of it. In a way, these questions are about the sidecars of the argument; even if you eliminate one of them, the argument will still ride.

Unlike the prior types of questions, which mostly dealt with the assumptions of an argument, inference questions can consider all aspects of the argument: the premises, the assumptions, the conclusion, or even how it applies to a related solution. Examples of this type of question are:

- If the statements above are true, which of the following must also be true?
- The statements above, if true, best support which of the following assertions?
- Which of the following can be correctly inferred from the statements above?
- If the statement above is true, then what might be the expected outcome if the plane left an hour earlier than expected?

Don't look for bold statements, but for very conservative steps forward in thinking. The correct answer will be the only one that has to be true if the statements in the passage are true.

Let's use our ongoing example to explore this idea. Here are two inferences you could draw from the passage:

- Athletic fields that are built lower than 100 feet above the flood plain are not necessarily in danger of flooding.
- Height above sea level may play a role in protecting athletic fields from damage due to flooding.

Notice, again, the moderate tone of these statements. These are hops, not leaps. Notice the language in use here: "not necessarily" and "may play a role." These make for weaker claims, but those are the kind the GMAT favors.

Explain/Resolve the Discrepancy

As we mentioned, the vast majority of questions that you'll see in the Critical Reasoning section are from the types we've covered so far. But every once in a while, you'll encounter an outlier, so we'll quickly review the other possibilities.

Sometimes the arguments in the passages don't wrap up with a clear conclusion. The premises presented might be incomplete, confusing, or even contradictory. The question will ask you to provide a logical explanation that resolves the confusion. Question stems from explain/resolve the discrepancy will look something like this:

- Which of the following, if true, would best explain the sudden decrease in energy consumption described above?
- Which of the following, if true, would help to explain the discrepancy above?
- Which of the following, if true, best accounts for the fact that Britain is not widely believed to be a leader in this field?

Questions of this type are quite closely linked to assumption questions, since the reasoning you'll need to use is very similar. Basically, you're being given a premise (or premises) and a conclusion that doesn't quite match up, and you'll need to figure out the assumption that connects the argument logically. Here's an example:

Over the past five years, Magda won several medals in running competitions. She was recently involved in a minor biking accident, however, and as a result of her injuries, she must wear a neck brace. Despite this fact, she is favored to win the big race in two months.

The question stem is:

Which of the following, if true, would help explain the apparent paradox described above?

Clearly, something's missing in this argument—the conclusion ("she is favored to win") is not supported by the premises (the biking accident, the neck brace), which seem to support the opposite conclusion.

Now let's consider what assumptions might make the above a logical argument; that is, what might explain the discrepancy?

- Magda wears a light neck brace at night but has full movement of her head during the day.
- The big race next month is an auto race.
- The neck brace will be removed next week, and Magda will have fully recovered before the big race occurs in two months.

Each of these statements, if true, could explain why the argument presented above must be true. They are not huge leaps in logic, but gentle hops. It's helpful to probe the passage for the unstated assumptions before you start looking at the answer choices. This will help you find the holes in the argument.

Ask the Right Question

Another infrequent type of Critical Reasoning question is the ask-the-right-question problem. In this type of question, you are asked to choose the answer choice that best explains what else you need to know in order to analyze or explain the situation presented in the problem. As you'll see, this question is like taking another step back from the argument, so you can consider it more carefully. Questions of this type often read like these examples:

- Which of the following must be studied in order to evaluate the argument presented above?
- Which of the following investigations is most likely to yield significant information that would help to evaluate the meteorologist's hypothesis?

This type of question is really just a variation on the questions that ask you to strengthen or weaken the argument. You'll want to look closely at one of the premises or assumptions upon which the argument you've been given is built. Unlike the more common types of questions, you're not asked to strengthen or weaken the argument, but to provide a question for which the answer will prove to strengthen or weaken the argument. That's why we suggest thinking of it as taking a step back and asking yourself, "What would help me improve (or attack) this argument?"

If we return to the most recent example, of Magda and the big race, and take a step back, we can hypothesize that knowing what kind of race the big race is would help us be able to strengthen or weaken the argument. So we'd look for an answer that's along the lines of "What type of race is the big race?" Notice how the answer is in the form of a question.

All of this makes for a fairly confusing question, indeed. Be glad that there aren't going to be too many of them on the GMAT.

The vast majority of practice Critical Reasoning questions we provide are about strengthening or weakening the argument, and the assumptions made within the argument. That's because you'll be asked those kinds of questions more than any others.

Parallel Reasoning

This type of question is not as difficult to think through but still requires careful thought. It's the "compare and contrast" question of the Critical Reasoning section. It asks you to understand the underlying logic of an argument you've been given, and then choose the argument that is most similar in some way. Here are examples of how parallel reasoning questions often read:

- Which of the following is most like the argument above in its logical structure?
- Which of the following supports its conclusion in the same way as the argument above?
- The logical flaw in the reasoning above is most similar to that in which of the following statements?

The only way to answer these questions without wasting a lot of time is to break down the passage you've been given into the parts that have been used to construct the argument. You'll have to block out all of the surrounding information and instead understand the logic. Let's look at a slightly different example of Magda and the big race again, one that eliminates the flaw in logic.

> Over the past five years, Magda won several medals in running competitions. She was recently involved in a minor biking accident, however, and as a result of her injuries, she must wear a neck brace. Therefore, when she competes in the big race next month, she's unlikely to win.

The question is: Which of the following is most like the argument above in its logical structure? So you'll need to break down the logic:

1. Magda has won several medals in running competitions.
2. Magda was recently involved in a biking accident and must wear a neck brace.
3. Because of her injury and the treatment for it, she probably will not win the big race.

This argument is essentially, because X (2) is true, Y (3) is unlikely to happen. (We strongly suggest trying to eliminate the specifics of the argument so that they don't distract you.)

Having broken down the argument into whatever shorthand works best for you, you're now ready to choose the argument in the answer choice that looks closest to this one:

- (A) The best runners are unlikely to be the best swimmers.
- (B) The journalist most likely will not finish her article on time because her computer isn't working.
- (C) Susan's lack of lower body strength will prevent her from becoming a strong runner.
- (D) Adelaide's decision to try body surfing led to her breaking her arm.
- (E) Millions of people entered the online contest, reducing the chances for any one of them to win.

The test-makers have a series of tricks they use on this type of question to trip you up. Notice that many of these answer choices deal with athletic endeavors, in the hope that since the argument was about running, you'll assume the answer must be, too. In fact, the exact opposite is true. When you see answer choices that seem very similar in subject matter to the original premise, it's likely that they are incorrect. They do not reflect parallel reasoning, because the same logic is not displayed.

If you cannot immediately identify the correct answer, you can help yourself by noting what the logic is in the argument. Eliminate the specifics of the passage and the answer choices. If you do that, it's clear that the choices are:

- (A) X is unlikely to be Y.
- (B) X is unlikely to happen because of Y.
- (C) X will never happen because of Y.
- (D) X happened.
- (E) Because X is true, Y is unlikely to happen to Z.

It's clear that B is the best choice, since it is the most similar (or parallel) argument to the passage.

If you're stumped, remember that it's OK to think about the logical structure in another way, especially if the X, Y, and Z just make things more confusing for you. Just be sure to contemplate the logic that's in use, because that is the key to answering this type of question correctly. You can always try using the X, Y, and Z shorthand in your practice with this book. It might become more comfortable for you.

Find the Conclusion

Another common question is the find-the-conclusion question. Much as assumption questions ask you to identify an assumption of the argument, this type, as the name implies, will ask you to draw a logical conclusion from the passage. Find-the-conclusion questions often are worded like these:

- Which of the following conclusions can properly be drawn from the information in the passage?
- The argument, as presented above, is structured to lead to what conclusion?

When you consider the answer choices provided, make sure you look for one that has to be true if the premises in the passage are true. There will be at least one other choice that might be true, but that's not the right choice. Here, yet again, you want to stick to hops in logic, not leaps.

Fill in the Blank

It's not hard to guess what to do with this type of question: you'll need to choose the answer that finishes the sentence the best! The blank will almost always represent the conclusion of the argument, so this type of question is similar to the find-the-conclusion question. It will read like this:

Which of the following best completes the passage above?

While it's probably a bad idea to call any of the questions on the GMAT easy, this type of question is quite straightforward. You'll have to read the passage and decide what's missing— usually a conclusion (although occasionally a premise). After you read the passage, note for yourself what the answer should look like. When you have that in your head, then you can look at the answer choices. Try to find the one that is closest to what you decided. And remember, once again, to keep your logic tight, making hops instead of leaps!

Structure of an Argument

This type of question is a relatively new one on the GMAT. You may find that your test doesn't include Critical Reasoning questions of this type, but just in case, do know that it exists. It's a bit like an inference question from Reading Comprehension, because you are asked to not just analyze the argument presented in the passage but also to think about the structure of the argument. Generally, one sentence in the passage will be in bold (a sure sign that the question will be a structure-of-an-argument question!), and you will be asked what role the bolded portion plays in the argument. In other words, you might be asked to identify it as a premise, evidence, or a conclusion. It will read something like this:

> In the passage above, what role does the second paragraph play?

Dialogue Questions

This, the last type we'll discuss, isn't actually a distinct form of question. Rather, you should be aware that occasionally questions that are presented as a dialogue—usually between two colleagues, or an employee and her supervisor—appear on the GMAT. Treat these as you would any other question, by reading them carefully and then deciding what information the question seeks to find. A dialogue passage will look something like this:

> Gayle: I can't believe we've been waiting this long for our food.
> Bernie: Well, it's very busy in this restaurant.
> Gayle: Of course it's busy. It's Friday night. Why didn't they plan for more business? They should have twice the waiters they have right now!
> Bernie: No, it's impossible to predict how many customers a restaurant will have at any given meal.

Problem-Solving Strategies

How to Approach Critical Reasoning Questions

Here's a basic strategy for all Critical Reasoning questions. You should:

1. **Read the question stem** (the first part of the question), which often begins something like "Which of the following if true . . . ."
2. **Read the passage carefully and critically.** As you do so, try to analyze the basic components of the argument in light of the question, using the question stem to guide you.
3. **Formulate a correct answer to the question** in your head or using the scrap paper (before you look at the answer choices).
4. **Review the answer choices.** If the correct answer is obvious, select that one (but still read the other choices, just to be sure); otherwise, try to eliminate choices until one is left.

It's helpful to read the question stem first because, unlike the Reading Comprehension passages where you're likely to be asked to look for several different things, you really only need to look for one answer in the passage. Knowing what it is beforehand can help you focus your reading. Do read carefully; in these passages, missing a "not" or other key word could affect your score.

Having the question stem in mind will also help you understand what you're looking for. The stem can point you in the direction of finding a flaw in the argument, uncovering an unstated assumption, or restating the argument's logic more generally.

Finally, sketching out your idea of the right answer is very helpful, because the answer choices are designed to confuse you. If you have an idea of what the correct choice should look like, you can pick out the correct answer much more quickly than if you have to consider, evaluate, and discard each answer choice.

Know How This Section Tries to Trick You

Just as the types of questions and the correct answers to those questions fall into patterns, so, too, do the wrong answers for a Critical Reasoning question fall into patterns. Sometimes, if you can identify an answer choice as falling into a pattern that other wrong answers follow, you'll be able to eliminate it immediately. Here are a few of those patterns:

Wrong answers tend to:

- **Come from Left Field.** If the answer choice seems wacky, it's wrong.
- **Go too Far.** This is the classic GMAT trick: there will be answers that seem to be true but require a leap in logic. The further you have to extend the logic, the more variables come into play. Instead, choose the answer that is closer to the premise in logic! A good tip is to avoid answer choices that have words such as *always, all, none,* or *never* in them. These terms are so broad that there's almost always an exception. Instead, look for words that qualify or limit the logic, such as *almost, usually, possibly, might,* and *could.*
- **Not Go Far Enough.** Answer choices like these are true, but only for one of the premises or part of the argument presented. There will be another choice that is true for the entire passage, which is the better choice. Keep looking!
- **Be Irrelevant.** Answer choices like these present a fact about (or even taken from) the argument but don't answer the question that is asked. Make sure you know what you're looking for before you start reading the answer choices!
- **Restate the Passage.** You just finished a section (Reading Comprehension) in which we suggested you look for familiar phrasing in answering your questions. That tip doesn't apply here, where you're asked to think beyond the passage. An answer choice that simply repackages part of the passage is probably wrong.
- **Appeal to Your Opinions or Values.** Sometimes the GMAT provides an answer choice that isn't logical, but that many people might feel is true or likely. As with all questions on the GMAT, though, you must stick to the presented argument and facts, no matter how the answer choices might want to sway you by appealing to your emotions.
- **Be the Opposite.** Remember, you'll be trying to read fast and move quickly through the test. The test-makers are counting on that, and thus are happy to provide you with an answer that is the exact opposite of what you're looking for, in hopes that you choose it while hurrying.

Problem-Solving Drills

Whew, that was a lot! Now that you have a good overview of the Critical Reasoning section, let's take a look at some practice questions. You'll find three sets of Critical Reasoning questions ahead, with 20 questions each. Each presents a number of passages and then one or two questions about each passage. Remember that on the GMAT, you will be asked only one question per passage, and you'll be asked about only 12 Critical Reasoning questions. As you use these drills to practice, try to time yourself to make sure that you're not spending more than 90 seconds on each question. After you complete each drill, check out the answers in the following section.

Critical Reasoning Drill 1

Each of the critical reasoning questions is based on a short argument, a set of statements, or a plan of action. For each question, select the best answer of the choices given.

The Good Manufacturing Consortium has received complaints about the quality of the products in their Books Made Simple product line. To eliminate these complaints, the operations director has decided to adopt a quality assurance program similar to that of the Highbrow Manufacturing Company, which has a high customer satisfaction rate.

1. Which of the following may most reasonably be inferred from the statements above?

    (A) The Highbrow Manufacturing Company is in danger of stealing all of the Good Manufacturing Consortium's business.

    (B) Products in the Books Made Simple product line do not deliver on promises made in their advertising.

    (C) The complaints about the Books Made Simple product line indicate a customer satisfaction rate that is lower than Highbrow Manufacturing's customer satisfaction rate.

    (D) The Books Made Simple line is a new one for Good Manufacturing.

    (E) The operations director at Good Manufacturing used to work at Highbrow in a similar capacity.

2. Which of the following, if true, offers the strongest support for the operation director's plan?

    (A) The quality assurance program that the operations manager is recommending will decrease the margins of the Books Made Simple line by 10 percent.

    (B) The Good Manufacturing Consortium and the Highbrow Manufacturing Company make similar products and market them to the same consumers.

    (C) The Good Manufacturing Consortium has been in business for twenty years longer than the Highbrow Manufacturing Company.

    (D) Highbrow Manufacturing provides consumers with a toll-free hotline that can be called during business hours for help.

    (E) Despite the complaints about the Books Made Simple line of products, the Good Manufacturing Consortium has a high customer satisfaction rate based on industry standards.

A school is considering changing its daily schedule. Currently, this school requires all students to arrive for class at 8:30 a.m. The proposed policy would permit each student to decide when to arrive from as early as 6 a.m. to as late as 10 a.m., beginning class when they are ready.

3. The adoption of this policy would be most likely to increase students' attendance if the following were true:

   Ⓐ Students were allowed to leave the school campus for lunch.
   Ⓑ Student attendance was shown to be directly connected to their after-school job work hours.
   Ⓒ Students recently voted to stagger their class schedules so that they could arrive earlier or later so long as they attended their required classes.
   Ⓓ The school band already gathers at 6:30 a.m. and has perfect attendance.
   Ⓔ In prior years, school began at 7:45 a.m.

4. The argument presented is most vulnerable to which of the following arguments?

   Ⓐ Students may dislike having a different schedule than their friends and classmates.
   Ⓑ Teenagers generally have a great deal of trouble staying awake at 6 a.m.
   Ⓒ Studies show that mixing grade levels weakens the academic environment.
   Ⓓ Teachers have criticized the plan as unfeasible; they say they must have a set schedule and class roster in order to teach effectively.
   Ⓔ There are only 50 parking spots in the student parking lot.

A city newspaper experienced a major drop in subscriptions in the month following its coverage of a controversial new building downtown. The newspaper also received a flurry of complaints via reader letters, e-mail, and tweets. The newspaper, however, maintains that the negative reactions to its coverage of the building had nothing to do with the cancelled subscriptions.

5. Which of the following, if true, most strongly supports the newspaper's stance?

   Ⓐ The other newspaper in the city reported a similar spate of complaints from their readers during the same month.
   Ⓑ The readers who wrote in to complain were all yearly subscribers.
   Ⓒ Newspapers publicly attribute drops in readership to their news coverage only when they receive complaints about that coverage.
   Ⓓ This was not the first series of stories on the controversy surrounding the new building that inspired readers to complain.
   Ⓔ Most readers rely on local television news as their primary source of information regarding the local controversy.

Fisherman: "**Most people blame fishermen for the decline over the last 15 years in freshwater trout found in Ohiopyle State Park.** But fishermen alone aren't the problem. In the past 15 years, Ohiopyle has been inundated with grizzly and black bears that are natural consumers of trout."

6. In the fisherman's argument, the portion in bold plays which of the following roles?

- Ⓐ It is the conclusion of the argument.
- Ⓑ It is a finding that the argument seeks to explain.
- Ⓒ It is an explanation that the argument concludes is correct.
- Ⓓ It provides evidence in support of the main conclusion of the argument.
- Ⓔ It introduces a premise that the argument goes on to oppose.

7. Which of the following, if true, would provide the best support for the argument?

- Ⓐ The deer popular in Ohiopyle State Park has declined.
- Ⓑ Bears eat berries and other plant-based foods as well as fish and game.
- Ⓒ Hunting black and grizzly bears was banned about four years ago.
- Ⓓ Autopsies of bears found dead in the woods showed that nearly all of them had recently consumed trout.
- Ⓔ Fishermen alone aren't the problem.

Last year, the rate of inflation was about 1 percent, but for the current year, it has been 3 percent. We can conclude that inflation is on an upward trend and the rate will be as high as 7 percent next year.

8. Which of the following, if true, most seriously weakens the conclusion above?

- Ⓐ Last year, a dip in crude oil prices dropped inflation temporarily below its stable level of 3 percent for recent years.
- Ⓑ The inflation figures were computed using a sample of data rather than all the available data.
- Ⓒ Increases in the pay of some workers are tied to the inflation level, constituting a force causing further inflation.
- Ⓓ The 1 percent rate of inflation last year represented a five-year low.
- Ⓔ Intervention by the Federal Reserve cannot affect the rate of inflation to any significant degree.

Avocado farmers get a higher price for their crop when avocados are more difficult to find in grocery stores. However, the price of avocados drops when the crop is abundant. Therefore, it makes sense that when a large avocado crop comes in, farmers should hold back a portion of it in refrigerated warehouses, hoping for a higher price in the future. This year's avocado crop is the smallest since the late 1990s. Nonetheless, avocado farmers may hold back a portion of their crops because _____.

9. Which of the following best completes the passage?

   (A) The practice of storing part of the year's crop was not widely practiced in the late 1990s.
   (B) The quality of this year's avocado crop is no better than the quality of the last five years' worth of crops.
   (C) Each of the last three years has produced record-breaking avocado crops.
   (D) For some avocado growers, this year's crop yielded the same harvest as last year's.
   (E) Avocado prices have not fluctuated much in recent years.

In order to measure the effect of environmental factors on attitudes and behaviors, students at a local high school were given a survey in their Social Studies class. The results of that survey indicated that students who spend a minimum of two hours on social media such as Facebook are more likely to indulge in online bullying. Therefore, spending time on Facebook encourages bullying among teens.

10. Which of the following is most like the argument above in its logical structure?

   (A) A video game company knows that most of its buyers are 18- to 30-year-old males, so it markets its games in stores where that demographic is most likely to shop.
   (B) A developing country gained access to televisions on a widespread basis for the first time, and, as a consequence, the people of that country are more interested in entertainment.
   (C) A recent census shows that more highly educated people tend to live in areas of lesser water pollution than in nearby areas; therefore, educated people are less likely to pollute.
   (D) A motorcyclist's education course offered at a local insurance company uses a video game to teach driving skills to students; only after winning at the game will their premiums on motorcyclist's insurance be lowered.
   (E) A survey of local homeowners indicated a strong preference for property taxes to be reduced by 20 percent over the next three years. Thus, the upcoming proposal to reduce property taxes will most likely pass.

11. Which of the following is an assumption that is made in the argument presented in the passage?

    (A) That the students taking the test are likely to lie about the answers
    (B) That students who spend time on Facebook are more likely to be bullies
    (C) That Facebook is a popular social media site
    (D) That bullying can be defined
    (E) That there is a connection between the amount of time spent on Facebook and the likelihood that a student will engage in bullying behavior

Andrew is a student at a local college. In order to improve his grades, he has decided to study for a minimum of two hours per night and to take vitamins to improve his memory.

12. Which of the statements below, if true, weakens Andrew's likelihood of success?

    (A) The campus library is not open every day.
    (B) Andrew works a part-time job with irregular hours.
    (C) Andrew has trouble remembering when his assignments are due.
    (D) Taking vitamins is not proven to help improve memory.
    (E) Andrew is not happy with his current grades.

13. Which of the following, if true, offers the strongest support for Andrew's plan?

    (A) Andrew's mother suggested the plan based on her own experience in college 30 years ago.
    (B) Andrew's doctor prescribed the vitamin regime based on its success with other patients of the same age and general health.
    (C) Andrew will also learn to write down his assignments.
    (D) The campus pharmacy had the vitamins in stock the day Andrew turned in his prescription for them.
    (E) Andrew needs to improve his grades in order to keep his scholarship.

In the week before a local election, a news website polled registered voters in the area to ask them which candidate they planned to vote for. **10 percent of registered voters were polled**, and 48 percent of them said they would vote for the incumbent, Jane Smith, in the election. Based on the poll results, the website concluded that Smith would win the election.

14. Which of the following is the most significant flaw in the premises of the argument presented above?

    (A) Only 10 percent of registered voters were polled.
    (B) Forty-eight percent is not a majority of registered voters.
    (C) Jane Smith is an incumbent.
    (D) The website concluded that Smith would win the election.
    (E) The website worked from an outdated roster of voters.

15. In the argument presented above, what role does the portion presented in boldface play?

    Ⓐ It provides evidence to support the website's conclusion.
    Ⓑ It is an assumption that does not provide support for the conclusion.
    Ⓒ It is a premise that is used to support the argument.
    Ⓓ It provides evidence to support a premise of the argument.
    Ⓔ It is a conclusion that must be proven for the argument to be valid.

A zoologist with extensive knowledge and experience working with North American snakes attempted to rally local public interest in saving the endangered Watersmith snake, native to the region. She eventually concluded that although she had attempted to make clear the vital role that Watersmith snakes play in preserving the ecology of the local river system, people could not find it in themselves to make an effort to save creatures they found so repellent.

16. The zoologist's opinion would be most strengthened by which of the following statements?

    Ⓐ The Watersmith snake population has been in decline for over 10 years.
    Ⓑ A recent survey of local newspaper readers found that Watersmith snake attacks are more feared than panther or poisonous toad attacks.
    Ⓒ Conservation efforts have been ongoing in the area since the 1960s.
    Ⓓ The zoologist had recently moved into the area.
    Ⓔ Watersmith snakes, although endangered, are not as much in risk of extinction as other species of snake.

17. Which of the following, if true, most clearly points to a flaw in the zoologist's reasoning?

    Ⓐ Conservation efforts in the area have been ongoing since the 1960s.
    Ⓑ Recent efforts by locals have helped stabilize the population of mountain panthers, a much-feared area predator.
    Ⓒ The zoologist did not keep track of daily visits to her website about saving Watersmith snakes.
    Ⓓ Watersmith snakes are principally aquatic.
    Ⓔ The local newspaper failed to run a story on the zoologist's efforts.

In Gortown, there are many shops that sell postal stamps as one of the items available at the counter. Yet Gortown also has two major post offices, which offer a variety of services. One of the post offices is open 24 hours a day. It is strange that people continue to buy stamps at the shops when the post offices are available.

18. Which of the following is an assumption made in drawing the conclusion above?

    Ⓐ People in Gortown do not often need to buy stamps.
    Ⓑ Gortown is a large city.
    Ⓒ There are no advantages to buying stamps at a small shop rather than at the post office.
    Ⓓ The post offices do not provide the kind of customer service a small shop can.
    Ⓔ Gortown needs more than two post offices.

19. Which of the following should be studied in order to evaluate the validity of the conclusion presented above?

    Ⓐ Do the majority of people who buy stamps buy them in large amounts?
    Ⓑ How far apart are the post offices from each other?
    Ⓒ Which of the other services offered by the post offices are most popular?
    Ⓓ What do people give as the reason they prefer buying stamps in the shops?
    Ⓔ What other products do the shops often sell at the same time as stamps?

Many recent scientific studies have found that preservatives can be harmful when added to food. That's why here at Hansen Foodstuffs, we make sure that all of our food is produced without preservatives. You can be sure you are doing the right thing for your family's health when you buy our products.

20. If the statements above are true, what must also be true?

    Ⓐ It is possible to produce food without preservatives that is safe to consume.
    Ⓑ Hansen Foodstuffs is an organic food company.
    Ⓒ Preservatives cause numerous health problems.
    Ⓓ Hansen Foodstuffs uses natural preservatives.
    Ⓔ Scientific studies are often subject to interpretation.

Answers

1. **C** is the best answer. You are asked to apply what you've read into a reasonable assumption in this inference question. Remember to take a hop instead of a leap. We are not given the reason for why the Books Made Simple line isn't successful. While B and D both provide explanations for why the line isn't doing well, neither is justified by the passage given. A is a broad statement that could be true, but requires a leap to get to, while E might also be true but isn't indicated in any way. C is the hop in logic that makes sense, and thus it is the best answer.

2. **B** is the best answer. This argument in the passage hangs on the idea that Good and Highbrow are similar companies who can benefit from the same practices. The only answer that speaks to that is B. C mentions both companies, but the comparison made does not speak to any benefit of the shared practices. A, D, and E mention only one of the companies. Even if they are true, they don't support the argument being made.

3. **C** is the best answer, because it strengthens the argument presented. If students have already asked for what the argument suggests, there is a better chance that they will respond positively to its implementation. A, D, and E seem like they're connected to the argument but are actually quite a leap—after all, a moment's thought shows that the band's perfect attendance at practice has nothing to do with the rest of the student body's arrival at school. B is a better choice but still does not seal the deal; we don't know what about attendance at school is related to after-school jobs.

4. **D** This is a question of extending the logic. You must figure out which of the premises given in the answer choice provides the largest detriment to the plan's success. Therefore, you must focus only on what you know to be true. Thus, A can be eliminated because you don't know if students will be separated from their friends. B can't be right, since it doesn't account for students starting class later in the morning, and C doesn't work either, because there's no mention of mixing class levels. E is one of those answers that's so clearly wrong it could almost convince you it's correct, just because it's so simple. But D is the best choice.

5. **A** is the best answer. If another organization experienced the same outcry but did not report cancelled subscriptions, that indicates that the newspaper may have lost subscribers for another reason. Remember, you're extending the logic here. It is not necessary to prove the newspaper's case. Notice, too, that C is one of those answers that simply restate something from the passage in hopes that you will choose it.

6. **E** In this structure-of-the-argument question, you must decide what role the first (bolded) sentence plays in the construction. It is not the conclusion (A), or a finding (B). D can't be right because it doesn't present evidence. That leaves E and C, and a moment's thought reveals that it is more of a premise than an explanation.

7. **D** is the best answer. C seeks to help prove why bears are more prevalent in the park, which is not the argument under consideration. A has no connection, and B could be seen as arguing against the stated opinion (If bears eat berries and plants, why do they need to eat the trout?). As for E, it is a restatement of a sentence in the question.

8. **A** is the best answer because it provides an explanation for why the argument presented will not hold true. It suggests that last year's inflation rate was a blip in a relatively stable inflation rate of 3 percent per year. Be careful not to bring your outside knowledge into this question. You may feel that government intervention (as mentioned in E) can affect the rate of inflation, or have a good argument for why a representative sample of data (B) is a good way to calculate. But the GMAT is only interested in information presented on the GMAT.

9. **C** is the best answer for this fill-in-the-blank question. It is the only answer that provides an explanation as to why the crop would be held back in a smaller harvest by suggesting that a large portion of last year's harvest is still available. The other answers change the premises of the argument or offer additional, tangential information.

10. **C** is the best answer in this parallel reasoning argument. Remember to take the time to sketch out the argument first. Here, the passage indicates that two things are true (the time spent on Facebook and the rise in bullying) and then connects them (as one causing the other) without good logic. Both can be true without a de facto connection. The argument in B does the same thing, concluding that people with higher educations are less likely to pollute without considering the myriad of other reasons why water might be less polluted in that area.

11. **E** is the best answer. This is a straightforward assumption question, but there is some trickiness in approaching it. Notice that A is a statement of the opposite, as you've been warned about. The survey-givers are assuming the exact opposite—that students are not lying in their answers. C and D are assumptions but seem broader than the passage. And B is the conclusion of the passage, not the assumption. That leaves E, a better choice than C or D.

12. **D** is the best answer in this weaken-the-argument question. Although it does not use the word *argument* to describe Andrew's plan, it is still that type of question. You can eliminate C as another example of the problem Andrew wishes to address, and E as another way of describing the problem. A and B sound like they could be impediments, but because there's no direct statement about when Andrew intends to study for two hours in the passage, they cannot be correct. D presents a true problem with Andrew's plan.

13. **B** is the best answer. This question simply reverses the request of question 12, now asking you to find the best support for the argument in the passage. The proven success of the vitamins (B) supports the idea that this will be a successful plan. A seems similar, but the doctor's word about a health matter carries more weight than Andrew's mother's, and the doctor's argument is based on more current evidence.

14. **A** This is a tough question that looks easy. D probably seems like the best answer—after all, it is a flawed conclusion—but look at the question stem. It is asking you what the flaw in the argument's premises is, not how the conclusion of the argument is flawed. C presented a fact, and E is not part of the passage (again, the question stem is key, because it is not asking you "which of the following if true . . ."). That leaves B and A. The bigger problem is the smaller representation of polled voters; 90 percent of possible voters haven't been asked their opinion, making the conclusion highly suspect. Remember to read the question stem carefully and choose only the answer that works.

15. **D** is the best answer for this structure-of-the-argument question. You must read the answer choices carefully to find the one that best describes what the bold portion is doing. It isn't a premise, conclusion, or assumption, but it is a factual detail, so D is the closest answer.

16. **B** This is a strengthen-the-argument question, so be sure to look for the answer that strengthens the zoologist's argument (called an "opinion" in the passage). B is the best support for the idea that people in the area are afraid of Watersmith snakes, which, in turn, helps prove her belief that they don't wish to aid Watersmith snakes. While all of the other answer choices may be true, their veracity does nothing to support her argument.

17. **B** This is a find-the-weakness question, and again, you must think about the argument presented. If it is true that local residents had recently helped save a frightening, unlikable regional animal, the zoologist's belief that they didn't want to help save Watersmith snakes because they are frightening and unlikable isn't logical. Notice that E is a good argument against a different opinion—if the zoologist had claimed that people didn't know about her efforts, for example. But for this argument, B is best.

18. **C** This question wants you to look at the assumptions being made by the creator of the argument. The argument expresses surprise that people would prefer to go to a small shop for stamps rather than visit a large post office. Only C directly points to that assumption, mentioning that there might be mitigating factors that make the small shop preferable to larger post office.

19. **D** This question is most similar to the ask-the-right-question genre. You need to take a step back and consider what else you need to know in order for the argument to work. While the other answer choices may provide part of the needed information, what you really want to find out is D.

20. **A** With this inference question, you need to follow the argument to its logical conclusion. If everything in the passage is true—as dubious as we may find it—that means that A must be true, and the company has figured out how to safely produce food without preservatives. B might seem like a natural inference, but it is a leap, not a hop. C is a restatement of information in the argument, and D contradicts the passage. That leaves E, which is generally true but not particularly supported by the passage. Remember to stick very close to what you're sure you know!

Critical Reasoning Drill 2

Each of the critical reasoning questions is based on a short argument, a set of statements, or a plan of action. For each question, select the best answer of the choices given.

A community college is experiencing a high turnover rate among its journalism faculty members. To rectify this problem, the chairperson of the journalism department has proposed to the dean that beginning next year, starting salaries for journalism instructors be increased by 10 percent to provide a more competitive pay package.

1. Which of the following, if true, indicates a flaw in the department head's plan?

   (A) There are several nearby universities that offer a similar pay scale.
   (B) The journalism faculty has generally indicated satisfaction with the number and type of courses they keep.
   (C) The college is located in a community with a high mortality rate.
   (D) Political science instructors receive approximately 15 percent more pay at the same college than what is proposed by the chairperson.
   (E) The chairperson joined the college two years ago, after the last chairperson resigned under pressure.

2. What statement, if true, would support the chairperson's plan the best?

   (A) The journalism classes at the community college are so popular that they are often overenrolled.
   (B) Student dissatisfaction with the journalism instructors is high.
   (C) In the last year, four journalism instructors from the community college have taken jobs at nearby universities that require longer hours but pay a higher salary.
   (D) When polled, journalism professors at the community college report general satisfaction with the numbers of courses they teach.
   (E) The community college dean stated that she was open to new proposals from department chairpersons.

The most popular style of batting helmets for baseball players provides protection of the top and back of the head as well as protection for the player's ear that's turned toward the pitcher. However, little to no protection is provided for the player's other ear and temple. A study of head injuries to baseball players at bat shows that a large proportion were caused by blows to the unprotected temple area. Therefore, if batting helmets protected both ears and temples, the risk of serious head injury to players at bat would be greatly reduced, especially since _____.

3. Which of the following most logically completes the passage?

    (A) baseball pitchers do not wear helmets on the mound

    (B) baseball players report that helmets with two ear coverings are uncomfortable to wear

    (C) the bone in the temple area of the skull is delicate and thus more susceptible to breaking and causing brain damage

    (D) batters are more likely to be hit on the side or arm

    (E) a batter's hearing could be compromised by the wearing of such helmets

In most factories, improving the technology of the assembly line increases labor productivity, the amount of goods a worker can produce per hour. In Libertore Factory, labor productivity is 20 percent higher than in Koltun Industries. Therefore, Libertore Factory must be further advanced technologically than Koltun Industries.

4. The argument above is most vulnerable to which of the following criticisms?

    (A) It presents a conclusion that ignores the facts stated in the argument.

    (B) It presents a possible cause of a condition as the only cause of that condition without considering other possible causes.

    (C) It presents as fact the author's opinion regarding Koltun Industries.

    (D) It presents a numerical fact as a premise leading to a false conclusion.

    (E) It fails to consider the other mathematical means of calculating labor productivity.

5. Which statement, if true, would best support the argument made in this passage?

    (A) Koltun Industries and Libertore Factory do not work in the same industry.

    (B) There is only one way to calculate labor productivity.

    (C) Until five years ago, Libertore Factory far outpaced Koltun Industries.

    (D) Koltun Industries was recently taken over by a foreign company.

    (E) A survey of Libertore Factor workers about their productivity revealed that 85 percent would like to see technological improvements on the assembly line.

Italian espresso is the gold standard for the beverage. People from all over the world purchased espresso machines made in Italy in hopes of learning to brew a perfect cup at home. Yet all over Italy, American coffee shops are on the rise. Many Italians prefer to start their day with a to-go cup of American coffee instead of the classic espresso. It is a shameful reduction of a culture to consume such a far inferior product.

6. Which of the following, if true, provides the most support for the argument made above?

   (A) Italians prefer the lower caffeination found in American-style coffee.
   (B) It is much more difficult to produce a good cup of espresso than a good cup of coffee.
   (C) Espresso is not as portable as coffee.
   (D) Consumer surveys show a 35 percent reduction in the consumption of espresso since the first American coffee shop opened in Italy.
   (E) American-style coffee shops are staffed by people who are generally bilingual.

7. If the statements above are true, which of the following must also be true?

   (A) Italians consume more American products in general these days.
   (B) American-style coffee shops should add espresso to their menus.
   (C) The convenience of carrying out a coffee may trump the national pride in producing great espresso for some consumers.
   (D) Italians prefer to consume Italian products.
   (E) Espresso shops would do a brisk business in America.

Basilburg shop owner: "If we want to save our downtown shopping area, we need to rally together to protest the opening of a DiscountPalace on the outskirts of town! Why, I looked into this issue, and did you know that DiscountPalace opened stores in the last five years in Mosora, Miggeville, and St. David? And all three of those towns experienced the bankruptcies of at least 20 percent of their downtown shopping area stores! They didn't rally to protect their small businesses. Do we want that to happen in Basilburg?"

8. The shop owner quoted above could strengthen her argument with which of the following facts, if true?

   (A) Another town in the same part of the state, Fayetteburg, successfully protested to keep DiscountPalace out of its area.
   (B) DiscountPalace is a company from overseas.
   (C) Most of the people in Basilburg do their shopping downtown already.
   (D) It is not unusual for a downtown shopping area to see a 20 percent turnover in stores over the course of a few years.
   (E) DiscountPalace has a record of ignoring local resident protests.

9. The conclusion presented above is based on the assumption that

   (A) DiscountPalace doesn't want bad publicity.
   (B) More people would shop in downtown Basilburg if they knew of the choices there.
   (C) DiscountPalace is unlikely to build near a community that has openly stated that the company isn't welcome.
   (D) People tend to feel closer to each other when they work together.
   (E) Bankruptcy is a natural part of running a business.

10. Which of the following is most like the passage in its logical structure?

   (A) If shoppers don't tell shops what products they like to buy, shops will buy whichever products they want, which are generally the cheapest available.

   (B) If the residents of Pittstown don't protest the construction of a new amusement park just down the highway, the arcade and carnival in downtown Pittstown may go under.

   (C) The townspeople in Ketcham protested the opening of a strip club downtown and were successful in having it moved outside of the town line.

   (D) When downtown shopping areas fail, the entire town is diminished.

   (E) Most runners need to hear detailed feedback on their running style in order to improve.

In the last five years, there has been a significant decrease in smoking. At the same time, the portrayal of smoking in movies and on television has decreased as well. Therefore, the decrease in smoking must have been caused by the decrease in the portrayal of smoking in media.

11. Which of the following, if true, most seriously weakens the argument made above?

   (A) More people watch cable television than ever before.

   (B) People who smoke are routinely shown to be more vulnerable to addiction than their peers.

   (C) Fewer teenagers watch network television than five years ago.

   (D) Smoking has been on decline for the last 25 years, although movies and television frequently portrayed it until about 10 years ago.

   (E) Information about the health hazards that come from smoking is not widely available.

12. Which of the following is an assumption on which the argument depends?

   (A) People who smoke watch a great deal of television.

   (B) There is a direct correlation between seeing an activity in the media and taking part in that activity.

   (C) Advertisements for smoking ran until the 1980s.

   (D) People who do not smoke are not as easily influenced as those who do.

   (E) The movement to remove smoking from television and film has affected the artistic quality of the works in question.

Casey: "We have 20 teachers sharing a photocopy machine in the second floor teachers' lounge. The machine is always breaking down, which means that 20 people is too many people to make use of one machine."

Corey: "I don't agree. We have 25 teachers sharing the copy machine in the first floor teacher's lounge. However, our copy machine almost never breaks down. Our machine must be better made than yours."

13. Which of the following, if true, would support Corey's argument the most?

    (A) The copy machines are of the same make and model.
    (B) There are more teachers who use the copy machine on the third floor.
    (C) There are 20 teachers who use the copy machine on the second floor.
    (D) No one makes a concerted effort to maintain either of the copiers in good running order.
    (E) The machine on the first floor is designed for higher volume than the model on the second floor.

14. Corey's argument is most vulnerable to the objection that it fails to

    (A) provide support for Casey's argument
    (B) come to a conclusion
    (C) use statistics to prove why 20 people using a copier is not too many
    (D) provide evidence that the first-floor copier is better made than the second-floor copier
    (E) uncover and dismiss Casey's hidden assumption

The highway bypass was supposed to relieve traffic in East Allegheny County. Although the bypass opened last year, traffic in the county has gotten worse over the last year. To relieve the traffic situation in East Allegheny County, therefore, the traffic commission should order the highway bypass to be free to all travelers.

15. Which of the following, if true, gives the most support to the conclusion of the passage above?

    (A) The bypass currently charges a large toll for every vehicle that uses it.
    (B) The bypass currently is free to all travelers.
    (C) The traffic in East Allegheny County has increased due to a large shopping complex that opened six months ago.
    (D) East Allegheny County will hold a surplus in highway repair funds due to good fiscal management.
    (E) The bypass runs along the length of the East Allegheny River.

16. Which of the following, if true, most weakens the conclusion above?

    (A) The bypass shaves 15 minutes off most commutes in East Allegheny County.
    (B) The tolls for the bypass are much higher than the state average for toll roads.
    (C) A survey published in the East Allegheny Times shows that 85 percent of people think the bypass tolls are fair.
    (D) A shopping complex that recently opened in East Allegheny County has several public transportation stops.
    (E) Many locations in East Allegheny County are not reachable by public transportation.

Julie's horse, a tall gelding named Louis, can respond to over 50 commands. Julie cites this fact as evidence for her claim that Louis can understand the English language.

17. Which of the following, if true, casts the most doubt on Julie's claim that Louis can understand the English language?

- (A) Louis does not respond to the same commands when spoken to him by Julie's husband in Italian.
- (B) Julie also claims that her gerbil, Marie, can understand English.
- (C) Horses are widely considered to be less intelligent than dolphins.
- (D) Each of the 50 commands to which Louis responds involves both a spoken word in English and a distinctive hand sign.
- (E) Scientists have demonstrated conclusively that horse vocal chords are incapable of replicating many of the sounds used in the English language.

18. Julie's argument is based on which of the following assumptions?

- (A) That Louis responds to her voice specifically
- (B) That horses are more intelligent than other animals
- (C) That being able to respond to a verbal command and understanding English are the same thing
- (D) That Louis is unique among horses
- (E) That it is unusual for an animal to be able to learn more than 20 commands

Excavation of the ancient city of Kanala in western Ghana revealed a pattern of debris and collapsed buildings typical of towns destroyed by earthquakes. Archeologists have hypothesized that the destruction was due to a major earthquake known to have occurred in the area in AD 56.

19. Which of the following, if true, most strongly supports the archeologists' hypothesis?

- (A) Modern histories of Ghana often mention that an earthquake occurred there in AD 56. *Doesn't prove anything*
- (B) No coins minted after AD 56 were found in Kanala, but coins minted before then are frequently found.
- (C) The people of Kanala did maintain a calendar.
- (D) Archeologists have uncovered several pieces of buildings from Kanala that are clearly in the style popular after the second century AD.
- (E) An earthquake was known to occur in Ghana in 56 AD. *Restates question = NO*

20. Which of the following would it be most useful to know in order to evaluate the argument?

- (A) Whether Kanala has been excavated
- (B) Whether the pattern of debris and collapsed buildings found in Kanala has any other known cause
- (C) Whether the people of Kanala maintained a calendar
- (D) Whether an earthquake was known to have occurred in the area in AD 56 *Already know it's true*
- (E) Whether modern historians of Kanala are basing their assumptions on known facts or tradition

Answers

1. **A** is correct. You must find the statement that will weaken the argument made. While C and E might be disconcerting, they don't argue against paying instructors more to keep them at the college. B and D seem like reasonable facts to consider, but A is more to the point of the chairperson's suggestion.

2. **C** This question is the opposite of the first. Now you're asked to find a sentence that would support the chairperson's proposal. C provides information that clearly shows that the salary is an issue for instructors at the community college. A and B are opposite answers, which generally indicates that neither one can be right. D doesn't support the chairperson's argument clearly, and E simply reports a fact that might have caused the chairperson to make his proposal.

3. **C** is the best way to complete this fill-in-the-blank question. The passage reads as an argument building toward approving of the helmets. Thus, B and E, which make an argument against such helmets, would be out of place. A and D may be true but are irrelevant to the issue under discussion.

4. **B** is the answer in this difficult question. The argument is clearly flawed, but finding how it is most flawed is tricky. To do so, you must consider how the argument is constructed. The biggest problem is the way it jumps to a conclusion without considering any other factors, so B is the best answer. A and C might be true, but are not enough to condemn the entire argument. D is gobbledygook, presented in hopes that you choose it while skimming the test, and E—while it may or may not be correct—does not speak to the larger problem of the argument's conclusion.

5. **E** is the best answer, since it speaks directly to the argument. You need to find something that supports the idea that Libertore Industries has fallen behind Koltun because of technological problems. E is the only answer that supports that. The other answers would require too great a leap in logic to be true. Remember to stay cautious in your logic!

6. **D** This question wants you to strengthen the argument, and D is the best way to do it because it speaks directly to the idea that consumption of espresso is down in favor of American-style coffee. A, B, C, and E are all reasonable, so there's no clearly wacky answer to eliminate. But notice that they all speak to arguments other than the one being made here. That's why it's so important to have a clear idea of what the argument is before you begin to look at the answer choices.

7. **C** This inference question asks you to extend the argument. If you believe that the entire paragraph is true, what else must be true? The statement most closely tied to the passage is C. Remember, hop, don't leap. It's quite a leap to say that Italians consume more American products (A) or prefer Italian products (D). The other answers are opposites: there's no reason why espresso shops would do well in America (E), and B suggests practically the same thing. Remember that when you have two answers that are essentially identical, they're almost always wrong!

8. **A** This is another question that asks you to further the argument being made, so you must be clear on the passage. Here, the shop owner wants to convince her fellow townspeople to rally. The best way to do that is to convince them that rallying has been effective in similar situations (A). E will do the exact opposite. B isn't connected to the argument, and C and D are facts that do not particularly help or hurt the argument being made.

9. **C** is the best answer for this assumption question because it ties directly into the solution the argument has proposed (which you can also think of as the conclusion!). A and D are general statements that might be true but are not specifically tied to this argument. E doesn't sound right (and certainly isn't an assumption that can be drawn from this passage). B might be true, but isn't connected to the main logic of this passage.

10. **B** Oh no! A parallel reasoning question! Remember our advice: if it sounds too close to the subject matter of the passage, it's probably not the right answer. And you can see that's true with answer choices A and D. E is tempting because it seems disconnected from the passage, but it's not right either. That leaves C and B. C seems similar. But if you read B (if X doesn't happen, Y will happen), you can see that the logic is exactly the same, whereas C is closer to X happened and caused Y to happen resulting in Z.

11. **D** You need to find the answer that most weakens the argument, which is that the decline in smoking is because of the decline in its portrayal on TV and in movies. D is the only answer that weakens the specific argument, by demonstrating that smoking has been on the decline for some time, long before it was eliminated from television and movies.

12. **B** This question asks to unpick the logic made in the passage and find the assumption within it. B is the only answer that points out that a connection is made between smoking and seeing people on television smoke. Now, you may argue with that connection—and with the passage itself, for that matter—but that is the working assumption in the passage.

13. **E** is the best answer. Remember, the dialogue form of question is relatively rare on the GMAT, but it does occasionally appear. This one is actually a strengthen-the-argument question—you're asked to choose the sentence that would make Corey's argument better. A and D don't help the argument at all, and B is irrelevant. That leaves C, which simply restates a sentence from the passage, or E, the correct answer.

14. **D** This is another question that requires you to make a hop, but not a leap, in logic. It is certainly possible that, as in E, there is a hidden assumption in Casey's argument that Corey has not attacked. But it is more probable that Corey's argument is vulnerable because he hasn't provided any evidence to sustain it.

15. **A** is the correct answer for the support-the-argument question. You're looking to support the idea of eliminating tolls on the bypass so that traffic use of it will increase. D seems connected, but if you think about it, a surplus in funds doesn't logically lead to the decision to make the bypass free. That logic is best connected to A.

16. **C** The question is flipped from question 15. Now you need to figure out what most weakens the argument. Again, remember that the argument is to eliminate tolls on the bypass so that traffic use will increase. Only C, which indicates that people are not avoiding using the bypass for monetary reasons, weakens that argument.

17. **D** is the best answer for this weaken-the-argument question. It's easy to get distracted by what seems like a fairly silly argument. There might be many reasons why you think it cannot possibly be true. But you still need to be sure to attack the logic that Julie is employing, not just pile up the reasons why she's nuts! D provides the best argument against her specific claim that her horse understands (not speaks, as in E) English.

18. **C** is the best answer. Here you are asked to find the assumption, making sure that you find the assumption that supports the argument. That's key, because several answer choices (such as A and D) certainly seem like the kind of assumptions someone like Julie might make. However, only C is an assumption on which her argument is built, because she is conflating the horse's ability to follow commands with his ability to understand English.

19. **B** This question requires slow reading to understand, and the answer choices are misleading. You need to find support for the argument. D does the opposite—it provides evidence against the argument—so the hope is that you'll choose it quickly because you're in a hurry. You can eliminate A since modern histories are of no help in *proving* ancient events, and E just restates a sentence from the question. That leaves C, the kind of fact that seems like it's going to be helpful, but in fact, doesn't budge the argument one inch. B supports the hypothesis.

20. **B** This is a rare ask-the-right-question problem. You are being asked to explain what would be most helpful to know in order to evaluate the logic of the argument presented. You have to remember (or reread) the argument in order to do this, of course. If you do, you'll see that B, which questions whether one of the assumptions of the argument is always correct, is the best answer. Watch out for D: that information is in the question, so you already know it is true. And it's a fact, not an assumption, so there's no point in questioning it!

Critical Reasoning Drill 3

Each of the critical reasoning questions is based on a short argument, a set of statements, or a plan of action. For each question, select the best answer of the choices given.

A recent report published in the local newspaper determined that 80 percent of drivers on Colorado highways regularly use their seat belts. However, 65 percent of drivers pulled over on routine traffic stops were NOT using their seat belts. Clearly, drivers who drive recklessly often also do not wear their seat belts.

1. The conclusion drawn above depends on which of the following assumptions?

   (A) Police were not targeting drivers who were not wearing seat belts.
   (B) Many of the drivers ticketed had been pulled over more than once in the time period covered by the report.
   (C) Drivers pulled over by police on Colorado highways for routine traffic stops are more likely to be engaging in reckless behavior including not wearing a seat belt.
   (D) There is no way to determine the connection between routine traffic stops and not wearing a seat belt.
   (E) That a "routine traffic stop" means that the driver was driving recklessly.

Gordon: "I found three comic books at the store that I wanted. But they cost more than I wanted to pay, so I left them for now."

Ryan: "What do you mean, "for now"?"

Gordon: "Well, I'll go back in a week when the new issues have come out and buy the comics I wanted at 50 percent off."

2. Which of the following, if true, would strengthen Gordon's logic?

   (A) The comic book store turns over merchandise frequently.
   (B) The comic book store has a policy of selling past issues for 50 percent off.
   (C) The comic book store has fierce competition from a larger comics shop that opened two blocks away.
   (D) Gordon is good friends with the owners of the comic book shop.
   (E) Gordon has memorized the delivery dates for new issues of his favorite comics.

3. Which of the following would best serve as a logical conclusion to Gordon's argument?

   (A) "I go to that store every week, anyway."
   (B) "That comic book store isn't the only one in town that sells the series that I like."
   (C) "I usually wait a week to buy my comics since they always drop the price when the new editions come out."
   (D) "They probably won't sell out of the series I like to read."
   (E) "Maybe they will still have them at full price."

A rare disease, Tabies, is diagnosed with increasing frequency. The diagnosis rate is four times what it was five years ago. The government should act now to provide greater funding to diagnose and treat Tabies.

4. Which of the following, if true, most weakens the argument that the government should provide greater funding to diagnose and treat Tabies?

   Ⓐ There is no known cure for Tabies.
   Ⓑ Tabies is never fatal and only occasionally forces the patient to spend more than three days recovering.
   Ⓒ Tabies is highly contagious.
   Ⓓ Funds to diagnose and treat Tabies have been provided by the government for the last three years.
   Ⓔ Early testing indicates that a potential Tabies vaccine is within six months of being ready to distribute.

5. The conclusion drawn above depends on which of the following assumptions?

   Ⓐ That lack of funds is what's keeping scientists from being able to find ways to help diagnose and treat Tabies
   Ⓑ That Tabies is a small-scale disease without global repercussions
   Ⓒ That Tabies is an unpleasant disease
   Ⓓ That there are no other diseases that should be studied before Tabies
   Ⓔ That people who have Tabies suffer greatly from the disease

Many people, especially children, suffer an allergic response when they consume peanuts or food that has been in contact with peanut dust. However, some factories that make food products have entirely banned peanuts from their premises. Therefore, people who have peanut allergies (and their parents) can safely buy and consume food from those companies.

6. Which of the following is an assumption on which the argument depends?

   Ⓐ Not all people have the same level of peanut allergies; some are much worse than others.
   Ⓑ The people who work in those factories have a clear understanding of what can cause an adverse reaction in someone who has a peanut allergy.
   Ⓒ People are willing to pay more for food products that were prepared in peanut-free factories.
   Ⓓ It takes a tremendous effort to create a peanut-free environment.
   Ⓔ It is possible to create and consistently maintain a peanut-free environment.

7. Which of the following is most like the argument above in its logical structure?

   (A) Many drugstores have banned all animals except service animals on their premises because of people who have allergies. Therefore, people who have allergies can safely shop at those drugstores.

   (B) Many people are allergic to bee stings, so they should avoid going outside when bees are active.

   (C) It is difficult to completely eliminate any chance of an accident at an amusement park, so people who go to them must be careful.

   (D) Cell phones create a huge distraction at concerts; therefore, cell phones are banned.

   (E) Some people are allergic to sulfites found in wine. Thus, some wineries do not add sulfites to their products, and they are safe for those with allergies to consume.

Joshua: "I have spent a lot of time in Europe on tour with the men's choir I am a part of. Having stayed at hotels throughout Scandinavia, I have noticed that there is a large discrepancy in the quality of the woodwork between hotels that were built before 1950 and those built after. It's clear that carpenters who worked on hotels built before 1950 were far more skilled and took greater pride in their work than carpenters who worked on hotels built after 1950."

8. Which of the following, if true, most seriously weakens Joshua's argument?

   (A) Joshua is not an expert on woodwork.

   (B) Homes with superior woodwork among other attributes are far less likely to be demolished than homes constructed with shoddy workmanship.

   (C) Carpenters working since 1950 have many more tools that they can use in their work.

   (D) The quality of woodwork in hotels is generally inferior to that found in private homes.

   (E) The changing weather patterns of the region make it difficult for woodwork to survive for more than 100 years.

Principal Ellington: "If the student body wants to have more parking spots available to them, **they need to raise money to buy the field next to the school so that it can be turned into a parking lot**. There are no other options. The existent staff and faculty parking lot takes up half of the rear schoolyard area, with the student parking lot as it is now to the side. The front parking lot of the school must be left for visitors and parents."

9. In the argument presented above, what role does the boldfaced portion play?

   (A) It presents evidence that supports the argument.

   (B) It presents a premise upon which the argument is based.

   (C) It presents facts that support the premise of the argument.

   (D) It is the conclusion to the argument.

   (E) It presents an inference used in the creation of the argument.

10. Which of the following, if true, most seriously weakens Principal Ellington's argument?

   (A) The faculty and staff parking lot is only three-quarters full on most school days.
   (B) The majority of the student body walks or takes a bus to school.
   (C) The owner of the adjacent field has offered to allow it to be used for parking, free of charge.
   (D) The school football coach has often stated his desire to have the adjacent field turned into a practice ground for the team.
   (E) The parking at the front of the school is insufficient on Parent/Teacher Night and other events that many parents or guardians attend.

Justin is an excellent amateur swimmer and is unbeaten in college swimming competitions. Last school year, he won the all-around title at the Meyersville University Invitational. A month ago, Justin was in a minor car accident that caused him to break his wrist. It will be in a cast for the remainder of the school year. Consequently, when the Meyersville University Invitational is held next month, _____.

11. Which of the following best completes the passage?

   (A) Justin definitely will not win the all-around title.
   (B) Justin will most likely not win the all-around title.
   (C) The best plan is for Justin to drop out of the competition.
   (D) It is unlikely that Justin will be allowed to participate.
   (E) Justin's chief rival, Sam, will finally have a shot at winning.

For a ban against the overprescription of a certain narcotic to succeed, both the FDA and the medical community must work together to prohibit over-prescription of that drug. While the FDA has recently prohibited its doctors from overprescribing Narvia medication, many doctors are continuing to prescribe it in what the FDA terms "excessive amounts." Therefore, the ban against overprescribing Narvia is unlikely to be effective.

12. Which of the following, if true, most strengthens the argument in the passage above?

   (A) The FDA has not provided clear guidelines for what is an appropriate amount.
   (B) There are no criminal repercussions to doctors who overprescribe Narvia, despite the prohibition.
   (C) The prohibition is based on a small disagreement between the head of the FDA and the head of the company that makes Narvia, too obscure for most patients to understand.
   (D) Narvia is an inexpensive and fast-acting medication.
   (E) Prior bans of medicines similar to Narvia have been effective.

13. Any of the following, if true, is a valid reason to believe the ban will not be successful EXCEPT:

    Ⓐ Doctors will not be fined for prescribing Narvia for those who wish to take it.

    Ⓑ The company that makes Narvia has not agreed to the ban and rejects the premise of it.

    Ⓒ Congress has declined to help enforce the ban.

    Ⓓ The language of the FDA's ban is vague and difficult to enforce.

    Ⓔ Compliance with the FDA's ban is voluntary.

Moore Rocks Town Council recently decided to consider the removal of all fire alarm boxes. The Moore Rocks Fire Department reports that 90 percent of all fire alarms emanating from fire alarm boxes turn out to be false. Since virtually everyone has a personal mobile phone now, the usefulness of the fire alarm boxes has passed and they are now merely a nuisance. The fire department recommends that the Council authorize the removal of all fire alarm boxes, which will reduce the number of false alarms without affecting people's ability to report a fire.

14. Which of the following, if true, most strongly supports the idea that the fire department's proposal will have the desired effect?

    Ⓐ Responding to all fire alarms, even those that turn out to be false, costs a great deal of money.

    Ⓑ The Moore Rocks Fire Department owns technology that allows it to trace all calls made by private phone and record crucial information about where the calls were made.

    Ⓒ Not every resident of Moore Rocks Town Council owns a mobile phone.

    Ⓓ The fire alarm boxes date from the late 1800s and are quite charming.

    Ⓔ In the past, the fire department has been unable to promptly respond to an actual fire because the department has been out on a false alarm.

15. Which of the following is an assumption that enables the fire department to reach the conclusion that fire alarm boxes should be removed?

    Ⓐ People are reluctant to take action if they see that no one else is doing so.

    Ⓑ People in Moore Rocks will not protest the removal of the fire alarm boxes.

    Ⓒ Cellular phone technology will never get to the point wherein most calls are untraceable.

    Ⓓ The majority of people who make false alarms would be less likely to do so if there was a greater chance that they would be caught.

    Ⓔ The removal of fire alarm boxes will significantly alter the downtown Moore Rocks area.

Since 1970, the town of Hotspur, New Mexico, has drawn water from the Makalesh River, which feeds Lake William. If the town's water use continues to grow at its present rate, in about 10 years the water level of Lake William will inevitably decrease to the point that it can no longer support its biologically fragile population of fish.

16. The prediction above is based on which of the following assumptions?

 Ⓐ The town of Hotspur will be able to reverse its trend of increasing water use if it implements an aggressive water conservation program.

 Ⓑ The amount of water that the lake loses to evaporation each year will increase over the next 10 years.

 Ⓒ There are multiple sources of water besides the Makalesh River that feed into Lake William.

 Ⓓ Since 1970, the lake's population of fish has become more biologically fragile.

 Ⓔ As the town's water requirements grow, it will not be able to meet those requirements by drawing on water sources other than the Makalesh River.

17. Which of the following presents the best conclusion to the argument above?

 Ⓐ It is vital that Hotspur make plans to transport the fish population of Lake Williams to another viable body of water.

 Ⓑ Therefore, the town of Hotspur's city council is immediately putting water conservation efforts in place.

 Ⓒ If the town of Hotspur wants to preserve the fragile fish population in Lake William, it will need to consider other sources for water.

 Ⓓ Malakesh River feeds into Lake William.

 Ⓔ Malakesh River is a freshwater river, and Lake William is a freshwater lake.

Ambiance Hotels has a customer loyalty program that rewards customers with a paper coupon for a free night at an Ambiance Hotel after spending four nights in one. The marketing department of the hotel chain notices that people have begun selling these coupons on the Internet for less than the cost of a night at an Ambiance Hotel. Therefore, the marketing department has advised that the hotel chain begin issuing web-based vouchers that are nontransferable.

18. What is the assumption underlying the marketing department's logic in its plan?

 Ⓐ Web-based vouchers are more difficult to sell than paper coupons.

 Ⓑ It's important to keep this customer loyalty program up and running, even if the hotel chain must make a financial sacrifice to do so.

 Ⓒ Tying the free night to one person via technology will cut back on customers' ability to sell those free nights.

 Ⓓ Not all Ambiance hotels charge the same price per night.

 Ⓔ Ambiance hotels' closest competitor also has a customer loyalty program.

19. Which of the following, if true, would present the best argument for the marketing department's plan?

    (A) Most Ambiance customers do not participate in the customer loyalty program.
    (B) It is virtually impossible to transfer a web-based voucher to anyone other than the person to whom it was issued.
    (C) Ambiance managers have stated that they do not have the time to trace every coupon before accepting it.
    (D) Some Ambiance customers have stated that they prefer the paper coupons because the web is not always easily accessible.
    (E) The marketing department feels it will be easier to encourage customers to sign up for additional cost items, such as breakfast, through the use of the loyalty program.

Nutritionists advise people to eat as many vegetables as possible in the day, saying that there is no limit to how many one should consume. However, some people have contracted a nearly fatal disorder from eating an abundance of carrots. Therefore, nutritionists should caution against the overconsumption of carrots while allowing the consumption of all other vegetables.

20. What can be said to be an underlying assumption in the argument above?

    (A) Eating too much of any other vegetable will not lead to disorders.
    (B) Carrots are not really vegetables.
    (C) When nutritionists advise people to eat many vegetables, they really meant fruits and vegetables.
    (D) Carrots can be overconsumed.
    (E) Nutritionists often exaggerate for effect.

Answers

1. **E** This is a confusing question with a shaky logic in the passage and a couple of numbers, too. Not to mention that the first answer choice, A, includes a double negative that will take you a while to figure out. That said, E is still the best choice because it is the only answer choice that reveals how an assumption supports the conclusion. Watch out for C, by the way: it's just a restatement of the passage.

2. **B** It's clear that Gordon's argument has an assumption that's not being shared in his conversation with Ryan. You need to decide which of the answer choices best strengthens his statement. B makes the best case because it would mean that there is a past policy that Gordon is assuming will be in place now. D seems tempting, but there's no actual connection between that fact and Gordon's assumption.

3. **C** Because Gordon's argument doesn't really come to a conclusion, this question is essentially asking for you to find one. C is the answer that best provides the conclusion to his logic, by explaining why he thinks waiting a week will allow him to buy the comics at 50 percent off. Don't be fooled by how other answer choices (such as D) sound like something someone might say. You're not writing a realistic dialogue, but rather wrapping up the argument that is presented.

4. **B** Here's a weaken-the-argument question. You're asked to think about what would most weaken the conclusion that the government should give more money to Tabies research. B is the best argument presented because it indicates that Tabies isn't a serious threat. E is an opposite answer choice: it reads as if it was correct, but only if you're trying to strengthen the argument. D also seems tempting, except that the passage already makes clear that some funding already exists for Tabies diagnosis and treatment, so the answer choice is really just a restatement.

5. **A** You're asked to find the assumption here, and it's the very first answer. As you know, you want to always focus on the argument's conclusion and find the underlying assumptions that got you there. A is the only answer choice that speaks to this particular argument.

6. **E** Here is a question that employs information you may have an opinion on already! Be careful not to let what you think leach into your answers. You're trying to find the assumption that the conclusion rests upon. The other answer choices are appealing depending on your opinion (if, for example, you think a company might charge more for peanut-free foods, C might appeal). E, however, is based only on the premises of the argument, which only holds if maintaining a peanut-free environment is possible. Stick to logic!

7. **E** This is a parallel reasoning question, and one that breaks the rules we mentioned, because the correct answer is fairly similar in subject matter to the original argument. That's why it's important to read carefully and take your time. Do notice that A and B also use allergies in their arguments. You just have to carefully pick your way through to find the right answer. Don't forget that sketching out the argument presented beforehand makes it easier to find the correct answer choice.

8. **B** You're finding the weakness in Joshua's argument. It is based on the premise that hotels built later in the 20th century are inferior, overall, to hotels built earlier. But B points out that the rate of attrition of hotels built before 1950—that is, the number of hotels destroyed—is unknown. If hotels with shoddy workmanship are more likely to be

torn down (remember, all the premises are presented as true), then B must be the correct answer.

9. **D** This is a structure-of-the-argument question, and a perplexing one, for the correct answer is counterintuitive. We are used to seeing the conclusion at the end of the passage (after all, it *concludes* the argument), but here it is presented at the beginning. Principal Ellington leads off with her conclusion, making D the best choice.

10. **C** Most of the answer choices in this weaken-the-argument question suggest that there's something wrong with using the field next to the school as a parking lot. But that isn't actually the principal's argument. She is suggesting that students need to raise money for the conversion of the field into a parking lot; only answer choice C raises a red flag, since it suggests that payment isn't needed. This seriously weakens her argument.

11. **B** is the best answer to this fill-in-the-blank question. You're really wrapping up the argument with the conclusion here, so you need to carefully consider what you actually know about the premises. A can be rejected because, after all, you can't be absolutely sure that he'll lose. What if no one else shows up?

12. **A** This is a strengthen-the-argument question, in which you're asked to find the answer that makes the argument stronger. A is the best choice because it shows that the ban cannot be effective because the basic facts—such as what constitutes an appropriate prescription—have not been established. B, D and E provide information that might weaken the argument. C builds an argument that isn't germane.

13. **B** Here, you're asked to find the reason that doesn't work against the ban's success. This is a tricky question, because the correct answer isn't one that helps to make the ban succeed, as you might be expecting. Instead, B merely offers further information—that the company that makes Narvia doesn't agree with the ban. Of course, there stand is neither here nor there. So while this answer choice doesn't oppose the ban, it also doesn't help it. Still, it's the correct choice. All of the others are reasons to believe the ban won't succeed.

14. **B** Here you must figure out which of the answer choices provides the best support for the argument in question. The fire department wants to do away with the fire alarms because prank calls so often come from them. The best support for this argument is not about the cost of the calls (A and E), whether in money or time, but B, which points out that calls from mobile or home phones can be traced. People are less likely to make a prank phone call if they know they will be caught. C and D, by the way, argue—or sort of argue—against the proposal. You'd only choose them if you weren't reading closely.

15. **D** is the correct answer. This question is quite similar to 14, but here you are asked to find the assumption that the fire department has used in building its case. It is obviously assuming that being able to trace false alarms back to those who placed them will be a deterrent to those who might otherwise make them by yanking a fire alarm on a street. You may disagree with this assumption, but that's what is underneath the argument!

16. **E** is the best answer for this assumption question. Remember, you're looking to find the unspoken assumption in the passage, something that the argument is built upon but is unstated. The argument clearly assumes that there's no way for Hotspur to get water except from the Makalesh River. It would be an entirely different concern if the town had multiple choices for water.

17. **C** is the best answer. The passage as presented doesn't quite come to a conclusion about what should be done, so the question asks you to do so. You can eliminate D and E immediately, since D is a restatement of a fact in the passage and E simply adds in a new

fact. A is a conclusion that could be reached based on the passage—but it's not a very good conclusion. It requires that leap in logic you always want to avoid. B is the same thing—a leap when you want to hop, as in C.

18. **C** is the best answer. You're looking for the assumption contained within the argument. Here, the argument is not just toward web-based coupons (as in A) but also that the coupons be tied to one person's name, as in C. That makes it the best choice because it is the most specific.

19. **B** This is a strengthen-the-argument question, and B provides the best support. The argument is that switching to Internet vouchers will help eliminate the selling of free night coupons. This argument is only valid if the Internet vouchers are better at stopping graft than the coupons. B indicates that they will be. Notice that D argues against the idea.

20. **A** This is an odd question, but actually quite tricky. Your instinct is to second-guess the passage, which takes a hyperbolic statement and then applies faulty logic to its interpretation. But the question asks you to take it seriously. If you do, you'll find that A is the assumption underlying the passage, because it suggests that other vegetables can be eaten in any quantity.

CHAPTER 14

GMAT Sentence Correction Questions

Introduction

There's only one type of question left in the GMAT Verbal section: Sentence Correction questions. There will be about 15 Sentence Correction questions in the 40 or so Verbal questions you'll be asked on the GMAT. In other words, there are slightly more Sentence Correction questions than Critical Reasoning or Reading Comprehension questions. Remember, you have 75 minutes to complete the Verbal section of the test.

This type of question is both good and bad news. The good news is that because the English language employs a limited number of grammar and mechanical conventions, there are only so many varieties of Sentence Correction questions that you can be asked. That means that more than any other Verbal question, you can actually *study* for this part of the test: that's why you'll find a thorough, if brief, review of the relevant grammatical and mechanical rules of the English language in this chapter. We also strongly suggest casual reading in the weeks before your test: choose a novel or book of nonfiction written in standard American English. Just having those sentences running under your eyes will help.

The bad news is that for many people, just mentioning the rules of English grammar is off-putting. And even if you feel fairly confident, it's easy to get confused when you have to answer multiple questions about them. Do keep in mind that there are basically three ways a sentence can be wrong on the GMAT: It could violate a rule of grammar. It could be worded in an unclear way. Or it could be worded in a nonstandard way (in other words, it sounds funny).

As with every other part of the test, steady work will win the race: be as well prepared as you can, and then move carefully and diligently through the questions. Don't panic, make your best guess and keep going!

Instructions

Before we dive into those grammatical rules, let's take a look at the instructions you'll receive on your computer screen as you begin the Sentence Correction portion of the GMAT:

The following questions present a sentence, part of which or all of which is underlined. Beneath the sentence you will find five ways of phrasing the underlined part. The first of these repeats the original; the other four are different. If you think the original is best, choose the first answer; otherwise choose one of the others.

These questions test correctness and effectiveness of expression. In choosing your answer, follow the requirements of standard written English; that is, pay attention to grammar, choice of words, and sentence construction. Choose the answer that produces the most effective sentence; this answer should be clear and exact, without awkwardness, ambiguity, redundancy, or grammatical error.

To review these directions for the subsequent questions of this type, click on HELP.

As you can see from reading the instructions, this is going to be yet another very dry section of the test. The questions test you on your knowledge of formal written English. This isn't the English we use in talking with each other or writing a quick e-mail; this is the kind of English you would use in writing a business report.

As the instructions suggest, you will be looking at an entire sentence, or a part of a sentence, that has been underlined. Your job is to spot the grammatical error in the underlined section and choose the answer choice that is the best way of saying the same thing in more precise, formal English.

You may be given a sentence or sentence part that actually is correct as presented. If that's the case, just choose answer choice A, because that is always the same as whatever is presented in the prompt. Approximately 20 percent of the Sentence Correction questions will not contain an error, so A will be your choice. You should expect to choose it about three times on the test!

It bears extra emphasis: the sentences you're given on the GMAT will not always need to be corrected. Expect to choose A at least twice and possibly up to four times on your test!

A Review of Grammar and Mechanics

Few people look eagerly at the task of reviewing grammar rules, but doing so will truly improve your score on the GMAT. Not only will you be better prepared for the Sentence Correction questions, but your ability to do well in writing your Analytical Writing Assessment will improve, too. Remember, a computer grades the AWA (along with a human reader). Computers can't pick up a lot of nuances in writing, but they can be programmed to pick up on grammatical errors. Eliminate those, and the computer will like your essay a bit more!

Let's take a look at some of the grammar and mechanics conventions you'll need to know on the GMAT.

This chapter can't substitute for a thorough overview of grammar and mechanics if you are totally at sea. We suggest reading a good book on grammar rules such as *The Elements of Style* for that level of help.

Verbs

A large proportion of the GMAT's Sentence Correction questions will be about verb usage. Incorrect verb tense and lack of subject-verb agreement are distressingly common errors, and they make writing look inexpert. Luckily, while these errors are very easy to make, they're also pretty easy to spot! Let's look at the most common type of error you'll have to correct on the GMAT, subject-verb agreement.

A verb is a word that describes action (like *eating*, *running*, *reading*) or a state of being (*am*, *is*, *was*, *were*).

Subject-Verb Agreement

You remember from your high school English classes that the subject of a sentence is the person, place, or thing taking action, while the verb tells you what action is being taken. These, the subject and the verb, must be in agreement. Forget about trying to remember a complicated rule about words ending in -*s*. Instead, focus on this: If your subject is plural, your verb must be plural. Likewise, if your subject is singular, your verb must be singular:

I was
We were
They are
She is

The dogs ran
The dog ran

The clowns sing
The clown sings

Remember that *you* is an exception. It's always plural, even when you're talking only about one *you*. So:

You lift me as a person.
You lift me as a class.

Of course, the GMAT is rarely that easy. Take a look at this sentence:

Elsie, like many cows, eat a great deal of hay.

On first glance, you might think that there's no problem here, probably because "cows eat a great deal of hay" sounds correct. The problem is that while the verb is *eat*, the subject isn't *cows*. It's *Elsie*! And her name is singular, so the sentence should read:

Elsie, like many cows, eats a great deal of hay.

Notice how the GMAT has deliberately tried to trick you by putting the word *cows*, a plural noun, into the sentence. It's hard to catch those easy mistakes, especially when you're in a hurry. This use of a modifying clause or phrase (such as *like many cows*) is a common trick on the GMAT.

The subject of the sentence is the noun that is taking action in the sentence.

Sometimes the GMAT tricksters use *either . . . or* or *neither . . . nor*. This is confusing because when *either* and *neither* introduce multiple nouns, it seems they would need a plural verb, such as in this example:

Either Susan or David tell the story.

This seems like it might be OK, because *Susan or David* is more than one noun. But *either* renders the noun singular, no matter how many singular nouns follow. So the correct form is:

Either Susan or David tells the story.

When *either* and *neither* are used with plural nouns or pronouns (or with both singular and plural nouns), the verb should agree with the noun closest to it, as in the following example:

Either Susan or the boys are riding the bus.

Another way the GMAT test-makers will try to trip you up in subject-verb agreement is with collective nouns—such as *audience, council, group, majority, series*—which are almost always treated as singular nouns on the test. (This is not always the case in real life, so be careful.) In other words, the GMAT favors a sentence such as this:

The audience was euphoric.

over this:

The audience were euphoric.

They do the same thing with singular collective pronouns such as *each, everyone, everybody, nobody*. Again, there are rare exceptions when the way a sentence is phrased might make the verb plural, but on the GMAT, you can count on these words being singular:

Each member of the audience was euphoric.
Nobody wants to do that again.

No matter how the GMAT tries to trip you up, the key is to find the subject in the sentence—the person, place, or thing taking action—and determine whether it is plural or singular. Then make your verb match.

Verb Tense

Verb tense tells readers when the action in the sentence happened or will happen. The three most common forms of verb tense are past (*We played.*), present (*We are playing.*), and future (*We will play.*). There are three more commonly used verb tenses beyond the basics: present perfect (*We have played.*), past perfect (*We had played.*), and future perfect (*We will have played.*). Figuring out verb tense can be overwhelming—this explanation barely scratches the surface—but the good news is that the GMAT does not ask you to identify verbs or the tense in which they appear. Rather, it is interested in your ability to use verbs correctly in a sentence, particularly in matching their tense throughout an example sentence. If the sentence begins with action in the past, the rest of the sentence (on the GMAT, anyway) should also be in the past.

You don't have to identify parts of speech or types of verb tense on the GMAT. You just need to be able to make words work together as smoothly as possible.

It is quite common to find that in the underlined portion of a GMAT Sentence Correction question there is more than one verb, and the tenses of the verbs do not match:

Sheila gave Rachel the key to the house after Rachel would stop by.

We can see what the sentence means, and it may be written in a way that is familiar to us in casual conversation. But the sentence is grammatically incorrect, combining past tense (*gave*) and conditional (*would stop*). A better form of the sentence is:

Sheila gave Rachel the key to the house after Rachel stopped by.

Now the two verbs (*gave* and *stopped*) agree in their tense.

Pronouns

Since the GMAT mimics the mistakes we most frequently make in real life, it makes sense that pronoun problems would be the second-most-common form of error that needs to be corrected on the test. We make a lot of pronoun mistakes! Pronouns are the words we use to replace nouns or proper nouns (names), including *he*, *she*, *it*, *they*, and *them*. There are other pronouns (technically, *there* is often a pronoun), but you will not see many GMAT questions concerned with them.

Pronouns replace nouns in sentences. Proper nouns are names used as nouns. They usually begin with capital letters. The word *princess* is a noun. *Princess Elise* is a proper noun. *She* is a pronoun.

There are two basic forms of pronoun mistakes that you'll have to correct on the GMAT. The first is called a pronoun reference error. This error occurs when the sentence does not make clear to the reader what or who the pronoun is referring to because the related noun (called the referent or antecedent) is unclear or missing. Here's an example:

According to Victoria, Kate and Louis wanted to take Mark shopping for a new car, <u>but he didn't know which one of them to choose</u>.

Here, we don't know if the *he* refers to Mark or Louis, and whether *them* refers to the people in the sentence or to cars.

This error is fairly easy to spot. If you see pronouns in the underlined portion of the sentence, ask yourself if it is immediately clear which noun they are referring back to, keeping in mind that your initial impression may not be the correct response. Just be sure to look for the answer that best improves the sentence. In that example, you'll need to find the answer that corrects for both *he* and *them*.

Another common form of pronoun error that the GMAT is fond of throwing at you is the pronoun number error, in which a plural pronoun replaces a singular object or vice versa. These sentences seem correct because they reflect the reality of how most of us talk at least some of the time, but they are incorrect in formal written English. Here's an example:

Manuel likes his coworkers, <u>but they do not socialize with colleagues outside of work functions</u>.

You see the problem: the subject of the sentence, *Manuel*, is singular, but the rest of the sentence refers to him as *they*. In a verbal conversation, it would most likely be clear that the speaker means Manuel and his wife or partner, but in written English, it's unclear. You'd need to fix that, looking for an answer choice that replaces *they* with *he*.

By the way, you may be thinking, wouldn't it be easier to write, "Manuel and his partner"? The answer to that is yes, that makes sense. However, you can only adjust the underlined portion of the sentence, so you'll have to choose the best fix for that.

Modifiers

Another common form of error is the misplaced modifier. While pronoun problems in the GMAT's Sentence Correction section are often about a misapplied pronoun, modifiers are more often misplaced than misused. A modifier is a phrase that modifies the subject of another phrase (almost always a noun). Modifiers should almost always come right before or right after the subject that they're modifying. If they aren't, the reader could think that the modifier is describing a different noun than what was intended. Here's an example:

Eating everything in sight, Jennifer tried to snap a photo of the black bear.

The sentence is trying to say that Jennifer tried to take a photo of a black bear who was eating everything in sight, but as you can see, the misplaced modifier makes it sound as if Jennifer was the one who couldn't stop eating!

Although Jennifer is the subject of the sentence, the black bear is the subject of the modifier, so it should read like this:

Jennifer tried to snap a photo of the black bear eating everything in sight.

This isn't the best sentence of all time, but it is certainly much more clear and correct.

Sentences with this type of error often happen in first drafts, before the writer has gone back to smooth out his or her writing. But because the meaning is clear to the writer, sometimes this type of sentence slips by a revision. Luckily for you, these errors are much easier to catch when you aren't the author!

Here are a few more misplaced modifier mistakes to look out for on the GMAT:

▪ **Adjectives:**

Sad and scared, the hotel looked welcoming to our young heroine.

Clearly, the adjectives *sad and scared* are supposed to modify *our young heroine*, not the hotel.

- **Adjectival Phrases:**

    A cook with a master's degree in criminology, the food made by Jack Smith was exquisite.

    Here, the adjectival phrase *A cook with a master's degree in criminology* is describing Jack Smith, not the food.

- **A Participial Phrase Introduced with a Preposition:**

    After swimming for hours, the cabin on the shoreline finally was in Wei's sight.

    The phrase *After swimming for hours* modifies Wei, not the cabin.

Don't be turned off by the grammatical labels above. If it makes you queasy to think of words like "a participial phrase," then don't! Just know to look for what the underlined portion of the sentence is referring to, and then check to make sure it is in the right place to modify the noun it describes.

Parallelism

While parallelism is not as common a mistake to be corrected on the GMAT Verbal, it is one that is tricky to spot. Many people don't understand the rules behind parallelism and thus do not know what to fix on the test. It's very easy to read through a sentence with a parallelism error and assume that A is the right choice—that is, that the sentence has no mistakes. Be on guard that you don't flub this type of question. Let's take a look at the rules, first.

Parallelism is a principle of formal written American English that states that if a sentence presents multiple related items or phrases, then each of those items or phrases should be presented in parallel grammatical structures. The key here is that idea of parallelism: everything should get listed in the same way. Looking at a few examples will help you understand this better.

> Rules of parallelism are so often violated that we barely notice them. That makes this type of question especially challenging. Stay alert for them.

The most common GMAT question about this grammatical idea presents items in a list and asks you to decide whether they are presented in parallel form. Here's what we mean:

Meredith, an award-winning scientist, is known for her research into blood clotting, anatomical intervention, and the applying of sutures to more efficiently heal wounds.

The list has a problem: the first two items in the list are nouns (*blood clotting, anatomical intervention*), but the third is a gerund (*applying of sutures . . .*). If you don't know what a gerund is, don't worry about it. Instead, just look at the list: two nouns, followed by a phrase beginning with a verb. They're not parallel. This would be a better form of the same sentence:

Meredith, an award-winning scientist, is known for her research into blood clotting, anatomical intervention, and the application of sutures to more efficiently heal wounds.

Here, *application of sutures* is now in noun format, and the entire sentence is parallel.

This type of error in a list doesn't only happen with a verb inserted into a list of nouns. The nonparallel structure could be a list of verbs with a misplaced noun:

> Grace, a dedicated teacher, is always taking her students to plays, inviting them on hikes, and she makes it a point to talk to their parents at least once a week.

As you can see, the error here is *she makes it a point . . .*, which doesn't fit with the other two parts of the list. They are in verb format, so it should be too. The sentence should be something more like this:

> Grace, a dedicated teacher, is always taking her students to plays, inviting them on hikes, and talking to their parents at least once a week.

While the mistake in parallelism is most commonly made in the last part of the sentence, after the *and* or *or*, it can appear anywhere, so read very carefully before deciding there's no error in a sentence that contains a list!

Along with list errors, parallelism can trip you up in another kind of sentence. The GMAT is also fond of two-part sentences in which the first half creates an expectation that the second half will be similarly constructed. Here's an example of a poorly formed sentence of this type:

> To say that Gloria is an exceptional mother is giving credit where credit is due.

We know: that sentence sounds perfectly fine to the ear. But it is technically incorrect. Because the sentence begins with the infinitive (*To say . . .*), the rest of the sentence should take that form as well:

> To say that Gloria is an exceptional mother is to give credit where credit is due.

The best advice we can give you on this kind of question is that when you see a sentence with a list or a two-part structure, you can be fairly sure that there's going to be a parallelism error. Look carefully for it!

Idiomatic Expressions

This type of question is a real doozy. There are thousands of idiomatic constructions (meaning the specific ways we match words together, often comparative words and/or prepositions) in the English language, and there's no way to prep you for all of them. That said, we tried to include as many of them as possible in the test questions that end this chapter, so take the time to work through them.

The further bad news is that there aren't any rules guiding idiomatic expressions, so if you run into one that you don't know on the GMAT, you'll be stuck with choosing the answer that sounds right. That said, there's good news, too: you WILL be familiar with many idiomatic expressions. Also, if you know the expression, they're not hard to figure out: if they sound correct, they're correct, and if not, the answer choice that you need should be immediately apparent. More good news: with only 15 Sentence Correction questions per GMAT, there's a good chance that the questions you receive about idiomatic expressions will be on familiar terms.

Here's an example of an idiomatic expression question:

Since I don't like football, I would prefer tickets to the Pirates rather with the Steelers.

The chances are pretty good that you immediately thought, wait, the answer should be "rather than." All you would then need to do is choose that expression from the answer choices.

Idiomatic expressions aren't colloquialisms, that is, regional sayings like "I just about fell out." The GMAT isn't interested in those, but in the broader range of quirks in American English.

As you can tell, this type of question responds particularly well to being spoken aloud, silently, so that you have a sense of what it would sound like aloud. It only takes one read-through to know that "rather with" sounds very awkward.

Here's a table of idiomatic expressions you can look for on the test:

According to	Because of	A dispute over	Rather than
Appear to	Choose from	Different from	Regard as
As great as	Conclude from	In danger of	Result of
As good as, or better than	Contribute to	In regard to	See . . . as
Attributed to	A debate over	Not only . . . but also	Subject to
Based on	Defined as	Prohibit from	Think of . . . as
	Determined by		

False Comparisons

You're no doubt familiar with the old phrase "comparing apples and oranges." Well, keep that in mind for the next type of question you can find on the GMAT, which looks for incorrect, or invalid, comparisons. There are two kinds of this question. The first compares two things that are not comparable. Here's an example:

The sweaters stored in this drawer are <u>larger than the other drawer</u>.

Now, of course, we understand that the writer of the sentence intends to say that the sweaters in this drawer are larger than the sweaters stored in the other drawer. But the sentence doesn't actually say that; instead, it compares the *sweaters* to the *other drawer*. To fix the sentence, you'll have to fix the underlined portion to better reflect the actual comparison. The sentence should be something like this:

The sweaters stored in this drawer are larger than those stored in the other drawer.

Nouns are not the only false comparisons, which leads us to our second type of false comparison question, which incorrectly compares actions:

After visiting the zoo, Gretel and I agreed that elephants move <u>more gracefully than ostriches</u>.

We know, we know. The example above sounds exactly like something you would say. That's the trick with these questions, because formal written English doesn't match the way we speak. Although it may seem silly, the above is actually a false comparison because it is comparing how elephants move to ostriches. Here's the correct sentence:

> After visiting the zoo, Gretel and I agree that elephants move more gracefully than ostriches move.

The way this type of sentence violates our "if it sounds right, it probably is right" guideline is why we've particularly pointed it out to you. Be alert for it and the other false comparisons on the test. Words to watch out for include *like*, *as*, *than*, *similar to*, and any other construction that shows a comparison is being made.

Quantity

Another tricky, and possibly unfamiliar, form of Sentence Correction question is the sentence that describes quantity. Even if you learned these rules in school, you may not remember them now, or often hear people employ these words with complete accuracy. Let's review them.

Basically, English has a number of different words for quantity, and those words are split between those that describe quantities of two and those that describe quantities of more than two. Here's a table of those words:

TWO ITEMS	MORE THAN TWO ITEMS
Better	Best
Between	Among
Less	Least
More	Most

Thus, if you have five answer choices, you choose *among* those choices. But if you're only trying to decide whether to choose B or D, you would choose *between* them. Similarly:

> I'm trying to decide who is the *better* of the two singers who auditioned yesterday, because I want to choose the *best* of all the people who tried out.

We often use these words interchangeably when speaking, but in written English, they should be used with more care. It's worth your time to memorize the table above.

There's another kind of quantity question, which asks you to look at the distinction between countable and noncountable items. The distinction is instinctive: if you would usually be able to count the number of items, then it's countable; if not, you wouldn't. So, for example, the number of people in your car is countable, while the amount of traffic is noncountable. The kind of number you are working with determines which kind of words about quantity you should use. Here's a quick overview:

COUNTABLE	NONCOUNTABLE
Fewer	Less
Many	Much
Number	Amount, Quantity

And here are a couple of example sentences:

> Madeline gave me fewer cookies than she gave Matteo.

> There wasn't much discussion about the amount of work we had to do before we continued.

In one of those quirks of English that can drive you crazy, while there are different words for smaller quantities, depending on whether they are countable or noncountable, there's only one word for a greater number or larger amount for both countable and noncountable quantities. That word? *More.*

> It took us more time than we expected, but we were able to buy more towels at the sale.

Look at the reverse of the above:

> It took us less time than we expected, and we were able to buy fewer towels at the sale.

English is a puzzling language. Just be ready for this mistake on the test! When you see numbers or quantities—really, any of the words in the tables above—that should be a warning to you that there's likely a mistake ahead.

Rare Errors

The previous sections covered the kinds of question you are most likely to find in the GMAT's Sentence Correction portion. Your best plan is to know the rules from those sections inside and out, but if you have time, you can learn this handful too. They are not very likely to be the main question, but they may help you eliminate answer choices.

■ **Split Infinitives:** They look like this:

<u>To carefully pick</u> out the crab meat

<u>To angrily complain</u> about the service

These are technically incorrect, because they split the infinitive (To . . . [verb]) with an adverb. Do not choose an answer choice that splits the infinitive.

The two most frequently cited grammatical rules are not to end a sentence with a preposition and not to split infinitives. Interestingly, while the GMAT is less concerned about the first (more on that soon), it is definitely interested in catching you on the latter.

■ **The Subjunctive Mood:** This verb tense expresses things that the speaker or writer wishes were true, but which are not true, as in this sentence:

<u>If Kate were younger,</u> she would qualify for that award.

The wish is in the first part: were Kate younger than she is, which is impossible to achieve, something could have happened. Every once in a while, the GMAT will try to trip you up with a sentence like this:

If Jim <u>was a nice guy,</u> he would have asked for forgiveness.

Seems OK, right? Well, the subjunctive verb is always *were*, no matter how many people or things make up the subject. So it should read:

If Jim <u>were a nice guy,</u> he would have asked for forgiveness.

▪ **Possessives:** Sometimes the GMAT will test you to see if you use possessives properly. The one that's most likely to trip you up is *it's*. Remember that *it is* = *it's*. If you want to say "something belonging to it," write it as in this example:

   The dog chewed <u>its</u> leash when left alone.

▪ **Terminal Prepositions:** This grammatical rule has somewhat fallen out of favor lately, but some grammarians say that you shouldn't end a sentence with a preposition:

She didn't know who to go with.

He wasn't sure what to do as there wasn't anyone to talk to.

Because this rule is no longer so steadfastly enforced, it's unlikely you'll see it as a main question. However, we suggest avoiding any answer choices that force the sentence to end in a preposition.

Other Answers to Avoid

Here are a few more tips about which answers to avoid. We suggest avoiding any answer that includes the word *being* if it isn't referring to a *human being*. In conversation, people are fond of using *being* incorrectly as follows:

   Being that I'm the head teacher, I need to get there first.
   She was early for the interview, being that she was nervous.

These sentences aren't exactly wrong, but they're not great. Don't choose them. Also, avoid complex verb constructions like this one:

   Marie will have been teaching at the school for 20 years next year.

A better choice is:

   Marie has been a teacher at the school for 20 years next year.

Try to choose active verb constructions in your answer. Avoid:

   The book was moved.

And choose:

   Andrew moved the book.

Again, these aren't ironclad rules. There might be a question or two that requires a passive verb, or the use of *being* in some odd way. But overall, these are good guidelines, especially when trying to choose between two answer

choices that seem equally correct. Remember, Sentence Correction questions
are asking you to consider effective expression as well as correctness. It stands
to reason that you may need to ask yourself, "What is the most effective way to
state this, as well as the grammatically correct way?"

Problem-Solving Strategies

If you're familiar with our suggestions for other portions of the Verbal part of the GMAT, you
won't be surprised by our suggestions here:

- **First read the entire question.** Some of the sentences are quite long, even stretching
  to what looks like a paragraph. (While you're at it, make sure you're on a Sentence
  Correction portion of the test and not a Critical Reasoning passage; they can look very
  similar!) Don't just read the underlined portion of the sentence. It won't make sense
  without the entire passage.
- **Before you look at the answer choices, try to figure out if there's something wrong with
  the underlined portion of the question.** (A hint: it might be helpful to say the sentence
  silently, since you can't say it aloud. Errors are sometimes easier to spot that way.) If you
  think there is an error—still before looking at the answer choices—try to articulate to
  yourself what the problem is. Is it a subject-verb disagreement? The wrong verb tense?
- **Test all of the answer choices.** On the other hand, if you think the sentence is correct
  as is, make a note, but you'll still need to test all of the answer choices to make sure that
  they are not somehow more correct. It's helpful to articulate to yourself why you think
  the sentence is correct as it is so that you do not get confused.
- **Next, try out the answer choices.** You want to attempt to eliminate them as quickly
  as possible. Obviously, if you've found an error, that rules out A, so now you have a
  25 percent chance of being correct, even if you guess! If you can, choose the one answer
  choice you think is correct.
- **If you're stuck between two answer choices, compare them to each other.** They can't
  be identical, so one will fix one aspect of the underlined passage and the other will fix
  something else. Which seems better? That's the one you choose.

Sentence Correction Drill 1

Directions: The following questions present a sentence, part of which or all of which is underlined. Beneath the sentence you will find five ways of phrasing the underlined part. The first of these repeats the original; the other four are different. If you think the original is best, choose the first answer; otherwise choose one of the others.

These questions test correctness and effectiveness of expression. In choosing your answer, follow the requirements of standard written English; that is, pay attention to grammar, choice of words, and sentence construction. Choose the answer that produces the most effective sentence; this answer should be clear and exact, without awkwardness, ambiguity, redundancy, or grammatical error.

1. In 1980, lack of precipitation reduced Costa Rica's coffee production to about 30 million tons, nearly 20 percent <u>less than those of the 1979 harvest.</u>

   - Ⓐ less than those of the 1979 harvest.
   - Ⓑ less than the 1979 harvest.
   - Ⓒ less than 1979.
   - Ⓓ fewer than 1979.
   - Ⓔ fewer than that of India's 1979 harvest.

2. Veronica needs to buy a new dress, resole her dancing shoes, <u>and the visit to the doctor needs to be rescheduled.</u>

   - Ⓐ and the visit to the doctor needs to be rescheduled.
   - Ⓑ and visiting the doctor needs to be rescheduled for later in the day.
   - Ⓒ and reschedule her visit to the doctor.
   - Ⓓ and doctor's visiting needs to be rescheduled.
   - Ⓔ and visit the doctor.

3. After I called all of your friends, <u>you was surprised</u> when they showed up for the party.

   - Ⓐ you was surprised
   - Ⓑ you were surprise
   - Ⓒ you was surprising
   - Ⓓ you were surprised
   - Ⓔ surprised was your feeling

4. Nancy, like many nurses, <u>work long hours.</u>

   - Ⓐ work long hours.
   - Ⓑ work long hour.
   - Ⓒ works long hours.
   - Ⓓ work for long hours.
   - Ⓔ work for longer hours.

5. The audience, already amazed by the special effects, <u>gasp when the curtain rose</u> on the second act's new set.

   - (A) gasp when the curtain rose
   - (B) gasped when the curtain rose
   - (C) gasp when the curtain roses
   - (D) gasp upon seeing the curtain rise
   - (E) gasps when the curtain rose

6. Once we realized that the polar bear wasn't going <u>to try to find its toys again</u>, we were ready to move on to another part of the zoo.

   - (A) to try to find its toys again
   - (B) to try to find it's toys again
   - (C) to try to find their toys again
   - (D) to try to find it's toys once more
   - (E) to tries to find its toys again

7. From what Mellie told me, Rick and Shanna took Nathan to the amusement park, <u>but he got scared and didn't want to go on the roller coaster.</u>

   - (A) but he got scared and didn't want to go on the roller coaster.
   - (B) but he got scared, and therefore didn't want to go on the roller coaster.
   - (C) but he got scared, making Rick not want to go on the roller coaster.
   - (D) but he got scared, being then that he did not want to go on the roller coaster.
   - (E) but Nathan got scared and didn't want to go on the roller coaster.

8. <u>Screaming like a banshee for his team to win, Grandma escorted Jeffrey from the stadium.</u>

   - (A) Screaming like a banshee for his team to win, Grandma escorted Jeffrey from the stadium.
   - (B) Because he would not stop screaming like a banshee for his team to win, Grandma escorted Jeffrey from the stadium.
   - (C) Because she would not stop screaming like a banshee for her team to win, Grandma escorted Jeffrey from the stadium.
   - (D) Jeffrey and Grandma had to be escorted from the stadium.
   - (E) Since Jeffrey was unable to stop screaming at every play his team made, and because his screams were like those of a banshee, Grandma felt she had to escort him from the stadium.

9. Marie Curie was a gifted scientist, <u>but they did not know the dangers of radiation at that time.</u>

    (A) but they did not know the dangers of radiation at that time.
    (B) but they did not know the dangers of radiation back then.
    (C) but he did not know the dangers of radiation at that time.
    (D) but neither she nor anyone else knew the dangers of radiation at that time.
    (E) but not gifted enough to say she knew the dangers of radiation.

10. <u>Leaping up to grab the phone, the entire office turned to watch Alfonso's actions.</u>

    (A) Leaping up to grab the phone, the entire office turned to watch Alfonso's actions.
    (B) As Alfonso leapt to grab the phone, the entire office turned to watch him.
    (C) The entire office was turning to watch as Alfonso was leaping to grab the phone.
    (D) It felt as if the entire office leapt to grab the phone, not just Alfonso.
    (E) Having leapt up to grab the phone, the entire office turned to watch Alfonso's actions.

11. <u>To say that Michelle is a voracious reader is understating the case!</u>

    (A) To say that Michelle is a voracious reader is understating the case!
    (B) To say that Michelle is a voracious reader was understating the case!
    (C) Michelle is a voracious reader, it isn't understating the case to say it!
    (D) To say that Michelle will be a voracious reader, is saying that the case is understated!
    (E) To say that Michelle is a voracious reader is to understate the case!

12. The Austrian princess had to choose <u>the best of two suitors' offers</u>: that of the Duke from Hungary and that of the Viscount of England.

    (A) the best of two suitors' offers
    (B) the best of both suitor's offers
    (C) the better of two suitors' offers
    (D) the best of each suitors' offers
    (E) the best of two suitor's offers

13. The presidential debate <u>dissolved into a debate over</u> which of the candidates should drop out of the race.

    (A) dissolved into a debate over
    (B) dissolved for a debate over
    (C) dissolving into a debate over
    (D) dissolved into a debate around
    (E) dissolves into a debate regarding

14. <u>If she was shorter</u>, Hannah could have been a gymnast.

    Ⓐ If she was shorter
    Ⓑ If she was short
    Ⓒ If she were shorter
    Ⓓ Had she been shorter than she is
    Ⓔ Shorter

15. The report indicated that the rise in inflation was attributable <u>to the rising in costs the bank will notice.</u>

    Ⓐ to the rising in costs the bank will notice.
    Ⓑ to the rising in costs that the bank will notice.
    Ⓒ to the rising in cost the bank noticed.
    Ⓓ to the rise in cost the bank noticed.
    Ⓔ to the rising in the costs that the bank noticed.

16. Natalia asked the reporters <u>to quietly wait by the steps</u> for the press conference to begin; of course, they ignored her.

    Ⓐ to quietly wait by the steps
    Ⓑ to quietly go to the steps and wait
    Ⓒ to the steps to go to wait quietly
    Ⓓ to wait by the quiet steps
    Ⓔ to wait quietly by the steps

17. <u>Less students came to the show</u> than Paulo was expecting, which was a disappointment to him; he thought that at least half of his class of 16 would show up.

    Ⓐ Less students came to the show
    Ⓑ Fewer students came to the show
    Ⓒ Lesser students came to the show
    Ⓓ Less students coming to the show
    Ⓔ Few students came to the show

18. The ban enacted by the World Space Association last week <u>will prohibit member countries from</u> contributing to space debris, among other provisions.

    Ⓐ will prohibit member countries from
    Ⓑ will be prohibiting member countries from
    Ⓒ will prohibit all of the member countries from
    Ⓓ will prohibit the countries that are members from
    Ⓔ will have prohibited member countries from

19. Although I cannot tell them apart, Christine <u>can always differentiate between the four flavors.</u>

        Ⓐ   can always differentiate between the four flavors.
        Ⓑ   can always differentiate between all of the four flavors.
        Ⓒ   can always differentiate among the four flavors.
        Ⓓ   can often differentiate between the four flavors.
        Ⓔ   can usually differentiate between the four flavors.

20. "We can poll all of the voters in the country," Takeya said, <u>"But until we know what he thinks, we're at a loss."</u>

        Ⓐ   But until we know what he thinks, we're at a loss.
        Ⓑ   But until we know what they think, we're at a loss.
        Ⓒ   But until we know what they thinks, we're at a loss.
        Ⓓ   But until we know what he thinks, we are at a loss.
        Ⓔ   But until we know what he thinks, a loss is where we're at.

Answers

1. **B** is the right answer. This looks like a quantity question, but you actually need to look at word choice, so it ends up being more of an idiomatic expression question. *Those* is not a necessary word in the sentence.
2. **C** is the right answer in this parallelism question. All parts of the sentence should be parallel.
3. **D** This is a subject-verb agreement question, which isn't too difficult if you recollect that *you* is always paired with *were*, not *was*, even when it is singular.
4. **C** Another subject-verb agreement question. Don't get thrown off by the modifying phrase. The subject is *Nancy*, not *nurses*.
5. **B** This is a verb tense question. The verb *rose* is past tense, so the verb *gasped* needs to be past tense as well.
6. **A** This sentence is correct as written. *Its* is the possessive form of the word. *It's* stands in for *it is*. A quick way to check is to substitute *it is* into the sentence. If that makes sense, you need the apostrophe.
7. **E** is correct. This is a question of pronoun reference. It's not clear in the sentence which male is meant by *he*. E corrects that.
8. **B** This is a misplaced modifier. Jeffrey is the one screaming like a banshee, not Grandma. B best fixes this out of the choices.
9. **D** is the correct answer in this pronoun number question. *They* seems to refer back to Marie Curie, but she is a *she*, not a *they*.
10. **B** fixes the misplaced modifier. The office didn't leap up, Alfonso did.
11. **E** fixes the parallelism mistake in the sentence. The infinitive at the beginning of the sentence means that there must be one later in the sentence.
12. **C** is the answer for this question of quantity. When two people are involved, the correct word is *better*. You'd need one more person to have *best* in the sentence.
13. **A** This is an idiomatic expression question. The expression is *a debate over*. While other answers provided may sound acceptable, this question wants you to choose the most likely standard English expression.
14. **C** This is an example of that tricky subjunctive mood question we warned you about! Remember that the subjunctive verb is always *were*, never *was*, even with a singular subject.
15. **D** This answer fixes both the parallelism and subject-verb agreement problems within the sentence. If you notice two problems in the underlined portion of the sentence, look for the answer that solves both of them.
16. **E** Don't split infinitives!
17. **B** *Fewer* goes with countable numbers. The rest of the sentence proves that Paulo's class was small enough to be countable!
18. **A** There aren't any problems with this sentence. The verbs line up with the subjects, and the idiomatic expression, *prohibit from*, is used correctly.
19. **C** When there are two flavors, *between* is correct; here, with four, *among* is better.
20. **B** is the best answer. The pronoun *he* used later in the sentence is unclear. The only noun it could refer to is *the voters*, which means that *he* has to be incorrect. By the way, we hope you didn't fall for E, which ends in a preposition!

Sentence Correction Drill 2

Directions: The following questions present a sentence, part of which or all of which is underlined. Beneath the sentence you will find five ways of phrasing the underlined part. The first of these repeats the original; the other four are different. If you think the original is best, choose the first answer; otherwise choose one of the others.

These questions test correctness and effectiveness of expression. In choosing your answer, follow the requirements of standard written English; that is, pay attention to grammar, choice of words, and sentence construction. Choose the answer that produces the most effective sentence; this answer should be clear and exact, without awkwardness, ambiguity, redundancy, or grammatical error.

1. Adam felt that the water pressure in the 747's cabin was <u>stronger than the other plane.</u>

   (A) stronger than the other plane.
   (B) stronger than the water pressure on the other plane.
   (C) stronger than he expected.
   (D) strongest of the two water pressures.
   (E) stronger than what he had experience on the other plane.

2. Tabies, a disease first identified in the hospitals of Cleveland, Ohio, <u>believed to be</u> the first snake-borne illness that manifests in humans.

   (A) believed to be
   (B) believes to be
   (C) will be believed to be
   (D) is believed to be
   (E) should be believed to be

3. <u>In danger for being arrested,</u> Susan B. Anthony insisted on leading the protest for Women's Voting Rights anyway.

   (A) In danger for being arrested,
   (B) In danger and being arrested,
   (C) In danger of being arrested,
   (D) In danger despite being arrested,
   (E) In danger or being arrested,

4. The number of zebras <u>was more than</u> the horses.

   (A) was more than
   (B) was lesser than
   (C) being greater than
   (D) were greater than
   (E) was greater than that of

5. Upon visiting the church where the murder had taken place, the grotesque brickwork unnerved the Duke.

 - Ⓐ Upon visiting the church where the murder had taken place, the grotesque brickwork unnerved the Duke.
 - Ⓑ Upon visiting the church where he knew the murder had taken place, the grotesque brickwork unnerved the Duke.
 - Ⓒ As he visited the church where the murder had taken place, the Duke was unnerved by the grotesque brickwork.
 - Ⓓ The grotesque brickwork, visiting the church, unnerved the Duke, for it was where the murder had taken place.
 - Ⓔ The murder having taken place in the church with the grotesque brickwork, the Duke was unnerved.

6. The corporation sells both stocks and bonds, but they do not offer any financial security.

 - Ⓐ but they do not offer any financial security.
 - Ⓑ but they do not offer much in the way of financial security.
 - Ⓒ but he does not offer any financial security.
 - Ⓓ but it does not offer any financial security.
 - Ⓔ but they does not offer any financial security.

7. Skipping past the house that was supposedly haunted, the old woman who lived inside stared at the little girl as she went by.

 - Ⓐ Skipping past the house that was supposedly haunted, the old woman who lived inside stared at the little girl as she went by.
 - Ⓑ As the little girl went skipping by, the old woman who lived inside the house that was supposedly haunted stared at her.
 - Ⓒ The old woman who lived in the house stared at the little girl who went skipping by the supposedly haunted house.
 - Ⓓ Supposedly haunted, the old woman stared at the little girl who skipping by her house.
 - Ⓔ As the little girl went skipping by, the old woman who lived inside stared at the house that was supposedly haunted.

8. Although Wellington feared a French invasion, he was confident that the coastal defenses could handle anything that the French threw at them.

   (A) Although Wellington feared a French invasion, he was confident that the coastal defenses could handle anything that the French threw at them.
   (B) Although Wellington feared that the French would invade, he confidently knew that the coastal defenses could handle anything that Wellington threw at them.
   (C) Although Wellington feared a French invasion, he was confident that the coastal defenses could be sure to handle anything that the French threw at them.
   (D) Although Wellington feared a French invasion, he was at the same time confident that the coastal defenses could handle anything that they threw them.
   (E) Although Wellington feared a French invasion, he was confident that the coastal defenses could handle anything that they threw at him.

9. Either the girls or the boys are the winners; we'll have to check the results to be sure.

   (A) Either the girls or the boys are the winners;
   (B) Either the girls or the boys will be the winners;
   (C) Either girls or boys are the winners;
   (D) Either the girls or the boys is the winner;
   (E) Either the girls or the boys is the winners;

10. I bought Julie, Cindy, Irina, and Melissa the quarterly reports they asked for, but she thinks the font is too small to be easily read.

    (A) but she thinks the font is too small to be easily read.
    (B) only she thinks the font is too small to be easily read.
    (C) but she thought the font was too small to be easily read.
    (D) but she thinks the font is too small.
    (E) but Cindy thinks the font is too small to be easily read.

11. To say that Emerson founded transcendentalism is to say that the movement came to life in the woods of Concord.

    (A) is to say that the movement came to life in the woods of Concord.
    (B) is saying that the movement came to life in the woods of Concord.
    (C) is a way of saying that the movement came to life in the woods of Concord.
    (D) was to say that the movement came to life in the woods of Concord.
    (E) says that the movement came to life in the woods of Concord.

12. Because Ronald does not enjoy vegetables, he would <u>rather than</u> cook them for his children.

    (A) rather than
    (B) rather not
    (C) rather
    (D) then rather
    (E) but not also

13. <u>A king with a reputation for social justice, Edward the II's reign was a long and happy one for most of its span.</u>

    (A) A king with a reputation for social justice, Edward the II's reign was a long and happy one for most of its span.
    (B) As a king with a reputation for social justice, Edward the II's reign was a long and happy one for most of its span.
    (C) For most of its span as a king with a reputation for social justice, Edward the II's reign was a long and happy one.
    (D) Edward the II was a king with a reputation for social justice; his reign was a long and happy one for most of its span.
    (E) Since he was a king with a passion for social justice, and his reign was a long and happy one, Edward II was a king.

14. <u>Who do you think is the best writer</u>, Michael or Peter?

    (A) Who do you think is the best writer
    (B) Who do you think is the better writer
    (C) Who do you think is the good writer
    (D) Who do you think is well writer
    (E) Who do you find to be the best writer

15. The newly inaugurated president turned her attention to her three campaign goals: <u>reducing poverty, improving the nation's schools, and an end to war overseas.</u>

    (A) reducing poverty, improving the nation's schools, and an end to war overseas.
    (B) reducing poverty and improving the nation's schools and an end to war overseas.
    (C) reducing poverty, improving the nation's schools, and ending war overseas.
    (D) reducing poverty, improving the nation's schools, and an end to overseas wars.
    (E) reduction in poverty, improving the nation's schools, and an end to war overseas.

16. <u>Much of the team's players</u> did not bother to read the newspaper.

   - Ⓐ Much of the team's players
   - Ⓑ Many of the team's players
   - Ⓒ Few of the team's players
   - Ⓓ All of the team's players
   - Ⓔ An amount of the team's players

17. Once a new astrological body is located, <u>astronomers choose from</u> a database of names to give it.

   - Ⓐ astronomers choose from
   - Ⓑ astronomers choose amongst
   - Ⓒ astronomers choose between
   - Ⓓ astronomers choose
   - Ⓔ astronomers choose to

18. Kristen went to the bank <u>for speaking among</u> Siovhan.

   - Ⓐ for speaking among
   - Ⓑ to speak among
   - Ⓒ to speak with
   - Ⓓ to speak nearby
   - Ⓔ to speak

19. Unlike the <u>United States, the president of the Philippines are</u> elected to a six-year term in office.

   - Ⓐ United States, the president of the Philippines are
   - Ⓑ United States, the president of the Philippines is
   - Ⓒ the president of the United State, the president of the Philippines is
   - Ⓓ United States, the people of the Philippines elect a president
   - Ⓔ the president of the United States, the president of the Philippines is

20. <u>Being that we were the first to leave the Council meeting,</u> we missed the argument that broke out over the proposition on the ballot.

   - Ⓐ Being that we were the first to leave the Council meeting
   - Ⓑ Being that we were the first to take our leave from the Council meeting
   - Ⓒ Being that we were the first to leave the Council meeting that we were attending
   - Ⓓ Because we were the first to leave the Council meeting
   - Ⓔ Being that we would have been the first to leave the Council meeting

Answers

1. **B** This is a false comparison question. If you look at the sentence, you'll see that the way it was originally written implies that the water pressure in the 747 is stronger than the other *plane*, not the other plane's water pressure. B does the best job of fixing that.

2. **D** This is a question of subject-verb agreement, made somewhat tricky because you'll have to identify the subject of the sentence. It's *Tabies*, which sounds plural because of the *s* at the end, but as a disease, is singular.

3. **C** This is an idiomatic expression question. The common American English phrase is *in danger of . . .* , and that is the only correct choice here.

4. **E** This is a quantity question. When the word *number* is part of the equation, the answer is never *more*, but always *greater*.

5. **C** is the best rewording of this sentence. The problem within it was the participial phrase modifying the wrong noun—*the Duke*, instead of *the church*—is fixed in this version, and it is less wordy than any other answer to boot.

6. **D** A corporation isn't a *they*, it's an *it*. This is a pronoun reference error.

7. **B** This is a mess of a sentence, but the real error is in the misplaced modifier. The woman isn't haunted; the house is. Answer choice B best fixes that problem.

8. **A** This is a pronoun reference question. It's correct as written. Although E might look acceptable, it uses *they* without a clear referent. Who would *they* be? Only the original sentence makes this clear.

9. **A** The original sentence is correct. When *either . . . or* is used with plural nouns, the verb needs to match the noun closest to it, which in this case is plural, *boys*.

10. **E** This is another pronoun reference question. It's impossible to tell which of the four women mentioned in the sentence is *she* in the underlined portion. Only E fixes this problem.

11. **A** This sentence is correct as it is written, matching the parallelism of the infinitive structure begun with the first part of the sentence.

12. **B** In this question of idiomatic expression, the correct phrase is *rather not*.

13. **D** The original sentence has a misplaced modifier, in which Edward's *reign* is described as being a king for social justice. While E technically fixes this problem, D does so with more economy of expression and style.

14. **B** When directly comparing two people, you can have only the "better" of the two. "Best" can be used only when three or more people are being compared.

15. **C** This is a question of parallelism. All the phrases used in the end of the sentence must match. Only C accomplishes this by making sure they all begin with a verb.

16. **B** is the best answer. When you have a countable number (as we can presume the team is), you use *many* instead of *much*, which is used for an uncountable number.

17. **A** It's correct as written: the idiomatic expression is *choose from*.

18. **C** The only phrase that makes sense out of the choices (including that already placed in the sentence) is *to speak with*.

19. **E** The original sentence—although it seems correct—compares the United States to the president of the Philippines. E presents a proper comparison and fixes the parallelism error.

20. **D** Remember our tip: the alternative to using *being* is almost guaranteed to be correct.

Sentence Correction Drill 3

Directions: The following questions present a sentence, part of which or all of which is underlined. Beneath the sentence you will find five ways of phrasing the underlined part. The first of these repeats the original; the other four are different. If you think the original is best, choose the first answer; otherwise choose one of the others.

These questions test correctness and effectiveness of expression. In choosing your answer, follow the requirements of standard written English; that is, pay attention to grammar, choice of words, and sentence construction. Choose the answer that produces the most effective sentence; this answer should be clear and exact, without awkwardness, ambiguity, redundancy, or grammatical error.

1. <u>Since the average rate of high school graduations were rising,</u> the school board concluded its plan had been effective.

   (A) Since the average rate of high school graduations were rising,
   (B) Since the average rate of high school students who were graduating were rising,
   (C) Because the average rate of high school graduations were rising,
   (D) Since the average rate of high school graduations was rising,
   (E) Since the average rate of high school graduation were rising,

2. Noted for its voracious appetite, <u>the Belgian goat, having originally been bred for its creamy-tasting milk, but now is celebrated for the low fat content of the milk.</u>

   (A) the Belgian goat, having originally been bread for its creamy-tasting milk, but now is celebrated for the low fat content of the milk.
   (B) the Belgian goat is now celebrated for the low fat content of its milk, although it was originally bred for the milk's creamy taste.
   (C) the Belgian goat is now celebrated for it's creamy-tasting and low-fat milk.
   (D) the Belgian goat, celebrated for the low-fat content of its milk now, was originally bred for that milk because it was creamy-tasting.
   (E) the Belgian goat gives milk which can be described as creamy-tasting and low-fat.

3. <u>Rising tides of foreclosures</u> across the state has led the governor to declare the housing market to be a source of "perpetual crisis."

   (A) Rising tides of foreclosures
   (B) Rising tides of foreclosure
   (C) The rising tide of foreclosures
   (D) The rising tide of foreclosuring
   (E) All of the foreclosures

4. "Three qualities I can bring to the job?" Xi said. "Easy. <u>I'm good at analyzing stock movements, applying the rules of the market to transactions, and writing reports that put this information in a highly readable form.</u>"

    (A) I'm good at analyzing stock movements, applying the rules of the market to transactions, and writing reports that put this information in a highly readable form."

    (B) I'm good at the analysis of stock movements, applying the rules of the market to transactions, and writing reports that put this information in a highly readable form."

    (C) I'm good at the analysis of stock movements, the application of the rules of the market to transactions, and writing reports that put this information in a highly readable form."

    (D) I'm good at analyzing stock movements, the application of the rules of the market to transactions, and the writing of reports that put this information in a highly readable form."

    (E) I'm good at: analyzing stock movements; applying the rules of the market to transactions; written reports that put this information in a highly readable form."

5. <u>Running to catch the train,</u> the people on the platform stared at Francisco as he screamed for the conductor's attention.

    (A) Running to catch the train,

    (B) Running as he was to catch the train,

    (C) As they ran to catch the train,

    (D) As he ran to catch the train,

    (E) Seeing him running to catch the train,

6. "<u>This group of students tend to ignore instructions,</u> which is frustrating," said the professor.

    (A) This group of students tend to ignore instructions,

    (B) This group of students tend to ignores instructions,

    (C) This group, comprised of students, tend to ignore instructions,

    (D) This group of students tends to ignore instructions,

    (E) The group of students tend to ignore instructions,

7. Five SteadyCam digital cameras were sold last week, <u>and it brought</u> to 15 the number of these popular cameras sold this month.

    (A) and it brought

    (B) and this brought

    (C) bringing

    (D) but it brought

    (E) and will bring

8. She <u>wanted to safely and quiet</u> ask him for his identification.

    Ⓐ wanted to safely and quiet
    Ⓑ wanted to safely and quietly
    Ⓒ wanted to safe and quiet
    Ⓓ wanted, safe and quiet
    Ⓔ wanted safely and quietly

9. Kate loves Bubbles, Julie, and Magritte, the birds she looks after for her mother, <u>but she can be difficult to feed.</u>

    Ⓐ but she can be difficult to feed.
    Ⓑ but she might be difficult to feed.
    Ⓒ but feeding her is difficult.
    Ⓓ but Magritte can be difficult to feed.
    Ⓔ but she finds feeding her difficult.

10. General Grant left for the front <u>after it was clear</u> the troops were in place.

    Ⓐ after it was clear
    Ⓑ after it would be clear
    Ⓒ until it was clear
    Ⓓ until it was going to be clear
    Ⓔ after it was clearly

11. Neither Mr. Garland nor Mrs. Sloat <u>were aware of the fight in the cafeteria.</u>

    Ⓐ were aware of the fight in the cafeteria.
    Ⓑ were aware of the fighting in the cafeteria.
    Ⓒ were aware that there was fighting in the cafeteria.
    Ⓓ were not aware of the fight in the cafeteria.
    Ⓔ was aware of the fight in the cafeteria.

12. <u>After it had stopped raining,</u> we will take the boat out on the lake to watch the sunset.

    Ⓐ After it had stopped raining,
    Ⓑ After it will stop raining,
    Ⓒ After it stops raining,
    Ⓓ After it is stopping raining,
    Ⓔ By the time it stop raining

13. The experiment seems promising, <u>but it is subject to further tests</u> to be sure.

    Ⓐ but it is subject to further tests
    Ⓑ but it is going to be subject to further tests
    Ⓒ but it is subjecting to further tests
    Ⓓ but it is the subject of further tests
    Ⓔ but these tests will subject it

14. <u>The waiter gave me fewer biscuits than I had ordered.</u>

   (A) The waiter gave me fewer biscuits than I had ordered.
   (B) The waiter gave me less biscuits than I had ordered.
   (C) The waiter presented me with less biscuits that I had ordered.
   (D) I had ordered three biscuits, but the waiter gave me less.
   (E) The ordering was for three, but the waiter gave me less biscuits.

15. <u>Because to</u> my allergy to shellfish, I will not enjoy the seafood banquet.

   (A) Because to
   (B) Because on
   (C) Because
   (D) Because only
   (E) Because of

16. <u>The amount of soup</u> that was consumed far surpassed what we were expecting.

   (A) The amount of soup
   (B) The number of soup
   (C) The pounds of soup
   (D) The reservoir of soup
   (E) All of the soup

17. Miki'ala <u>was asked to carefully review</u> the questions before taking the test.

   (A) was asked to carefully review
   (B) was asked to, with care, review
   (C) were asked to carefully review
   (D) was asked to review carefully
   (E) was asked carefully to review

18. <u>Being that the company went bankrupt,</u> it's difficult to tell who owns the rights to their products.

   (A) Being that the company went bankrupt,
   (B) Because the company went bankrupt,
   (C) Although the company went bankrupt,
   (D) Being the bankrupt company,
   (E) Bankrupted, the company,

19. <u>I wish I had given you better advice</u> about the merger.

  Ⓐ I wish I had given you better advice
  Ⓑ I wished I had given you better advice
  Ⓒ I have wishes that I had given you better advice
  Ⓓ I wish I gave you better advice
  Ⓔ I gave you advice than I wished

20. If that group of senior citizens <u>don't quiet down,</u> the group will have to be asked to leave the restaurant.

  Ⓐ don't quiet down
  Ⓑ don't quiets down
  Ⓒ quiets down
  Ⓓ quiet down
  Ⓔ doesn't quiet down

Answers

1. **D** The best answer matches the verb in the second part of the sentence (*concluded*). You also must adjust for a singular subject (*rate*).

2. **B** This is a whale of a sentence, and the real error is probably in trying to pack so much information into it. That said, B does the best job of presenting the information as clearly as possible, without changing the meaning intended.

3. **C** This is an idiomatic expression question. The phrase should be *The rising tide*. Notice that the rest of the question includes a singular verb, and that cannot be altered. Thus, you must choose the finishing phrase that best matches.

4. **A** The sentence is correct as it is. The parallelism is in order throughout.

5. **E** As the sentence is written, the opening phrase does not modify the subject of the sentence (*the people on the platform*). E fixes the mistake in the best way.

6. **D** The problem here is one of subject-verb agreement. The subject is *group*, not *students*, so you must choose the singular form of the verb.

7. **C** is the best answer out of those offered.

8. **B** While the words in question are adverbs, you can still apply the rules of parallelism here: both forms of *safe* and *quiet* should end in *-ly*. B does that. If you're not sure, mouthing the sentence should tell you which sounds best.

9. **D** In this question of pronoun reference, it's not clear who *she* refers to at the end of the sentence. D makes this clear.

10. **A** The verbs match in this sentence; there are no verb tense errors!

11. **E** The essential problem in this sentence is the lack of subject-verb agreement. When a writer uses *neither . . . nor . . .* with two or more singular nouns, he must also use a singular verb.

12. **C** The sentence lacks clear use of verb tense. C fixes this in the simplest way.

13. **A** The sentence is correct, as the idiomatic expression is *subject to*.

14. **A** The sentence is correct. The number of biscuits is a countable number, so *fewer* is correct. We only use *less* when the number is noncountable.

15. **E** The popular expression is *Because of*, making it the right answer here.

16. **A** This sentence is correct as written. Soup is a noncountable quantity, and *amount* goes with noncountable quantities.

17. **D** Don't split infinitives! That's the major problem with this sentence. D fixes it by removing *carefully* from *to review* and leaving the meaning of the sentence the same.

18. **B** is the best answer. Remember that you want to avoid *being* if you possibly can. B does the best job of that while keeping the meaning of the sentence the same.

19. **A** There's nothing wrong with the sentence as it is. It's in the subjunctive mood and done well, too. The other choices change the meaning of the sentence, even if they are grammatically correct as well. If the sentence works as it is, don't change it!

20. **E** In this final subject-verb agreement question, the subject is *the group*, not *senior citizens*. Therefore, the singular form of the verb must be used, as in E.

PART 8

GMAT Practice Tests

GMAT PRACTICE TEST 1

GMAT PRACTICE TEST 2

The following practice tests recreate the range of questions you are likely to encounter when you take the GMAT. Working through these practice tests under test-like conditions will help you gain the knowledge and confidence you will need to achieve your goals on the GMAT. Each of the practice tests is composed of four parts:

1. Analytical Writing Assessment: "Analysis of an Argument"		30 minutes
2. Integrated Reasoning section	12 questions	30 minutes
3. Quantitative section	37 questions	75 minutes
4. Verbal section	41 questions	75 minutes

To maximize the benefits you gain from these practice tests, make your practice experience as similar as possible to the conditions you will experience on the actual test:

- Find a quiet and comfortable place where you will not be interrupted.
- Take an entire test in one sitting if you can find the time. If not, try to clear time to complete at least an entire section in one sitting.
- Time yourself and stick to the time limit. If you run short on time, force yourself to make educated guesses; you may need to make guesses on the real test.
- Have your testing materials—answer sheet, scratch paper, and pencils—in hand before you begin the test. Remember, you can use a calculator only on the Integrated Reasoning section.
- Answer the questions in order. You cannot skip around on the GMAT, so make sure not to get into the habit of doing so.
- Write on scratch paper, not the test itself. You will not be able to write on the computer screen (!), so get into the habit of using scratch paper.
- Be sure to type your response to the Analytical Writing Assessment.

Don't forget that there are **six additional practice tests** available online or on the app. See page 8A in the Welcome section for details.

GMAT PRACTICE TEST 1

Analytical Writing Assessment

Analysis of an Argument

Time—30 minutes

Directions: In this section, you will be asked to write a critique of the argument presented below. You may, for example, consider what questionable assumptions underlie the thinking, what alternative explanations or counterexamples might weaken the conclusion, or what sort of evidence could help strengthen or refute the argument.

Read the argument and the instructions that follow it, and then make any notes that will help you plan your response. Write your response on a separate sheet of paper. If possible, type your essay on a computer or laptop. Observe the 30-minute time limit.

A spokesman for a dairy company issued the following statement:

Many consumers buy organic milk because they are concerned about the consequences of widespread use of recombinant bovine growth hormone and antibiotics in conventional dairy industry. These concerns, however, are unfounded. While bovine growth hormone has been shown to produce significant developmental effects in cattle, no study has ever shown that its presence in commercial milk has had any developmental effects on human consumers. Regarding antibiotics, while it has been argued that large-scale, preemptive use of antibiotics in cattle feed can interfere with the animals' immune systems and can lead to the proliferation of antibiotic-resistant strains of bacteria, neither of these effects alter the quality of the milk produced by cattle that are fed antibiotics. Therefore, there is no reasonable justification for a consumer to pay $5 for a gallon of organic milk when a perfectly good gallon of conventional milk can be had for half the price.

Discuss how well-reasoned you find this argument. In your discussion, be sure to analyze the line of reasoning and the use of evidence in the argument. For example, you may need to consider what questionable assumptions underlie the thinking and what alternative examples or counterexamples might weaken the conclusion. You can also discuss what sort of evidence would strengthen or refute the argument, what changes in the argument would make it more logically sound, and what, if anything, would help you better evaluate its conclusion.

Integrated Reasoning

Time—30 minutes

Select the best answer or answers for the questions below. You may use a calculator for this section of the test only.

On the actual test, you will be provided with an online calculator. You will NOT be permitted to bring your own calculator to the test.

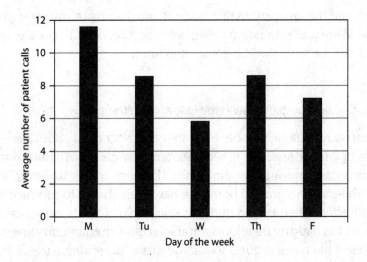

The graph above is a bar graph with five bars, each representing the average number of hourly calls received by a medical clinic from its patients. The clinic answers calls during the weekdays, from Monday through Friday. The total number of calls was recorded and an average determined for each day based on calls received over a 1-year period. Select the best answer to fill in the blank for each of the statements below, based on the data shown in the graph.

1. The average number of calls received on Wednesdays is closest to _____% of the average number of calls received on Mondays.

   (A) 6
   (B) 12
   (C) 50
   (D) 60
   (E) 200

The number of weekdays in which the average number of calls falls between 6 and 10 is _____% of 5, the number of weekdays.

- (A) 30
- (B) 40
- (C) 60

2. Based on the information shown in the bar graph, if the clinic wishes to reduce the cost of maintaining its office staff while minimizing disruptions in service to its patients, it should cut down on the number of staff assigned to answer phone calls on _____.

- (A) Mondays
- (B) Tuesdays
- (C) Wednesdays
- (D) Thursdays
- (E) Fridays

Read the sources below before answering the question that follows.

Source #1: Car rebates

Car manufacturers often provide a rebate on new car purchases. The offer of a cash reward for purchasing a car is often enough to convince consumers to prefer one American-made model over another.

A certain car manufacturer, a large retailer of luxury cars, has several manufacturer rebate promotions on popular car models in 2017. To qualify, a person must purchase specific vehicles and subscribe to the rules of the Access Program.

Manufacturer Rebate

Car Model A	Up to $1,500
Car Model B	Up to $1,000
Car Model C	Up to $2,000
Car Model D	Up to $750

Source #2: Price list for cars

Car Model A	$38,000–$42,000
Car Model B	$31,000–$45,000
Car Model C	$46,000–$60,000
Car Model D	$42,000–$57,000

Source #3: Access Program levels of benefit

Business Partners: Those who join the car company's Business Partners program or who are members of the Associated Builder's and Contractor's Union are eligible for 100% of the rebate amount.

Adaptive Equipment Partners: Those who require adaptive equipment or other customizations for health reasons, and who submit the appropriate paperwork and medical documentation at the time of purchase, are eligible for 100% of the rebate amount.

Customer Loyalty Partners: Purchasers who hold credit cards with the car company, who work for the company, or who have a trade-in that was purchased from the same dealership are eligible for 75% of the rebate amount.

Cash Earns Cash Bonus: Purchasers who have a trade of significant value, who trade a car made by the car manufacturer but purchased from a different dealership, or who are paying cash for the car are eligible for 50% of the rebate amount.

3. Consider each of the items listed below. Select *Yes* if the item can be determined based on the information given in the three sources. Otherwise, select *No*.

Yes	No	
○	○	The maximum rebate amount given to eligible Business Partners who purchase Car Model A
○	○	The exact rebate amount given to eligible Customer Loyalty Partners who work for the company and purchase Car Model C
○	○	The exact vehicle price paid by an Adaptive Equipment Partner who purchases Car Model B and submits the appropriate paperwork and medical documentation at the time of purchase

This table displays data on coffee sold by a Guatemalan producer in 2017.

On the actual exam, you will be able to sort the table by any of its columns. (Columns can be sorted in ascending order only.) The following table is shown sorted in different ways to mirror the test.

Sorted by Variety (Column 1)

VARIETY	SALES, NATIONAL SHARE (%)	SALES, NATIONAL RANK	EXPORTS, NATIONAL SHARE (%)	EXPORTS, NATIONAL RANK
Coarse ground	18	4	7	5
Dark roast	31	1	60	1
Espresso roast	12	4	87	1
Fine ground	20	5	15	4
French roast	53	2	49	2
Light roast	21	2	32	2
Medium ground	36	1	15	3
Medium roast	71	1	58	1
Whole bean	50	3	22	4

Sorted by Sales, National Share (Column 2)

VARIETY	SALES, NATIONAL SHARE (%)	SALES, NATIONAL RANK	EXPORTS, NATIONAL SHARE (%)	EXPORTS, NATIONAL RANK
Espresso roast	12	4	87	1
Coarse ground	18	4	7	5
Fine ground	20	5	15	4
Light roast	21	2	32	2
Dark roast	31	1	60	1
Medium ground	36	1	15	3
Whole bean	50	3	22	4
French roast	53	2	49	2
Medium roast	71	1	58	1

Sorted by Exports, National Share (Column 4)

VARIETY	SALES, NATIONAL SHARE (%)	SALES, NATIONAL RANK	EXPORTS, NATIONAL SHARE (%)	EXPORTS, NATIONAL RANK
Coarse ground	18	4	7	5
Fine ground	20	5	15	4
Medium ground	36	1	15	3
Whole bean	50	3	22	4
Light roast	21	2	32	2
French roast	53	2	49	2
Medium roast	71	1	58	1
Dark roast	31	1	60	1
Espresso roast	12	4	87	1

4. For each of the following statements, select *Yes* if the statement can be shown to be true based on information in the table. Otherwise, select *No*.

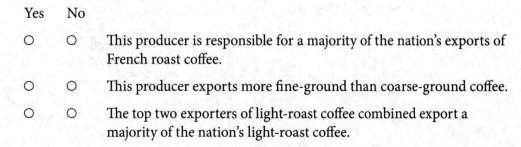

Yes   No

○   ○   This producer is responsible for a majority of the nation's exports of French roast coffee.

○   ○   This producer exports more fine-ground than coarse-ground coffee.

○   ○   The top two exporters of light-roast coffee combined export a majority of the nation's light-roast coffee.

GO ON TO NEXT PAGE ➤

5. Arden spent his vacation touring London and Paris. On his first day in London, he boarded a double-decker bus, which traveled 30 miles through the city at an average speed of 15 miles per hour. He then boarded a tour bus and traveled 30 miles outside the city. The bus stopped at a museum outside of London for lunch for 60 minutes before returning to its original location in the city. The bus traveled an average of 60 miles per hour.

Arden then took a van tour of the chapels in the city. The van traveled at an average of 10 miles per hour and covered 50 miles. The van then returned Arden to a Tube station, where he traveled 15 minutes by Tube to his hotel. He returned to his hotel 9 hours and 15 minutes after boarding the double-decker bus.

In the table below, indicate how much of Arden's journey was spent traveling by bus, and indicate the amount of time Arden spent exploring specific locations of interest during his tour of the London area. Make only two selections, one in each column.

TIME SPENT TRAVELING BY BUS	TIME SPENT EXPLORING LOCATIONS OF INTEREST	TIME (HOURS AND MINUTES)
○	○	2 hours, 0 minutes
○	○	3 hours, 0 minutes
○	○	3 hours, 30 minutes
○	○	4 hours, 45 minutes
○	○	5 hours, 15 minutes
○	○	6 hours, 0 minutes

6. A target practice weapon can fire a maximum of X rounds per minute. Ammunition is distributed by the case. Each case contains 18,000 rounds.

In terms of the variable X, select the expression that represents the number of rounds used in 1 hour of practice, when the weapon is used to its maximum capacity, and select the expression that represents the number of shooting practice hours that a full case of ammunition can cover. Make only two selections, one in each column.

NUMBER OF ROUNDS IN 1 HOUR	NUMBER OF PRACTICE HOURS COVERED BY ONE CASE	EXPRESSION
○	○	$60X$
○	○	$\dfrac{60}{X}$
○	○	$\dfrac{18,000}{60X}$
○	○	$\dfrac{X}{18,000}$
○	○	$18,000 + 60X$

Percentage of Population Attending Selected Sports Events, Single Year

Sorted by City (Column 1)

CITY	BASEBALL	FOOTBALL	BASKETBALL	HOCKEY
Baltimore, MD	35	42	28	39
Dayton, OH	9	35	17	8
Houston, TX	20	32	19	16
Las Vegas, NV	8	5	2	7
Newark, NJ	18	7	16	21
Philadelphia, PA	33	32	23	37
Seattle, WA	27	11	19	26

7. For each of the following statements select *Would help explain* if it would, if true, help explain some of the information in the preceding table. Otherwise select *Would not help explain.*

Would help explain	Would not help explain	
○	○	Visitors to Las Vegas prefer indoor gambling to attending sporting events.
○	○	Seattle's football team recently lost some key players.
○	○	Philadelphia's high schools have an excellent hockey program.

The source that follows accompanies questions 8 and 9. Select the best answer to fill in the blank for each of the statements below, based on the data shown.

A group of 1,000 people filing for unemployment were asked to provide information about their age and education level. Refer to the Venn diagram below of the survey results. Each symbol represents 10 people in the sample of 1,000.

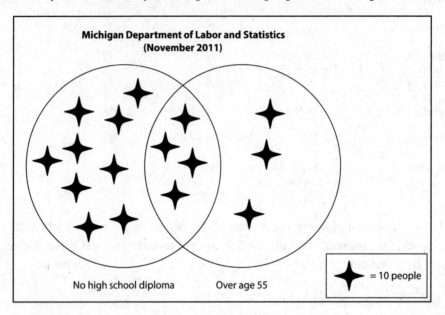

8. Out of the entire sample, the probability that a randomly chosen person over age 55 has no high school diploma is _____.

    Ⓐ 1 out of 4
    Ⓑ 3 out of 4
    Ⓒ 4 out of 7
    Ⓓ 7 out of 16

9. Out of the entire sample, the probability that a randomly chosen person with no high school diploma is over the age of 55 is _____.

    Ⓐ 1 out of 4
    Ⓑ 4 out of 9
    Ⓒ 4 out of 13
    Ⓓ 9 out of 16

10. The Rogers family is planning a vacation on a very tight budget. They cannot spend more than $300 per day on activities. They elect to go to the Kitty Hawk area of North Carolina and rent a beach house, which comes complete with bikes, surf gear, and beach toys. They also have a neighborhood pool and sand volleyball court in the area with free access. They want to include exactly two activities per day that are physically active and no more than two activities per day at the beach. They also want to include no more than two events per day costing more than $5.00 per person. There are four family members: two adults and two children.

Below is their tentative schedule for the first two days.

DAY ONE	DAY TWO
Picnic at the beach—Free	Ride bikes down the boardwalk—Free
Tour the Elizabethan Gardens at Historic Fort Raleigh—Adults, $8; Children, $6	Parasailing—$49 per person
Wright Brothers Historic Site—Adults, $4; Children, Free	Build a sandcastle—Free
Volleyball game—Free	Surfing—Free
Lost Colony Theater—$24 each seat	Mini-golf—$10 per person

In the table below, select the activity that could be added to the schedule for either day, and then select the activity that could not be added for either day. Make only two selections, one in each column.

EITHER DAY	NEITHER DAY	ACTIVITIES AVAILABLE
O	O	Swimming at the pool—Free
O	O	Make homemade ice cream—Free
O	O	Sunbathing at the beach—Free
O	O	Hot air balloon ride—$80 per person
O	O	Tennis game—Free
O	O	Water skiing—$4 per person

GO ON TO NEXT PAGE ➤

The source that follows accompanies questions 11 and 12.

The table below gives information on total warranty repairs and total nonwarranty repairs provided in 2016 by a national appliance chain store. The 20 appliances were included in the table because they fall among the top 25 appliances repaired by the company in terms of both total warranty repairs and total nonwarranty repairs. In addition to listing the total warranty repairs and total nonwarranty repairs for each appliance type, the table also gives the percent of increase or decrease over the 2015 warranty repair and 2015 nonwarranty repair numbers, and the rank of each appliance type for total warranty and total nonwarranty repairs.

On the actual exam, you will be able to sort the table by any of its columns. (Columns can be sorted in ascending order only.) The following table is shown sorted in different ways to mirror the test.

Sorted by Manufacturer (Column 1)

APPLIANCE			WARRANTY REPAIRS			NONWARRANTY REPAIRS		
MANUFACTURER	TYPE	COLOR	NUMBER	% CHANGE	RANK	NUMBER	% CHANGE	RANK
KitchenAid	Dishwasher	Stainless	1,401	−8.0	19	13,462	−2.3	5
KitchenAid	Stove	Black	4,573	−4.7	3	13,014	−6.0	9
KitchenAid	Dryer	White	3,789	−6.2	5	12,968	−0.7	10
LG	Dryer	White	2,403	1.7	12	13,671	−3.5	2
LG	Microwave	Black	1,247	−3.1	21	13,579	−0.9	4
LG	Washer	Red	3,610	1.2	7	13,272	−0.1	7
LG	Stove	Black	1,599	9.6	18	12,541	−8.1	12
Norseman	Refrigerator	Stainless	3,663	0.4	6	13,952	−2.0	1
Norseman	Stove	Stainless	1,612	0.7	17	12,520	−3.2	14
Norseman	Washer	Stainless	1,321	9.7	20	12,011	−4.0	17
Ovenmaid	Refrigerator	White	1,977	9.2	15	13,602	−7.0	3
Ovenmaid	Stove	Black	2,628	−0.3	10	12,950	−0.8	11
Ovenmaid	Dishwasher	Red	4,721	3.4	1	11,928	−0.3	18
Ovenmaid	Dryer	White	2,376	−0.3	22	11,903	−0.1	20
RCS	Stove	White	1,982	7.8	14	13,321	−0.4	6
RCS	Refrigerator	White	4,703	2	2	13,065	−2.5	8
RCS	Washer	White	3,509	−2.9	9	11,907	−2.0	19
Whirlpool	Washer	Black	4,513	1.3	4	12,478	−6.1	15
Whirlpool	Dishwasher	Red	1,937	1.2	16	12,403	−2.0	16
Whirlpool	Microwave	Black	2,604	6	11	11,890	−1.9	21

Sorted by Type (Column 2)

APPLIANCE			WARRANTY REPAIRS			NONWARRANTY REPAIRS		
MANUFACTURER	TYPE	COLOR	NUMBER	% CHANGE	RANK	NUMBER	% CHANGE	RANK
KitchenAid	Dishwasher	Stainless	1,401	−8.0	19	13,462	−2.3	5
Whirlpool	Dishwasher	Red	1,937	1.2	16	12,403	−2.0	16
Ovenmaid	Dishwasher	Red	4,721	3.4	1	11,928	−0.3	18
LG	Dryer	White	2,403	1.7	12	13,671	−3.5	2
KitchenAid	Dryer	White	3,789	−6.2	5	12,968	−0.7	10
Ovenmaid	Dryer	White	2,376	−0.3	22	11,903	−0.1	20
LG	Microwave	Black	1,247	−3.1	21	13,579	−0.9	4
Whirlpool	Microwave	Black	2,604	6	11	11,890	−1.9	21
Norseman	Refrigerator	Stainless	3,663	0.4	6	13,952	−2.0	1
Ovenmaid	Refrigerator	White	1,977	9.2	15	13,602	−7.0	3
RCS	Refrigerator	White	4,703	2	2	13,065	−2.5	8
RCS	Stove	White	1,982	7.8	14	13,321	−0.4	6
KitchenAid	Stove	Black	4,573	−4.7	3	13,014	−6.0	9
Ovenmaid	Stove	Black	2,628	−0.3	10	12,950	−0.8	11
LG	Stove	Black	1,599	9.6	18	12,541	−8.1	12
Norseman	Stove	Stainless	1,612	0.7	17	12,520	−3.2	14
LG	Washer	Red	3,610	1.2	7	13,272	−0.1	7
Whirlpool	Washer	Black	4,513	1.3	4	12,478	−6.1	15
Norseman	Washer	Stainless	1,321	9.7	20	12,011	−4.0	17
RCS	Washer	White	3,509	−2.9	9	11,907	−2.0	19

Sorted by Rank in Warranty Repairs (Column 6)

APPLIANCE			WARRANTY REPAIRS			NONWARRANTY REPAIRS		
MANUFACTURER	TYPE	COLOR	NUMBER	% CHANGE	RANK	NUMBER	% CHANGE	RANK
Ovenmaid	Dishwasher	Red	4,721	3.4	1	11,928	−0.3	18
RCS	Refrigerator	White	4,703	2	2	13,065	−2.5	8
KitchenAid	Stove	Black	4,573	−4.7	3	13,014	−6.0	9
Whirlpool	Washer	Black	4,513	1.3	4	12,478	−6.1	15
KitchenAid	Dryer	White	3,789	−6.2	5	12,968	−0.7	10
Norseman	Refrigerator	Stainless	3,663	0.4	6	13,952	−2.0	1
LG	Washer	Red	3,610	1.2	7	13,272	−0.1	7

Sorted by Rank in Warranty Repairs (Column 6) (*Continued*)

APPLIANCE			WARRANTY REPAIRS			NONWARRANTY REPAIRS		
MANUFACTURER	TYPE	COLOR	NUMBER	% CHANGE	RANK	NUMBER	% CHANGE	RANK
RCS	Washer	White	3,509	−2.9	9	11,907	−2.0	19
Ovenmaid	Stove	Black	2,628	−0.3	10	12,950	−0.8	11
Whirlpool	Microwave	Black	2,604	6	11	11,890	−1.9	21
LG	Dryer	White	2,403	1.7	12	13,671	−3.5	2
RCS	Stove	White	1,982	7.8	14	13,321	−0.4	6
Ovenmaid	Refrigerator	White	1,977	9.2	15	13,602	−7.0	3
Whirlpool	Dishwasher	Red	1,937	1.2	16	12,403	−2.0	16
Norseman	Stove	Stainless	1,612	0.7	17	12,520	−3.2	14
LG	Stove	Black	1,599	9.6	18	12,541	−8.1	12
KitchenAid	Dishwasher	Stainless	1,401	−8.0	19	13,462	−2.3	5
Norseman	Washer	Stainless	1,321	9.7	20	12,011	−4.0	17
LG	Microwave	Black	1,247	−3.1	21	13,579	−0.9	4
Ovenmaid	Dryer	White	2,376	−0.3	22	11,903	−0.1	20

Sorted by Rank in Nonwarranty Repairs (Column 9)

APPLIANCE			WARRANTY REPAIRS			NONWARRANTY REPAIRS		
MANUFACTURER	TYPE	COLOR	NUMBER	% CHANGE	RANK	NUMBER	% CHANGE	RANK
Norseman	Refrigerator	Stainless	3,663	0.4	6	13,952	−2.0	1
LG	Dryer	White	2,403	1.7	12	13,671	−3.5	2
Ovenmaid	Refrigerator	White	1,977	9.2	15	13,602	−7.0	3
LG	Microwave	Black	1,247	−3.1	21	13,579	−0.9	4
KitchenAid	Dishwasher	Stainless	1,401	−8.0	19	13,462	−2.3	5
RCS	Stove	White	1,982	7.8	14	13,321	−0.4	6
LG	Washer	Red	3,610	1.2	7	13,272	−0.1	7
RCS	Refrigerator	White	4,703	2.0	2	13,065	−2.5	8
KitchenAid	Stove	Black	4,573	−4.7	3	13,014	−6.0	9
KitchenAid	Dryer	White	3,789	−6.2	5	12,968	−0.7	10
Ovenmaid	Stove	Black	2,628	−0.3	10	12,950	−0.8	11
LG	Stove	Black	1,599	9.6	18	12,541	−8.1	12
Norseman	Stove	Stainless	1,612	0.7	17	12,520	−3.2	14

Sorted by Rank in Nonwarranty Repairs (Column 9) (*Continued*)

APPLIANCE			WARRANTY REPAIRS			NONWARRANTY REPAIRS		
MANUFACTURER	TYPE	COLOR	NUMBER	% CHANGE	RANK	NUMBER	% CHANGE	RANK
Whirlpool	Washer	Black	4,513	1.3	4	12,478	−6.1	15
Whirlpool	Dishwasher	Red	1,937	1.2	16	12,403	−2.0	16
Norseman	Washer	Stainless	1,321	9.7	20	12,011	−4.0	17
Ovenmaid	Dishwasher	Red	4,721	3.4	1	11,928	−0.3	18
RCS	Washer	White	3,509	−2.9	9	11,907	−2.0	19
Ovenmaid	Dryer	White	2,376	−0.3	22	11,903	−0.1	20
Whirlpool	Microwave	Black	2,604	6.0	11	11,890	−1.9	21

11. Review each of the statements below. Based on the information provided in the table, indicate whether the statement is true or false.

   True   False

   ○   ○   Norseman washers experienced an overall increase in repairs between 2015 and 2016.

   ○   ○   In 2016, more LG washers were repaired than LG dryers.

   ○   ○   The appliance with the highest rank based on nonwarranty repairs and the appliance with the lowest rank based on nonwarranty repairs are the same brand.

   ○   ○   In 2016, more KitchenAid stoves were repaired than LG stoves.

12. Suppose that Whirlpool changes its washer warranty policy, resulting in an increase in the number of black washer warranty repairs performed in 2017 over those performed in 2016. If the percent increase is 5.7% over warranty repairs performed in 2016, the number of black washer warranty repairs performed in 2017 would be closest to:

   ○   4,256

   ○   4,570

   ○   4,770

   ○   5,003

   ○   7,085

STOP.

Quantitative

Time—75 minutes

Solve the problem and indicate the best of the answer choices given.

NUMBERS: All numbers used are real numbers.

FIGURES: A figure accompanying a problem-solving question is intended to provide information useful in solving the problem. Figures are drawn as accurately as possible EXCEPT when it is stated in a specific problem that its figure is not drawn to scale. Straight lines may sometimes appear jagged. All figures lie in a plane unless otherwise indicated.

1. Jim's Taxi Service charges an initial fee of $2.25 at the beginning of a trip and an additional charge of $0.35 for each 2/5 of a mile traveled. What is the total charge for a trip of 3.6 miles?

   (A) $3.15
   (B) $4.45
   (C) $4.80
   (D) $5.05
   (E) $5.40

2. If the area of a square with sides of length 8 centimeters is equal to the area of a rectangle with a width of 4 centimeters, what is the length of the rectangle, in centimeters?

   (A) 4
   (B) 8
   (C) 12
   (D) 16
   (E) 18

3. A beaded necklace has white and brown beads only. If 2/3 of the beads are white and there are 13 brown beads in the necklace, how many beads in total are in the necklace?

   (A) 39
   (B) 33
   (C) 26
   (D) 21
   (E) 10

4. If $x = \dfrac{a}{3} + \dfrac{b}{3^2} + \dfrac{c}{3^3}$, where a, b, and c are each equal to 0 or 1, then x could be each of the following EXCEPT:

    (A) $\dfrac{1}{27}$

    (B) $\dfrac{1}{9}$

    (C) $\dfrac{4}{27}$

    (D) $\dfrac{2}{9}$

    (E) $\dfrac{4}{9}$

SCORE	NUMBER OF APPLICANTS
5	2
4	12
3	21
2	7
1	8

5. Fifty applicants for a job were given scores from 1 to 5 on their interview performance. Their scores are shown in the table above. What was the average score for the group?

    (A) 2.79
    (B) 2.86
    (C) 2.91
    (D) 2.99
    (E) 3.03

GO ON TO NEXT PAGE ➤

The following data sufficiency problems consist of a question and two statements, labeled (1) and (2), in which certain data are given. You have to decide whether the data given in the statements are <u>sufficient</u> for answering the question. Using the data given in the statements <u>plus</u> your knowledge of mathematics and everyday facts (such as the number of days in July or the meaning of *counterclockwise*), you must indicate whether

Ⓐ Statement (1) ALONE is sufficient, but statement (2) alone is not sufficient.
Ⓑ Statement (2) ALONE is sufficient, but statement (1) alone is not sufficient.
Ⓒ BOTH statements TOGETHER are sufficient, but NEITHER statement ALONE is sufficient.
Ⓓ EACH statement ALONE is sufficient.
Ⓔ Statements (1) and (2) TOGETHER are NOT sufficient.

NUMBERS: All numbers used are real numbers.

FIGURES: A figure accompanying a data sufficiency problem will conform to the information given in the question, but will not necessarily conform to the additional information given in statements (1) and (2). Lines shown as straight can be assumed to be straight, and lines that appear jagged can also be assumed to be straight. You may assume that the position of points, angles, regions, etc., exist in the order shown and that angle measures are greater than zero. All figures lie in a plane unless otherwise indicated.

NOTE: In data sufficiency problems that ask for the value of a quantity, the data given in the statements are sufficient only when it is possible to determine exactly one numerical value for the quantity.

6. Carrie, Lisa, and Aniyah all make purchases at a music store that sells all records for a certain price and all CDs for a certain price. How much does Carrie pay for 1 record and 2 CDs?

   (1) Lisa bought 3 records for $22.50.
   (2) Aniyah bought 2 records and 4 CDs for $55.00.

7. N and P are points on the number line below 20. Is P closer to 10 than N is?

   (1) P is greater than the average of 10 and N.
   (2) $\dfrac{P}{N} = 3$

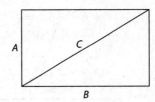

8. What is the area of the rectangular region depicted above with sides A and B and diagonal C?

   (1) $C^2 = 9 + A^2$

   (2) $A + B = 7$

9. Do at least 20 percent of the people in country X who are over the age of 25 possess a college diploma?

   (1) In country X, among the population over the age of 25, 26 percent of the male population and 16 percent of the female population possess college diplomas.

   (2) In country X, women account for 55 percent of the total population.

10. If $C = \dfrac{5r}{2s}$ and $s \neq 0$, what is the value of C?

   (1) $r = 4s$

   (2) $r = \dfrac{2}{5}$

Solve the problem and indicate the best of the answer choices given.

11. If $8a = 9b$ and $ab \neq 0$, what is the ratio of $\dfrac{a}{9}$ to $\dfrac{b}{8}$?

   (A) $\dfrac{64}{81}$

   (B) $\dfrac{8}{9}$

   (C) 1

   (D) $\dfrac{9}{8}$

   (E) $\dfrac{81}{64}$

12. Two hundred multiples of seven are chosen at random, and 300 multiples of eight are chosen at random. Approximately what percentage of the 500 selected numbers are odd?

   (A) 20%

   (B) 25%

   (C) 40%

   (D) 50%

   (E) 80%

GO ON TO NEXT PAGE ➤

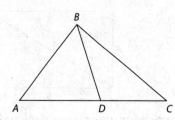

13. In triangle *ABC* above, if ∠*BAD* and ∠*ADB* have measures of 4*n*°, ∠*ACB* has a measure of *n*°, and ∠*DBC* has a measure of 45°, what is the measure of ∠*ABC*? (Figure not necessarily drawn to scale.)

  Ⓐ 45°
  Ⓑ 60°
  Ⓒ 90°
  Ⓓ 105°
  Ⓔ 120°

14. A coed soccer team has *W* women and *M* men on the team. If 4 women and 2 men are added to the team roster, and if one person on the team is selected at random to serve as team captain, then the probability that the team captain will be a woman can be represented as

  Ⓐ $\dfrac{W+4}{W+M+6}$

  Ⓑ $\dfrac{W+4}{W+M+2}$

  Ⓒ $\dfrac{W+4}{M+2}$

  Ⓓ $\dfrac{W+4}{W+M}$

  Ⓔ $\dfrac{W}{M}$

15. What is the twenty-third digit to the right of the decimal point when the fraction $\dfrac{23}{24}$ is written in decimal notation?

  Ⓐ 1
  Ⓑ 2
  Ⓒ 3
  Ⓓ 4
  Ⓔ 5

16. If Scott has earned x dollars by working 3 days a week at a constant daily rate for w weeks, which of the following represents his daily wage?

    (A) $3xw$

    (B) $\dfrac{3w}{x}$

    (C) $\dfrac{w}{3x}$

    (D) $\dfrac{xw}{3}$

    (E) $\dfrac{x}{3w}$

17. $\left(\dfrac{1}{3} - \dfrac{1}{2}\right) - 1 =$

    (A) $\dfrac{-7}{6}$

    (B) $\dfrac{-5}{6}$

    (C) $\dfrac{-1}{6}$

    (D) $\dfrac{5}{6}$

    (E) $\dfrac{7}{6}$

18. In a certain conservative mutual fund, 70 percent of the money is invested in bonds, and of that portion, 40 percent is invested in highly rated corporate bonds. If at least $1.4 million in this fund is invested in highly rated corporate bonds, what is the smallest possible total value for the mutual fund?

    (A) $4 million
    (B) $5 million
    (C) $6 million
    (D) $7 million
    (E) $8 million

19. If the diameter of a circle is 14, then the area of the circle is

    (A) 7π
    (B) 14π
    (C) 28π
    (D) 49π
    (E) 196π

The following data sufficiency problems consist of a question and two statements, labeled (1) and (2), in which certain data are given. You have to decide whether the data given in the statements are <u>sufficient</u> for answering the question. Using the data given in the statements <u>plus</u> your knowledge of mathematics and everyday facts (such as the number of days in July or the meaning of *counterclockwise*), you must indicate whether

Ⓐ   Statement (1) ALONE is sufficient, but statement (2) alone is not sufficient.
Ⓑ   Statement (2) ALONE is sufficient, but statement (1) alone is not sufficient.
Ⓒ   BOTH statements TOGETHER are sufficient, but NEITHER statement ALONE is sufficient.
Ⓓ   EACH statement ALONE is sufficient.
Ⓔ   Statements (1) and (2) TOGETHER are NOT sufficient.

20. If a is an integer, is b an integer?

(1) The average (arithmetic mean) of a and b is an integer.
(2) The average (arithmetic mean) of a, b, and $b + 4$ is a.

21. Did Alberto pay more than N dollars for his new stereo, excluding the sales tax?

(1) The price Alberto paid for the stereo was $1.05N$, including the sales tax.
(2) Alberto paid \$35 in sales tax on the purchase of his new stereo.

22. Is $r < 1$?

(1) $r > 0$
(2) $r^2 < 1$

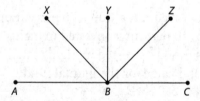

23. In the figure above, with B a point on the line AC, what is the measure of $\angle XBZ$? (Figure not necessarily drawn to scale.)

(1) BX bisects $\angle ABY$, which is a right angle, and BZ bisects $\angle YBC$.
(2) $m\angle ABX = m\angle XBY = m\angle YBZ = m\angle ZBC$

24. If P and Q are both positive, what is the value of P?

(1) PQ is a positive multiple of 5.
(2) 300 percent of P equals 500 percent of Q.

25. MegaTech and UltraCorp are considering a merger to form the MegaUltraTech Corporation. Does MegaTech have more employees than UltraCorp?

    (1) The average (arithmetic mean) age of UltraCorp employees is 32.8, while the average age of MegaTech employees is 27.2.
    (2) If the merger goes through and all employees from both companies remain employed, the average (arithmetic mean) age of the MegaUltraTech employees will be 31.4.

Solve the problem and indicate the best of the answer choices given.

26. In a sample of 800 high school students in which all students are either freshmen, sophomores, juniors, or seniors, 22 percent are juniors and 74 percent are not sophomores. If there are 160 seniors, how many more freshmen than sophomores are there among the sample of students?

    (A) 42
    (B) 48
    (C) 56
    (D) 208
    (E) 256

27. The time it took car P to travel 600 miles was 2 hours less than the time it took car R to travel the same distance. If car P's average speed was 10 miles per hour greater than that of car R, what was car R's average speed, in miles per hour?

    (A) 40
    (B) 50
    (C) 60
    (D) 70
    (E) 80

28. For any numbers a and b, $a \bullet b = ab(3 - b)$. If a and $a \bullet b$ both represent positive numbers, which of the following could be a value of b?

    (A) −5
    (B) −2
    (C) 2
    (D) 4
    (E) 7

29. Marcella has 25 pairs of shoes. If she loses 9 individual shoes, what is the greatest number of matching pairs she could have left?

    (A) 21
    (B) 20
    (C) 19
    (D) 16
    (E) 15

30. If Finn was 18 months old one year ago, how old was he, in months, x months ago?

    (A) $x - 30$
    (B) $x - 12$
    (C) $18 - x$
    (D) $24 - x$
    (E) $30 - x$

31. A restaurant orders 150 kg of pumpkins from the farmer's market. The farmer fills the order with 23 pumpkins. The average mass of the first 20 pumpkins is 6.5 kg. What must be the minimum average mass of the remaining 3 pumpkins to fill the order?

    (A) 5.5 kg
    (B) 5.67 kg
    (C) 6.67 kg
    (D) 7 kg
    (E) 11.5 kg

32. The square root of 636 is between which set of integers?

    (A) 24 and 25
    (B) 25 and 26
    (C) 26 and 27
    (D) 27 and 28
    (E) 28 and 29

33. In a forest 150 deer were caught, tagged with electronic markers, then released. A week later, 50 deer were captured in the same forest. Of these 50 deer, it was found that 5 had been tagged with the electronic markers. If the percentage of tagged deer in the second sample approximates the percentage of tagged deer in the forest, and if no deer had either left or entered the forest over the preceding week, what is the approximate number of deer in the forest?

    (A) 150
    (B) 750
    (C) 1,250
    (D) 1,500
    (E) 2,500

The following data sufficiency problems consist of a question and two statements, labeled (1) and (2), in which certain data are given. You have to decide whether the data given in the statements are <u>sufficient</u> for answering the question. Using the data given in the statements <u>plus</u> your knowledge of mathematics and everyday facts (such as the number of days in July or the meaning of *counterclockwise*), you must indicate whether

- Ⓐ Statement (1) ALONE is sufficient, but statement (2) alone is not sufficient.
- Ⓑ Statement (2) ALONE is sufficient, but statement (1) alone is not sufficient.
- Ⓒ BOTH statements TOGETHER are sufficient, but NEITHER statement ALONE is sufficient.
- Ⓓ EACH statement ALONE is sufficient.
- Ⓔ Statements (1) and (2) TOGETHER are NOT sufficient.

34. If $5a = 9b = 15c$ where a, b, and c are all nonzero, what is the value of $a + b + c$?

   (1) $3c - a = 5c - 3b$
   (2) $6bc = 10a$

35. Stanley has gained 8 pounds a year ever since he turned 18. How much weight has Stanley gained since he turned 18?

   (1) Stanley now weighs twice what he weighed when he turned 18.
   (2) Stanley is now twice the age he was when he turned 18.

36. What is the value of the greater of two numbers if one of the numbers is three times the smaller number?

   (1) One of the numbers is 12.
   (2) The sum of the two numbers is 16.

37. If $\sqrt{r}$ is a positive integer, what is the value of r?

   (1) $r < 70$
   (2) $\sqrt{r} > 7$

———————————————— STOP. ————————————————

Verbal

Time—75 minutes

The following questions present a sentence, part of which or all of which is underlined. Beneath the sentence, you will find five ways of phrasing the underlined part. The first of these repeats the original; the other four are different. If you think the original is best, choose the first answer; otherwise choose one of the others.

These questions test correctness and effectiveness of expression. In choosing your answer, follow the requirements of standard written English; that is, pay attention to grammar, choice of words, and sentence construction. Choose the answer that produces the most effective sentence; this answer should be clear and exact, without awkwardness, ambiguity, redundancy, or grammatical error.

1. The gap in the ozone layer over the North Pole can expand each summer enough that it exposes regions as far south as Sweden by heightened UV radiation, also increasing rates of skin cancer in the northern regions by as much as 50 percent.

    (A) that it exposes regions as far south as Sweden by heightened UV radiation, also increasing
    (B) that regions as far south as Sweden have been exposed to heightened UV radiation, as well as having increased
    (C) to expose regions as far south as Sweden to heightened UV radiation, increased
    (D) to expose regions as far south as Sweden to heightened UV radiation and increase
    (E) that exposure to heightened UV radiation in regions as far south as Sweden, as well as increasing

2. In winning the 1998 Kentucky Derby, Swiftilocks showed a burst of speed as that of Man o'War, who won 20 of 21 races in 1919 and 1920.

    (A) as that of Man o'War, who won
    (B) not unlike that of Man o'War, who won
    (C) not unlike Man o'War, who won
    (D) like that of Man o'War for winning
    (E) like Man o'War and his winning

3. Rising tides of unemployment claims across the state has led the governor to declare the economy to be in a state of emergency.

    (A) Rising tides
    (B) Because the rising tide
    (C) The tide is rising
    (D) The rising tide
    (E) The rising of the tide

4. Seeking to decrease the incidence of tooth decay, <u>the American Dental Association is to spend $45 million over the next seven years promoting good dental hygiene</u>.

    Ⓐ the American Dental Association is to spend $45 million over the next seven years promoting good dental hygiene

    Ⓑ the American Dental Association will spend $45 million over the next seven years to promote good dental hygiene

    Ⓒ over the next seven years the American Dental Association is to spend $45 million promoting good dental hygiene

    Ⓓ good dental hygiene will be promoted by the American Dental Association, which is spending $45 million over the next seven years

    Ⓔ $45 million will be spent by the American Dental Association over the next seven years on the promotion of good dental hygiene

5. Some paleontologists claim that the discovery of what appear to be feathers in the fossil of an Archosaur could force a revision of current theories on the phylogeny of Archosaurs, alter conceptions of dinosaur skin surfaces, and <u>require scholars to credit birds with a far earlier origin than previously thought</u>.

    Ⓐ require scholars to credit birds with a far earlier origin than previously thought

    Ⓑ scholars may be required to credit birds with a far earlier origin than previously thought

    Ⓒ require a crediting by scholars of birds with a far earlier origin than previously thought

    Ⓓ compared to what was previously thought, require scholars to credit birds with a far earlier origin

    Ⓔ crediting birds with a far earlier origin than scholars had previously thought

For the following questions, select the best of the answer choices given.

6. Covington College has four full-time Classics professors, but only 12 Classics majors. This three-to-one student-to-professor ratio is the lowest in the college. Since the school is facing financial difficulties, and the tuition fees from just 12 students are not sufficient to pay the salaries of 4 full-time professors, the college should cancel the Classics program to reduce expenses.

Which of the following, if true, most weakens the conclusion above?

    Ⓐ Professors in the Classics department teach popular language and literature classes that are attended by hundreds of students who are not Classics majors.

    Ⓑ Students at Covington College pay, on average, $22,500 per year in tuition and fees, while the average professor of humanities receives a salary of $61,500 per year.

    Ⓒ A well-regarded Classics program adds prestige to a college or university.

    Ⓓ The Classics department has already decreased in size from six full-time professors 10 years ago.

    Ⓔ The study of classical literature and languages is increasingly irrelevant to the high-tech workplace of today.

7. A pharmaceutical company tested a new diet drug over a two-month period. The test group of 100 dieters lost an average of five pounds per person during the first month, but gained an average of two pounds per person in the second month.

   All of the following could help explain the results of the experiment except:

   (A) The second month of the test occurred during the winter holiday season, when people are more likely to gain weight.

   (B) The diet drug has unpleasant side effects, causing many of the subjects to stop using it after the first month.

   (C) The pharmaceutical company provided low-calorie diets to the test subjects in the first month, but let the dieters choose their own food in the second month.

   (D) The pharmaceutical company selected for the test people who were 20 to 40 pounds over their ideal weights.

   (E) The diet drug relies on a metabolic effect that loses efficacy the longer a person takes the drug.

8. The Tricounty Bridge was supposed to relieve traffic in East Countway County. Although the bridge was opened last year, traffic in the county has gotten worse. To relieve the traffic situation in East Countway, therefore, the traffic commission should order the Tricounty Bridge closed.

   Which of the following, if true, gives the most support to the conclusion of the passage above?

   (A) The increased traffic seen in East Countway over the last year is largely attributable to a large casino and resort hotel that opened for business shortly after the opening of the Tricounty Bridge.

   (B) The Tricounty Bridge allows inhabitants of heavily populated West Countway County to reach East Countway in less than a half-hour, as opposed to the two hours the trip required before the opening of the bridge.

   (C) The bridge is only open for the periods between 7–9 a.m. and 3–5 p.m. on weekdays.

   (D) Ship captains on the Countway River have complained that the bridge disrupts traffic on the river, thereby hurting the local economy.

   (E) The bridge is unlikely ever to pay for itself with the current low toll payment.

9. Alcohol-control advocates argue that television advertising plays a large role in leading teenagers to drink. In Hungary, however, where television advertising of alcoholic beverages has been prohibited since 1980, teenage alcohol use is higher than in some other European countries where such advertising is legal.

Which of the following statements draws the most reliable conclusion from the information given above?

(A) Hungarian culture, in general, views alcohol use more positively than do most other European cultures.
(B) Television advertising is the most effective way to encourage consumers to try a new alcoholic beverage.
(C) Television advertising cannot be the only factor that affects the prevalence of teenage drinking.
(D) Alcohol use among Hungarian teenagers has increased in recent years.
(E) Alcohol abuse is the greatest threat facing Hungarian teenagers.

The questions in this group are based on the content of a passage. After reading the passage, choose the best answer to each question. Answer all questions following the passage on the basis of what is <u>stated</u> or <u>implied</u> in the passage.

The complex life cycle of the *Plasmodium* protozoan, the causative agent of malaria, has contributed to the difficulty of devising effective public health measures to combat the disease. It took scientists centuries to deconstruct the basic relationship between protozoan, mosquito vector, and human host. Modern physiologists and epidemiologists are still working out the intricacies of malarial infection.

The disease is transmitted by the bite of a female *Anopheles* mosquito infected with the *Plasmodium* parasite. Only *Anopheles* mosquitoes are capable of transmitting the disease, and only females take blood meals from humans. To become infected with *Plasmodium*, the female mosquito takes a blood meal from a human carrying the parasite in his or her blood. Once ingested, the parasite matures in the mosquito's gut for approximately a week, after which it migrates to the insect's salivary glands. By mixing with the mosquito's saliva, the parasite facilitates its transmission to a human host when the mosquito bites that human.

Once in a human's bloodstream, the parasite travels to the human's liver. At this initial stage, the *Plasmodium* parasite is called a sporozoite. Within the liver, the sporozoite can form 30,000 to 40,000 daughter cells, called merozoites, which are released into the host's bloodstream at a later date, sometimes within a week of the initial infection and sometimes as much as several months later. The merozoites seek out and attach themselves to red blood cells, in which they incubate 8 to 24 daughter cells over the next two days. When the daughter cells are mature, the red blood cell ruptures and the new parasites are released into the bloodstream to seek out red blood cells of their own. Some of the new merozoites become male and female gametocytes; if these gametocytes are ingested by a mosquito feeding on the host's blood, they will fertilize in the mosquito's gut to produce new sporozoites, and the cycle will continue.

The symptoms that we associate with malaria—a high, recurring fever; joint pain; a swollen spleen—are caused by toxins released from the red blood cells ruptured by merozoites. The human spleen can destroy these infected blood cells, but the *Plasmodium* parasite counters this effect by increasing the stickiness of proteins on the blood cells' surfaces so that the cells stick to the walls of blood vessels. If the sticky surface proteins affect a particularly large number of cells, the malaria can transform into a hemorrhagic fever, the most deadly form of malaria.

A further complicating factor in the natural history of malaria is the many variants of the *Plasmodium* protozoan. Scientists now recognize that malaria is caused by at least six different species: *P. falciparum, P. vivax, P. ovale, P. malariae, P. knowesli,* and *P. semiovale.* Of these species, *P. falciparum* accounts for the majority of infections and approximately 90 percent of malarial deaths in the world.

10. The passage is primarily concerned with which of the following?

   Ⓐ Describing the life cycle of the *Plasmodium* protozoan as it relates to the disease malaria
   Ⓑ Comparing and contrasting the life cycles of the six variants of the *Plasmodium* protozoan known to cause malaria
   Ⓒ Addressing the public health implications of the life cycle of the *Plasmodium* parasite
   Ⓓ Providing information on how a person can avoid infection with malaria
   Ⓔ Describing the life cycle of the *Anopheles* mosquito as it relates to the transmission of the *Plasmodium* protozoan to humans

11. Which of the following most accurately states the role of the first paragraph in relation to the passage as a whole?

   Ⓐ It summarizes two theories, the relative merits of which are debated in the passage.
   Ⓑ It puts forth an argument that the rest of the passage is devoted to refuting.
   Ⓒ It introduces a new concept that the rest of the passage expands upon.
   Ⓓ It frames the background and relevance of the material to follow.
   Ⓔ It outlines the major themes of each of the four paragraphs to follow.

12. If a mosquito were to bite a person, and that person were later to develop malaria and die of the disease, it is most likely that the person was infected with which of the following?

   Ⓐ *Anopheles gambiae*
   Ⓑ *Anopheles semiovale*
   Ⓒ *Plasmodium malariae*
   Ⓓ *Plasmodium vivax*
   Ⓔ *Plasmodium falciparum*

13. The relationship of a merozoite to a sporozoite is most like which of the following?

    Ⓐ A mother to a daughter
    Ⓑ A brother to a sister
    Ⓒ One of several subsidiaries spun off from a large corporation
    Ⓓ A computer program to a computer
    Ⓔ Orange juice to an orange tree

14. Based on the information given in the passage, which of the following would be most effective in preventing a person infected with malaria from developing a hemorrhagic fever?

    Ⓐ Surgical removal of the spleen
    Ⓑ A medicine that prevents changes to the surface proteins of red blood cells
    Ⓒ An effective vaccine against malaria
    Ⓓ A potent pesticide that reliably kills the *Anopheles* mosquito without producing any negative consequences for the environment or for human health
    Ⓔ A small infusion of a weaker variant of the *Plasmodium* protozoan that will then compete with the existing parasitic infection

For the following questions, select the best of the answer choices given.

15. In fisheries in general, when a large harvest is taken one year, there will be fewer fish available to be harvested in the following year, leading to decreasing yields of most fish species over time. The Maine lobster is an anomaly, however. Even though the vast number of lobster traps covering the New England coast pull in more lobsters every year, the number of lobsters in the water has shown no signs of decreasing.

Which of the following, if true, most helps to explain the apparent anomaly concerning the number of Maine lobsters?

    Ⓐ The decline of other fish species in the region has deprived the lobster of its natural food source of scavenged fish.
    Ⓑ The bait in lobster traps provides abundant food for young lobsters, which are still small enough to swim out of the traps, leading to much higher survival rates among young lobsters than would be expected in nature.
    Ⓒ As global warming heats the waters of the Atlantic coastline, the Maine lobster has been able to extend its viable environment well past Nova Scotia, further north than ever before.
    Ⓓ The ever-increasing demand for lobsters in seafood restaurants and steakhouses across the country has driven a corresponding increase in the supply of the product.
    Ⓔ The increased lobster harvest has resulted in many juvenile lobsters but very few breeding-age lobsters, which could result in a crash in lobster numbers in the near future.

GO ON TO NEXT PAGE ➤

16. Federal tax evasion is a serious crime that places an unfair tax burden on those members of society who pay their fair share. To reduce the incidence of tax evasion, the government needs to prosecute a handful of high-profile individuals whose cases will receive substantial media attention.

    The argument above relies on which of the following assumptions?

    Ⓐ The tax system is so complicated that even people who try to comply with it may not pay some of their taxes inadvertently.
    Ⓑ The average citizen will be less likely to evade taxes after he or she sees a high-profile individual prosecuted for tax evasion.
    Ⓒ Tax revenues collected from high-profile tax evaders will help alleviate the unfair tax burden on honest citizens.
    Ⓓ Although it is difficult to secure a conviction on a charge of tax evasion, if the government focuses its efforts on a small number of high-profile individuals, the odds of obtaining a conviction will increase.
    Ⓔ While there is no universal measure for determining whether a taxation system is "fair" or "unfair," the current system was constructed by Congress to represent the societal priorities and values of the American people.

17. Adam's dog, a golden retriever named Hans, can respond to over 150 different commands. Adam cites this fact as evidence for his claim that Hans can understand the English language.

    Which of the following, if true, casts the most doubt on Adam's claim that Hans can understand the English language?

    Ⓐ Each of the 150 commands to which Hans responds involves both a spoken word in English and a distinctive hand sign.
    Ⓑ Hans does not respond to the same commands when spoken to him by Adam's French and Italian friends in their own languages.
    Ⓒ Scientists have demonstrated conclusively that canine vocal chords are incapable of replicating many of the sounds used in the English language.
    Ⓓ Animal behaviorists have demonstrated that even very young dogs surpass both wolves and chimpanzees—animals that are thought to be more intelligent than dogs—in the ability to understand human nonverbal communication.
    Ⓔ The golden retriever is widely considered to be less intelligent than the border collie, and no border collie has ever been shown to truly understand the English language.

18. The Comfocar company manufactures a sedan that can drive comfortably at 80 miles per hour. A rival company, Turbocar, recently introduced a comparably equipped sedan that can drive comfortably at up to 110 miles per hour. Turbocar claims that its sedan will outsell Comfocar's sedan because the Turbocar sedan can get customers to their destinations in comfort much faster than can the Comfocar sedan.

Which of the following, if true, casts the most doubt on Turbocar's claims?

   (A) Customers in surveys consistently rank comfort among the most important criteria in purchasing a car.

   (B) Many road surfaces are engineered to allow comfortable driving at speeds up to 120 miles per hour.

   (C) Automotive safety experts state that it is not safe for any car to be driven faster than 100 miles per hour.

   (D) Comprehensive research has determined that while the Turbocar model has faster acceleration and a higher top speed than the Comfocar sedan, both cars show approximately the same fuel efficiency.

   (E) Nowhere in the main marketing areas for these two car companies is it legal or practical to drive faster than 70 miles per hour.

The following questions present a sentence, part of which or all of which is underlined. Beneath the sentence, you will find five ways of phrasing the underlined part. The first of these repeats the original; the other four are different. If you think the original is best, choose the first answer; otherwise choose one of the others.

These questions test correctness and effectiveness of expression. In choosing your answer, follow the requirements of standard written English; that is, pay attention to grammar, choice of words, and sentence construction. Choose the answer that produces the most effective sentence; this answer should be clear and exact, without awkwardness, ambiguity, redundancy, or grammatical error.

19. <u>Blues musician Paul "Poboy" Smith, born in Tupelo, Mississippi, in 1936, has since 1958 been a fixture on the southern blues scene after the release of his debut album in that year.</u>

   (A) Blues musician Paul "Poboy" Smith, born in Tupelo, Mississippi, in 1936, has since 1958 been a fixture on the southern blues scene after the release of his debut album in that year.

   (B) Being born in 1936 in Tupelo, Mississippi, blues musician Paul "Poboy" Smith released his debut album in 1958 and has been a fixture on the southern blues scene since then.

   (C) Born in Tupelo, Mississippi, in 1936, blues musician Paul "Poboy" Smith has been a fixture on the southern blues scene since the release of his debut album in 1958.

   (D) Having been a fixture on the southern blues scene since 1958 when he released his debut album, Paul "Poboy" Smith is a blues musician who was born in 1936 in Tupelo, Mississippi.

   (E) Since the release of his debut album in 1958, blues musician Paul "Poboy" Smith has been a fixture on the southern blues scene; he was born in Tupelo, Mississippi in 1936.

GO ON TO NEXT PAGE ➤

20. SEC regulations require that <u>a public company disclose to their</u> potential investors any legal, technological, or financial complications that could endanger their investments.

    (A) a public company disclose to their
    (B) a public company discloses to its
    (C) a public company disclose to its
    (D) public companies disclose to its
    (E) public companies have disclosed to their

21. The genius of Beethoven can be seen in the widely observed phenomenon that his music has the same appeal to an illiterate shepherd wandering the steppes of <u>Kazakhstan as to</u> a professional musician sipping her latte in Paris.

    (A) Kazakhstan as to
    (B) Kazakhstan, just as to
    (C) Kazakhstan; just as it would to a
    (D) Kazakhstan, as it would to a
    (E) Kazakhstan as a

22. <u>Mary, just as did the other students, objected to</u> the squash casserole.

    (A) Mary, just as did the other students, objected to
    (B) Like the other students, Mary was objectionable to
    (C) Mary, like the other students, objected to
    (D) Mary objected, in the manner of the other students, to
    (E) Mary, as the other students, objected

23. At the MegaTek Corporation, an inexperienced financial analyst mistook the <u>rising cost of semiconductors as a seasonal fluctuation</u> in the market.

    (A) the rising cost of semiconductors as a seasonal fluctuation
    (B) rise in price of semiconductors as a seasonal fluctuation
    (C) rising cost of semiconductors for a seasonal fluctuation
    (D) rising of the cost of semiconductors for a fluctuation by season
    (E) rise of semiconductors in price to a seasonal fluctuation

The questions in this group are based on the content of a passage. After reading the passage, choose the best answer to each question. Answer all questions following the passage on the basis of what is *stated* or *implied* in the passage.

The collapse of the stock "bubble" of Internet-related companies in 2000–2001 resulted in more than its fair share of analysis, hand-wringing, and finger-pointing. A panel discussion at a recent Technology Today conference in Santa Monica produced a heated debate between two former luminaries of the dot.com world: investment banker Pat Verhofen and Sue Mickelson, founder and CEO of Internet retailer Frizbeez.com.

Verhofen fired the opening shot by placing blame for the collapse of Internet stocks on the shoulders of Internet entrepreneurs who aggressively promoted ideas without viable business models. These entrepreneurs were both irresponsible and deceptive, Verhofen argued, to take investors' money to fund operations that could not reasonably turn a profit, such as giving computers away for free or selling bulky objects, such as dog food or furniture, over the Internet. Many of these companies, he suggested, were little more than arrangements of smoke and mirrors designed to separate investors from their money.

Mickelson responded that Verhofen was like a fox in a henhouse blaming the rooster for all the dead chickens. Entrepreneurs cannot be blamed, she argued, for trying to make money for themselves and other people, because that is what entrepreneurs do. She also stated that it's impossible to know what ideas will work until they are tried; contemporaries of the Wright brothers said that a heavier-than-air aircraft could never work, and look at the skies today.

Mickelson instead placed the blame on the unscrupulous bankers and fund managers who hyped Internet stocks in order to cash in on fees from IPOs and trades. In contrast to entrepreneurs, these financial types actually do have a responsibility to offer only sound financial advice to their clients. If anyone should bear the blame, she argued, it should be people like Pat Verhofen.

Indigo Smith, the moderator of the panel, responded that perhaps the true fault lay with the common investors, who should not have invested in technology stocks in the first place if they lacked the knowledge to do so properly. While she expressed sympathy for those elderly investors who lost substantial portions of their retirement savings on flimsy Internet stocks, she observed that no one forced them to invest in those stocks.

24. Which of the following best describes the structure of the passage?

    (A) It mentions a puzzling situation, and then describes three approaches people have taken to help understand that situation.
    (B) It presents an argument for why something took place, and then offers a refutation of that argument.
    (C) It introduces a past phenomenon and then presents three explanations for why the phenomenon took place.
    (D) It describes a problem, offers a solution to the problem, and then offers reasons why the solution could not work.
    (E) It offers three explanations for a phenomenon and then summarizes what all three have in common.

25. Which of the following statements presents the strongest conclusion one could draw based on the information given in the passage?

  (A) The collapse of the Internet stock "bubble" drove thousands of investors into bankruptcy.

  (B) People involved with the Internet do not all agree on which party bears the most responsibility for the collapse of the Internet stock "bubble."

  (C) Of all parties involved with the Internet, financial professionals such as investment bankers and fund managers derived the most profits from the stock "bubble."

  (D) The Internet stock "bubble" would not have occurred if entrepreneurs had been honest about the true financial prospects of their companies.

  (E) The average investor has no one to blame but himself or herself if he or she invested in an Internet stock without adequately understanding the true financial prospects of the companies in question.

26. Which of the following best captures the meaning of the simile attributed to Mickelson that Verhofen "was like a fox in a henhouse blaming the rooster for all the dead chickens"?

  (A) As an entrepreneur, Mickelson understands that similes and other figures of speech can help convey complex ideas to audiences.

  (B) Verhofen, as an investment banker, was personally responsible for promoting businesses that he knew were not viable from a long-term perspective.

  (C) Foxes, unlike roosters, have no legitimate business in henhouses, and are far more likely than roosters to kill chickens.

  (D) As an investment banker, Verhofen was more likely to be the culprit of the crime than those he identified as responsible.

  (E) Entrepreneurs cannot be blamed for trying to make money for themselves and other people because that is what they do.

27. If Mickelson had not used the example of the Wright brothers in her argument, what other example might have illustrated her point as well?

  (A) Despite widespread public opinion that the sun revolves around the earth, Galileo Galilei published findings showing that the earth revolved around the sun; he later retracted this assertion as a result of pressure from the Roman Catholic Church.

  (B) A tobacco company chose to market cigarettes to children despite widespread public opinion that such marketing is unethical; over the following decade, the company expanded its share of the tobacco market.

  (C) A home electronics company devoted substantial development resources to eight-track audio technology despite widespread industry opinion that cassette tapes were the wave of the future; eight-tracks were soon replaced by cassette tapes, which in turn were replaced by compact discs.

  (D) A newspaper chose to publish a story that government lawyers said it could not print; the newspaper won its case against the government lawyers in a federal court, and the writer of the story won a Pulitzer Prize.

  (E) A computer company initiated research into manufacturing a computer for home use when widespread public opinion held that computers could be useful only for large corporations or government agencies; personal home computers became a multibillion-dollar market.

28. If Verhofen's arguments and statements are all correct, which of the following statements can accurately be inferred?

   (A) Biotechnology executives who aggressively raise investment capital for bioengineered products with no conceivable market should be held responsible if biotechnology stocks crash.

   (B) Investors should make financial decisions only with the advice of qualified financial advisors, such as investment bankers or fund managers.

   (C) If people lose money on investments that they inadequately researched, they have only themselves to blame.

   (D) If insurance companies provide home insurance for homes built in a hurricane zone and those homes are subsequently all destroyed by a major hurricane, the insurance company should be blamed for any investment losses suffered by its shareholders.

   (E) The collapse of Internet stocks would not have occurred if companies had not attempted to sell bulky items, like dog food, over the Internet.

The following questions present a sentence, part of which or all of which is underlined. Beneath the sentence, you will find five ways of phrasing the underlined part. The first of these repeats the original; the other four are different. If you think the original is best, choose the first answer; otherwise choose one of the others.

These questions test correctness and effectiveness of expression. In choosing your answer, follow the requirements of standard written English; that is, pay attention to grammar, choice of words, and sentence construction. Choose the answer that produces the most effective sentence; this answer should be clear and exact, without awkwardness, ambiguity, redundancy, or grammatical error.

29. While some military planners claimed that it would be possible to win a war fought with nuclear weapons, many scientists argued that such a war could not truly be won, because the fallout from nuclear warfare would create a nuclear winter and it also would be rendering the earth uninhabitable.

   (A) it also would be rendering the earth uninhabitable
   (B) rendering the earth uninhabitable
   (C) might have uninhabitably rendered the earth
   (D) render the earth uninhabitable
   (E) would also have rendered the earth uninhabitable

30. Providing adequate public health-care facilities is a crucial task in a county like Travis, where more than 60 percent of household incomes are below the poverty line.

   (A) where more than 60 percent of household incomes are
   (B) where more than 60 percent of household income is
   (C) which has more than 60 percent of the household incomes
   (D) where they have more than 60 percent of household income
   (E) where more than 60 percent of them have household incomes

GO ON TO NEXT PAGE ➤

31. Noted for its tenacity and courage, <u>the English bulldog, having originally been bred for the brutal sport of bull-baiting, but now is cherished</u> as a loyal animal companion.

    Ⓐ the English bulldog, having originally been bred for the brutal sport of bull-baiting, but now is cherished

    Ⓑ English bulldogs were originally bred for the brutal sport of bull-baiting, but they are now cherished

    Ⓒ English bulldogs were originally bred to bait bulls in a brutal sport, but it is now cherished

    Ⓓ the English bulldog was originally bred for the brutal sport of bull-baiting, but it is now cherished

    Ⓔ the English bulldog, originally bred to bait bulls for a brutal sport, is now being cherished

32. Advanced market research for the MegaTek Corporation predicts that launching a MegaTek Superstore in a given city <u>would only succeed should the density of repeat customers have been greater than</u> 200 per square mile.

    Ⓐ would only succeed should the density of repeat customers have been greater than

    Ⓑ will succeed only should the density of repeat customers be more numerous than

    Ⓒ will succeed only if the density of repeat customers is greater than

    Ⓓ should only succeed with a repeat customer density of greater than

    Ⓔ will succeed only with repeat customer density being greater than

For the following questions, select the best of the answer choices given.

33. In order to increase revenues, a cell-phone company has decided to change its fee structure. Instead of charging a flat rate of $20 per month and $0.05 for every minute over 200 minutes, the company will now charge $50 per month for unlimited usage.

Which of the following is a consideration that, if true, suggests that the new plan will not actually increase the company's revenues?

    Ⓐ A rival company, which charges no start-up fee, offers an unlimited calling plan for $40 per month.

    Ⓑ Two-thirds of the company's customers use less than 500 minutes per month.

    Ⓒ Studies have shown that customers using unlimited calling plans will increase their monthly usage of minutes by over 50 percent.

    Ⓓ One-fifth of the company's customers use in excess of 1,000 minutes per month.

    Ⓔ In recent months the company has received several complaints of insufficient signal strength and poor customer service.

34. A real estate developer in Florida, desiring to protect his high-rise apartment building on the beach from hurricane damage, has planted sea oats in two rows in front of his building in order to encourage the development of sand dunes between the water and his building.

    Which of the following, if true, casts the most doubt on the probable effectiveness of the developer's plan?

    (A) Sand dunes provide little protection for tall buildings against the wind, which is sufficiently powerful even in minor hurricanes to cause serious damage to buildings.

    (B) Sand dunes have been shown to provide effective protection against the storm surge, the pounding waves driven by hurricane-force winds onto dry land.

    (C) Although sea oats will lead to the growth of sand dunes over many years, it would be far faster to build concrete bunkers between the building and the water.

    (D) Hurricane insurance has become so expensive that many owners of beachfront property choose not to buy it.

    (E) The developer has invested in reinforced steel girders and shatterproof glass as a way of minimizing damage to his building in the event that a hurricane hits the area.

35. According to local tradition, Sultan Abu ibn al-Hasan founded the East African trading state of Kilwa in the mid-tenth century. Professor Ascalon, however, argues that Sultan al-Hasan did not rule in Kilwa until at least a century later.

    Which of the following, if true, provides the strongest support for Professor Ascalon's position?

    (A) The Hunsu Kubwa Palace, the largest stone structure in sub-Saharan Africa prior to the eighteenth century, dates to the rule of Sultan Sulaiman in the fourteenth century.

    (B) The oldest mosque on the island, which has traditionally been attributed to the reign of Abu ibn al-Hasan, has a foundation dating to ca. 800 C.E.

    (C) The Kilwa Chronicle, a document based on Kilwa oral history that has been shown to be unreliable on matters of chronology, dates the rise to power of Sultan al-Hasan to the year 957 C.E.

    (D) Silver and copper coins bearing the name of Abu ibn al-Hasan have been found in archeological sites dating from the late eleventh to the fourteenth centuries, but none have been found in sites dating earlier than the late eleventh century.

    (E) Archeological records suggest that the island of Kilwa enjoyed a period of economic prosperity beginning in the mid-eleventh century.

36. In theory, Ecuador could be a major exporter of shrimp. In actuality, it is not. The explanation is that 80 percent of the country's rich estuaries are owned by the government. This hurts Ecuador's shrimp production, because the government does not have the flexibility necessary for efficient shrimp farming that private industry possesses.

The answer to which of the following questions would be most relevant to evaluating the adequacy of the explanation given above?

- (A) Who owns the 20 percent of estuaries that are not owned by the government?
- (B) What percentage of Ecuador's production of shrimp is consumed domestically?
- (C) Has the government stated any plans to sell any of its estuaries to private industry, provided that the price is sufficient?
- (D) Is Peru, Ecuador's neighbor to the south, actually better suited for commercial shrimp farming than Ecuador, which is a substantially smaller country?
- (E) How does Ecuador's shrimp production on government-owned estuaries compare to that on comparable land owned by private industry?

The questions in this group are based on the content of a passage. After reading the passage, choose the best answer to each question. Answer all questions following the passage on the basis of what is <u>stated</u> or <u>implied</u> in the passage.

One of the best sources modern scholars have for learning about Hellenistic Egypt is the large supply of papyrus fragments that have turned up in the Egyptian desert over the last century. Papyrus is a thick type of paper made from a reedy plant found in Egypt. Papyrus is much tougher than the wood-pulp paper used in modern society; whereas a book produced today will most likely fall apart within a century, there are papyrus fragments that are still legible over 2,000 years after scribes wrote on them.

It is primarily by accident that any of these fragments have survived. Most of the surviving fragments have been found in ancient garbage dumps that were covered over by the desert and preserved in the dry heat. The benefit of this type of archeological find is that these discarded scraps often give us a more accurate picture of the daily lives of ancient Egyptians—their business affairs, personal correspondence, and religious pleas—than the stone engravings and recorded texts that were intended to be passed down to later generations.

One of the most important papyrus discoveries of recent years was the revelation in 2001 that a scrap of papyrus that had been discarded and used to wrap a mummy contained 110 previously unknown epigrams (short, witty poems) by the Hellenistic poet Posidippus (ca. 280–240 B.C.). Posidippus lived in Alexandria and benefited from the support of King Ptolemy II Philadelphos (ruled 284–246 B.C.). These new epigrams have yielded fascinating insight into the court culture and literary sensibilities of early Hellenistic Egypt.

King Ptolemy, of course, was also a sponsor of the famous library of Alexandria, the greatest depository of knowledge in the ancient world. According to the twelfth-century Byzantine writer John Tzetzes, the ancient library contained nearly half a million papyrus scrolls. If that library had not burned down, maybe archeologists today would not have to spend so much of their time sorting through ancient trash!

37. The author's primary intention in this passage appears to be which of the following?

    (A) To shed light on the underappreciated work of the Hellenistic poet Posidippus

    (B) To compare the relative merits of papyrus and wood-pulp paper as media for recording information

    (C) To discuss the ways in which papyrus fragments help scholars learn about Hellenistic Egypt

    (D) To answer the questions regarding the burning of the library of Alexandria, one of the great mysteries of the ancient world

    (E) To suggest possibly fruitful paths for future archeological research into Hellenistic Egypt

38. Which of the following would best illustrate how a discarded fragment of papyrus might give us a more accurate picture of the daily lives of ancient Egyptians than a record intended to be permanent?

    (A) A poet such as Posidippus may have composed rough drafts of his epigrams on papyrus fragments prior to writing them in their final form.

    (B) Grocery lists, which give insights into the diets of ancient people, would never be included in stone inscriptions but could be scribbled on scraps of papyrus.

    (C) The Hellenistic monarchs employed some of the finest historians of the Greek world to provide chronicles of their reigns.

    (D) Some papyrus fragments may have been used for purposes other than writing, such as binding wounds or wrapping small packages.

    (E) Stone inscriptions describing military events often embellish the truth to favor whoever is paying for the inscription.

39. The mention of the discovery of 110 previously unknown epigrams by the poet Posidippus serves what purpose in the passage?

    (A) Revealing insights into the nuances of court culture in Hellenistic Egypt

    (B) Demonstrating how durable a material papyrus can be

    (C) Arguing for a greater appreciation of this little-known Hellenistic poet

    (D) Highlighting the importance of royal patronage in the development of arts and literature in the Hellenistic world

    (E) Illustrating the kind of discovery that can be made from researching papyrus fragments

40. According to information given in the passage, which of the following locations would probably yield the highest probability of finding a previously undiscovered papyrus fragment?

   (A) The ship of a royal messenger that sank off the Egyptian coast of the Mediterranean Sea in the third century B.C.

   (B) The charred remnants of an ancient Egyptian palace that was burned by Roman troops in the first century B.C.

   (C) The refuse heap of an ancient Egyptian town that was buried in the desert in the fifth century A.D.

   (D) The private collections of French and British explorers from the nineteenth century A.D. who first uncovered many of the principal sites of Egyptian archeology

   (E) The library of a Hellenistic fishing village that sank into the marshes of the Nile Delta in the third century A.D.

41. What does the author imply by the final statement: "If that library had not burned down, maybe archeologists today would not have to spend so much of their time sorting through ancient trash!"?

   (A) The author implies that if the library had not burned down, archeologists would be able to appreciate the full cultural legacy of King Ptolemy II Philadelphos.

   (B) The author implies that if the library had not burned down, scholars today would have not only the full works of Posidippus, but also those of Aeschylus, Sophocles, and Euripides.

   (C) The author implies that if the library had not burned down, the scrolls contained within the library would have decomposed before modern times in any event, because they would not have been preserved in the dry heat of the desert.

   (D) The author implies that if the library had not burned down, it might have contained more complete details about the life and culture of Hellenistic Egypt than can be found in the papyrus fragments from ancient refuse dumps.

   (E) The author implies that if the library had not burned down, the cultural awakening of the Renaissance might have occurred centuries earlier.

——————————— STOP. ———————————

Answer Key

See page 607 for answers to the Integrated Reasoning section.

QUANTITATIVE	VERBAL
1. E	1. D
2. D	2. B
3. A	3. D
4. D	4. B
5. B	5. A
6. B	6. A
7. E	7. D
8. C	8. B
9. E	9. C
10. A	10. A
11. C	11. D
12. A	12. E
13. D	13. C
14. A	14. B
15. C	15. B
16. E	16. B
17. A	17. A
18. B	18. E
19. D	19. C
20. D	20. C
21. E	21. A
22. B	22. C
23. D	23. C
24. E	24. C
25. C	25. B
26. B	26. D
27. B	27. E
28. C	28. A
29. B	29. D
30. E	30. A
31. C	31. D
32. B	32. C
33. D	33. A
34. B	34. A
35. B	35. D
36. B	36. E
37. C	37. C
	38. B
	39. E
	40. C
	41. D

Answers and Explanations

Analytical Writing Assessment
Model Response

The dairy company spokesman claims that consumers have no reasonable justification to pay a price premium for organic milk, because their reasons for buying such milk are unfounded. Though this author may have valid reasons for supporting the conventional milk industry, his argument is based on an incorrect application of scientific research and weakened by vague, misleading language. Additionally, and perhaps most significant, while the spokesman's argument may apply to a small subset of consumers, it cannot be expanded to the general public as he claims.

The dairy spokesman claims that many consumers buy organic milk solely due to concerns about the consequences of widespread RBGH and antibiotic usage, and their potential side effects on humans. From this he concludes that "there is no reasonable justification for a consumer to pay $5 for a gallon of organic milk." Regardless of the effects of RBGH and antibiotics, this is an improper jump in logic, since consumers have many other reasons to choose organic milk over its conventional counterpart. Thus, even if everything else the author writes is true, he cannot draw conclusions for all consumers based on the preferences of a small subset of the population.

Additionally, in addressing the concerns of this group of consumers, the spokesman draws incorrect conclusions from scientific research. He claims "no study has ever shown that its [RGBH] presence in commercial milk has had any developmental effects on human consumers." However, there is a significant difference between "no study has ever shown" and "studies have proven that." Using the latter phrase would indicate that researchers had studied the issue and proven RBGH harmless. Instead, the author's wording leaves open the possibility that no studies have even been conducted on this topic.

Finally, the author states that the quality of milk is not affected by cows that are fed antibiotics, which eliminates this as a reason for concern. However, *quality* is a subjective term. Consumers who choose to purchase organic milk may define quality through many different attributes such as taste, shelf life, or the way the cows are treated during milk production. Thus, the author's narrow definition of quality ignores a wide range of logical reasons that could explain differing consumer preferences.

For the reasons above, the dairy spokesman's argument is weak. His statement could have been more persuasive had he used scientific sources that actively prove conventional milk is safe, rather than trying to adapt tangentially related studies. Further, while the author's claims may hold for a set of consumers, he should be careful when drawing conclusions about the entire population.

Integrated Reasoning

1. The answer to the first blank is **C**. About 12 calls an hour are received on Mondays and about 6 calls an hour on Wednesdays, so about 50% as many calls are received on Wednesdays as on Mondays.

    The answer to the second blank is **C**. The number of weekdays in which the average number of calls falls between 6 and 10 is 3, which is 60% of 5.

2. The correct answer is **C**. The fewest calls are received on Wednesdays, so that would be the best day for the clinic to assign fewer staff members to answering the phone.

3. The correct answers are shown below.

Yes	No	
●	○	The maximum rebate amount given to eligible Business Partners who purchase Car Model A
○	●	The exact rebate amount given to eligible Customer Loyalty Partners who work for the company and purchase Car Model C
○	●	The exact vehicle price paid by an Adaptive Equipment Partner who purchases Car Model B and submits the appropriate paperwork and medical documentation at the time of purchase

Source #3 indicates that eligible Business Partners receive 100% of the rebate amount associated with their purchased vehicle. Purchasers of Car Model A are eligible for a rebate of up to $1,500 according to Source #1, so the maximum rebate can be determined from the information given.

Source #3 indicates that eligible Customer Loyalty Partners receive 75% of the rebate amount associated with their purchased vehicle, but the other sources do not provide enough information to determine the exact dollar amount of the rebate.

Source #2 gives a range of costs for each vehicle model, but exact prices are not specified. This third item cannot be determined based on the information given.

4. The correct answers are shown below.

Yes	No	
○	●	This producer is responsible for a majority of the nation's exports of French roast coffee.
○	●	This producer exports more fine-ground than coarse-ground coffee.
●	○	The top two exporters of light-roast coffee combined export a majority of the nation's light-roast coffee.

This producer is responsible for 53% of the nation's sales of French roast coffee, but only 49% of its exports.

This producer has a bigger share of the nation's exports of fine-ground coffee, but without knowing the actual amounts exported, it is impossible to tell which type this producer exports more of.

The grower shown in the table exports 32% of the nation's light-roast coffee and is the nation's second-biggest exporter of that type of coffee. Therefore, the biggest exporter must export more than 32%, so the top two exporters together export more than 64% of the nation's total.

5. The correct answers are **3** hours spent traveling by bus and **6** hours spent exploring locations of interest.

TIME SPENT TRAVELING BY BUS	TIME SPENT EXPLORING LOCATIONS OF INTEREST	TIME (HOURS AND MINUTES)
○	○	2 hours, 0 minutes
●	○	3 hours, 0 minutes
○	○	3 hours, 30 minutes
○	○	4 hours, 45 minutes
○	○	5 hours, 15 minutes
○	●	6 hours, 0 minutes

Arden traveled by bus twice during the day. The first time was on a double-decker bus in the city. The bus traveled for 30 miles at 15 miles per hour, so Arden spent 2 hours on this bus. The second bus was a tour bus outside the city. The tour bus traveled 60 miles round trip at 60 miles per hour, so Arden spent 1 hour on this bus. He spent 3 hours total on the two buses.

Arden explored locations of interest twice: the museum outside of London and chapels within London. He spent 60 minutes at the museum and toured chapels for 50 miles. The chapel van traveled 10 miles per hour, so the chapel tour took $50 \div 10$, or 5 hours. Altogether, Arden spent 6 hours exploring locations of interest.

6. The correct answers are **60X** rounds used in 1 hour and $\dfrac{18,000}{60X}$ practice hours covered by a full case.

NUMBER OF ROUNDS IN 1 HOUR	NUMBER OF PRACTICE HOURS COVERED BY ONE CASE	EXPRESSION
●	○	$60X$
○	○	$\dfrac{60}{X}$
○	●	$\dfrac{18,000}{60X}$
○	○	$\dfrac{X}{18,000}$
○	○	$18,000 + 60X$

The weapon fires a maximum of X rounds per minute. There are 60 minutes in an hour. So the weapon fires $60X$ rounds per hour.

There are 18,000 rounds in a case. Each hour of shooting practice uses $60X$ rounds of ammunition. To find the number of hours covered by one full case, divide the total rounds per case (18,000) by the number of rounds used per hour ($60X$).

7. The correct answers are shown below.

Would help explain	Would not help explain	
○	●	Visitors to Las Vegas prefer indoor gambling to attending sporting events.
●	○	Seattle's football team recently lost some key players.
●	○	Philadelphia's high schools have an excellent hockey program.

The preferences of visitors to Las Vegas don't explain the behavior of the people who live there, so they don't explain why such a low percentage of Las Vegas's actual population attends sporting events.

Seattle's football team having become weaker could explain why other sports have become more popular in Seattle.

If many high school students in Philadelphia play hockey, they and their families might come to be more interested in watching it than in watching other sports.

8. The correct answer is **C**. Altogether, 70 people in the sample are over age 55; of those 70, 40 have no high school diploma. The probability 40 out of 70 is equal to 4 out of 7.

9. The correct answer is **C**. Altogether, 130 people in the sample have no high school diploma; of those 130, 40 are over the age of 55. The probability 40 out of 130 is equal to 4 out of 13.

10. The correct answers are making ice cream on either day and the hot air balloon ride on neither day.

EITHER DAY	NEITHER DAY	ACTIVITIES AVAILABLE
○	○	Swimming at the pool—Free
●	○	Make homemade ice cream—Free
○	○	Sunbathing at the beach—Free
○	●	Hot air balloon ride—$80 per person
○	○	Tennis game—Free
○	○	Water skiing—$4 per person

Homemade ice cream could be made on either day, because it is free and does not involve physical activity or the beach. The hot air balloon ride could not be scheduled for either day, because it would exceed the daily budget, and both days already have two activities costing more than $5 per person.

Swimming, sunbathing, tennis, and water skiing could be scheduled for Day One, but not Day Two. Day Two already has two physical activities and two activities at the beach.

11. The correct answers are shown below.

True	False	
○	●	Norseman washers experienced an overall increase in repairs between 2015 and 2016.
●	○	In 2016, more LG washers were repaired than LG dryers.
○	●	The appliance with the highest rank based on nonwarranty repairs and the appliance with the lowest rank based on nonwarranty repairs are the same brand.
●	○	In 2016, more KitchenAid stoves were repaired than LG stoves.

A 9.7% increase in warranty repairs of Norseman washers means there were 1,321/1.097, or about 1,204 warranty repairs in 2015. So there was an increase of 1,321 − 1,204 = 117 warranty repairs in 2016. A 4% decrease in nonwarranty repairs means there were 12,011/0.96, or about 12,511 nonwarranty repairs in 2015. So there was a decrease of 12,511 − 12,011 = 500 nonwarranty repairs in 2016. Therefore, the total number of repairs was less overall.

A total of 16,882 LG washers and 16,074 LG dryers were repaired.

Based on nonwarranty repairs, the highest-ranking appliance is the Norseman refrigerator and the lowest-ranking appliance is the Whirlpool microwave.

KitchenAid stoves rank higher in both warranty repairs and nonwarranty repairs than LG stoves, so more KitchenAid stoves were repaired overall.

12. The correct answer is **4,770**. In 2016, there were 4,513 warranty repairs performed on Whirlpool black washers. If this number increases by 5.7% in 2017, the total number of warranty repairs performed in 2017 would be $4,513 \times 1.057$, or 4,770.

Quantitative

1. The answer to the first question is **E**. 3.6 miles divided by 2/5 equals 9, so the total charge is $2.25 + (9 \times \$0.35) = \$5.40$.

2. The correct answer is **D**. The square has an area of $8 \times 8 = 64$, so the length of the rectangle is $64/4 = 16$ (the area of a rectangle is its width times its length).

3. The correct answer is **A**. Brown beads make up 1/3 of the beads in the necklace, so the total number of beads is $13 \times 3 = 39$.

4. The correct answer is **D**. The most direct way to address this problem, since there are only eight possible values for x, is to determine all the possible values and then check them against the possible answers. x could equal 0, 1/27, 3/27 (= 1/9), 4/27, 9/27 (= 1/3), 10/27, 12/27 (= 4/9), or 13/27. The only answer not among these choices is D, 2/9.

5. The correct answer is **B**. You can calculate this average score exactly the same way you would calculate a GPA—multiply each of the scores by the number of applicants with that score, add them all up, and divide the sum by 50. $10 + 48 + 63 + 14 + 8 = 143$; $143/50 = 2.86$.

6. The correct answer is **B**. (1) alone is insufficient because it tells you only the price of records, and does not give the price of CDs. (2) alone is sufficient, because the quantity of items is twice that of Carrie's purchase, so the purchase price is therefore half of what Aniyah paid—$27.50.

7. The correct answer is **E**. Both statements alone and combined are insufficient, because, for example, the values (9, 3) for (P, N) meet all the conditions and yield an answer of "yes," while the values (18, 6) meet all the conditions and yield a "no."

8. The correct answer is **C**. You need to know the product of A and B to solve this question. (1) alone is insufficient because it does not give the value for A, although you can infer from the Pythagorean theorem that $B = 3$. (2) alone is insufficient because (A, B) could be (1, 6) or it could be (3, 4), there is no way to tell. If the statements are combined, you can take the value that $B = 3$ and determine from the equation in statement 2 that $A = 4$; therefore, the area of the rectangle is 12.

9. The correct answer is **E**. (1) is insufficient because it does not tell what percentage of the population over 25 is female. If the gender split is 50/50, then the answer to the question is "yes"; if the gender split is 25/75 with more females, then the answer is "no." (2) alone is insufficient, and although it appears to address the insufficiency in statement (1), it

actually does not, because we cannot infer that the gender split for the total population is the same as the gender split for the population over 25.

10. The correct answer is **A**. In order to answer this question, you need to remove both variables so that a numerical answer is left. (1) is sufficient because it allows you to restate the equation $C = \dfrac{20s}{2s} = 10$. (2) is insufficient, because a variable remains in the equation.

11. The correct answer is **C**. The ratio of these numbers is $(a/9)/(b/8) = (a/9)(8/b) = 8a/9b$; you can substitute $8a = 9b$ from the question, so $8a/9b = 9b/9b = 1$.

12. The correct answer is **A**. All multiples of 8 are even, and half of the multiples of 7 are odd; the multiples of 7 make up 2/5 of the total, so if 1/2 of those multiples of 7 are odd, then 1/5 of the total will be odd, or 20%.

13. The correct answer is **D**. The principle to remember here is that an exterior angle of a triangle—such as $\angle ADB$—is equal to the sum of the remote interior angles of the triangle, in this case $\angle DBC$ and $\angle DCB$ ($=\angle ACB$) of triangle BDC. Thus, $\angle DCB + \angle DBC = 4n$, or $\angle DBC = 3n = 45°$, and therefore $n = 15°$ and $4n = 60°$. The three angles of a triangle must equal 180°, so $\angle ABC = 180° - 60° - 15° = 105°$.

14. The correct answer is **A**. The probability is equal to the new number of women, i.e., $W + 4$, divided by the new total, which is $W + M + 6$. The answer, therefore, is $\dfrac{W+4}{W+M+6}$.

15. The correct answer is **C**. This would be an unreasonably difficult question except that the fraction in question is the repeating decimal $0.958\overline{33}$, so the digit to the right of anything after the third decimal place is 3.

16. The correct answer is **E**. His daily wage can be determined by dividing his total income by the total number of days he has worked. x is his income, and $3w$ is the total number of days he has worked, so $\dfrac{x}{3w}$ is his daily wage.

17. The correct answer is **A**. The statement $\left(\dfrac{1}{3} - \dfrac{1}{2}\right)$ equals $\dfrac{-1}{6}$; $\dfrac{-1}{6} - 1 = \dfrac{-7}{6}$.

18. The correct answer is **B**. If 40 percent of the amount invested in bonds is invested in highly rated corporate bonds, then the total amount invested in bonds is $1.4 million times 10/4 = $3.5 million. $3.5 million in bonds is 70 percent of the total fund, so the total fund is $3.5 million times 10/7 = $5 million.

19. The correct answer is **D**. The diameter of a circle is twice its radius, so if the diameter is 14, then the radius is 7. The formula for the area of a circle is πr^2, so the area of this circle is 49π.

20. The correct answer is **D**. (1) alone is sufficient; the statement can be restated as $(a + b)/2$ is an integer; no noninteger divided by an integer—in this case, 2—is going to yield an integer, so $a + b$ must be an integer, and therefore b must be an integer. (2) alone is sufficient; the statement can be restated as $a + 2b + 4 = 3a$, so $b + 2 = a$; we know that a is an integer, and any integer plus 2 is an integer, so b must be an integer.

21. The correct answer is **E**. (1) alone is insufficient because the answer could be "yes" or "no" depending on the percentage of the sales tax. (2) alone is insufficient because it gives no information about the price of the stereo relative to N. Combining the two statements yields no useful information, since neither the sales tax percentage nor the total purchase price is known, so the question cannot be resolved.

22. The correct answer is **B**. (1) alone is insufficient because r could equal any positive number, which could give either an affirmative or a negative response to the question. (2) is sufficient, because the only values of r for which the statement is true are those between -1 and 1, exclusive, which means that the answer is "yes," $r < 1$.

23. The correct answer is **D**. (1) alone is sufficient, because if ∠*ABY* is a right angle, then ∠*YBC* must also be a right angle. Given both right angles are bisected, the *m*∠*XBY* and *m*∠*YBZ* must both equal 45°, and therefore *m*∠*XBZ* = 90°. (2) alone is sufficient, because if all four angles have equal measure, and their sum is 180°, then each angle must have measure 45°, and therefore *m*∠*XBZ* = 90°.

24. The correct answer is **E**. Neither (1) nor (2) is sufficient, because there is an infinite number of values for *P* and *Q* that could meet either or both conditions [e.g., (5, 3), (10, 6), (15, 9), etc.].

25. The correct answer is **C**. (1) alone is insufficient, because it gives us no information about the number of employees at either company. (2) alone is insufficient for the same reason. If the two statements are combined, we are able to infer that there are more employees at UltraCorp than at MegaTech, because the average age of the employees of the combined company is closer to the previous UltraCorp average than to that of MegaTech.

26. The correct answer is **B**. 22% are juniors, 100% − 74% = 26% are sophomores, 160/800 = 20% are seniors, and therefore 100% − (22 + 26 + 20)% = 32% are freshmen. 32% of 800 = 256 freshmen; 26% of 800 = 208 sophomores; 256 freshmen − 208 sophomores = 48 more freshmen than sophomores.

27. The correct answer is **B**. You could set this up algebraically and eliminate a variable, but it might be faster to just set up a simple equation and plug in the answers until one fits the statements in the question. If car R is traveling at answer A's 40 miles per hour, then it will travel the 600 miles in 15 hours, while car P traveling at 50 mph will cover the 600 miles in 12 hours; this does not meet the 2-hour difference mentioned. If car R is traveling at answer B's 50 mph, then it will take 12 hours to cover 600 miles, while car P will cover it in 10 hours at 60 mph; this meets the 2-hour difference specified in the question, so B is the correct answer.

28. The correct answer is **C**. The most direct approach to this sort of problem is to plug in the answers and see which one works. Choices A and B are out because any negative value for *b* would result in a negative value for *a*•*b* if *a* is positive. C works because it gives the result *a*•*b* = 2*a*, which has to be positive. D and E do not work, because they result in negative values for *a*•*b*. Therefore, C is the only answer that provides a possible value for *b*.

29. The correct answer is **B**. The greatest number of matching pairs remaining will occur when the greatest number of lost shoes are part of matching pairs; if four matching pairs and one other individual shoe were lost, then Marcella would still have 20 matching pairs left.

30. The correct answer is **E**. If Finn was 18 months old 1 year ago, then he is now 18 + 12 = 30 months old. 30 − *x* represents his age *x* months ago.

31. The correct answer is **C**. The remaining three pumpkins must make up the difference between 150 kg and (20 pumpkins × 6.5 kg =) 130 kg, so 20 kg. For three pumpkins to fill 20 kg, each must have a minimum mass of 20 divided by 3, which equals 6⅔, which is best expressed here as 6.67 kg.

32. The correct answer is **B**. The best solution here is to plug in the numbers from the answers until you find one that works. 24 × 24 = 576, 25 × 25 = 625, 26 × 26 = 676 . . . therefore, the square root of 636 is between 25 and 26.

33. The correct answer is **D**. 5 out of 50 deer is 10 percent. If this is representative of the percentage of tagged deer in the forest, then the 150 tagged deer are 10 percent of the 1,500 total deer in the forest.

34. The correct answer is **B**. Statement (1) alone is insufficient; you can restate the equation as $3b = 2c + a$; if you multiply both sides of the equation by 3, you get $9b = 6c + 3a$; you can determine from the equation $5a = 15c$ that $a = 3c$, so all this restated equation tells you is that $9b = 15c = 5a$, which tells you nothing about the actual value of a or b. Statement (2) is sufficient. If you divide both sides of the equation by 2, you get $3bc = 5a$; you know that $5a = 9b$, so you can form the equation $3bc = 9b$, which you can reduce to $c = 3$. With this value you can determine that $a = 9$ and $b = 5$, and you can thereby find a definitive answer to the question posed.

35. The correct answer is **B**. (1) alone is insufficient because it does not tell us what Stanley weighed when he turned 18. (2) alone is sufficient, because it tells us that he has aged 18 years since then, meaning that he has gained 18×8 pounds = 144 pounds.

36. The correct answer is **B**. (1) alone is insufficient because the two numbers could be 4 and 12 or 12 and 36. (2) alone is sufficient because the only two numbers that meet the stated conditions are 4 and 12.

37. The correct answer is **C**. (1) alone is insufficient because r could be several numbers less than 70, such as 64 or 49. (2) alone is insufficient because r could be several numbers greater than 49, such as 64 or 81. When the statements are combined, the only number that meets both criteria is 64, so the answer is C.

Verbal

1. The correct answer is **D**. The construction "exposes . . . by heightened UV radiation" in A is unidiomatic. In B, the construction "that regions . . . have been exposed" makes "regions" the subject of the clause, and this does not work with the following clause, where it appears that the regions, rather than the radiation, are increasing rates of skin cancer. C and E both form sentence fragments. D is the clearest and most standard statement of the information.

2. The correct answer is **B**. A is incorrect because "like" rather than "as" should be used to compare two noun phrases. C and E are incorrect because they erroneously compare Man o' War to Swiftilocks's burst of speed. D fails to make clear whether Swiftilocks or Man o' War won the 20 races. B provides the clearest statement of the information.

3. The correct answer is **D**. A is incorrect because "tides" does not agree in number with "has led." B and C create sentence fragments. E is less idiomatic and concise than D. D is the best answer.

4. The correct answer is **B**. "the American Dental Association" is the subject of the introductory phrase "Seeking to decrease the incidence of tooth decay," so it should come immediately after that phrase; C, D, and E incorrectly place other phrases between the introductory phrase and its subject. D and E also unnecessarily use passive verb constructions. The construction "is to spend . . . promoting" in A is less idiomatic and forceful than "will spend . . . to promote" in B, because, in general, use of a declarative active verb is more forceful than use of a "to be" verb, and infinitives are generally more forceful than gerunds. B is the best answer.

5. The correct answer is **A**. A is grammatically correct and idiomatic, so it is the best choice. To maintain parallel structures with the other clauses in this sentence with an understood connection to the verb "could," the sentence should read "could force . . . , [could] alter . . . , and [could] require . . ."; thus, A and C are the only choices. The construction "require a crediting by scholars of birds" in C is awkward and confusing, so A is the best answer.

6. The correct answer is **A**. This answer directly counters the argument that the Classics professors are not cost-justified to the college, because their salaries are supported not only by Classics majors, but by hundreds of nonmajors as well.

7. The correct answer is **D**. This answer provides no explanation for the difference in weight loss experienced by the test subjects over the first and second months, while all of the other answers provide explanations.

8. The correct answer is **B**. This answer provides an explanation for the increase in traffic after the opening of the bridge, and supports the assertion that closing the bridge would reduce traffic in East Countway because it would discourage inhabitants of West Countway from entering the county.

9. The correct answer is **C**. If teenagers in Hungary drink more alcohol than teenagers in some countries that do permit advertising of alcoholic products, clearly there are other factors influencing the situation.

10. The correct answer is **A**. The first three paragraphs are all directly addressed to the life cycle of the *Plasmodium* protozoan, and the last two paragraphs discuss the implications of the parasite's life cycle for malaria in humans. Answer C is partially accurate, but the passage is certainly more focused on describing the life cycle of *Plasmodium* than on describing its public health implications, so A is the better answer.

11. The correct answer is **D**. The first paragraph mentions the background of the effort to understand the life cycle of the malaria parasite ("It took scientists centuries to deconstruct the basic relationship among protozoan, mosquito vector, and human host"), and it provides relevance to the following passage by linking the topic to human health ("has contributed to the difficulty of devising effective public health measures to combat the disease").

12. The correct answer is **E**. The passage states, "Of these species, *P. falciparum* accounts for the majority of infections and approximately 90 percent of malarial deaths in the world."

13. The correct answer is **C**. The passage states, "Within the liver, the sporozoite can form 30,000 to 40,000 daughter cells, called merozoites, which are released into the host's bloodstream at a later date," so the relationship should be that of descent from the latter to the former, and of many from one, which answer C captures. Answer A could be correct if the order were reversed.

14. The correct answer is **B**. The passage states, "If the sticky surface proteins affect a particularly large number of cells, the malaria can transform into a hemorrhagic fever, the most deadly form of malaria." Answer C is incorrect because a vaccination would not help an already infected person.

15. The correct answer is **B**. Answer B provides an explanation—the food in lobster traps leading to a higher survival rate among young lobsters—for the apparent anomaly that the lobster harvest can increase every year without decreasing the total population of lobsters.

16. The correct answer is **B**. Since prosecuting "a few high-profile individuals" can have little direct impact on the overall picture of federal tax collection, the only way in which this plan can meaningfully "reduce the incidence of tax evasion" is if it creates a widespread indirect impact by deterring a large number of citizens from attempting to evade taxes.

17. The correct answer is **A**. A provides an alternative explanation for the dog's ability to understand the 150 commands, suggesting that the dog may be responding to the "distinctive hand signs" instead of the English words.

18. The correct answer is **E**. If it is neither legal nor practical for either of the sedan models to be driven faster than 70 miles per hour, then it is not true that the Turbocar will be able to get customers to their destinations faster than can the Comfocar.

19. The correct answer is **C**. A is flawed because it is unclear what "that year" refers to and because the combination of "since" and "after" is redundant. B presents a bizarre chronology by referring to Smith's birth in 1936 in the present perfect "being born" and then using the simple past for a later event in 1958; also, the "has been a fixture ... since then" is awkward. D is somewhat redundant in identifying Smith as a "blues musician" after identifying him as a "fixture on the southern blues scene," and it presents the information in an illogical order by introducing Smith's name so late in the sentence. E awkwardly separates the final clause from the rest of the sentence, so that there is really no reason why these should not be separate sentences. C is the most concise and idiomatic of the answer choices, and it presents the information in the most logical way.

20. The correct answer is **C**. The subject and possessive pronoun of the underlined clause should agree in number, so A and D are out. B is incorrect because the construction "require that a public company disclose" must be in the subjunctive voice, and therefore must be "disclose" instead of "discloses." In E, it does not make sense here to use the past tense when talking about "potential investors." C is the clearest and most standard statement.

21. The correct answer is **A**. A is grammatically correct and reflects standard English usage of the construction "[subject] is the same to X as to Y." The other options are all less idiomatic than A, so A is the best answer.

22. The correct answer is **C**. "Just as did the other students" is a less standard construction than answer C, which is the clearest and most concise of the choices.

23. The correct answer is **C**. The proper construction is "mistook . . . for," not "mistook . . . as." Of the two answers with this construction, C and D, D is awkwardly worded, so C is the correct answer.

24. The correct answer is **C**. The passage introduces the past phenomenon of the Internet stock collapse in the first paragraph and then presents three alternative explanations of who was responsible for that collapse. C is better than A because the stated positions are better characterized as "explanations" than as "approaches," and C is better than E because the passage provides no summary of what the three explanations have in common.

25. The correct answer is **B**. The passage provides three opposing viewpoints on this very question, so clearly this is an accurate statement based on the passage. Answers A and C might be true, but there is inadequate support for them in the passage. Answers D and E present opinions similar to those of Verhofen and Smith, respectively, in the passage, but the question does not state that the opinions expressed in the passage are necessarily true, so these statements cannot be taken as "strong conclusions." B is the best answer.

26. The correct answer is **D**. The passage states that Verhofen is an investment banker and that Mickelson places the blame for the Internet collapse on "unscrupulous bankers." Her metaphor implies that an investment banker blaming entrepreneurs is, like a fox found among a group of dead chickens, a more likely culprit than those he blamed. D captures this idea. B captures part of this idea, but it does not address the aspect of blaming others.

27. The correct answer is **E**. The answer should describe a business or technological innovation that a person or company pursued despite widespread opinion that the idea could not work, and that then turned out to be a great success. The example of personal home computers in E captures all of the relevant themes. C is wrong because the innovation failed, and B and D are wrong because people said that the idea *should* not be done, not that it *could* not be done. A is a weak answer because it is talking about

a concept rather than a business or technological innovation, and because Galileo retracted his cosmological statements. E is the best answer.

28. The correct answer is **A**. A provides the most similar circumstances to those of Verhofen's argument, in which Internet entrepreneurs "who aggressively promoted ideas without viable business models" should be blamed for the collapse of Internet stocks. B and C have no support in the text, D provides a different type of example that does not coincide well with Verhofen's argument, and E overstates Verhofen's position, since he identified companies that sell bulky items as one of the causes of the Internet stock collapse, but not the only cause. A is the best answer.

29. The correct answer is **D**. The correct answer should provide a parallel construction to "create a nuclear winter," since both phrases follow "nuclear warfare would"; answer D is parallel to "create a nuclear winter," and it is the most succinct of the available choices.

30. The correct answer is **A**. The sentence is grammatically and stylistically correct.

31. The correct answer is **D**. The answer has to refer to "the English bulldog" singular, because the final phrase refers to "a loyal animal companion" singular; therefore, B and C are out. Answer A is incorrect because the "but now" does not work with the phrasing of the sentence. Between D and E, the wording of E is somewhat awkward in that "is now being cherished" is less standard than the simpler "is now cherished"; D is the best answer.

32. The correct answer is **C**. Since the underlined passage is what "the MegaTek Corporation predicts," the underlined passage should take the future tense "will" rather than "would" or "should." Of the choices B, C, and E, C presents the most standard English construction.

33. The correct answer is **A**. If a rival company offers an apparently comparable plan for 20 percent less, it is likely that customers will switch to that rival company's plan, thereby reducing the company's revenue.

34. The correct answer is **A**. Answer A describes a form of hurricane damage—wind damage—that the developer's plan can do little to prevent.

35. The correct answer is **D**. Answer D does not provide proof that Sultan al-Hasan ruled in the eleventh century, but it does provide results that are consistent with that hypothesis. Moreover, the results cited answer exactly the sort of question that archeologists would ask in order to disprove the professor's hypothesis. None of the other answers offer support for the hypothesis, so D is the best answer.

36. The correct answer is **E**. The explanation in the passage hinges on the assumption that shrimp farming on government-owned estuaries will be less productive than shrimp farming on estuaries owned by private industry. E directly questions whether that assumption is correct, and, if it is, to what degree government ownership is holding back the potential production of Ecuador's estuaries.

37. The correct answer is **C**. The first sentence of the passage is: "One of the best sources modern scholars have for learning about Hellenistic Egypt is the large supply of papyrus fragments that have turned up in the Egyptian desert over the last century." Each of the first three paragraphs addresses this topic directly, while the fourth paragraph addresses it tangentially.

38. The correct answer is **B**. A grocery list provides the kind of information that could be important to archeologists today who want to learn about the daily lives of people in Hellenistic Egypt, but Hellenistic scribes would not have thought that information of this sort was important enough to mention in records intended for posterity.

39. The correct answer is **E**. The passage mentions the Posidippus discovery in order to give an example of the kind of new material that is being found in these discarded papyrus fragments. Statements A, B, C, and D may be accurate to an extent, but they do not address how the mention of Posidippus relates to the overall theme of the passage.

40. The correct answer is **C**. The passage states: "Most of the surviving fragments have been found in ancient garbage dumps that were covered over by the desert and preserved in the dry heat." The location described in answer C conforms closely with the type of place mentioned in the passage as where "most" of the fragments have been found, so this type of location will probably be the most fruitful place to look for more fragments.

41. The correct answer is **D**. The passage previously stated that the papyrus fragments, which are generally found in ancient refuse dumps, provide insights into daily life that cannot be found in more permanent sources. To reduce the need for archeologists to search for these papyrus fragments, the lost collection of the library would have to provide more complete information of the type found in the fragments than can be found in the fragments themselves; answer D suggests that the library would have contained such information.

GMAT PRACTICE TEST 2

Analytical Writing Assessment

Analysis of an Argument

TIME—30 MINUTES

Directions: In this section, you will be asked to write a critique of the argument presented below. You may, for example, consider what questionable assumptions underlie the thinking, what alternative explanations or counterexamples might weaken the conclusion, or what sort of evidence could help strengthen or refute the argument.

Read the argument and the instructions that follow it, and then make any notes that will help you plan your response. Write your response on a separate sheet of paper. If possible, type your essay on a computer or laptop. Observe the 30-minute time limit.

A speaker at an electronic entertainment conference made the following statements:

Video games have been widely criticized for having a negative effect on the nation's youth. If one looks at the facts, however, over the last 25 years, the period in which the use of video games became common among the nation's youth, math scores on the most commonly used college aptitude test have risen consistently, and entry-level salaries for college graduates have also risen significantly. This evidence suggests that video games are actually providing young people with the skills they need to succeed in college and in the workplace.

Discuss how well-reasoned you find this argument. In your discussion, be sure to analyze the line of reasoning and the use of evidence in the argument. For example, you may need to consider what questionable assumptions underlie the thinking and what alternative examples or counterexamples might weaken the conclusion. You can also discuss what sort of evidence would strengthen or refute the argument, what changes in the argument would make it more logically sound, and what, if anything, would help you better evaluate its conclusion.

---

12 QUESTIONS

Integrated Reasoning

TIME—30 MINUTES

Select the best answer or answers for the questions below. You may use a calculator for this section of the test only.

> On the actual test, you will be provided with an online calculator. You will NOT be permitted to bring your own calculator to the test.

1. The Eurostar is a line of high-speed trains that provide fast, efficient, and eco-friendly travel all over Europe. Under normal travel conditions, the Eurostar produces fuel emissions of CO_2 at a rate of E kilograms per kilometer (E kg/km) when it is traveling at a constant speed of T kilometers per hour (T km/hr).

   In terms of the variables E and T, select the expression that represents CO_2 fuel emissions produced in 1 hour by the Eurostar traveling at a constant speed, T, under normal traveling conditions, and select the expression that represents the amount of CO_2 emitted by the Eurostar traveling at a constant speed, T, under normal traveling conditions, for 200 kilometers. Make only two selections, one in each column.

CO_2 EMITTED IN 1 HOUR	CO_2 EMITTED IN 200 KILOMETERS	EXPRESSION
○	○	$200E$
○	○	$\dfrac{E}{200}$
○	○	ET
○	○	$\dfrac{T}{200}$
○	○	$\dfrac{T}{E}$

Read the sources below before answering the question that follows.

Source #1: Article about hardwood consumption

Currently the global economy consumes roughly 15 billion cubic feet of hardwood per year. This is nearly 2.5 times the amount of hardwood consumed annually in the 1950s. This causes a number of environmental issues, including loss of watersheds, destruction of habitats, increased air pollution, and landfill crowding.

Global hardwood consumption is expected to steadily increase, growing by roughly 20% in the 2010s and by more than 50% by 2050. The effects of the growth will be devastating to the world's hardwood forest. It is estimated that currently 10 times more trees are lost annually to wood consumption than are replanted, resulting in a net destruction of 40 million forest acres annually.

Source #2: Analysis of hardwood industrial paths

All wood consumption flows through two industry paths: construction use and stationery consumption. Construction use wood begins at sawmills and becomes lumber, plywood, veneer, wood paneling, construction material, and furniture stock. Stationery wood goes to the paper mills and becomes paper, cardboard, and fiberboard.

Generally, 50% of all cut hardwood goes to sawmills for whole-wood projects; 20% goes to chip mills for fuel consumption, particle board creation, and other semiwood products; and the remaining 30% goes to pulp mills. Unfortunately, roughly 25% of the wood that is cut never actually reaches consumers, because wasteful manufacturing practices render it useless and send it straight to landfills.

Source #3: Article on tree use

The United States is the greatest global consumer of hardwood products, using more than 17% of the 15 billion cubic feet cut annually. This is roughly twice the consumption rate of other industrialized nations and three times that of developing countries.

The average American consumes 886 pounds of paper per year. This is twice that of most European residents and more than 200 times that of Chinese persons, who consume only 3 pounds of paper per year.

2. Consider each of the items listed below. Select *Yes* if the item can be determined based on the information given in the three sources. Otherwise, select *No*.

Yes	No	
○	○	The amount of hardwood, in cubic feet, consumed annually by the United States, other industrialized nations, and developing countries
○	○	The amount of paper, in pounds, consumed annually by residents of most European countries
○	○	The amount of hardwood cut annually, in cubic feet, that goes to sawmills for whole-wood projects

3. The following table gives information for 2011 on total cancelled flights and total passengers rebooked. The 19 airports included in the table are among the top 25 airports throughout the United States in terms of both total cancelled flights and total rebooked passengers. In addition to listing the total cancelled flights and total rebooked passengers for each airport, the table also gives the percent of increase or decrease over the 2010 cancelled flights and rebooked passengers, and the rank of each airport for total cancelled flights and total rebooked passengers.

> On the actual exam, you will be able to sort the table by any of its columns. (Columns can be sorted in ascending order only.) The following table is shown sorted in different ways to mirror the test.

Sorted by State (Column 2)

AIRPORT			CANCELLED FLIGHTS			PASSENGERS REBOOKED		
CODE	STATE	WIND ZONE	NUMBER	% CHANGE	RANK	NUMBER	% CHANGE	RANK
SMF	CA	I	149,621	3.7	11	1,156,374	−1.3	13
SFO	CA	I	129,294	−0.9	18	1,121,738	1.2	15
LAX	CA	I	127,339	4.3	19	1,006,845	−4.8	20
DEN	CO	II SWR	187,905	2.1	1	1,372,490	7	6
DCA	DC	II HSR	151,583	−3.6	8	1,290,757	8.6	11
TPA	FL	III HSR	145,009	−0.5	13	1,332,105	0.6	7
MIA	FL	III HSR	155,114	−2.5	5	1,295,682	3.9	10
ORD	IL	IV	165,030	−3.0	3	1,429,764	−5.2	5
BWI	MD	II HSR	176,558	5.3	2	1,632,008	0.4	2
STL	MO	IV	151,592	9	7	1,542,367	0.1	3
BOS	MA	II HSR	163,908	1.2	4	1,300,768	0.2	9
EWR	NJ	II HSR	123,812	0.2	20	1,109,334	4.2	17
LAS	NV	I	109,867	0.6	22	1,439,008	−0.7	4
LGA	NY	II HSR	133,545	3.2	17	1,802,389	−2.0	1
JFK	NY	II HSR	139,009	2.5	15	1,102,938	−4.8	18
PIT	PA	IV	148,453	1.8	12	1,300,982	3.4	8
IAH	TX	III HSR	122,729	−2.7	21	1,002,377	2.2	21
SLC	UT	I	154,772	−2.9	6	1,272,314	−5.8	12
SEA	WA	I	150,776	−4.0	9	1,008,452	−4.0	19

Sorted by Wind Zone (Column 3)

AIRPORT			CANCELLED FLIGHTS			PASSENGERS REBOOKED		
CODE	STATE	WIND ZONE	NUMBER	% CHANGE	RANK	NUMBER	% CHANGE	RANK
LAS	NV	I	109,867	0.6	22	1,439,008	−0.7	4
SLC	UT	I	154,772	−2.9	6	1,272,314	−5.8	12
SMF	CA	I	149,621	3.7	11	1,156,374	−1.3	13
SFO	CA	I	129,294	−0.9	18	1,121,738	1.2	15
SEA	WA	I	150,776	−4.0	9	1,008,452	−4.0	19
LAX	CA	I	127,339	4.3	19	1,006,845	−4.8	20
LGA	NY	II HSR	133,545	3.2	17	1,802,389	−2.0	1
BWI	MD	II HSR	176,558	5.3	2	1,632,008	0.4	2
BOS	MA	II HSR	163,908	1.2	4	1,300,768	0.2	9
DCA	DC	II HSR	151,583	−3.6	8	1,290,757	8.6	11
EWR	NJ	II HSR	123,812	0.2	20	1,109,334	4.2	17
JFK	NY	II HSR	139,009	2.5	15	1,102,938	−4.8	18
DEN	CO	II SWR	187,905	2.1	1	1,372,490	7	6
TPA	FL	III HSR	145,009	−0.5	13	1,332,105	0.6	7
MIA	FL	III HSR	155,114	−2.5	5	1,295,682	3.9	10
IAH	TX	III HSR	122,729	−2.7	21	1,002,377	2.2	21
STL	MO	IV	151,592	9	7	1,542,367	0.1	3
ORD	IL	IV	165,030	−3.0	3	1,429,764	−5.2	5
PIT	PA	IV	148,453	1.8	12	1,300,982	3.4	8

Sorted by Rank in Cancelled Flights (Column 6)

AIRPORT			CANCELLED FLIGHTS			PASSENGERS REBOOKED		
CODE	STATE	WIND ZONE	NUMBER	% CHANGE	RANK	NUMBER	% CHANGE	RANK
DEN	CO	II SWR	187,905	2.1	1	1,372,490	7	6
BWI	MD	II HSR	176,558	5.3	2	1,632,008	0.4	2
ORD	IL	IV	165,030	−3.0	3	1,429,764	−5.2	5
BOS	MA	II HSR	163,908	1.2	4	1,300,768	0.2	9
MIA	FL	III HSR	155,114	−2.5	5	1,295,682	3.9	10
SLC	UT	I	154,772	−2.9	6	1,272,314	−5.8	12
STL	MO	IV	151,592	9	7	1,542,367	0.1	3

(continued)

Sorted by Rank in Cancelled Flights (Column 6) *(continued)*

AIRPORT			CANCELLED FLIGHTS			PASSENGERS REBOOKED		
CODE	STATE	WIND ZONE	NUMBER	% CHANGE	RANK	NUMBER	% CHANGE	RANK
DCA	DC	II HSR	151,583	−3.6	8	1,290,757	8.6	11
SEA	WA	I	150,776	−4.0	9	1,008,452	−4.0	19
SMF	CA	I	149,621	3.7	11	1,156,374	−1.3	13
PIT	PA	IV	148,453	1.8	12	1,300,982	3.4	8
TPA	FL	III HSR	145,009	−0.5	13	1,332,105	0.6	7
JFK	NY	II HSR	139,009	2.5	15	1,102,938	−4.8	18
LGA	NY	II HSR	133,545	3.2	17	1,802,389	−2.0	1
SFO	CA	I	129,294	−0.9	18	1,121,738	1.2	15
LAX	CA	I	127,339	4.3	19	1,006,845	−4.8	20
EWR	NJ	II HSR	123,812	0.2	20	1,109,334	4.2	17
IAH	TX	III HSR	122,729	−2.7	21	1,002,377	2.2	21
LAS	NV	I	109,867	0.6	22	1,439,008	−0.7	4

Sorted by Rank in Passengers Rebooked (Column 9)

AIRPORT			CANCELLED FLIGHTS			PASSENGERS REBOOKED		
CODE	STATE	WIND ZONE	NUMBER	% CHANGE	RANK	NUMBER	% CHANGE	RANK
LGA	NY	II HSR	133,545	3.2	17	1,802,389	−2.0	1
BWI	MD	II HSR	176,558	5.3	2	1,632,008	0.4	2
STL	MO	IV	151,592	9.0	7	1,542,367	0.1	3
LAS	NV	I	109,867	0.6	22	1,439,008	−0.7	4
ORD	IL	IV	165,030	−3.0	3	1,429,764	−5.2	5
DEN	CO	II SWR	187,905	2.1	1	1,372,490	7.0	6
TPA	FL	III HSR	145,009	−0.5	13	1,332,105	0.6	7
PIT	PA	IV	148,453	1.8	12	1,300,982	3.4	8
BOS	MA	II HSR	163,908	1.2	4	1,300,768	0.2	9
MIA	FL	III HSR	155,114	−2.5	5	1,295,682	3.9	10
DCA	DC	II HSR	151,583	−3.6	8	1,290,757	8.6	11
SLC	UT	I	154,772	−2.9	6	1,272,314	−5.8	12
SMF	CA	I	149,621	3.7	11	1,156,374	−1.3	13
SFO	CA	I	129,294	−0.9	18	1,121,738	1.2	15
EWR	NJ	II HSR	123,812	0.2	20	1,109,334	4.2	17

(continued)

Sorted by Rank in Passengers Rebooked (Column 9) (*continued*)

AIRPORT			CANCELLED FLIGHTS			PASSENGERS REBOOKED		
CODE	STATE	WIND ZONE	NUMBER	% CHANGE	RANK	NUMBER	% CHANGE	RANK
JFK	NY	II HSR	139,009	2.5	15	1,102,938	−4.8	18
SEA	WA	I	150,776	−4.0	9	1,008,452	−4.0	19
LAX	CA	I	127,339	4.3	19	1,006,845	−4.8	20
IAH	TX	III HSR	122,729	−2.7	21	1,002,377	2.2	21

Review each of the statements below. Based on the information provided in the table, indicate whether the statement is true or false.

True	False	
○	○	All the airports in wind zone III HSR experienced a decrease in the number of cancelled flights.
○	○	Each of the airports in Florida (FL) had more passengers rebooked than any of the airports in New York (NY).
○	○	Three of the five airports with the most cancelled flights had fewer cancelled flights than the previous year.
○	○	Altogether, the airports in wind zone II SWR had fewer than 200,000 cancelled flights.

4. Top Trucks has two major custom lines: mud-truck improvements and low-rider packages. Last spring, the company completed roughly 200 customizations. This fall, market analysts suspect that the number of customizations will rise significantly. Specifically, they expect customizations to increase by roughly 170 customizations. For the first time, mud-truck improvement sales will exceed low-rider packages.

   In the table below, identify the minimum number of mud-truck improvements Top Truck's employees should expect to complete during fall sales and the total number of customizations Top Trucks will complete next spring, if growth continues at its current rate. Make only two selections, one in each column.

MUD-TRUCK IMPROVEMENTS THIS FALL	TOTAL CUSTOMIZATIONS NEXT SPRING	NUMBER OF CUSTOMIZATIONS
○	○	170
○	○	186
○	○	200
○	○	370
○	○	443
○	○	540

GO ON TO NEXT PAGE ➤

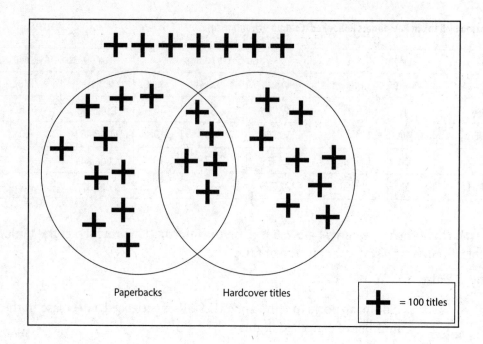

Paperbacks   Hardcover titles

✚ = 100 titles

5. Refer to the preceding Venn diagram of an inventory of book titles sold by Marshall Books. Each symbol represents 100 titles in a total inventory of 3,000 distinct book titles. Select the best answer to fill in the blanks for each of the statements below, based on the data shown.

If one title is selected at random out of the total inventory, the chance that the title is available in print as either a paperback or hardcover or both is _____.

A 5 out of 30
B 7 out of 30
C 18 out of 30
D 23 out of 30

If one title is selected at random out of the total inventory, the chance that the title is available in print in both paperback and hardcover is _____.

A 5 out of 30
B 7 out of 30
C 18 out of 30
D 23 out of 30

Percentage of Venues Offering Performances in Selected Musical Genres, Single Year

Sorted by State (Column 1)

STATE	CLASSICAL & OPERA	ROCK/POP	JAZZ	COUNTRY
California	47	61	58	37
Florida	19	34	26	23
Illinois	24	45	68	13
Minnesota	18	25	36	8
New York	37	51	36	23
Ohio	32	18	26	30
Texas	19	12	17	63

6. For each of the following statements select *Would help explain* if it would, if true, help explain some of the information in the above table. Otherwise select *Would not help explain*.

Would help explain	Would not help explain	
○	○	Texas has a large number of venues specifically devoted to country music.
○	○	In general, Minnesota's concertgoers prefer rock music to jazz.
○	○	The most famous classical violinist in the country comes from Florida.

7. In 2010, New York was the number one tourist destination in the United States. After achieving this ranking, city officials set a goal of hosting 50 million visitors in the 2012 tourist season. The graph below shows the number of domestic and international visitors to visit New York between 2000 and 2010. Select the best answer to fill in the blanks for each of the statements below, based on the data shown in the graph.

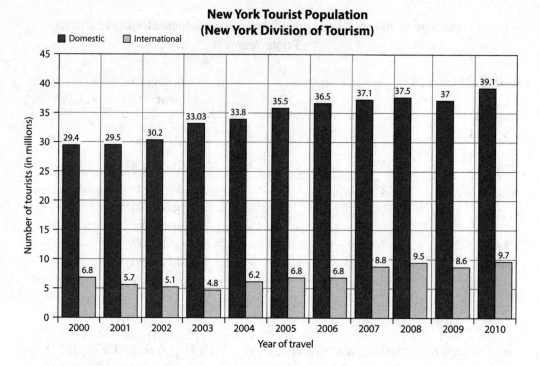

The relationship between year of travel and number of domestic tourists is best described as _____.

   (A) negative
   (B) no relationship
   (C) positive

The number of international tourists in 2010 was closest to _____ % of the number of domestic tourists in 2010.

   (A) 5
   (B) 10
   (C) 20
   (D) 25
   (E) 30

The sources that follow accompany questions 8 and 9.

E-mail #1—E-mail from the *director of the training department* to the technical publications manager

September 12, 8:03 A.M.

We are preparing our schedule for the November 1st training of new clients for our EXM software. To date we have received 23 reservations and expect the class will close at 35 students, the capacity of our training room. Our training manuals are currently in production and will be ready for content review on September 15th. Allowing a two-week turnaround for the developer's review, we should have a three-week window for your department to provide the necessary formatting, standard company information, and printing. Can you provide the date you could deliver 35 manuals prior to the 21st of October? We will need a week to 10 days to allow adequate time for our trainers to prepare their computer-based exercises.

E-mail #2—E-mail from the *technical publications manager* in response to the director of the training department

September 12, 9:12 A.M.

Thank you for the update regarding the training schedule. We have a very heavy schedule to meet in the month of October, and we will add your manual to our calendar. Please provide the approximate number of pages of the manual you are creating. Standard company information is fixed at 3 pages. We will charge your department on a per-page basis, plus the fixed costs of collating and preparation, which is currently $2.00/manual. Color graphics will add an extra $.50/page to our normal $.25/page of black and white text. If your manual is less than 100 pages, we should be able to deliver by your deadline.

E-mail #3—E-mail from the *director of the training department* in response to the technical publications manager

September 12, 9:46 A.M.

The manual for this three-day training will exceed 100 pages and may run as long as 115 pages, with 5 pages of color graphics. I will know the exact number once the review is completed on October 1.

8. If the information contained in all three e-mails is correct, the total cost of the requested manuals will be closest to which of the following?

   ○ $1,060

   ○ $1,080

   ○ $1,100

   ○ $1,120

   ○ $1,190

9. Consider each of the following statements. Does the information in the three sources support the inference as stated?

   Yes   No

   ○   ○   The director of the training department believes that the software training class will be filled to capacity.

   ○   ○   The director of the training department expects that printing of the training manual will exceed the department's printing budget.

   ○   ○   The technical publications department will most likely be able to deliver 35 copies of the training manual by October 21st.

The following table displays data on animals in an African zoo in 2017.

On the actual exam, you will be able to sort the table by any of its columns. (Columns can be sorted in ascending order only.) The following table is shown sorted in different ways to mirror the test.

Sorted by Animal (Column 1)

ANIMAL	POPULATION, NATIONAL SHARE (%)	POPULATION, NATIONAL RANK	BORN IN CAPTIVITY, NATIONAL SHARE (%)	BORN IN CAPTIVITY, NATIONAL RANK
Bear	74	1	33	1
Elephant	32	3	35	2
Giraffe	16	5	5	4
Gorilla	93	1	48	1
Lion	14	5	18	4
Monkey	24	3	19	5
Ostrich	20	4	58	1
Tiger	29	2	71	1
Zebra	87	1	48	2

Sorted by Population, National Share (Column 2)

ANIMAL	POPULATION, NATIONAL SHARE (%)	POPULATION, NATIONAL RANK	BORN IN CAPTIVITY, NATIONAL SHARE (%)	BORN IN CAPTIVITY, NATIONAL RANK
Lion	14	5	18	4
Giraffe	16	5	5	4
Ostrich	20	4	58	1
Monkey	24	3	19	5
Tiger	29	2	71	1
Elephant	32	3	35	2
Bear	74	1	33	1
Zebra	87	1	48	2
Gorilla	93	1	48	1

Sorted by Born in Captivity, National Share (Column 4)

ANIMAL	POPULATION, NATIONAL SHARE (%)	POPULATION, NATIONAL RANK	BORN IN CAPTIVITY, NATIONAL SHARE (%)	BORN IN CAPTIVITY, NATIONAL RANK
Giraffe	16	5	5	4
Lion	14	5	18	4
Monkey	24	3	19	5
Bear	74	1	33	1
Elephant	32	3	35	2
Gorilla	93	1	48	1
Zebra	87	1	48	2
Ostrich	20	4	58	1
Tiger	29	2	71	1

10. For each of the following statements, select *Yes* if the statement can be shown to be true based on information in the preceding table. Otherwise, select *No*.

Yes	No	
○	○	More gorillas than lions were born in this zoo in 2017.
○	○	In 2017, this zoo had more ostriches born in captivity than any other zoo in the country.
○	○	More giraffes in this zoo were born in the wild than in captivity.

11. The number of people in the world who natively speak Language A is 330 million. The number of people in the world who natively speak Language B is 260 million. Language experts who chart the growth of both languages claim that in five years, the number of persons who natively speak Language A will be approximately 450 million, and the number of persons who natively speak Language B will be approximately 300 million.

In the table below, identify the average annual rate of growth of Language A native speakers, and then identify the difference between Language A's and Language B's average annual growth rates. Make only two selections, one in each column.

LANGUAGE A	DIFFERENCE IN LANGUAGE A AND LANGUAGE B	AVERAGE RATE OF GROWTH (NATIVE SPEAKERS PER YEAR)
○	○	6,000,000
○	○	8,000,000
○	○	12,000,000
○	○	16,000,000
○	○	24,000,000
○	○	48,000,000

GO ON TO NEXT PAGE ➤

12. The diagram shows, in two column groupings, various divisions of human gestation, with a total length of approximately 308 days. In the leftmost column, the full pregnancy is divided into its trimesters. In the second graphic area, the zygote stage is magnified and shown in greater detail. Select the best answer to fill in the blanks for each of the statements below, based on the data shown.

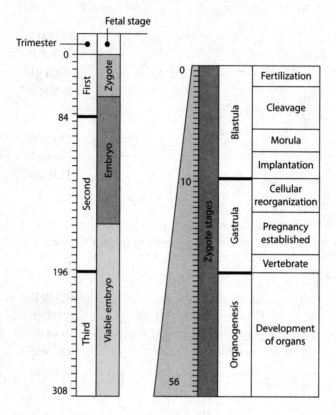

Cellular reorganization accounts for closest to _____ % of the zygote phase.

  Ⓐ 7
  Ⓑ 12
  Ⓒ 25

The second trimester is closest to _____ % as long as the first.

  Ⓐ 75
  Ⓑ 112
  Ⓒ 133

—————————————————— **STOP.** ——————————————————

37 QUESTIONS

Quantitative

TIME—75 MINUTES

The following data sufficiency problems consist of a question and two statements, labeled (1) and (2), in which certain data are given. You have to decide whether the data given in the statements are <u>sufficient</u> for answering the question. Using the data given in the statements <u>plus</u> your knowledge of mathematics and everyday facts (such as the number of days in July or the meaning of *counterclockwise*), you must indicate whether

- (A) Statement (1) ALONE is sufficient, but statement (2) alone is not sufficient.
- (B) Statement (2) ALONE is sufficient, but statement (1) alone is not sufficient.
- (C) BOTH statements TOGETHER are sufficient, but NEITHER statement ALONE is sufficient.
- (D) EACH statement ALONE is sufficient.
- (E) Statements (1) and (2) TOGETHER are NOT sufficient.

NUMBERS: All numbers used are real numbers.

FIGURES: A figure accompanying a data sufficiency problem will conform to the information given in the question, but will not necessarily conform to the additional information given in statements (1) and (2). Lines shown as straight can be assumed to be straight, and lines that appear jagged can also be assumed to be straight. You may assume that the position of points, angles, regions, etc., exist in the order shown and that angle measures are greater than zero. All figures lie in a plane unless otherwise indicated.

NOTE: In data sufficiency problems that ask for the value of a quantity, the data given in the statements are sufficient only when it is possible to determine exactly one numerical value for the quantity.

1. If x is an integer, is $\dfrac{18+54}{x}$ an integer?

    (1) $18 < x < 54$

    (2) x is a multiple of 18

2. If $a > 0$ and $b > 0$, is $\dfrac{a}{b} > \dfrac{b}{a}$?

    (1) $a = b - 2$

    (2) $\dfrac{a}{4b} = \dfrac{1}{5}$

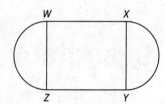

3. The figure above shows the shape of a flowerbed. If arcs *WZ* and *XY* are semicircles and *WXYZ* is a square, what is the area of the flowerbed?

   (1) The perimeter of square *WXYZ* is 24.
   (2) The diagonal $WY = 6\sqrt{2}$.

4. A total of 72 passengers are on a ship, and they go out on an excursion in boats R and Q. How many of the ship's passengers are female?

   (1) There are 13 females on boat Q.
   (2) There are equal numbers of women on boats R and Q.

5. In the *xy* plane, is the point (4, −2) on the line *l* ?

   (1) Point (1, 1) is on line *l*.
   (2) The equation $x = 2 - y$ describes line *l*.

Solve the problem and indicate the best of the answer choices given.

NUMBERS: **All numbers used are real numbers.**

FIGURES: **A figure accompanying a problem-solving question is intended to provide information useful in solving the problem. Figures are drawn as accurately as possible EXCEPT when it is stated in a specific problem that its figure is not drawn to scale. Straight lines may sometimes appear jagged. All figures lie in a plane unless otherwise indicated.**

6. A type of extra-large SUV averages 12.2 miles per gallon (mpg) on the highway, but only 7.6 mpg in the city. What is the maximum distance, in miles, that this SUV could be driven on 25 gallons of gasoline?

   Ⓐ 190
   Ⓑ 284.6
   Ⓒ 300
   Ⓓ 305
   Ⓔ 312

7. The ratio of 2 quantities is 5 to 6. If each of the quantities is increased by 15, what is the ratio of these two new quantities?

   Ⓐ 5:6
   Ⓑ 25:27
   Ⓒ 15:16
   Ⓓ 20:21
   Ⓔ It cannot be determined from the information given.

8. $\sqrt{6^2 + 8^2 - 19} =$

(A) $3\sqrt{2}$
(B) 8
(C) 9
(D) 10
(E) $\sqrt{119}$

9. In an animal behavior experiment, 50 tagged white pigeons and 200 tagged gray pigeons were released from a laboratory. Within one week, 88 percent of the white pigeons and 80.5 percent of the gray pigeons had returned to the laboratory. What percent of the total number of pigeons returned to the laboratory?

(A) 80.5
(B) 82
(C) 82.5
(D) 85
(E) 86.5

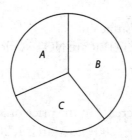

10. In the circular region shown above, sections A and B represent $\dfrac{3}{8}$ and $\dfrac{5}{11}$, respectively, of the area of the circular region. Section C represents what fractional part of the area of the circular region?

(A) $\dfrac{15}{88}$

(B) $\dfrac{2}{11}$

(C) $\dfrac{5}{22}$

(D) $\dfrac{45}{88}$

(E) $\dfrac{73}{88}$

11. At the wholesale store you can buy an 8-pack of hot dogs for $1.55, a 20-pack for $3.05, and a 250-pack for $22.95. What is the greatest number of hot dogs you can buy at this store with $200?

    (A) 1,108
    (B) 2,100
    (C) 2,108
    (D) 2,124
    (E) 2,256

The following data sufficiency problems consist of a question and two statements, labeled (1) and (2), in which certain data are given. You have to decide whether the data given in the statements are <u>sufficient</u> for answering the question. Using the data given in the statements <u>plus</u> your knowledge of mathematics and everyday facts (such as the number of days in July or the meaning of *counterclockwise*), you must indicate whether

(A) Statement (1) ALONE is sufficient, but statement (2) alone is not sufficient.
(B) Statement (2) ALONE is sufficient, but statement (1) alone is not sufficient.
(C) BOTH statements TOGETHER are sufficient, but NEITHER statement ALONE is sufficient.
(D) EACH statement ALONE is sufficient.
(E) Statements (1) and (2) TOGETHER are NOT sufficient.

12. What was the percent decrease in the price of MegaTek (MGTK) stock during the market decline of March 1, 2001, to March 1, 2002?

    (1) The price of MGTK was $56.20 on March 1, 2001.
    (2) The price of the stock on January 1, 2002, was only one-quarter of its price as of March 1, 2001.

13. Aran's long-distance telephone plan charges him $0.50 for the first 4 minutes of a call, and $0.07 per minute for each subsequent minute. Aran made a call to Lupe for x minutes, where x is an integer. How many minutes long was Aran's call?

    (1) The last 7 minutes of Aran's call cost $0.22 less than the first 7 minutes of the call.
    (2) The call did not cost more than $1.05.

14. If x and y are both positive numbers, is x greater than 75% of y?

    (1) $5x > 4y + 1$
    (2) $x = 6$

15. Is $xyz = 1$?

    (1) $x(y^z) = 1$
    (2) $5z = 0$

16. What is the average (arithmetic mean) of x and y ?

    (1) The average of $x + 3$ and $y + 5$ is 14.
    (2) The average of x, y, and 16 is 12.

Solve the problem and indicate the best of the answer choices given.

17. One day a car rental agency rented 2/3 of its cars, including 3/5 of its cars with CD players. If 3/4 of its cars have CD players, what percent of the cars that were not rented had CD players?

    (A) 10%
    (B) 35%
    (C) 45%
    (D) 66.7%
    (E) 90%

18. If x is 20 percent greater than 88, then $x =$

    (A) 68
    (B) 70.4
    (C) 86
    (D) 105.6
    (E) 108

19. A farmer with 1,350 acres of land had planted his fields with corn, sugar cane, and tobacco in the ratio of 5:3:1, respectively, but he wanted to make more money, so he shifted the ratio to 2:4:3, respectively. How many more acres of land were planted with tobacco under the new system?

    (A) 90
    (B) 150
    (C) 270
    (D) 300
    (E) 450

20. $\sqrt{144} + \sqrt{225} + \sqrt{324} =$

    (A) 18
    (B) 33
    (C) 36
    (D) 42
    (E) 45

21. What is the perimeter of a square with area $\dfrac{9P^2}{16}$?

    Ⓐ $\dfrac{3P}{4}$

    Ⓑ $\dfrac{3P^2}{4}$

    Ⓒ $3P$

    Ⓓ $3P^2$

    Ⓔ $\dfrac{4P}{3}$

22. If a three-digit number is selected at random from the integers 100 to 999, inclusive, what is the probability that the first digit and the last digit of the integer will both be exactly two less than the middle digit?

    Ⓐ 1 out of 900

    Ⓑ 7 out of 900

    Ⓒ 9 out of 1,000

    Ⓓ 1 out of 100

    Ⓔ 7 out of 100

23. Which of the following inequalities is equivalent to $-4 < x < 8$?

    Ⓐ $|x-1| < 7$

    Ⓑ $|x+2| < 6$

    Ⓒ $|x+3| < 5$

    Ⓓ $|x-2| < 6$

    Ⓔ None of the above

24. $\dfrac{80 - 6(36 \div 9)}{\dfrac{1}{4}} =$

    Ⓐ 416

    Ⓑ 224

    Ⓒ 188

    Ⓓ 104

    Ⓔ 56

25. Three different lumberjacks can chop W amount of wood in 30 minutes, 45 minutes, and 50 minutes according to their different levels of skill with the axe. How much wood, in terms of W, could the two fastest lumberjacks chop in 2 hours?

   (A) $6\frac{2}{3}W$

   (B) $6W$

   (C) $4\frac{2}{3}W$

   (D) $3W$

   (E) $2\frac{2}{3}W$

The following data sufficiency problems consist of a question and two statements, labeled (1) and (2), in which certain data are given. You have to decide whether the data given in the statements are <u>sufficient</u> for answering the question. Using the data given in the statements <u>plus</u> your knowledge of mathematics and everyday facts (such as the number of days in July or the meaning of *counterclockwise*), you must indicate whether

   (A) Statement (1) ALONE is sufficient, but statement (2) alone is not sufficient.
   (B) Statement (2) ALONE is sufficient, but statement (1) alone is not sufficient.
   (C) BOTH statements TOGETHER are sufficient, but NEITHER statement ALONE is sufficient.
   (D) EACH statement ALONE is sufficient.
   (E) Statements (1) and (2) TOGETHER are NOT sufficient.

26. In what year was Edward born?

   (1) In 1988, Edward turned 17 years old.
   (2) Edward's sister Lisa, who is 14 months older than Edward, was born in 1970.

27. Is $rs = rx - 2$?

   (1) r is an odd number
   (2) $x = s + 2$

28. A CEO is building an extra-wide garage in which to park his limousines. The garage is x feet wide, and at least 2 feet of space is required between each two cars and between the cars and the walls. Will all 9 limousines fit in the garage?

   (1) The average width of the limousines is the square root of x.
   (2) $x = 100$.

29. If $q + r + s = 45$, what is the value of qr?

   (1) $q = r = s$
   (2) $q - r - s = -15$

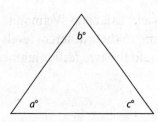

30. Is the triangle depicted above isosceles? (Figure not necessarily drawn to scale.)

    (1) $180 - (a + c) = 60$
    (2) $a = 2b - c$

Solve the problem and indicate the best of the answer choices given.

31. Last year Jackie saved 5% of her annual salary. This year, she made 10% more money than last year, and she saved 8% of her salary. The amount saved this year was what percent of the amount she saved last year?

    (A) 56%
    (B) 76%
    (C) 158%
    (D) 176%
    (E) 188%

	P	Q	R	S
P	0	144	171	186
Q	144	0	162	X
R	171	162	0	Y
S	186	X	Y	0

32. The table above shows the one-way driving distance, in miles, between four cities: P, Q, R, and S. For example, the distance between P and Q is 144 miles. If the round trip between S and Q is 16 miles farther than the round trip between S and R, and the round trip between S and R is 24 miles less than the round trip between S and P, what is the value of X?

    (A) 174
    (B) 182
    (C) 186
    (D) 348
    (E) 364

33. If 35 percent of 400 is 20 percent of x, then x =

    (A) 200
    (B) 350
    (C) 700
    (D) 900
    (E) 1,400

34. $(2^3 - 1)(2^3 + 1)(2^6 + 1)(2^{12} + 1) =$

    (A) $(2^{24} - 1)$
    (B) $(2^{24} + 1)$
    (C) $(2^{48} - 1)$
    (D) $(2^{96} + 1)$
    (E) $2^6(2^{12} - 1)$

35. To be considered for "movie of the year," a film must appear in at least ¼ of the top-10-movies lists submitted by the Cinematic Academy's 765 members. What is the smallest number of top-10 lists a film can appear on and still be considered for "movie of the year"?

    (A) 191
    (B) 192
    (C) 193
    (D) 212
    (E) 213

36. In a sample of associates at a law firm, 30 percent are second-year associates, and 60 percent are not first-year associates. What percent of the associates at the law firm have been there for more than two years?

    (A) 10%
    (B) 20%
    (C) 30%
    (D) 40%
    (E) 50%

37. Which of the following fractions has the greatest value?

    (A) $\dfrac{48}{(2^5)(3^2)}$

    (B) $\dfrac{12}{(2^4)(3^3)}$

    (C) $\dfrac{6}{(2^3)(3^2)}$

    (D) $\dfrac{144}{(2^4)(3^4)}$

    (E) $\dfrac{81}{(2^3)(3^5)}$

––––––––––––––––––––– STOP. –––––––––––––––––––––

Verbal

The questions in this group are based on the content of a passage. After reading the passage, choose the best answer to each question. Answer all questions following the passage on the basis of what is <u>stated</u> or <u>implied</u> in the passage.

Forget hostile aliens. According to a forthcoming book by noted astrophysicist Egbert Larson, the intrepid humans who first attempt interstellar space travel will face far more daunting challenges before they ever meet angry Little Green Men.

Larson begins with the problem of relativistic time dilation. If you travel all the way to Alpha Centauri, you'd like to come back and tell your friends about it, right? It's not too likely to happen, though. If Mr. Einstein was right about relativity—and we're not going to say he wasn't—then time slows down when you approach the speed of light. A person traveling at any velocity near the speed of light will age only days for every week, month, or even year that passes on earth. Relativity does not present a problem for interstellar space travel, per se, but it does mean that interstellar civilizations or even just interstellar communications will require a mind-boggling amount of calendar juggling.

Did we mention that you'd have to travel at near the speed of light? That's because the distance between stars is so vast that even if you could travel at the speed of light—which, Larson reminds us, you can't—it would take more than four years to reach our closest star neighbors, Alpha Proxima and Alpha Centauri, and decades or centuries to reach the other stars in our "immediate neighborhood." And if you tried to accelerate directly to the speed of light like they do in the movies, you'd be instantly splattered on the back of your theoretical spacecraft. Achieving anything close to light speed will require sustained acceleration at a level that human bodies can withstand—say, a crushing two gravities—for over a year. Better hope somebody brings some potato chips.

Speaking of chips, food is going to be a problem. Since it is economically, if not physically, impossible to accelerate 200 years' worth of food to nearly the speed of light, and since you're not likely to find any grocery stores along the way, someone will have to figure out how to make food in space. Keeping a crew alive on the way turns out to be the trickiest part of all. Once you've got the nearly impossible physics of space travel worked out, you still have to figure out the chemistry and biology of keeping your air and water clean and keeping your crew fed and safe from radiation and infection, and—did we mention the 200 years?—you'll probably need several generations of crew members to complete the trip. Ever been on a bus for more than 24 hours? It's not a pretty picture.

We applaud Larson for his insightful writing and his scrupulous attention to scientific detail. For those of you seeking a cold, hard look at the reality of interstellar space travel, this is a wonderful read. But be warned: Larson doesn't let you down gently. For those of you sincerely hoping to beam up with Scotty—and you know who you are—you might want to give this one a pass.

1. Which of the following would make the most appropriate title for this passage?

   Ⓐ Going Boldly Where No One Has Gone Before: The Promise and Peril of Interstellar Space Travel

   Ⓑ The Day the Earth Stood Still: Why Interstellar Space Travel Is Essential to Human Survival

   Ⓒ The Wrath of Larson: Egbert Larson's Quest to Build an Interstellar Spacecraft

   Ⓓ A Busted Flat in Beta Regulus: The Crushing Challenges of Interstellar Space Travel

   Ⓔ Say It Isn't So, Mr. Einstein: Egbert Larson's Challenge to the Theory of Relativity

2. Based on the tone and content of the passage, it is most likely which of the following?

   Ⓐ A book review in a journal intended for astrophysics professionals

   Ⓑ A movie review in an entertainment industry publication

   Ⓒ A book review in a science magazine aimed at a general audience

   Ⓓ A book review in a newspaper

   Ⓔ A transcript of a talk given at a science fiction convention dedicated to "celebrating a popular television show's anniversary"

3. The passage implies that all except which of the following could be threats to human health during extended interstellar voyages?

   Ⓐ Meteor impact

   Ⓑ Radiation poisoning

   Ⓒ Accelerating too fast

   Ⓓ Starvation

   Ⓔ Old age

4. According to the passage, which of the following will present the most difficult challenge for humans attempting interstellar space travel?

   Ⓐ Achieving velocities near the speed of light

   Ⓑ Withstanding the acceleration necessary for traversing interstellar distances

   Ⓒ Maintaining clean air and water on a journey that could last centuries

   Ⓓ Accommodating the effects of relativistic time dilation

   Ⓔ Enabling the humans on board to survive during the journey

5. According to the information given in the passage, if two 20-year-old twins lived on earth, and one of them left on a journey for Alpha Centauri at very close to the speed of light, then managed to survive the journey and return to earth having aged 40 years during the journey, what could she expect to find upon her return to earth?

   Ⓐ Her great-grandmother
   Ⓑ Her twin at the age of 20
   Ⓒ Her twin at the age of 40
   Ⓓ Her twin at the age of 60
   Ⓔ Her twin's great-grandchildren

6. Which of the following inventions, if it could be perfected and manufactured at a viable cost, would address the most challenges to human interstellar space travel, as presented in the passage?

   Ⓐ A ram-scoop drive that can accelerate a spacecraft of any size to four-fifths of the speed of light within 24 hours
   Ⓑ A cold-sleep capsule that essentially halts the passage of time for human inhabitants while protecting them from all physical harm
   Ⓒ A sustainable biosphere that reliably generates healthy food and automatically cleans air and water
   Ⓓ A neutrino-based communications system that permits instantaneous communication across any distance without any relativistic time dilation
   Ⓔ An impervious force field that protects the ship and its inhabitants from radiation, meteor strikes, or hostile alien attacks

7. The author of the passage most likely mentions "Little Green Men" in the first paragraph for what purpose?

   Ⓐ To poke fun at the ignorance of most science fiction readers
   Ⓑ To introduce a daunting challenge that will have to be addressed before human interstellar space travel can become possible
   Ⓒ To draw a comparison between the attempts of humans to voyage in space and the more successful attempts of other civilizations
   Ⓓ To draw an amusing distinction between a supposed danger of space travel, as presented in the popular media, and the actual challenges posed by interstellar space travel, as perceived by scientists
   Ⓔ To suggest that the concept of human interstellar space travel is as much of a myth as the "Little Green Men" that appear in science fiction movies and television programs

For the following questions, select the best of the answer choices given.

8. A wholesale fruit distributor, in an effort to increase its profit margins, has proposed cutting the tops off of the pineapples it ships in order to increase the number of pineapples that can fit in a standard-size truck.

   Which of the following, if true, gives the strongest evidence that the fruit distributor's plan will increase its profit margins?

   - (A) Pineapples with the tops cut off have been shown to rot three times faster than uncut fruit.
   - (B) Customers buy whole pineapples in part because of their exotic, spiky appearance.
   - (C) Cutting the tops off of pineapples may inadvertently remove some of the fruit within.
   - (D) The fruit distributor ships primarily to a fruit canning company that has no use for pineapple tops.
   - (E) Pineapple juice has been shown to be an even more potent source of vitamin C than orange or cranberry juice.

9. A brand of cough syrup comes with a measuring cup attached so that customers can measure the proper dosage. A consultant has pointed out that this cup is unnecessary, since most customers have measuring cups at home. Since the cups increase the cost of packaging the cough syrup and reduce the total number of units that can be shipped in a standard package, the consultant advises that the company can increase its net revenue on this product (total revenue minus total costs) by selling the cough syrup without the measuring cups.

   Which of the following, if true, provides the strongest evidence that the company should not follow the consultant's advice?

   - (A) Studies have shown that customers who use cough syrup without a measuring cup frequently take either too little or too much of the medicine, rendering the dosage either ineffective or, in cases of overdose, dangerous.
   - (B) The company has included a measuring cup with each bottle of cough syrup for the last 18 years.
   - (C) Studies have shown that 85 percent of consumers possess at home either a measuring cup, a set of measuring spoons, or both.
   - (D) Many customers neglect to follow the recommended dosage of cough syrup even when the measuring cup is packaged along with the bottle of cough syrup.
   - (E) Shipping the cough syrup bottles without the measuring cups will provide a marginal improvement in the number of cough syrup bottles that can be shipped in a standard package.

The following two questions are based on the following passage:

A study by a group of dentists has concluded that regular use of a certain brand of mouthwash is as effective as flossing in preventing gum disease. The mouthwash company has released a television ad suggesting that people who do not like flossing can now rely solely on mouthwash and brushing to maintain good dental health. A leading manufacturer of dental floss brought a lawsuit against the mouthwash company demanding that the advertisement be discontinued on the grounds that it is misleading.

10. Which of the following, if true, provides the strongest support for the dental floss company's claim that the advertisement is misleading?

   (A) The dental floss manufacturer is concerned that it will lose market share in the dental health market because the advertisement encourages people to switch from dental floss to mouthwash.
   (B) The dental floss company claims in its own advertisements that brushing and flossing after every meal is the most effective way to maintain good dental health.
   (C) Although mouthwash is an effective deterrent to gum disease, it is less effective than dental floss at removing plaque and preventing cavities between teeth.
   (D) Per usage, mouthwash is three times more expensive than dental floss, if the recommended amounts of both products are used.
   (E) The dentists who conducted the study on the effectiveness of mouthwash in preventing gum disease obtained their funding for the study from a company that manufactures mouthwash.

11. Which of the following, if true, most supports the mouthwash company's defense that its advertisement promotes greater public health?

   (A) Since the dental floss company is protesting the advertisement only to protect its own economic self-interest, it cannot be seen as representing greater public health.
   (B) Greater public health is best served if people use both mouthwash and dental floss, a combination that has been shown to be more effective than either method used alone.
   (C) Many people object to flossing because it is painful and causes their gums to bleed.
   (D) Since, on average, people are twice as likely to use mouthwash regularly as to floss regularly, the advertisement will increase the number of people who take effective action against gum disease, a serious public health problem.
   (E) Gum disease has been proven to have links with the early onset of heart disease, one of the top three threats to public health in terms of mortality.

12. An electrical appliance company has submitted a new model of washing machine for stress and durability testing. After the conventional round of tests, 26 of the 90 machines tested no longer functioned. Observing these results, the company determined that the washing machine model was acceptable for the consumer market.

Which of the following, if true, most strongly supports the company's decision regarding the washing machine?

(A) When the number one rated washing machine was submitted for stress and durability testing, 96 out of 100 machines were still functioning at the end of the test.

(B) Because of the extreme stress of the testing process, any model that has more than two-thirds of its machines functioning at the end of the test process is considered sufficiently durable for the consumer market.

(C) Most consumers will tolerate a washing machine that functions only 64 times out of 90 attempts.

(D) Although the model tested is less durable than other models on the market, its projected price is considerably lower than that of the most durable models.

(E) The electrical failure that brought down most of the 26 washing machines that ceased functioning could probably be avoided if the machine were redesigned.

The following questions present a sentence, part of which or all of which is underlined. Beneath the sentence, you will find five ways of phrasing the underlined part. The first of these repeats the original; the other four are different. If you think the original is best, choose the first answer; otherwise choose one of the others.

These questions test correctness and effectiveness of expression. In choosing your answer, follow the requirements of standard written English; that is, pay attention to grammar, choice of words, and sentence construction. Choose the answer that produces the most effective sentence; this answer should be clear and exact, without awkwardness, ambiguity, redundancy, or grammatical error.

13. <u>Having accounted for</u> only 13 percent of the student body at Northlake High, students who attended Megalopolis Middle School dominate the Northlake High student government.

(A) Having accounted for
(B) With
(C) Despite having been
(D) Although accounting for
(E) As

14. Because the key witness died just prior to the start of the trial, <u>Detectives Mack and Smith were not able in determining the extent of</u> administrative corruption.

    Ⓐ Detectives Mack and Smith were not able in determining the extent of
    Ⓑ therefore the detectives, Mack and Smith, were unable to determine the extent of
    Ⓒ Mack and Smith, the detectives, were not able of determining the extent to
    Ⓓ Detectives Mack and Smith were not able to determine the extent of
    Ⓔ the extent was unable to be determined by Detectives Mack and Smith of

15. Health Department statistics demonstrate that children <u>reading high on glucose with family histories of diabetes</u> are twice as likely as the general population to develop diabetes.

    Ⓐ reading high on glucose with family histories of diabetes
    Ⓑ with high glucose readings whose families have a history of diabetes
    Ⓒ with high glucose readings and who have a diabetic history in the family
    Ⓓ having high glucose readings and also having histories of diabetes in their family
    Ⓔ with a history of diabetes running in the family and with high glucose readings

16. Medical experts have amassed evidence concluding that users of smokeless tobacco <u>be more prone to heart disease, hypertension, and mouth cancers</u> than people who do not use smokeless tobacco.

    Ⓐ be more prone to heart disease, hypertension, and mouth cancers
    Ⓑ are proner to heart disease, hypertension, and mouth cancers
    Ⓒ are more prone to heart disease, hypertension, and mouth cancers
    Ⓓ experience heart disease, hypertension, and mouth cancers at heightened rates
    Ⓔ suffer heart disease, hypertension, and mouth cancers at a higher risk

17. Chef Sylvia Bostock's eclectic offerings at her new restaurant, Sylvia's, range from an Asian-inspired tuna tartelette in a soy-ginger demiglace <u>with</u> a succulent cowboy rib-eye served atop a small mountain of fried onions.

    Ⓐ with
    Ⓑ to
    Ⓒ in addition to
    Ⓓ and
    Ⓔ and to

18. The governing board of the new league has modified its rules so that preexisting teams can stay together even though <u>not all their members meet the new minimum age requirement</u>.

    Ⓐ not all their members meet the new minimum age requirement
    Ⓑ the new minimum age requirement has not been met by all their members
    Ⓒ not all their members have met the new minimum age, as required
    Ⓓ all their members have not met the new minimum age requirement
    Ⓔ all their members do not meet the new minimum age requirement

For the following questions, select the best of the answer choices given.

19. Since 1960, the fast-growing town of Hotstone, Arizona, has drawn water from the Gray River, which feeds Lake Mudfish. If the town's water use continues to grow at its present rate, in about 20 years the water level of Lake Mudfish will inevitably decrease to the point that it can no longer support its biologically fragile population of fish.

    The prediction above is based on which of the following assumptions?

    (A) As the town's water requirements grow, it will not be able to meet those requirements by drawing on water sources other than the Gray River.
    (B) Since 1960, the lake's population of fish has become more biologically fragile.
    (C) The amount of water that the lake loses to evaporation each year will increase over the next two decades.
    (D) There are multiple sources of water besides the Gray River that feed into Lake Mudfish.
    (E) The town of Hotstone will be able to reverse its trend of increasing water use if it implements an aggressive water conservation program.

20. Public protests can cause even the most powerful companies to change their policies. For example, an activist group recently staged a demonstration in front of the HydraBore corporate headquarters to protest the company's use of the chemical Ectomazathol. Within three months of the demonstration, HydraBore replaced Ectomazathol in its production plants with another chemical.

    Which of the following, if true, casts the most doubt on the connection between the public protest and the decision of the company to change chemicals?

    (A) Preliminary studies show that the new chemical may be more carcinogenic than Ectomazathol.
    (B) The recently introduced chemical that is replacing Ectomazathol is less expensive and more effective in its industrial application than Ectomazathol.
    (C) HydraBore devoted no publicity efforts to announce its switch from Ectomazathol to the new chemical.
    (D) As protests against HydraBore have become more frequent, the company has subsequently increased its public relations budget.
    (E) The activist group that staged the demonstration has been linked to illegal acts of theft and sabotage within other corporate headquarters.

21. A recent spate of art thefts at a major museum has led to a drastic increase in the insurance premiums that the museum must pay to insure its collection. Many art fans are concerned that the museum, which traditionally has no entrance fee, will be forced to charge a high entrance fee in order to pay for the increased insurance premiums.

    Which of the following, if true, would most alleviate the concern of the art fans that the museum will be forced to charge high entrance fees?

    - (A) Law enforcement officials recently apprehended the Belgian Bobcat, a notorious art thief who has been linked to at least 20 art heists.
    - (B) Citing a dispute with the insurance company over the terms of its coverage, the museum has chosen to cancel its insurance policy.
    - (C) The majority of visitors to the museum are schoolchildren, who could not reasonably be expected to pay a high entrance fee.
    - (D) The museum pays for the majority of its total expenses from its large endowment, which is earmarked specifically for purchasing new art.
    - (E) The museum recently installed a state-of-the-art burglar alarm system that will make future thefts almost impossible.

22. Which of the following, if true, best completes the passage below?

    The traditional view of Homer is that of a blind bard who wrote down the epic poems known as the *Iliad* and the *Odyssey* in the eighth century B.C.E. We know now, however, that this picture cannot be true. The language used in the epic poems contains elements of the Greek language dating from the twelfth to the eighth centuries B.C.E., but the Greek writing system was not developed until the late seventh century, when it was used to record clerical notes. A more accurate statement regarding Homer, therefore, is that, if he existed, he most likely _____.

    - (A) wrote the poems down in the fifth century B.C.E., using a preexisting oral tradition of Greek epic poetry.
    - (B) was involved in the recording of clerical notes in Greek in the seventh century.
    - (C) composed the poems orally in the eighth century and then dictated them to a scribe in the late seventh century.
    - (D) composed the poems orally in the twelfth century, using a predecessor of the Greek language.
    - (E) composed the poems orally in the eighth century, using elements of preexisting Greek epic poetry.

The questions in this group are based on the content of a passage. After reading the passage, choose the best answer to each question. Answer all questions following the passage on the basis of what is <u>stated</u> or <u>implied</u> in the passage.

One of the biggest problems facing the art world today is the dilemma over the repatriation of cultural treasures. Although the subject has not been widely noted by the general public, in recent decades museums and art dealers have repeatedly faced off against the representatives of nations and ethnic groups whose cultural legacies have been robbed by the rapacious collecting of these so-called art experts. Advocates of repatriation have argued that cultural treasures should be returned to their nations of origin, both because of basic fairness and because the artwork and cultural artifacts in question are best understood within their local context.

Several prominent museums, most notably the British Museum in London and the Louvre in Paris, have defended themselves on the grounds that they can better protect and preserve these cultural treasures than can the developing nations and impoverished ethnic groups that frequently seek their return. They further argue that more people can see the treasures if they are proudly displayed in a major museum, as opposed to some poorly funded national museum in a backwater country; evidently, the quantity of viewers is more important than the relevance of the art and artifacts to the viewer.

The arguments of the museum curators fall apart in an instance such as the Elgin Marbles. These majestic marble sculptures, which once graced the Parthenon on the Acropolis in Athens, were stolen by Lord Elgin in the nineteenth century and given to the British Museum, which holds them to this day. The people of Athens have built a beautiful, modern museum on the Acropolis to display the Elgin Marbles and other treasures from the Greek cultural heritage, so there can be no valid argument that the Greeks are unable to house the sculptures properly. Furthermore, more people visit the Acropolis every day than visit the British Museum.

23. Of the following, the most appropriate title for the passage above would be:

    Ⓐ The Elgin Marbles: Timeless Symbols of the Glory That Was Greece
    Ⓑ The Role of Great Museums in the Preservation of Cultural Artifacts
    Ⓒ Repatriation of Cultural Treasures: The British Museum's Dirty Little Secret
    Ⓓ The Value of Cultural Treasures in Defining National Identity
    Ⓔ A Curious Curator: Lord Elgin and the Rise of the British Museum

24. The third paragraph plays what role in the passage?

    Ⓐ It summarizes all the points expressed in the first two paragraphs.
    Ⓑ It raises new arguments that expand on those previously expressed.
    Ⓒ It suggests a possible area for useful research in the future.
    Ⓓ It rejects the arguments expressed in the first paragraph.
    Ⓔ It provides concrete evidence against arguments expressed in the second paragraph.

GO ON TO NEXT PAGE ➤

25. The situation involving the repatriation of the Elgin Marbles to Athens is most similar to which of the following?

   (A) A Native American tribe in Oregon requests that a museum in Chicago return some ceremonial masks that could help in fundraising efforts to build a proposed museum in Portland.

   (B) The nation of Peru in South America threatens the nation of Ecuador with military action if Ecuador does not hand over various gold artifacts of the Inca Empire, which originated in Peru.

   (C) The National Archeology Museum of Cairo in Egypt requests that the Louvre return eight mummies from the time of Ramses the Great for the Cairo Museum's new exhibit hall dedicated to artifacts from Ramses' court.

   (D) The nation of Greece requests the nation of Turkey to provide Greek archeologists with free access to ancient Greek sites on the Ionian coast of Turkey, and to transfer any cultural artifacts found there to the National Archeology Museum in Athens.

   (E) A museum in Baton Rouge, Louisiana, requests that the Texas History Museum in Austin, Texas, loan the original "Lone Star" flag to Baton Rouge for a new exhibit entitled, "Texas: Our Neighbor to the East."

26. What is the purpose of the final sentence of the passage?

   (A) To express pride in the cultural treasures of Athens

   (B) To refute the argument that more people can see the Elgin Marbles at the British Museum than at the Acropolis

   (C) To comment on the relative number of tourists at two of Europe's most famous tourist attractions

   (D) To express concern that the large number of tourists on the Acropolis will damage the Elgin Marbles, should they be returned

   (E) To provide an appropriate end to a rousing debate

27. The author's attitude toward museum curators who oppose the repatriation of cultural treasures is best summarized as what?

   (A) Righteous indignation

   (B) Bemused sarcasm

   (C) Seething anger

   (D) Condescending approval

   (E) Grudging admiration

28. Which of the following, if true, would best support the position taken by the advocates of repatriation, as expressed in the first paragraph?

   (A) Of seven gold Inca statues sent from the Field Museum in Chicago to the National Archeology Museum in Lima, Peru, four were stolen within six months of being put on display.

   (B) Mummies taken from the dry heat of Egypt and relocated to the damp climate of London have shown disturbing signs of decay.

   (C) Operating a first-rate art and archeology museum is financially unfeasible for most developing nations, which face a difficult enough challenge feeding their people.

   (D) A type of sculpture from central Africa appears dull and nondescript in a museum setting, but when placed in the region of its origin can clearly be seen to replicate the colors and shapes of local rock formations.

   (E) British colonists in India in the nineteenth century felt that it was their right to claim the nation's artistic treasures as their own in exchange for importing the benefits of a modern industrial society.

The following questions present a sentence, part of which or all of which is underlined. Beneath the sentence, you will find five ways of phrasing the underlined part. The first of these repeats the original; the other four are different. If you think the original is best, choose the first answer; otherwise choose one of the others.

These questions test correctness and effectiveness of expression. In choosing your answer, follow the requirements of standard written English; that is, pay attention to grammar, choice of words, and sentence construction. Choose the answer that produces the most effective sentence; this answer should be clear and exact, without awkwardness, ambiguity, redundancy, or grammatical error.

29. According to government health statistics, <u>Americans born before 1925 develop obesity by the age of 65 only 8 percent of the time, but 35 percent of those born since 1950 did so by age 35.</u>

   (A) Americans born before 1925 develop obesity by the age of 65 only 8 percent of the time, but 35 percent of those born since 1950 did so by age 35.

   (B) only 8 percent of Americans born before 1925 developed obesity by the age of 65; if they are born since 1950, 35 percent develop obesity by the age 35.

   (C) only 8 percent of Americans born before 1925 developed obesity by the age of 65; of those born since 1950, 35 percent developed obesity by the age of 35.

   (D) obesity develops by the age of 65 in only 8 percent of Americans born before 1925, and by 35 by the 35 percent born since 1950.

   (E) of Americans born before 1925, only 8 percent of them have developed obesity by the age of 65, but 35 percent of those born since 1950 do by the age of 35.

30. In his groundbreaking work on special relativity, Albert Einstein displayed an intellectual boldness in the face of a reluctant scientific establishment that was <u>not unlike that of Galileo Galilei, who refused</u> to accept the intellectual limits placed on him by the censors of the Catholic Church.

   - (A) not unlike that of Galileo Galilei, who refused
   - (B) like Galileo Galilei and his refusal
   - (C) not unlike Galileo Galilei, who refused
   - (D) like that of Galileo Galilei for refusing
   - (E) as that of Galileo Galilei, who refused

31. <u>The rising of the rate</u> of tardiness among MegaTech employees has generated concern among management that the employees are not sufficiently focused on increasing shareholder value.

   - (A) The rising of the rate
   - (B) Rising rates
   - (C) The rising rate
   - (D) Because of the rising rate
   - (E) Because the rising rate

32. Increasingly over the last few years, corporations involved in patent litigation <u>have opted to settle the lawsuit rather than facing</u> the protracted legal expenses of a court battle.

   - (A) have opted to settle the lawsuit rather than facing
   - (B) have opted settling the lawsuit instead of facing
   - (C) have opted to settle the lawsuit rather than face
   - (D) had opted for settlement of the lawsuit instead of facing
   - (E) had opted to settle the lawsuit rather than face

33. The ManStop, Boston's hot new men's clothing store, offers a selection that <u>is on range from</u> conservative pin-striped suits for that day at the office to stylish cashmere pullovers for that night on the town.

   - (A) is on range from
   - (B) ranging from
   - (C) ranges to
   - (D) ranges from
   - (E) having ranged from

For the following questions, select the best of the answer choices given.

34. An agricultural cooperative wants to sell more of its less popular vegetables, zucchini in particular. A consultant has suggested that the cooperative's farmers should attempt to market a purple form of zucchini instead of the conventional green form, because people generally dislike green-colored vegetables.

   Which of the following, if true, casts the most doubt on the accuracy of the consultant's assertion?

   (A) Broccoli and green peas, which are both green vegetables, are among the most popular vegetables in the country.

   (B) Grapes and eggplants, which both have purple skin, are popular among consumers of all ages.

   (C) Summer squash, a yellow-colored cousin of the zucchini, is one of the most popular summer vegetables.

   (D) Green tomatoes are far less popular than red tomatoes.

   (E) A chewing gum company reports that its purple-colored grape gum is less popular than its green-colored sour apple flavor.

35. Homely Hotels has a customer loyalty program in which for every four nights a customer spends at a Homely Hotel, he or she receives a coupon good for one free night at any Homely Hotel. Recently people have begun selling these coupons on the Internet for less than the cost of a night at a Homely Hotel. This marketing of coupons has resulted in decreased revenue for the Homely Hotel chain.

   To discourage this undesirable trade in free-stay coupons, it would be best for Homely Hotels to restrict:

   (A) the number of coupons a customer can receive in one year

   (B) use of the coupons to the specific hotel in which they were issued

   (C) the valid dates of the coupons to only the month immediately following the date of issue

   (D) use of the coupons to the recipient or people with the same last name

   (E) use of the coupons to Homely Hotel franchises that charge an equal or lesser nightly rate than the franchise that issued the coupon

36. An American manufacturer of space heaters reported a 1994 fourth-quarter net income (total income minus total costs) of $41 million, compared with $28.3 million in the fourth quarter of 1993. This increase was realized despite a drop in U.S. domestic retail sales of space-heating units toward the end of the fourth quarter of 1994 as a result of unusually high temperatures.

Which of the following, if true, would contribute most to an explanation of the increase in the manufacturer's net income?

(A) In the fourth quarter of 1994, the manufacturer paid its assembly-line workers no salaries in November or December because of a two-month-long strike, but the company had a sufficient stock of space-heating units on hand to supply its distributors.

(B) In 1993, because of unusually cold weather in the Northeast, the federal government authorized the diversion of emergency funding for purchasing space-heating units to be used in the hardest-hit areas.

(C) Foreign manufacturers of space heaters reported improved fourth-quarter sales in the American market compared with their sales in 1993.

(D) During the fourth quarter of 1994, the manufacturer announced that it would introduce an extra-high-capacity space heater in the following quarter.

(E) In the third quarter of 1994, a leading consumer magazine advocated space heaters as a cost-effective way to heat spaces of less than 100 square feet.

The following questions present a sentence, part of which or all of which is underlined. Beneath the sentence, you will find five ways of phrasing the underlined part. The first of these repeats the original; the other four are different. If you think the original is best, choose the first answer; otherwise choose one of the others.

These questions test correctness and effectiveness of expression. In choosing your answer, follow the requirements of standard written English; that is, pay attention to grammar, choice of words, and sentence construction. Choose the answer that produces the most effective sentence; this answer should be clear and exact, without awkwardness, ambiguity, redundancy, or grammatical error.

37. Archeological excavations of Roman ruins on the Greek island of Crete show that securing control over the maritime trade routes of the Eastern Mediterranean was a primary goal of the Romans, <u>as it was of the Greeks</u> in preceding centuries.

(A) as it was of the Greeks
(B) like that of the Greeks
(C) as that of the Greeks
(D) just as the Greeks did
(E) as did the Greeks

38. The family's mood, which had been enthusiastic at the beginning of the trip, sank as the temperature <u>has risen, dramatically, but not enough for calling</u> off the whole trip.

   (A) has risen, dramatically, but not enough for calling
   (B) has risen, but not dramatically enough to call
   (C) rose, but not so dramatically as to call
   (D) rose, but not dramatically enough to call
   (E) rose, but not dramatically enough for calling

39. Although no proof yet exists <u>of the electromagnetic disturbances observed being the results of nuclear weapons testing</u>, diplomats are treating the situation with utmost delicacy.

   (A) of the electromagnetic disturbances observed being the results of nuclear weapons testing
   (B) regarding the observed electromagnetic disturbances having been the results of nuclear weapons testing
   (C) that the electromagnetic disturbances observed were the results of nuclear weapons testing
   (D) that nuclear weapons testing resulted in the electromagnetic disturbances having been observed
   (E) that the electromagnetic disturbance observed were resulting from nuclear weapons testing

40. Hip dysplasia is more common among German shepherds <u>than</u> dogs of other breeds.

   (A) than
   (B) than is so of
   (C) compared to
   (D) in comparison with
   (E) than among

GO ON TO NEXT PAGE ➤

41. The only lucid arguments printed in the newspaper concerning the new bond proposal was put forth by the high school principal who wrote a series of letters to the newspaper's editor.

   (A) The only lucid arguments printed in the newspaper concerning the new bond proposal was put forth by the high school principal in a series of letters to the newspaper's editor.

   (B) The principal of the high school wrote a series of letters to the newspaper's editor that put forth the only lucid argument concerning the new bond proposal that was printed in the newspaper.

   (C) In a series of letters to the newspaper's editor, the principal of the high school put forth the only lucid argument concerning the new bond proposal to be printed in the newspaper.

   (D) The high school's principal's series of letters to the newspaper's editor lucidly put forth the only arguments concerning the new bond proposal to be printed in the newspaper.

   (E) Putting forth the only lucid arguments concerning the new bond proposal to be printed in the newspaper, the series of letters to the newspaper's editor were written by the high school's principal.

─────────────── **STOP.** ───────────────

Answer Key

See page 661 for answers to the Integrated Reasoning section.

QUANTITATIVE	VERBAL
1. C	1. D
2. D	2. C
3. D	3. A
4. C	4. E
5. B	5. E
6. D	6. B
7. E	7. D
8. C	8. D
9. B	9. A
10. A	10. C
11. B	11. D
12. E	12. B
13. C	13. D
14. A	14. D
15. B	15. B
16. D	16. C
17. E	17. B
18. D	18. A
19. D	19. A
20. E	20. B
21. C	21. B
22. B	22. E
23. D	23. C
24. B	24. E
25. A	25. C
26. A	26. B
27. E	27. A
28. C	28. D
29. A	29. C
30. E	30. A
31. D	31. C
32. B	32. C
33. C	33. D
34. A	34. A
35. B	35. D
36. C	36. A
37. A	37. A
	38. D
	39. C
	40. E
	41. C

Answers and Explanations

Analytical Writing Assessment
Model Response

The conference speaker argues that video games provide young people with valuable skills needed to succeed in college and at work. While there may be a correlation between video game usage and increased salaries, this argument is based on improper logic and is thus fundamentally flawed.

The speaker acknowledges that video games have been criticized for negatively affecting our nation's youth over the past few years, a fact that cannot be denied. He then claims that a correlation between frequent video game use and higher test scores and salaries implies that video games have led to these positive outcomes. Correlation, however, does not imply causation. There are many other things that have likely increased over the past 25 years, including, for example, cell phone use. However, just as it is unreasonable to conclude that the popularity of video games has caused increased cell phone use, it is unreasonable to conclude that it has increased salaries or test scores.

In order to properly conclude that video game usage provides young people with the skills needed for success, the speaker should either cite or conduct a scientific study that formally addresses the relationship between these activities. By including a control group, the speaker could demonstrate that this increase in test scores and salaries was indeed due to video game usage and was not the product of previously unrecognized factors.

Due to his lack of evidence, the speaker's claim is poorly argued. The statement would have been substantially more persuasive if he had demonstrated true causation instead of mere correlation. Causation can be proved, either by conducting his own research or citing other scientific papers, and either would go a long way to making him a more credible spokesman.

Integrated Reasoning

1. The correct answers are **ET** and **200E**.

CO$_2$ EMITTED IN 1 HOUR	CO$_2$ EMITTED IN 200 KILOMETERS	EXPRESSION
○	●	$200E$
○	○	$\dfrac{E}{200}$
●	○	ET
○	○	$\dfrac{T}{200}$
○	○	$\dfrac{T}{E}$

The total amount of CO$_2$ emitted equals the number of kilograms per kilometer times the number of kilometers. At a rate of T km/hr, the Eurostar travels T km in 1 hour, so the CO$_2$ emitted in that hour is E (the number of kilograms per kilometer) times T.

The total CO$_2$ emitted in 200 kilometers equals E (the number of kilograms per kilometer) times the number of kilometers, 200.

2. The correct answers are shown below.

Yes   No

● ○ The amount of hardwood, in cubic feet, consumed annually by the United States, other industrialized nations, and developing countries

● ○ The amount of paper, in pounds, consumed annually by residents of most European countries

● ○ The amount of hardwood cut annually, in cubic feet, that goes to sawmills for whole-wood projects

Source #1 indicates the total amount of hardwood consumed annually by the global economy, 15 billion cubic feet. Source #3 indicates the annual consumption rate for the United States, other industrialized nations, and developing countries. Enough information is provided to calculate the actual amounts consumed annually in cubic feet.

Source #3 provides the information necessary to determine the second item. The average American consumption amount is provided: 886 pounds of paper per person per year. This is twice that of most European residents, so the European amount can be calculated.

The third item can be determined by the information provided in Sources #1 and #2. Source #1 indicates the total amount of hardwood consumed annually in the world, and Source #2 gives the percentage of this amount that goes to sawmills for whole-wood projects.

3. The correct answers are shown below.

True   False

● ○ All the airports in wind zone III HSR experienced a decrease in the number of cancelled flights.

○ ● Each of the airports in Florida (FL) had more passengers rebooked than any of the airports in New York (NY).

○ ● Three of the five airports with the most cancelled flights had fewer cancelled flights than the previous year.

● ○ Altogether, the airports in wind zone II SWR had fewer than 200,000 cancelled flights.

There are three airports in wind zone III HSR, and each of them experienced a decrease in the number of cancelled flights.

All of the Florida airports ranked higher than all of the New York airports by number of cancelled flights, but not by number of passengers rebooked. The airport with the most passengers rebooked was a New York airport.

Out of the top five airports ranked by cancelled flights, only two experienced a decrease in cancelled flights compared to the previous year.

There is only one airport in wind zone II SWR, and that airport had 187,905 cancelled flights.

4. The correct answers are **186** fall mud-truck improvements and **540** total customizations next spring.

MUD-TRUCK IMPROVEMENTS THIS FALL	TOTAL CUSTOMIZATIONS NEXT SPRING	NUMBER OF CUSTOMIZATIONS
○	○	170
●	○	186
○	○	200
○	○	370
○	○	443
○	●	540

Last spring, the company completed roughly 200 customizations. This fall, the company expects to complete 170 more customizations than were completed last spring. The company should complete 370 total customizations this fall. Mud-truck improvement sales will exceed low-rider packages this fall. If Top Trucks sold an equal number of the two types of customizations, it would sell 185 of each type. If more mud-truck improvements are sold, the minimum number of mud-truck improvements would be 186.

If growth continues at its current rate, Top Trucks will sell 200 + 170 customizations this fall, or 370. It will sell 370 + 170 customizations next spring, or 540.

5. The answer to the first blank is **D**. The symbols inside either or both circles in the Venn diagram represent the titles available in either paperback, hardcover, or both. There are 23 such symbols, representing 2,300 titles out of 3,000, or 23 out of 30.

The answer to the second blank is **A**. The symbols inside the intersection of the circles in the Venn diagram represent the titles available in both paperback and hardcover. There are 5 such symbols, representing 500 titles out of 3,000, or 5 out of 30.

6. The correct answers are shown below.

Would help explain	Would not help explain	
●	○	Texas has a number of venues specifically devoted to country music.
○	●	In general, Minnesota's concertgoers prefer rock music to jazz.
○	●	The most famous classical violinist in the country comes from Florida.

If many concert venues in Texas offer only country music performances, that would help explain the relatively low percentage of venues overall that offer other kinds of performances.

The fact that Minnesota concertgoers prefer rock music to jazz does not help explain why rock performances are offered at fewer venues in the state than jazz performances.

The Florida birthplace of a famous violinist does not help explain why fewer Florida venues offer classical music performances than performances in other genres. It also does not help explain why the percentage of Florida venues that offer classical concerts is lower than the percentage of venues in most other states that offer classical concerts.

7. The answer to the first blank is **C**. There is a general upward trend in the number of domestic tourists over the years, so the relationship between year and number of domestic tourists is positive. The answer to the second blank is **D**. In 2010, there were close to 40 million domestic tourists and close to 10 million international tourists, or about 25% of 40 million.

8. The correct answer is **$1,190**.

    If the manuals run to 115 pages each, plus the three pages of standard company information, they will have a total of 118 pages, with five of those containing color graphics. The total cost of printing one manual will therefore be $0.25 × 118, plus an extra $0.50 × 5, plus $2.00, which equals $34.

    The cost of 35 manuals will be $34 × 35, or $1,190.

9. The correct answers are shown below.

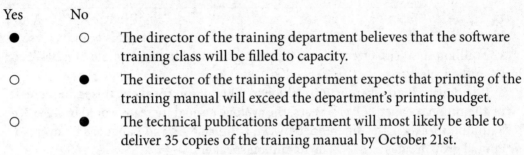

Yes	No	
●	○	The director of the training department believes that the software training class will be filled to capacity.
○	●	The director of the training department expects that printing of the training manual will exceed the department's printing budget.
○	●	The technical publications department will most likely be able to deliver 35 copies of the training manual by October 21st.

    The first inference is supported by the information in E-mail #1. The training director indicates that the class should have 35 registrants, the capacity of the training room.

    The second inference is not supported by the information in any of the three sources. The three sources do not mention the department's printing budget.

    Based on the information given in the three sources, the technical publications department is not likely to be able to deliver 35 copies of the training manual by the deadline of October 21st. E-mail #2 states that delivery should be on time if the manual is under 100 pages, but E-mail #3 indicates that the manual will exceed 100 pages.

10. The correct answers are shown below.

Yes	No	
○	●	More gorillas than lions were born in this zoo in 2017.
●	○	In 2017, this zoo had more ostriches born in captivity than any other zoo in the country.
○	●	More giraffes in this zoo were born in the wild than in captivity.

    The zoo had a greater share of the nation's gorillas, but that doesn't tell us how many gorillas or lions the zoo had in all.

    In 2017, this zoo ranked first in the country for ostriches born in captivity.

    The table compares giraffes at this zoo with the giraffe population at other zoos, but it does not compare giraffes at this zoo that were born in the wild with giraffes at this zoo that were born in captivity, so we can't be sure this statement is true.

11. The correct answers are **24,000,000** for Language A, and **16,000,000** for the difference between Language A's and Language B's average annual growth rates.

LANGUAGE A	DIFFERENCE IN LANGUAGE A AND LANGUAGE B	AVERAGE RATE OF GROWTH (NATIVE SPEAKERS PER YEAR)
○	○	6,000,000
○	○	8,000,000
○	○	12,000,000
○	●	16,000,000
●	○	24,000,000
○	○	48,000,000

If Language A grows from 330 million to 450 million speakers, this is an increase of 120 million speakers. Over 5 years, the average annual increase would be 120 ÷ 5, or 24 million speakers.

If Language B grows from 260 million to 300 million speakers, this is an increase of 40 million speakers. Over 5 years, the average annual increase would be 40 ÷ 5, or 8 million speakers. The difference between Language A's and Language B's average annual growth rates is 24 − 8, or 16 million speakers.

12. The answer to the first blank is **B**. The zygote phase lasts about 56 days, and about 7 of those days are devoted to cellular reorganization; 7 is 12.5% of 56. The answer to the second blank is **C**. The first trimester is about 84 days and the second is about 112 days; 112 is about 133% of 84.

Quantitative

1. The correct answer is **C**. (1) alone is insufficient, because if $x = 36$, then the answer is "yes," but if $x = 37$, then the answer is "no." (2) alone is insufficient, because if $x = 36$, then the answer is "yes," but if $x = 180$, then the answer is "no." If the statements are combined, however, then the only value of x that meets all the conditions is 36, for which the answer is "yes."

2. The correct answer is **D**. (1) alone is sufficient because it tells us that b is a larger number than a, which means that the answer to the question must be "no." (2) alone is sufficient; the statement can be simplified to $5a = 4b$, which means that b is larger than a, so the answer to the question must be "no."

3. The correct answer is **D**. (1) alone is sufficient; if the perimeter of the square is 24, then the length of each side is 24/4 = 6, and the radius of each of the semicircles is 6/2 = 3. The area of the square is 6 × 6 = 36, and since the formula for the area of a circle is πr^2, the area of the semicircles is $2 \times \frac{1}{2}[\pi(3 \times 3)] = 9\pi$; $36 + 9\pi$ is the area of the flowerbed. (2) alone is sufficient; the side of a square is the diagonal divided by $\sqrt{2}$ (this is derived from the Pythagorean theorem), so the sides are equal to 6; by following the same process used with statement (1), you can determine the area of the flowerbed.

4. The correct answer is **C**. (1) alone is insufficient because it gives no information about the number of females on boat R. (2) alone is insufficient because it does not give the number of women on either boat. If the statements are combined, we see that there are 13 women on each boat, or 26 in all.

5. The correct answer is **B**. (1) alone is insufficient because it offers information about only one point on the line. (2) alone is sufficient, because you can check whether the point (4, –2) satisfies the line's equation (and therefore lies on the line) by substituting its coordinates into the line's equation.

6. The correct answer is **D**. The SUV will reach its maximum distance only if driven only on the highway; $25 \times 12.2 = 305$.

7. The correct answer is **E**. With no idea of what the quantities actually are, there is no way to tell how adding 15 to each of them will affect their ratio; for example, if the quantities were 5 and 6, the new ratio would be 20:21, but if the quantities were 10 and 12, the ratio would be 25:27.

8. The correct answer is **C**. $\sqrt{6^2 + 8^2 - 19} = \sqrt{36 + 64 - 19} = \sqrt{81} = 9$.

9. The correct answer is **B**. 88% of 50 is 44, and 80.5% of 200 is 161. 44 + 161 = 205. 205/250 total pigeons = 0.82 = 82%.

10. The correct answer is **A**. Section C is equal to $1 - (3/8 + 5/11) = 1 - (33/88 + 40/88) = 15/88$.

11. The correct answer is **B**. You should start with the 250-packs, because that is the best value, with each hot dog costing less than 10 cents. Rounding 22.95 to 23 for simplicity, you can determine that you can afford 8 of the 250-packs, for a total of $183.60. The 20-packs are the next best value at around 15 cents per hot dog, so with the remaining $16.40 you can buy 5 of the 20-packs for $15.25, leaving $1.15. The $1.15 isn't enough for an 8-pack, so the total number of hot dogs is $8 \times 250 + 5 \times 20 = 2,100$.

12. The correct answer is **E**. (1) alone is insufficient because it gives only the value at the starting point of the period in question. (2) alone is insufficient because the price as of January 1, 2002, is irrelevant to the question. Combining the two statements yields no new insights.

13. The correct answer is **C**. (1) alone is insufficient; we know that the first 7 minutes cost $0.50 + 3 \times $0.07 = $0.71; the least the last 7 minutes could cost is $7 \times $0.07 = $0.49, which is exactly $0.22 less than the first 7 minutes, so we know that the last 7 minutes did not include the first 4 minutes, but that is all we can tell. (2) alone is insufficient, because the call could have lasted any length of time under 12 minutes (12 minutes cost $1.06, 11 minutes cost $0.99). If the two are combined, the only value that meets all the conditions is 11 minutes.

14. The correct answer is **A**. Dividing both sides of the equation in (1) by 5 implies that x is greater than 4/5 of y, which equals 80% of y, so the question is answered in the affirmative and (1) alone is sufficient. (2) is insufficient without providing any information about the relative value of y, so the answer is A.

15. The correct answer is **B**. (1) alone is insufficient, because x, y, and z could be (1, 1, 1) or (1, 1, 0) or other values, which give different answers to the question. (2) alone is sufficient, because if $z = 0$, it does not matter what the values are for x and y; $xyz = 0 \neq 1$.

16. The correct answer is **D**. (1) alone is sufficient; the statement could be restated to say that $x + y + 3 + 5 = 14 \times 2$, or $x + y = 20$; therefore, the average of x and y is 10. (2) alone is sufficient; the statement could be restated as $x + y + 16 = 12 \times 3$, or $x + y = 20$; therefore, the average of x and y is 10.

17. The correct answer is **E**. One way to approach this problem is to think of the fractions as actual cars. Since the given denominators are 3, 4, and 5, imagine that there are 60 cars. In this case, the agency rented 40 cars (2/3 of 60), 45 of the total cars have CD players (3/4 of 60), and 27 of its cars with CD players were rented (3/5 of 45). From these numbers, we can determine that 20 cars in total were not rented (60 – 40), and 18 cars with CD players were not rented (45 – 27). 18 out of 20 is 90 percent.

18. The correct answer is **D**. Eliminate A, B, and C because x is greater than 88. 120 percent of 88 is $1.2(88) = 105.6$.

19. The correct answer is **D**. The numbers in both sets of ratios add up to 9, so you can look at each of the ratios in terms of ninths of 1,350. In the original planting system, tobacco accounted for 1/9 of the total, so $1,350/9 = 150$. In the new system, tobacco accounts for 3/9, or 450. $450 - 150 = 300$.

20. The correct answer is **E**. The statement can be restated as $12 + 15 + 18 = 45$.

21. The correct answer is **C**. The area of a square is the square of its sides, so one of the sides of this square is $\sqrt{\dfrac{9P^2}{16}} = \dfrac{3P}{4}$. The perimeter of a square is its side times 4, so the perimeter is $3P$.

22. The correct answer is **B**. There are exactly 7 digits out of the 900 for which this statement is true: 131, 242, 353, 464, 575, 686, 797; that equals a probability of 7 out of 900.

23. The correct answer is **D**. $|x - 2| < 6$ implies $-6 < x - 2 < 6$, which is equivalent to $-4 < x < 8$. A is equivalent to $-6 < x < 8$, B is equivalent to $-8 < x < 4$, and C is equivalent to $-8 < x < 2$.

24. The correct answer is **B**. The statement is equivalent to $4[80 - 6(4)] = 4(56) = 224$.

25. The correct answer is **A**. The fastest lumberjack can chop W in 30 minutes, so in 2 hours = 120 minutes, he will chop $4W$. The next fastest can chop W in 45 minutes, so he will be able to chop $\dfrac{120}{45}W = 2\dfrac{2}{3}W$; $4W + 2\dfrac{2}{3}W = 6\dfrac{2}{3}W$.

26. The correct answer is **A**. (1) alone is sufficient because it gives 1971 as the only answer. (2) alone is insufficient, because the conditions stated could apply to either 1971 or 1972.

27. The correct answer is **E**. (1) alone can neither prove nor disprove the equation above because there are infinite values of r, s, and x for which the equation could be true or false. (2) alone is not sufficient. By plugging in $s + 2$ for x, you can determine that you can answer the question when $r = 1$, but you don't actually know that r does, in fact, equal 1. Putting both statements together, you still don't have enough information to answer the question, as there are values that could give you either true or false answers. So E is the correct answer.

28. The correct answer is **C**. (1) alone is insufficient because it gives us no actual measurements. (2) alone is insufficient because it gives us the width of the garage, but not the width of the cars. If the two are combined, we see that the cars cannot fit in the garage. The square root of $100 = 10$, so the 9 cars will require 90 feet of space, but the additional space required between and around the cars will be another 18 feet, so the cars will not fit in the garage.

29. The correct answer is **A**. (1) alone is sufficient, because the only value for q, r, and s that meets the conditions of the question and the statement is 15; thus, we can determine the value of qr. (2) alone is not sufficient; although it would work for the values $(q, r, s) = (15, 15, 15)$, it would also work for $(q, r, s) = (15, 14, 16)$.

30. The correct answer is **E**. A triangle is isosceles if two of its angles are equal. (1) tells us that $(a + c) = 120°$, which is not sufficient to prove whether or not the triangle is isosceles. (2) can be altered to $(a + c) = 2b$, which is not sufficient to prove whether or not the triangle is isosceles. If the two are combined, we have $2b = 120$, and therefore $b = 60$. Knowing the measure of one angle is still insufficient, since a could equal 59 and c could equal 61, so the question remains unresolved.

31. The correct answer is **D**. For simplicity, assume that she earned $100 last year and saved $5. This year she earned $110 and saved $110 \times 0.08 = \$8.80$. $8.80/5 = 1.76$ or 176%.

32. The correct answer is **B**. To find *X*, the distance between S and Q, start with a number you know; the distance between S and P is 186 miles, and the round trip therefore is 372 miles; 372 = the SR round trip + 24 miles, so SR round trip = 348 miles; SQ round trip = SR round trip − 16 miles, so SQ round trip = 364. *X* is the one-way SQ distance, so 364/2 = 182.

33. The correct answer is **C**. First, 35% of 400 = 140. If 140 = 0.2*x*, then *x* = 140/0.2 = 700.

34. The correct answer is **A**. Following the rules for multiplying two binomials and the rules for exponents, $(2^3 - 1)(2^3 + 1)(2^6 + 1)(2^{12} + 1) = (2^6 - 1)(2^6 + 1)(2^{12} + 1) = (2^{12} - 1)(2^{12} + 1) = (2^{24} - 1)$.

35. The correct answer is **B**. 765 times 1/4 equals 191.25, but the question states "at least 1/4," so the movie must appear on 192 lists.

36. The correct answer is **C**. The answer must be a subset of the 60 percent of associates that are not first-year associates. Of these, you must subtract the 30 percent that are second-year associates, leaving only 30 percent, so the answer is C.

37. The correct answer is **A**. This problem becomes much easier if you recognize that all of the fractions include $\dfrac{1}{\left[(2^3)(3^2)\right]}$; for purposes of comparison, you can multiply each of the fractions by $(2^3)(3^2)$ to simplify things. This leaves you with the following values: A = 12, B = 2, C = 6, D = 8, and E = 3; A is the greatest value.

Verbal

1. The correct answer is **D**. An ideal title would capture the idea that this is a review of a book by Egbert Larson concerning the daunting challenges of interstellar space travel. C and E both appear to be attractive choices because they mention Larson and they mention issues addressed in the passage, but they are both incorrect because they focus on topics that are *not* in the passage: there is no mention in the passage of Larson's building a spacecraft, and his work seems to build on the theory of relativity rather than challenging it. B is mostly off topic. A and D both address the central issue of the difficulty of space travel, but A is incorrect because it introduces the concept of "the promise" of space travel, which is not addressed in the passage. D is the best answer.

2. The correct answer is **C**. The passage is clearly talking about a book, so B is out. The passage assumes some knowledge of science—as shown by its reference to "Mr. Einstein" without any further identification that it is talking about the physicist Albert Einstein—but it does not assume a comprehensive knowledge of physics, as shown by its explanation of relativistic time dilation, a concept that no professional astrophysicist would need to have explained. Thus the very general audience of D and the very specific audience of A are both out. E is not obviously wrong, but the fact that the passage makes no mention of "poetry" and the fact that C specifically mentions a "book review" makes C the stronger choice.

3. The correct answer is **A**. The passage mentions the dangers of B, D, and E in the fourth paragraph (the statement that the mission will need several generations implies that the first generation will die of old age), and C is addressed with the statement: "And if you tried to accelerate directly to the speed of light like they do in the movies, you'd be instantly splattered on the back of your theoretical spacecraft." Meteor impacts, although in fact a serious issue for voyages of this nature, are not discussed in the passage.

4. The correct answer is **E**. The passage states: "Keeping a crew alive on the way turns out to be the trickiest part of all." This is a fair approximation of statement E.

5. The correct answer is **E**. The passage states: "If Mr. Einstein was right about relativity . . . then time slows down when you approach the speed of light. A person traveling at any velocity near the speed of light will age only days for every week, month, or even year that passes on earth." If the twin on the voyage was traveling at "very close" to the speed of light, we can assume that for her, time slowed down a great deal compared to time as experienced on earth. The twin on earth would most likely have died of old age long before the voyaging twin's return, leaving only the possibility that the earth twin's descendants might be there to greet her returning twin.

6. The correct answer is **B**. B addresses all the survival issues handled by C, and in addition its protection "from all physical harm" addresses the radiation mentioned in E and the acceleration problems that are inherent in A. B also protects against the daunting passage of time necessary for interstellar space travel. Based on the information in the third paragraph, the invention in A would not be usable without some other protective invention because humans could not withstand that rate of acceleration. D would be an astounding invention on its own, but it does not address as many of the challenges mentioned in the passage as B. B is the best answer. Why hasn't someone invented this thing yet?

7. The correct answer is **D**. The passage states: "Forget hostile aliens. According to a forthcoming book by noted astrophysicist Egbert Larson, the intrepid humans who first attempt interstellar space travel will face far more daunting challenges before they ever meet the Little Green Men." While the passage is light in tone, it does not suggest that the aliens are necessarily a "myth," as in E, or that those who believe in them are ignorant, as in A. On the other hand, it does not say that they exist or that humans are likely to contact them, which rules out C. The point of the introduction is that there are more daunting immediate problems than the theoretical risk of alien attacks, so B is out. D captures the essence of the introduction.

8. The correct answer is **D**. Answer D suggests that the company can reap the benefits of fuller trucks while bearing no ill consequences from cutting off the tops, Answers A, B, and C all give reasons *not* to cut off the tops. Answer E is irrelevant.

9. The correct answer is **A**. Answer A suggests that there will be consequences from selling the cough syrup without the measuring cup that could hurt the product's sales; if the product is perceived as ineffective or dangerous, fewer people will buy it, and that effect will most likely decrease net revenue.

10. The correct answer is **C**. If the advertisement suggests that "people who do not like flossing can now rely solely on mouthwash and brushing to maintain good dental health," but in actuality mouthwash is less effective than flossing at performing certain functions that are important to good dental health, then the advertisement is misleading.

11. The correct answer is **D**. If the advertisement does increase the number of people taking effective preventive measures against gum disease, then it is serving the public health. This argument is vulnerable to the criticism that the public health benefits of the ad are offset by the increased likelihood of plaque and cavities between teeth of people who stop flossing, but answer D is still stronger than any of the alternatives.

12. The correct answer is **B**. B suggests that the observed results of the durability testing are well within the acceptable range for tests of this sort; by this same standard, the washing machine model would have failed the test if 30 or more machines had stopped working.

13. The correct answer is **D**. The underlined passage should suggest that the dominance of student government by a group representing a small minority of the total student body is contrary to expectations, thus C or D. The past tense of C, however, does not agree with the present tense "dominate" used later in the sentence, so D is the best choice.

14. The correct answer is **D**. The "were not able in determining" of A and the "were not able of determining" in C are unidiomatic, so A and C are out. The passive voice of E—"unable to be determined"—is stylistically inferior to the active voice used in B and D, so E is out unless there are more serious problems with B and D. The use of "therefore" in B is redundant following the "because" at the beginning of the sentence, so B is out. D is the clearest and most standard of the options.

15. The correct answer is **B**. Answer B is the clearest and most concise formulation of the intended statement. The construction "reading high" in A is awkward; C is incorrect because "a diabetic history" is awkward; D is incorrect because "having high glucose readings" is stylistically inferior to "with high glucose readings"; E is less concise than B.

16. The correct answer is **C**. "be more prone" (A), "are proner" (B), and "at heightened rates than" (D) are all grammatically incorrect, while statement E does not really make sense; statement C is the clearest and most standard wording.

17. The correct answer is **B**. The idiomatic construction here is "{subject} ranges from X to Y." B completes the construction.

18. The correct answer is **A**. A is grammatical and idiomatic, so it is the best choice. A is preferable to B because B uses the passive voice and because the present tense used in A, "not all . . . meet", corresponds better with the preceding verb phrase "can stay together" than the past tense used in B. A is preferable to C because A uses the present tense and because the final phrase "as required" in C is somewhat awkward. D and E are incorrect because they imply that no one meets the requirements, rather than just some of the members.

19. The correct answer is **A**. If the town could meet its water requirements from sources other than the Gray River, then the depletion of Lake Mudfish would not necessarily be "inevitable"; since the prediction states that it is inevitable, statement A is an assumption upon which the prediction is based.

20. The correct answer is **B**. If B is true, then the company had sufficient reason to switch to the new chemical without taking the public protest into consideration.

21. The correct answer is **B**. If the museum has cancelled its insurance policy, it will not have to pay the increased premiums, so the stated reason for charging a high entrance fee will no longer be valid.

22. The correct answer is **E**. The statement in the passage that the "language used in the epic poems contains elements of the Greek language dating from the twelfth to the eighth centuries B.C.E." suggests that the poem was probably composed in the eighth century, using preexisting poetic material. If "the Greek writing system was not developed until the late seventh century," then the poem must have been composed orally if it was composed in the eighth century, because it could not have been written down at that time. The mechanism described in C is vaguely plausible, although it is very unlikely that a person who composed poems in the eighth century would be alive to dictate them in the late seventh century. E is the best answer.

23. The correct answer is **C**. The main subject of the passage is the debate over the repatriation of cultural treasures; the passage states that the subject is not widely noted by the outside world, hence "secret"; and the passage presents the British Museum in a negative light, hence "dirty little secret."

24. The correct answer is **E**. The example of the Elgin Marbles is used to poke holes in the arguments of museum curators expressed in the second paragraph.

25. The correct answer is **C**. In both C and the description of the Elgin Marbles issue in the text, there is an existing museum, presumably capable of both protecting and preserving cultural artifacts, that is seeking the return of cultural treasures to display in a newly created space among relevant cultural context.

26. The correct answer is **B**. The sentence specifically addresses one of the arguments against repatriation of the Elgin Marbles, i.e., that more people can see the sculptures in the British Museum.

27. The correct answer is **A**. The author's tone is certainly critical, as seen in terms such as "robbed" and "so-called art experts" and in the argument as a whole. The author's hostility to the museum curators does not rise to the level of "seething anger," however, and only one of the sentences ("evidently, the quantity of viewers. . .") could accurately be described as "bemused sarcasm," whereas the tone of the entire passage could be characterized as "indignant."

28. The correct answer is **D**. The passage states, "Advocates of repatriation have argued that cultural treasures should be returned to their nations of origin, both because of basic fairness and because the artwork and cultural artifacts in question are best understood within their local context." The African sculptures in question are clearly easier to understand within their local context.

29. The correct answer is **C**. A is confusing, both because of its wording and because of its confusion of tenses: "develop" and "did so." B and E also mix tenses. The presentation of facts in D is confusing, and its use of the present tense is inappropriate for data that concern the past. C is the best answer.

30. The correct answer is **A**. B and C are incorrect because they erroneously compare Galileo Galilei to Albert Einstein's intellectual boldness. D fails to make clear whether Albert Einstein or Galileo is doing the refusing. E is incorrect because "like" rather than "as" should be used to compare two noun phrases. A is the best answer.

31. The correct answer is **C**. A is less idiomatic and concise than C. B is incorrect because "rates" does not agree in number with "has generated." The "because" in D and E turns the first clause into a sentence fragment. C is the best choice.

32. The correct answer is **C**. A is incorrect because it employs a nonparallel construction with "to settle" and "facing." In B, "have opted settling" is unidiomatic. D and E both incorrectly use the past perfect tense ("had opted"), which is inappropriate because the introductory clause "over the last few years" implies that the action in question began in the past and has continued into the present; past perfect is used for actions that terminated in the past. C is the best answer.

33. The correct answer is **D**. The idiomatic construction here is "{subject} ranges from X to Y." D completes the construction.

34. The correct answer is **A**. Answer A offers evidence that directly counters the consultant's statement that people do not like green vegetables. E provides weak support for the idea that a green food could be more popular than a purple one, but the

difference between gum and vegetables is sufficiently distinct to make A the stronger answer.

35. The correct answer is **D**. Answer D presents a substantial impediment to unauthorized trade in the coupons, while still retaining the customer loyalty benefits for which the program was presumably created. The other answers either fail to address the unauthorized trade in a meaningful way or significantly reduce the value of the customer loyalty program.

36. The correct answer is **A**. Answer A describes a situation in which costs would be substantially decreased because of the savings on worker salaries, but also in which revenues could remain substantially the same because preexisting stock was on hand. The described situation provides a plausible explanation for the observed financial results.

37. The correct answer is **A**. A is the only response that makes clear that the goal was what the Romans and Greeks had in common. B and C lack clear referents for "that." D and E fail to make clear exactly what the Greeks "did." A is the best answer.

38. The correct answer is **D**. The verb form "has risen" is supposed to describe an action simultaneous with "sank," so it should be in the same verb form as "sank," and so "rose" is a better verb form for this sentence; this excludes A and B. C inaccurately implies that the sinking mood itself could call off the trip; D and E correctly suggest that the sinking of the family's mood is a possible justification for calling off the trip. Between D and E, D is preferable because the construction "not . . . enough to call off" is more concise and forceful than "not . . . enough for calling off." D is the best answer.

39. The correct answer is **C**. The construction "proof exists that x was y" is more idiomatic and direct than the constructions in A and B: "proof exists of x being y" or "proof exists regarding x having been y"; consequently, C is preferable to A or B. D incorrectly suggests that the observation of disturbances was the result of the nuclear testing, rather than the electromagnetic disturbances themselves. E contains an error in verb-subject agreement with the construction, "disturbance . . . were." C is the best answer.

40. The correct answer is **E**. The idiomatic construction used here is "more common among x than among y," as in answer E. Answer A leaves open the illogical possibility that hip dysplasia among German shepherds is a more common phenomenon than the existence of other breeds of dogs. B lacks parallelism, and C and D are unidiomatic.

41. The correct answer is **C**. C presents the most idiomatic and clearest statement of the facts. A contains a subject-verb disagreement with "arguments . . . was." B implies that the bond proposal, rather than the letters, was printed in the newspaper. D also has a subject-verb disagreement, because "series" is a collective noun and technically should take a singular verb, "series . . . puts forth" instead of "series . . . put forth"; the multiple possessives in D also make it awkward and hard to follow. The organization of information in E is confusing, and the passive construction leaves the natural subject of the sentence, the principal, as the object of a preposition at the end of the sentence. C is the best choice.

Sources for Reading Comprehension Passages

Reading Comprehension Drill 1

Questions 1–3	Walter W. Skeat, *English Dialects from the Eighth Century to the Present Day*
Questions 4–7	T. Martin Wood, *Whistler: Masterpieces in Colour Series*
Questions 8–10	Shannon Reed
Questions 11–14	Jennie Hall, *Viking Tales*
Questions 15–17	Shannon Reed
Questions 18–20	Thomas Roger Smith and John Slater, *Architecture: Classic and Early Christian*

Reading Comprehension Drill 2

Questions 1–4	Shannon Reed
Questions 5–7	H. Irving Hancock, *The High School Boys' Training Hike*
Questions 8–11	Shannon Reed
Questions 12–15	Shannon Reed
Questions 16–19	Shannon Reed
Questions 20–22	Shannon Reed

Reading Comprehension Drill 3

Questions 1–4	Frank M. Chapman, *What Bird Is That? A Pocket Museum of the Land Birds of the Eastern United States Arranged According to Season*
Questions 5–7	Elizabeth Cady Stanton, Susan B. Anthony, and Matilda Joslyn Gage, *History of Woman Suffrage*, Volume III (of III)
Questions 8–11	Shannon Reed
Questions 12–14	John Lingard and Hilaire Belloc, *The History of England from the First Invasion by the Romans to the Accession of King George the Fifth*, Volume 8
Questions 15–18	Shannon Reed
Questions 19–21	Shannon Reed